THE PAPERS OF

WOODROW WILSON

VOLUME 14

1902-1903

SPONSORED BY THE WOODROW WILSON
FOUNDATION
AND PRINCETON UNIVERSITY

THE PAPERS OF
WOODROW
WILSON

ARTHUR S. LINK, EDITOR

DAVID W. HIRST AND JOHN E. LITTLE
ASSOCIATE EDITORS

JEAN MACLACHLAN, CONTRIBUTING EDITOR

M. HALSEY THOMAS, CONSULTING EDITOR

JOHN M. MULDER, EDITORIAL ASSISTANT

Volume 14 · 1902-1903

PRINCETON, NEW JERSEY
PRINCETON UNIVERSITY PRESS
1972

INTRODUCTION

THE period covered by this volume—mid-July 1902 to early September 1903—reveals the new President of Princeton University laying the groundwork for the transformation of that institution into a university in fact as well as in name. In his inaugural address, "Princeton for the Nation's Service," Wilson states his philosophy of a liberal education for the first time, and in subsequent speeches we see him striving to refine that still inchoate philosophy. He startles the trustees and alumni by revealing that Princeton is at a point of crisis because of inadequate endowment and income, the absence of a coherent curriculum, and uninspiring teaching methods. He then calls for a rapid quadrupling of endowment and projects bold goals for the near future, among them a revolutionary new method of undergraduate instruction, a great graduate school, a school of law and jurisprudence, and the strengthening of the university's scientific departments.

The academic year 1902-1903 was for Wilson a time of planning and trying to find his bearings. Aside from re-forming the standing committees of the faculty and appointing Henry B. Fine as the new Dean of the Faculty, he undertook no important changes in the university. This was true in part because, as the news reports printed in this volume repeatedly show, he spent a large portion of his time on the alumni circuit, both getting to know his "constituents," as he called them, and rallying them to the support of his plans for Princeton. Moreover, he had become more than ever in demand as a public lecturer.

Wilson and his wife spent separate vacations during the summer of 1902 to enable one of them to remain in Princeton to help care for his ailing father, Joseph Ruggles Wilson. Their letters during this prolonged separation are full of details about their daily lives and the renovation and furnishing of Prospect, then the residence of the President of Princeton University. During the following summer, in 1903, they realized their dream of a trip together to Great Britain and the Continent. Wilson's daily record of this trip, printed herein for the first time, gives a detailed view of their itinerary and activities.

Prominent in this volume are a large number of reviews of Wilson's *A History of the American People*, which Harper and Brothers published in the autumn of 1902. The text of *A History of the American People* is not printed in this series, and these reviews are included to provide the reader with detailed descriptions of the contents of this most widely read of Wilson's historical works. In addition, a number of them shed light on Wilson's strengths and weaknesses as an historian. In fact, taken all together, they constitute an excellent editorial note on *A History of the American People.*

Just as the twelfth volume of *The Papers of Woodrow Wilson* marked the end of one stage in Wilson's career, so this fourteenth volume inaugurates another. As President of Princeton, he was intimately involved in every phase of the university's life. Since documents in this and succeeding volumes will disclose that involvement in every significant aspect, the volumes covering the Princeton presidency will constitute in part a documentary history of Princeton University from 1902 to 1910.

Work on Volume 13, which will be a cumulative table of contents and index of the first twelve volumes, is well along, so that it will soon see the light of day.

Readers are again reminded that *The Papers of Woodrow Wilson* is a continuing series; that persons, institutions, and events that figure prominently in earlier volumes are not re-identified in subsequent ones; and that the Index to each volume gives cross references to fullest earlier identifications. We reiterate that it is our practice to print texts *verbatim et literatim*, repairing words and phrases only when necessary for clarity or ease of reading, and that we make silent corrections only of obvious typographical errors in typed copies.

We are grateful to Miss Mary Yates of Rydal, England, for information about Wilson's visits to the lake district of England in 1906 and 1908; to Miss Marjorie Sirlouis for transcribing Wilson's shorthand; and to Mrs. Bryant Putney of Princeton University Press for continued help in copyediting.

THE EDITORS

Princeton, New Jersey
June 21, 1972

CONTENTS

ILLUSTRATIONS

Following page 276

TEXT ILLUSTRATIONS

ABBREVIATIONS

ALI	autograph letter initialed
ALS	autograph letter(s) signed
API	autograph postal initialed
att(s).	attached, attachment(s)
CCL	carbon copy of letter
EAW	Ellen Axson Wilson
enc(s).	enclosed, enclosure(s)
env.	envelope
hw	handwriting, handwritten
L	letter
PL	printed letter
S	signed
sh	shorthand
T	typed
TCL	typed copy of letter
tel.	telegram
TLS	typed letter signed
TRS	typed report signed
WW	Woodrow Wilson
WWhw	Woodrow Wilson handwriting, handwritten
WWsh	Woodrow Wilson shorthand
WWT	Woodrow Wilson typed
WWTD	Woodrow Wilson typed document
WWTLS	Woodrow Wilson typed letter signed

ABBREVIATIONS FOR COLLECTIONS AND LIBRARIES

Following the National Union Catalog of the Library of Congress

CSmH	Henry E. Huntington Library, San Marino, Calif.
CtHC	Hartford Seminary Library
CtY	Yale University Library
DLC	Library of Congress
ICU	University of Chicago Library
MB	Boston Public Library
MdBJ	The Johns Hopkins University Library
MdHi	Maryland Historical Society, Baltimore
MH	Harvard University Library
NhD	Dartmouth College Library
NHi	New York Historical Society, New York
NIC	Cornell University Library
NjP	Princeton University Library
NjR	Rutgers University Library
NN	New York Public Library
NNC	Columbia University Library
PBm	Bryn Mawr College Library
PHC	Haverford College Library

PP	Free Library of Philadelphia
PPAmP	American Philosophical Society, Philadelphia
RSB Coll., DLC	Ray Stannard Baker Collection of Wilsoniana, Library of Congress
TSewU	University of the South Library, Sewanee, Tenn.
UA, NjP	University Archives, Princeton University Library
Vi	Virginia State Library, Richmond, Va.
ViU	University of Virginia Library
WC, NjP	Woodrow Wilson Collection, Princeton University
WHi	State Historical Society of Wisconsin, Madison
WP, DLC	Woodrow Wilson Papers, Library of Congress
WWP, UA, NjP	Woodrow Wilson Papers, University Archives, Princeton University Library

SYMBOLS

[July 13, 1902]	publication date of a published writing; also date of document when date is not part of text
[*Dec. 18, 1902*]	latest composition date of a published writing
[[Nov. 29, 1902]]	delivery date of a speech if publication date differs

THE PAPERS OF

WOODROW WILSON

VOLUME 14

1902-1903

THE PAPERS OF
WOODROW WILSON

To Edith Gittings Reid

My dearest Friend,   Princeton, 12 July, 1902

Your letter from Cambridge[1] touched me very near the quick. I have received hundreds of letters about my election to the presidency of the University, and many of them have been from very dear friends, but yours struck a note unlike any of the rest, and roused in me a special sort of gratitude, a deep sense of the genuine affection of a nature deeper, of surer instinct for the heart of friendship, than the others. *You* were thinking of *me*,—of the office hardly at all; the rest of the office chiefly and of their pleasure that I should have been honoured with it. It is not egotism that I should like your way best. You give me a friendship which is for my*self*,—and that I crave more than all the honours and all the praises it were possible to win.

You need give yourself no concern about the History.[2] It was finished a couple of weeks ago (no,—one week ago) and my decks are clear; and, as for my health, that is firm and excellent. No doubt I shall have to give up writing for the next three or four years, and that is a heartbreaking thing for a fellow who has not yet written the particular thing for which he has been in training all his life; but when I can tell you the circumstances I am sure that you will say that it was my duty to accept. It was a singularly plain, a *blessedly* plain, case. You must help me to succeed by being glad that I did not hesitate.

It pleased me to find your letter written on the familiar paper of the Bull Hotel, where I have spent a good many days and where I could imagine your surroundings: and it delighted me to hear how the charm of Cambridge,—so familiar to you and yet so inexhaustible and so safe against ever growing stale,—was proving a veritable balm and blessing to you. I hope you are well and *strong*!

Mrs. Wilson joins me in the warmest love. Please thank Mr. Reid for his message and give him our most affectionate regards. Mrs. Wilson and I have set our hearts on having you both present at my inauguration Oct. 25.

Your devoted friend   Woodrow Wilson

ALS (WC, NjP).
    [1] Mrs. Reid was traveling in England and had written Wilson from Cambridge as soon as she received word of his election. Edith G. Reid to WW, June 22, 1902, Vol. 12.
    [2] That is, his *A History of the American People.*

From Ellen Axson Wilson

My own darling,   Clifton [Mass.]   July 12 1902

    Here we are safe and sound after a pleasant journey and a good nights rest.[1] We had a delightful surprise in New York, Ed & Florence[2] met us in Jersey City! They had been out to see Agnes two days before and learned our plans from her. So of course he piloted us across town, (and we did not need a cab) and we had a nice hour together. They start south today on the Savannah steamer,—will have a few hours there with such of the family as are at home and a day or two in Atlanta. And just think! Ed solved the problem [Thomas A.] Edison put him at in the two weeks he was there! In fact he did it in *one* week, for he had to wait a week for certain chemicals. Two or three other men had worked at it for two or three years. Isn't that fine! Still Ed doesn't think there is much "in it" at Edisons, and is going back to Mannie.[3] He can always have Edisons to fall back upon if the changes in the management at Mannie should make him wish to leave. It seems to me more than ever a pity that he isn't engaged in higher scientific work.

    Mr. Tedcastle met us a[t] the station and we made the 6.03 train *without* our trunks. Mr. T. has the checks and will send them over today but we can't get them 'till he comes back tonight. Rather inconvenient! eh? They have breakfast at half past seven on Mr. T's account & it is insisted that I have mine in bed so as to have a good rest. I did not get up till nine! Dear little Helen was here, but left with Mr. T. at eight for Bar Harbour.

    The place is all that it has been represented for beauty and the air is delicious. The house is pretty and dainty and well kept and I am sure it will do you good in your turn to be here.

    By the way, Salem is only two or three miles away & we are going there, and also to Boston antique stores in search of a handsome side-board;[4] so suppose you don't finally decide that question till you hear the result: we go to one of the places on Monday and suppose you look at "Bowles" on 4th Ave.[5] when you go in.

    I am of course in a hurry to get this first letter off, so no more now. It is better not tell you, *darling,* how much I want you, or

how hard I am fighting home-sickness. I love you, *dear* Woodrow,
beyond all words and am always and altogether

Your own   Eileen.

Dear love to all.

ALS (WC, NjP).
  [1] Mrs. Wilson and her sister, Margaret Randolph Axson, were visiting their
old friends, Agnes Vaughn Tedcastle and Arthur W. Tedcastle of Wellesley Hills,
Mass., at their summer place at Clifton on the Massachusetts North Shore. The
Wilsons were taking their vacations in turns so that one of them might be home
to care for the ailing Joseph Ruggles Wilson.
  [2] Her brother, Edward William Axson, and his wife, Florence Leach Axson.
  [3] That is, he was going to return to work for the Buffalo Iron Co. in Mannie,
Tenn.
  [4] As following documents will reveal in much detail, the Wilsons were very
busy during the summer of 1902 renovating and furnishing Prospect, then the
residence of the President of Princeton University.
  [5] Frank Bowles, antique dealer, 347 Fourth Ave., New York.

From Harrison Randolph[1]

Dear Sir: Charleston, S.C., 12 July, 1902

I beg to announce the vacancy in our department of History
and Economics, and ask that your Committee on Appointments
nominate a man for the place. The salary is $1200. Lecture and
recitation work to the amount of twelve or fourteen hours a week
is expected. It is thought, perhaps, that conditions in Charleston,
and the facilities afforded for the study of early colonial history
should render this work especially interesting and attractive.[2]

Respectfully yours,   Harrison Randolph

TLS (WP, DLC).
  [1] President of the College of Charleston.
  [2] Wilson's reply is missing, but he recommended William Garrott Brown of
Cambridge, Mass., former Lecturer in History at Harvard and prolific popular
American historian. See W. G. Brown to WW, Aug. 13, 1902, printed as an Enclosure with EAW to WW, Aug. 14, 1902.

From John Wesley Fielder, Jr.[1]

Dear Dr. Wilson: Princeton, N.J., July 12th, 1902.

I am sorry to report that Mr. & Mrs. McAlpin have, after full
consideration, decided not to take any house in Princeton this
year.[2]

I am awaiting answer from Prof. Robbins[3] and, I shall use my
best efforts to get Mrs McLeod here from Buffalo, and in the
mean time, I will endeavor to find out more about her. Her name
is Elizabeth A. McLeod of New York City,[4] and she has been oc-

cupying the same residence that Mrs. Cleveland once occupied in New York City, and from her conversation, I concluded she was well acquainted with Mrs. Cleveland. However, I may be wrong in this, and I feel if you could write Mrs. Cleveland yourself, she no doubt would gladly give you any information she can about her social standing. Mrs. Cleveland would treat your letter in confidence. I think that Mrs. McLeod would make you a good tenant judging from my impression of her. Kindly let me know if you will write Mrs. Cleveland.[5]

Respectfully yours,   J. W Fielder Jr.

TLS (WP, DLC).

[1] Real estate agent and insurance broker in Princeton.

[2] That is, the Charles Williston McAlpins, who were living at the Princeton Inn, had decided not to rent the Wilson house on Library Place.

[3] Edmund Yard Robbins, Professor of Greek at Princeton.

[4] Elizabeth Atkins McLeod, widow of Archibald Angus McLeod. Her son, Archibald A. McLeod, Jr., entered Princeton in the autumn of 1902.

[5] Wilson did indeed write to Mrs. Cleveland, as Frances F. Cleveland to WW, Aug. 10, 1902, discloses.

To Ellen Axson Wilson

My own sweet darling,   Princeton, 13 July, '02

Sunday has come and all goes well. All day yesterday I was busy with the stenographer and with callers, with errands and with college business. I enclose dear little Margaret's first letter.[1]

The lunch went off beautifully on Friday. Miss Garrett came with "M. Carey" (*Mother* Carey?),[2] and we had a most affable time. They seemed genuinely pleased with everything. They were here from 12:23 to 3:50. First we went into some rooms in Blair, then into Alexander Hall, then into the Library (seminary rooms included, of course, for Bryn Mawr is about to build a Library as well as an additional dormitory), and finally into the Chapel. Miss Garrett had never seen the window to Horatio.[3] Then I took them a little drive down Prospect Ave. to the athletic grounds, &c. Jessie presided at the table very prettily. Father did not come down.

Anna[4] arrived yesterday, a lively and pleasing piece. She seems, so far as *I* can tell, to be falling into harness very easily, and the servants seem to like her. She is to go to church with us this morning,—and sit with us, I suppose. My man's wit is unable to devise otherwise.

I saw about the chimneys[5] yesterday. Measurements are to be made at once and the bricks ordered at once. Mr. Matthews, the superintendent,[6] whom I saw about it, fears that it will take some time to get the moulded brick, because they are slow to bake and the kiln is by no means run expeditiously. But he will order at once, and I have authorized him to go ahead with the work as soon as possible.

I have written to our two furniture firms in New York[7] that I expect to be in to see them to-morrow (Monday). I am afraid that will cut me out of writing to my darling to-morrow, but I will find a few minutes if I can. The errands I have ought not to take the whole day.

We are all perfectly well. I do not dare to think about you much,—but my heart keeps at it all the while, and I am in every drop of my blood   Your own   Woodrow

All join in warm regards to the Tedcastles and in warmest love to Madge. I wrote to sister[8] saying just what you suggested I should say.

ALS (WC, NjP).

[1] The enclosure is missing.

[2] Mary Elizabeth Garrett of Baltimore, daughter of John Work Garrett (1820-1884), founder of the Bryn Mawr School of Baltimore and a major benefactor of the Johns Hopkins University School of Medicine; and Martha Carey Thomas, President of Bryn Mawr College. The two women had been close friends since girlhood.

[3] Horatio Whitridge Garrett, Princeton 1895, died on October 2, 1896. His mother, Mrs. Thomas Harrison Garrett of Baltimore, presented the university with a stained glass window in his memory. Designed by Louis C. Tiffany of New York, it was installed in the Marquand Chapel in December 1897. After this building burned in 1920, the Garrett family donated a second window in memory of Horatio Garrett. It is located in the Marquand Transept of the Princeton University Chapel.

[4] Anna C. Ericksen, a nurse for Dr. Wilson.

[5] Of the Wilsons' house on Library Place, which were to be rebuilt.

[6] William R. Matthews, in the construction business in Princeton.

[7] James Fay, antiques, 438 Fourth Ave., and the Antique Furniture Exchange, 156 West 34th St.

[8] Annie Wilson (Mrs. George, Jr.) Howe, who was in Germany with her son, George Howe III, a Ph.D. candidate in classics at the University of Halle.

From Ellen Axson Wilson

My own darling,   Clifton   Sunday   [July 13, 1902]

I hope you will excuse pencil; there seems to be no ink except at the desk in the sittingroom, and I want to write here and now, —in this quiet after dinner hour when I am supposed to be resting. We had a glorious two hour drive this morning to Nahant, behind two fine horses and partly on the hard beach,—a *particularly* delightful thing to do as I learned when a girl at Old Orchard. Both sea and land were exquisitely beautiful and the day absolutely perfect, with a *soft* sea breeze without a touch of chill in it[,] the sort we had at Sagg.[1] It was a drive to be remembered always. We brought up short & turned about at the great stone gates of Henry Cabot Lodge's estate. He has a noble park &c. covering all the outer point of the Nahant peninsula. People are allowed to walk but not drive through it. I didn't know he was so rich; he seems to be, like Roosevelt, one of fortune's all round favourites!

The wind has suddenly changed now & it is much cooler—not quite so much to my taste here, but better if it lasts for our excursion to Boston tomorrow. Besides the sea from the window where I sit has grown superb in colour,—green close by, deepest blue beyond, with white caps and "breaking waves" on the rocks below me. Yesterday it was rather pale and washed out in tint.

Last night I went to a ball! Unexpected! eh? It was at the swell hotel & Mr. Tedcastle as one of the "cottagers" had been invited with his family. So he insisted the girls should go "to see what it was like," and I must chaperone them. They sat there, perfect wall-flowers of course, for an hour or so, but perhaps mildly amused "sizing up" the dancers,—a remarkably ugly crowd.

I wonder what my darling is doing this Sunday afternoon with no Ricketts nor Hibbens to divert him. Chiefly sleeping I hope. Ah, how I wish I were there!—or better still that he were here. That would be absolutely perfect. I am really afraid I ought to write short letters; there is no incident with which to fill four pages even, and when I begin to grow personal I find myself beyond measure oppressed at the situation—at my being away and you there alone. I wouldn't feel it half so bad if you could only loaf during the two weeks. But that inauguration address[2] when I let my mind dwell on it gets on *my* nerves, I *hope more* than on yours. Oh, my darling! You *are* so precious, to me first, and to so many others too! Why didnt you let me stay & try to take care of you? I love you! *love* you! I idolize you, my own darling! As ever—   Your little wife,   Eileen.

ALS (WC, NjP).
    [1] Sagaponack, Long Island, where the Wilsons had vacationed in 1890 and 1893.
    [2] "Princeton for the Nation's Service," printed at Oct. 25, 1902.

From John Gresham Machen[1]

Dear Sir: Baltimore, Md.   July 13, 1902.

After the celebration at Northfield on the evening of the Fourth of July, the very natural enthusiasm of the Princeton men was such that we did not have a good opportunity to speak to you.[2] I therefore write on behalf of the leader and other members of the Johns Hopkins delegation to express our deep appreciation of the honor you bestowed upon us in publicly making known your connection with an institution otherwise so humbly represented at the conference. It is, indeed, a cause of pride and congratulation to us all that there is one among the alumni of our own University to whom we can join others of greater age and more honorable position in always giving such sincere respect and admiration.

Yours very respectfully,   J. Gresham Machen.

ALS (WP, DLC).
    1 Identified in Mary G. Machen to WW, June 28, 1902, Vol. 12, n. 2.
    2 When Wilson spoke at the Northfield, Mass., Student Conference, about which see C. H. Dodge to WW, Jan. 3, 1901, n. 1, Vol. 12. The text of Wilson's address is printed at July 4, 1902, *ibid*.

To Ellen Axson Wilson

Everett House, Union Square,
My own darling,   New York.   14 July, 1902

I have had lunch here, and have a few minutes to loaf and chat with my sweet one.

I have been to Fay's and ordered the dining room furniture, all but the serving table. He sent me the photograph of a seven-foot sideboard which was obviously just the thing we wanted—a beautiful swell in the centre between the columns,—carved capitals on plain columns, and bird claw feet like the table (on a smaller scale, of course),—price $210. He explained to me how he could make a heavier pedestal table of the sort we most admired, 20 ft. long and yet abundantly strong,—a nest of legs within the pedestal,—price $125. I ordered it and the side-board both. Total for dining room, without serving table, $635. I also ordered the 3 bed-room chairs.

At the Antique Furniture Co's I ordered the parlour furniture prepared, packed, and held for orders, and secured an option on the screen for $50. That, I believe, completes my part in the furniture business for the present.

The pangs of loneliness got hold upon me most promptly, my love. You are my *life*,—but I'm not dwelling on that. I am well and serene, and to-morrow shall plunge into my inaugural. I am slowly accumulating ideas wherewith to clothe my ideals. Love to Madge, warmest messages to the Tedcastles, and for yourself the whole life force of   Your own   Woodrow

ALS (WC, NjP).

From Ellen Axson Wilson

My own darling,   Clifton   July 14 1902

We went into Boston this morning, starting at 8.26 and getting back at lunch time. Since lunch I have been resting, for it turned out a hot day and I reached home very tired: so now I write hurriedly before dressing for dinner.

I did not find any antique side-boards large enough, but I went to two places where they make perfectly lovely reproductions; better than Aimones[1] or anything we saw in New York. They will both send you drawings, and the one from "Bowker"[2] with four columns, price $223.00, I hope you will seriously consider. It is the same thing only better that Aimones offered for $268.00, and that Flint[3] was to send us a drawing of. I think Bowker's is the most artistic place I have been to. I should say he bears the same relation to *all* the New York ones that Caproni does to Castell-vechi[4] in casts. He does'nt keep the large pieces in stock,—makes them only to order, but the smaller furniture that he did have was exquisite. I forgot in my haste (for we went there late,) to ask about a lowboy to match. Will write to him. The side board would go to New York by water so the freight would not be *very* much more.

I also went to a place where I saw lovely drawing-room papers and textures, the cheapest of the latter, alas! $3.50 a yard!

I havn't had a word from my darling yet and oh! how I want it! Was so disappointed today when the letter—the one that you forwarded,—turned out to be from Mrs. *Simpson.*[5] I am very well indeed and as happy as I can be away from you. Agnes nearly talks me to death but I pretend to need a lot of rest and spend the afternoons in my room.

I love you *passionately*!—I am in every heart throb,

Your own   Eileen.

Dearest love to all.

ALS (WC, NjP).
   [1] Aimone's Manufacturing Co., 430 East 23rd St. and 433 East 22nd St., New York.
   [2] Lyman A. Bowker, interior decorator, 120 Tremont St., Boston.
   [3] George C. Flint Co., furniture, with various locations in New York.
   [4] P. P. Caproni & Brother, Boston art dealers specializing in reproductions of sculpture, and L. Castelvecchi & Co., casts, 225 Fourth Ave., New York.
   [5] Her letter is missing, and she is unknown to the Editors.

From Day Allen Willey[1]

Dear Sir: Baltimore, July 14th [1902].

The article I sent you appeared as an ostensible interview with you in the Sunday edition of the Philadelphia Press a few days after the announcement of your selection as President at Princeton.[2] I regret that I did not preserve the clipping from which it was taken or I would inclose it.

I know that the editor of the Independent[3] would deeply appreciate your courtesy in allowing the publication of your views.[4] The fact that it has never been given the press in any way, you wi[l]l admit has restricted its publicity. It touches upon a topic of such vital interest to the people at large that it seems to me its publication would really be very valuable from an educational standpoint.

If you would prefer to furnish your views in another form this would of course be equally acceptable, but I have thought that the article returned might save you valuable time as well as effort.[5]

I trust you wil[l] pardon my further reference to the matter but I feel its importance is a sufficient excuse.

                     Very Respectfully   D Allen Willey

TLS (WP, DLC).
[1] A free-lance journalist of Baltimore.
[2] The article, which appeared, actually, in the Philadelphia *North American*, June 15, 1902, was entitled "Princeton's New President Would Reorganize U.S. Government" and consisted of a series of quotations from Wilson's "Leaderless Government," printed at Aug. 5, 1897, Vol. 10.
[3] William Hayes Ward, editor from 1896 to 1914.
[4] That is, concerning the need for stronger executive leadership in the national government, the subject of "Leaderless Government."
[5] Nothing came of this suggestion to reprint "Leaderless Government" in part or in whole.

To Ellen Axson Wilson

My own precious darling,   Princeton, 15 July, 1902

I cannot say how your sweet letter of Sunday has delighted me. It is so full of the exhilaration of your fine drive along the coast, of the wholesome air that comes in at your windows, of the changing colour of the sea,—of vacation refreshment and quietness of thought, that it does me more good, a thousand times, than any outing I could take myself. My heart fairly sang as I read it. *This* is what makes me happy! You are to start home, my sweetheart (I know you will do this for the sake of the love you bear me!) on Monday, the 28th, *not* at the close of the preceding week. I want to finish my address before you get home, and I shall not be able to do so sooner. All day today, for example, I have been answering letters. To-morrow I begin the address (D. V.). I *must* have the happiness of having my own way if I am to write it with free spirits; and you must not deny me this. You do not know from what a depth of preference I speak. It will really be balm to my mind. I am perfectly well, not a bit jaded, and everyway fit for my writing, if only you will *let* me be perfectly content. I shall get off myself just as soon.

I felt very guilty when I read in the letter which came yesterday that you thought that I had better not order the sideboard until you had looked in Boston and Salem. Your memorandum said "Decide about table and sideboard," and so I decided, and ordered both yesterday, as I wrote to you from New York. Probably your letter came yesterday morning, but after I left the house for the 9:05, and I did not read it until I got back in the evening, when the deed was done. I am very sorry. But I did not feel that the order could properly be withdrawn from Fay. I think you will be satisfied with the board, whatever you may think of my too prompt obedience.

Ah, how I love you, how I live in your love and in your happiness, how intensely I am   Your own   Woodrow

We are all well. Love to Madge and to the Ts.

ALS (WC, NjP).

To Edward Graham Elliott

My dear Mr. Elliott: Princeton, N. J.   July 15th, 1902.

Your letter of June 16th[1] gave me a great deal of gratification. I dare say that the change in my engagements will result in a somewhat heavier burden falling on you next year, but you may be sure that I shall make it as bearable a burden as possible. It is not my intention to give up my courses of lectures. I cannot tell until I experiment in the matter how long it will be possible for me to carry them; but I should hope that it would never become necessary for me to lose this direct contact with the men, or the intellectual stimulation which comes from class room work.[2] There is not likely next year, therefore, to be any radical change in the general program of work, which I have already indicated to you. It will be a pleasure to see you back again, and I hope that you will come in good health and spirits.

Very sincerely yours,   Woodrow Wilson

TLS (WC, NjP).

¹ E. G. Elliott to WW, June 16, 1902, Vol. 12.

² As this letter indicates, Wilson did not anticipate that his assumption of the presidency would require any immediate or substantial changes in his own course work. Indeed, when the *Catalogue of Princeton University, 1902-1903* appeared in February 1903, the description of Wilson's courses was virtually identical with the one that he had prepared for the catalogue of 1897-98 (see Wilson's New Course Program in Political Science and Jurisprudence, printed at Dec. 1, 1897, Vol. 10). Having given the courses "Outlines of Jurisprudence" (described in the Editorial Note, "Wilson's Teaching at Princeton, 1891-92," Vol. 7) and "The Elements of Politics" (see the notes for this course printed at March 5, 1898, Vol. 10) in the autumn and spring terms, respectively, of the academic year 1901-1902, he offered the following year the two courses which he customarily alternated with them, namely "Constitutional Government" (see the notes for this course printed at Sept. 19, 1898, Vol. 11) in the autumn term and "American Constitutional Law" (see the notes for this course printed at March 2, 1894, Vol. 8) in the spring term. In addition, in 1902-1903, Wilson gave—for the last time, as it turned out—his full-year senior elective course in English common law (see the Editorial Note, "Wilson's Teaching at Princeton and the Johns Hopkins, 1893-97," Vol. 8, and, for Wilson's decision to expand the course to cover a full year, WW to F. L. Patton, June 8, 1897, Vol. 10).

The announcement of Wilson's courses in the catalogue for 1903-1904 remained as before, except that the course in English common law was omitted. In the spring of 1904, the faculty of Princeton University under Wilson's leadership undertook a wholesale revision of the undergraduate curriculum. (See the Editorial Note, "The New Princeton Course of Study," Vol. 15.) In part as a result of this action, and also because the burdens of the Princeton presidency were growing too heavy for him to continue to carry a full teaching load, Wilson abandoned his courses "The Elements of Politics" and "American Constitutional Law." The courses in jurisprudence (now retitled "The Elements of Jurisprudence") and constitutional government remained. In the new curriculum, both courses were required of all juniors concentrating in the Department of History, Politics, and Economics. Wilson revised his course in constitutional government to include some of the lectures and readings of his discarded course in American constitutional law. He continued to give "Elements of Jurisprudence" in the autumn term and "Constitutional Government" in the spring term each year to the end of his career at Princeton in 1910.

To Clarence Valentine Boyer

My dear Mr. Boyer,   Princeton, New Jersey, 15 July, 1902.

I am a little puzzled, I find, just what selections to make for your first purchase of books in Political Science:¹ but I think that probably the following will give you as broad a variety and as various a stimulation of thought as any list I can think of:

Montesquieu, "The Spirit of the Laws" (Bohn's ed.).

Walter Bagehot, "The English Constitution." (AppleTon).

Sir Jas. Fitzjames Stephen, "Liberty, Equality, Fraternity." (Henry Holt).

Anthony Trollope, "The Life of Cicero." (Harpers).

The Federalist. There are numerous editions, but all give the text of the papers themselves, and that is chiefly what you want.

    Edmund Burke, "Letter to the Sheriffs of Bristol," Speech on
      "Conciliation with America," and Speech on "Taxation in
      America." These three can be found separately published, or
      published together. See catalogues, e. g., of D. C. Heath,
      Ginn and Co., etc.
    James Bryce, "The American Commonwealth" (Macmillan), if
      you already have de Tocqueville's "Democracy in America,"
      for the two should be read together.
    Elisha Mulford, "The Nation." (Houghton and Mifflin).
    J. Lawrence Lowell, "Essays on Government" and ["]Govern-
      ments and Parties of Continental Europe," both published
      by Houghton & Mifflin.
    Sir Charles Dilke, "Greater Britain." (Macmillan).
    The En[g]lish Citizen Series (Macmillan), the two volumes of
      the Series entitled "Central Government" and "Local Govern-
      ment."
    Woodrow Wilson, "Congressional Government" (Houghton &
      Mifflin), to be read along with
    Henry J. Ford, "The Rise and Growth of American Politics"
      (Macmillan).

Hoping that these will be of real service to your thought,
             Yours with much regard,   Woodrow Wilson

WWTLS (WP, DLC).
  [1] Wilson was replying to C. V. Boyer to WW, June 25, 1902, Vol. 12.

To Daniel Coit Gilman

My Dear Dr. Gilman: Princeton, N. J., July 15th, 1902.

    Your letter from Berlin[1] has given me the deepest gratification.
I do not know any one whose support and Godspeed I should
more desire in the circumstances. I feel that a great deal of my
university training has come from you and from my association
with the men at the Hopkins. And just now, at the outset of my
new duties, while I feel myself painfully untried in the things
I am about to undertake, there is a peculiar value to me in finding
that you, who know men and understand the work to be done,
have confidence in my success. I wish that I *could* hope that a
day would come when some one could stand up and say in public
to me, as truthfully as I had the pleasure of saying to you, that
my work—a great work covering many years of achievement—
had been thoroughly well done.[2] I shall strive and pray for that

end, and letters like yours will help me forward in the arduous business. With warmest regards both to Mrs. Gilman and yourself.

Gratefully yours,   Woodrow Wilson

Printed in Fabian Franklin, *The Life of Daniel Coit Gilman* (New York, 1910), pp. 380-81.
    [1] D. C. Gilman to WW, June 21, 1902, Vol. 12.
    [2] See Wilson's presentation address to Gilman at the celebration of the twenty-fifth anniversary of the founding of The Johns Hopkins University, printed at Feb. 21, 1902, Vol. 12.

To Jabez Lamar Monroe Curry

My dear Dr. Curry: Princeton, N. J.   July 15th, 1902.

I hope that you knew when you were writing me your letter of the 22nd of June,[1] that you were about to communicate not only a pleasure, but strength and courage to the man whom you were addressing. You must realize, I hope, how much it means to a younger man to receive the encouragement and Godspeed of a veteran who has won the honor of the whole country in his field of work. It is a sort of laying on of hands, and certainly not only my love for the University I have undertaken to serve, but also the confididence [confidence] and generous sympathy of men like yourself (if there are any other men like yourself) will make my task, if not an easy one, at least one which gives joy and satisfaction in the doing. I thank you with all my heart.

Quite apart from the message your letter bore, it was very delightful to hear from you and to know of your health and prosperity; and may they be continued indefinitely. With warmest regard and appreciation,   Faithfully yours,   Woodrow Wilson

TLS (J. L. M. Curry Papers, DLC).
    [1] J. L. M. Curry to WW, June 21, 1902, Vol. 12.

From Ellen Axson Wilson

My own darling,   Clifton   July 15 1902

The letters came at last this morning,—two of them[,] Sundays and yesterdays; I cant say how glad I was to get them and dear little Margaret's too. It was rather hard to wait so long to hear even of her safe arrival,—thanks to leaving so soon after she did.[1]

We have just been through such a startling experience, that I can hardly compose my mind to write. Dear little Annie Beatty had a frightful attack of something like heart failure as the result of her bath in the surf. She and Madge went in together; I was writing to Margaret here at the window and Francis[2] & I decided they had been in long enough so they were called and came up to the house feeling pretty well. But all at once while taking off her shoes she became rigid, perfectly purple, and practically unconscious, though all the time uttering the most distressing cries in her effort to get her breath. Agnes was in the third story with a sempstress, but I called for the whiskey bottle and poured it down her, the maids carried her bodily upstairs & with great difficulty we got off her wet things, rubbed her with whiskey and rolled her in blankets and hot water bags. She came to fairly soon and seems quite herself again now. Agnes thinks it was caused by her going in too soon after being unwell. She went down to the station and telephoned to the doctor in Boston. He says the danger is over and that we did all we should except that we ought to keep up the whiskey at intervals for some hours.

But I don't know why I should write you so many details, except of course that out of the abundance of the heart the mouth speaketh.

It is very satisfactory indeed about the side-board; I am glad you ordered it. It seems from your description to be practically the same as Bowkers, and $15.00 cheaper besides the saving on freight. Suppose you don't order the serving table at all until we get possession of the house, can measure the wall spaces between "openings," and see what size will look best. I am glad it is all right about the table too; everything is entirely satisfactory including the prices. Of course you will send back the drawings to the Boston men.

I am delighted that the chimneys are to be done; *how* I shall enjoy the sight of them! Mr. Tedcastle says we ought to sell our house & invest the money! We would save some three hundred a year & lots of trouble! Tell me what Mr. Feilder hears from his letters.

I am *so* glad the inaugural promises to take shape easily, dearest.

We are both as well as well can be, and I *love* you *passionately* and am always and altogether,   Your own,   Eileen.

Will you send me the funny editorial from the Santa Cruz paper?[3] It is in the pasteboard box on my chest of drawers. The letter from Phila. was from Mr. Henry enclosing the "barber" letter.[4]

The doctor has just been here and says Annie's heart action is still very bad and that she must stay in bed an indefinite time.

Agnes says he thinks it may be a permanent injury, but she is *so* rattled that I cannot help hoping she misunderstood. It all makes me nervous about the children though. One trouble was their eating (popcorn) just before going in. But Madge was & is "perfectly all right."

ALS (WC, NjP).

[1] Margaret Wilson had gone to Baltimore to visit her cousin, Mary Eloise Hoyt.

[2] Frances Snell, a music teacher, who was also visiting the Tedcastles.

[3] This was an editorial in the Santa Cruz, Calif., *Surf*, June 27, 1902, commenting on the letter from "Old-Fashioned Democrat" to the Editor of the *Indianapolis News*, May 1, 1902 (printed at this date in Vol. 12), suggesting Wilson for the Democratic presidential nomination in 1904. "With Cleveland and Hill clasping hands in New York," the *Surf* said, "Colonel Watterson in Kentucky and Colonel Bryan in Nebraska rearing upon their hind legs and Mr. Gorman in Maryland sawing wood, it is a pleasant diversion of thought, to say the least, to turn towards the man from Princeton."

[4] This letter from Bayard Henry is missing.

To Ellen Axson Wilson

My own darling,   Princeton, 16 July, 1902

Your letter which came this morning thoroughly convinced me of my indiscretion in ordering a side-board (though the one I ordered is, I am sure, much better than any we could get at Flint's and much more artistic than the one at Aimone's, to judge by the photographs). I therefore wrote at once to Fay, asking him to hold on (if he could without actual loss to himself) until I could exchange letters with you. I will wait till the sketch comes from Boston and then obey the memorandum over again and "decide," —though I am so well satisfied with Fay's photograph that I expect to keep faith with him after all if I can. I feel a little badly, as it is, over having asked him to suspend operations after a definite order.

I know that you will be pleased with the letter and the reports[1] which I enclose. They made dear Jessie's face shine. She will write the good news to Margaret.

I set out on my inaugural this morning and got very satisfactorily started,—writing half a history stint (about 650 words). Having allowed myself ten days in wh. to complete the address, and 650 words being about one tenth of the whole, this may count, on this undertaking, as a *whole* stint. I shall not drive myself.

I shall be glad if my indiscretion in buying the sideboard keeps you out of the hot and tiresome city. What you need now is to *keep still* and *loaf*, you dear thing. Those are your orders.

I have just had a cable message from Elliott[2] which says "Passed summa," which, being interpreted, means that he has passed for his Doctor's degree "summa cum laude," with the highest distinction. There are, ordinarily, three degrees of excellence: "cum laude," "magna cum laude," "summa cum laude." Hurrah for the boy!

We are all perfectly well; the weather is fine and cool; Anna seems to be getting on famously; and everything is all right. Of course, so long as you are not every moment accessible, my heart goes at low pressure; but I am as steady as a church and my love for you only does me good. I am alive because I am

Your own   Woodrow

Love fr. all to all.

ALS (WC, NjP).
  [1] From Miss Fine's School in Princeton, a girls' school founded in 1899 by May Margaret Fine, which Jessie was attending. The enclosures are missing.
  [2] This cable is missing.

From Ellen Axson Wilson

My own darling,   Clifton   July 16 1902

This morning brought me a delightful budget of letters,—yours, dear little Jessies, and Margarets, and I have been very happy over them. All is well here too. Annie is all right though the doctor is keeping her in bed another day. She is a pupil nurse, you know, here on her vacation, and was *very* tired,—a fact which was probably the true cause of the trouble yesterday. The doctor has no idea that the heart was permanently injured. Agnes was really prostrated longer than Annie,—was awake all night,—in spite of the fact that we did not let her know yesterday till the danger was over and Annie quite herself again. She was, *very* naturally, angry with us all for "taking the responsibility" of *not* calling her!

And to think that after all that excitement in the morning I should have seen two boys almost drown in the afternoon! Just after finishing my letter to you I went down on the great rock that juts far out below the bluff to watch the breakers. There was a thunder-storm on the way and the waves were much higher than they have been since we came, and were dashing grandly against the rock with spray as high as a house. All at once I heard a great shouting and saw a black-bearded man on the beach gesticulating wildly. I looked about and saw not far from me two boys struggling in the water in the heaviest part of the waves. They were trying to swim to land but the undertow was so strong that they could make no headway. The little one kept screaming "I can't get in, I can't get in!" while the older struggled doggedly. They were very near me,—and the rock,—but a quarter of a mile from the beach, and the father did not go in after them—being it seems already exhausted by a struggle with the waves himself. Suddenly the little one turned about and made straight for the rock: "Oh! I thought he will surely be dashed to pieces." But fortunately it had a long sloping weatherworn side just there, and, to make a long story short, first one and then the other got safely up on the rock, only a little bruised and cut. Mr. Tedcastle says I will be going around all the rest of the time with a whiskey bottle under one arm and a life preserver under the other.

After yesterday's storm, today is finer than ever and the sea more "deeply, darkly, beautifully blue." I seem to have never fully realized before what an exquisite colour *blue* is;—have even decided to keep my little boudoir blue!

Dear heart, you put my staying longer in such a way that I shan't be able to say 'no' unless you will withdraw the request,—but oh! *please do!* I was counting the days until the 24th and will be so miserably disappointed if you keep me here longer. I thought you would not get off until the 28th and I do *so* want to have a few days with you before you leave. Besides—to be practical—I ought to go to Phila. no later than that to see about wall-papers &c., and I wanted you to make one trip with me to look at them too, for I care more for your taste and judgment than for Mr. Holmes',[1]—besides the obvious importance that you should have colours and patterns in the house that *you* will enjoy living with!

So won't you *please* be kind and say that it will be all right—*"perfectly* all right!"—for me to come home on the 24th?

Tell darling little Jessie how very glad I was to get her letter and that I want "more," like the little Oliver. With dear love to them all, and for my darling a heart full to overflowing from his own,   Eileen.

ALS (WC, NjP).
[1] An interior decorator in Philadelphia.

To Thomas Raynesford Lounsbury[1]

My dear Mr. Lounsbury,   Princeton, New Jersey, 16 July, 1902

I must try to get just a line to you to tell you of the genuine pleasure your cordial note[2] brought me from over sea. It is no burden, it is a genuine self-indulgence to acknowledge such a letter,—a letter of real, spontaneous friendship. A man lives, I take it, not to make acquaintances and receive compliments, but,—besides his work,—to make friends and keep the cockles of his heart warm. The rewards of my presidency seem to be coming to me now (lest they should lack at the end?). Hereafter come hard work, the deep waters of responsibility, for Princeton is to be handled at a crisis in her development; but now at the outset come these delightful voices of friendship, which sing courage and good cheer to me. I thank you from the bottom of my heart!

Gratefully and faithfully Yours,   Woodrow Wilson

ALS (T. R. Lounsbury Papers, CtY).
[1] Professor of English Language and Literature and Librarian of the Sheffield Scientific School at Yale University.
[2] It is printed as an addendum in this volume.

From Frederic John Paxon[1]

My dear Mr. Wilson: Atlanta, Ga., 7/16/02.

Accept many thanks for your favor of the 12th. We should be pleased to accept your proposition for $100.00 and expenses for a lecture to be delivered late this Fall or in the early Spring of 1903, and shall be pleased to leave the matter open until the latter part of November.[2]

We have a selfish motive in having you come with us, we have such a large proof of Princeton graduates and we all admire the present President of Princeton, and are anxious to hear a lecture from him.

The undersigned was for many years in the Book business and he always watched with great interest anything emanating from your pen.   Sincerely yours,   F J Paxon

TLS (WP, DLC).
[1] Retail merchant of Atlanta and chairman of the executive committee of the Atlanta Lecture Association.
[2] Further correspondence between Paxon and Wilson is missing, but Wilson did not speak in Atlanta in 1903 or 1904.

To Ellen Axson Wilson

My own darling,   Princeton, 17 July, 1902

The sketches of sideboards came from Boston this morning. I am afraid that they *are* a little more artistic than Fay's; but the difference is not great enough, I think, to justify me in withdrawing a definite order from Fay. I have just written to him, therefore, to go ahead. I suspect that a good deal of the difference of impression made on my eye by the Boston sketches and Fay's photograph was due to the sketchiness of the sketch,—the suggestions it makes to the imagination. I think you will be satisfied with what Fay makes. The part below the drawers has a sweeping swell like this (you are supposed to be looking down on the board from the ceiling, and *through* the drawers!). The squares are the tops of the capitals of the columns.

It was deeply distressing to hear of what poor little Annie Beatty went through with,—and of all the excitement and anxiety that went along with it. I trust that you[r] next letter will bring reassuring reports. Please express my warm interest and sympathy.

Alas, our chimneys have been measured, and are too small, by three feet, for the Blair Hall tops. If reduced to our size and made to contain our big flues, they would be too frail to stand the heavy winds. The superintendent and I are to discuss other plans this afternoon, and I will report in to-morrow's letter.

Annie[1] left for her vacation to-day, and Anna seems to fall into her place very easily, though with a little embarrassment. Her name, by the way, is Anna Ericksen. I wonder if she is descended from Lief.

Another (half) stint was salted down this morning, and I had enough of the forenoon left for a number of other things, such as the paying of bills. I find that I can do that much on the address without any sense of strain, and there is no need to do more.

I am perfectly well and manage, by not thinking of you *too* much to keep in excellent spirits. It is delightful to think of you a *little*! You are *so* sweet, *so* delightful, so precious, so altogether desirable! I am heart and mind   Your own   Woodrow

Love from all to all.

ALS (WC, NjP).
[1] Annie M. McLauchlin, a servant.

To Robert Bridges

My dear Bobby,   Princeton, New Jersey, 17 July, 1902.

It is just as I supposed. The contemptible creature who edits the Popular Science Monthly[1] has begun his quotation from me this time,[2] as he did last,[3] in the middle of a paragraph; has left out the whole of a strong eulogy of science; and has misrepresented me just as much as possible. I have a great mind to write to him and tell him just what I think of him.

Thank you for the copy of the Monthly. I like to know what the cur is about.

I am hard at work on my inaugural address.

             , With all affection,   Woodrow Wilson

WWTLS (WC, NjP).
  [1] James McKeen Cattell.
  [2] In an editorial on Wilson's election to the Princeton presidency, Cattell said that there was no reason to believe that scientific study at Princeton would flourish any more under Wilson than it had under Patton. *Popular Science Monthly*, LXI (July 1902), 286-87. To prove Wilson's bias against science, Cattell reprinted, on pages 269-71 of the volume just cited, the concluding paragraphs of Wilson's Sesquicentennial address, "Princeton in the Nation's Service," beginning with the sentence "I have no laboratory but the world of books and men in which I live; but I am much mistaken if the scientific spirit of the age is not doing us a great disservice, working in us a certain degeneracy."
  [3] In *Science*, New Series, IV (Dec. 18, 1896), 908-10.

From Ellen Axson Wilson

My own darling,   Clifton   July 17 1902

Madge and I are quite excited over Ed Elliots extraordinary success. Aren't you astonished? I knew he was a fine fellow and a good worker, but I had no idea there was anything remarkable about him; yet there must be to accomplish such a feat as this. Hurrah for him indeed!

I am very much pleased too at the letters from Baltimore.[1] Not that it makes any real difference, but the children will be happy about it.

We have been in to Boston again this morning,—just the day for it,—very cool, almost cold. Madge's trunk came perfectly *smashed*, with a "received in bad order lable [label]" on it. You know we feared it wouldn't last the journey. So we had to get her another, *big* one to hold all her possessions,—also shoes for her & some other things—total, to be put on her account, $21.64. That with $17.00 for my linen has left me with $7.00. So please, dear, send me some more; enough for the journey home for the two of us.

I had a good time looking at wall-papers this morning. I have some lovely samples,—just what I want for several of the rooms, so that if the Phila. ones don't suit me exactly I will know where to go. It is also an advantage to see something beforehand and give my ideas as to the house time to form,—as with *you* and the *inaugural*! In fact I know so exactly what I want, that if Mr. Holmes doesn't agree with me,—so much the worse for Mr. Holmes! He will be dismissed with just so much less compunction!

I am *so glad* that you have made a satisfactory beginning on the inaugural, darling. I know how much there is to you and to all artists in a good beginning. And I am equally glad that you have no sense of hurry in doing it.

I am sorry to have given you the extra trouble about the sideboard; but by this time my letter has reached you expressing my entire satisfaction with what you did. We are *perfectly* well and I am having as good a time as is possible away from my darling. I won't say anything to Agnes about staying longer until you answer my last. With love unspeakable,

Your little wife   Eileen.

Please excuse incoherence, &c, People have been talking all about me. Why won't people provide their guests with ink!

Dear love to Father and the children. My greetings to Anna. I am glad to hear such good accounts of her.

ALS (WC, NjP).

¹ Presumably letters from Margaret Wilson, which are missing.

From Andrew Fleming West

Dear Wilson,   Princeton, N. J.   July 17 1902

The appended documents include all the official papers on the Graduate School to date,—excepting only the action recorded in the minutes of the Trustees. Notices of these are pasted in my record book & the Trustees Committee on the Graduate School in my desk. As you may possibly have occasion to refer to these papers during my absence,¹ I attach copies to this letter. I have written Magie saying you desire him to act in my place till I return.   Ever Yours   Andrew F. West

ALS (WP, DLC). Encs.: printed documents relating to the Graduate School of Princeton University, Dec. 1900-May 26, 1902.

¹ West was about to leave for Europe for the purpose, principally, of making such observations on European residential colleges for higher liberal studies as might be useful in preparing a report on the subject of a residential graduate college for Princeton. Abroad, he stayed longest in Oxford, where he devoted six weeks to a study of every aspect of academic life in that city. He also examined carefully, but for shorter periods, various colleges at Cambridge, the University of Berlin, and the École Normale Supérieure and the Fondation Thiers in Paris. Other institutions visited included Durham, Edinburgh, St. Andrews, Trinity College (Dublin), Leyden, Leipzig, Halle, Bologna, and the American School in Rome. For these and other details, see the article, "Professor West's Trip," *Daily Princetonian*, Jan. 14, 1903.

To Ellen Axson Wilson

My own darling,   Princeton, 18 July, 1902

Would you be willing to close the flues to the fire-places in the two spare rooms and in the night nursery? Mr. Matthews, the superintendent of the Little Hall work, whom I am consulting about the chimneys, thinks that very likely the tops we want, or at any rate tops very like them, could be put on our chimneys if in each chimney one flue,—and therefore one top,—could be cut out, or, rather stopped up to make more space for the others. That would give two of the chimneys three tops, or "stacks," each, and the other, the kitchen chimney, two. The trouble is that each of the chimneys lacks the necessary breadth by about three feet. The chimneys on Blair look small and slender because the building is so large.

Two of your letters came yesterday, by some whim of the mails, and so I am going without any at all to-day. The second letter recounted your painful experience in watching the two boys who came so near drowning. You poor darling,—what a day. I hope you have suffered no ill effects from it.

Here we are all well except poor Father. He is having one of his attacks to day,—one with the long, savage, wearing pain. It began about eleven this morning and is still unbroken (3 o'clock). The paregoric seems to have lost its effect.

The address advanced by a little more than its daily stint, nevertheless. My old hack mind is a most reliable beast, and can apparently be counted on to do its task whenever bidden! I am in the thick of its thesis now.

I find that the trouble with me when you are away is that I *think* too much,—even after I go to bed. There are none of these delightful periods in my day when I can go to you as a tired boy would go to his mother, to be loved and petted. The close, un-argued sympathy of these dear intervals is unspeakably sooth-ing and refreshing to me. Not that I am in the least worried or fretted over anything: my days are perfectly equable, but, ah, for my darling—   Your own   Woodrow

Of course you could choose any flues you pleased.

As for the day of your coming back, sweet love, if you come on the 28th we will still have several days together,—you may be sure that I will see to that. Because of money arrangements (made with the Treasurer) I *cannot* leave town before August 2nd. Does not that make a difference,—all the difference?   Your W.

ALS (WC, NjP).

From Ellen Axson Wilson

My own darling,   Clifton   July 18 [1902]

I find myself again reduced to a pencil, as the desk is in use; I hope it is not illegible when it reaches you.

We have had a visitor—all the morning,—Mrs. Hidden.[1] It has been a threatening day and we have been quietly sewing and chatting; but now it shows signs of clearing with interesting cloud and water effects. I must hasten out to walk on the beach so as not to miss them. It will be rather good fun to run away alone while Agnes is still busy with her dress-maker and to remain invisible until four o'clock! She somewhat mars our enjoyment of "nature" by her incessant flow of "languidge." I do well to write such spiteful things with a pencil if I must write them at all, eh? They will perish the sooner.

I am excessively disappointed about the chimneys! There is no denying it! What *is* to be done! I am very eager for tomorrow's letter.

The curve you draw of the side-board is charming. I am sure I shall like it as well as any.

I have been intending for several days to send you the enclosed cuttings, though doubtless you have seen one of them,—Andover's "*Answer*" (save the mark.) *Won't* Stockton be furious when *he* sees it! Did you ever see anything so utterly damning as the "inside view" of Andover given in the letter?[2] I also saw "Princeton's answer" but did not secure the paper; but of course you saw that.

By the way, I have only $3.00 instead of seven! I had forgotten that certain purchases were on Agnes bill and not yet settled!

I am *so* glad you are well and getting on well with the speech. How is Father? Give my dear love to him & the girls, and keep for yourself all you want, darling;—more than I dare express now even if I could. With passionate love,

Your own   Eileen.

Keep this "inside view." It may comfort poor Stockton to see it!

ALS (WP, DLC). Encs.: various clippings from the Boston *Herald*.
1 Isabel McKee (Mrs. William Henry) Hidden of Cambridge, Mass.
2 Princeton University, on July 2, 1902, issued a statement revealing that of the thirty-one students of Phillips Academy, Andover, who had taken the examinations in June for entrance to Princeton, twenty-two had been rejected for cheating. "This is the most flagrant cribbing that has ever come under our notice . . ," the statement said. "The cribbing in several instances was so obvious that only very ignorant students would have attempted it. . . . And, further, on the whole, the papers were easily the poorest lot we have examined this year." *New York Times*, July 3, 1902. This statement was widely circulated by the Associated Press and of course caused considerable comment.
The clippings from the Boston *Herald*, which Mrs. Wilson enclosed in her letter, included a letter to the Editor dated July 10, 1902, by Dr. Arthur W. Ryder.

He declared that, both as a student and later as a faculty member at Andover, he had observed that cheating of all kinds had been an accepted practice among most Andover students for at least twelve years.

The second clipping was a statement, dated July 13, 1902, by Alfred Ernest Stearns, Vice-Principal of Andover. Stung by Princeton's charges, he retorted that Princeton bore the major share of the responsibility for the incident because of its alleged policy of permitting anyone to take the entrance examinations, no matter how ill-prepared they were. Thus, he continued, poor students took the Princeton exams with no intention of actually entering Princeton but rather in hope that, by passing some of the subject tests, they could use these results to enter other colleges. Moreover, Stearns said, the professor sent from Princeton to conduct the examinations did so in a very lax manner, making no effort to prevent cheating.

The third clipping was an editorial in the *Herald* of July 15, 1902, commenting on Stearns's statement. This editorial suggested that the Vice-Principal was saying in effect that Andover students with no intentions of entering Princeton took the Princeton exams because they found them "dead easy." It also condemned the methods alleged to have been followed by the Princeton examiner. However, it pointed out that Stearns's statement did not really answer Ryder's charge that cheating was an accepted practice at Andover and called for "stern discipline . . . for the creation of a right public sentiment in the student body."

Mrs. Wilson's remark about Stockton Axson suggests that he may have been the Princeton professor who conducted the examinations at Andover.

From John Kelman[1]

Dear Sir,   Niagara Falls, N.Y.   July 18. 1902.

I had the great pleasure of hearing you at Northfield, on the fourth of July, and hoped to meet you on the fifth, but found to my regret that you were gone. I had an introduction to you from Professor [James] Seth[2] of Edinburgh, who asked me to convey to you his very kind remembrances. He has been a very good friend to me in Edinburgh, and he very specially desired me to give you his message. I have been hoping to have the chance of visiting Princeton, but find now that that will be out of my power. Will you allow me to say how deeply your words in Northfield impressed me, and how much they inspired me for my own work there on the subsequent days?

With kind regard

I am   Yours sincerely   John Kelman

ALS (WP, DLC).
[1] John Kelman (1864-1929), Presbyterian minister, pastor of the New North United Free Church, Edinburgh, 1897-1907; St. George's United Free Church, Edinburgh, 1907-19; and the Fifth Avenue Presbyterian Church in New York, 1919-29. Author of numerous books on religion in life.
[2] Identified in WW to EAW, June 25, 1899, n. 3, Vol. 11.

To Ellen Axson Wilson

My own darling,   Princeton, 19 July, 1902

I went over to Harry Fine's to dinner last night. Rudolph Schirmer[1] was there, a fine fellow, though you did not find it out when we lunched with them at West's. West and Dulles were the other guests. It was in part a consultation. We wanted Schirmer's advice as to the music on the programme at my inauguration. His taste and judgment in such matters are excellent. The evening went most agreeably.

This morning I got, I believe, to the mid-point in my address. The task grows harder as the argument thickens, but with the modest stint to which I confine myself I get through, copying and all, by half past eleven or twelve, and have time enough before lunch to grind off the business letters of the day,—so that I feel quite like a gentleman of leisure and realize that it is vacation. Fortunately, I never worked out the argument on liberal studies, which is the theme of my inaugural, before, never before having treated myself as a professional "educator," and so the matter is not stale but fresh and interesting. I am quite straightening out my ideas!—and that amuses me. I feel like a new prime minister getting ready to address his constitutents. I trust I shall seem less like a philosophical dreamer than Mr. Balfour does.[2]

Dear father had an unusually hard time,—a long, stubborn attack,—yesterday, and is weaker than usual to-day; but otherwise he seems all right again; and the rest of us are *in statu quo*. Of course there is a difference in my case. When I say that I am "perfectly all right" when you are away you understand that I don't mean it exactly. There is nothing the *matter*, but there is something *lacking*,—a sort of *blank* feeling, as if one of the *aims* of life were removed,—as if a function of the heart were suspended. I do not see how I am going to manage to go away myself almost at once when you come back, having just had a taste of what it means to be separated from you and yet to be in every pulse   Your own   Woodrow

Love from all to all.

ALS (WC, NjP).
   [1] Rudolph Edward Schirmer, Princeton 1880, president and son of the founder of the internationally famous New York music publishing firm of G. Schirmer, Inc.
   [2] Arthur James Balfour, who had become British Prime Minister on July 12, 1902.

From Ellen Axson Wilson

My own darling,   Clifton   July 19 1902

I do not think it would be a *very* serious matter to close the three flues you mention; *we* have had no occasion for a fire in them since the house was built. It would certainly be better to sacrifice those flues than to leave the chimneys permanently as they are with those hideous tin stove pipes,—if that is the only alternative. It would make *no* difference as regards the little yellow room for that chimney was not "cured" and will not draw as it is;—and the little night nursery is always well heated by the furnace. I am quite willing to decide it so. I suppose there *is* the alternative of some sort of terra cotta tops, and if you think it would be wiser to have them I will resign myself cheerfully,—though of course the brick chimneys are better to look at. Do you think with the reduced number that the stacks will have the desired tall slender effect on our smaller house? There is one comfort in the situation viz., that it will be much cheaper to build seven tops than ten. There is also one question that occurs to me, and we must be *very* sure of the answer before we proceed;—we must be *very* sure that the changes at the top do not alter the draughts in the flues and cause them to smoke again. Will it not make angles or other complications in the flues? Since Mr. Whitley[1] is to come almost immediately to examine the "Prospect" chimneys, (has he been written to?) I would strongly advise questioning him on this point. He will not charge for his opinion. You remember closing those very flues was what he planned to do first. The trouble seems to be that from the first too many flues were crowded into each chimney. I should be very glad if the matter ended in our getting the flues themselves in a safer condition. I am always uneasy about them, lined as they are with so perishable a stuff as sheet iron,—that can't stand coal fires at all. Query,—can we forbid tenants to use coal fires? It is of course only a question of time before they burn out; and doesn't that mean constant danger to the house from fire?

Since you insist, dearest love, there is nothing for me to do but to stay over till Monday, but oh how I hate it! More than ever since getting your letter today which reveals more plainly than the others that you are missing me. If you would only believe it I will have got all the good possible to me from the trip in the two weeks. I came to *rest* you know; how will it help me then if I grow *restless* to the point of nervousness. I am threatened with that already today & I don't see how I can prevent its being worse in another week. Oh, how I long for my darling.

I am so sorry about Father's severe attack. Give him my love & sympathy. Dear love to the children. Agnes is talking to Annie and sometimes to me so I hardly know what I am writing. Excuse everything.

I love you, I *love you*, tenderly, passionately, devotedly.

Your little wife,   Eileen.

ALS (WC, NjP).
1 Probably Joseph Whitley of Trenton, listed as a "steamfitter" in the Trenton
city directory for 1901 and as an "engineer" in 1903.

To Ellen Axson Wilson

My own darling,   Princeton, 20 July, '02

A passage in a letter which I received yesterday[1] will interest
you: "I remember you distinctly as an infant of a few months
old, very plump and fat and remarkably quiet. Dr. Woodrow
said to me once: 'that baby is dignified enough to be Moderator
of the General Assembly.'" What do you think of that as an example of a remarkably early case of "feeling one's oats"?

To-day feels like a genuine piece of midsummer with us, not
only because it's very hot indeed, but also because there is nothing
to do. The town is at last almost empty. When I have been to see
Mrs. Brown there will be nothing to do but sleep the rest of the
day. I am thinking of looking in on the Harpers late this afternoon; but meanwhile I shall sleep, sleep, sleep, to get ready for
the thick of my argument to-morrow. These are the days, ah,
these are the days when it goes hardest to be without my darling.
My heart has nothing to do but brood. It is sweet brooding: no
man had ever sweeter memories to dwell upon, let his thoughts
run near or far; but to think of what *all* our days together have
been is only to realize the more acutely what it is to have the
blessed succession even for a little while broken. You have stolen
so deep into my heart, dear, that you have become part almost
of my consciousness! I often marvel at the circumstances of my
life, there has been so much sweetness and unmarred good fortune in it, so much love and deep content, so much quiet delight. I thank God from the bottom of my heart! I have been so
trusted and loved and honoured. It is marvelous. What deep ingratitude it would be should I repine or fret at anything. And you,
my darling, are at the centre of it all,—all the greatest delights,
all the deepest content, centre in you. Nothing but happiness
has come to me since the day I married you. And, ah, how I delight in making love to you,—it is a sort of self-indulgence, for
all that is best in me seems to spring then into full consciousness
and joyous action. I wonder if I have brought you any such delights as you have brought me? *Can* it be as delightful to be mine
as it has always been and must always be to be

                                        Your own   Woodrow

All well.

ALS (WC, NjP).
1 It is missing.

To Winthrop More Daniels, with Enclosure

My dear Daniels,   Princeton, 20 July, '02

Would you feel like undertaking the collaboration proposed in M. Boucard's letter. I am manifestly not fitted for the part, even if I were likely to have time for it, and yet I have a decided weakness for seeing things of this kind come Princeton's way, and would be gratified if you could undertake it.

M. Boucard has translated two of my books and seems a man in excellent scientific standing and in request by the publishers. He is a Maitre des Requèttes in the Council of State; and Gaston Jèze is "Chargé de Cours à la Faculté de Droit" in the University of Aix-Marseille.[1] They have been joint editors of a valuable series of volumes under the general title Bibliothèque Internationale de Droit Public,—translations of foreign works.[2]

I hope you are all well and getting full refreshment.

Cordially Yours,   Woodrow Wilson

Will you kindly return the letter

ALS (Wilson-Daniels Corr., CtY).
[1] Actually, at this time Jèze was Professor at the University of Lille.
[2] For further correspondence about this matter, see WW to W. M. Daniels, July 31, 1902; and WW to W. M. Daniels, Sept. 6, 1902, with its Enclosure, M. Boucard to WW, Aug. 11, 1902.

E N C L O S U R E

From Max Boucard

Cher Monsieur,   Paris   le 3 Juillet 1902

Mon ami Jèze et moi désirons fonder une revue trimestrielle de science et de législation financières, dans laquelle seront traitées toutes les matières concernant les finances de france et de l'etranger.

Nous ne pourrions pas avoir de meilleur *collaborateur que vous*, et nous venons vous demander votre concours.

Il ne s'agirait pas d'un bien gros travail, mais seulement de quelques *chroniques très rares*, et de *beaucoup de documents* avec quelques courts commentaires, permettant au public français de suivre un peu le mouvement scientifique financier américain.

Nous serions très heureux de vous voir accepter notre proposition, et en même temps très reconnaissants.

Si, cependant, vous ne vouliez pas accepter, nous vous demanderions de nous indiquer quelque autre collaborateur de vos amis qui pourrait se charger de ce travail.

Voulez-vous bien, cher Monsieur, recevoir tous nos remercie-
ments anticipés et croire à mon bien sincère dévouément.

Boucard

ALS (WP, DLC).

From Ellen Axson Wilson

My own darling,   Clifton   July 20, 1902

We are having an unmistakably rainy day and very chilly too,
and are spending it, as we did yesterday, close about the fire
reading aloud, &c. We are having a pleasant time yet it is disappointing too, for had it been bright we would have had another
lovely drive today. Sunday is the only time Mr. Tedcastle has time
for it. I hope the cold weather here means that it is cool even in
Princeton.

While I think of it, I promised to ask you if you could give
Francis [Frances] Snell two or three letters of introduction to
people in Indianapolis. Of course you could to Mrs. Tarkington[1] at
any rate. Francis goes there this fall to be music teacher in a
"select" church school. She is a *very* fine girl, and attractive and
good looking too, so that I am quite willing to have you introduce
her as "a young friend of your wifes"! There is no hurry about the
letters though, I only promised to ask if there was anyone there
to whom you could write them.

By the way, you have told me nothing about the correspondence with "Harper" regarding the special edition.[2] I am very
anxious to hear all about it. Have you had any other interesting
letters? I suppose that is the only source from which there could
be any "news" in these quiet summer days. I really have nothing
whatever in the shape of a fact to communicate. I heard a,—
to me,—fresh witticism of [A. Lawrence] Lowells, which I must
record before I forget it. He said "Harvard *must* be the wisest
place in the world because the freshmen *bring* so much wisdom
to it and the seniors take none away"!

Give my dear love to Father and the children. I shan't say
much about my regard for *you*, lest I break down and cry here
"before fowk,"—for there is no denying the fact that I am homesick today,—fairly wearying for my darling's arms about me.

Your own   Eileen.

ALS (WC, NjP).
 [1] Laura Louisa Fletcher Tarkington, who had married [Newton] Booth Tarkington of Indianapolis, former Princeton student and friend of Wilson, on June
18, 1902.

2 She meant regarding Wilson's royalties on the subscription edition of *A History of the American People*, about which see WW to EAW, July 22, 1902, and Harper and Bros. to WW, Oct. 4, 1902.

From Richard Heath Dabney

My dear Woodrow: Nahant, Mass., 20 July, 1902.

Who would have "thunk" it?! Who could have guessed that an Illimitable Idiot would ever be selected as the President of a great university?! Yet the deed is done, and it's not "mesilf" that's sorry! I was too busy to write to you when the news reached me, and hence had to telegraph instead,[1] but hope that briefer form of congratulation showed as well as a lengthy epistle how rejoiced I was to hear of so well-deserved a promotion. In a way it was no surprise except in the apparent suddenness of President Patton's resignation. For I had heard for some time that you were slated as his successor. You have a great opportunity and will, I have no doubt, make an enduring mark upon Princeton & upon education in general. The only thing I don't like about it is that I fear you are now out of our reach if the Univ. of Va. should adopt the presidential system.

It is not difficult to imagine that you have your hands full of work, now that you have just assumed these new & great responsibilities, and I therefore hesitate considerably to make a request of you that will entail upon you any expenditure of time. And yet, knowing the sterling quality of your friendship, and knowing also how well qualified you are to assist me, I am going to ask you to do it. The circumstances are these.

In spite of the enormous load on my shoulders (all the History & Economics taught at the U. of Va.) I have made up my mind to attempt something more. I have been long hoping that the Univ. authorities could do something to relieve me of part of my burden, and I still hope for it. But I have concluded not to wait any longer, but to make an effort, at least, to do some historical investigation on my own account. Possibly I may kill myself in the attempt, but I am tired of deferring the attempt to the Greek calends. It has always been my desire to do some work in American History, but unfortunate circumstances of various sorts caused me to delay the attempt for years. It is probably too late for me to achieve even such success as might have been possible under more favorable auspices, but I believe it will be more manly to go ahead now and do what I can than to wait any longer for fortune's favors.

I have contracted with publishers to write a thick volume on Reconstruction by August, 1904.[2] It is a terribly short space of time, and I am fearful lest it was very rash in me to agree to it. I have been here at Nahant with my wife & baby & nurse for 3 weeks, & for the last 2 weeks have been going daily to Boston to study in the Public Library. Realizing how absolutely essential every saving of time will be, I have determined to ask you, who have had so much experience in historical investigation & writing, to give me a few points as to methods of saving time. I do not wish to burden you too greatly, but will be thankful for the smallest hint.

My idea of procedure is about as follows. First to read the most available works on Reconstruction (I have already read here your article in the Atlantic Monthly[3] with great profit, as well as the others in the series)[4] and then to construct a tentative outline or table of contents in the shape of chapter headings. Next, to go to the sources (as far as I can get at them,) of the subject of each chapter, and make as copious extracts from them as possible in the time at my disposal. Then to go over these extracts, study them thoroughly, and finally write my narration based upon them.

Is this your method? Or, do you make your extracts for the whole subject before writing anything at all?

Moreover, do you take notes in note-books, or upon separate slips of paper? The latter, I should think, would be the better way, so that the slips might be arranged after the manner of the cards in a Library card-catalogue. Would you sometimes make out more than one slip for the same item? For example, would you make out 2 slips for an extract from a speech, say, by Charles Sumner on the Ku Klux Klan, one slip headed *Charles Sumner*, & the other *Ku Klux*?

If you use slips, what are the most practical dimensions for them?

Can one buy any special receptacle for holding such slips? If so, where?

But I will not trouble you further—being confident that you will do what you *can* for me, and not wishing you to do one particle more than you are able without seriously interfering with your work.

This is a beautiful place & a cool one. I wish you were here.

With regards to Mrs. Wilson, I remain

Faithfully yours,   R. H. Dabney.

ALS (WP, DLC).

[1] His telegram is missing.

[2] Dabney never published this work.

[3] "The Reconstruction of the Southern States," printed at March 2, 1900, Vol. 11.

[4] See WW to EAW, Feb. 25, 1900, n. 2, *ibid*.

From John Grier Hibben

Grove Cottage

My dear Woodrow   Gorham, N. H., July 20 1902

Beth & I reached here last Tuesday, Jenny being detained in Elizabeth on account of her Aunt who is not well. We are expecting Jenny tomorrow. Mr Philbrook[1] was at first doubtful about arranging for a room that would [be] comfortable for you, & feared he might not have one by the first of August. He now informs me that he can give you a comfortable room on Aug. 1st. I have been waiting for him to give me some definite information before writing to you. I hope that nothing will prevent your joining us by Aug 1st. Beth is very desirous that you bring one of the girls with you. It would be delightful if you could arrange to do so. Give our love to Mrs. Wilson if she is now with you, though I suppose she has left by this time for Boston.

We will give you a hearty welcome when you arrive. In haste
Affectionately yours   John Grier Hibben

ALS (WP, DLC).

[1] Charles M. Philbrook, proprietor of Grove Cottage.

From Bliss Perry

My dear Wilson: Greensboro, Vt.   20 July, 1902

I was very sorry to miss the opportunity of seeing Mrs. Wilson at Clifton on Thursday. But an unexpected office emergency kept me in town. On my present schedule of keeping office hours every other week, I find the "busy" week is likely to be very crowded.

But I should like the long gossip with her or with you. Daniels, who is here, and Winans, whom I saw as he passed through Boston, have given me some side-lights upon "the great transaction" —as the pious hymn has it—of last month. I confess that my chief sensation, next to the pride and delight I felt in your election, was a sort of "ninth wave" of homesickness. I never used to like to fight in faculty-meetings, even for good causes, but I own that the thought of you sitting in the chair made me want to buckle on the old armor and take a hand. But you will always have enough men "on the Lord's side," I am sure, and better men than I am.

May Heaven bless you, & keep you from the woes that are lugubriously foretold for those of whom all men speak well. No-body, surely, ever entered upon such an office as yours with so general and sincere a chorus of praise and good wishes. And please think of me, in these Hyperborean regions, as waving my hat as heartily as any one can & wishing I knew how to sing "Old Nassau."

Take care of yourself, & let me know whenever you come within hand-grasping distance.   Yours,   Bliss Perry

ALS (WP, DLC).

To Ellen Axson Wilson

Princeton, 21 July, 1902

Of course, my sweet darling, if Mrs. T. and the place are getting on your nerves come away when you originally planned to come, –if I have not already spoiled things and made it impossible. It was for your sake altogether that I was insisting. I am *so* anxious that you should get *full* rest and refreshment before coming back to the labours of house decoration and preparations to move, and so convinced that two weeks were too short a time, that I felt justified in insisting, my heart to the contrary, notwithstanding; and, if you *can* get two more days of rest or ease out of it I hope with all my heart that you will. But act on your own best judgment in the matter. Ah, how I love you, and how gladly I would give all I have to make you happy and keep you well. I sometimes think that you are absolutely all that I have in the world that I really care for and live for!

I sent the cheque, dearest, before I got your second statement of your finances, and made the amount $21.64,–the amount of your purchases for Madge,–merely for convenience in my own book keeping. If it is not enough please send me a telegram, say-ing "Will come when I can," and I will send more at once.

It is still before lunch; the morning's stint is done and the morning's mail answered; is not that evidence of work done with-out strain? I am perfectly well. I do not greatly admire what I am writing: it seems rather commonplace as compared with what I had *meant* to say! but it will do for lack of a better inspiration.

Mr. Matthews seems quite certain that the deflection of the flues at the top of the chimneys will make absolutely no difference in the draught, and he speaks with the intelligence and confidence of a man who knows. It remains to be seen whether, even with a reduction of one flue, the remaining flues can be made big enough if the Blair Hall bricks are used for the stacks. Mr. Matthews has not yet completed his calculations and drawings. If not, I will go down to Phila. and see what can be had in terra cotta. We will not give it up now that we are in for it.

Ah, sweet one, how your messages of love comfort and delight me. Your love keeps me happy, keeps me alive—it is everything to me that I am *accepted* as   Your own   Woodrow

All well, and all send deepest love.

ALS (WC, NjP).

From Ellen Axson Wilson

My own darling,   Clifton, July 21 1902

I am glad you have had such a pleasant evening at the Fines. I am glad West and Dulles are still in town too. I hope you see a great deal of them all. I wish too that I could communicate to you my feeling about the Conovers[1] so that you would *enjoy* them as I do; for they I know are in town. I can't help believing that you would enjoy them if you took the pains to know them, that is to get on easy terms with them.

It is still a grey day but several lighter shades of grey than on the last two days, and it has not rained today. I think it is going to clear. There is to be a flower parade today in honour of the fiftieth anniversary of Swampscott, so the weather is of some importance. We are starting out to see it in half an hour.

We took a walk this morning, not on the beach for it was high tide, but among the villas above. I saw one very beautiful house in the style of ours but much more elaborate, and the chimneys all except one were perfectly plain square chimneys, yet they did not look badly. One rose from the outside of the house and was made from bottom to top of large *pebbles*, so to speak, such as those we brought home from Gloucester.[2] It was most picturesque. All the stone work of the house was of the same sort. The stone chimney too was plain and square. It suggested to me that perhaps we could do very well without "stacks"; almost anything would *do* that rid us of the stove-pipes. But I think if we have plain ones they should be like those here,—*very* plain;—to differentiate them in *some* way from the ordinary type. Those here are plastered over like the house. You will find that book of Mrs.

Aikens,—the English homesteads,[3]—on the library table. Suppose you look it over and see if you get an idea.

I can't tell you how glad I am, dear, that the work is going so well. It is the best thing I have heard for some days, it makes me very happy. With dear love to all & with a a [*sic*] *passion* of love for my darling.   Your little wife   Eileen.

I had to close hastily to get this mailed, for it is time to go to the *pee*-rade.

ALS (WC, NjP).

[1] Helen Field (Mrs. Francis Stevens) Conover and her children, Juliana and Thornton, of 10 Bayard Lane.

[2] That is, East Gloucester, Mass., where they had vacationed in 1898.

[3] She was probably referring to a book belonging to Sarah Elizabeth Noyes Aiken, widow of Professor Charles Augustus Aiken of the Princeton Theological Seminary, then living at 10 Bank Street. The Editors have been unable to identify it.

From William Libbey

My dear Wilson,   London Eng.   July 21/02.

I heard some days ago of the changes which had taken place in Princeton but have not had time to write you my feelings on the subject before now.

You can feel sure of my hearty congratulations and my earnest wishes for all success in your new sphere and your new responsibilities.

It is certainly a grand opportunity and one of which any man might justly feel proud, particularly after the flattering manner in which the introduction to it came, in your case. I only hope that your health will allow you to really *enjoy* the work.

You know my feelings on the subject of Princeton; I think that I can truthfully say that I have been willing to work for her at any hour of the day or night, and that shall be my ambition in the future. So, as long as you do not upset all of the "basal concepts" of a liberal education, and knock the bottom out of the Princeton curriculum for purely utilitarian purposes, you can count upon me as a steady lieutenant, since I should always be pleased to cooperate with you in any way to promote the true interest of our Alma Mater—but remember this I shall sometimes insist upon my right to call you "Tommy" as usual.

Please give our kind regards to Mrs Wilson and with best personal wishes believe me to be

                    Yours as ever   William Libbey

ALS (WP, DLC).

To Ellen Axson Wilson

My own darling,   Princeton, 22 July, 1902

Has Margaret written you how she went into Philadelphia, with Will.,[1] to see Dr. Küsel, and found that he had married the lady dentist who was his neighbour and gone off on a wedding journey, forgetting all about his engagement?[2] There's an amusing bit of news for you!

And, faith, you seem to need it. This dear, doleful little Sunday letter of yours that came this morning shows you ill enough off for amusement and for the occupations that cheer. I must admit, with contrition, that such homesick, woebegone letters please me. They make me feel so complacent and stuck up that it should be "all on account o' me,"—*such* a dear little lady, so sweet, so charming, and so fond of me! It's a delicious sensation. And yet, seriously, my precious one, how it cuts, and how it deepens my own longing, to have these sweet cries for home and for me come to my ears,—"wearying for my darling's arms about me," and how do you suppose your darling is feeling in that same matter?

I am ashamed to have to confess that I have not written to the Harpers about the terms of subscription to the "edition of looks." The more I thought of it the more it looked like having an unpleasant time with them with no substantial object in view. They *could* not change the terms of subscription when once the circulars had gone out without all sorts of embarrassments which have since been made plain to my thought,—and they would probably be forced to say "Very sorry, but we cannot." And so I have let it go, and must beg my dear little mentor not to be vexed.

The writing went a little hard to-day. I am nearing the wind-up and the difficulties, the artistic difficulties, seem to increase with every paragraph,—but at least there is only a (new) stint and a half to be done. Probably Thursday will see the thing finished. I will then read it to my friends and put it away to soak till September.

I love, admire, honour, dote upon you beyond measure, but not beyond reason,—the reason being your sweet self,—and am overwhelmingly   Your own   Woodrow

ALS (WC, NjP).
[1] William Dana Hoyt, Mrs. Wilson's first cousin, who was visiting his sisters, Mary Eloise Hoyt and Florence Stevens Hoyt, in Baltimore.
[2] G. C. Küsel to WW, July 20, 1902, ALS (WP, DLC), apologizes for the vagueness about his office hours which caused Margaret to make a useless trip.

From Ellen Axson Wilson

My own darling,   Clifton   July 22 1902

I have your two letters today—Sundays and Mondays as well as dear little Nell's and a postal from Margaret so I am rich indeed and very happy.

Did Margaret tell you of her trip to Phila? The time came when the dentist said he would be back and would like to see her, so she and Will went in unfortunately without writing first. So they had their trip for nothing for he was still away and on his *wedding tour*! He had married the woman dentist in the next apartment! Is'nt it funny.

I have plenty of money, dear, for my return trip. As for the day, you were so urgent that I thought I would *have* to stay until Monday and told Agnes so,—then all at once found I simply *couldnt* wait so long, and resolved to split the difference and come on Sat. That is settled now with Agnes and I will not open the question again. Madge & I, thinking you would expect us Monday, were rather planning a "surprise" Saturday night! But it is better, after this morning's letter to let you know.

Don't think poor dear Agnes "gets on my nerves"; it isn't as bad as that though she does bore me sometimes. The restlessness came altogether from the thought of my darling left there at home with his work, and Father ill, and nobody and nothing to amuse him and the heat, and *everything*! It really would be *intolerable* to stay away longer, with all these things tormenting my mind. You don't know how suddenly my spirits rose when Saturday was finally settled upon.

We spent the morning in Boston again and had a good time. The weather is cold, so it did not fatigue us but was really a spree. We saw more wall-papers both for "Prospect" and for Agnes "suite," also Gruby ware &c. &c., and the public gardens and more antiques.

They are all waiting for me to go on with a book they are reading so perhaps I had better stop. With dear love for all & love unspeakable for my darling Woodrow, I am always & altogether
                                  Your own   Eileen

As to the "terra cotta tops" see my yesterday's letter. I think a plain square brick chimney would do as well & of course be much cheaper. And *it* would hold the four flues. I have seen more of the rough stone chimneys, some of them *not* outside chimneys. They are *charming*. I wonder if they are expensive.

ALS (WC, NjP).

To Ellen Axson Wilson

My own darling,   Princeton, 23 July, 1902

To-day, at high noon, the address was finished, copying and all. How is that for a good journey for the faithful old hack? And, so far as I can see, I'm none the worse for wear. I am a bit tired, of course, for to squeeze the last passage out (which, by the way, is purely Wilsonian, not a touch Miltonic)[1] rather put me to it; but it's not much of a passage, after all, and the cost of production was not excessive. I shall not know just what the whole thing amounts to until you read it. Shall I know then, I wonder?

Mr. Matthews has made his drawings and calculations (of space) for the chimneys and finds that, minus one flue per chimney, they work out perfectly. He has now sent off to get the prices on the bricks. That looks hopeful, does it not. It's a pity, though, that we had to wait to make the house beautiful for somebody else! And yet, for the next decade or two we shall probably see chiefly, if not only, the outside of it, and the new chimneys will comfort us as artists.

Now and again an interesting letter straggles in, but my mail seems now to have dropped to the business level. There is "nothing doing." Yesterday I received, not the proofs from Pirie MacDonald,[2] but a finished photograph[3] from the plate from which the Review of Reviews portrait was taken.[4] I must say it seems to me excellent,—the true fact of the man, and I think that you will yourself like it, even if it isn't quite so "sweet" as your favourite of Pach's.

How good it seems that I should be within but little more than half a week of my darling! I think the writing of my address has emphasized the separation for me. I am so in need of your constant sweet sympathy and appreciation when I work. My fund of vitality and good cheer seems doubled when you are beside me at every turn of the day. Now I shall live in the delight of the expectation of your return. I live in you, my sweet one.

I am well, in excellent spirits, and rejoice every minute in being   Your own   Woodrow

All are well, and all send love to all.

ALS (WC, NjP).
[1] Wilson remembered Edmund Clarence Stedman's characterization of the closing paragraph of his Sesquicentennial address as "really Miltonic in nobility of cast and diction." See E. C. Stedman to WW, Nov. 22, 1896, Vol. 10.
[2] A New York photographer, identified in Albert Shaw to WW, June 12, 1902, Vol. 12.

3 It is printed in the photographic section of Vol. 12.
4 It appeared in the New York *Review of Reviews*, XXVI (July 1902), 37.

From Ellen Axson Wilson

My own darling,   Clifton, July 23 1902

Hurrah, we actually have some *blue* sky this morning again, and some sunshine, rather pale as yet but evidently determined to prevail! We began to fear we would not see his face again while we were here. It seems that it rained on "St. Swithin's day" and therefore was predestined to rain for forty days. But I think now our visit will end in the same blaze of glory with which it began.

And to think you have nearly finished the inaugural already! How remarkable! You certainly are wonderful! I can scarcely wait till Sunday to read it. *Arn't* you glad,—honour bright,—that I was insubordinate and declined to stay over this Sunday? *I* am so glad that my heart fairly sings. We would have had no Sunday together otherwise before you left. Now it is only three days more before I see my darling, and tomorrow I can say "it is the day after tomorrow." I am really happy and content now to wait—so long and no longer!

I am about to go out to return *calls, Calls!*—think of it! An unexpected infliction during a seashore outing! One was a Yale professor and his wife whose cottage is just back of this one,—Prof Gooch, a chemist.[1] He seems an attractive man,—but his wife! oh his *wife*! But two of the other women are really entertaining, Mrs. Hidden, you know, and a Mrs. Gooding, a large lively dame who has a pretty wit & whose manner is singularly laughter-moving, even more than what she says. I must write to the children this morning before I am called off, so will cut this a little, —not *very*,—short. With devoted, passionate love

                                        Your own   Eileen.

ALS (WC, NjP).
1 Frank Austin Gooch and Sarah Wyman Gooch. He was Professor of Chemistry at Yale.

To Ellen Axson Wilson

                                        Princeton, 24 July, 1902

Ah, my darling, how my heart leaped within me when I read this morning in your sweet letter of yesterday that you were coming to your lover on Saturday! My pulses have been quicker ever since. You may be sure that I have been urging you to stay longer only that I might see just so much more bloom in your cheeks: my love for you is not *wholly* selfish (if it is meself that says it!),—but, ah, the joy of this disappointment! It makes a *boy* of me again at a stroke! And the dear letter in which the good news came was pitched in so sweet a key of high spirits. Your love for me intoxicates me, my Eileen, mavourneen. It will make a man of me yet! Finishing my address yesterday did not give me one tithe of the sense of release that a single page of that letter gave me. Ah, sweetheart, *wont* you let me make *my* vacation two weeks and come back, a happy lover, to you? That will be true mercy. I hate going away more than ever, now that everybody is so durned polite to me as a great personage! Ah, how delicious it would be to go quietly off, just you and I, on a bridal trip together to some place where nobody would know us! We cannot; but merely to dream of it does me good!

Dear little Jessie is having a touch of diarrhoea, but it seems light and not worth consulting a doctor about. I've begun giving her the chalk mixture. Except for that we are all well. Dear Father is about as usual, and sits out-of-doors more than he did, the weather being for the most part delightful. We have had only one or two days that were at all trying to bear, and I, for one, do not feel the least need or desire for a change of air.

"Day after to-morrow"! How my heart sings to think of it, and of all that it means! What a sweet Sunday we will have together. Jessie and Nellie were so delighted with your letter, darling,—it was a pleasure to see how their faces shone.

Good-bye till you are in my arms again, and the happiest man in the Union,   Your own   Woodrow

Love from all to all.

ALS (WC, NjP).

From Ellen Axson Wilson

My own darling,   Clifton   July 24 1902

This is my last letter and, I find, my last sheet of paper; that shows careful calculation, does'nt it? I am certainly happy to know it is the last and that day after tomorrow I will be in my darlings arms. Ah *won't* it be good to be together. We will have a few days of perfect holiday-making since you can't leave at once. What shall we do to celebrate the completion of all that work,— the history and the inaugural? We must think of something.

Alas! that coy sunshine has deserted us again, it is a grey day and *cold*! I am shivering in my jacket. Surely it can't have been *very* hot even in Princeton with such constant low temperature here.

I am *very* much disappointed that Pirie McDonald did not send all the proofs. Won't you *please* write and ask him for them? It would be very strange, if there were no really good ones in all that lot, and I can't bear the idea of their being altogether lost, without our even seeing them. If that thing was really the best he can do then I don't think much of him as an "artist-photographer." Since I am to be back so soon suppose you do not finally settle about the chimneys until my return. You have not answered my questions about Mr. Whitley. I do *hope* he has been written to about "Prospect."

And will you ask them,—Mr. Pyne I suppose[1]—to write to Sloanes[2] about that discount on carpets *at once*, so that it will be arranged for before we go in early next week. We will certainly need as big a one as possible for Wiltons *are* $2.50 a yard.

I am perfectly well and thoroughly rested,—mind as well as body by a course of novel-reading which served well its purpose of taking me out of my own life temporarily with its, present, necessity for planning so many things. The planning seemed wearisome before I left home, but now I am looking forward to the work at Prospect next month with real eagerness and pleasure. I can already *see* the completed rooms in my mind's eye, and they are beautiful. I have the most *beautiful* tapestry paper for the guest room and Morris hangings in cotton to go with it, *so* artistic and so rich and dignified looking. The carpet will be solid mahogany red with one of our fine rugs at the hearth.

Give my dear love to Father & the girls. I love you, dear, more than tongue can tell,—you are the well-spring of all joy in my life; I am always and altogether,   Your own   Eileen.

ALS (WC, NjP).
  1 Moses Taylor Pyne and Cornelius Cuyler Cuyler had raised a special "Woodrow Wilson Fund" of $500 for the furnishing of Prospect, and Cuyler's secretary, Alexander Bell, administered the money. See WW to EAW, Aug. 27, 1902, and its Enclosure, Alexander Bell to WW, Aug. 23, 1902.
  2 W. & J. Sloane, carpets, 884 Broadway, New York.

To William Laurence Ledwith[1]

My dear Dr. Ledwith,   Princeton, 29 July, '02

I thank you most sincerely for your generous letter of yesterday.[2] Every such cordial greeting and hearty Godspeed from men whom I respect and who love Princeton goes to the quick with me, and adds to my strength to a degree it would be hard to estimate but which my heart distinctly registers. There is a vast deal to do for Princeton, but, surely, with such backing, there ought to be nothing but hard work needed to accomplish it.

I thank you both for the letter and for the generous impulse which led you to write it.

With much regard,

Sincerely Yours,   Woodrow Wilson

ALS (WC, NjP).
[1] Princeton 1874; D.D., 1895. Pastor of the Tioga Presbyterian Church of Philadelphia and Librarian of the Presbyterian Historical Society.
[2] It is missing.

From Richard Heath Dabney

Dear Woodrow: Nahant, Mass. 30 July, 1902

Many, many thanks for your letter.[1] I am too busy for a reply but send a p.c. to say how delighted I am at the prospect of seeing you in Boston soon. Let me know when you will be there. Any day will suit me. If you come before you can let me know, you will find me upstairs in the Public Library in the room known as the Barton-Ticknor Library.

Hastily but cordially   R. H. D.

API (WP, DLC).
[1] It is missing.

To Winthrop More Daniels

My dear Daniels,   Princeton, New Jersey, 31 July, 1902.

I am sincerely glad that you are willing to collaborate with M. Boucard.[1] It seems to me an interesting project, and I do not know of any man who is more entirely fitted to do what M. Boucard asks than you are. I will write to him at once.

I am glad, too, to hear of your camping trip away from all possible interruption. I hope it has set you up every way. My own vacation is to begin on Saturday. I hope to have all of August.

We have had only a scribbled note from Stock, to tell us of his arrival at his destination, and, alas! of an attack of grippe.

Mrs. Wilson joins me in warmest regards to Mrs. Daniels, yourself, and the Perrys.

Cordially and faithfully Yours,   Woodrow Wilson

WWTLS (Wilson-Daniels Corr., CtY).
[1] Daniels' letter is missing.

From James MacNaughton Thompson[1]

Dear Dr. Wilson: [Princeton, N.J., July 31, 1902]

On the eve of the day when you become Princeton's President, I wish to add my congratulations and heartiest best wishes to the many that will come to you. Somehow when I am talking with you, I find it difficult to express myself but the best means of denoting my pleasure is to tell you that, as an undergraduate, you were my "inevitable" President; the wish was father to the thought and now that the wish has developed into a reality, I am just about the most pleased alumnus in the great body of very much pleased alumni.

To feel that I can talk to you from time to time about the various matters that particularly concern my department, is a very great pleasure and satisfaction.

We have *such* a chance here in Princeton, in every way, and I want to do my share by pulling every pound in my power.

I presume letters, to you, are not without their drawbacks especially at this time when you are so heavily taxed, so please consider this note as tho' you had read my mind and that's the end of it; but I could not refrain from some expression of my feelings to you.

With renewed congratulations, and sincere well-wishing, believe me,   Faithfully yours,   J. MacN. Thompson.

ALS (WP, DLC).
   [1] Princeton 1894; Curator of Grounds and Buildings at Princeton University, 1901-1904.

From George Madison Priest[1]

Dear Dr. Wilson: Jena.   31 July 1902.

Your letter of the 15th inst. reached me last Monday and after careful consideration of the subject you broach, I am prepared to write an affirmative answer. It is naturally somewhat disappointing to return without having attained the object of my coming to Germany but since you think I can be of service to Princeton, I am glad to waive personal considerations and glad to serve, however imperfectly. I shall stay in Jena as long as possible for the good of work in hand but shall sail in time to reach Princeton by Sept. 16, wind and wave permitting, and conduct the entrance examination in German in the School of Science on that day.

Before closing allow me to take this opportunity to express my great pleasure and satisfaction in knowing that Dr. Patton's large mantle has fallen upon your shoulders, a pleasure and satisfaction which all Princetonians feel. In fact Craig[2] and Beam,[3] who are now in Jena, desire expressly to be included in the above "my."

With best regards to yourself and hoping that you will have no reason to regret the confidence which you suggest, believe me as ever—   Sincerely yours—Geo. M. Priest.

ALS (WP, DLC).
    [1] Princeton 1894, Instructor in German at Princeton University. He had spent the academic year 1901-1902 studying at the Universities of Leipzig, Marburg, and Jena. He received the Ph.D. from Jena in 1907.
    [2] Hardin Craig, born in Owensboro, Ky., June 29, 1875. A.B., Centre College of Kentucky, 1897; A.M., Princeton, 1899; Ph.D., Princeton, 1901. Instructor in English, Princeton, 1901-1905; Edgerstoune Preceptor in English, 1905-10. Professor of English, University of Minnesota, 1910-19, State University of Iowa, 1919-28, Stanford University, 1928-42, and the University of North Carolina, 1942-49. Visiting Professor of English, University of Missouri, 1949-61. Author and editor of many books and articles on English literature, including an edition of the complete works of Shakespeare. He also wrote an interpretive study, *Woodrow Wilson at Princeton* (Norman, Okla., 1960). Died Oct. 13, 1968.
    [3] Jacob Newton Beam, Princeton 1896, Instructor in German. He was studying for the Ph.D. at Jena and received the degree in 1903.

From Robert Harris McCarter

My Dear Tommy   Newark, N.J. Aug. 1, 1902
    I believe you are today assuming your new duties & responsibilities and I only write to wish you God speed & Every good fortune in this your new & exalted position. Dont feel that you must answer this. I know how busy you are, & want you to know I am thinking of you.
                    Ever your sincere friend   Robert H. McCarter

ALS (WP, DLC).

From Frank Howard Lord

Dear Tommy: New York, August 1, 1902.
    Billy Wilder handed me your letter *in re* portrait and I called on the photographer this forenoon. While the photograph is undeniably a fine one, the clothes are not dignified enough and I wish you would immediately have another photograph taken in your gown. The picture is for the drawing room of the Princeton Club[1] and is to be placed alongside those of Dr. McCosh, Dr. Patton and other presidents of the University, and you will therefore see the propriety of your being photographed in your royal robes.

We are fast completing the improvements to the Club House and hope to be in by the first of September, so I would very much like to have this matter fixed up before that time.[2]

Billy Wilder, Wood Halsey and myself foregathered at Billy Isham's last evening and enjoyed a heart-to-heart talk about sundry matters, among them your approaching coronation.

With very best wishes and hoping this will find you enjoying health and happiness, I am always,

Faithfully yours,   Frank H. Lord

TLS (WP, DLC).
    [1] The Princeton Club of New York, then located at 72 East 34th St.
    [2] The photograph is not now at the Princeton Club of New York; perhaps it was never made.

From Richard Watson Gilder

Private   (Lee)

My dear President Wilson,   New York, 2nd Aug. 1902

I should have said that if you can do this[1]—of course the remuneration should be of an extra quality.

The fact that you *are* to make a study of the subject leads me to hope that you can expand that study into something longer including a narrative of events,—the whole divisable into three parts, of say from five to seven thousand each.

Sincerely   R. W. Gilder

ALS (WP, DLC).
    [1] Gilder had apparently talked recently with Wilson about the possibility of a brief biography of Robert E. Lee for serialization in the *Century Magazine*.

Francis Landey Patton to Moses Taylor Pyne

My dear Sir: [Princeton, N.J.] August 2, 1902

I am in receipt of your kind favour of July 30 advising me of the arrangements that had been made for the payment of my salary.[1]

I desire to express to you and through you to those who have been associated with you in this matter my very grateful appreciation of the generous treatment I have received through means of which my retirement from the Presidency of the University has been attended with so much comfort.

It is I assure you my sincere desire to serve the University under the new administration to the best of my ability.

I am very faithfully yours   Francis L. Patton

ALS (Patton Letterpress Books, UA, NjP).
¹ These "arrangements" are the subject of much correspondence in Vol. 12.

Francis Landey Patton to Cuyler, Morgan and Company

Dear Sirs: [Princeton, N.J.] August 2, 1902

I am in receipt of your esteemed favour of July 31 advising me that the sum of $31,500 has been placed to my credit on your books.

I shall be seeking an investment for most of the money in the near future and shall be glad to have it remain on deposit with you in accordance with your kind suggestion until I need it from time to time for the purpose referred to.

I shall probably give myself the pleasure of calling at your office in reference to the matter on Monday August 4.

I am very truly yours   Francis L. Patton

ALS (Patton Letterpress Books, UA, NjP).

To Ellen Axson Wilson

My own darling,   Clifton, Mass., 3 August, 1902

Here I am, safe and sound, and very comfortable. I am sorry to say I have not seen Mrs. Tedcastle yet. The doctor has ordered her to keep to her room and give herself a complete rest cure, in order to avoid, instead of having to cure, acute nervous trouble. It seems that the adhesions are giving her trouble again, and the doctor fears that, if she does not surrender to their warnings now, she may have a complete breakdown. The rest are very well.

I was a little wayworn when I arrived last night, but was quickly rested, and am feeling "perfectly all right" to-day. My trains were late all the way along,—even the train to New York, which I never knew to be noticeably behind time before, was half an hour late getting it [in]. Something seemed to be wrong with the engine: they stopped several times to work at it. I had something of a rush, therefore, to catch the twelve o'clock train at 42nd. St.,—and *it* was half an hour late at Boston. Because it was Saturday, I suppose, we took on five extra coaches, fell behind at our stopping places, and could not make up lost time. I felt very badly at the thought of making Mr. Tedcastle miss his 6:03 train; but he didn't miss it! Not he! Finding that my train was reported half an hour late, and knowing that I could shift for myself, he went on out home. I went over to the North Station very demurely, took something to eat (chicken broth and sliced peaches!), and boarded the 7:50 for Clifton, where I found Mr. Tedcastle and my trunk waiting for me on the platform.

This morning we drove over to Nahant in a sea fog, which only now and again lifted to let us see the water about us, but which did not prevent our seeing the charming roads and country houses. I found Heath Dabney, and made an appointment to meet him to-morrow in Boston and take lunch together. It was a real pleasure to see him again.

I can't get over my guilty feeling, my pet, at being away. I am so well, so able-bodied, so fit for physical work, so free of even the thoughts of literary work, that there is no real, only a theoretical reason, for my taking a vacation, and it seems to me a case of mere self-indulgence. And yet,—and yet,—I don't know, either. To judge by my present feelings, it is no self-indulgence to be away from the one person in all the world whom I perfectly love. I am *painfully*   Your own   Woodrow

ALS (WC, NjP).

From Ellen Axson Wilson

My own darling,   Princeton   Aug 3 1902

I enclose the notes,—though I don't know why there should be *two*. Mr. Howe[1] said he could not send a letter of credit because people have to sign their *own* letters of credit; that the thing to do was to get a draught on Berlin or Dresden, then Sister Annie if she wished could buy her letter of credit there. So I came back to the house and told Father and he said it was all right; to get the draught on Dresden, which I did. There is a receipt which I am to keep, so that if the letter miscarries we can recover the money from this end. I will write to her and enclose the draught as soon as I finish this.

The passage for each of them,—full fare for a child over ten,— by the slower steamers,—about eight days,—was $80.00 *before* the first of Nov. and *after* that time $65.00, a saving of $30.00. So Father after reading her letter, decided to send the $130.00. He said he thought she *wanted* to stay until Nov. and that anyhow it would be foolishness to waste $30.00! The draught therefore is for $930.00 [$130.00]—only it is in marks.

I saw Mr. Thomson[2] about Mr. Cope[3] and then went on to Prospect about the shades. Mrs. Patton was very kind and nice insisting upon taking me *all* over the house. There are fire places in all the bedrooms;—and there is no furnace heat *at all* in our room! Isn't that dreadful? The "state bed" room is a beautiful room, if anything larger than the study. A great many of the Patton things are out and they are ready to move the rest, but the other house isn't ready; the plumbers are detaining them. They hope to be out in a few days, but Mrs. Patton insists that in the meantime the workmen should begin on the rooms that are empty; so I will have them measured at once and the paper ordered.

I certainly had a busy day yesterday—was out all the morning seeing to these various things, and in the afternoon packed the children's trunks[4] and looked after Father, for the poor dear came down with an attack. It was not a bad one however, he declined to take any paragoric, and is all right today. We are all well of course. Equally of course I am lonely, but happy to think you are actually *resting* at last.

How I wish I hadn't to send you these silly letters![5] Don't you think I might just tell people like those Geo. & Tex. stupids that you are absent,—and inaccessible? My love to all the family. Tell Agnes I will send the receipts[6] just as soon as I can find time to copy them.

With love unspeakable, believe me, darling, always and altogether,   Your own   Eileen.

ALS (WC, NjP).
  [1] Edward Howe, president of the Princeton Bank.
  [2] James MacNaughton Thompson.
  [3] Walter Cope, the distinguished architect of Philadelphia, a pioneer in the development of collegiate Gothic in the United States, who had designed Blair Arch, Blair Hall, and Stafford Little Hall at Princeton.
  [4] The three girls would soon join Mary Eloise Hoyt at Bay Head, N. J.
  [5] They are missing.
  [6] That is, recipes.

From Jenny Davidson Hibben

My dear President Wilson,   Shelburne [N.H.] August 3, 1902.

This is to ask you *when* you are coming to Shelburne? We wish to know because we want very much to see you and also because Mr. Philbrook whose rooms are in great demand would like to know from what date to reserve your room.

We have found a nice quiet one for you, where you may rest undisturbed. The country is heavenly, the people *most* "morally attractive"—the house plain and comfortable. The Westcotts are here & are charming, & we hope soon to have you.

Your address I have found in the Boston Herald—where your plans for August were chronicled. I hope that it is correct, and that this reaches you.

We are very well. Jack shaved off his mustache in July, looked like Dr. Patton, & has promptly allowed it to grow again, & is beginning to look like himself. I hope that Mrs. Wilson's weeks at the seashore benefited her—she will have busy months now I know. Jack sends his love to you, and I am, my dear President, with all good wishes for a happy and successful administration,

Ever yours,   Jenny Davidson Hibben

Address care Mr. Chas Philbrook   Gorham, N. H.

ALS (WP, DLC).

Two Letters to Ellen Axson Wilson

The Thorndike

My own darling,   Boston, Mass   4 August, 1902

I have not deserted the Tedcastles and moved into town. I have come in to meet Heath Dabney, am a little early (I don't like to interrupt his work at the Public Library until lunch time is at hand) and stop in here for a chat with the sweetest, most charming little woman in the world. How long it seems since I left her! Of course the mail brought no letter from her this morning,—it's too soon, and I did not expect any,—it brought only a roll of proof[1] and the package from Marsh & Burke[2]; and these first days always seem like days of isolation. The change of scene adds to the sense of distance and of separation, and a fellow's heart cries out for home.

They are certainly kindness itself at the Tedcastle's; the position of the house is ideal; there is everything there to make me feel perfectly comfortable and at home; and I am happy. The holiday quietness of mood is on me, too, and all my faculties are at rest. But the wrench is too recent, my heart is still sore with the parting. It will take me several days to get my equilibrium and adjustment. My pulses can't beat full until I am with you again, but things will be as well appointed with me as I deserve.

I saw Mrs. Tedcastle yesterday afternoon for a few minutes just before tea,—in her own room. She looked very well indeed, I thought, and of course talked without effort, or any evidence of nervousness. She is certainly *perfectly* hospitable, and her thoughtfulness for my convenience and comfort are shown morning, noon, and night. I find the young ladies every way sweet and admirable. There is a Miss Curtin[3] visiting Miss Frances,—a Barnard College woman,—who is also most interesting and very attractive. Mr. Tedcastle is,—himself!

Give unmeasured love to all, my sweet one, and dream of me all you can. I live upon your love; thoughts of you keep me young and bouyant. Love me as I love you!

Your own   Woodrow

[1] Of *A History of the American People.*
[2] Princeton druggists.
[3] Margaret Higgins Curtin of Hoboken, N. J., B.S., Teachers College, Columbia University, 1902.

My own darling,   Clifton, Mass., 5 Aug., '02

No letter this morning! The mails are provokingly slow and tardy, and are no doubt treating you the same way at your end of the line. It will be easier for our hearts when we are in regular communication again!

Mr. and Mrs. Pollard[1] called last night, with a naval lieutenant of quite unintelligible name; and so did Professor Gooch. Mr. and Mrs. P., Mr. Tedcastle, and I were in one group, Professor G., the young ladies, and the lieutenant in another. I do not know the professor as yet any better than you do, therefore. Mrs. Pollard is very good to look at, has attractive manners, and laughs at one's jokes with a hearty abandon which is wholly to her credit. I subscribe to your good opinion of her, and shall take pleasure in returning the call. Professor Gooch, being so near at hand, will be easily got at.

After writing to you yesterday I went to the Public Library, looked about a little at its paintings, and then found Dabney in his quiet retreat upstairs hard at work. We went off to lunch together, at a place with a *very* scant bill of fare, and then sat the rest of the afternoon in the open court of the library talking over things new and old: the old days, college work, politics, history, till it was time for him to catch his boat and me my train. I enjoyed it very thoroughly and in true holiday spirit. I had intended to make some little purchases, but it was five o'clock before I got down to the shops, and they were closed! You see how irresponsible I have become already, like a man with nothing to do or to think of.

I feel very well and vigourous,—and wish for you with every breath I draw. It is almost painful, almost provoking, at this distance to think how sweet you are, how altogether engaging and desirable! How a man can have such a wife as I have and *leave* her for so much as twenty-four hours, is something that quite passes my comprehension. He must be under the stress of some direful necessity (as I am *not*) or he must be a fool! Ah, darling! how I love you!   Your own   Woodrow

Love, a great deal of love, to all.

ALS (WC, NjP).
    1 Probably Alonzo Wilder Pollard, Harvard 1883, and Elise Welch Pollard, of Brookline, Mass. He was a member of the firm of Wood, Pollard & Co., importers and grocers.

From Ellen Axson Wilson, with Enclosure

My own darling,   Princeton   Tuesday morn. [Aug. 5, 1902]
    I am distressed to think that you must go one day without a letter but it was unavoidable. A truck broke down across the car tracks on 23 St. yesterday and delayed the cars for half an hour. I finally got out and walked half a mile to the Ferry but missed the boat and my train by ten minutes. So I reached home at bed-time and *very* tired; so as I could not get the letter mailed any-how I did not sit up to write it but am doing it early in the morn-ing instead. The children got off in good shape. I found all the Harpers going to Bay Head so they took charge of the children and Madge did not go. I think it helped the children over the crisis to have the "cute" little Harper babies[1] to amuse them on the way. Even Nellie was more philosophical than Margaret was. But, dear me!—it is lonely here without them,—not to mention *you*!
    Your two dear letters have just come, and *how* good it was to get them! I am sorry Agnes is laid up but it will make you all the more completely your own master while there. I don't see why you shouldn't have the most absolute and refreshing rest and get lots of good out of it. These tiresome letters are the only draw-back. Won't you,—*to please me*—let them accumulate and just once or twice while there go to a stenographer and do them all up? I dare say you could do it just over at the hotel. If you were not teased daily with them you would have nothing to worry you, —for *I* am doing *finely* and am enjoying the business. Had a real good time yesterday, but can't tell you about it now as I am ex-pecting Mr. Thomson every minute & there are some business letters to write.

I love you, dear, devotedly, passionately,—I am altogether
Your own　Eileen.

Mr. Osborn's mss. has not come; shall I send it on when it does?

ALS (WC, NjP) with WWhw notations on letter.
[1] Isabel Westcott Harper, born Dec. 1, 1896, and George McLean Harper, Jr.,
born Sept. 19, 1899.

E N C L O S U R E

From Henry Fairfield Osborn

My dear Wilson:　　　　　　　　　　　　New York, August 2, 1902.

I want to extend to you my warm congratulations upon the
chorus of welcome which your election has aroused in all parts
of the country. Your task will be an easy one because of the
enthusiastic and united support of the alumni and I trust of the
general public. I feel confident that the Augustan age is opening
for Princeton; and you may always count upon me as one of
your warmest supporters.

I feel that there is a vast amount of work to be done, especially
in the curriculum, in the faculty, and in the social life of the
students. As regards the last, I feel especially that the Freshman
and Sophomores should receive far more attention, particularly
as regards their surroundings in boarding houses, etc. The food
is bad, and many young men form bad habits in early years in
consequence.

The course of study is still more important. I venture to send
you a random discourse on this subject which I have been composing during the last few months, and which represents the
results of years of thought on the matter. I hope it will be of some
service to you; yet I have no doubt you have already reached very
similar conclusions in certain directions.

I have thought of printing it for private distribution among certain of the trustees and faculty, and then omitting all references
to Princeton and publishing it with some modifications as an
article either in the *Century* or *Atlantic*. What do you think of
this?[1]

You see I am very severe on the Princeton course of study,
and have not stopped to praise the many strong points. As you
know, I am deeply interested in the College; and all my criticisms
are written in the most friendly spirit.

With kindest regards to Mrs. Wilson, and hoping to see you in
September, I am

Always faithfully yours,　Henry Fairfield Osborn

P.S.

Will you kindly hold this manuscript till early in September, when it may be returned to Garrison.[2] H.F.O.

In the meantime kindly show it to West before he sails.

For the English Department—the youngest brother of Prof. Bliss Perry,[3] formerly at Lawrenceville, now at Williams College is a fine fellow & doing admirable work, I am informed.

TLS (WP, DLC).
   [1] He published it anonymously under the title of *The Mediaeval and the True Modern Spirit in Education* (Lancaster, Pa., 1903).
   [2] Or Garrison-on-Hudson, where he had a summer home.
   [3] Lewis Perry, A.B., Williams, 1898; A.M., Princeton, 1899. Master of English and Elocution at the Lawrenceville School, 1899-1901, at this time Instructor in English and Elocution at Williams College. He was later Professor of English at Williams and, from 1914 to 1946, Principal of Phillips Exeter Academy.

From Ellen Axson Wilson

My own darling,   Princeton, Aug 5 1902

   This is the second letter today!—it is the only way I can manage to get one off tomorrow since I go to New York on the 9.05. I hope after this I won't have to make another trip for some little time. That will finish up the draperies and furniture and get some linen and muslin curtains to be working on. The china, glass and silver I wont get of course until I see *exactly* how much has been spent on other things.

   Mr. Thompson and I had a conference at Prospect today and settled many things. The bathroom problem works out beautifully. The lovely little tower-room does not have to be sacrificed. Indeed *it* is a *long* way from the guest room, with the third story staircase in between. But the little room over the entrance, which is smaller than the tower room, can be cut in two and a bath room made *connecting* with the state room,—a door cut in the partition wall. It would be our bath room when there were no guests, for there are, oddly enough, two hall doors already to this little room, so that it could be cut in two with the greatest ease. Does that suit you? We could have a *good* bath room without sacrificing any chamber, for the dressing room connecting with Paul's room[1] has also a hall door and is just the right size and shape for a bath room, but it would be a Sabbath day's journey from the "state room." Paul's is the room over the breakfast room. Tell me which of these two plans you prefer.

   Mr. Thompson discouraged me by saying that we could not actually move into the house before the *first* of Oct! It is the steam work that is going to take the time. But he thinks we will find it much easier in the long run to have it all done at once before we "settle." If you think that is an impossible program for you now is the time to make your protest to him. All this work does not mean steam *heat* this winter but only empty pipes and radiators! But it *would* be a great thing not to be torn up with it later.

I am sorry, dearest, to fill a letter with business; it couldn't be helped. I won't do it often. Mrs. Fine came in and spent the evening so that I began writing at bedtime, and I am so tired I must go to bed now.

By the way, I wanted to get all bills together to settle, and in looking for them among the loose letters on your desk I came upon the enclosed,[2] and I wondered if you had thought of Wm. Garrott Brown in connection with them,—with the Charleston one especially of course. Did you recommend anyone for them? How would you like to ask Mr. Brown to come out to Clifton to see you? Mr. Osborn's mss. has come.

We are all perfectly well. Father seems very serene and cheerful. The weather is good,—nights perfect. I love, *love, love* you, my *darling*, beyond all words, I am in every heart-throb.

Your own   Eileen.

ALS (WC, NjP).
  [1] That is, the room formerly occupied by Paul Richard Patton, Dr. Patton's son.
  [2] Harrison Randolph to WW, July 12, 1902.

From Pirie MacDonald

My Dear Doctor: New York   Aug. 5/02
   With the exception of the one submitted none of the first lot were up to the scratch I had set, and I hope that you will forgive me in not sending the others.

   I want very much to make some studies of you in your gown and will be very glad to make some others in your private capacity for Mrs. Wilson at that time.

   I will be away Aug 7-21[.] Wont you arrange to come in for an hour some day soon?   Very truly   Pirie MacDonald

ALS (WP, DLC).

To Ellen Axson Wilson

My own darling,   Clifton, Mass., 6 August, 1902
   I enclose the note. The *date* will have to be written in the day you obtain the loan. Thank you for attending so well to the busi-

ness for sister Annie. What you did seems to me very satisfactory in every way.

If Mac. Thompson succeeds in getting the steam in this autumn at Prospect the defect with regard to our bed-room will, of course, be remedied. By the way, when you next see him will you not ask him to make a note to run the steam pipes into the *third* storey of the tower so that that room can be used; and, if you decide to divide the second storey tower room, to get a bath room out of it, remind him to arrange for heating both halves of it. The same would apply to any other room you should decide to cut in two.

Your sweet letter comforted me greatly, my pet. It came yesterday afternoon just as I was starting for Salem. I had no errand there, except to make the one or two little purchases I had *meant* to make in Boston; but went over chiefly for amusement and an outing. We are having fogs and dull, showery weather for the most part, but the afternoons have shown an inclination to be clear and bright. I don't much care what the weather is, you know. I rather welcome the rain. Yesterday I had a snug snooze of a couple of hours, the fruit of sheer laziness, without any rain at all for pretext. I think a good deal about college affairs these quiet hours, but not to fatigue. The right to *plan* is so novel, the element of vexation, the sense of helplessness we had for so long, is so entirely removed, that it is a pleasure to think out the work that is to be done. If it did not have the incalculable money element in it, there would be no touch of worry about any of it. There is something, too, in doing the thinking where there are no Princeton people! When I get with the Hibbens and Westcotts I shall stop planning and insist upon playing, taking nothing seriously! How fine it is that nobody about here knows or cares about universities and their presidents! By the way, Mr. Pollard turns out to be a Harvard man, and a very intelligent dissentient from Mr. Elliott's [Eliot's] ideas, bred under them though he was.

Ah, my sweet one, what a comfort it is merely to write words which you are to see! It seems somehow to bring me *almost* into your presence. I almost see your dear, loving eyes as you read, and the precious love in them for   Your own   Woodrow

A great deal of love to all.

ALS (WC, NjP).

To Richard Watson Gilder

My dear Mr. Gilder,   Clifton, Massachusetts, 6 August, 1902.

If this were to be the second year of my presidency, I might think the thing a possibility; it being about to be the first (as they say in the Latin grammars), I have too much knowledge of what lies before me to attempt what you suggest. It is very kind of you; I know how to appreciate the compliment; but how I am to get even the address[1] written is more than I now see. If I come with credit through that, I shall be grateful.

Thank you very much; forgive me for declining; and believe me,

With warmest regards,

Faithfully Yours,   Woodrow Wilson

WWTLS (Berg Coll., NN).
    [1] An obvious reference to his inaugural address, a draft of which he of course had completed.

From Richard Heath Dabney

Nahant, Mass.,
My dear Woodrow: Wednesday Night [Aug. 6, 1902].

I had to make such a rush on Monday to catch my boat (which I succeeded in doing) that I couldn't make any arrangements with you. I now scribble a hasty line to ask that you come over Sunday & take dinner with us. I should like very much for Mrs. Dabney to meet you, and I am hankering to see you again myself. I enjoyed our conversation so much the other day & was so stimulated by it that I could hardly sleep at all that night! I was thinking about our topics of discussion & didn't care much whether I slept or not. Next time I can be cooler about it. Do come if you can, & drop me a line letting me know when to expect you & whether by boat or "barge" as they call the omnibus from Lyme to Nahant. If you have not walked out on the Nahant rocks, you have still a treat in store.

Hastily but cordially,   R. H. Dabney.

P.S. Come as early in the day as possible & stay as late as ditto.[1]

R. H. D.

ALS (WP, DLC).
    [1] About Wilson's visit to the Dabneys, see WW to EAW, Aug. 11, 1902.

From Hopson Owen Murfee[1]

My dear Sir: Marion, Alabama.   6 August 1902

I write to ask you to visit Alabama during the next autumn, winter, or spring in the interest of the cause of education. Education is now beginning to receive attention throughout the South; and, in this state especially, there is need of intelligent interest and a proper public sentiment. To insure this we desire to secure the aid of those who have rendered distinguished service to the cause in other sections of the country, and who can speak from experience and with the voice of authority. The leaders of education and public affairs in Birmingham, Huntsville, and Mobile have already assured me of their active support in the matter, and have promised to raise the necessary funds for the cost of addresses by eminent educators. In Montgomery and Anniston also we purpose to make similar arrangements.

It is our earnest desire to have you come to Alabama in this connection. Especially do we desire to have you come to deliver an address at the Institute before our students. The chief function of the Institute is to train boys for the great universities, and to induce them to go on to these universities for advanced study. We believe that an address from you will be a source of lasting inspiration to our boys and of inestimable service to the cause of education in the state. This address we should like to publish in the quarterly bulletins of the Institute for distribution throughout the South. In addition to our one hundred or more boys, the audience here will contain over three hundred girls from the two schools for girls in Marion.

I sincerely hope that you will be able to come South to speak throughout the state and at the Institute. I shall be glad to arrange the details of your tour to suit your wishes.[2]

Yours very respectfully   H. O. Murfee
Assistant Superintendent

TLS (WP, DLC).
[1] Assistant Superintendent of the Marion, Ala., Military Institute.
[2] Wilson's reply is missing; however, he declined Murfee's invitation.

From Penrhyn Stanley Adamson[1]

My Dear Professor,   Dundee Scotland   Aug 6th 02.

The news of your election has just come to me, and I cannot refrain from letting you know the affectionate memories I have of our new president.

Over here, in Scotland one has time to think. Among these hills I find that memories grow mellow and dear. One that I have learned to love is that of a platform whereon stands a lean man buttoning his coat preparatory to the fray. Alas, I am idle minded! I recollect one morning wondering—as I watched the long fingers reaching for their accustomed grip—wondering, what would happen should someone surreptitiously cut away the buttons. The idea fa[s]cinated me and, in my mind's eye, I developed the picture; it was very funny and I chuckled. Suddenly I felt that the room was very quiet, and looking up I found the professor's eye fixed sternly upon me; I had laughed aloud.

So it is that each one takes something different from your class-room. Some—the immortal few, perhaps—the makings of great jurists: many the basis of good citizenship, and all a finer sense of right—a clearer sense of honour, and a deep respect and love for you my dear Professor.

I am,   Sincerely and indebtedly   Yours
                          P. Stanley Adamson.

ALS (WP, DLC).
    ¹ Penrhyn Stanley Adamson, of Dundee, Scotland, was an "academic special student" at Princeton from 1899 to 1901. He later became well known in the United States under the name of "Penrhyn Stanlaws" as an illustrator, portrait artist, playwright, and motion picture director.

To Ellen Axson Wilson

My own darling,   Clifton, Mass., 7 August, 1902

You must not worry about the letters you have to forward to me. It is rather a relief to have *some*thing to do in the morning,—and with my typewriter it is no effort. It *would* be a burden if I had to answer them all with my pen; but, doing nothing for the rest of the day, it is rather a comfort to have an hour's work or so with which to give zest to the loafing that follows. I could enjoy nothing if I were to let the letters accumulate.

I forgot yesterday to give you the safe combinations[.] The mortgage which is to be deposited as security with the note is in the little wooden drawer in the safe next the window, which is opened as follows: Turn the disc to the right till the mark at the top is opposite 79; then in the reverse direction till 22 reaches the mark *the third time*; then to the right again until 90 is reached *the second time*; then in the reverse direction until it stops. The handle will then turn and the door open.

There is something in the other safe which Mac Thompson may ask for: the forms for invitations for my inauguration with which West furnished me. They are alongside my inaugural address, between dark cardboards held together by a narrow band of rubber. That safe is opened thus: Turn to the right several times (the number is immaterial) till 84 is opposite the mark; then the other way till 17 is reached *the third time*; then to the right again until 87 is reached *the second time*; then the other way to 32 *the first time*, when the door will open if you turn the disc, which is also the handle, to the right again till it stops.

Yes, dear, please send me Osborn's Mss. when it comes. I may get a good deal out of it.

It makes me deeply uneasy, my pet, to hear of the long, fatiguing days of business, in town and at home, on which you have entered. As you love me take it quietly and slowly. I know how lonely you will feel with the children away, and how free you will feel yourself to work as you please; but *remember me* and prove your love for me in the way in which it is hardest for you to prove it.

All send you the most affectionate and admiring messages. I am perfectly well, having a good, sleepy time, and dead in love with you.   Your own   Woodrow

Dear love to Madge and dear Father.

ALS (WC, NjP).

From Ellen Axson Wilson, with Enclosures

My own darling,   Princeton, Aug. 7 1902.

I have had two delightful letters since I wrote you last;—letters which have made me very happy because they conveyed the impression that you were really enjoying yourself and getting thoroughly rested and relaxed. You *dear* thing! *How glad* I am to think of you actually having time to loaf at last,—history and speech both done. Everytime I think of it, it gives me fresh pleasure as if I had just shaken off a great load myself.

I am having a good time too. The weather is *delicious*—cool and bright, and I am thoroughly enjoying the business I am about.

By the way, was the 4th Ave. man to *cover* the furniture,—drawing-room—that we bought from him? If it has not been settled so, would you give him the job or let Wanamaker send up there for it and do it? I should say it would depend a little on whether it was in the first man's bargain to pack and ship the goods without extra charge. But then I suppose Wanamaker would do the same.

Wasn't that a nice letter from Finley? And this one from Wilbur is'nt bad; is'nt he the drinking one. Who is this "Arthur Goodrich" who wrote you from the "World's Work"? It is odd he should have the same name as my old friend.[1] Did you ever meet him? Won't you try a Boston photographer for the "Worlds Work"? They make such good reproductions in that magazine, that I should like them to have one of you.

I was at "Prospect" most of the morning with the electric light man and Mr. Thompson, and have been writing business letters ever since lunch,—think I must stop now and rest a bit. The children are safe and well and happy, and we are all well.

With devoted love,   Your little wife,   Eileen.

ALS (WC, NjP).

[1] Mrs. Wilson was referring to the Arthur Goodrich who courted her unsuccessfully in New York in 1884-85 and was the subject of much correspondence printed in Vols. 3 and 4 of this series. Wilson's correspondent was Arthur Frederick Goodrich (1878-1941), at this time managing editor of *World's Work*.

ENCLOSURE I

From John Huston Finley

My dear Friend: August 1, 1902

Before the first day of your administration ends I must send you a word of greeting. The wireless telegraphy of our friendship has already made you conscious of my affectionate good-will and of my supreme confidence, but I send this in confirmation.

It has been the most gracious of fates that has (at your prompting) led me to Princeton. The "position" is almost ideal in the opportunities and associations it has given and now promises; for it is with an even greater pleasure that I look forward to service under your generalship.

I do not need to pledge you what my affection could not withhold. What I have to give, I am glad it is the right of one for whom I have unmixed admiration to command.

Here's to you my dear friend,
> Expounder of the Constitution,
> "Expander" of Princeton University,
> Exponent of our hopes and
> Exemplar of best desires;

May you come late to the Ex-presidency.

                        Yours sincerely,   John H. Finley

ALS (WP, DLC).

From George Franklin Fort Wilbur[1]

My Dear Wilson: Asbury Park, N.J., Aug. 6/02

When I saw a little item in the Sun of recent date to the effect that you had become President of Princeton College I thought it would be a proper time to add my congratulations to the number with which you must have by this time been almost overwhelmed, and I do this, Wilson, with a warm heart and with best wishes for your success, as must be the feeling of all your classmates. For now that one of their number has actually become President of the College, they feel that it is an additional honor to be a member of the class which has turned out to have been a famous one. How proud your classmates are of you! And, Wilson, when you in your quieter moments recall all the honors that have so continuously flown toward you since those early days of '75 when the roll call of Wilbur, Wilder, Wilson, was a familiar sound of Freshman year, it must almost make you hold your breath to realize that you have actually reached that highest of honors—the Presidency. And as you could not help recognizing your growing fame, it must have been a memorable moment when you first realized that you had become what the world calls great. To my mind your honor is higher than that of being President of the country and that you may be guided to do what is best for Princeton University is the prayer of your classmate,

G. F. Wilbur

ALS (WP, DLC).
[1] Princeton 1879; M.D., University of Pennsylvania, 1882. Physician in Asbury Park, N. J.

From Arthur Frederick Goodrich

Dear Sir: New York   August 5th, 1902.

"The World's Work" would like to print in its October number, apropos of your inauguration as president of Princeton University, an entirely new portrait of you. Would it be possible for you to give time to a photographer we can send from New York, or is there some man at Princeton you would care to go to for such a purpose?

You may be sure we appreciate that you are busy, and that

every infliction upon your time is bothersome, but it will be a great favor to us if you will let us arrange this little matter.[1]

Very truly yours,   Arthur Goodrich

TLS (WP, DLC).
    [1] Actually, Wilson had the photograph taken by James E. Purdy of 146 Tremont St., Boston. It appeared in *World's Work*, IV (Oct. 1902), 2585. This portrait appears in the photographic section of this volume.

From David Benton Jones

My Dear Mr. Wilson: Chicago   August 7th, 1902.

I have been wanting to send you a note for some days to tell you how much the University is to be congratulated upon the fact that you are now its President, and not merely its President-elect.

There was an element of unreality about the situation for some time after the change had been brought about that made it difficult for me to feel that an actual change was impending.

I am sure every Princeton man will now feel renewed zeal and enthusiasm for the place and for the life it holds.

You are not greatly to be congratulated upon the change that has come to you. The task is burdensome even if it were entirely clear just what should be done. It is always a matter of great perplexity to be made responsible for any large undertaking during a period of uncertainty or of transition. It seems reasonably clear that university work has not been reduced to its final terms.

I take it for granted that there must have been some controlling reason for changing the date of your installation from Commemoration Day, October 22nd, to Saturday, October 25th. I am sorry this should be so. I could be present on Wednesday, the 22nd, but cannot on Saturday, the 25th, and I should greatly enjoy witnessing what I am sure will be an impressive ceremony. A fixed engagement here on the 25th makes it impossible for me even to hope that I can be present.

With my heartiest wishes for you and for Princeton, I remain

Very sincerely yours,   David B. Jones.

TLS (WP, DLC).

To Ellen Axson Wilson

My own, precious sweetheart,   Clifton, Mass., 8 Aug., 02

Your letters do me *so* much good! They come to me like daily confirmations of your love,—and that is the real source of all my pleasure, as of all my happiness. God bless you and keep you!

No, dear, the people of whom we bought the drawing room furniture were not to cover it; they were only to pack it ready for shipment and store it until we ordered it forwarded. I fear it is already boxed. By the way, we were to have the option on a screen at $50.00 only until Aug. 15, they wrote me.

This *is* a *delightful* letter from Finley. He certainly has a gift for friendship, and can make his affection tell in a way that is beautiful.

Yes, Wilbur is "the drinking one." I did not know that he could express himself so well and with so much feeling. I shall be constrained to think better of him.

I dont know who the Arthur Goodrich can be who writes from the *World's Work*. The name is certainly very suggestive. [Walter Hines] Page was with Houghton, Mifflin, & Co.; perhaps he took Mr. Goodrich down with him or sent for him. I've never been in Doubleday and Page's office. I shall ask about Boston photographers and perhaps try my luck with one.

Yesterday was a *dies non*, so far as happenings were concerned. After my letters were written I just amused myself, and did nothing to be remembered. An amusing thing happened when I went to the station for my mail at noon. Prof. Münsterberg, of Harvard,[1] who has a cottage here, came in while I was there, and the station master, seeing that we did not speak, came promptly out of his little office and, saying "You gentlemen ought to know one another," cheerily introduced us! Münsterberg is thoroughly well worth knowing, but I was a little bored. I'd rather, for the time being, keep an absolute *incog*. The incident was none the less a most diverting one. It seems Mr. Chapman, the station agent, is a quite a character,—a "general utility" man, and a friend of all men.

I spent a good part of the afternoon riding on the trolley between Marblehead and Salem.

I am perfectly well, capable of incalculable periods of sleep, and busied all the while with delightful thoughts of my incomparable little partner. She is the source of all my rest of spirit, of all that makes my life a thing to be desired. With love deep, devoted, unspeakable   Your own   Woodrow

Dear love to Father and to Madge

I think the way you have settled the bath-room question excellent. Alas, about the 1st. of October; but Thompson is right. It cannot be helped. The news that we are to have pipes but no heat is distressing,—but must be borne with philosophy.

ALS (WP, DLC).
    [1] Hugo Münsterberg, Professor of Psychology at Harvard.

To John Huston Finley

My dear Friend,   Clifton, Mass., 8 August, 1902

Your letter touched me to the quick. Such friendship, so generous and without qualification, and so delicately and affectionately expressed, makes me feel rich indeed in the best elements of strength and of success, and I thank you for it with all my heart.

I have mislaid your address and must send this the long way around, by Princeton; but it cannot grow cold for keeping, any more than yours did, which reached me only this morning. It is a source of deep happiness to me that I should have found for you a work and a home which you find so congenial, and that I should have brought to my side such a friend.

May God bless you and yours,

Your sincere friend,   Woodrow Wilson

ALS (J. H. Finley Papers, NN).

Two Letters from Ellen Axson Wilson

My own darling,   Princeton   Aug 8 1902

I have been exceedingly inconvenienced this morning by a very natural mistake of Mrs. Hightmans;[1] she has shut the top of your desk and I can't get in! Will you please send me the key by the very first mail? I could have *sworn* that the duplicate key was in the basket on my bureau but it has disappeared. Could you have taken it?

I have spent half the morning ransacking the house for it, and now I have engagements with Mr. Thompson and others which makes it impossible for me to write a real letter to my darling,—since this *must* go on the first mail. I enclose a card[2] which the bearer wanted me to send you,—why I don't know. He came from New York to see you.

The weather is still superb. All well. Father very cheerful.

With love unspeakable.   Your little wife,   Eileen.

ALS (WC, NjP).
    [1] She is unknown to the Editors.
    [2] This enclosure is missing.

My darling, [Princeton, N.J., Aug. 8, 1902]

I have found the duplicate key, just ten minutes after mailing my letter to you. It was in the little china box on my bureau.

Lovingly, Your own Eileen.

ALS (WP, DLC).

From James MacNaughton Thompson

My dear Dr. Wilson: [Princeton, N.J.] August 8th, 1902.

Your favor of the 7th came to me this morning and I have sent for the forms of the invitations and will get them under way as soon as possible. It was my intention to notify the gentlemen whom Mr. Cuyler had appointed on the Inauguration Committee, about September 1st, so that we can get their acceptances and be ready for business by the time Mr. Cuyler returns on the 15th of September. I will write Mr. Pyne for the necessary authority.

Hoping that you are enjoying the rest which you so well deserve and that you will return well stored with health and energy for the coming year, believe me,

Faithfully yours, J MacN. Thompson, Curator.

TLS (WP, DLC).

To Ellen Axson Wilson

My precious darling, Clifton, Mass., 9 Aug., '02

I am going into town to-day, to make inquiries about a Princeton millionaire[1] who lives in these parts, upon whom I wish to call, if he is accessible, and invite him to my inauguration. He is an old gentleman of the Class of '48, without heirs, and ought to be thinking of his duty to his alma mater. This is to be just a preliminary skirmish, to get acquainted. I hope he is not off somewhere where I cannot get at him.

The weather is glorious, and "going to town" suggests nothing but a most comfortable jaunt. I always get more amusement, you know, out of a crowded town than out of any other place,—when I have the leisure to look about and see what is entertaining,—and to-day I shall probably have plenty.

You often think, my sweet one, that my judgments about you are not sober judgments of truth, but surely, when I get away

from home and no longer see your dear eyes or feel the charm
that has held me all these nineteen years, I am in possession of
my calm senses. And at no other time do I realize so definitely or
so vividly the beauty, grace, strength, and tenderness of my darling's nature, or the delight there is in the action of her mind. I
love to think of you! Nothing rests or delights me more: it is the
one subject that leads to no worry or disappointment. And I wonder about you with as romantic a wonder as I used to feel when
I was not yet your accepted lover. Ah, my pet, all that I am, all
that has come to me in my life, I owe to you. If there is anything
that commends me to the admiration of other men it is a certain
poise and elevation of spirit,—that I know from what they say to
me—and that I get from my deep content and happiness with you.
It is not natural to me. Deep purturbations are natural to me,
deep disturbances of spirit. I could not make the impression I do,
I could not be what I am, if I did not take such serene happiness
from my union with you. You are my spring of content; and so
long as I have you, and you too are happy, nothing but good and
power can come to me. Ah, my incomparable little wife, may God
bless and keep you! I am altogether and with deep delight

Your own   Woodrow

Dear love to Father and Madge.

ALS (WC, NjP).
  [1] Isaac Chauncey Wyman of Salem, Mass.

From Ellen Axson Wilson

My own darling,   Princeton, Aug. 9, 1902.

I have been for a large part of the morning at "Prospect" with
the steam man settling where the registers and radiators are to
be. It is to be all indirect radiation on the first floor; isnt that
good? The papers are on the way and the carpet man and shade
man are to be down on Monday to measure; so I hope work will
really *begin* on Monday. Mr. Krespach[1] told me this morning that
the Pattons would really go out Monday.

I have a little joke on you. I found on your desk a letter from
Kate Wilson to me, date July 13, which *I* had never seen or heard
of though it had been opened![2] I had quite a laugh about it;—
shall I tell Kate on you? She was, you remember, pleading for
news about the presidency. It seems they are quite aggrieved at
"knowing no more about it all than the general public." I shall
try and write to her tonight; but I am getting a frightful number

of letters these days most of them requiring prompt answers for one reason or another,—seven yesterday, four today, &c. I am getting quite desperate about it! *You* are fairing better just now.

I wish there were some way of finding out whether *my* Mr. Goodrich is or is not the dead one so as to get him off my mind! I am afraid the chances are against him; can you think of any way to settle it?

Arn't the enclosed about Central R. R. interesting?[3] Instead of selling out my $2000 I would like to buy two more!

Your tale of the station master was very entertaining. I should think from his writing, Prof. Münsterberg would be very interesting and possibly amusing. We are all well including Father. The weather is glorious. I enclose today's letter from Jessie that you may have the latest news from the children.[4] Your letters, dear, breathe an air of quiet enjoyment that does my heart good. God bless you! I *love* you!—love you with every heart throb and am altogether   Your own,   Eileen.

ALS (WC, NjP).
  [1] Frank L. Krespach, upholsterer and furniture repairer, 7 and 9 Nassau St.
  [2] This letter from Mrs. Joseph R. Wilson, Jr., is missing.
  [3] Clippings or circulars about the Central Railroad of Georgia, which are missing.
  [4] This enclosure is missing.

From Ira Winthrop Travell[1]

Dear Sir: Plainfield, New Jersey.   August 9, 1902.

The Annual Meeting of the New Jersey High School Teachers' Association will be held on Dec 5-6 in Newark. It has been our custom to invite a representative of one of the neighboring colleges to address the Association after the banquet on Friday evening. On such occasions Dr. Patton, Dr. Low, and Dr. Butler have been our guests of honor. Will you not be our guest this year?

It is altogether fitting that the New Jersey High Schools should sustain the most cordial and loyal relations to Princeton. This banquet affords a most favorable opportunity for you in the beginning of your administration to meet the teachers of the high schools of this state and to strengthen the bonds of friendship which exist between you and us.

Hoping that you will honor us by a favorable reply,[2]
I am,   Very truly yours,   I. W. Travell
        President N. J. High School Teachers' Association.

TLS (WP, DLC) with WWhw notation on letter: "Accepted W. W."

1 Principal of Stillman High School, Plainfield, N. J., and president of the New Jersey High School Teachers' Association.
2 Wilson spoke to the association in Newark on Dec. 5, 1902. A report of his address is printed at Dec. 6, 1902.

To Ellen Axson Wilson

My own darling,   Clifton, Mass., 10 Aug., '02

I have the house to myself. It is Sunday morning, and Mr. Tedcastle and the two young ladies, Miss Snell and Miss Curtin, have gone off for a walk along the beach. Miss Beatty left on Friday to resume her work in Philadelphia. This afternoon I am going over to Nahant to spend an hour or two with Heath Dabney, and meet Mrs. Heath (No. 2).[1] I got a glimpse of their baby boy last Sunday,—as fine, handsome a brown-eyed little darling as ever I saw,—a really splendid little fellow.[2] I should think that his mother must be extremely good looking—or else have the particular sorts of homeliness that (in a mixture) offsets her husband's,—though I must say that Heath has improved in looks immensely.

I spent an idle, pleasant day in Boston yesterday. Mr. Wyman I did not find (the alumnus of '48), and, after making a few small purchases (such as the typewriter shields) and taking a leisurely lunch (and looking up a Greek word at the Public Library!) I went to Keith's theatre and sat for almost three hours and a half enjoying music, songs, dances, horse play, and gymnastics. It was all of the most respectable kind, and a look around on the audience made me feel quite at home,—not at all out of my class. They were the most solid, wholly genteel, cultivated looking set I ever saw in such a place: old gentlemen who looked like clergymen, bank presidents, railway directors; old dowagers who looked like patrons of society. I stayed till train time! Nothing like being far away from home to get a chance to indulge my old bohemian instincts!

I could have the real vacation spirit in it all, and be a veritable boy, if only my sweetheart were with me! Ah, there's the rub! I am having a good time and getting excellent refreshment, but if *she* were here there would be deep joy instead of mere pleasure. I find, now that I get a certain remove, that my election to the presidency has done a very helpful thing for me. It has settled the future for me and given me a sense of *position* and of definite, tangible tasks which takes the *flutter* and restlessness from my spirits. If I could have *you*, therefore, I could be so *serene*, your sweetness and the stimulation of your charm added to the sense of settled duty! Ah, but you are the most subtly charming of all women. It is very life to me to be   Your own   Woodrow

A great deal of love to dear Father and dear Madge

ALS (WC, NjP).
1 Dabney's second wife, Lily Davis Dabney.
2 Virginius Dabney, born Feb. 8, 1901.

From Ellen Axson Wilson

My own darling,   Princeton, Aug. 10 1902

I have been to church and been to see Mrs. Brown and now I will write my little letter to you before going up to loaf a little. It is a pleasure not to be so driven as I have been all last week; especially to have plenty of time for Father. I have been with him most of the day when not at church. He seems cheerful though he had an attack yesterday. But it was not one of the painful ones. I was surprised, for he had seemed so very well before, walking a good deal for him. I think it was possibly due to too much fruit. We are getting *fine* peaches now and with the rich cream we are living high.

Mr. Thompson sent a mason who is going to estimate on plain chimney-tops; and Mr. T. will have his workmen put up the scaffolding at cost price, which will save us quite a good deal. Tell me what you think of the plain chimneys that you see about there. The one I am having him estimate on is like those on Mr. Thompson's house [at 48 Mercer St.] which I like very well. It is something like this.[1] I am afraid that doesn't give the idea! It is just one row of brick projecting a little below the top. I think it can be done cheaper and more promptly now than later. Shall I let him go ahead? I really *prefer* it to terra-cotta tops.

If you feel like it, it would be quite a help to go to Caproni's, select the "faun" and see if the plaster pedestals will do. They are like a piece of fluted column. The figures ought to stand rather high in that high-ceiled hall; as high as your Washington[2] whose pedestal is 3 ft 11 in. Of course it is *the* "Marble Faun," of Praxiteles,—and Hawthorne! You could have it shipped at once, & the *two* pedestals if you like them.

There is no news either in town or college,—except indeed this item in the paper which interested me though I don't know the people. "Mrs. Van Doren of Van Deventer Ave. is visiting her *husband* who lives in Peekskill N.Y."[3] I hope it will prove a joyful occasion.

Mac Thompson told me a queer thing, viz., that "C. C." [Cuyler] told him in *May* that "Dr. Patton was to be crowded out at Commencement and you put in,"—and that he also told him the *whole* story! A very foolish, imprudent C. C.! He said to Thompson, "Mac, *you* must keep it a dead secret, though I just *can't*! I've *got* to tell you!" He said that after the election he happened to go up to the Inn with C. C., and that he and Miss Cuyler[4] rushed into each others arms and embraced passionately on the strength of it. You ought to hear how Thompson talks about you. He says he is going to have that letter you wrote him lately *framed*!

Madge and I have had the greatest fun reading "Abner Daniel."[5] I wish you had it with you; that household would enjoy it especially. *Rome* is the *metropolis* of the country! Rome girls visiting in the place overawe the natives with their smart costumes and city ways. And there is a good joke on Mr. Tedcastle; one of the minor characters is named, Tedcastle, (called Teddy) and is the greatest fool in the book! All the people have the familiar old names. We are in love with Abner himself,—such an improvement on "David Harum,"[6]—just as witty and *so* much more mellow, wholesome, honest & *good*.

I am *perfectly* well,—not tired at all,—and I love you, my darling, unspeakably. You are the very life of me. I literally think of you all the time; nothing else ever crowds you out.

(Love to all from M. & me.)   Your own   Eileen

ALS (WC, NjP).

[1] At this point she drew a chimney.

[2] About the presentation of this statue to Wilson, see the news report printed at March 18, 1897, Vol. 10.

[3] E. Gertrude and John V. Van Doren of 34 Van Deventer St. who were, actually, in process of moving to Peekskill.

[4] Eleanor de Graff Cuyler, sister of Cornelius Cuyler Cuyler, who lived with him until his marriage in 1906.

[5] William Nathaniel Harben, *Abner Daniel* (New York and London, 1902). Harben specialized in dialect novels set in his native region of northern Georgia.

[6] Edward Noyes Westcott, *David Harum, A Story of American Life* (New York, 1898).

From Frances Folsom Cleveland

Dear Mr Wilson: [Buzzards Bay, Mass.] 10 Aug. 1902.

It is curious that I never suspected that Mrs McLeod would one day serve me so good a turn as to bring me so pleasant a letter from you! I wish I could reward her and you, by telling you something about her. I met her at a luncheon in Buffalo a good many years ago. At that time her husband was a high up official in the

Reading Road, possibly President. I had no acquaintance with her, and they followed us at [as] tenants of Mr Benedict's[1] house in 51st St. next his own, and I heard of them occasionally through the Benedicts, who knew them slightly, as being very nice people. Mr Benedict spoke to me of her last week, and of the possibility of her going to Princeton to live, as her boy was to enter Princeton, and I imagine from what he said, that he could tell you some of the things which you would wish to know about her, better than we could do. Her husband died in the spring, and I saw her one day in Princeton, shortly after, looking for a house.

I have made a longer story than necessary out of the very little knowledge I have. The impression I have received from what little I do know is that she is a nice quiet pleasant sort of person who would probably be a desirable tenant. I feel pretty sure that she has not a large income but that she is perfectly reliable.

As to ourselves, we are not having just the sort of summer we had planned as we have had bad weather and a good deal of sickness, though not severe, among the children, and I have had two bad coughs myself; but Mr Cleveland has kept well and kept fishing! And now that the weather has improved we hope for better health along with it.

I thank you for your good wishes, and I trust the vacation will do all for you that you need or wish, (perhaps both!)

Mr Cleveland joins me in all good wishes, and I am

Yours very sincerely   Frances F. Cleveland.

Should you care to write Mr. Benedict, his address is E. C. Benedict (Indian Harbor,) Greenwich, Conn.

ALS (WP, DLC).
[1] Elias Cornelius Benedict, stockbroker, long-time friend of Grover Cleveland.

To Ellen Axson Wilson

My own darling,   Clifton, Massachusetts, 11 August, 1902

My plan is to get to Northeast Harbor by Friday evening, and spend Saturday and Sunday with the Morgans, leaving for the White Mountains on Monday, the 18th. It will not be worth while, therefore, for you to mail me any letter addressed to Clifton which leaves Princeton later than Wednesday; and I think that, if I were you, I would send only those to Northeast Harbor (Care Mrs. Junius S. Morgan) which you can get off on Thursday. After that address me at "Grove Cottage," Gorham, New Hampshire. By the way, you have not yet sent me Osborn's Mss. The Osborn's are with the Morgan's and I should like to be able to talk the lucubration over with O. when I get there.

I apologize about Kate's letter! It came one day when you were away; I had just written to Josie a letter which had crossed Kate's and which constituted a virtual answer to it; and so her plaint passed out of my mind. I hope you will not tell her: she would be hurt.

I noticed in the paper a day or so after leaving home that there had been big sales of Georgia Central securities at advanced figures, and did not understand what it meant. This reported deal probably explains it. I am glad you did not act at once upon your resolution to sell.

I went over to Nahant yesterday, as I planned, but had only an hour with the Dabneys. I went over by trolley and "barge," and the way was so round-about, the pace so slow, the route of the barge so remote from the place I wanted to get to, that it was indeed a Sabbath Day's journey, and I had to turn back almost as soon as I arrived. Mrs. Dabney is *not* pretty, as I had conjectured she must be,—neither is she the opposite. She is just plain,—and pleasant. I spent a very enjoyable hour with them. The day was so glorious that moving about in it was a refreshment, and to-day we are paying for it with a rain storm out of the southeast.

I have no plans for to-day, therefore, except to take a long snooze and renew my youth. But, for that matter, I can never grow *essentially* older while you love me. Every time I think about you or see your dear eyes or touch your lips I am a boy again, and a lover all over. I live on the *romance* of being your husband and beloved chum,—on the pride and delight of being, acceptably to you,   Your own   Woodrow

Abundant love to dear Father and dear Madge.

ALS (WC, NjP).

To David Benton Jones

My dear Mr. Jones,   Clifton, Massachusetts, 11 August, 1902.

Your kind letter of the seventh has been forwarded to me here, where I am spending part of my short vacation. I came away from Princeton the day after my term as president began: that was the first use I made of my privileges. Such is the force of precedent with men of our race!

I deeply appreciate your letter. I take my chief hope of what is to come from the support and friendship of men like yourself, who know me and whom I trust down to the ground; and I feel sure that I shall take the better part of my success from your counsel. I feel particularly near to you, if you will let me say so, because I have learned your courage and your zest in unselfish action. I wish you could have heard what has come to me from very unexpected quarters in the way of hearty praise and deep appreciation of the services you have already rendered the University. You know what I think. I could not add now to what I have already had the privilege of saying to you, at Princeton, without seeming to praise you for my own advancement!

I feel the weight of the responsibility that has come upon me, and feel it very solemnly; but I am glad to say that I do not feel it as a burden. I am glad to give all that is in me to the task now to be undertaken. There is a vast deal to be done, and it is impossible yet to plan it wisely all the way through. It will be wisest to make our general purpose distinct to ourselves, and the outline of the means by which we mean to seek its attainment, and then attack the details one at a time. I find the outlines forming in my mind with a good deal of definiteness and certainty. In fact we have so long talked them over in a little circle in Princeton that they are easily to be compounded out of common counsel. Hitherto they have been in our minds as a sort of abstract thesis; now, if men with money are generous to us, they may come into shape as real achievements.

I am more sorry than I can say that the change of date for the inauguration means that you cannot be present. I had promised myself the most helpful talks with you and the real pleasure and comfort of seeing you. The twenty-fifth was chosen for the sake of the majority, because more men can get to Princeton on a Saturday than on a Wednesday. The men who planned the change seemed so confident that it was the best thing to do that I fear they cannot be changed back.

Hoping that you are well, and with warmest regards both to your brother and for yourself,

Faithfully and cordially Yours,   Woodrow Wilson

WWTLS (Mineral Point, Wisc., Public Library).

From Ellen Axson Wilson

My own darling,   Princeton, Aug. 11 1902

I was drawing one or two little checks just now and I found to my amusement that I didn't know how to draw one for less than a dollar! If this one will work will you please send it on to its destination. I don't believe we will need to borrow until your return; there is $256.00 in Bank; and of bills that have come in and are unpaid only Leighs[1] is of any size.

I was at Prospect all the morning with the carpet and shade man, also seeing Krespach and Titus;[2] since lunch I have written business letters steadily. I am afraid that means a bald little note for my darling, for it is now 4 P.M. and *very* hot and humid, and my mind is a perfect blank. How I would like to write a letter that would make you as happy as the *beautiful* one that came to me this morning has made me! How can you wonder that to be so loved by you,—so believed in—is almost too good to be true. But "the thoughts that arise in me" as I read such words are far far beyond the power of *my* tongue to express. I love you darling with every heart-throb and I am as always,

Your own   Eileen.

A letter has just come from China to Sister Annie. Shall I forward it? It is very large and thick. It is evidently from Jeanie.[3]

ALS (WC, NjP).
    [1] There were grocers, tailors, merchants, etc., in Princeton named Leigh, and it is impossible to identify this one.
    [2] Nelson W. Titus, cabinet maker, 17 Alexander St.
    [3] Jeanie Woodrow (Mrs. Samuel Isett) Woodbridge, Wilson's first cousin.

To Ellen Axson Wilson

My own darling,   Clifton, Mass., 12 Aug., '02

I am going into Boston this morning to have my picture "took" for the *World's Work*. I hope I shall have better luck than (in your opinion) I had at Pirie MacDonald's. I wish I had my gown here.

It makes me a bit anxious, my pet, to read in your letters how hard, how fast, how continuously you are working; but the sweet air of good sense, the zest in the work, the love between the lines, the fine spirit of a splendid little woman in every line you write both stimulates and calms me. After all, perhaps I need not be afraid that *such* a little woman will be foolish, forget the *obligations* of her love for me, and spoil her splendid strength. Ah, my sweet one, how my heart yearns for you, and over you, all the time!

I had a long call yesterday afternoon from Professor Münsterberg (in consequence of our introduction at the station!). He is writing a book,—a German book,—on American characteristics,[1] and our talk ran all the while on America. It proved very interesting. He talks extremely well, as he writes, and is a man of quite extraordinary powers of observation. I enjoyed the interview very much indeed.

We donned our best bibs and tuckers last night, Mr. Tedcastle, the young ladies, and I, and called on the Pollards, but they were out. No matter: I had told them all my best stories! No use marring the impression!

By the way, I have exchanged calls with Professor Gooch, next door, and found him both interesting and attractive,—a man, evidently, of fine nature.

I shall lunch in town with Heath Dabney. It is quite like old times to have these long chats with him.

I don't wonder that you were startled to learn what C. C. had been telling. That was most indiscreet. But it's all over now. I have just heard, from Morgan, that C. C. has come out of his illness all right. Isn't that good?

Yes, dear, by all means go ahead with the chimneys. I am sure that I shall like the plain well enough. I like those about here very well indeed,—though most of them are more slender than ours. I have not been able to draw anything that suited me better.

I love you unspeakably. I am altogether and with a joy for which there is no measure,   Your own   Woodrow

Love to dear Father and Madge

ALS (WC, NjP).
[1] Hugo Münsterberg, *Die Amerikaner* (2 vols., Berlin, 1904); *The Americans*, Edwin B. Holt, trans. (New York, 1904).

From Ellen Axson Wilson

My own darling,   Princeton, Aug. 12, 1902

I enclose with your letters Mr. Thompson's note about the chimneys;[1] if [it] is satisfactory to you,—as it is to me,—please drop me a line by the next mail to that effect and I will tell them to go ahead.

The Pattons went out yesterday turning over the keys to me. Today the paperers have begun scraping the walls, the papers being all in the house. Mr. Titus and I also settled about the blue carpet and he begins work on it tomorrow. It will cover Father's room and the back hall. It is a comfort to have something actually begun.

I also enclose a note from Mr. Cope.[2] Isn't it kind in him? I of course begged him to set his own time, so he came today at two, and we had our consultation at "Prospect." He says the most important thing is to get out that mantle, and of about equal importance to take out that high wash-board panelling. He wants just a heavy chair rail a good deal lower. I think it is ugly too but I told Mr. Thompson I would not take the responsibility of ordering it taken out without at least consulting some one member of the committee; so he is going to speak to Mr. Henry. Mr. Thompson is eager for these changes and says he has the money to pay for them, and also for *all* the painting, saved from some other sum he had control of for work on "Prospect." Mr. Cope asked Mr. T. who was our decorator, and was told that we were trying to do it ourselves to save money. He offered to make the little drawings of mouldings, &c. Mr. Thompson it seems thanked him but intimated that we had no money for such purposes, and Mr. Cope was quite surprised, and said he had not had the slightest idea of charging for his advice or assistance,—that it was a great pleasure to render it & begged him to tell Mrs. Wilson so. I was much relieved for I had been a little afraid when he came down especially on this business that I had got myself into trouble. It is a great load off my mind to have his authority to support me in these changes.

Just after my return from Prospect Dr. Elmer[3] came in. He and his wife had driven over for pleasure, and he very kindly stopped to see how my shoulder was doing. He looked at it and said it was all right.

I go into New York tomorrow just for some odds and ends and to look in those 4th Ave. shops for a mirror. Mr. Cope thinks that all-important. Mr. Thompson is having a friend look for one in Georgetown and Alexandria. Then I must go to Flints about the washstand; we won't need it, you know, now that we are to have a bath-room. What do you think I ought to get for the room instead?—a solid handsome table or a pierglass? I shall look tomorrow but not decide till you give me your opinion.

I enclose dear little Nells letter received today.[4]

Just here young Sloane[5] called and stayed *late*! I shall *have* to stop. All are well, weather *glorious* again; a storm yesterday put an end to the humidity that was oppressing us.

With love unspeakable   Your own,   Eileen.

ALS (WC, NjP).
    [1] It is missing.
    [2] This note is missing.
    [3] Probably William Elmer, M.D., Princeton 1861, of 44 W. State St., Trenton.
    [4] This enclosure is missing.
    [5] James Renwick Sloane, Princeton 1900, a student at the Columbia University Law School and son of William Milligan Sloane of Princeton.

From Charles Scribner

My dear Mr. Wilson: New-York   Aug 12th 1902

Ever since your election I have been intending to write my congratulations and good wishes. As you know, I am very deeply interested in all that concerns Princeton and, in company with all the alumni whom I know, very much pleased that you are now at the head. No doubt the feeling of responsibility is great and it must be a source of great satisfaction to be sure that you have the support of a large body of loyal alumni. Please take this note therefore as evidence that you have mine. If there is ever any way in which I can be of service to you, do not hesitate to call upon me.   Yours sincerely   Charles Scribner

ALS (WP, DLC).

To Ellen Axson Wilson

My own darling,   Clifton, Mass., 13 Aug., '02

I went to Caproni's yesterday,—a really beautiful art gallery!— and found the pedestals just what we want, except for height. Three feet, six inches is the best we can do. Don't you think that enough? We could get nothing else half so ornamental and satisfactory. The marble faun, alas, is not made in the right size,—is seven or eight inches too short to serve as a companion piece to the victory. Besides, it is not particularly well reproduced. The piece which seems to me most suitable,—altogether suitable, indeed, in subject, pose, and size (the extended arm gives it somewhat the same effect as the spread wings of the victory) is the full length Apollo belvidere. It is beautifully reproduced in exactly the same height as the victory, and seems to me to have exactly the grace and spirit desirable for the place it is to occupy. I have the catalogue, with the things I looked at marked, and, if you approve, please send me a blank cheque (from the *back* of the cheque book) and I will send the order on from Gorham. I did not like to depart from your choice without consulting you.

I had a very pleasant day in town: found Heath at work in the Library, lunched with him, and then sat with him an hour or more in the public garden, talking of things new and old,—chiefly of questions of American history associated with Reconstruction, the subject upon which he is to write a volume. He is in the deep waters of general reading on the subject, and is in search of points of view.

We are having brilliant weather, clear and cool, in which it is a pleasure to be at large. How I hope you are getting some taste of the same quality at Princeton! I go in to-day to lunch with Perry. This is his week (or four days, rather) in town, and this lunch is by appointment from Greensboro, Vermont. It will be a pleasure to see him again.

I have daily, hourly pangs of homesickness, my sweet, sweet pet. Really, at bottom, I am a fool to leave *you* in search of pleasure. The thing is absurd on the face of it, as I have so often said, and I smile sardonically at the effort a hundred times a day. A change of air, no doubt, I get, but the real tonic for me is companionship, at leisure, with you, and the touch of your lips. But then you are not at leisure!   Your own   Woodrow

Deep love to the dear ones.

ALS (WC, NjP).

From Ellen Axson Wilson

My own darling,   Princeton, Aug. 13, 1902.

I have got back from New York, tired, but very triumphant having found at an auction room a stunning mantle mirror six feet wide (just the width of the chimney breast) and eight feet high in fine condition with good plate glass for $40.00 *dollars*! There will be $8.00 more for hauling and crating so that it will cost delivered I suppose about $50.00. Is'nt that fine? I feel as if the room were made now. The mantle is to be unpacked early tomorrow morning. Mr. Fay told me he could get such a mirror for me for a hundred to a hundred and fifty dollars. I suppose that represents the difference between the price one pays when one bids for a thing and when it is thrown on the market.

I also found at Fays a *gem* of a table for the guest room for $20.00, genuine antique, a perfect beauty. I found that there were only *two* chairs at Prospect for the reception room, so I decided we were obliged to have more than the five, or we couldn't seat an ordinary dinner party in the room. So I got two more of the same reduced lot at $25.00 each instead of the screen, another big square arm chair and an *exquisite* small one with carved back all wood. I have been pricing that style of furniture everywhere and I am more impressed than ever with the bargain we got. There is not the smallest, plainest chair of that sort to be had anywhere else for less than $35.00. (Flint has taken back the washstand.) And by the way the five chairs will be uphol-

stered there for $11.50; they had not packed them. Do excuse
this incoherent scrawl; it will sound natural at least! I am "sure"
writing just as I talk after a day in New York. I must stop though
for I find several letters to be answered tonight and I walked a
great deal today. With love unbounded,

Your devoted little wife,   Eileen.

ALS (WC, NjP).

From William Francis Magie

My dear Wilson,   Altrincham, England   Aug. 13, 1902

(I shall use this address for my official correspondence, though
I confess it seems rather formal). West has informed me of your
desire that I should take charge of his work in his absence.[1] Of
course I shall do so gladly; there is only one difficulty. To save
money we have taken passage on a slow steamer that will not,
I fear, reach New York until Sept. 21 or 22d. A little matter
like that didn't matter in the old regime—but I regret coming back
late now, very much—for I want to be with you at the opening
of College—& I don't like to begin by doing what I admit is cen-
surable. But the chief trouble arises from this—that the Dean
of the Graduate School ought to be on hand early to meet the
new men who come from other Colleges—so as to make them
feel at home & to start them off promptly and pleasantly. This I
shall not be able to do. I don't think it would be possible for me
to change my passage now—& I know I could not do it without
cutting off more of my stay here than I am willing to lose. Now
I can suggest either of two courses. Either put someone else to
do the Dean's work—[Henry Dallas] Thompson would do it very
well—for one; or if you are willing to wait for me to come back—
make some arrangement by which the really new Graduates—not
the Seminary men—who can wait just as well as not—but the few
who come to give their whole time to us—can be sent to you for
a short interview. You need do nothing more than shake hands
& welcome them & ask them to wait for my coming—but that
little will make all the difference between their feeling dis-
gruntled and being contented. I don't like to suggest anything
which will sent [send] you more callers than you would otherwise
have, but I really think you would do the Graduates a service
if you could manage to do this—that is, provided you want me to
do the work enough to keep the place open till I can return.
West's secretary, Mrs. Creasy[2] will be at his office after Sept. 15 &

will carry out your orders. I shall write to her & give her full instructions on the supposition that you will adopt the second plan—which she can discard if you appoint someone else.

I saw Paul van Dyke in London, & we agreed that the Com. on Scholarship[3] ought to resign. No doubt we all will agree on that. If you constitute a new committee to get up a course of study, I hope you will act as its chairman, as the President ought to do.

It was a great pleasure to get your letter, which supplemented what I had heard from my father [W. J. Magie] & from Fine. I cannot tell you with what a feeling of relief I look forward to the years to come. I feel as if my fighting days were over—not I hope my working days—but that I can now pursue the glorious acts of peace—& do my duty without irritation of mind.

Paul van Dyke was in a curiously mistified condition of mind about the resignation. He was very cordial in his expressions of satisfaction with your election. Of course I couldn't explain matters; but could only surmise that some other cause than the one made public might have influenced Dr. Patton in his decision. Paul has been working hard & successfully, I should judge. He has of course reached conclusions diametrically opposed to those of the other authors who have worked on the same subject—if he hadn't he wouldn't have been Paul. But he is at work writing— so that his department will have something of output to show.[4]

We have been travelling up from Italy through Switzerland & down the Rhine to Holland—& are now staying with the Mac-Larens[5] at their house in one of the suburbs of Manchester—a very pretty little country town. We shall travel a little in England before sailing, but we are here—that is in England, mostly for this visit.

I am glad to hear that you & Mrs Wilson are well. We are improved in mind—if not in body—so far as I can see we are just as well as when we left home & no better—by this trip. I am longing to get back—I lie awake nights thinking about Princeton & how my laboratory work will go—& wondering what we shall do in the Faculty. The loafing time I have had is long enough for me. If I can arrange it I shall go to the British Association. Libbey is going to read a paper there on Petra which he visited & photographed this summer.

Now I don't seem to have written quite so official a letter after all—& instead of filing it you had better make a note of the Graduate School business & then burn it.

Yours faithfully W. F. Magie

ALS (WP, DLC).

¹ "I asked Tommy Wilson what arrangement he wished made for attending to the business of the Graduate School during my absence. He promptly selected you for that task, and I sincerely hope you will be able to undertake it." A. F. West to W. F. Magie, July 17, 1902, TLS (Miscellaneous Correspondence and Files of the Dean of the Graduate School, 1902-48, UA, NjP). About West's absence, see A. F. West to WW, July 17, 1902, n. 1.

² Anna B. Creasey, long-time secretary to Dean West.

³ About this committee, see the notes for a talk to the St. Louis Alumni, Nov. 21, 1901, n. 2, and Minutes of the Princeton University Faculty, April 16, 1902, n. 1, both printed in Vol. 12.

⁴ Van Dyke was probably working on his *Renascence Portraits* (New York, 1905).

⁵ Probably the family of Donald Campbell MacLaren, a member of Wilson's and Magie's Class of 1879.

To Ellen Axson Wilson

My own darling,   Clifton, Mass., 14 Aug. '02

By all means have Thompson go ahead with the chimneys. The figures are very satisfactory.

If you are sure that the bath room will really make a washstand unnecessary (sometimes, as, for example, when man and wife occupy the room together, a washstand in addition to the bath room arrangements would be very convenient) I incline to a pier glass rather than a table,—though the glass is really not necessary, and a table, which would cost less, would furnish more. Please follow your own taste and judgment in the matter, my sweet one.

Hurrah for Mr. Cope! He seems the right stuff, and no doubt he will help you a great deal.

The proofs I inclose are those I did *not* take (for the *World's Work*) but they have elements of excellence which were successfully combined in the one I *did* take, which I feel pretty sure you will like very much.

I had a most pleasurable time with Perry, and my inference from his letter was confirmed! *This is in the profoundest confidence.* He told me that he thought it quite probable,—at any rate more than possible,—that in a couple of years (say) he would feel like breaking away from his present occupations and going back to college work (and of course to Princeton). He told me another piece of good news. Mrs. Perry is strong and plump again and tramps about the golf links with him in a way which evidently makes him deeply happy. She went to a hospital a few weeks last Spring and was very much benefitted by the treatment, and has been growing stronger and happier ever since. If you get her back, therefore, you will get her back restored to her normal self again. The prospect is most attractive any way you look at it.

I am afraid, my sweet love, that I cannot write you a letter to-morrow. It takes *all day* to get to Northeast Harbor. I leave here at 6:53 in the morning and reach there about seven in the evening. But of course I will write on Saturday. Ive just declined a telegraphic invitation from Mrs. Charles E. Green to lunch with her at Bar Harbor on Monday!

Ah, my love, my love, what bliss it would be to hold you, if only for a moment, in my arms! I love you with a quite painful intensity, and am altogether   Your own   Woodrow

Deep love to all,—the precious children included.

ALS (WC, NjP). Encs. missing.

To Mary Livingston Potter Green[1]

My dear Mrs. Green,   [Clifton, Mass., Aug. 14, 1902]

I confidently had hoped to have an opportunity to thank you for your kind intentions with regard to my entertainment while at Mt. Desert.[2] I was very much disappointed that I did not. I was very sorry not to be able to fall in with your interesting plans for luncheon in my honor tomorrow, and very much appreciate the preparations you had made for my pleasure.

I was surprised that you had not communicated with me before issuing your other invitations, but take for granted that there must have been some good reason for your not doing so. My plan to leave for Mt. Desert tomorrow had been formed some weeks ago, and could not possibly have been changed on such short notice.

Let me again express my warm appreciation of your kindness, and my sincere regret that you were put to any trouble or embarrassment by my inability to accept your invitation.

Very sincerely Yours,   Woodrow Wilson

Transcript of WWshLS (WP, DLC).
 1 Widow of Charles Ewing Green.
 2 Mount Desert Island on the Maine coast.

To John Wesley Fielder, Jr.

My dear Mr. Fielder,   Clifton, Massachusetts, 14 August, 1902.

I have had a letter from Mrs. Cleveland about Mrs. McLeod, which is very satisfactory indeed; and I think it would be very agreeable to us to rent the house to her, if she feels like taking it.

Mrs. Wilson writes me that there is no likelihood of the work on "Prospect" being finished before the end of September. I am afraid, therefore, that you will have to name the first of October as the date at which possession of our little house can be given.

With much regard,

Sincerely Yours,   Woodrow Wilson

WWTLS (WC, NjP).

To Charles Scribner

Clifton, Massachusetts,

My dear Mr. Scribner,   14 August, 1902

Your kind letter of the twelfth has been forwarded to me here. I thank you for it most sincerely.

It puts me more in heart than I can say to have the support and cordial confidence of men like yourself, who stand near the University in taste and interest and near the intellectual forces of the country. I know that your interest in the University, moreover, is not sentimental merely, but that you have proved it in the most substantial manner by gift and counsel. I shall feel it an element of real strength that you have given me leave to come to you, and shall look forward to many a helpful conference with you,—especially about our English Department, in which, I know, you are especially interested.

With warmest regard and appreciation,

Sincerely Yours,   Woodrow Wilson

ALS (Charles Scribner's Sons Archives, NjP).

From Ellen Axson Wilson, with Enclosure

My own darling,   Princeton, Aug 14 1902

I enclose the blank check for the Apollo. It will be fine[.] I am so much obliged to you for looking at them. The 3-6 pedestals will do perfectly well.

I saw the mantle this morning and it is in most respects much handsomer than we thought. The pilasters (?) that support the shelf are carved *beautifully* and in excellent style, and the marble is lovely. But the three-cornered spaces on either side of the opening are carved in low relief with hideous natural roses and morning-glories. But it *is* simple low relief and we think there will not be any difficulty in having them smoothed off. Mr. Thompson is to see a marble cutter at once.

Just one more business matter. How do you think the dining room ought to be lighted? The electric light man says with such a large room a central light, chandelier or something like the Finley's have, is the only thing. I think he is probably right. Mr. Cope says side lights will be *much* more beautiful, with the table lighted only by candles, &c. The electric man says he *must* put in the central wire for he is *sure* when we try it we will find the other does not work practically, but he can put in the others too. But that will add with fixtures $40.00, and of course I don't want that. *Please* decide it! Of course our two low candelabra would not light the 20 ft. table.

Father has been very anxious to go and see "Prospect" so we went this morning. He was perfectly delighted; says it is the most beautiful private house he ever saw. He would go all over it in his enthusiasm and I fear has overtired himself.

I am glad you have such fine weather. It is just the same here. Am glad too that you met & enjoyed Prof. Münsterberg, and that you are to see Mr. Perry. Mr. Dabney of course was best of all; I have been delighted that you had his companionship. Will he be able to write a sane book on "reconstruction"? I wonder why Mr. Brown can't go to Charleston? I hope that means he is well provided for.

All perfectly well.

With love beyond words,   Your own   Eileen.

Love to the Hibbens & Westcotts.

Tell me the size of the check you draw please, that I may know if it becomes necessary to use that note.

ALS (WC, NjP).

From William Garrott Brown

My dear Sir,   Cambridge, Mass. Aug. 13, 1902.

A letter comes to me from the President of the College of Charleston inviting me to apply for the chair of History and Economics there. To my surprise, President Randolph tells me that it was you who suggested my name. I cannot see my way to apply for the place, but am very much gratified that without even a personal acquaintance you should have been moved to think of me in that connection.

Will you let me add that we are all wishing for you the utmost success in your present high enterprise?

Very truly yours,   William Garrott Brown.

TLS (WP, DLC).

From George Hutcheson Denny

My Dear Sir: Lexington, Virginia Aug. 14. 1902.

It is not too late, I trust, to extend to you and to Princeton University the cordial greetings of Washington & Lee, kindred in sources & in aims.

Your election gave us all great pleasure. Virginia is proud of her son. I wish for you many happy years of useful service in your distinguished position.

Please accept my thanks for sending us Dean West last June.[1] We never celebrate an important event here without the help of Princeton.

With great regard,

Yrs very sincerely   George H. Denny

I believe your election will give Princeton a stronger hold on the South than ever before. Do not expect too much *at once*, however. The Southerners move slowly.

ALS (WP, DLC).
[1] To attend his inauguration as President of Washington and Lee University. See G. H. Denny to WW, March 24, 1902, n. 3, Vol. 12.

From Ellen Axson Wilson

My own darling,   Princeton, Aug. 15, 1902

I am *so delighted* with these "proofs" that I feel as if I couldn't *bear* to have the plates destroyed! Are you perfectly *sure* that the one you selected is better? People arn't always good judges of their own pictures. Won't you at least write at once to the photographer asking him, if it isn't too late, to keep these plates until I see the finished one? If I only knew the name of the man so as [to] hurry off a note to him direct! I am really excited on the subject.

Just at this point it occurred to me that I would do better to send a note to Agnes asking her to save the plates if possible, since you will be so far from Boston. So I hurried off a note to her and am resuming this at night. How I *hope* those plates are not destroyed! There are two of them, the one in the "Pach" position,

¾ face, square shoulders & the full face which we think *splendid*! By the way the class of '91 has out a book with the Pirie Mc-Donald picture as frontispiece and it is *much* better than the photo; the eyes are superb and some little change in the shadows has made the mouth better. Odd, is'nt it?

I am perfectly delighted at what you tell me about the Perrys. Both at the prospect of having them here and at her improved health.

That reminds me somehow of our house. I told Mr. Fielder that we could not get out of it until Oct. and also that we would not *lease* it at present but only rent by the year as we might sell. I said "we aren't anxious to sell but every house has its price you know. I understand for instance that Mr. Davis[1] wants a little place in town." He said "that's so, he is in my hands at present." So I said, "well if he will pay enough he can have ours,—say $25,000" and he exclaimed, (which is why I repeat the conversation) ["]Oh you are putting the price too *low*! You should ask $30,000,—at least to begin with!" What do you think of that? $30,000 would mean an addition of $1500 a year to our income,—counting the $300.00 that this costs us.

Father is all right again today. He was so tired and excited yesterday afternoon from his visit to "Prospect," that he was t[h]reatened with an attack and took the medicine. But he escaped it.

I am just as well as possible, never felt better. The weather keeps all the time at *exactly* the temperature best suited to my physical well-being, and I feel fit for anything. In the morning I wake rather early and,—having nothing better to do!—take a hot bath and go back to bed and read for a while. Then I get up and do my exercises in a leisurly and exhaustive manner and come down to breakfast feeling *fine*.

Ed Elliot turned up last night, leaving this morning. He was very natural & attractive but had spoiled his looks with a horrid little Frenchy mustache.

With love unbounded, believe me, dear heart, always and altogether,   Your own   Eileen.

You will laugh at the letter from Gibbs.[2] Do make the "Harpers" allow the poor dear to waste his money if he wants to. He doesn't realize how much cheaper it would be to ask you some silly questions and get a whole autograph letter instead of a signature.

ALS (WP, DLC) with WWhw notations on letter.
  [1] He is unknown to the Editors.
  [2] It is missing.

From Edward Ingle

Dear Wilson: Baltimore, Aug. 15th, 1902.

A little sketch in this week's issue of the Manufacturers' Record may interest you.[1] I have sent you a copy.[2] In writing this sketch, which makes no pretense to thoroughness, I was impressed with the wonderful influence of Princeton upon the early Southern educational history. And I thought that, perhaps, an interesting study might be made under your auspices by the Princeton student in Princetonian educational genealogy. I enclose a clipping bearing upon your election to the Presidency of Princeton.[3]

I have kept a close watch upon the field since I last wrote you, but this clipping is the only one that I have discovered.[4] I am
                    Sincerely yours,   Edward Ingle

TLS (WP, DLC).
[1] Edward Ingle, "New England and the North in Early Southern Life," *Manufacturers' Record*, XLII (Aug. 14, 1902), 59-61.
[2] It is missing in WP, DLC.
[3] This enclosure is missing.
[4] Mrs. Wilson, in a postscript to WW to E. Ingle, June 19, 1902, Vol. 12, had said that she would be grateful for additional clippings about her husband.

Two Letters to Ellen Axson Wilson

My own darling,   North East Harbor [Me.], 16 August, 1902

I must scribble a little note before breakfast (on a very shaky table) to tell you of my safe arrival. I am, as you may suppose, plunged here into the midst of "life" again. It promises to be very interesting and enjoyable, and there will be a great deal to tell about it,—but not in letters. I am perfectly well; the Morgans are delightful; but they have planned so many things for me that I am to have no time to chat with my sweet love. Even a little note, nevertheless, can carry the great love that is in my heart. My sweetheart is in my thoughts all the while,—I could not find pleasure anywhere if she were not,—there would be no cheer or song in the world! My solace, my delight! You are worth all other things and all other thoughts put together! That's the reason I can rest and keep young. I have always a theme in my heart that makes it leap and in my mind that soothes and satisfies it!
        Dear love to all,   Your own   Woodrow

My own darling,   North East Harbor, Me.   17 Aug., 1902

Again it is before breakfast. If to-day should run as yesterday did, without breaks (as it probably will, though Sunday), there would be no chance of finding space for a letter when once it is under way. Yesterday we put on old clothes (I put on a suit of Morgan's!) and went out some six or seven miles to fish for cod. The party consisted of Morgan, Harry Osborn, Pyne, [Laurence] Hutton, and myself. I caught nothing, but the sail and the fine air of the open sea were delightful,—the party most congenial and interesting. We had a jolly, boyish time, took a picnic lunch on the boat, and did not get back till a little after four o'clock. Then we had to dress immediately for a reception. Some fifty or sixty people had been invited in to meet me,—some of them old friends, most of them (interesting) strangers. After that there was a dinner: the guests a Mr. and Mrs. Parkman[1] and Monsignor Doane,[2] the Roman Catholic brother of the Episcopal "William of Albany,"[3] whom I met at the reception. Both of them are thoroughly worth meeting. I went to bed at eleven none the worse for wear. The sail saved the day,—and everybody I met was most agreeable. Perhaps, after several years of practice, I may be able to get myself into the spirit of the thing! The Morgans are delightful. You *must* like Junius, dear; he really is true stuff.

Your sweet letter did me deep good. Hurrah for the mirror! Your bargain luck certainly stands by you! How I adore you,— how I love you!   Your own   Woodrow

Dear love to Father and Madge.

ALS (WC, NjP).
    [1] Henry and Frances Parker Parkman of Boston, who had a summer home at Northeast Harbor.
    [2] The Rt. Rev. George Hobart Doane of Newark, N. J.
    [3] The Rt. Rev. William Croswell Doane, Protestant Episcopal Bishop of Albany.

From Ellen Axson Wilson

My own darling,   Princeton, Aug. 17 1902

I was out on business all yesterday morning; and Father had an attack in the afternoon (not a very bad one,—he is all right today) so I could not write until night, and that was not worth while of course. But Friday's letter was mailed yesterday morning so there will be no break in my letters.

I enclose a bill for you to send to New York to have paid at once as it is owing to a perfect stranger.[1] I was tempted to send *your* check for it, but I don't want to use that note if I can help it! This little stand is the quaintest, most delightful thing, and exactly matches the bed, &c.,—those massive compound curves.

It is a rather rare antique;—it is perfectly square, not a "washstand" at all but a "bedstand." The candle and snuffers, &c., stand on top, then there is a little drawer and a closet below. This and the table are $45.50, the discarded washstand was $42.00. These will "furnish" much more. I am delighted with them both.

We are still having *glorious* weather; and I have enjoyed loafing in the sunshine hugely. I meant to write you this afternoon, for tonight I must also write the children and one or two other people, but somehow I was too lazy, and the sun and air were too fine to leave.

There has come in the "Shield" the organ of your Greek letter fraternity one of the best articles that I have seen about you yet. It is by "N. Wilbur Helen" an instructor here.[2] He gets in Mr. Hadley's bi-centennial speech[3] and also the nice paragraph from "Harpers Weekly."[4] But among the notes at the back was the enclosed; is'nt it provoking?[5] To be held up as an encouragement to dawdlers! It was a "big break" to tell that to a reporter!—for of course the item is more spicy without your explanation!

I wonder if you are not half frozen at "Northeast"! At any rate you are seeing *glorious* scenery I know. Ah, me! how good it would be to be with my darling there!—or *any*where! All perfectly well, I love you, dear, tenderly, passionately,—I am altogether,

Your own   Eileen.

ALS (WC, NjP).
  1 This enclosure is missing.
  2 N. Wilbur Helen [Nathan Wilbur Helm, Instructor in Latin at Princeton], "Princeton University and Her New Phi Psi President," *The Shield of Phi Kappa Psi*, xxii (August 1902), 507-13.
  3 That is, President Arthur Twining Hadley's citation when he conferred the Litt.D. on Wilson at the Yale Bicentennial on Oct. 23, 1901. For the citation, see the news report printed at Oct. 26, 1901, n. 2, Vol. 12.
  4 It appeared in *Harper's Weekly*, xlvi (June 21, 1902), 777.
  5 The enclosure is missing. However, she was referring to the following item on page 533 of the issue of *The Shield* just cited: "Bro. Woodrow Wilson, president-elect of Princeton, consoles those students who lag behind the leaders in the class room by telling them that he himself stood fortieth in a class of a little over one hundred."

To Ellen Axson Wilson

My own darling,   North East Harbor, 18 Aug., 1902

This rush in a summer household is death to lover's plans. To-morrow I can write you a real letter; to-day, just a message of devotion. I leave at 11.45 A.M. and reach Gorham 11.50 P.M. I am well and happy,—happy in nothing so much as being

Your own   Woodrow

ALS (WC, NjP).

From Ellen Axson Wilson

My own darling,   Princeton, Aug. 18, 1902

What do you think of the enclosed sample for the diningroom chairs? I was in there last week and selected a lighter, *greener* piece from his sample book,—a beautiful colour. Now he writes as you see.[1] I should be disappointed to be obliged to have this, especially since it wears darker he says. But if *you* like this I will let it go.

I find myself not a little embarrassed by having to go through with so much red tape in making college purchases. It is all very well for the large bills like Wanamakers, but it is absurd to have to send little casual ones at auction rooms, &c. to you and Pyne and Cuyler before they can be paid. There is no sense in it, and it subjects me to mortification. I have already had to send your private check to two, and shall probably have to do the same for the mirror. Can't you explain this to Cuyler or Pyne and have,— say—$300.00 put in the bank here that I can draw from for such purposes? By the way, Whitley's men arrived today! Isn't that good?

I am truly delighted to hear that the Morgan visit is turning out such a success. I don't wonder that you enjoyed the fishing with such a pleasant party; but am agreeably surprised that you also liked the reception and the dinner on top of it! Are you developing a taste for "Sassiety" in your old age?—I was interrupted just here by the Fines who have just gone. Mr. Fine was most interesting. By the way he was telling me what an interesting community North East Harbour is and how different from Bar Harbour,—all "gebildete Leute"—with Eliot at the fore—as usual. Was he at the reception?

It is rather late and I go to town tomorrow, for bedding, blankets, muslin curtains, &c. so must stop. Mrs. Stowell[2] says they will have an important sale of china beginning the 2nd of Sept.—Tuesday & begs me to be there that day as the good things go very fast. All perfectly well. Love unbounded from,
                    Your little wife,   Eileen.

The [Robert McNutt] McElroys have another little girl born yesterday morning. Both doing well. Her name is Louise.

ALS (WC, NjP).
[1]. This enclosure is missing.
[2] The Editors have been unable to identify her.

To Ellen Axson Wilson

My own darling, Gorham, N. H. 19 Aug. '02

I arrived here last night, or, rather this morning, immediately after midnight, after an uneventful journey. The Hibbens and Wes[t]cotts are well; it is delightful to see them again; and I am revelling in getting hold of letters from you again. One,—one dear letter, I received at North East Harbor; but here I have had three and am happy. Ah, how you do dominate my life! How my heart slackens or bounds as it loses or obtains hold of you. I cannot *breathe* without the support of your love and the thought, at least, of your presence!

I must answer at once your business questions: I should think that *enough* side lights would abundantly light the dining room (say four), but put in a central wire *without* fixtures.

The photographic plates (I am delighted that you are so much pleased) will be kept one month (i.e. until about Sept. 12). The one I sent to the *World's Work* was distinctly the best, both in my opinion and in Perry's, though we hesitated between it and the full face one. You will not see the *World's Work* picture until October 1st. If you like these others, therefore, order some at once, addressing Purdy, Photographer, 146 Tremont St., Boston, and asking him to send you the bill. Send the proof at the same time, to avoid mistake. I hope you will select the full face. There is something unusual about it.

By all means let Fielder charge $30,000 for the house, if he chooses. We are not anxious to sell and that price, if we got it, would reconcile us to parting with it.

Hurrah for the little antique bed table. You are a genius at looking for things. I will start the bill through its routine at once.

This place is beautiful, exceedingly delightful. I never saw a more engaging, a more satisfying view. It will be a deep comfort to be within sight of it for two weeks. And the house is comfortable and well kept. But, dear me, how the mountains do make me dream, dream, dream of you, of the sweet, dear, beautiful little lady whose passion is for such scenes as these! My heart aches, to see them alone. I feel lonely, not only, but selfish as well. I am consumed with thoughts of you. Your own Woodrow

ALS (WC, NjP).

From Ellen Axson Wilson

My own darling,   Princeton, Aug. 19 1902.

I have been to New York today, and since my return have sat a long time with Father and written several business letters, so I fear I must put you off with no more of a letter than the one I received! A very sweet little note however and quite sufficient under the circumstances!

I have just written long letters of explanation to Mr. Alexander Bell enclosing the bill for the mirrors and to the auctioneer who sold them to me. It is a very humiliating business for me! We decided on Mr. Cope's advice to get *two* mirrors, since the two cost less than we had expected to pay for the one, and since I found I could afford it. The second one is to go where the plain one is now and the plain one, stained to match the woodwork, is to go over the dining room mantle. The two mirrors are the same price and style,—indeed came out of the same room. Mr. Cope said, just as Mr. Holmes did, that what the room wanted most to carry out the style was "glass and gold"! It will be stunning, will it not?—with the two. And so perfectly consistent

Please tell Mr. Lavake[1] that his design is *perfectly hideous*, for it certainly is. Imagine two heads in those little cramped-spaces! Tell him if he must have the two heads to have one on one side, one on the other, & leave off Old North.[2] Don't be weakly good-natured and allow him to perpetrate, (and perpetuate) some horror on such an occasion!

All well; the weather still perfect.

With love inexpressible, believe me, darling, always and altogether,   Your own,   Eileen.

ALS (WC, NjP).
    [1] Myron E. LaVake, jeweler of 172 Nassau St., who was designing the inaugural medal.
    [2] That is, Nassau Hall.

To Ellen Axson Wilson

                                        Gorham, New Hampshire
My own sweet darling,   20 August, 1902

I *like* the colour of this piece of leather, though I do not think that I would *select* it *de novo*. It is a fine piece of colour in itself, and I shall be *very* well satisfied with it in case you do not feel like going elsewhere for the colour you really want.

I sympathize with your embarrassment about small bills, and will write to Mr. Bell, Cuyler's secretary, asking him to get Pyne's authority to put $300 at your disposal, as you suggest. How like a selfish dog I feel that you should be having *all* the trouble of this complicated business! Never mind,—week after next!

My warm congratulations to the McElroys. I am very happy to hear the good news.

No, Mr. Eliot was *not* at the reception. He was not bidden. The Morgans, I believe, do not know him. I am not growing fond of "Sassiety," but the people Mrs. Morgan invited seemed one and all interesting,—not mere society folk.

I am delighted with this place. The house and and [*sic*] the housekeeping are like those at Sagg in its first, its good estate, and, instead of the sea, there are, on every hand, glorious mountains which it is an elevation, an inspiration to look on. A better selected spot than that which the house stands on I think I never saw; and yet it was originally only a farm house, and the farm work still goes on all about it. Aside from the Hibbens and Westcotts and a Professor and Mrs. Child[1] (Prof. Child is an old friend of Stock's at Philadelphia) the people here, though for the most part "gebildete Leute," are indisputably ordinary and uninteresting. But they do not worry me. Apparently it is not necessary to have anything to do with them. How happy I could be here if only I could look out upon these mountains with your eyes,—with your hand in mine! I enjoy everything so much more through you. Nothing that I do not share with you seems now entirely real to me or entirely my own: so integral, so indispensable a part of me does my love seem,—so completely am I

Her own   Woodrow

Love, real love, to dear Father and dear Madge.

ALS (WC, NjP).
[1] Clarence Griffin Child and Elizabeth Reynolds Child. He was at this time Assistant Professor of English at the University of Pennsylvania.

To Arthur W. Tedcastle

Gorham, N. Hampshire,

My dear Mr. Tedcastle,   20 August, 1902

Never go to North East Harbor for rest. Go for fun, but never for quiet! I did not have one moment of my own. This is the first afternoon I have felt my own master. Monday I travelled; yesterday I rested and pulled myself together.

I am very well, and perfectly delighted with this place. My stay at Clifton prepared me to enjoy things with full zest,—for I do not know when I have enjoyed a visit more or taken more refresh-

ment from it. If Mrs. Tedcastle had only been well and I might
have enjoyed her, too, it would have been ideal. I shall keep the
good taste of those quiet, friendly days in my heart for many a
day!

Please give my affectionate regards to Mrs. Tedcastle, Miss
Snell, and Miss Curtin (both of whom I thoroughly enjoyed
knowing), and believe me

Cordially and gratefully Yours,   Woodrow Wilson

ALS (WP, DLC).

To John Wesley Fielder, Jr.

Gorham, N. Hampshire,
My dear Mr. Fielder,   20 August, 1902.

Thank you for your letter of information about renting the
house. Mrs. Wilson told me of your suggestion that we make
$30,000 the price asked for the house, and I have written her
that I would like you to use that figure instead of the one we
named at first, $25,000.

Sincerely Yours,   Woodrow Wilson

WWTLS (WC, NjP).

To Edward Ingle

My dear Ingle,   Gorham, N. Hampshere, 20 August, 1902.

Thank you very much for your letter of the fifteenth, which has
been forwarded to me here. I shall look forward with a great deal
of interest to reading your sketch in the Record when I return
home; and I very much appreciate your suggestion that Princeton's influence in the South be made a special subject of study.
I shall act upon it as soon as possible.

Cordially Yours,   Woodrow Wilson

WWTLS (E. Ingle Papers, MdHi).

From Ellen Axson Wilson

My own darling,   Princeton   Aug. 20 1902

Your dear letter from Gorham came tonight,—apparently it is
a longer journey. I am delighted that you find it so beautiful, and
comfortable and pleasant; you will surely be willing to stay in
such a place,—with trips to other points of interest for a change,—
for three weeks. And you know there is absolutely no reason why

you should come home; there will be nothing doing the first week in Sept.; we won't have begun to think about moving.

McClure[1] telegraphed this afternoon for an "exclusive" picture,—wanted to send a photographer out tomorrow. I answered that you were out of town, and then wrote him tonight about the "full face" Purdy plate. I like it very much, there is something individual in a marked degree about it. You will laugh to hear that I have fallen in love with the Pirie McDonald picture! I simply hang over it and doat upon it! The eyes are so splendid; I toned down the light on the lip with very tender pencil touches, which much improved the mouth.

I have had a very busy day; it is past bed-time and I must still write a letter after this, so must stop now. Have been trying for days to write a long letter on a special subject and can never somehow get the time. We have had visitors this evening or rather Madge has, which detained me. Think of three young men calling at once (but not together) in Princeton in the summer! Mr. Conover,[2] young Sloane, and Aleck Alexander's freshman brother.[3] Young Sloane is rather attentive!

I send a nice budget of letters from the children which Beth will enjoy too. Is'nt Mary's satisfactory?[4] *Isn't* it funny to think of Jessie and Nellie playing at robbers and longing for pistols? Love to all the friends, and to my darling love unspeakable from

Your little wife,   Eileen.

ALS (WC, NjP).
  [1] Samuel Sidney McClure, editor of *McClure's Magazine*.
  [2] Perhaps Thornton Conover of 10 Bayard Lane.
  [3] Claude Aitcheson Alexander, brother of Alexander John Aitcheson Alexander '97.
  [4] All these enclosures are missing. "Mary" was Mary Eloise Hoyt.

To Ellen Axson Wilson

Gorham, N. Hampshire,
My own sweet darling,   21 August, 1902

I quite agree with your verdict with regard to La Vake's proposed medal, and I will write to him accordingly. I shall suggest that he get Howard Butler[1] to make a design for it, and that there be only one head on it,—my own. Nothing like taking the bull by the horns, disagreeable as it may be!

The cheque I sent to Caproni, dear, was for $35.00. Each of the pedestals cost $7.00, the Apollo Belvidere cost $20.00, and the packing $1.00.

The rain has come upon us to-day, chill and drear, out of the East. I have slept, as usual in such circumstances; and we have sat by the fire and talked and talked, and the day goes by easily and pleasantly enough. Westcott and Hibben chafe and are restless when they cannot be out on the mountains. Their delight is to get up a[t] six and tramp until seven in the evening. But a rainy day, as you know, deprives me of nothing. It but makes the loaf more complete. And somehow it seems to bring me nearer to you, when we are separated. When I walk about in unfamiliar scenes you seem far, far away,—*so* far away, and the scenes so foreign, because you do not know them; but, shut within a quiet room you seem so real and so near! It is as if you must surely walk presently to my side and kiss me! Ah, if I could only touch your lips and look into your eyes once a day, what cheer and tonic there would be for me in that brief moment, to support me the long day through! It is happiness to *think* of you, but it is *life* to be with you; and, if I knew that we should never see one another again, it would be torture to think of you, even though I knew you loved me. How would these long separations be possible if we did not know that they were but for a little, and that presently,—very soon,—we should be in each other's arms again? You are busy, and do not, cannot let thoughts of me disquiet you as they did while you were at Clifton, but I,—what is there for me to do but to dream of you, and realize the last detail, till I am driven almost from my self command, how vacant my life is without you? It is a sweet despair, because I know it is not to last,—that I am to have you again close against my heart; but, sweet as it is, it strains my heart to the utmost, and I am ready to cry out because I am   Your own   Woodrow

Love without stint to dear Father and dear Madge.

ALS (WC, NjP).
  [1] Howard Crosby Butler, Princeton 1892, Lecturer on Architecture at Princeton.

To Cyrus Hall McCormick

My dear Cyrus,   Gorham, N. Hampshire, 21 August, 1902.

   I very much want a good photograph of your father, the one you think best, for my History of the American People, which is soon to come from the press. Will you not have one sent me* at once? The volume into which it should go is being made up; I am very much dissatisfied with the portrait they have reproduced (which I saw for the first time yesterday); and unless we can get another practically at once it will be too late to reproduce and substitute it.

I am having a bit of a vacation up here in the White Mountains, and am enjoying it very much; but shall be more than ready, shall be eager, to get back to work by the first of September.

With warmest regards to Mrs. McCormick and yourself,

Faithfully Yours,   Woodrow Wilson

*Please have it sent direct to Harper & Brothers, Franklin Square, New York City, marked in such a way as to identify it.

WWTLS (WP, DLC).

From Ellen Axson Wilson

My own darling,   Princeton, Aug. 21. 1902

I have been in New York all day and came back to find Father sick so that it is now 10.40 P.M. and I havn't had a chance to write. He is perfectly quiet now; it was a light attack,—no pain.

Madge also leaves in the morning which is another reason why I could not write. She expected to go Tuesday, and I had made this engagement for today with Mrs. Stowell who came from the country to meet it, so I had to go. It was to finish the business of curtains and hangings. The man in charge of them is just back from his vacation so nothing has been done about them since you left until today. They will be *lovely*. I also got the bedding.

I found here a print of the accepted photo. from Purdy. It is *splendid* in pose and line of nose, face, &c.,—just my favourite angle. It would be *perfect* if the shadow were not so flat on the shadow side,—scarcely a suggestion of a line at the corner of the mouth or running from the nose. It makes the mouth look *just* a *little* short, though the expression is fine in spite of it. Did it have that fault in the proof? It looks to me like a picture that had been too much retouched. But I am delighted with it never-the-less.

But I must go to bed. No letter from my darling today, alas!

With devoted love   Your little wife,   Eileen.

ALS (WC, NjP).

From James MacNaughton Thompson

Dear Dr. Wilson: Princeton, Aug 21st [1902].

After talking to you about the Woodhull lectures,[1] I wrote Judge [James Hay] Reed of Pittsburg and yesterday received his check for $500., which was the sum you said would be needed. I knew you would be glad to know that this matter was cared for.

Shall I send you the check or deposit it with the Treasurer for "Woodhull Lecture Fund" or whatever title you see fit to name?

If you could find time to write Judge Reed personally, I am sure he would appreciate it deeply. His son, David, graduated in 1901 and his son, James, is in 1904. His address is "Hon. James H. Reed, Carnegie Bldg. P'burg., Pa."

"Prospect" at present looks as tho' some baby tornadoes had been playing hide-and-seek but order is scheduled to arrive out of this chaos about October 1st.

When you return, I should be much gratified if you could give me an hour or two in which to go over existing conditions in our buildings because I feel very strongly the necessity of having you and the Trustees realize, from actual observation, what the necessities of our present conditions are for, as a business proposition, we must stop decay and deterioration as soon as possible.

Hoping that you will return to us full to the brim of strength and energy, believe me, with best wishes.

Faithfully yours,   J MacN. Thompson.

ALS (WP, DLC).
 ¹ A new course in personal hygiene, required for freshmen, to be inaugurated in the coming fall term by Alfred Alexander Woodhull, M.D., Princeton 1856, Colonel, U. S. Army Ret. Colonel Woodhull was also to give a second-term elective course in general sanitation for seniors.

To Ellen Axson Wilson

My own darling,   Gorham, N. Hampshire, 22 August, 1902

You argue, in the sweet letter received to-day, that there will be nothing doing in Princeton the first week in September and that I ought to stay here a third week. Two will be quite enough, thank you. The truth is, that I am getting quite uneasy,—about you. If you work hard all day and then sit up writing letters till after bed-time every evening, as you evidently do, it is high time I was at home again to prevent your seriously overdoing the business,—if necessary, to send you off, for another rest. I am not sure that I can keep myself here the two weeks. I hate myself and the whole vacation business when I sit down and think. These beautiful mountains, which would be your delight, seem to rebuke me when I think of you drudging at home! This is the very last experiment of this kind that I shall ever try. It is deeply, abominably selfish.

The clouds are clearing away to-day, the sun is making more and more headway against them, and probably by to-morrow we shall have glorious weather once more.

I am delighted, as well as deeply amused, that you should have come to like the Pirie MacDonald picture. I have liked it from the first. I *wanted* to look like that. And I quite agree with your judgment about the full-face Purdy photograph. "There is something individual, in a marked degree, about it." Perry and I had a great deal of difficulty in deciding whether it or the one we chose was the better.

Thank you ever so much, my sweet one, for sending the children's and Cousin Mary's letters. They interested and delighted me *very* deeply. Bless the dear, thoroughbred darlings! How I love them! And, as for their mother, I am nearly dying for the love of her. Her sweet image haunts me day and night: I grow feverish with longing at every thought of her; nothing satisfies me because she is not here. Her influence disturbs me; I know not which way to turn for relief from the intense loneliness that dogs me! I was meant to live *with* her, not away from her. No man who had once had the blessing of her love and the infinite sweetness of possessing her could ever feel anything but bereaved every moment he misses that might be spent with her. I am with all the patience of an exile,　　　　Her own　Woodrow

Love to dear Father and dear Madge.

ALS (WC, NjP).

From Ellen Axson Wilson

My own darling,　　　　　　　　　　Princeton, Aug. 22 1902

Another unlucky evening in the matter of writing to you! I had just told father good-night and come down stairs intending to spend the evening writing letters when Mrs. Fine came in to spend the evening reading aloud to me,—bringing her own literature,—an article by Swinburne. She has just gone and it is after ten and I am overwhelmingly sleepy. It was very good in her to think of it, realizing how lonely I would be without Madge who left this morning. I certainly do miss her; we have had more real companionship,—been more intimate, than we ever were before and we have enjoyed each other. Now I have nothing but your pictures, five of which I carry about the house with me and prop up before me if I am sewing, or writing! The more I look at the "Purdy" the more I feel that it was a splendid thing spoiled in the retouching. I wonder if they couldn't take off the touches that have so softened and flattened it! I should think they would wipe off the glass plate.

Was'nt that a dear little letter from Nellie? How very naturally she writes! I am expecting Mary down in a few days.

I have actually been to a "tea" this afternoon,—at the Leavitt Howes[1] to meet Mrs. Venable who remains here with her boy.[2] I enjoyed *going to it* extremely—the drive I mean! It has been a glorious day,—as usual!

I am perfectly well;—and Father is quite over yesterday's little attack. He has a good many but they are all mild. They may be due to his eating so much fruit. For dinner he has a large saucer of blanche mange, a larger of apple, and a largest (sometimes two) of peaches and cream besides chicken potatoes rice and tomatoes. Then he eats peaches between meals & a cantaloupe for breakfast! He is perfectly delighted with his room at "Prospect,"—says it is the best room in the United States. Love to all the friends. With love inexpressible for my darling, I am as ever,

Your own,   Eileen.

ALS (WC, NjP).

[1] Leavitt and Rosalie Howe of Snowden Lane, near Princeton. Howe was a gentleman farmer.

[2] Helen Skipworth Wilmer (Mrs. Edward Carrington) Venable of Petersburg, Va. Edward Carrington Venable, Jr., was about to enter Princeton with the Class of 1906.

A News Report

[Aug. 23, 1902]

PRINCETON AT NORTHFIELD.

The Rev. H. A. Brigham of Boston has written an exceedingly graphic description of the Fourth of July celebration at the Student Conference at Northfield. . . . A huge Princeton Tiger was suspended above the space in the auditorium assigned to the large delegation from the University and Princeton receives [received] the "place of honor" in the singing of favorite college songs with "Old Nassau." When President-elect Woodrow Wilson, the orator of the day, entered the Princeton delegation were instantly on their feet and greeted him by singing the following new stanza of the Faculty Song:

> "Here's to Wilson our President,
> In Princeton college he pitched his tent;
> Now he's the boss of the wonderful show,
> Here's to Woodrow Wilson, O!"

After his oration[1] four Princeton men ascended the platform, put on President Wilson a Princeton sash and then in great state

escorted him to a conspicuous place among the Princeton delegates. When beginning his oration President Wilson was the
target for wild cheers throughout the house and fully captured
the crowd by saying he had come to the conclusion that they left
off building the tower of babel on the Fourth of July.

Printed in the *Princeton Press*, Aug. 23, 1902.
 1 "Religion and Patriotism," printed at July 4, 1902, Vol. 12.

Two Letters to Ellen Axson Wilson

My own darling,   Gorham, N. Hampshire, 23 August, 1902

Please, as you love me, do *not* write any more letters to me
after bed-time, and on the days when you go to New York *do not
write at all*. I will understand perfectly, and will not be alarmed.
I'd a thousand times rather go without a letter altogether than
see in every line of it my darling's pale cheeks and tired eyes,
and break my heart with the image. Every letter for the past two
weeks has been written after bed time. I think another one will
bring me home next week! And I must know that you are *not*
doing it. You must not simply write and say nothing about the
hour or the circumstances. I have visions enough of you now
worn out and sadly in need of rest,—and hate myself and all that
I do accordingly. Remember, my love, I am not your husband
merely: I am your *lover* and fill my mind every hour of the day
with thoughts of how you are faring. I *live* upon thoughts of you,
and if they are anxious and full of foreboding how can it go well
with me? I am not asking that you hurry some task of the day or
evening and steal an hour from other things which are pressing
and necessary for your letter to me; I am begging that you *omit
the letter altogether*. When it is an extra burden to you I do not
want it, I can't stand it! I'd rather go without for a week. And now
Madge is away and there is no companionship of any sort for
you,—nothing but work, killing work! What a fool I have made of
myself!

I am perfectly well: nothing seems to knock me up,—not even
eating anxiety about you. I ought to find something to do. The
only occupation I have is writing letters and reading proofs. To-
day they have sent me ninety-five pages of proof and I have work
cut out for a whole morning,—and hard work at that.

You need not wonder at the irregularity of my letters. They are
written at the same hour every day, but we are three miles from
the post office and they are sent in at no regular time. They have

to wait for errands in the village. Ah, my darling, how eagerly, how tenderly, how painfully I love you!

Your own Woodrow

Dear love to father.

Gorham, N. Hampshire,

My own precious darling,   24 August, '02

Almost everyone else in the house has gone into the village to church, to hear one of our fellow boarders who is a Unitarian,—or a Universalist, I am not clear which. The difference is not important; and, from the systematic way in which he does *not* bring up his children, I judge that he is either imperfectly religious or else a fool,—and he does not seem to be a fool.

Speaking of phases of religion reminds me that Jack Hibben spends part of every day, when he is not out tramping in the mountains, revising his book on Hegel, which he is about to publish through the Scribners.[1] Mrs. Hibben evidently thinks it much the most serious and successful piece of work he has done; and I dare say you will find it interesting and helpful. It is a systematic statement and (I believe critical) exposition of Hegelian doctrine. He is evidently putting a deal of his best force into it.

These quiet hours by myself fix my thoughts more than ever, if possible, on my dear little wife, the quite incomparable little woman upon whom my life depends, and all that concerns her. What concerns her interests me more than anything else in the world: and it is as easy as it is delightful to conjure images of so individual, so invariably engaging and interesting a person. I never knew any one who more pleased the imagination or provoked the idealizing powers of the mind. You are such a woman as Tennyson or Mrs. Browning might have invented, but could never have made quite so complete and perfect as the reality which excites me to deepest happiness. There is something spiritual and ideal about you, my darling, which I never saw in any other human being, and yet (this is the consummation of the marvel) there goes along with it a *physical* charm which would conquer even those who had no eyes for the element of spirit. I worship, I adore you; I take virtue and spirit and pleasure from you and am altogether bound to you as

Your own Woodrow

Deep love to dear Father.

ALS (WC, NjP).
[1] John Grier Hibben, *Hegel's Logic: An Essay in Interpretation* (New York, 1902).

From Ellen Axson Wilson

My own darling,   Princeton, Aug 24 1902

Last night just after my solitary supper there came a ring a[t] the bell and it turned out to be Mary Hoyt! Wasn't that nice? She is going to stay until Wednesday night. But it prevented my writing last night; and I have not had much chance today either. I went to church as usual and on my return found Father with an attack just coming on. So I was with him nearly all the rest of the day, and have naturally given the evening to Mary. Am a little tired now and I fear must cut this short. It was delightful to have Mary come and tell me *all* about the children. Certainly everything seems to be going well with them in every respect. She had just seen Uncle Tom[1] too and found him doing finely. This cool summer has been a godsend to him. It is just as usual today,— perfectly beautiful. I am perfectly well of course, but so tired I can hardly write,—so sorry. Father is resting quietly now; it was not a bad attack. Love to all friends. I love you, my darling, inexpressibly. Ah, for the great heart's word that would tell you *how* I love you!   Your own   Eileen.

ALS (WC, NjP).
[1] The Rev. Dr. Thomas Alexander Hoyt of Philadelphia.

To Ellen Axson Wilson

My precious darling,   Gorham, N. Hampshire, 25 Aug., 1902

It is Monday morning! *Next* Monday morning I shall start for home, and by night,—if my train fulfils its schedule and reaches the Grand Central Station at 7:10 P.M.,—shall be again in my darling's arms. How it makes my blood leap to think of it,—I shall dream of it all the week through,—and the dreaming will grow less and less painful for longing as the week goes by and I am on my way toward the delightful goal. I know of no one who is better to dream of than my darling. Most dreams that are sweet work a deep dissatisfaction in the mind because they can never come true, but dreams of you are less sweet than the reality. The *fact* of you is sweeter still. The summer days of idleness are, with me, always days of self-examination and self-distrust,—days of weakness when I do not feel equal to the tasks set for me the rest of the year,—and all that is intensified when I am alone, and too much with myself. What a source of steadying and of strength it is to me in such seasons of too intimate self-questionings to have one fixed point of confidence and certainty,—the even, unbroken, excellent perfection of my little wife, with her poise, her easy capacity in action, her unfailing courage, her quick, efficient thought,—and the womanly charm that goes with it all, the sweetness, the feminine grace,—none of the usual *penalties* of efficiency,—no hardness, no incisive sharpness, no air of command or of unyielding opinion. Most women who are efficient are such terrors,—have some touch of Mrs. Hutton about them,—of the Mrs. Hutton we do *not* like,—and *manage* where you only dominate by charm and sweet convincingness. Mrs. Hibben was telling me only to-day how Mrs. McCosh loves and admires you and counts on you. What a sweet old age *you* will have, my queen. How proud I shall be of your grey hairs—the crown of your years of love and service!   Your own   Woodrow

Deep love to dear Father

ALS (WC, NjP).

To William Morrison Coates[1]

My dear Sir,   Gorham, New Hampshire, 25 August, 1902.

It is really very hard to have to decline such an invitation as you have extended to me to be present at the annual dinner of the Haverford Alumni. I feel that there is every reason why it would be delightful to accept. But I foresee that this first year of my presidency is going to be so full, to overflowing, with engagements which it will be my plain official duty to make that it would be a mere imprudence to add any others, whatever the temptation.

Please accept my very warm thanks, my warmest expressions of regard and appreciation, and my sincerest regrets.
                    Very cordially Yours,   Woodrow Wilson

WWTLS (PHC).
  [1] Haverford College 1863, a wool dealer of Philadelphia.

From Ellen Axson Wilson

My own darling,   Princeton, Aug. 25, 1902

It is just twelve o'clock and I have just come in from a nice little drive with Mary. We went to "Prospect" for her to see it and then on to the aqueduct. It is a glorious morning; the swamps about Stony Brook are a mass of the beautiful, rosy hibiscus, and the road-sides pink and white with ironweed and Queen Ann's lace,—*beautiful*! We had a charming drive.

I am *so* sorry, dear, that you are worried about me,—and so unnecessarily! How badly I have managed! It was just that I kept thinking I would have a quieter, more uninterrupted time,— (above all a more *unhurried*)—for writing to you if I put off till night,—and every night for a week (not *two* weeks, I am *sure*!) something came up to disarrange that little plan and postpone the letter until late. I shall certainly write in the day from now on and do nothing but amuse myself in the evening. That is a promise. When I go to the city only a line to let you know I am back safely. I am not going to be so full of business now for a time, for the reason that everything is under weigh. Plumbing, heating, lighting, painting, papering, carpets, shades, bedding, hangings, upholstering, refinishing are all settled in *detail* and contracted for, and everything begun, and I can rather rest on my oars. I am going in Wednesday to get some odds and ends of silk, muslin, &c., to recover cushions, make bureau covers, &c. while I have time. There is a *quantity* of linen to hem but fortunately Anna does it beautifully, by hand, and is spending practically all her time at it. It was a severe shock to find that none of my table clothes would do on the new wide table; they would hang over the sides only two inches. So besides the two long ones I had to get ten others, costing about $15.00. Just beginning housekeeping over again! Isn't it dreadful? The old ones must be put away for the first trousseau!

If you could see me you would certainly not be anxious about me, for I never felt better in my life, or less tired as a rule. And everyone speaks of how well I look. You know you have frequently observed that running about, going to the city, &c. agrees with me better than sitting at home sewing, even when the severe weather makes it a trial to me; and in this weather it is really a pleasure.

(You know if you come home exactly at the end of four weeks you will find the same reason to be bored that you had when you left.)

How long a journey is it? I suppose it is a day from there to New York. I told you, I think, that I am to be in New York on Tuesday the second for the sake of the china sale. If you *must* return the first of the month it would be good to have you meet me there that morning; for I would *much* prefer your help in selecting the china; we could get the silver too. I am assuming that you would reach N. Y. late the night before. But I *wish* you *would* stay through that week. I really don't expect them to have the sort of china we want at that sale.

Father is as well as usual today.

Mary stays till Wed. morning.

With love inexpressible believe me darling,

Your own   Eileen.

To whom did you send that extra "Harper" with your picture? I can't remember and I have three or four others to give away, and don't want to make a mistake.

ALS (WC, NjP).

Frederick A. Steuert[1] to Harper and Brothers

Gentlemen: [Chicago] August 25th, 1902.

Herewith please find a photograph of Mr. Cyrus H. McCormick, which I am sending you at the request of Mr. Woodrow Wilson, of Princeton N.J.[,] understanding from him that it is to be used in place of one which you already have, and from which the proper reproductions will be made for the "History of the American People" which is about to go to press. When the photograph has served your purpose will you kindly return same to me, greatly obliging.

I am,

Very respectfully yours,   F. A. Steuert   Secretary.

CCL (C. H. McCormick Papers, WHi).
[1] Confidential secretary to Cyrus H. McCormick.

To Ellen Axson Wilson

My own darling,   Gorham, N. Hampshire, 26 August, 1902

It is a very amusing picture you sketch for my imagination, of Mrs. Fine reading Swinburne to you the evening through. It is a deep vexation to me that she should have kept you up till after ten and thrown your letter writing on till after bed-time; but very likely it was good for you to be kept, even so, from loneliness, and intellectual amusement for *you* from Mrs. Fine is a most pleasing idea! It is high time that I should hurry home now that Madge is gone. It has quieted my thoughts about you to know that you had Madge. I foresaw the new intimacy you speak of, and rejoiced in it. I knew the pleasure you would get from it. But now, nothing but work and loneliness. It's neither safe nor wholesome. I must be at hand to coax you away from being busy overmuch. I think it is one of the chief satisfactions of my life that my mere companionship brings pleasure into your life and lightens your thought of burdens. I do not understand why it should, as you know, but there is no need that I should understand it. A little mystery, a little standing wonder and inexhaustible surprise, add to the zest of the happiness I get from it. My darling has a genius for loving, and there is an element almost of detachment in my enjoyment of her exercise of it: the display of it is so sweet, so delicate, so full of natural charm, so instinctively artistic,—like herself; and she is never so much or so characteristically herself as when displaying it. That is why you are so often an unconscious artist in words, because you are such an inevitable artist in acts, when your whole heart is engaged. And so I speak and write better to you than to anyone else in the world, with a freer release of my powers, with a more intimate discovery of the poet that is in me, with a more complete marriage of mind and heart. It is, and must all my life be, a deep inspiration to be

Your own   Woodrow

Deepest love to dear Father

ALS (WC, NjP).

From Ellen Axson Wilson

My own darling,   Princeton, Aug. 26, 1902

It is a beautiful morning. I have been strolling about the garden and will now write to you before settling down to sew. I am having as I predicted quite a lull in "business"; everybody is at work; even the masons have begun on our chimneys this morning, and Mr. Thompson must be away for I have not seen or heard of him for some three days. Yesterday Mary and I spent a quiet afternoon out of doors, she reading aloud, I sewing and we will probably do the same today—unless we "go trollying"! I am perfectly well, Father is all right and there is no news at all.

It is a good time to tell you about a matter that is making me very sick at heart,—has given me several sleepless nights in the last two weeks. I will not have to write the whole story because the enclosed letter from Mamie Erwin will tell it.[1] You saw her first letter,[2]—did you not?—telling me of little Hamilton's death?

When I answered I begged her to write me all about the family, speaking of how I had begged in vain for letters before, and how it had distressed me to be so helplessly ignorant of them all. This came in reply,—this miserable story of a broken household. Isn't it *terrible*? I always knew that everything depended on Beth, but even I did not expect such a complete demonstration of that fact. Think of *three* of the children dead, and the rest scattered;— and, worst of all, none of them getting any education, and sinking down even in the social scale. It is Ellie,[3] of course that I am chiefly distressed about because, owing to her age (fifteen) and sex, her needs are most pressing.

I was interrupted by the unexpected arrival of Will Hoyt to spend the rest of the day and night. Have had no chance to go on with my letter today. Tomorrow we all leave together on the 9.05, I to New York.

That adorable love letter this morning, dearest, made me happy beyond words. Ah *how* I love you!

Your own   Eileen.

ALS (WP, DLC).
   [1] Mamie, daughter of Hamilton Erwin of Morganton, N. C., and the late Elizabeth ("Beth") Adams Erwin, Mrs. Wilson's girlhood friend, whose letter is missing.
   [2] It is missing.
   [3] Ellen Woodrow Erwin.

Harper and Brothers to Frederick A. Steuert

Dear Sir: New York City   Aug. 26. 1902

We beg leave to acknowledge the receipt of the photograph of the portrait of Mr. McCormick, which we shall return to you, as requested after the reproduction is made.

Thanking you for your courtesy in the matter, we are

Yours very truly   Harper & Brothers

ALS (C. H. McCormick Papers, WHi).

To Ellen Axson Wilson, with Enclosure

My own darling   Gorham, N. Hampshire   27 August, 1902

The enclosed letter, from C. C. Cuyler's secretary, means that C. C. left in such a hurry (he was no doubt already ill,—for his illness declared itself almost at once on the steamer) that only $500.00 of the subscription was definitely provided for; and that Mr. Bell can send you *now* only about $180.00 (he is away from his office and gives the figures only approximately). C. C. is expected back by the 15th, quite well, I am delighted to hear, from Morgan, and will of course take the matter up at once and get it in shape. The big bills, at Wanamaker's and Flint's, need not be settled before the 1st. of October. Meanwhile, Mr. Bell has laid the matter before Pyne.

I think that you had better not send anything off to me, my pet, after the first mail on Friday. The delivery of mail here on Sunday is very uncertain.

How glad I am that Mary Hoyt turned up. Your loneliness after Madge's departure had got on my spirits. Now there will be only half a week's interval between cousin Mary's return to the shore and my arrival home. If my train is late getting in to New York (I have a margin of but 40 minutes) I fear I shall miss the last train out for Princeton (8 o'clock) Monday evening. But, if I have to stay in town over night, I can at least get back home by a quarter past ten Tuesday morning.

I am perfectly well; the Westcotts and Hibbens are as good to me as you,—even you,—could desire, and, if I were not a forlorn lover, I could be quite happy here. If *you* were only here *how* happy I could be! The weather has been for the most part fine during this week. To-day Westcott and Hibben have gone off for a twenty-mile tramp along the shoulders of the presidents, Adams and Washington. I have no such ambitions. I am such a loafer that I rather think my fellow boarders think me lazy and inefficient! All send warmest love, and I am, with deep joy, altogether   Your own   Woodrow

Warmest love to poor, dear Father.

ALS (WC, NjP).

From Alexander Bell

Dear President Wilson: Warren Co., N. Y.   Aug 23d 1902

Your favor of 20th inst. has been forwarded to me here where I am on my vacation until Sept. 1st—hence the delay.

I am today writing Mr Pyne at Bar Harbor enclosing your letter and asking him to authorize me by wire to have our office in N. Y. instructed to send Mrs. Wilson a cheque for the balance remaining in the "Woodrow Wilson Fund." As soon as Mr Pyne telegraphs me I will at once wire C. M. & Co accordingly.

A bill arrived from you the other day for about $24. & the same day one from Mrs. Wilson for $96. so the account (relying on my memory alone) should stand something like this:

Cash paid in		$500.
One bill already paid about	$200.	
Bills on hand unpaid say	120.	320.
Approximate balance say		$180.

so that in any event I fear we could not send Mrs Wilson the $300. unless some additional subscriptions come in very soon. You may be sure I shall gladly do whatever I can to facilitate Mrs. Wilson's convenience in the matter as well as your own, & as soon as I hear from Mr Pyne will advise you of the result.
            Yours very truly   Alexander Bell.

ALS (WP, DLC).

To Henry Norris Russell, with Enclosure

                        Gorham, New Hampshire,
My dear Mr. Russell,   27 August, 1902.
    It gives me real pleasure to enclose such a letter as you ask for, and to express the warmest good wishes, for your success and happiness while studying over sea.[1]
            Cordially and sincerely Yrs.,   Woodrow Wilson

    [1] Russell, an old friend of the Wilsons and a member of the Class of 1897, was to be a research student in astronomy at King's College, Cambridge, during the academic year 1902-1903.

        E N C L O S U R E

To the Registrar of Cambridge University

My dear Sir,   Gorham, N. Hampshire, 27 August, 1902.
    I take real pleasure in introducing to you Mr. Henry Norris Russell, a graduate of Princeton, University, who purposes undertaking advanced study and research at Cambridge. I can commend him to you as one of the most capable men of recent years at Princeton, and a man who will make the best use of the opportunities afforded him; and I ask for him your kindest attention.
            Very truly Yours,   Woodrow Wilson
            President, Princeton University.

WWTLS (H. N. Russell Papers, NjP).

From Ellen Axson Wilson

My own darling,   Princeton, Aug. 27 1902

Back from New York safe and well and not very tired. Have just come from discussing the latest developments of the coal strike[1] with Father,—our usual evening occupation! (Do you see the papers up there? Have you read Hewitt's letter?[2] That seems the most important thing that has happened in the matter for some time.)

But I must keep my word and *not* write a letter. Yours of this morning tells me that you are coming Monday,—and I see from your tone that it is no use urging you to "bide a wee." If we could only count on its remaining cool it would not matter, but I am afraid we must make up for all this in the first weeks of Sept. There is *nothing* for you to do here,—as you see not even any mail of consequence. Don't you think you *ought* to try and content yourself for another week?

Of course if you *will* come then you won't want to stay in New York overnight if it isn't necessary,—if you can make the half past nine train. So I told Mrs. Stowell I would not be in on Tuesday, but would perhaps come on Wednesday for the sake of the sale.

How do you expect me to keep my head, you dear thing, when you send me such letters as you have done recently—when you lavish upon me such delicious praise? Surely there was never such a lover before, and even after all these years it seems almost too good to be true that you are *my* lover. All I can say in return is that I love you as you deserve to be loved,—as much as you can possibly *want* to be loved by

                              Your own   Eileen

ALS (WC, NjP).

[1] The strike of the United Mine Workers, under the leadership of John Mitchell, against the anthracite coal operators of Pennsylvania, which had begun on May 12, 1902.

[2] A statement issued on August 25, 1902, by Abram Stevens Hewitt, New York industrialist and philanthropist, saying that the basic issue of the strike was not hours or wages but the union's demand for recognition. Concession of this demand, Hewitt continued, would deny the right of every man to sell his labor in a free market and make Mitchell dictator of the coal industry and give him enough political power to decide the next presidential election. "The only solution for the trouble," Hewitt concluded, "is for Mr. Mitchell to order the strike off without delay." *New York Times*, Aug. 26, 1902.

From Thomas St. Clair Evans[1]

East Northfield, Mass.

My dear President Wilson,   Aug. 27th, 1902

In response to your suggestion made to me at the Student Conference[2] I have found that the following are the most efficient college preachers in the middle eastern section of the country—

√Rev. G. Campbell Morgan D.D. Address in care of W. R. Moody East Northfield, Mass. Congregationalist from London now speaking throughout the U.S. on Mr Moody's invitation. He is probably the best teacher and preacher on practical christianity of our day. His engagements are made very far ahead so that he will be hard to secure.

√Robert E. Speer A.M. Secretary Presbyterian Board of Foreign Missions, 156 fifth Avenue New York. He could help the fellows more than any other man if you can get around the lack of Rev &c. He has been one of the Yale Preachers for several years.

Rev Alexander McKenzie D.D. "The First Church in Cambridge," Cambridge, Mass. Congregationalist.

√Rev. Wilton Merle Smith D.D. '77 New York. Presbyterian.

Rev C. C. Albertson D.D. First Methodist Church, Germantown

Rev Floyd W. Tomkins S.T.D. Holy Trinity Episcopal Church Philadelphia.

Rev A. C. Dixon D.D. Ruggles St. Baptist Church, Boston.

Rev Wm. Patterson D.D. Bethany Presbyterian Church, Philadelphia.

Rev R. H. Nelson D.D. St. Peter's Episcopal Church, Philadelphia

√Rev A. F. Schauffler D.D. New York City Mission Society, Presbyterian

Bishop Cyrus D. Foss D.D. L.L.D. 2043 Arch St. Philadelphia Methodist Church.

Rev C. A. R. Janvier, Holland Memorial Pres. Church, Philadelphia—a Princeton man. Very good.

√Rev J. Ross Stevenson D.D. Fifth Avenue Pres. Church, New York City.

Rev S. J. McPherson D.D. Lawrenceville.

Rev E. Walpole Warner, St. James Episcopal Church, Madison Ave. and 71st St. New York.

Bishop Ethelbert Talbot D.D. L.L.D. Central Pa Diocese of Episcopal Church, South Bethlehem, Pa.

√President Charles Cuthbert Hall D.D. L.L.D. Union Theological Seminary, New York.

√President W. H. P. Faunce D.D. L.L.D. Brown University.

Of course I would include Dr Patton and Dr Van Dyke among the very first.

I have checked those who are specially fine.

If I can be of any assistance in securing any of the Philadelphia men I shall be delighted to do so.

I want to see Princeton with the strongest list of preachers in the country.

As you enter upon your new duties I want to assure you of my heartiest good wishes and prayers. I have every confidence that you are the man for the place.

Yours very cordially,   Thomas St Clair Evans

Recommended Preachers cont'd

Rev. Dr. Campbell Morgan   Northfield, Mass.
Rev. Dr. Geo. A. Gordon of Old South Ch. Boston
Dr. S. Parkes Cadman of Brooklyn, N.Y.
Rev. James E. Freeman,   Yonkers.
Dr. [William Stephen] Rainsford of New York.
Dr. Patton.

ALS (WP, DLC).
  ¹ Princeton 1897, Secretary-Treasurer of the Y.M.C.A. of the University of Pennsylvania.
  ² That is, the Northfield Student Conference at which Wilson had spoken on July 4, 1902.

From Frederick A. Steuert

Dear Sir: [Chicago] August 27, 1902.

At the request of Mr. Cyrus H. McCormick I forwarded on August 25th to Messrs. Harper Bros., Franklin Square, New York City, an additional photograph of Mr. McCormick's father. Mr. McCormick thanks you for bringing this matter to his attention and wonders if you had all the information which you desired in preparing the article you mentioned.

I am,

Very respectfully yours,   F. A. Steuert   Secretary

CCL (C. H. McCormick Papers, WHi).

To Ellen Axson Wilson

My own darling,   Gorham, N. Hampshire, 28 August, 1902

I do not remember sending the *Harper* with my picture in it to any one. Perhaps you did give me an address to which to send it (I have a vague recollection that you did), but if so I do not recall what it was. Was it Uncle Will?[1]

I had thought, until I read your letter which came yesterday, that if I missed the connection for Princeton Monday evening I would take a train for Trenton and try to get home by the trolley. But, of course, if you are to be in New York the next day, I will not try the round about way, but will stay in New York and meet you at the Jersey City station. If I do not turn up at home, therefore, by ten o'clock Monday night (the train is scheduled to arrive at about 9.40) you may expect to see me as you come through the Exit gate at Jersey City. How can I bear to meet you and not take you in my arms and kiss you?

That was an infinitely sweet and soothing letter that came yesterday (to-day's mail is not in yet) with its narrative of quiet drives and work carried forward to an interval of leisure. It did me more good than any amount of mountain air could do me. I am so made that every benefit or damage seems to be to my spirit, and to my body only indirectly *through* my spirit; and when my heart is at ease about you it seems real vacation time and I am full of vigour. When my heart is not at ease nothing goes well with me,—the very air I breathe seems tainted! The trouble is that in summer, with all strain of pressing business taken off, I have *time* to be unhappy, and, separated from you, am easily upset. I ought not to let you *see* my disturbed spirits; but what can I conceal from you? These four weeks, though they have been full of refreshing rest and pleasure, have seemed four *months* for length. The good they have done me physically will probably appear best when I get home and have again what is indispensable to me, your companionship and all the sweet comforts which go with it. You see I cannot be weaned: I am hopelessly in love with you and incorrigibly

Your own   Woodrow

Tender love to dear Father.

ALS (WC, NjP).
[1] William Dearing Hoyt, M.D.

From Ellen Axson Wilson

My own darling   Princeton, Aug. 28, 1902

Two dear letters from you today, which was certainly delightful only it means a blank day tomorrow.

The check from the Cuylers came this morning and for $300.00. About half an hour after came a regular *dun* from Mrs. Swann[1] for the $100.00! The maid was to wait for an answer, and did wait while I wrote the check. And this afternoon she sent me a formal receipt without another word. She is certainly unique.

I have had a very busy day again for reasons which I havn't time to mention,—busy *out*side and *in*—writing letters and directing Mr. Titus,—and chiefly taking care of Father who has had another attack, poor dear. It is now nine o'clock and he is not yet asleep, so I am scribbling this in great haste (while Annie watches for me.)

A letter came to him from Sister Annie. She says she will sail on the 4th of Oct. All as well as usual[.] So this is actually to be my last letter—or note rather,—I havn't written you *any* letters! I wish I had had time to make this a decent one. But I must keep my word and not sit up late,—for I *am* a little tired tonight.

Goodnight, dear, May God bless and keep you and bring you safely home! Oh, how I hope you won't miss that train!

With love, tender, devoted, passionate,—I am as ever,
                    Your little wife,   Eileen.

ALS (WC, NjP).
[1] Josephine Ward Thomson Swann, who was married first to John Renshaw Thomson, United States Senator from New Jersey from 1853 until his death in 1862. In 1878, she married Thomas Swann, President of the Baltimore & Ohio Railroad, 1848-53; Mayor of Baltimore, 1856-60; Governor of Maryland, 1865-69; and congressman from Maryland, 1869-79. He died in 1883. Mrs. Swann moved to Princeton about 1892 and lived at 50 Stockton St. The dun was probably for Mrs. Wilson's contribution to some charity, about which no evidence can be found.

Two Letters to Ellen Axson Wilson

My own darling,   Gorham, N. Hampshire, 29 August, 1902

You must not change your plan about spending Tuesday in New York. Please write to Mrs. Stowell again that you will carry out your original plan. If I catch my train for Princeton and get there Monday evening, I would a great deal rather turn right around and go back to New York on Tuesday, *before* settling down, than wait, restless, *un*settled, until Wednesday. If I *miss* my my [*sic*] train, I will stay in town over night and the whole thing will be as convenient as possible. I shall consider that as settled.

That was, indeed, the saddest of letters you sent me, from poor Mamie Erwin. We might have known that *he*[1] would act in that way,—but no knowledge of him takes away from the pathetic tragedy of the situation. Had you thought of doing something for little Ellie, your namesake?[2]

It will hardly be worth while for me to write more than one more letter to you. If I miss my train Monday night, I will telegraph you, so that you may know that I am at least safe in New York. I shall have an all day's ride. I leave North Gorham station, five miles from here, at 7:21 in the morning, taking a quarter past six breakfast to catch the train, and travel till 7.10 in the evening, the hour at which the schedule says I ought to arrive at 42nd. St. station. That's a long pull: twelve hours solid. But I am not easily fatigued now,—at any rate more than superficially.

I have to hold myself in hand very carefully now, as during the *first* days of an absence, to guard my emotions from painful overflow,—from dangerous, demoralizing overflow. Alas, I am too intense! If you did not love me so in return I do not know what would become of me. It seems to *heal* such emotions as mine to get such complete, such *soothing* love in return. It is my life that I am   Your own   Woodrow

Deep love to dear Father

[1] That is, Hamilton Erwin.
[2] Correspondence concerning the matter is missing, but Wilson's bank register for 1902-1903 (MS. in WP, DLC) discloses that the Wilsons acted at once, secured Ellen Erwin's enrollment at Salem Academy in Salem, N. C., and assumed responsibility for all her expenses.

My own darling,   Gorham, N. Hampshire, 30 August, 1902

It seems like winning *very* near the goal to be able to say that this is my last letter before *seeing* you and being happy again. May I be spared from spending a vacation without you again! No doubt we did the wisest thing in sight this summer, and everywhere I have gone everything possible has been done to make me both comfortable and happy. The Hibbens and Westcotts, have been lovely to me, as the Tedcastles and the Morgans were, and have fully won all over again their right to be called dear friends: you would love Mr. and Mrs. Hibben more than ever if I could tell you how sweet they have been to me. It is not what has happened to me that I am bewailing: I have been blessed and petted. It is what I have lacked. I have lacked what only my own sweet, intimate darling can give me, and what I cannot do without,—how shall I define it? It is a sort of spiritual reinforcement, and renewal too, which comes from absolute communion of thought, from having every motion of the spirit shared in, shared with an intimacy and an instinctive zest which means more than trust or confidence or even love,—an indefinable singleness of heart and life, in which the very breath seems to be shared. No doubt I ought not to *depend* on that; no doubt I ought to have independent strength enough to live without daily taste of that unspeakable happiness. But apparently I have not. Having once had it, it has entered into my soul and become indispensable to the full exercise of the other qualities of my nature,—many of which, I fancy most of which, it has discovered and brought to perfection.

But I must pull up,—that way lies intolerable impatience! I am coming, my darling, God willing; and when I have you I shall be happy.   Your own   Woodrow

Deep love to dear Father

ALS (WC, NjP).

A Memorandum for a Report to the Board of Trustees of Princeton University

31 Aug. '02

Mem. Report to Board of Trustees, October, 1902.[1]

Essential soundness and splendid *esprit* of the present College.

But insufficiently capitalized

(1) Too much work
Research choked

(2) Too little pay

(3) Insufficient
equipment

Not attractive to ambitious men who desire gentle *status.* Men now preparing for college positions. Our own part in preparing teachers.

What is necessary (besides reorganization of studies):

New methods (the tutorial system)

Strengthening of weak departments, e.g., History, Economics, Biology.

Equipment: Recitation Hall—Physical Laboratory—Biological Laboratory.

Mem. Report to Board of Trustees, October, 1902.

Essential soundness and splendid esprit of the present College.
But insufficiently capitalized:
    (1) Too much work
        Research choked
    (2) Too little pay
    (3) Insufficient Equipment

} Not attractive to ambitious men or to men who desire quiet status. Men now preparing for college positions. Our own part in preparing teachers.

What is necessary (besides reorganization of studies):
    New methods (the tutorial system)
    Strengthening of weak departments, e.g., History, Economics, Biology.
    Equipment: Recitation Hall — Physical Laboratory — Biological Laboratory.
    Increase of Salaries
    School of Science: Re-endowed, reorganized.
        Equipment and Support.
            Remarks on depending on fees.
    Schedule of minimum Cost.

Not to be classed with its immediate rivals as a University in
    Either development or equipment. Not classed with them any longer,
as a matter of fact, in academic circles.
    Comparative Statistics.
What is necessary: Graduate School. (What it would mean besides mere
                        building and additional Courses of instruction.)
                        Our own in the schools.
            School of Jurisprudence (explained)
                Electrical School (Reputation already gained).
    Schedule of minimum Cost.

Housing and feeding of the Students. (Reputation of Princeton for expensiveness
    and bad food, esp. in Freshman and Sophomore years.)
.. ys via Means.

31 Aug. '02

*Wilson's handwritten outline of his first report to the Board
of Trustees as President of the University*

Increase of Salaries

School of Science: Re-endowed, reorganized.

Equipment and Support.

Remarks on depending on *fees.*

Schedule of minimum *Cost.*

Not to be classed with its immediate rivals as a *University* in either development or equipment. *Not* classed with them any longer, as a matter of fact, in academic circles. *Comparative statistics.**

What is necessary: Graduate School. (What it would mean besides mere building and additional courses of instruction.

☞ *Our* men in the schools.)

School of Jurisprudence (explained)

Electrical School (Reputation already gained).

Schedule of minimum *Cost.*

Housing and feeding of the students. (Reputation of Princeton for expensiveness and bad food, esp. in Freshman and Sophomore years.)

Ways and means.

*	History	Economics	Biology
Harv.	15	13	16
Yale	10	8	3
Pa.	6	5	8
Col.	9	7	20
Pr.	3	2	3

WWhw memorandum (WP, DLC).

1 This was Wilson's first outline of his report to the Board of Trustees printed at Oct. 21, 1902.

To Jenny Davidson Hibben

Gorham, Sunday evening,

My dear Mrs. Hibben,   31 August, 1902

This is just a line of good-bye. I need not say how distressed I have been by your illness. Yesterday and to-day have been as hard to get through with, I believe, as any days I have ever known,—but not because I was lonely,—only because you were ill; not because I was *bored* but because distress had full time and opportunity to bite in. Jack and you have been so good, so exceptionally kind and sweet to me since I got here that I had pleased myself with the thought that, though I must turn away to the masquerade that lies before me, I should at least turn to it straight from idyllic days. We must try to forget the last two days. Perhaps if you get back to Princeton before the play begins, we can manage to recreate a few days of our old lives to take the place of these!

I am so glad that you are better. May complete recovery come at once! Good-bye.

Faithfully and affectionately Yours,   Woodrow Wilson

ALS (photostat in WC, NjP).

A Pocket Notebook

[c. Sept. 1, 1902-c. Aug. 31, 1903]

Inscribed "Woodrow Wilson 1902-1903," with WWhw notes, reminders, names and addresses, and one bibliographical reference.

Pocket notebook (WP, DLC).

To Frederick A. Steuert

Princeton, New Jersey,

My dear Mr. Steuart,   5 September, 1902.

Please thank Mr. McCormick for his note to me about the photograph of his father sent to the Harpers. It was not wanted for any article particularly dealing with Mr. McCormick Sr's career, but only to accompany a reference to his great invention which I had made in my History of the American People which the Harpers are about to publish. I did not at all like the portrait they had already put into the text, and asked them to send to Mr. McCormick for the better one which he has so kindly sent.

Very truly Yours,   Woodrow Wilson

WWTLS (WP, DLC).

From Charles Williston McAlpin

[Princeton, N. J.]

My dear Dr. Wislon [Wilson]:   September 5, 1902.

. . . At the October meeting of the Trustees last year it was voted that the Faculty should appear in full Academic costume at the opening of the University. A notice to this effect was sent to each member of the Faculty and to all the instructors. Shall I send a postal card notice to the same effect a few days before the opening of college?

I remain,

Sincerely yours,   [C. W. McAlpin]   Secretary.

CCL (McAlpin File, UA, NjP).

From John Wesley Fielder, Jr.

Dear Dr. Wilson: Princeton, N. J., Sept. 5th, 1902.

I delivered the contracts for the sale of your property, Library Place, which you signed this morning, to Mr. Robert Garrett, and retain in my safe the extra copy of said contract which you also signed in order to meet any contingency that might arise in the loss of the originals, should that ever occur in the mails.

Mr. Garrett stated to me that he considered the transaction closed as to its purchase, and that he would forward the contracts signed, together with the check of $2500, on Monday next, and we should receive them by Tuesday at the latest.

I spoke to him in regard to the shades and the stair and hall carpets and told him what Mrs. Wilson desired me to say, and he has expressed a desire to consider the purchase of them as soon as he returns from Europe, and wished me to say to you and Mrs. Wilson that if you can arrange to leave the shades up and the stair and hall carpet and any other carpet in the bed rooms down until his return, he should like very much to look at them with the idea of purchasing. I presume you and Mrs. Wilson can arrange in your moving to leave these things spoken of until the last, and should Mr. Garrett after the 15th of October decide that he will not take them, they can be then removed, however, I believe he intends fully to accept of the proposition Mrs. Wilson wished me to make to him, and that is to take the above articies [articles] at a price that is fair and equitable.

Respectfully yours,   J. W. Fielder, Jr   agent

TLS (WP, DLC).

To John Huston Finley

My dear Friend,   Princeton, 6 Sept., 1902

I came back home to find your note of Monday[1] lying on my desk. You may be sure I appreciated it. You may be equally sure that I will take advantage of its generous offer of assistance.

Come around to see us before the rush of the term sets in and catch up with the summer talk.

Faithfully & cordially Yours,   Woodrow Wilson

ALS (J. H. Finley Papers, NN).
1 It is missing.

To Winthrop More Daniels, with Enclosure

My dear Daniels,   Princeton, New Jersey, 6 September, 1902.

The enclosed letter, so far as it is legible, explains itself. M. Boucard will write you soon as to the detail of his plans for the journal and the exact assistance expected of col[l]aborators.

I hope that you have had the most refreshing sort of summer and that Mrs. Daniels and the boy[1] are as well as possible.

Faithfully Yours,   Woodrow Wilson

WWTLS (in possession of R. Balfour Daniels).
1 Robertson Balfour Daniels, born August 6, 1900.

E N C L O S U R E

From Max Boucard

Cher Monsieur: Paris, Aug 11. 1902

Je vielle vous adresser tous mes compliments sur votre élection à la Présidence; j'en suis très heureux, et on ne pouvait faire un meilleur choix. Tous vos amis français se joignent à moi pour vous féliciter.

Nous savons avec regrets que vous ne puissiez pas collaborer à notre révue, mais nous comprenons parfaitement que vous seriez trop occupé pour cela.

Je vais écrire à Monsieur M. Daniels aussi que vous me le conseillez, et j'espère que avec votre aide il voudra bien devenir notre collaborateur, mais je desirais vivement que vous soyez assez aimable pour vouloir bien lui annonçer ma prochaine lettre.

Adieu, cher Monsieur, viellez bien croire à mes trés dévoués sentiments   Boucard

ALS (in possession of R. Balfour Daniels).

To Charles Williston McAlpin, with Enclosure

Princeton, New Jersey,

My dear Mr. McAlpin, 6 September, 1902.

. . . Thank you for calling my attention to the action of the Board of Trustees about academic costume at the opening of the University. I would be obliged to you if you would have the enclosed notice printed, not on postal cards, but on sheets of paper suitable for mailing, and have a copy sent to each member of the Faculty not later than the twelfth.

With much regard, and hoping that you have had your full share of summer refreshment,

Sincerely Yours,   Woodrow Wilson

WWTLS (McAlpin File, UA, NjP).

ENCLOSURE

At the stated meeting of the Board of Trustees of the University held October 15, 1901 the following resolution was passed:

(Here insert the Resolution)

You are requested to be present in full academic costume at the Chancellor Green Library at 2.45 P.M., sharp, on the afternoon of Wednesday, September 17, 1902.

Woodrow Wilson, President.

WWT MS. (McAlpin File, UA, NjP).

From Charles Baker Wright[1]

Dear Wilson: Middlebury, Vermont, Wed., Sept. 10, 1902.

My pleasure in your new honor is none the less sincere because my expression of it is somewhat tardy; I simply chose to come later that I might avoid the rush. I have rejoiced in all your successes since the old days when I used to watch the MS of "Congressional Government" growing thicker, and now I count it a special good-fortune that I can wish you happiness in the larger field.   Sincerely yours,   C. B. Wright.

ALS (WP, DLC).

[1] Who had roomed in the same boardinghouse as Wilson when both were graduate students at The Johns Hopkins University. At this time, Wright was Professor of Rhetoric and English Literature at Middlebury College.

From Henry Fairfield Osborn

My dear Wilson: New York, September 10, 1902.

I am very glad to receive your letter of September 8th; and take pleasure in sending you my views regarding the biological work at Princeton, in which I take the warmest interest; in fact, I shall be only too glad to give you from time to time any assistance I can in this and other matters, and shall not feel in the least injured if you do not agree with me or adopt my suggestions.

To begin with, we have the *making of a strong department in the offices already established,* although I feel that some changes in personnel are very desirable and will have to be brought about gradually. As arranged now, Professor McCloskie teaches invertebrate zoology and botany. Rankin is his 'under-study' in invertebrate zoology. McClure teaches comparative anatomy; Dahlgren histology and cytology; Scott vertebrate palaeontology; Baldwin biology, evolution, etc. McClure is assisted by [Silvester], who is a young man of unrivaled capacity as a preparator.[1]

So far as I can see, only two new positions need to be created, namely, a full or associate chair of botany and a full or associate chair of physiology, in order, with rearrangement of personnel of our present staff, to constitute a really strong biological department, so far as officers are concerned. This would bring an organization something like the following:

for preparatory medical work   undergraduate
for general zoological work   "
for advanced research   graduate

			Salary	
		Mini-mum	Medium	Maxi-mum
I	Head professor of invertebrate zoology, cytology, experimental zoology, etc. (Macloskie.)	3,400	$4,000.	4,000
	Asst. professor or instructor of the same, (Rankin)	1,000	1,000. to	1,500
II	Head professor of comparative anatomy, vertebrate zoology, etc. (McClure)	3,000	4,000.	4,000
	Assistant in the same subjects, also in charge of histology, (Dahlgren)	1,000	1,000. to	1,500
III	Associate or full professor of botany,†	1,500.	2,500. to	4,000

A staff, capable of conducting College & University work

IV Associate or full professor of physiology†	1,500.	2,500.	to 4,000
Assistants at $750. each	750.	1,500	1,500
Preparator	1000.	1,000.	to 1,250
	$13,150.††	$17,500	$21,750

V Palaeozoology and vertebrate palaeontology, provided for by present Blair professor of zoology (Scott)

VI Biology, evolution, etc., provided for by present professor of psychology, (Baldwin)

To the above should be added maintenance & apparatus, increase of collections, renewals &c	3,500	4,500	5,500

The net increase over the present annual expenditure in the University, for the re-organization and strengthening of the department, would not exceed [blank] $ You have the figures at hand.

A *Museum of Natural History* seems to me one of the greatest needs of the University, to house the splendid collections in Nassau Hall† (I understand Professor Libbey assents to this) and the collections in the Green School of Science;†† also to provide ample laboratory spaces for the various biological and geological branches. Such a museum should be built in the very simplest style of rectangular construction, on the unit system, that is, with movable partitions; and should be accompanied by an endowment for its maintenance. I think that $500,000. would amply provide both the museum and the endowment. This would give an enormous impetus to the biological courses.

With such an equipment and a sympathetic departmental organization, Princeton would immediately take rank with any of the universities excepting Harvard, Chicago, and Columbia, which are still more strongly equipped.

I think it not at all improbable that we can find some benefactor who would enjoy presenting a natural history museum with the idea that his name should be connected with it. McClure

† In the institution of Botany[,] now taught by Professor Macloskie[,] and Physiology, as new branches, it might well be understood that the incumbents would be younger promising men expected to do the entire teaching, with the assistance of junior assistants receiving from $500. to $750. each. Very able men could be found but could not long be retained at the minimum salary.

†† Columbia devotes $14,000 to Zoology, in addition to expenditures in Botany & Physiology.

has at present no space for graduate work; Scott & Dahlgren are also greatly overcrowded and badly quartered.

I hope to be down at the opening. I look forward to vigorous freshening of the entire *morale* of the institution under your direction and guidance. I feel that you understand student human nature thoroughly, and the students will rapidly respond to your leadership. Tradition is so strong at Princeton that changes must naturally be introduced very gradually; but I am certain that before the end of the year there will be a reasonable amount of study pervading the whole institution—and an increase of refinement and the culture spirit.

We are all happily reassembled at Garrison for a week or ten days before the boys[2] go off to school and college.

Always most faithfully yours,   Henry F. Osborn.

† releasing this building as a historical, students, and organization hall—similar to Higginson Hall at Harvard.

†† releasing spaces in this building for other departments.

P.S.

I send you a few lines in addition, which I ask that you kindly tear up, regarding the personnel of the department.

Professor McCloskie is a man of natural ability, but too discursive either as a teacher or organizer of the studies of the department.

McClure is very strong in his preparation for medicine and as an original investigator in comparative anatomy. He seems to me to have the best idea of organization, sequence of courses, etc.

Rankin is a man of moderate ability, and while a very pleasant fellow, it would be a mistake to have him look forward to succeeding McCloskie, as a very strong man is needed in that department of biology in the present development of science, a man somewhat of the newer lines of investigation of my colleague Professor E. B. Wilson;[3] and such a man can be had.

Dahlgren is a naturally able fellow, but needs stimulating in the line of original investigation, where he has not sustained his earlier promise. His work should also be more closely co-ordinated with that of McClure.

Scott is a brilliant and inspiring teacher, but has not shown much capacity for organization, although always willing and ready to co-operate.

Baldwin is becoming a great authority on the principles of biology, and one of his courses should certainly appear in the biological programme.

I have in mind one or two young men of great ability and promise whom I would recommend for your consideration in case an opening occurs at Princeton.

Even with our present staff exactly as it is, without any augmentation, a great deal can be accomplished by the infusion of the university spirit and by a proper correlation and sequence of courses.   H. F. O.

TLS (WP, DLC).
  [1] George Macloskie, Professor of Biology; Walter Mead Rankin, Professor of Invertebrate Zoology and Curator of the Zoological Museum; Charles Freeman Williams McClure, Professor of Comparative Anatomy; Ulric Dahlgren, Assistant Professor of Histology; William Berryman Scott, Blair Professor of Geology; James Mark Baldwin, Stuart Professor of Psychology; and Charles Frederick Silvester, Assistant in Anatomy.
  [2] Alexander Perry Osborn and Henry Fairfield Osborn, Jr.
  [3] Edmund Beecher Wilson, Professor of Zoology at Columbia University.

From Oliver B. Babcock[1]

My dear Sir: Minneapolis, Minnesota, Sept. 11, 1902.

I write to ask whether you would be willing to come to Minneapolis some time next winter and deliver an address for us on some theme of general interest which is near to your own heart.

"The New Century Lectures" are maintained for the purpose of affording this community an opportunity to hear the leading speakers of the country on various topics, and we wish we might include you on our program this year.

The date does not necessarily have to be decided upon now, if you will only agree to come *some* time during the season, but we would prefer it not to be earlier than December; almost any time, however, after the first of December up to early spring, would suit us. We thought we had our program about completed for the coming season, but have decided that you are wanted here and wanted badly. We are therefore going to hold back our program for a few days in order to hear from you, although it should already be in the printer's hands. May I not ask you to telegraph me at my expense, as soon as possible after the receipt of this, whether you can come (leaving if you prefer, the date open), on what terms you would be willing to deliver the address, and what subject you would like to speak upon.

Assuring you of a warm welcome in the event of your coming, and hoping sincerely that we will receive a favorable reply, I am
                              Cordially yours,   O. B. Babcock.

P.S.—We of course realize perfectly that you do not do much

lecturing, but we do know you make occasional addresses, and a great many people here would like to see this city favored with one from you. Minneapolis is a somewhat spoiled child. It is in the habit of getting many things denied to other cities. We trust you will be indulgent like the rest, and come.[2]   O. B. B.

TLS (WP, DLC).
[1] Secretary of the New Century Lectures Committee and businessman of Minneapolis.
[2] Wilson's reply is missing, but he accepted the invitation and spoke in Minneapolis on April 25, 1903. A report of his speech is printed at April 26, 1903.

From Charles Williston McAlpin

My dear Dr. Wilson: [Princeton, N. J.] September 12, 1902.

I have received a letter from Mr. Charles B. Alexander[1] of which the following is a copy:

"23 August 1902.

Dear Sir:

Please see that an invitation is sent to the Inauguration of President Wilson to Thomas Walsh, Esq., LeRoy & Phelps Place, Washington, D. C.[2] It would be a great stroke of policy that the new President would express a wish for their presence and to let them know that two seats would be at their disposal in Mrs. Alexander's pew.

They are horribly rich and are interested in Princeton, and know the new President and are to send their son here.[3]

With kind regards,

Truly yours,   (Signed) C. B. Alexander."

I have written to Mr. Alexander that I would lay the matter before you.

I remain,

Sincerely yours,   [C. W. McAlpin] Secretary.

CCL (McAlpin File, UA, NjP).
[1] Charles Beatty Alexander, Princeton trustee since 1898.
[2] Wealthy mine owner and mining engineer.
[3] The son did not attend Princeton.

To Charles Williston McAlpin

Princeton, New Jersey,
My dear Mr. McAlpin,   13 September, 1902.

I am not sure that there is any "literature" at your disposal on the subject of Prof. Barringer's[1] inquiry; but, if you can give him some definite information about our several [alumni] associations (their organization and dinners) and about our league of western clubs, it will be what he wants.

  With much regard,

                    Sincerely Yours   Woodrow Wilson

Thank you for the copy of Mr. Alexander's let[ter.] I will reply to it. It will be easy, and I think wise, to do what he asks.

WWTLS (McAlpin File, UA, NjP).
  [1] Paul Brandon Barringer, M.D., Professor of Physiology and Materia Medica and Chairman of the Faculty at the University of Virginia, whose letter is missing.

To Henry Cooper Pitney, Jr.[1]

                              Princeton, New Jersey,
My dear Mr. Pitney,   15 September, 1902.

  I shall be very glad indeed to see you on Saturday, the twentieth. I expect to be at home (on Library Place) throughout the forenoon and from 2.30 to 4 in the afternoon. I shall hope to see you at your convenience.

                    Very sincerely Yours,   Woodrow Wilson

WWTLS (Washington Association of N. J., Morristown, N. J.).
  [1] Princeton 1877, a prominent lawyer of Morristown, N. J., who was coming to invite Wilson to deliver the address at the annual banquet of the Washington Association of New Jersey in Morristown in February 1903. A stenographic report of the address is printed at Feb. 23, 1903.

To Daniel Moreau Barringer

My dear Moreau,   Princeton, New Jersey, 16 September, 1902.

  You forgot that I am now responsible for the chapel services on Sunday, and must from now on be all but a minister in charge.[1] But I have invited Wood. Halsey[2] for the twenty-eighth; he can take care of himself. If he accepts, therefore, you may expect me to come to you for the night of the twenty-seventh. If you do not hear from me again, you may know that I am coming. It is a most delightful idea. For my pleasure it is as important to see you as to incorporate the Jefferson,[3] and I thank you most warmly for the invitation.

  With all affection,

                    Faithfully Yours,   Woodrow Wilson

WWTLS (D. M. Barringer Papers, NjP).
  [1] He meant not only that he was responsible for inviting guest preachers for services in Marquand Chapel on Sunday mornings, but that, following im-

memorial custom, as President of Princeton University he was expected usually to conduct or preside at these services.

2 The Rev. Dr. Abram Woodruff Halsey of the Class of 1879, at this time Secretary of the Board of Foreign Missions of the Presbyterian Church in the U.S.A.

3 To incorporate the Thomas Jefferson Memorial Association of the United States, about which see the news item printed at Feb. 16, 1903, n. 1.

A News Report

[Sept. 18, 1902]

IMPRESSIVE EXERCISES

Attendant Upon the Opening of the
University for the Year.

The exercises in connection with the formal opening of the University were held at three o'clock yesterday afternoon, in Marquand Chapel. President Wilson presided, and after reading the first and ninth Psalms and leading in prayer, addressed the faculty and students on the opening of the one hundred and fifty-sixth college year. He said that among the thoughts suggested by the new year was this, that we are only passing figures here, but that for the time being we are the University, and what we are it is.

He said that the following elements of reassurance at the outset of his leadership were particularly vivid in his own mind—a sense of comradeship with the faculty and with the undergraduates, and a sympathy with the latter's play as well as with their work.

"But," he said, "we are men in the midst of a world of men. We have put off short clothes, and the mere life of play. We are in the midst of a strenuous age, and must fill ourselves with the sense of it. There was never more to understand, to ponder, to master, and the world demands of us expert advice or nothing. Scholarship, he said—broad luminous, thorough catholic, masterful scholarship—is our chief duty and our chief glory."

He then extended a welcome to the Freshmen into this free world, and advised them that the effort of the university was to show them how to rightly use it.[1]

The exercises were closed with the benediction by ex-President Patton.

Printed in the *Daily Princetonian*, Sept. 18, 1902.
[1] There is a WWhw outline of this talk in WP, DLC.

Notes for a Talk to Princeton Freshmen[1]

Philadelphian[2] Welcome to the Freshmen. 20 September, '02.

The gentlemen who are to follow will tell you what our life here
  is; it is my pleasant function to bid you welcome to it.

This place the natural clearing house for the various interests of
  our college life. *Everything* should enter into a man's religion.

You may not *feel* welcome just now, but it is the natural introduction to a world where a man has no protection except his own
  character and the good opinion of his fellows,—and no advantage

Here a man frees his powers and strips his prejudices away.

He is free to live by principle or to live subject to influence

We love the place and expect you to love it.

WWhw MS. (WP, DLC).
  [1] A brief news report of this talk is printed at Sept. 22, 1902.
  [2] The Philadelphian Society, about which see n. 1 to the news item printed at
Nov. 1, 1890, Vol. 7.

Notes for a Talk at a Vesper Service

Chapel, Sunday Afternoon, 21 Sept., 1902

Phil. IV., 8. "Finally, brethren, whatsoever things are true, &c
  . . . think on these things."

The deliberate government of the thoughts, the theme.

A man may choose his thoughts as he may choose his company,—
  may choose his thoughts *by* choosing his company. *In the
  midst of labour* he may rest himself, *in the midst of excitement*
  calm himself, *in the midst of sorrow* soothe himself, *by a
  change of mental scene*

By books ⎫
By nature ⎬ may *cultivate high company*
By men   ⎭

WWhw MS. (WP, DLC).

A News Report

[Sept. 22, 1902]

FRESHMAN RECEPTION.
Entering Men Welcomed by
Philadelphian Society. Addresses Made.

The annual reception of the Philadelphian Society to the Freshman class was held from seven thirty until ten o'clock Saturday

evening, in Murray-Dodge Hall. The exercises of the evening were opened by John E. Steen 1903, President of the Society, in a speech of welcome to the entering men. . . .

President Wilson delivered the last address of the evening, welcoming the entering students on behalf of the Faculty and Alumni. He spoke of the undergraduate life, and urged the entering students to take the proper stand and make something of themselves here in the University, that they may become fitted to cope with the larger problems of life in the outside world.

Members of the Glee Club rendered several selections during the evening, and after the addresses refreshments were served in Murray Hall.

Printed in the *Daily Princetonian*, Sept. 22, 1902.

To Daniel Moreau Barringer

My dear Moreau,   Princeton, New Jersey, 26 September, 1902.

I am to meet the Inauguration Committee to-morrow morning here, but mean to take the early afternoon train which leaves here at 3.17 and reaches Philadelphia at 4.32. I do not know the schedule to Strafford, but I shall take the earliest train out that I can catch: you will know which that will be.

I am sorry to say that engagements here early Monday morning make it necessary that I should catch the train out from Philadelphia Sunday afternoon at 5.20; so that I cannot literally spend the whole day with you, but it is delightful to think how long I can stay.

Ever

Faithfully and cordially Yours,   Woodrow Wilson

WWTLS (D. M. Barringer Papers, NjP).

From the J. B. Lippincott Company

Dear Sir: Philadelphia. Sept. 26, 1902.

We have arranged for a new edition of Prescott's works to be reset with additional notes and published first as a limited edition with superior illustrations, etc.

We are desirous of inserting in this edition Introductions to the several Histories by a leading American historical scholar and we naturally turn to you. Our idea is a general Introduction relative to Prescott as an historian, etc. consisting of say twenty pages of about three hundred words per page, and special Introductions for each of the Histories and for the Miscellanies of say ten pages each, i.e.:

General Introduction
Introduction to Conquest of Mexico
Introduction to Conquest of Peru
Introduction to Ferdinand and Isabella
Introduction to Philip II.
Introduction to Charles V.
Introduction to Miscellanies.

About seventy five or eighty pages in all, which could be increased to one hundred pages if you desire.

We beg to inquire if you are willing to write such Introductions, and shall be glad to know the compensation which you would consider appropriate, unless the general figure we have had in mind, five hundred dollars, is satisfactory to you.

Hoping that we may receive an early reply indicating your willingness to undertake the work,[1] we are

Very truly yours,   J. B. Lippincott Co.   R

P.S. We should have stated in our letter that the new edition is to be published in twenty-two volumes and at monthly intervals two volumes each beginning early next year. Consequently all of the Introductions would not be needed at one time. The General Introduction and that for Mexico would be required in January next, and that for Peru a month later, the others following at intervals of one or two months.

TLS (WP, DLC).
[1] Wilson declined. The edition appeared under the title of *The Works of William H. Prescott*. Montezuma Edition. Edited by W[ilfred]. H[arold]. Munro and comprising the notes of the edition by J[ohn]. F[oster]. Kirk (22 vols., Philadelphia and London, 1904-1906).

From Arthur Twining Hadley

[New Haven, Conn.]

My dear President Wilson: Sept. 27th, 1902.

Perhaps this letter comes at just the wrong time, when you are so full of business that you do not wish to consider anything else; but the matter is of such importance that I do not feel that I ought to defer all mention of it until November.

Three years ago Mr. William E. Dodge gave us a fund bearing an income of $1200, to be paid for a course of about six lectures (in general, not less than five nor more than eight), on the Responsibilities of Citizenship. This constitutes much the most important lectureship of this kind which we have. It is not intended that each lecturer should cover the whole ground, but should take any special topic connected with this general subject which he wishes to treat. Each course of lectures is published at the expense of Yale University by Charles Scribner's Sons, and it is intended that the volumes thus successively published shall form a series of importance. The first course of lectures was by Mr. Justice Brewer, the second by Bishop Potter.[1]

It is our most earnest wish that, if your engagements will possibly permit, you should give the course during the spring of 1903. We appreciate very fully the many claims upon your time, and should be guided mainly by your convenience in the choice of dates. Bishop Potter preferred to put his course rather late in the year, and delivered his lectures in the last week of April and the first week of May. But if you desired to put them earlier, they could advantageously be spread over a longer range of time. Your studies are so exactly in the line contemplated by Mr. Dodge in his letter of gift, of which I enclose a copy, that I feel sure that you must have material which, with relatively little labor, could be put in shape suitable for this purpose. We should doubly welcome your coöperation at this time as an earnest of yet further increase in the cordiality and closeness of the relations which have bound Princeton and Yale together. This must serve as my apology for introducing a suggestion of an additional burden in a year which is sure to be so full of burdens.

I am looking forward with the utmost pleasure to the chance of attending your inauguration on the twenty-fifth of October. Pray give my kindest remembrances to Mrs. Wilson, and believe me,   Faithfully yours,   [Arthur T. Hadley]

CCL (Hadley Letterbooks, Archives, CtY).
  [1] David J. Brewer, *American Citizenship* (New Haven, Conn., 1902); Henry Codman Potter, *The Citizen in His Relation to the Industrial Situation* (New York, 1902).

To Arthur Twining Hadley

                                          Princeton, New Jersey,
My dear President Hadley,   1 October, 1902.

It goes exceeding hard to have to decline the kind invitation you have just sent me to be the next Yale Lecturer on the Responsibilities of Citizenship. I esteem it a very great compliment that you should wish to have me; the subject attracts me deeply;

and my strong instinct in such matters draws me to it. But it is a sheer case of necessity that I should decline. Before my new duties were put upon me I had made literary engagements of a very exacting kind and my problem now is how to get through the winter with credit, doing two things at once. In declining I know that I decline a great privilege and a real pleasure.

I am delighted to hear that you will be able to attend my inauguration. Mrs. Wilson and I join most heartily in the hope that you will come on Friday, that Mrs. Hadley will come with you, and that you will be our guests.

With warmest regard and appreciation,

Faithfully Yours,   Woodrow Wilson

WWTLS (A. T. Hadley Papers, Archives, CtY).

From the Minutes of the Princeton Academic Faculty[1]

5 p.m. October 1st, 1902.

The Faculty met, the President presiding. . . .

Resolved, that a committee be appointed to draft resolutions expressing the sorrow of the Faculty for the death of Professor Humphreys.[2]

The President appointed on this Committee Professors Hoskins, Vreeland, and Robbins.[3]

Resolved, that a Committee be appointed to draft rules of order for the Academic Faculty.

The President appointed on this Committee Professors Finley, Fine, and Magie, to act with the President.[4]

The Faculty then adjourned.

Attest,   W. F. Magie
                                                      Clerk.

"Minutes of the Academic Faculty of Princeton University, 1898-1904," bound minute book (UA, NjP).

[1] The Princeton University Faculty had been divided in 1898 into the Academic Faculty and the Science Faculty (consisting of those members whose main duties lay with the School of Science). However, both faculties met jointly as the University Faculty to consider common problems.

[2] Willard Humphreys, Professor of German, died at his home on Bayard Lane on September 26, 1902, at the age of thirty-five years. He had succumbed to an overdose of chloral hydrate taken for a toothache.

[3] John Preston Hoskins, Assistant Professor of German; Williamson Updike Vreeland, Assistant Professor of Romance Languages; and Edmund Yard Robbins, Professor of Greek.

[4] For the report of this committee, see the extract from the Academic Faculty Minutes printed at Dec. 3, 1902.

From Arthur Twining Hadley

[New Haven, Conn.]

My dear President Wilson: October 2d, 1902.

I feared very much that the pressure of your duties might compel you to render such answer as you have given. Let us hope that the pleasure of hearing you in New Haven is only deferred for a year or two, and not put wholly out of the question.

I wish with all my heart that it were possible for me to accept your very kind invitation. I specially want Mrs. Hadley to see you and Mrs. Wilson. Unfortunately, I have a fixed engagement of long standing for an address on the evening of Friday, the twenty-fourth, which will only just allow me to make connections with your inauguration, and will not admit of our accepting your hospitality for the night. I shall trust that this pleasure also, like the other, is only deferred, and that we may have in the future many opportunities of becoming better acquainted not only with one another, but with one another's households.

Faithfully yours,   [Arthur T. Hadley]

TCL (Hadley Letterbooks, Archives, CtY).

A News Report

[Oct. 4, 1902]

MASS MEETING.
Professors Carter and Axson Speak
in the Interests of the Halls.

The annual mass meeting in the interests of Whig and Clio Halls was held at eight o'clock last evening in Murray Hall. President Wilson presided over the meeting and delivered a short address of welcome, in which he stated that both as an alumnus of one of the Halls and as President of the University he was glad to recommend the entering men to take up work in the Halls.

President Wilson then introduced Professor Jesse Benedict Carter, representing Clio Hall. Professor Carter said that our duty to ourselves, our duty to those who sent us here, and our duty to the University all urged us to join one of the Halls. He mentioned as the advantages of Hall work, proficiency in debating, which is yearly becoming more prominent in University life, proficiency in extempore speaking, which is of such great benefit in the outside world, and a knowledge of parliamentary law. He closed by stating that the Halls in drawing out the Greek

Letter fraternities from the University have helped to preserve the democratic spirit of Princeton.

Professor Axson spoke on the responsibility resting upon a man who is deciding how he shall spend four years in college, and impressed upon the entering men the necessity of joining Hall immediately. Professor Axson said that while we cannot all be orators, it is a man's duty to be able to express himself clearly. In conclusion, he urged all men with the slightest oratorical ability to take advantage of the training in oratory which the Halls afford.

Printed in the *Daily Princetonian*, Oct. 4, 1902.

To Benjamin Lawton Wiggins[1]

My dear Sir: Princeton, N. J. Oct. 4th, 1902.

It is a real gratification to me to know that you will be able to be present at my inauguration.[2] I, of course, very well remember our pleasant meeting at Professor Gildersleeve's[3] and I shall look forward to the renewal of our acquaintance with real pleasure.

Let me thank you very warmly for the cordial words of congratulation contained in your letter. I think it gives a man the best sense of strength that he can have to find that men of judgment and leading [learning] believe in him, and I have been greatly heartened by your kind words.

With much regards,
Very sincerely yours, Woodrow Wilson

TLS (TSewU).
[1] Professor of Greek at and Vice-Chancellor of the University of the South.
[2] Wiggins' letter is missing.
[3] In Baltimore, on February 20, 1902.

From Andrew Fleming West

Dear Wilson, Oxford. October 4 1902

If I could forget Princeton anywhere, it would be here in Oxford. But as I can't,—why, then, just a short letter. This time I am getting well with the life of the University, though the term has not yet begun. Everyone is coming back, the new students or 'freshers' are wandering about taking examinations, buying gowns, & furnishing their rooms with extra bric-a-brac. "Still by the gateway flits the gown" of one and another Master of the Schools who is examining in Responsions. The Vice Chancellor[1] is here and was kind enough to have me drink tea with him in Oriel. Then I have dined with the Fellows of Magdalen, & have met several men well worth meeting, among them Reginald Lane Poole, the historic student,—lecturer in "Diplomatic."

I have read everything recommended by Mr. Gerrans[2] as worth reading on Oxford organization of studies, and am to meet some of the best tutors to have the working of the tutorial system explained in detail. Oxford requires far more daily work of her 'Passmen' than your predecessor supposed. Their *daily work is supervised*[,] checked up at intervals (I mean valued and marked, not 'checked' in the mere common meaning). The *"industry"* of the Passmen is a matter of incessant care and stimulation. What Oxford calls "obstacles to idleness" are thrown freely in the Passman's path.

I now conclude my discourse with some pictures,—just wee glimpses of the loveliness of Oxford as seen in Magdalen.

[picture of the outdoor pulpit of Magdalen College Chapel]   The *"Out Door Pulpit"* close by the chapel

[picture of Magdalen College tower]   By *moonlight*, what a dream in silvery grays and whites!

[picture of Magdalen College from the River Cherwell]   Here Billy & Mrs. Magie & I rowed. That is Billy rowed. I steered. This is called the Division of Labor in modern economics.

[picture of the west door of Magdalen College Chapel]   True Gothic as distinguished from the "fake" Gothic of your sanctuary—the 2d Church of Princeton. Billy, I think, likes the architecture of the 1st Church—the best specimen of 'fake' Greek now extant.

With kind regards to Mrs Wilson & strenuous wishes for a splendid Inauguration,

Ever yours   Andrew F West

ALS (WP, DLC).
  [1] David Binning Monro, Provost of Oriel College.
  [2] Henry Tresawna Gerrans, Tutor and Mathematical Lecturer at Worcester College.

From Harper and Brothers

Dear Mr. President: New York City October 4th, 1902.

We have your letter of the 2nd inst.[1] and, in response to your inquiries, we beg leave to submit the following:

Our present *net* price is substantially the same as the old *list* price. The arrangement referred to, which was entered into by leading publishers and booksellers, was made primarily with a view to regulate discounts, so as to protect small dealers against large department stores. If the History were published under the old list system, the price would still be the same—$17.50. All that "net" means is, substantially, that the retailer is not permitted to cut the price.

Now, as to royalties: You may remember that originally you thought to issue the work in two volumes, in which case the retail price for the set would have been about $7.50. Subsequently, the work grew into five volumes. The expansion was due, was it not, as much to our method of manufacture as to additional material on the part of the author. In other words, it is possible to put creditably the history as it now stands into two or, at most, three volumes. Following Green closely, this would have been done, and, of course, the list price would decline with the lesser number of volumes. So, the price as fixed seems to yield as much royalty as we had ever hoped for.

It is the custom to pay royalties on the regular edition price, except in the case of books sold by subscription, when the universal custom is to reduce the royalty. (Of course, we do not suggest and would not consent to this.)

In the case of your History, it was decided to bring out three editions, and thereby endeavor to cover the field thoroughly. The editions are:

Alumni Edition............$40.00 (Limited to 350 copies)
Subscription Edition....$25.00
Trade Edition.............$17.50

Our estimates on the work, for illustrations, manufacture, royalties to be paid, etc., resulted in the above prices.

The reasons why it seems just and equitable to pay royalty upon one price only ($17.50) are these: the alumni edition costs so much more to issue, that, to pay additional royalty upon the retail price would make the cost so excessive, the plan might have to be abandoned. The careful attention to minutest detail of manufacture takes away largely from the apparent profit, and, frequently, the chief reason for issuing a limited edition is one of policy and advertising—not of profit. In the matter of the subscription edition at $25.00, the net returns to us are materially smaller than on the trade edition at $17.50. We must pay agents, commission and expenses, must pay expenses of collection of accounts running over a year, must bear the inevitable losses occasioned by failure to continue payments—(a fixed ratio)—and, in addition, give away with each set sold a year's subscription to HARPER'S MAGAZINE or WEEKLY. With all other authors except one, the royalty on subscription editions is lower, and in this exceptional case we have been forced to discontinue the sale by agents. Thus, you see how the subscription edition makes up for the apparent injustice of the alumni edition.

We write thus fully and frankly in the full assurance that you will understand, and we beg that you will read into the letter nothing that is not set forth. We feel that we are equal partners in a great work, that our interests are one, and that unless we both do well neither will do well.

We confidently believe that the sales of this very important work will prove entirely satisfactory to you, and that your kindly expressed views of our dealings with authors will be emphasized as time goes on.

Very truly yours,   Harper & Brothers.

TLS (WP, DLC).
 1 Wilson's letter is missing.

To Henry Cooper Pitney, Jr.

My dear Mr. Pitney: Princeton, N. J.   Oct. 7th, 1902.

I am ashamed to say that I had allowed a rush of duties to postpone my writing to Mr. Meigs[1] about my obligation to the Hill School for the 22nd of February. I will write to him at once, and let you know the consequence. I greatly appreciate your interest in having me in Morristown at that time.

Very sincerely yours,   Woodrow Wilson

TLS (Washington Association of N. J., Morristown, N. J.).
 1 John Meigs, Headmaster of the Hill School in Pottstown, Pa.

To Daniel Coit Gilman

My dear Mr. Gilman,   Princeton, New Jersey, 10 October, 1902

Mrs. Wilson and I are looking forward with the greatest pleasure to seeing Mrs. Gilman and you at my approaching inauguration, and I write to ask if you will not come on Friday, the twenty-fourth, dine with us that evening, and be our guests over night,—over Sunday, if you will be so generous.

We shall hope to see the refreshing effects of your European trip shine in you both.

Cordially Yours,   Woodrow Wilson

ALS (D. C. Gilman Papers, MdBJ).

From Richard Heath Dabney

[Charlottesville]

My dear Woodrow: Univ. of Va. 11 Oct., 1902

Though much pressed for time, I cannot resist the invitation of the Trustees of Princeton to be present at your "blow-out." The Faculty have appointed me their official representative, and I shall take great pleasure, both in this capacity and as an individual, in giving you the Virginia "Yell" in true Comanche fashion. Of course I hardly hope to get much more than a glimpse of you in your triumphal toga, but it will give me great satisfaction to line up with the representatives of other institutions and whoop you up.

You are probably too busy to do it yourself, but I should be greatly obliged if you would get your secretary to let me know whether it will be expected of me to don any official rig, such as cap & gown, etc., &, if so, whether it be possible to rent such duds in Princeton or elsewhere. You know we have no such costume here. If caps & gowns are not to be worn, will a Prince Albert coat with stove-pipe hat be the proper caper?

As it is not very likely that the through trains stop at Princeton Junction, I suppose I shall have to spend the previous night at, say, Trenton; and should be glad if you would send me a schedule of the local trains. I suppose that the "Princeton Inn" is the best place to put up at.

Mrs. Dabney regrets very greatly her inability to accept the invitation of the Trustees. I wish she could meet Mrs. Wilson & your daughters. Please give them our regards.

Well, tra-la-la-la! I wish you joy & lots of it.

Most sincerely & cordially yours,   R. H. Dabney.

ALS (WWP, UA, NjP) with WWhw notation on letter: "Can entertainment be provided for Prof. Dabney for Friday Night? W.W."

To Henry Cooper Pitney, Jr.

My dear Mr. Pitney: Princeton, N. J. Oct. 13th, 1902.

I have just received a letter from Mr. Meigs[1] of the Hill School, in which he generously releases me from my obligations to him in respect of Washington's birthday. I, therefore, write to say that it will give me great pleasure to address the Washington Association on that day.

With much regard and appreciation,
                    Very sincerely yours,   Woodrow Wilson

TLS (Washington Association of N. J., Morristown, N. J.).
  [1] It is missing.

The Finance Committee's Report to the Board of Trustees of Princeton University

New York City, October 14, '02.

The Committee on Finance met at the office of Mr. M. Taylor Pyne, 52 Wall Street, at 3 P.M.

Present:

The chairman, Mr. Pyne, President Woodrow Wilson, Mr. John A. Stewart, Mr. C. C. Cuyler, Mr. J. W. Alexander, Mr. B. Henry.

Excuses were received from Mr. McCormick and Mr. Green.

The minutes of the last meeting were read, corrected, and approved.

The Treasurer's report and the Budget received.

On motion it was directed that of the uninvested funds, at least $20 000. be invested in the Union Pacific 4% Convertible bonds

Moved and carried that the salary of the President be made $8 000. a year, and that there shall be no additional fees.

Moved and carried that an appropriation of $2 000. a year be made to the President for entertainment and for expenses in caring for the property.[1]

Moved and carried that the salary of Mr. Robbins be increased $500. a year as recommended by Dr. Patton at the meeting of the Board of Trustees held June 9th, '02.

Moved and carried that the request of the Clerk of the Faculty for a sum not to exceed $300. to defray expenses in connection with his office be referred to the Chairman and President Wilson with power.

Moved and carried that the salary of Prof. H. C. Cameron be

made $2 000. a year to be continued during the pleasure of the Board of Trustees.

Moved and carried that the bills which had already been contracted for the entertainment of the School Masters in May '02, be paid, and that no further bills should be contracted.

Moved and carried that the salaries of the Registrar's assistants, Mr. Olden and Mr. Kerr,[2] be increased to $50. each per month.

Moved and carried that Mr. H. C. Bunn[3] be recommended to the Board as Assistant Treasurer.

Upon motion, bill of Tiffany & Company for Oxford Letter was ordered paid; bill for envelopes for Alumni Directory was also ordered paid.

Upon motion, the President was authorized to engage a secretary at a salary of $500. a year.[4]

Moved and carried that the salary of Prof. Humphreys (deceased), be paid to Nov. 1st.

Upon motion, the President was authorized to engage an instructor in the German Department in place of Prof. Humphreys [at] a salary of $600.[5]

Upon motion, the appointment of Dr. Rettger,[6] as instructor in mathematics in the School of Science in place of Mr. Brooks[7] at a salary of $800. a year, was approved.

Upon motion the same amount as last year was authorized for the Department of Psychology, as follows:

For Demonstrator, F. S. Wrinch[8] $300
"   Laboratory expenses 150
"   Psychological Review 150

to be charged to the School of Philosophy Fund.

Moved and carried that Mr. E. G. Elliott be appointed instructor in Politics at a salary of $1 000. a year.

Moved and carried that the salary of G. W. P. Silvester (bottle washer for Prof. Neher) be made $250. a year.

The Treasurer reported that fifteen bonds of the St. Louis, Iron Mountain & Southern Railroad Company were still registered in the name of The Trustees of The College of New Jersey, change of the registry name having been overlooked at the time the other securities were transferred from The Trustees of The College of New Jersey to the Trustees of Princeton University. Whereupon, it was

RESOLVED, That Henry G. Duffield, Treasurer of the Trustees of Princeton University be and he is hereby authorized to transfer the fifteen bonds of the St. Louis, Iron Mountain & Southern Railroad Company standing in the name of The Trustees of The College of New Jersey to The Trustees of Princeton University, the present corporate title of the Institution.

The question of paying eight students for singing in the Chapel choir as was done last year was discussed by the Chairman and the President, and it was agreed that students should not be paid for singing in the Chapel choir.

On motion the meeting adjourned.

H G Duffield   Secretary.

TRS (Trustees' Papers, UA, NjP).

[1] That is, Prospect.

[2] Frank G. Olden of Mercer Heights and Wilbur Kerr of 26 Edgehill St.

[3] Henry Conrad Bunn served as Assistant Treasurer from 1902 to 1904, when he became Curator of Grounds and Buildings.

[4] At about this time, Wilson engaged McQueen Salley Wightman '04 as his part-time secretary.

[5] Charles Edward Lyon, a doctoral candidate at the Johns Hopkins, was employed for the year 1902-1903. However, in 1903 John Preston Hoskins was promoted from Assistant Professor to Professor of German, and Max Friedrich Blau was appointed Assistant Professor of German.

[6] Ernest William Rettger.

[7] John Milton Brooks, Instructor in Mathematics, had resigned in 1902.

[8] Frank Sidney Wrinch, Demonstrator in Experimental Psychology.

From Edith Gittings Reid

My very dear Friend   [Baltimore] Oct. 16th [1902]

Here we are at home again and thinking of you and the 25th. Harry & I are going to your Inauguration.

Will you ask Mrs Wilson if she would be so very good as to secure us one double room & one single room at the Inn for the evening of the 24th? Miss Goodwillie[1] wishes to go with us.

Tell Mrs Wilson that I am not at all a particular person. I would be delighted with the best rooms & equally delighted with the worst!

What do I care about rooms! I want to see you & the delight of the students in their Master.

I have so much to tell you.

Give my love to Mrs Wilson

Ever faithfully yours   Edith Gittings Reid

By the way Oliver Cromwell is alive again. He was our Ship's Steward on the return voyage[.] Here is our last menu—

Weak Irish

Chops à la reform

Black Cap Pudding.

ALS (WP, DLC).
  1 Mary C. Goodwillie, pioneer social worker of Baltimore, at this time a volunteer worker for the Federated Charities.

A News Item

[Oct. 18, 1902]

President Wilson has finally moved into Prospect, which has been renovated and redecorated and refurnished for his occupancy. His former home on Library Place, which he built about ten years ago, has been bought by John and Robert Garrett of Baltimore, of the classes of '95 and '97, respectively, who with their mother, Mrs. T. Harrison Garrett, will use it as a Princeton home.

Although moving and writing his inaugural are but a part of what President Wilson has heen [been] doing in these busy days, he has not missed one of his lectures, it is said—and he has not given up riding his bicycle to and from them.

Printed in the *Princeton Alumni Weekly*, III (Oct. 18, 1902), 52.

To Daniel Coit Gilman

My dear Dr. Gilman: Princeton, N. J.   Oct. 18th, 1902.

It is all right. I had conferred with [Allan] Marquand, and he had generously consented to let us have you, and I knew that the matter would straighten itself out in due time, so that your room with us has been kept unmortgaged. We are looking forward with the greatest pleasure to having you in our house.

With all cordial regards,
                    Very sincerely yours,   Woodrow Wilson

TLS (D. C. Gilman Papers, MdBJ).

From Theodore Roosevelt

My dear President Wilson: [Washington] October 18, 1902.

I have kept hoping that I might be able to get on to see you inaugurated, but the doctors are positive that for at least ten days I ought not to take a railway trip.[1] I have now begun to ride a little, but I am not allowed to do any walking outside of the house as yet. I had a bad bruise on the leg-bone which nearly caused serious trouble, and I ought not to take any chances. I am very, very sorry. I hope to see you on here this winter.

Faithfully yours,   Theodore Roosevelt

TLS (Letterpress Books, T. Roosevelt Papers, DLC).

1 While on a speaking tour, the President had narrowly escaped death in a serious accident near Pittsfield, Mass., on September 3. A trolley car, going at a high rate of speed, collided with the open, horse-drawn carriage in which he was riding. A Secret Service man was killed, and Roosevelt was thrown out of the carriage, striking his right cheek and injuring his leg. He continued the tour until September 24, when an abscess that had formed on the injured leg forced his return to the White House and confinement to a wheel chair.

To Theodore Roosevelt

Princeton, New Jersey,

My dear Mr. President,   20 October, 1902

It is a deep disappointment that we are not to have you with us next Saturday, but of course the reason is imperative. We would a great deal rather have you take care of yourself than have you confer an honor and pleasure on us,—and it is no small compensation to us to know that by being careful you are sure to escape serious trouble from the wound which has caused us so much anxiety.

Thank you most sincerely for the cordial words in which you speak of your own disappointment.

We have all watched with the deepest interest your courageous and patriotic course in regard to the coal strike, and have rejoiced, as the whole country has, in your triumph.

With warmest regard, and a deep regret tempered with thankfulness that you are making strides toward recovery,

Faithfully Yours,   Woodrow Wilson

ALS (T. Roosevelt Papers, DLC).

From Maurice Francis Egan[1]

My Dear Sir: Washington, D. C.   October 20, 1902.

I have not had the honor of meeting you since we dined some time ago at our late friend, Mrs. Winthrop's;[2] but I have remembered with genuine satisfaction many things you said on the occasion, and I have followed, with equally genuine satisfaction, your writings ever since and have taken every occasion to recommend them to my students at the Catholic University. Permit me to congratulate you and Princeton on the coming occasion, you on your enlarged sphere of righteousness, (not unmingled with humor, wit,— *esprit* is a better word, after all,—for your sphere will be made by you,) and Princeton on the opening of a new epoch. I am   Yours sincerely   Maurice Francis Egan.

ALS (WP, DLC).
¹ Professor of English Language and Literature at the Catholic University of America.
² On February 19, 1898, at the home of Alice Worthington (Mrs. William Woolsey) Winthrop in Washington. See WW to EAW, Feb. 20, 1898, Vol. 10.

Cornelius Cuyler Cuyler to the President and Board of Trustees of Princeton University

[New York]
DATED OCTOBER 20*th*, *1902*.

Mr. President and Gentlemen of The Board:

. . . In connection with the subject of dormitories, it is a great pleasure as a Princetonian and with intense satisfaction as a member of the class of 1879 to have the honor to read the following letter:

> My dear Cuyler: New York, October 8th, 1902.
>
> I am authorized by the class committee of '79 to inform the Committee of the Trustees on Grounds and Buildings, of which you are chairman, that the Class has decided to present to the University as a memorial of the 25th anniversary of its graduation, a building to be known as the Seventy-Nine Dormitory. The class committee therefore apply to the Committee on Grounds and Buildings to designate a suitable site for the erection of such a building in the near future. It is our intention to break ground officially on October 25th, the day of President Wilson's Inauguration.
>
> This action is taken with the full approval of President Wilson.
>
> Faithfully yours,   (Signed) Robert Bridges, '79.
>
> To C. C. Cuyler, Esq.

At the recent meeting of the Committee on Grounds and Buildings, it was decided to recommend to this Board that the gift of this class to the University be accepted with the hope that other classes may emulate its example and with the hearty thanks for this splendid manifestation of loyalty. It was also directed that the Board be asked to ratify the action of the Committee as to the site selected, namely, the west side of Washington Road at its intersection with Prospect Avenue. The arch of the building will thus furnish an imposing entrance to "Prospect" and greatly improve the street where our Clubs are situated.

"PROSPECT"

This building has been completely renovated and re-decorated; direct and indirect radiation installed and made a part of the Central Power Plant. Electricity has been introduced, many new fixtures placed and the old gas fixtures remodeled for electricity. One new bath room has been made, another completed and a lavatory on the main floor provided. Door-ways have been cut for greater convenience. Considerable planting has been done about the grounds. All flues have been overhauled and general plumbing repairs effected. . . .

Respectfully submitted,   C C Cuyler, Chairman

TLS (Trustees' Papers, UA, NjP).

To the Board of Trustees of Princeton University

PRINCETON, NEW JERSEY,
GENTLEMEN OF THE BOARD OF TRUSTEES: 21 October, 1902.

I feel that the most serviceable way in which I can begin my administration is to render to you a somewhat detailed account of the position and needs of the University.

It is only candid to say that its position is, in many respects, critical, and that its needs are great and numerous; but it is reassuring to know that the critical situation has arisen, not out of any essential unsoundness or out of any demoralization that has touched the spirit of the place, but only out of its imperfect development and its insufficient resources. I never knew a body of men who, taken as a whole, were more worthy of trust and confidence than the Faculty of this University. They have the real spirit of devotion and of unselfish service; they are seriously and intelligently interested in the welfare and improvement of the University; and they are ready to advance its interests in any way that may afford them a hope of realizing their ideals. It is no small part of our strength that they hold for the most part the same ideals and seem one and all to have taken on the wholesome spirit of the place. The institution is in all its *personnel* and action sound and vigorous.

But the first thing that struck me when I came to look closely into its affairs was, that it is insufficiently capitalized for its business. I find that during the last fiscal year of the University $27,-613.27 were subscribed for its current expenses. Here are the items:

For assistant librarians, ...	$ 3,000 00
For seminaries, ...	10,360 93
For the purchase of books, ...	1,119 99
For salaries, ...	7,466 68
For fellowships and prizes, ...	890 00
For general expenses, ...	4,775 67
	$27,613 27

A portion of the $10,360.93 subscribed for seminaries went toward their permanent furnishing and equipment and may be deducted from what will be needed another year; but most of this large amount was contributed to defray expenses which must be repeated every year if the seminaries are to be kept in a condition of efficiency. Practically the whole sum of $27,613.27, therefore, represents expenditures which, once undertaken, must be continued from year to year, unless the work of the University is to be seriously curtailed. $27,613.27 represents the interest, at four *per cent.*, on $690,331.75. We are in effect, therefore, using a capital of some $700,000 which we do not own or control. This is evidently a very unsound, a very unsafe business situation.

From one point of view, it is true, it is a situation which is full of hope and calculated to give us the greatest possible encouragement for the future. This large sum annually subscribed to defray the expenses of the University represents in concrete form the extraordinary zeal and open-handed generosity of the alumni and friends of Princeton. It is heartening to think how many men there are who every year give large sums out of their private incomes to keep the University they love in a position to do its present work without embarrassment. It ought, moreover, to be remembered that these sums do not include what is given almost from year to year for the purchase of property contiguous to the grounds of the University, for the enlargement of its boundaries and the beautification of its campus. But, delightful as it is to think of that side of the matter, mere business prudence renders it imperative that we should think of the other side and take steps to make the foundations under us solid, secure against accidents. We are using $690,331.75 more capital than we own.

Moreover, even with the use of this additional capital our staff is overworked and underpaid, and the University lacks necessary equipment in almost every department. The effect of too much work and too little pay upon university instructors is very serious indeed. It has been noticed of late years, with a great deal of well-founded alarm, that the quality of the men who are preparing themselves for university positions is sharply falling off, the country over,—both the social and the intellectual quality. A university career is, in this country, becoming, not more, but less and less attractive to men of real capacity and strong ambition. That is not true in older countries, but it is true here; and the reason is that, with too little pay and too much work, the university career is no career at all, but mere obscure drudgery. Too little pay makes a mean way of living necessary which deprives a scholar of his natural place among gentlemen; too much work cuts him off from independent study and therefore from scholarly reputation, the two things the hope of which draws him into the profession. A true university is a place for research as well as for instruction. It cannot keep alive without research; it cannot serve the country properly if it does not do its part in widening the boundaries of knowledge and making ideas a power among men. It merely fulfils its necessary function by making itself a place where teachers can live without anxiety and prosecute their studies without physical exhaustion. The question of salaries and of the number of class-room hours required of a faculty is as much a question of efficiency and equipment as the building of laboratories and the purchase of scientific apparatus. Indeed, the subtle spirit of the place depends on these things.

I believe that some part of the strain of routine work we are now under can be removed by a thorough-going readjustment. The University has had a remarkable growth in the last thirty years, but it has been a growth which has resulted, I dare say, from the necessity of the case, in a miscellaneous enlargement rather than in a systematic develop[m]ent. It has consisted in a multiplication of courses which have in large part remained uncoördinated. The order of studies, their sequence, their relation to one another, their grouping, their respective values: all these things need immediate reconsideration. The Faculty is inclined to take these questions up with zeal and in the best spirit, and I believe that before the end of the year we shall have thrown the whole schedule of studies into the new and better scheme, which may be expected to effect a real economy both of time and of effort. It may be that we shall discover, besides, some unexceptionable way of shortening the baccalaureate course without weakening or cheapening it.

But what we need more than mere reorganization is in many

things a radical change of method. The method of the drill subjects which can be taught by the recitation of small groups of men in a class-room is sufficiently ascertained and fixed; and the laboratories need little reconsideration of method. Give them but apparatus and space enough and they are made efficient. But there are whole groups of subjects in which our methods of instruction need to be fundamentally altered, and these are the subjects which the majority of men in the upper years of study pursue: philosophy, the great modern literatures, history, politics, jurisprudence, economics,—the studies which, outside the field of the sciences, contain the thought of the modern world. We have tried to teach these by lectures and have failed. They are essentially reading subjects. They cannot be learned from the mouth of any one man or out of the pages of any one book. Their students must be reading and thinking men.

Lectures in such subjects are useful,—useful in proportion as the lecturer is stimulating or able to impart by example the zest and the method of exact enquiry. Lectures in such subjects, it seems to me, ought to be of two kinds, and of two kinds only: those which exhibit the whole broad field of the subject and draw the student to all its outlooks and lines of suggestion, putting him under the stimulation of seeing all its broad significance and of realizing all the interesting questions which lie involved in it, and those which illustrate for the student the exact, intensive way in which a scholar should thoroughly canvass some one question or phase of a subject and illustrate the intimate methods of research. For the rest, university men should be made to get up *subjects*, not lectures, for examination,—and get them up for themselves. The examinations should not be on the contents of a course of lectures or on any single discussion of a subject, but on the subject itself as a whole, as it may be got up out of a library of books. If our Juniors and Seniors idle their time away and get little or no stimulation and culture out of the closing years of their course, it is because there is nothing for them to do but to listen to lectures. They read only if they please. The evil will be remedied only when they are made to read and cover great subjects by their own efforts, under the stimulation of lectures.

The way to do this is to make use, in a modified form, of the English tutorial system. Under that system men are examined, not on particular courses of lectures (they may attend the lectures of distinguished lecturers or not, as they please) nor on particular books, but upon subjects which they are expected to get up for themselves, and upon which they are tested by outside examiners. Tutors superintend and assist their reading, show them the best books in which to get at the subjects assigned, act as their coaches and advisors in their preparation for the general tests which await them. The trouble with the English tutorial system is that the tutors go to seed. What I would propose for Princeton is that in each department in which it may be said to be of the very gist of education to be acquainted with the central literature of the subject a sufficient number of competent young men, not mere youngsters who have just taken their first degree in the arts, but men who have taken on the serious spirit of advanced study, be employed as tutors, as superintendents and coaches, as companions, of the men's reading, with the task of seeing to it that the reading is done, and is done thoroughly. I would keep a tutor at such a task for not more than five years, only while he retained the freshness and enthusiasm of the first years of teaching. After five years of that sort of work he would have shown what else he was fit for and should be put at something else. He should be employed from year to year; should receive at least a thousand dollars the first year; and, if retained, an increase of salary each year until a maximum of two thousand dollars was reached in his fifth year. No less than fifty such tutors would be necessary to make our present work in Junior and Senior year efficient; and fifty tutors of this kind, at an average salary of fifteen hundred dollars, would do more to make educated men out of our students than fifty full professors at an average salary of four thousand who did nothing but lecture to large classes. Ordinary class-room and lecture work cannot accomplish the purpose at all. This one thing is our central and immediate need.

There are other needs, self-evident and very pressing, which call for no explanation or argument. We are particularly weak in the departments of history, economics, and biology, in which our immediate rivals are especially strong. The following brief table shows the number of teachers in the several departments named in Harvard, Yale, Columbia, the University of Pennsylvania, and Princeton:

	History.	Economics.	Biology.
Harvard	15	13	16
Yale	10	8	3
Columbia	9	7	20
University of Pennsylvania.	6	5	8
Princeton	3	2	4

The department of biology needs, with us, both an increase of equipment and an increase of corps. Of this I shall speak again. The department of history needs at least two more men for an average development, and the department of economics two. There is immediate need for a complete physical laboratory. The need of a new recitation and lecture hall is so pressing that it is becoming next to impossible to arrange class schedules for our present limited number of available rooms. Equally notorious among us is the need for a very substantial endowment for the library. The library is at the heart of every study, and until it is sufficiently endowed to provide for the free purchase of books every department in the University will be hampered in its work. The need for a sufficient increase in the general endowment funds in order that there may be a somewhat general and not illiberal increase in the salaries of the existing teaching staff of the University is recognized on all hands as lying very near the centre of every question of efficiency. It is quite as obvious that, with the growth of the University, we need also a very considerable enlargement of the general administrative staff.

And when all these needs have been mentioned there remains the School of Science, the most imperfectly developed part of the University. The invested funds of the School of Science amount to a total of only $438,120, and with only that slender capital nothing effectual can be done to put the School upon the same plane of efficiency and reputation that the scientific departments of other great universities occupy. Something can be done, and, I hope, done at once, to reorganize the scientific as well as the academic department, but when the reorganization shall have been effected the radical defect of the School of Science will remain,—its insufficient corps, equipment, and support. It has proved an extremely demoralizing circumstance that the School of Science has had to depend for its support chiefly upon the fees of students. So long as that is the case there can be no true independence exercised in determining the right standards of admission, of work, or of attainment on that side of the University. It is perfectly evident to me, however, that an increase of excellence and a proper stiffening of standards would, in the long run —if only we were able to stay out the long run—add very greatly to the number of students. We lack students now only in proportion as we lack reputation. I would call attention to the fact that the great majority of the students who now enter the School of Science enter for the B.S. degree, and pursue, after entrance, not a strictly scientific course, but what is in most cases virtually an academic course without Greek. These men would in other institutions be classed as academic students. In other words, they come in by the door of the School of Science, not because they wish to become scientific students, but because they wish to enter Princeton without Greek. With the proper endowment and equipment of the School of Science, we could draw men to us in large numbers for veritable scientific study; and I reckon that a proper endowment could not possibly fall below a minimum of one million dollars.

I ask your attention, therefore, at this point, to the following recapitulation:

Present resources of the University:
General endowment (including the
  School of Science), ... $1,021,404 70
Special endowments, ... 1,856,318 90
Productive property, ... 963,000 00

$3,840,723 60

The Treasurer of the University estimates that there is, besides, unproductive property of the University aggregating $2,440,000 in value.

Present needs of the University, to put existing work on a proper basis:

Increase of salaries, ... $250,000
Maintenance of present expenses, ... 690,332
Fifty tutorships at $45,000 each, ... 2,250,000
Two Professorships of History, ... 200,000
Two Professorships of Economics, ... 200,000
Library endowment, ... 500,000
Recitation Hall, ... 150,000
Physical Laboratory, ... 200,000
Biological Laboratory, ... 150,000
Additional Biological instruction, ... 212,000
School of Science, ... 1,000,000
Business offices of the University, ... 200,000

$6,002,832

I feel that it would be impossible to overemphasize the gravity and the pressing character of these needs. They should be met, and met at once, if only to fulfill our moral obligations to the public. Without these things we are not doing honestly what we advertise in our catalogue. If we cannot add at least this much within a reasonable length of time I shall earnestly advocate a sufficient curtailment of our present work to put it on a business-like basis of efficiency.

And yet, if all these immediate needs were met, we should still lack as much more to put us upon an equality with the institutions with which we must always be compared. No institution can have freedom in its development which does not stand at the top in a place of real leadership. If Princeton should ever come to be generally thought of as standing below Harvard and Yale in academic development her opportunity for leadership and even for independent action within her own sphere would be gone. She would inevitably be relegated to a rôle of imitation. And I must in mere candor say to you that, if she be not re-endowed and systematically built up upon such a scale as I here suggest, and that practically at once, she has that lot in store for her in the immediate future. There was a time when Harvard, Yale, and Princeton was the list in everyone's mouth when the leading colleges of the country were spoken of; but since the greater colleges were transformed into universities Princeton has fallen out of the list. At least when academic men speak; and they must be the ultimate judges. Persons who stand outside academic circles still speak of Harvard, Yale, and Princeton together, but those who are informed know that Princeton has not kept pace with the others in university development, and that while she has lingered, other, newer, institutions, like Columbia, the Johns Hopkins, and the University of Chicago have pressed in ahead of her. One or the other of two courses is open to us. Either we may withdraw from the university competition and devote ourselves to making what we have solid and distinguished, or we must find money enough to make Princeton in fact a great university. The first course, I take it, no true Princeton man would seriously consider for a moment; and yet it is the honest course, morally the necessary course, if we do not take the other. And the other means a great sum of money.

On the side of university growth our first and most obvious need is a Graduate College. Professor West has made us familiar with the plans for such a college which he has conceived. Those plans seem to me in every way admirable and worthy of adoption. To carry them out would unquestionably give us a place of unique distinction among American universities. He has conceived the idea of a Graduate College of residence: a great quadrangle in which our graduate students should be housed like a household, with their own commons and their own rooms of conference, under a master whose residence should stand at a corner of the quadrangle in the midst of them. This is not merely a pleasing fancy of an English college placed in the midst of our campus to ornament it. In conceiving this little community of scholars set up at the heart of Princeton, Professor West has got at the real gist of the matter, the real means by which a group of graduate students are most apt to stimulate and set the pace for the whole University.

And of course the School with its endowment would mean a multiplication of the courses of study, for undergraduates as well as for advanced students. We none of us believe that the graduate and the undergraduate work ought to be divorced. The men who lead graduates forward into the methods of advanced study and research should keep themselves always in vital touch with the world of ordinary thought outside the University by teaching undergraduates also, who are preparing to be, not scholars, but such men as can serve the country best in the ordinary walks of citizenship.

The possession of a Graduate College of real distinction would do more than increase courses of study and fill Princeton with men who would infect the place with the real spirit of scholarship. It would restore Princeton to her place in the preparatory schools. One of our most critical weaknesses at the present moment is that there are so few Princeton men on the teaching staffs of the preparatory schools. The better preparatory schools will no longer willingly take as teachers men who have received only the first degree in the arts or the sciences. They wish men definitely trained for their task after graduation; and we cannot supply them. So long as we cannot supply them, so long as the preparatory schools of the country are conducted and governed and given their spirit by men from other universities, we can play no real part of leadership in American education.

We cannot have a medical college in Princeton, and my present judgment is that it would not be wise to effect an organic connection with any medical school at a distance from Princeton, because such a school could not be wholly dominated by the spirit of the University or become in character an essential part of it. No doubt the best we can do for those of our graduates who go into the medical profession will be to supply the preliminary scientific training necessary for preparation for the practice of medicine and make such arrangements as may turn out to be feasible for the full recognition of that work in the medical schools to which our graduates principally resort.

We can have a school of jurisprudence. I do not call it a law school, though it might very properly be called that. I call it a school of jurisprudence because I want to emphasize my conception of what a law school ought to be. It is possible in a three years' course built upon university studies to teach law in a thoroughly scholarly fashion and yet rob it of no practical feature that it ought to have. But what is quite as necessary is that law should be set forth in the light of its historical derivations and of its full significance as a scheme of institutional thought. A school in which law was taught only to university graduates and by men who could give it its full scholarly scope and meaning without rendering it merely theoretical or in any sense unpractical,—men who could, rather, render it more luminously practical by making it a thing built upon principle, not a thing constructed by rote out of miscellaneous precedents,—would at once command the respect of the entire profession on both sides of the water, and put legal study upon the highest plane. No more appropriate place than Princeton could be found for such a school, and Princeton alone is likely to establish it.

The other immediate addition to the University which I propose is a fully equipped electrical school. The reputation which Professor Brackett has already given to our instruction in electrical engineering, without endowment, almost without apparatus, is an earnest of what might be done to put Princeton in the way of equipping men for the service of the country in the profession which is sure to be chief among the practical professions of the immediate future; and I know of no endowment which would be of more practical and immediate benefit to Princeton in the field of science than an endowment for a thorough school of electrical engineering.

Add a law school and an electrical school and a museum of natural history such as is absolutely indispensable to the proper development of the great group of biological sciences, and Princeton's claim to equal standing with universities of the first rank would no longer be open to question. A biological laboratory would, after all, be of little use without the full outfit for biological study which only a properly supplied museum of natural history can supply.

I append a table of the estimate cost of these additions, necessary to create a real university in Princeton:

Graduate School, ... $3,000,000
School of Jurisprudence, ... 2,400,000
Electrical School, ... 750,000
Museum of Natural History, ... 500,000
_____
$6,650,000

This total, added to the total sum needed to make our work sound and honest as it stands, makes a grand total (if the biological laboratory of the first list be omitted, which would be united with the Museum of Natural History of the second list) of $12,-502,832.

I have touched each item of this important catalogue of needs in the briefest possible way, but every item is of the most vital consequence. I have put in nothing which is not a real and imperative need; and I have estimated each item at what I believe to be its minimum cost. I cannot dwell with too much emphasis on the immediate necessity of securing these funds. I do not hesitate to say that the reputation and the very success of the University are staked upon obtaining them soon. I shall myself use my best and most diligent efforts to obtain them, and I must ask the hearty, the vigilant, the continued assistance and co-operation of every member of the Board in the undertaking. We work in this matter for the very life of the institution we love and have pledged our duty to.

There are other matters, vital also in their kind, to which I feel that we ought to pay the most careful and systematic and immediate attention. The dormitory accommodations of the University have fallen so far behind the number of students that there is too much crowding in the dormitories and the prices for lodgings in the town have risen much too high. Princeton is in danger of becoming regarded, to her great detriment and discredit, as one of the most expensive places in the country at which a student can take up residence, at any rate for the first years of his course. Moreover, it is high time that something were done to secure wholesome and well cooked food for the Freshmen and Sophomores, especially. The boarding houses of the town do not supply such food as might easily be supplied at the prices they charge. I have made some general suggestions to the Committee on Grounds and Buildings with regard to these matters with which I will not trouble the Board at this time. I wish now simply to call attention to the very great importance of these matters to the health and comfort, and even to the morality, of the students, and to say that it will be my hope to see a satisfactory solution worked out at no distant day.

I have laid before you great matters, involving sustained and trying effort, but with the confident expectation that they will prove easier in the accomplishment than we can now foresee, and with the full assurance that we shall find genuine and deepening satisfaction and reward in mastering a difficult task because of the spirit of love and devotion in which we shall undertake and prosecute it.

WOODROW WILSON.[1]

Printed document (WP, DLC).
  [1] There is a WWsh draft of this report, entitled "Report to Trustees, October, 1902," in WP, DLC.

From the Minutes of the Board of Trustees of Princeton University

[Oct. 21, 1902]

. . . The President-elect of the University stated that as his Report had been printed and sent to the Trustees he would not read it at this time. He spoke on parts of it, however, and made some suggestions. . . .

SUGGESTIONS BY PRESIDENT-ELECT

The President-elect referred to the presence as presiding officer at the Inauguration Exercises on October 25th of His Excellency Franklin Murphy, Governor of New Jersey and *ex-officio* President of the Board, and suggested the consideration of the propriety of conferring the honorary degree of LL.D. on him *in Camera* Saturday morning, October 25th.

NOMINATION FOR HONORARY DEGREE

Dr. [Elijah R.] Craven nominated the Hon. Franklin Murphy, Governor of the State of New Jersey, for the honorary degree of LL.D. The nomination was seconded by Dr. [David R.] Frazer and Mr. [Samuel B.] Dod.

BALLOTING ON CANDIDATE FOR HONORARY DEGREE

The By-Laws were suspended by unanimous consent. The Board then proceeded to ballot. Trustees Bayard Henry and [Simon John] McPherson acted as tellers and reported that all the ballots were in favor of Governor Murphy. It was thereupon voted to confer the honorary degree of LL.D. on His Excellency Franklin Murphy, *in Camera*, Saturday morning, October 25th. . . .[1]

"Minutes of the Trustees of Princeton University, June 1901-Jan. 1908," bound minute book (UA, NjP).
[1] See the Minutes of the Princeton Board of Trustees printed at Oct. 25, 1902.

Two Resolutions by Grover Cleveland

[Oct. 21, 1902]

Resolved

That the President of the University be fully authorized by the Board of Trustees in reorganizing the teaching force to create such vacancies in such force as he may deem for the best interest of the University.

Resolved.

That the Board approves the President's suggestion that he be at liberty to exhibit his report this day made to such persons as he may deem best in his efforts to carry out its recommendations.[1]

Hw MS. (Trustees' Papers, UA, NjP).
[1] These resolutions were adopted by the Board.

Samuel Ross Winans to the Board of Trustees' Committee on Morals and Discipline

Gentlemen: Princeton, N. J., October 21st, 1902.

Since my last report the cases of discipline of sufficient importance to be enumerated are twenty-five in number. I will take them up and comment upon them in groups.

I *Drinking*. Sixteen of the twenty-five are cases of intoxication, more or less serious. Ten of them occurred at Commencement time, too late for report then. Seven of the men involved were Sophomores ('04, becoming Juniors) and three were Freshmen ('05). Two of them (Freshmen) got their drink at the class headquarters of classes holding reunions, where the drink, they affirmed, was practically forced upon them. The prominence of general drinking, with open house for all comers, as a feature of these class re-unions is greatly to be deplored. It not only causes scandal and injures the reputation of the University, but also the example, the license of this custom, affects the tone of the undergraduate and counteracts our discipline. Some reasonable reform here is urgent. Possibly a direct communication from the Trustees of the University to the several class organizations through the Secretaries might prove effective. Personal presentation of the matter also to influential alumni might secure their interest and aid in abating this evil.

Another serious matter is again brought forcibly to our attention by the fact that in six of the foregoing cases the students were overcome by drink served at the annual upper-class Club banquets on the Friday before Commencement. The use of all malt or alc[o]holic liquors upon the premises is prohibited in the charter of these Clubs. This provision, however, has come to be violated because no suitable outside place can be had for this annual dinner, at which numerous alumni are guests. The new members also are introduced at that time. Every year cases of excess are reported by the Proctor, while others no doubt escape his notice.

This Autumn two Seniors and two Sophomores have been suspended, and two Sophomores reprimanded and put on probation —for drinking. If we can secure, by persuasion or by threats, prompter closing of saloons at the legal hour, 11 P.M., it will be a great gain for good order and sobriety.

II *Hazing.* For the first two weeks there was the customary guying and "horsing" of the Freshmen,—bidding them run, take off their hats, etc,—which the undergraduate conceives is not hazing within the meaning of the hazing regulations, and is a thing to be winked at and tolerated. On the whole, there has been somewhat less of this practice than usual, and it stopped, as student tradition demands, after the Sophomore-Freshman ball game.

The President at the very opening addressed the Sophomores on hazing;[1] and an effort was also made to arouse the Student Hazing Committee to a sense of its responsibilities under the regulations of four years ago.[2] In the last week or two, however, the Sophomores have been reviving general hazing in the old fashion, —taking Freshmen from their beds at midnight and later out to remote spots, where they are put through various performances. In most cases no physical violence is perpetrated. In some cases very objectionable things have been required, endangering health and causing physical ill. All of this is in direct violation of the

[1] The Editors can find no report of this address.

[2] The Student Hazing Committee was constituted at a mass meeting of students on December 1, 1898, called to consider the problem of hazing at Princeton. After considering resolutions prepared by a committee from the junior and senior classes, the mass meeting approved the resolutions, outlawed hazing at Princeton, and established a Student Hazing Committee, consisting of the vice presidents of the two upper classes, the editor-in-chief of the *Daily Princetonian*, and the manager and assistant manager of the baseball team, to enforce the ban. The student committee had the power to refer violators to the faculty Discipline Committee for appropriate action. *Daily Princetonian*, Dec. 2, 1898.

letter and the spirit of the student regulations. A party about to take a Freshman out at midnight recently was surprised by one of the proctors. The student Committee sitting on the case has reported four men for indefinite suspension. Meanwhile we are anxious to see how far the Committee will have the support of the student body; whether the students will sustain the action and the imposition of an effective penalty, or whether the anti-hazing feeling has quite disappeared, or active interest in the matter so weakened that the Faculty must itself once more essay the suppression of hazing by such measures as it can apply. There is now no one of the classes in College which was here when the Hazing Resolutions were discussed and adopted. The action and present attitude of the Committee itself is encouraging. As long as there is any prospect or real desire and effort on the part of the students to suppress hazing, it is, I believe, wise to encourage them and to bear patiently some annoyances conspicuous, but not very serious. The situation is now critical as to the continuance of the system of student control of hazing.

III *Proctors*. A new assistant proctor, Linton Earl, was engaged this Fall in place of Titus,[3] who was engaged last year, but proved unsuited to the work. The new assistant was last year in private employ about the University and has the great advantage of understanding College ways and knowing most of the students individually. He is doing good work. A special proctor was engaged for about two weeks. With the increasing numbers and the distribution of the students about the town I think the time may soon come when it will be necessary to have proctors on duty all night, one on the main street and one on University Place. The town police are useless as far as students are concerned. Our proctors retire after 12 p.m. as soon as quiet prevails. Often a disorderly party will turn up later and create disturbances. A third year Special is now under suspension for such midnight disorder.

IV. *Scholarship*. At the June examinations the reports of the Committee on Examinations and Standing, Academic and Scientific, showed fifty six (56) men to be dropped under the Rules, for failures and earlier deficiencies in their studies. Fourteen (14) were Academic (an unusually small number): 1 Junior, 5 Sophomores, 6 Freshmen, 2 Specials. Forty two (42) were Scientific: 10 Juniors, 9 Sophomores, 18 Freshmen, 5 Specials. These numbers were unusually large, this being due in a meas-

[3] The only Titus listed in the Princeton town directory for 1902 was Nelson W. Titus, the cabinetmaker.

ure to the application of a stricter rule adopted last year, by which neglected arrearages of work were given more weight. As this was the first year in which the rule took effect, the Committee exercised some discretion in its application—especially in the upper-class cases. Out of the forty two (42), more than half were allowed to take examinations in the Fall. Nineteen (19) accordingly have succeeded in keeping on with their classes. Twenty-three (23) have been dropped,—ten (10) entering a lower class, thirteen (13) withdrawing from the University.

Of the fourteen (14) Academic cases, Eight (8) continue in their classes: One (1) enters a lower class; five (5) withdraw. At the February Examinations seventeen (17) men Academic and seventeen (17) Scientific (mostly Freshmen) were dropped out and withdrew at that time. Sixteen (16) of them,—11 Academic and 5 Scientific,—re-enter this Fall in a lower class.

The net loss of students, therefore, from the February Examinations is, Academic 6, Scientific 12; from the June Examinations Academic 5, Scientific 13. Total 36 for the year,—not an excessive number out of 1237 undergraduates. I append to this report a tabulated conspectus by classes.[4]

V. *Entrance Examinations.* At the June Entrance Examinations there were a number of cases of cheating. Most of them were at Phillips Academy, Andover.[5] The publicity given the affair in the newspapers was not intentional on our part, and the matter was explained to the Principal, who nevertheless continued to misrepresent our action to the public. Hereafter it is intended to give clear, printed notice in the examinations that evidence of dishonesty in the papers, alike the giving and receiving of aid, will permanently debar applicants from Princeton. All papers showing collusion were rejected in June. In view of all the circumstances, however, it was deemed best this Fall to allow a re-trial of the examinations, when requested. One student only availed himself of the privilege; and he passed.

At our Fall Examinations in Princeton, emphatic notice was given of our position. One student found guilty of copying was permanently excluded.

VI. *Matriculation.* The Matriculation list shows that the numbers on the Freshman roll of new students admitted and actually here are about thirty (30) short (20 Academic, 10 Scientific) of the numbers of last year's class.

For the first time I had the matriculants enter not their age in

4 This conspectus is not printed.
5 See EAW to WW, July 18, 1902, n. 2.

round numbers, but their birthday. From these data, using years and months, I have ascertained carefully the average age at entering. When this was done, 186 Academic and 144 Scientific students had matriculated.

The Academic average is 18 years and 6 months; or throwing out half a dozen very old men, as really vitiating the statistics, the average age of the Academic Freshman is *18 years and 4 months*. The average of the Scientific Freshman is just *19 years*. While the Freshmen entering the C.E. course[6]—(a little more than one third of the Scientific students)—average *19 years and 4 months*. While this is so, it is to be observed that the Scientific requirements demand usually a year less time in preparation.

By the traditional custom the religious denomination of the matriculants is recorded. The Presbyterians constitute about one half of the whole,—and more than half on the Academic side. Episcopalians make one fifth of the Academic students, one third of the Scientific. Methodists make about 10% in each department. There are 14 Roman Catholics, (10 of these in the Scientific department); 2 Jews, and 2 Christian Scientists. Three fifths of the whole number set themselves down as communicants in their respective denominations. In this particular there is a strong contrast between the Academic and the Scientific student. On the Academic side the Presbyterian communicants outnumber the non-communicants in the remarkable proportion of 7 to 2, the proportion for all Academic students being 2 to 1. On the Scientific side the non-communicants are slightly in the majority; and again the C.E. students make the poorer showing. I append a tabular conspectus of these statistics.[7]

Owing to the delay in passing on the proposed revision of the Rules and Regulations it was necessary to reprint the pamphlet as it was for distribution to matriculants. Inasmuch as it sometimes becomes necessary to put a sharp penalty on men neglecting summons to a Committee, it might be well not to omit, as proposed, Section 7 of Chapter IX.[8] Three men have been suspended this Fall for this offence.

Respectfully Submitted   S. R. Winans—Dean

TLS (Trustees' Papers, UA, NjP).
   [6] That is, the course in Civil Engineering.
   [7] This conspectus is not printed.
   [8] "7. If any student shall refuse to appear personally before any officer of the University, when required so to do, he shall be punished for contempt of authority." *Princeton University*[,] *Rules and Regulations* (n.p., 1902), p. 18.

To Edith Gittings Reid

My dearest Friend,   Princeton, 22 Oct., 1902

I *ought* to be considering what I am going to say in one of the informal speeches (the most exacting kind) which will be expected of me on Saturday, but I mean to give my heart leave and steal a minute or two to tell you that I,—that *we*,—have set our hearts on having you stay over Sunday. I shall be absorbed by "functions" *all* day,—and far into the night Saturday,—from Friday afternoon on, indeed, far into Sunday morning, and I simply *must* have *some* time in which to see and enjoy you. If you will only stay into the next week a bit, we shall be quit of our official guests by Monday morning and can have the delight,—it would be nothing less,—of bringing you and Mr. Reid over here to "Prospect" to be our own! Be generous to us and stay as long as you can!

Mrs. Wilson joins me in warmest love and urgency.

Always   Your devoted friend,   Woodrow Wilson

ALS (WC, NjP).

To Irving Strong Upson[1]

My dear Sir: Princeton, N. J.   Oct. 23rd, 1902.

Allow me to thank you for the LL.D. diploma, which came today by Adams Express, as the permanent record of the honor conferred upon me last June by Rutgers College.[2]

I have already taken occasion to express my high appreciation of the honor which I so much value.

                    Very truly yours,   Woodrow Wilson

TLS (University Archives, NjR).
    [1] Librarian, Registrar, and Secretary of the Faculty of Rutgers College.
    [2] See David Murray to WW, June 20, 1902, Vol. 12.

Two Letters from Charles Williston McAlpin

My dear Sir: [Princeton, N. J.] October 24, 1902.

I have the honor to inform you that at a meeting of the Trustees of Princeton University held October 21, 1902 on recommendation of the Finance Committee the following resolutions were adopted:

"RESOLVED that the salary of the President of the University be made $8000 a year and that there shall be no additional fees."

"RESOLVED that an appropriation of $2000 a year be made to the President of the University for entertainment and for expenses in caring for the property."

"RESOLVED that the President of the University be authorized to engage a Secretary at a salary of $500 per annum."

"RESOLVED that the President of the University be authorized to engage an Instructor in the Greek [German] Department in place of Professor Humphreys at a salary of $600 per annun [annum]."

On the recommendation of the Committee on Morals and Discipline it was voted that a committee of five members of this Board be appointed to confer with one representative from each of the existing Clubs upon the whole question of the relation of the Clubs to the University and its light [life] and report to this Board. This committee was also directed to consider that part of the Report of the Dean of the Faculty which has reference to drinking.

If you will advise me of the names of this committee I will notify them of their appointment.[1]

On motion of Mr. Cleveland seconded by Mr. John A. Stewart the following resolution was adopted:

"RESOLVED that the President of the University be fully authorized by the Board of Trustees in reorganizing the teaching force to create such vacancies in such force as he may deem for the best interest of the University."

On motion of Mr. Cleveland seconded by Mr. Davis the following resolution was adopted:

"RESOLVED that the Board approves the President's suggestion that he be at liberty to exhibit his Report this day made to such persons as he may deem best in his efforts to carry out its recommendations."

I have the honor to remain,
Very sincerely yours,   [C. W. McAlpin]   Secretary.

[1] This committee consisted of Moses Taylor Pyne, chairman, James Waddel Alexander, Henry Woodhull Green, Rev. Dr. Charles Wood, and John David Davis. Their report is printed at June 8, 1903.

My dear Sir: [Princeton, N. J.] October 24, 1902.

At a meeting of the Trustees of Princeton University held October 21, 1902 a letter from the Class Committee of '79 was read stating that the Class of '79 has decided to present to the University, as a memorial of the Twenty-fifth Anniversa[r]y of its graduation, a building to be known as The Seventy-Nine Dormitory. On motion of Mr. John A. Srewart [Stewart] duly seconded Mr. Bayard Henry was appointed a committee to prepare a vote of thanks which was presented by him to the Board and unanimously adopted. I enclose a copy of the same and would ask you to present it to the Class of '79 on behalf of the Trustees of Princeton University.

I remain,

Very sincerely yours,   [C. W. McAlpin]   Secretary.

CCL (McAlpin File, UA, NjP).

From the Minutes of the Board of Trustees of Princeton University

[Oct. 25, 1902]

Pursuant to the adjournment of October 21st. the Trustees met in the University Library at ten o'clock on Saturday morning, October 25, 1902. . . .

HONORARY DEGREES CONFERRED

President-elect Wilson presented His Excellency Franklin Murphy, Governor of New Jersey, for the honorary degree of LL.D. and the degree was conferred on him *in camera.*

GOVERNOR MURPHY QUALIFIES AS PRESIDENT OF THE BOARD

Governor Murphy having taken and subscribed to the oaths required by the Charter qualified as a Trustee of Princeton University, and took the chair.

INAUGURATION OF PRESIDENT WILSON

It was ordered to attend the Inauguration of Woodrow Wilson as President of Princeton University. . . .[1]

[1] For an account of the inauguration and the events of the day, see the news report printed at Nov. 1, 1902.

An Inaugural Address[1]

[Oct. 25, 1902]

PRINCETON FOR THE NATION'S SERVICE.

Six years ago I had the honor of standing in this place to speak of the memories with which Princeton men heartened themselves as they looked back a century and a half to the founding of their college. To-day my task is more delicate, more difficult. Standing here in the light of those older days, we must now assess our present purposes and powers and sketch the creed by which we shall be willing to live in the days to come. We are but men of a single generation in the long life of an institution which shall still be young when we are dead, but while we live her life is in us. What we conceive she conceives. In planning for Princeton, moreover, we are planning for the country. The service of institutions of learning is not private but public. It is plain what the nation needs as its affairs grow more and more complex and its interests begin to touch the ends of the earth. It needs efficient and enlightened men. The universities of the country must take part in supplying them.

American universities serve a free nation whose progress, whose power, whose prosperity, whose happiness, whose integrity depend upon individual initiative and the sound sense and equipment of the rank and file. Their history, moreover, has set them apart to a character and service of their own. They are not mere seminaries of scholars. They never can be. Most of them, the greatest of them and the most distinguished, were first of all great colleges before they became universities; and their task is two-fold: the production of a great body of informed and thoughtful men and the production of a small body of trained scholars and investigators. It is one of their functions to take large bodies of young men up to the places of outlook whence the world of thought and affairs is to be viewed; it is another of their functions to take some men, a little more mature, a little more studious, men self-selected by aptitude and industry, into the quiet libraries and laboratories where the close contacts of study are learned which yield the world new insight into the processes of nature, of reason, and of the human spirit. These two functions are not

[1] A WWsh draft, dated July 23, 1902, and an undated WWT draft, heavily emended, of this address are in WP, DLC. The following text is printed from Wilson's reading copy. "Princeton for the Nation's Service" was printed many times, "official" versions appearing in the *Daily Princetonian*, Oct. 25, 1902; the *Princeton Alumni Weekly*, III (Nov. 1, 1902), 89-98; and the *Princeton University Bulletin*, XIV (Dec. 1902), 17-33.

to be performed separately, but side by side, and are to be informed with one spirit, the spirit of enlightenment, a spirit of learning which is neither superficial nor pedantic, which values life more than it values the mere acquisitions of the mind.

Universities, we have learned to think, include within their scope, when complete, schools of law, of medicine, of theology, and of those more recondite mechanic arts, such as the use of electricity, upon which the skilled industry of the modern world is built up; and, though in dwelling upon such an association of schools as of the gist of the matter in our definitions of a university, we are relying upon historical accidents rather than upon essential principles for our conceptions, they are accidents which show the happy order and system with which things often come to pass. Though the university may dispense with professional schools, professional schools may not dispense with the university. Professional schools have nowhere their right atmosphere and association except where they are parts of a university and share its spirit and method. They must love learning as well as professional success in order to have their perfect usefulness. This is not the verdict of the universities merely but of the professional men themselves, spoken out of hard experience of the facts of business. It was but the other day that the Society for the Promotion of Engineering Education indorsed the opinion of their president, Mr. Eddy,[2] that the crying need of the engineering profession was men whose technical knowledge and proficiency rest upon a broad basis of general culture which should make them free of the wider worlds of learning and experience, which should give them largeness of view, judgment, and easy knowledge of men. The modern world nowhere shows a closeted profession shut in to a narrow round of technical functions to which no knowledge of the outside world need ever penetrate. Whatever our calling, our thoughts must often be afield among men of many kinds, amidst interests as various as the phases of modern life. The managing minds of the world, even the efficient working minds of the world, must be equipped for a mastery

2 Henry Turner Eddy, Professor of Engineering and Mechanics at the University of Minnesota, was President of the Society for the Promotion of Engineering Education in 1896-97. In his presidential address, delivered at the fifth annual meeting in Toronto on August 16, 1897, he deplored what he said was the growing demand by engineering colleges that "courses of engineering instruction shall be exclusively devoted to engineering." "The culture studies," he asserted, "are of fundamental importance." At this and at subsequent annual meetings of the society, there were discussions of committee reports on entrance and graduation requirements; however, nothing in the society's *Proceedings* indicates that Eddy's opinion that an engineer's education should rest upon a broad basis of general culture was specifically endorsed by the society.

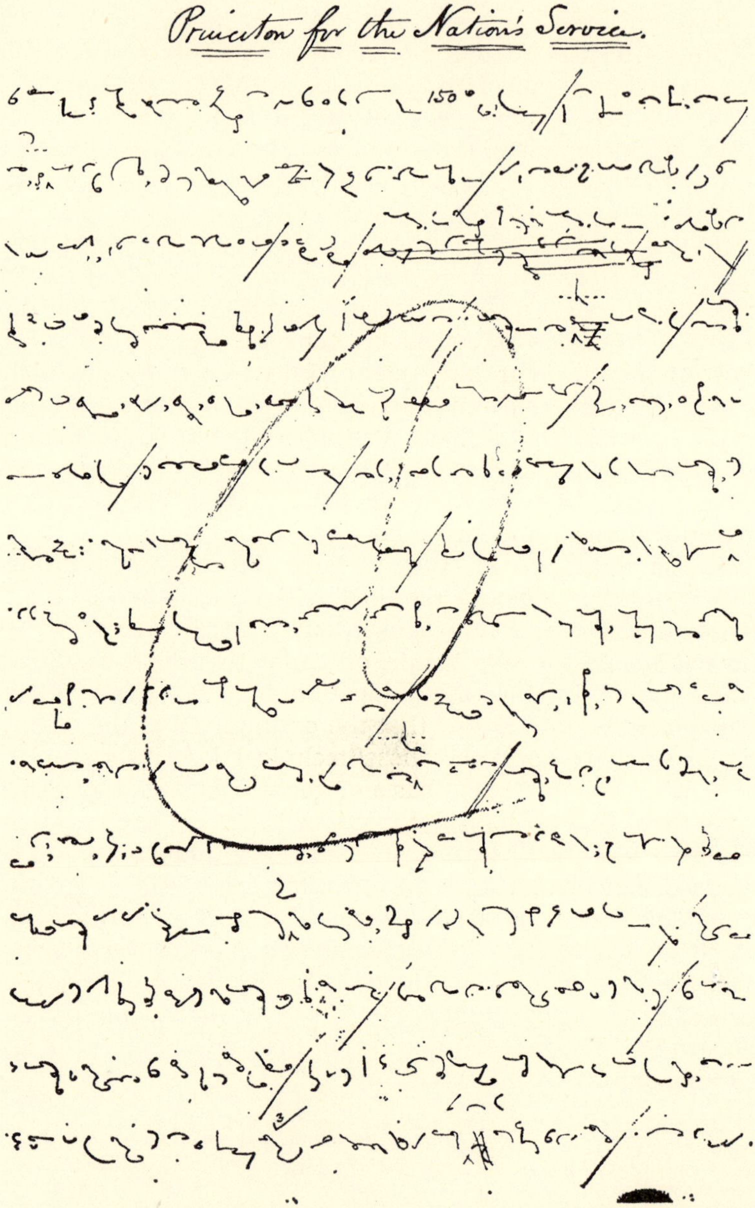

Princeton for the Nation's Service.

[shorthand text]

The first page of Wilson's shorthand draft of his inaugural address

PRINCETON FOR THE NATION'S SERVICE

Six years ago I had the honour of standing in this place to speak of the

memories with which Princeton men heartened themselves as they looked back.

a Century and a half,
~~one hundred and fifty years~~ to the founding of their college. To-day my

task is more delicate, more difficult. Standing here in the light of those

older days, we must now assess our present purposes and powers and sketch

the creed by which we shall be willing to live in the days to come. We

are but men of a single generation in the long life of an institution which

shall still be young when we are dead, but while we live her life *is* in us.

What we conceive she conceives. In planning for Princeton, moreover, we

are planning for the country. The service of institutions of learning is

not private, but public. It is plain what the nation needs as its affairs

grow more and more complex and its interests begin to touch the ends of the

earth. Its needs efficient and enlightened men. The universities of the

country must take part in supplying them.

American universities serve a free nation whose progress, whose power,

whose prosperity, whose happiness, whose integrity depend upon individual

initiative and the sound sense and equipment of the rank and file. Their

history, moreover, has set them apart to a character and service of their

own. They are not mere seminaries of scholars. They never can be. Most

of them, the greatest of them and the most distinguished, were first of all

great colleges before they became universities; and their *task* ~~problem~~ is two-

fold: the production of a great body of informed and thoughtful men and the

production of a small body of trained scholars and investigators. It is

one of their functions to take large bodies of young men up to the places

of outlook whence the world of thought and affairs is to be viewed; it is

The first page of Wilson's typed copy of his inaugural address

whose chief characteristic is adaptability, play, an initiative which transcends the bounds of mere technical training. Technical schools whose training is not built up on the foundations of a broad and general discipline cannot impart this. The stuff they work upon must be prepared for them by processes which produce fibre and elasticity, and their own methods must be shot through with the impulses of the university.

It is this that makes our age and our task so interesting: this complex interdependence and interrelationship of all the processes which prepare the mind for effectual service: this necessity that the merchant and the financier should have traveled minds, the engineer a knowledge of books and men, the lawyer a wide view of affairs, the physician a familiar acquaintance with the abstract data of science, and that the closeted scholar should throw his windows open to the four quarters of the world. Every considerable undertaking has come to be based on knowledge, on thoughtfulness, on the masterful handling of men and facts. The university must stand in the midst, where the roads of thought and knowledge interlace and cross, and, building upon some coign of vantage, command them all.

It has happened that throughout two long generations,—long because filled with the industrial and social transformation of the world,—the thought of studious men has been bent upon devising methods by which special aptitudes could be developed, detailed investigations carried forward, inquiry at once broadened and deepened to meet the scientific needs of the age, knowledge extended and made various and yet exact by the minute and particular researches of men who devoted all the energies of their minds to a single task. And so we have gained much, though we have also lost much that must be recovered. We have gained immensely in knowledge but we have lost system. We have acquired an admirable, sober passion for accuracy. Our pulses have been quickened, moreover, by discovery. The world of learning has been transformed. No study has stood still. Scholars have won their fame, not by erudition, but by exploration, the conquest of new territory, the addition of infinite detail to the map of knowledge. And so we have gained a splendid proficiency in investigation. We know the right methods of advanced study. We have made exhaustive records of the questions waiting to be answered, the doubts waiting to be resolved, in every domain of inquiry; thousands of problems once unsolved, apparently insoluble, we have reduced to their elements and settled, and their answers have been added to the commonplaces of knowledge. But, meanwhile, what of the preliminary training of specialists, what of the general foundations of knowledge, what of the general equipment of mind which all men must have who are to serve this busy, this sophisticated generation?

Probably no one is to blame for the neglect of the general into which we have been led by our eager pursuit of the particular. Every age has lain under the reproach of doing but one thing at a time, of having some one signal object for the sake of which other things were slighted or ignored. But the plain fact is, that we have so spread and diversified the scheme of knowledge in our day that it has lost coherence. We have dropped the threads of system in our teaching. And system begins at the beginning. We must find the common term for college and university; and those who have great colleges at the heart of the universities they are trying to develop are under a special compulsion to find it. Learning is not divided. Its kingdom and government are centred, unitary, single. The processes of instruction which fit a large body of young men to serve their generation with powers released and fit for great tasks ought also to serve as the initial processes by which scholars and investigators are made. They ought to be but the first parts of the method by which the crude force of un-trained men is reduced to the expert uses of civilization. There may come a day when general study will be no part of the function of a university, when it shall have been handed over, as some now talk of handing it over, to the secondary schools, after the German fashion; but that day will not be ours, and I, for one, do not wish to see it come. The masters who guide the youngsters who pursue general studies are very useful neighbors for those who prosecute detailed inquiries and devote themselves to special tasks. No investigator can afford to keep his doors shut against the comradeships of the wide world of letters and of thought.

To have a great body of undergraduates crowding our class-rooms and setting the pace of our lives must always be a very wholesome thing. These young fellows, who do not mean to make finished scholars of themselves, but who do mean to learn from their elders, now at the outset of their lives, what the thoughts of the world have been and its processes of progress, in order that they may start with light about them, and not doubt or darkness, learning in the brief span of four years what it would else take them half a life-time to discover by mere contact with men, must teach us the real destiny with which knowledge came into the world. Its mission is enlightenment and edification, and these young gentlemen shall keep us in mind of this.

The age has hurried us, has shouldered us out of the old ways, has bidden us be moving and look to the cares of a practical generation; and we have suffered ourselves to be a little disconcerted. No doubt we wcre [were] once pedants. It is a happy thing that the days have gone by when the texts we studied loomed bigger to our view than the human spirit that underlay them. But there are some principles of which we must not let go. We must not lose sight of that fine conception of a general training which led our fathers, in the days when men knew how to build great states, to build great colleges also to sustain them. No man who knows the world has ever supposed that a day would come when every young man would seck [seek] a college training. The college is not for the majority who carry forward the common labour of the world, nor even for those who work at the skilled handicrafts which multiply the conveniences and the luxuries of the complex modern life. It is for the minority who plan, who conceive, who superintend, who mediate between group and group and must see the wide stage as a whole. Democratic nations must be served in this wise no less than those whose leaders are chosen by birth and privilege; and the college is no less democratic because it is for those who play a special part. I know that there are men of genius who play these parts of captaincy and yet have never been in the classrooms of a college, whose only school has been the world itself. The world is an excellent school for those who have vision and self-discipline enough to use it. It works in this wise, in part, upon us all. Raw lads are made men of by the mere sweep of their lives through the various school of experience. It is this very sweep of life that we wish to bring to the consciousness of young men by the shorter processes of the college. We have seen the adaptation take place; we have seen crude boys made fit in four years to become men of the world.

Every man who plays a leading or conceiving part in any affair must somehow get this schooling of his spirit, this quickening and adaptation of his perceptions. He must either spread the process through his lifetime and get it by an extraordinary gift of insight and upon his own initiative, or else he must get it by the alchemy of mind practiced in college halls. We ought distinctly to set forth in our philosophy of this matter the difference between a man's preparation for the specific and definite tasks he is to perform in the world and that general enlargement of spirit and release of powers which he shall need if his task is not to crush and belittle him. When we insist that a certain general education shall precede all special training which is not merely mechanical in its scope and purpose, we mean simply that every mind needs for its highest serviceability a certain preliminary orientation, that it may get its bearings and release its perceptions for a wide and catholic view. We must deal in college with the spirits of men, not with their fortunes. Here, in history and philosophy and literature and science, are the experiences of the world summed up. These are but so many names which we give to the records of what men have done and thought and comprehended. If we be not pedants, if we be able to get at the spirit of the matter, we shall extract from them the edification and enlightenment as of those who have gone the long journey of experience with the race.

There are two ways of preparing a young man for his life work. One is to give him the skill and special knowledge which shall make a good tool, an excellent bread-winning tool of him; and for thousands of young men that way must be followed. It is a good way. It is honorable, it is indispensable. But it is not for the college, and it never can be. The college should seek to make the men whom it receives something more than excellent servants of a trade or skilled practitioners of a profession. It should give them elasticity of faculty and breadth of vision, so that they shall have a surplus of mind to expend, not upon their profession only, for its liberalization and enlargement, but also upon the broader interests which lie about them, in the spheres in which they are to be, not breadwinners merely, but citizens as well, and in their own hearts, where they are to grow to the stature of real nobility. It is this free capital of mind the world most stands in need of,—this free capital that awaits investment in undertakings, spiritual as well as material, which advance the race and help all men to a better life.

And are we to do this great thing by the old discipline of Greek, Latin, Mathematics, and English? The day has gone by when that is possible. The circle of liberal studies is too much enlarged, the area of general learning is too much extended, to make it any longer possible to make these few things stand for all. Science has opened a new world of learning, as great as the old. The influence of science has broadened and transformed old themes of study and created new, and all the boundaries of knowledge are altered. In the days of our grandfathers all learning was literary, was of the book; the phenomena of nature were brought together under the general terms of an encyclopaedic Natural Philosophy. Now the quiet rooms where once a few students sat agaze before a long table at which, with a little apparatus before him, a lecturer discoursed of the laws of matter and of force are replaced by great laboratories, physical, chemical, biological, in which the pupil's own direct observation and experiment take the place of the conning of mere theory and generalization, and men handle the immediate stuff of which nature is made. Museums of natural history, of geology, of paleontology stretch themselves amidst our lecture rooms, for demonstration of what we say of the life and structure of the globe. The telescope, the spectroscope, not the text book merely, are our means of teaching the laws and movements of the sky. An age of science has transmuted speculation into knowledge and doubled the dominion of the mind. Heavens and earth swing together in a new universe of knowledge. And so it is impossible that the old discipline should stand alone, to serve us as an education. With it alone we should get no introduction into the modern world either of thought or of affairs. The mind of the modern student must be carried through a wide range of studies in which science shall have a place not less distinguished than that accorded literature, philosophy or politics.

But we must observe proportion and remember what it is that we seek. We seek in our general education, not universal knowledge, but the opening up of the mind to a catholic appreciation of the best achievements of men and the best processes of thought since days of thought set in. We seek to apprise young men of what has been settled and made sure of, of the thinking that has been carried through and made an end of. We seek to set them securely forward at the point at which the mind of the race has definitely arrived, and save them the trouble of attempting the journey over again, so that they may know from the outset what relation their own thought and effort bear to what the world has already done. We speak of the "disciplinary" studies through which a boy is put in his school days and during the period of his introduction into the full privileges of college work, having in our thought the mathematics of arithmetic, elementary algebra, and geometry, the Greek and Latin texts and grammars, the elements of English and of French or German; but a better, truer name for them were to be desired. They are indeed disciplinary. The mind takes fibre, facility, strength, adaptability, certainty of touch from handling them, when the teacher knows his art and their power. But they are disciplinary only because of their definiteness and their established method: and they take their determinateness from their age and perfection. It is their age and completeness that render them so serviceable and so suitable for the first processes of education. By their means the boy is informed of the bodies of knowledge which are not experimental but settled, definitive, fundamental. This is the stock upon which time out of mind all the thoughtful world has traded. These have been food of the mind for long generations.

It is in this view of the matter that we get an explanation of the fact that the classical languages of antiquity afford better discipline and are a more indispensable means of culture than any language of our own day except the language, the intimate language, of our own thought, which is for us universal coin of exchange in the intellectual world, and must have its values determined to a nicety before we pay it out. No modern language is definite, classically made up. Modern tongues, moreover, carry the modern babel of voices. The thoughts they utter fluctuate and change; the phrases they speak alter and are dissolved with every change of current in modern thought or impulse. They have, first or last, had the same saturations of thought that our own language has had; they carry the same atmosphere; in traversing their pleasant territory, we see only different phases of our own familiar world, the world of our own experience; and, valuable as it is to have this various view of the world we live in and send our minds upon their travels up and down the modern age, it is not fundamental, it is not an indispensable first process of training. It can be postponed. The classical literatures give us, in tones and with an authentic accent we can nowhere else hear, the thoughts of an age we cannot visit. They contain airs of a time not our own, unlike our own, and yet its foster parent. To these things was the modern thinking world first bred. In them speaks a time naïve, pagan, an early morning day when men looked upon the earth while it was fresh, untrodden by crowding thought, an age when the mind moved as it were without prepossessions and with an unsophisticated, childlike curiosity, a season apart during which those seats upon the Mediterranean seem the first seats of thoughtful men. We shall not anywhere else get a substitute for it. The modern mind has been built upon that culture and there is no authentic equivalent.

Drill in the mathematics stands in the same category with familiar knowledge of the thought and speech of classical antiquity, because in them also we get the lifelong accepted discipline of the race, the processes of pure reasoning which lie at once at the basis of science and at the basis of philosophy, grounded upon observation and physical fact and yet abstract, and of the very stuff of the essential processes of the mind, a bridge between reason and nature. Here, too, as in the classics, is a definitive body of knowledge and of reason, a discipline which has been made test of through long generations, a method of thought which has in all ages steadied, perfected, enlarged, strengthened and given precision to the powers of the mind. Mathematical drill is an introduction of the boy's mind to the most definitely settled rational experiences of the world.

I shall attempt no proof that English also is of the fundamental group of studies. You will not require me to argue that no man has been made free of the world of thought who does not know the literature, the idiomatic flavor and the masterful use of his own tongue.

But, if we cannot doubt that these great studies are fundamental, neither can we doubt that the circle of fundamental studies has widened in our day and that education, even general education, has been extended to new boundaries. And that chiefly because science has had its credentials accepted as of the true patriciate of learning. It is as necessary that the lad should be inducted into the thinking of the modern time as it is that he should be carefully grounded in the old, accepted thought which has stood test from age to age; and the thought of the modern time is based upon science. It is only a question of choice in a vast field. Special developments of science, the parts which lie in controversy, the parts which are as yet but half built up by experiment and hypothesis, do not constitute the proper subject matter of general education. For that you need, in the field of science as in every other field, the bodies of knowledge which are most definitively determined and which are most fundamental. Undoubtedly the fundamental sciences are physics, chemistry and biology. Physics and chemistry afford a systematic body of knowledge as abundant for instruction, as definitive almost, as mathematics itself; and biology, young as it is, has already supplied us with a scheme of physical life which lifts its study to the place of a distinctive discipline. These great bodies of knowledge claim their place at the foundation of liberal training not merely for our information, but because they afford us direct introduction into the most essential analytical and rational processes of scientific study, impart penetration, precision, candour, openness of mind, and afford the close contacts of concrete thinking. And there stand alongside of these geology and astronomy, whose part in general culture, aside from their connection with physics, mechanics and chemistry, is to apply to the mind the stimulation which comes from being brought into the presence and in some sort into the comprehension of stupendous, systematized physical fact,—from seeing nature in the mass and system of her might and structure. These, too, are essential parts of the wide scheme which the college must plot out. And when we have added to these the manifold discipline of philosophy, the indispensable instructions of history, and the enlightenments of economic and political study, and to these the modern languages which are the tools of scholarship, we stand confused. How are we to marshal this host of studies within a common plan which shall not put the pupil out of breath?

No doubt we must make choice among them, and suffer the pupil himself to make choice. But the choice that we make must be the chief choice, the choice the pupil makes the subordinate choice. Since he cannot in the time at his disposal go the grand tour of accepted modern knowledge, we who have studied the geography of learning and who have observed several generations of men attempt the journey, must instruct him how in a brief space he may see most of the world, and he must choose only which one of several tours that we may map out he will take. Else there is no difference between young men and old, between the novice and the man of experience, in fundamental matters of choice. We must supply the synthesis and must see to it that, whatever group of studies the student selects, it shall at least represent the round whole, contain all the elements of modern knowledge, and be itself a complete circle of general subjects. Princeton can never have any uncertainty of view on that point.

And that not only because we conceive it to be our business to give a general, liberalizing, enlightening training to men who do not mean to go on to any special work by which they may make men of science or scholars of themselves or skilled practitioners of a learned profession, but also because we would create a right atmosphere for special study. Critics of education have recently given themselves great concern about over-specialization. The only specialists about whom, I think, the thoughtful critic need give himself any serious anxiety are the specialists who have never had any general education in which to give their special studies wide rootage and nourishment. The true American university seems to me to get its best characteristic, its surest guarantee of sane and catholic learning, from the presence at its very heart of a college of liberal arts. Its vital union with the college gives it, it seems to me, the true university atmosphere, a pervading sense of the unity and unbroken circle of learning,—not so much because of the presence of a great body of undergraduates in search of general training (because until these youngsters get what they seek they create ideals more by their lack than by their achievement), as because of the presence of a great body of teachers whose life-work it is to find the general outlooks of knowledge and give vision of them every day from quiet rooms which, while they talk, shall seem to command all the prospects of the wide world.

I should dread to see those who guide special study and research altogether excused from undergraduate instruction, should dread to see them withdraw themselves altogether from the broad and general survey of the subjects of which they have sought to make themselves masters. I should equally despair of seeing any student made a truly serviceable specialist who had not turned to his specialty in the spirit of a broad and catholic learning,—unless, indeed, he were one of those rare spirits who once and again appear amongst us, whose peculiar, individual privilege it is to have safe vision of but a little segment of truth and yet keep his poise and reason. It is not the education that concentrates that is to be dreaded, but the education that narrows,—that is narrow from the first. I should wish to see every student made, not a man of his task, but a man of the world, whatever his world may be. If it be the world of learning, then he should be a conscious and a broad-minded citizen of it. If it be the world of letters, his thought should run free upon the whole field of it. If it be the world of affairs, he should move amidst affairs like a man of thought. What we seek in education is full liberation of the faculties, and the man who has not some surplus of thought and energy to expend outside the narrow circle of his own task and interest is a dwarfed, uneducated man. We judge the range and excellence of every man's abilities by their play outside the task by which he earns his livelihood. Does he merely work, or does he also look abroad and plan? Does he, at the least, enlarge the thing he handles? No task, rightly done, is truly private. It is part of the world's work. The subtle and yet universal connections of things are what the truly educated man, be he man of science, man of letters, or statesman, must keep always in his thought, if he would fit his work to the work of the world. His adjustment is as important as his energy.

We mean, so soon as our generous friends have arranged their private finances in such a way as to enable them to release for our use enough money for the purpose, to build a notable graduate college. I say "build" because it will be not only a body of teachers and students but also a college of residence, where men shall live together in the close and wholesome comradeships of learning. We shall build it, not apart, but as nearly as may be at the very heart, the geographical heart, of the university; and its comradeships shall be for young men and old, for the novice as well as for the graduate. It will constitute but a single term in the scheme of coördination which is our ideal. The windows of the graduate college must open straight upon the walks and quadrangles and lecture halls of the *studium generale*.

In our attempt to escape the pedantry and narrowness of the old fixed curriculum we have, no doubt, gone so far as to be in danger of losing the old ideals. Our utilitarianism has carried us so far afield that we are in a fair way to forget the real utilities of the mind. No doubt the old, purely literary training made too much of the development of mere taste, mere delicacy of perception, but our modern training makes too little. We pity the young child who, ere its physical life has come to maturity, is put to some task which will dwarf and narrow it into a mere mechanic tool. We know that it needs first its free years in the sunlight and fresh air, its irresponsible youth. And yet we do not hesitate to deny to the young mind its irresponsible years of mere development in the free air of general studies. We have too ignorantly served the spirit of the age,—have made no bold and sanguine attempt to instruct and lead it. Its call is for efficiency, but not for narrow, purblind efficiency. Surely no other age ever had tasks which made so shrewdly for the testing of the general powers of the mind. No sort of knowledge, no sort of training of the perceptions and the facility of the mind could come amiss to the modern man of affairs or the modern student. A general awakening of the faculties, and then a close and careful adaptation to some special task is the programme of mere prudence for every man who would succeed.

And there are other things besides material success with which we must supply our generation. It must be supplied with men who care more for principles than for money, for the right adjustments of life than for the gross accumulations of profit. The problems that call for sober thoughtfulness and mere devotion are as pressing as those which call for practical efficiency. We are here not merely to release the faculties of men for their own use, but also to quicken their social understanding, instruct their consciences, and give them the catholic vision of those who know their just relations to their fellow men. Here in America, for every man touched with nobility, for every man touched with the spirit of our institutions, social service is the high law of duty, and every American university must square its standards by that law or lack its national title. It is serving the nation to give men the enlightenments of a general training; it is serving the nation to equip fit men for thorough scientific investigation and for the tasks of exact scholarship, for science and scholarship carry the truth forward from generation to generation and give the certain touch of knowledge to the processes of life. But the whole service demanded is not rendered until something is added to the mere training of the undergraduate and the mere equipment of the investigator, something ideal and of the very spirit of all action. The final synthesis of learning is in philosophy. You shall most clearly judge the spirit of a university if you judge it by the philosophy it teaches; and the philosophy of conduct is what every wise man should wish to derive from his knowledge of the thoughts and the affairs of the generations that have gone before him. We are not put into this world to sit still and know; we are put into it to act.

It is true that in order to learn men must for a little while withdraw from action, must seek some quiet place of remove from the bustle of affairs, where their thoughts may run clear and tranquil, and the heats of business be for the time put off; but that cloistered refuge is no place to dream in. It is a place for the first conspectus of the mind, for a thoughtful poring upon the map of life; and the boundaries which should emerge to the mind's eye are not more the intellectual than the moral boundaries of thought and action. I do not see how any university can afford such an outlook if its teachings be not informed with the spirit of religion, and that the religion of Christ, and with the energy of a positive faith. The argument for efficiency in education can have no permanent validity if the efficiency sought be not moral as well as intellectual. The ages of strong and definite moral impulse have been the ages of achievement; and the moral impulses which have lifted highest have come from Christian peoples,— the moving history of our own nation were proof enough of that. Moral efficiency is, in the last analysis, the fundamental argument for liberal culture. A merely literary education, got out of books and old literatures is a poor thing enough if the teacher stick at grammatical and syntactical drill; but if it be indeed an introduction into the thoughtful labors of men of all generations it may be made the prologue of the mind's emancipation: its emancipation from narrowness,—from narrowness of sympathy, of perception, of motive, of purpose, and of hope. And the deep fountains of Christian teaching are its most refreshing springs.

I have said already, let me say again, that in such a place as this we have charge, not of men's fortunes, but of their spirits. This is not the place in which to teach men their specific tasks,— except their tasks be those of scholarship and investigation; it is the place in which to teach them the relations which all tasks bear to the work of the world. Some men there are who are condemned to learn only the technical skill by which they are to live; but these are not the men whose privilege it is to come to a university. University men ought to hold themselves bound to walk the upper roads of usefulness which run along the ridges and command views of the general fields of life. This is why I believe general training, with no particular occupation in view, to be the very heart and essence of university training, and the indispensable foundation of every special development of knowledge or of aptitude that is to lift a man to his profession or a scholar to his function of investigation.

I have studied the history of America; I have seen her grow great in the paths of liberty and of progress by following after great ideals. Every concrete thing that she has done has seemed to rise out of some abstract principle, some vision of the mind. Her greatest victories have been the victories of peace and of humanity. And in days quiet and troubled alike Princeton has stood for the nation's service, to produce men and patriots. Her national tradition began with John Witherspoon, the master, and James Madison, the pupil, and has not been broken until this day. I do not know what the friends of this sound and tested foundation may have in store to build upon it; but whatever they add shall be added in that spirit, and with that conception of duty. There is no better way to build up learning and increase power. A new age is before us, in which, it would seem, we must lead the world. No doubt we shall set it an example unprecedented not only in the magnitude and telling perfection of our industries and arts, but also in the splendid scale and studied detail of our university establishments: the spirit of the age will lift us to every great enterprise. But the ancient spirit of sound learning will also rule us; we shall demonstrate in our lecture rooms again and again, with increasing volume of proof, the old principles that have made us free and great; reading men shall read here the chastened thoughts that have kept us young and shall make us pure; the school of learning shall be the school of memory and of ideal hope; and the men who spring from our loins shall take their lineage from the founders of the republic.

Printed document with WWhw emendations (WP, DLC).

From Henry Smith Pritchett[1]

My dear Dr. Wilson: Boston, Mass. [c. Oct. 25, 1902]

I cannot deny myself the pleasure to send a line on the part of the Institute of Technology to congratulate you on coming into your great office. You have, I am sure, the opportunity to do a great work, not only for Princeton, but for education in this country; and I am sure your interests are such as to make you wish to deal with the larger questions as well as with the more local ones.

With every good wish for your prosperity and for the usefulness and growth of Princeton under your leadership, I am,

Very sincerely yours,   Henry S. Pritchett

TLS (WP, DLC).
[1] President of the Massachusetts Institute of Technology.

From Adrian Hoffman Joline

My dear Dr. Wilson: New York   Oct 25, 1902

We took our humble part to-day in the ceremonies of the inauguration. The last one I attended was in 1868, when "Jimmie"[1] became Prex—and I hope to live long and never attend another. I write merely to send my congratulations and to express my delight in the address, which "rang true,"—also to say that Mrs. Joline and I would have presented ourselves to you & to Mrs Wilson this afternoon, but for the fact that the recent death of Mr. Larkin[2] has been so much of an affliction that Mrs Joline is not going anywhere at present & attended to-day only because of her very great admiration for one whom we are wont, (disrespectfully perhaps you may think it) to call "Tommy Wilson."*

Yours faithfully   Adrian H Joline

*This is Frank's[3] fault.

ALS (WP, DLC).
[1] That is, James McCosh.
[2] Francis Larkin, father of Mary Larkin (Mrs. Adrian H.) Joline.
[3] That is, Wilson's classmate, Francis Larkin, Jr.

From Abram Woodruff Halsey

My Dear Wilson,   New York City   Oct. 27, 1902.

Saturday was not only "a red letter day" for you, for the Class of '79, for Princeton, but also for each one of us who have known you so long and well[.] It was my greatest *Princeton* day. I wish to thank you personally for all that the day brought to me and for those masterful words of yours at the Class Dinner when you led us to the very heights.[1] It was a crisis for you, and the class as well. I think both stood the test. I was proud of the class—the number present, the rare combination of dignity and pleasantry exhibited, the sanity and heartfulness of word and act, and the spirit of comradeship which dominated the entire body from [Samuel] Alexander to [George Green] Youmans [Yeomans].

I was proud of you and shall carry to the end of my life journey your noble and inspiring words.

May your reign so auspiciously begun continue long with ever expanding influence and blessing.

Most Cordially   A. W. Halsey

ALS (WP, DLC).
[1] The only report of this speech is the brief characterization of it in the news report of Wilson's inauguration printed at Nov. 1, 1902.

From Stockton Axson

Richmond, Va.

My dear Brother Woodrow: Monday [Oct. 27, 1902]

In the crush and furor of Saturday I had no chance for even a hurried word after your monumental effort in Alexander Hall, and I left Princeton immediately after the game[1] that afternoon. So I am taking this opportunity to say the word I should have said had you been more accessible on Saturday.

I suppose few men have ever entered upon new and great phases of their careers with such universal approbation as you have won. There was but one opinion on all sides; sometimes expressed to me directly, but as frequently incidentally overheard by me as it was uttered between men who knew nothing of my identity—and that opinion was that in a masterly address, most impressively delivered, you had struck exactly the proper note. It was interesting to observe how this unanimous opinion was voiced by the wise and foolish alike, that is to say by men who have thought on the problems with which you were dealing and by men who in the nature of things could have given no thought to the subject. Princeton and its friends are certainly behind you in solid phalanx.

For myself, I figure that address as the keystone of a noble career, a symmetrical career sustained by genius *and* character. That life and health and joyous strength may be spared to you in order that you may embody your vision in realities, is, I am sure, the hope of all and the prayer of many.

With love and best wishes

Yours affectionately   Stockton Axson

ALS (WP, DLC).
[1] Princeton defeated Columbia in football by a score of 22 to 0 on Oct. 25, 1902.

To Charles William Kent

My dear Charlie: Princeton, N. J.   Oct. 27th, 1902.

Your letter of the 25th[1] has given me the greatest pleasure. It was very delightful to have Heath Dabney here, even though the crowding events of the day made it impossible for me to get more than a glimpse or two of him, and now to have this letter of yours completes my gratification, because it makes the greeting of the University of Virginia more than an official greeting, making it the greeting of old friends. I have retained undimmed the impressions of the old times at the University of Virginia, and the sense of comradeship with you men down there has been strong upon me ever since. I feel as if it were a Godspeed from the family, the academic family, to which I belong, that has come to me from you and Heath. Mrs. Wilson joins me in warmest regards to Mrs. Kent and yourself, and I am,

Faithfully and gratefully yours,   Woodrow Wilson

TLS (Tucker-Harrison-Smith Coll., ViU).
[1] It is missing.

To Seth Low

My dear Mr. Low,   Princeton, 28 Oct., 1902

Allow me to thank you for your kind letter of the twenty-sixth.[1] It would have been a great pleasure to have you here at my inauguration, but I quite appreciate the difficulty you must experience in breaking away from your many duties and engagements. Your kind greeting gratifies me very deeply.

Sincerely Yours,   Woodrow Wilson

ALS (S. Low Papers, NNC).
[1] It is missing.

To Anson Phelps Stokes, Jr.[1]

My dear Mr. Stokes: Princeton, New Jersey. 29 October, 1902.

I am sincerely sorry that you were prevented from attending my inauguration last Saturday, but I greatly appreciate the cordial letter received this morning,[2] containing your warm assurances of interest, and your kind congratulations. It is a great pleasure to me to feel this comradeship with Yale men, and to express in return my warmest feeling of identification with what they as well as we ourselves represent.

With warm regard and appreciation,

Very sincerely yours,   Woodrow Wilson

TLS (U. S. Presidents' Coll., CtY).
[1] Secretary of Yale University.
[2] It is missing.

To Richard Heath Dabney

My dear Heath: Princeton, New Jersey. 31 October, 1902.

Your letter[1] gave me the greatest pleasure. It was delightful to know that you had enjoyed yourself while in Princeton. I felt fairly inhospitable, letting you come and go without seeing you in any intimate and familiar manner, but, of course, I knew that you understood and would recognize the necessity of my submitting to publicity all day.

I am very much interested in what you say about the Presidency of the University of Virginia, and wish very much that I could suggest some man who would certainly have the qualifications you desire; but my affection for the University is such that I am not willing to name any but the very best man, and I must confess that at the moment no man of exactly the right type occurs to me. Administrative ability does not often go with deep rooted academic ideals and principles, and yet the two must be combined in the right man. I shall not fail to think of the matter, and write you again should the proper suggestion come to me.

I will forward the engraved address[2] to you today for Dr. Barringer's signature.

Mrs. Wilson joins me in warmest regards both to you and Mrs. Dabney, and I am, as ever,

Faithfully yours,   Woodrow Wilson

TLS (Wilson-Dabney Corr., ViU).
[1] It is missing.

2 The address from the University of Virginia to Princeton University upon the occasion of Wilson's inauguration, which Dabney had presented and Dr. Barringer, as Chairman of the Faculty, had neglected to sign.

To Ivy Ledbetter Lee[1]

My dear Mr. Lee: Princeton, New Jersey. 31 October, 1902.

Thank you most sincerely for your kind letter of yesterday.[2] I remember you very well indeed and with a great deal of pleasure, and was glad to learn that you had come back to our immediate neighborhood. It is delightful to have your assurances of interest and agreement in my views as expressed on Saturday. I believe that all men with true academic spirit will show themselves ready to support such views in the long run, and in the meantime Princeton must show them the way.

Let me see you whenever you are in Princeton, and let me express the hope that you are placed for your work in the way which you most desire.

With regards,

Very sincerely yours,   Woodrow Wilson

TLS (in possession of Henry Bartholomew Cox).
1 Princeton 1898, on the editorial staff of the *New York Times*.
2 It is missing.

To Richard Watson Gilder

My dear Mr. Gilder: Princeton, New Jersey. 31 October, 1902.

No, I have not given up the idea of the political work[1] to which I have all my life been looking forward, but I am sorry to say that it looks now as if it must be postponed a good many years. Writing on any extensive scale is for the present obviously impossible for me. I must for say three or four years be merely a business man. I feel, therefore, that I must let the arrangements for the publication of what I may write wait for the opportunity to do the writing itself. The whole thing is too problematical and distant to be handled now. I none the less appreciate your kind suggestion, and thank you for it most sincerely.

It was a great pleasure to see you here on Saturday.

Very sincerely yours,   Woodrow Wilson

TLS (Berg Coll., NN).
1 His projected *magnum opus*, "The Philosophy of Politics."

A News Report of Wilson's Inauguration

[Nov. 1, 1902]

The Inauguration of President Wilson was a distinguished success. The ceremonies had true dignity, the addresses were classic, the assemblage was notable, the arrangements were of machine-like nicety, and the weather was perfect, from a morning so balmy that even the venerable representatives of '32 found it comfortable to wait in line out of doors, to the brilliant sunset which cast a remarkable orange glow over the victorious football field.

The University banners, white field with the coat of arms in the college colors, were floating from the turrets and towers of Princeton above the gorgeous autumn tree-tops, as the academic procession filed slowly through the noble arches of the library. And it was a most resplendent procession the people lined up on either side gazed upon. We thought we were doing pretty well in the way of academic millinery at the time of the sesquicentennial celebration, but these seven divisions, each under a separate marshal, were quite as notable in colors, and certainly more so in numbers. There were more caps and gowns in this procession than in the bicentennial parade at New Haven; in fact, more than in any former academic procession in America, we believe, except at Columbia last year. In the seventh section three-quarters of a century was represented—from Dr. James Curtis Hepburn '32 to Louis James '06.

In the earlier divisions, beside representatives of the army, the government, the state, the church and finance, it was a novelty—at Princeton—to see marching along with the other academic dignitaries, a number of ladies—President Mary E. Wool[l]ey of Mount Holyoke, Professor Alice V. Brown of Wellesley, Dean Agnes Irwin of Radcliff[e], and others. But the most brilliant costumes were not, as at most public assemblages, worn by the women; the Oxford gown with its scarlet was perhaps the most radiant of all.

The Hon. Franklin Murphy, Governor of New Jersey, ex-officio President of the board of trustees, presided over the Inauguration, and the Hon. W. J. Magie '52, Chancellor of the state, administered the three oaths of office and presented the charter to the President for signing. The Rev. Dr. Henry van Dyke '73 made the opening prayer,[1] and the Right Rev. Dr. Henry Yates Satterlee, Bishop of Washington, pronounced the benediction.

The Governor occupied the baldachino. On his right was Mr.

---

[1] It is printed in the *Princeton University Bulletin*, XIV (Dec. 1902), 3-4.

Cleveland, on his left President Wilson. Farther along, next to Dr. van Dyke and Bishop Satterlee, sat the Right Rev. Dr. John Scarborough, Bishop of New Jersey. Dr. Patton sat in the front row on the opposite side of the platform to Dr. van Dyke. The rest of the high seats were occupied by the "delegates of universities, colleges, and learned societies in the order of seniority of charters under which degrees may be conferred"—as many of them as could get on the platform, that is; the rest were in the first orchestra seats.

Mr. Booker T. Washington was among these. Behind them came the invited guests who were not formal representatives of universities, including such men as the Hon. Thomas B. Reed, Gen. John M. Wilson, the Hon. Robert T. Lincoln, Dr. C. A. Briggs, Dr. H. C. Minton, Edmund Clarence Stedman, William Dean Howells, and other men distinguished in other than academic ways. One of the most interesting if not the most interested of the spectators was Mr. J. P. Morgan. Though a graduate of one of the German universities, he did not wear academic regalia or march with the procession. He sat with relatives in the horseshoe. Mark Twain's snowy mane was conspicuous, especially when he nodded, as he sometimes did during Dr. Patton's address. He once told a friend that he considered Dr. Patton the best after-dinner speaker he ever heard. Venerable Parke Godwin '34, one of our most illustrious graduates, was also distinguished among the distinguished guests.

The administering of the oaths was an impressive ceremony. We print below the full text of the new President's vows. He made his responses as if he meant them to serve for more than a quaint bit of symbolism. He then signed the charter, with all of us for witnesses, and the Chancellor handed over to him the keys of the university—at least one key, Witherspoon Hall's, because it is such a fine big one. Then began the addresses.[2] We print them elsewhere. That is the reason we can print very little else in this number. We wish ever[y] son of Princeton could have been there to hear these memorable speeches. A reading will show how significant they are, how basically significant, and how especially pertinent they are to the educational questions of this day and hour. President Wilson's inaugural will stand as an academic profession of faith. But only those who were present can realize the deep impression they made on the distinguished audience gathered there to hear these distinguished speakers, each of

[2] By Dr. Patton, Grover Cleveland, and Wilson. Patton's address is printed in *ibid.*, pp. 4-9; Cleveland's, in *ibid.*, pp. 9-17.

whom was at his very best that morning, and of whom Princeton is now more than ever proud.

Chancellor Magie '52 propounded the questions for the new President's vows, of which the following is a copy, taken from the Book of Charters, which Dr. Wilson and the Chancellor signed in the presence of the audience:

I do solemnly swear that I will support the Constitution of the United States.

I do sincerely profess and swear that I do and will bear true faith and allegiance to the Government established in this State under the authority of the people.

I do solemnly promise and swear that I will faithfully, impartially and justly perform all the duties of the office of President of Princeton University according to the best of my abilities and understanding.

Woodrow Wilson.

Sworn and subscribed at Princeton, New Jersey, this twenty-fifth day of October, A.D., 1902, before me,

W. J. Magie,
Chancellor of New Jersey.

The crowd, of course, was nothing like the crowd at the sesquicentennial celebration, but that was a three-days continuous performance containing many features calculated to bring greater crowds. But a goodly number flocked in on the special trains from New York and Philadelphia, notwithstanding the absence of President Roosevelt. It was deeply regretted that Princeton could not be honoured by his presence on this occasion, especially as he is a professed admirer of our new President, thereby resembling most of his countrymen, it seems.

Whether or not many of the alumni stayed away on account of the limited seating capacity of Alexander Hall, certainly every one who came gained admittance if he sought it. Though we took pains to make a number of inquiries, we have yet to hear of anyone's failing to get in. The actual seating capacity may be limited, but the standing room does not seem to be. And the more people there are in the galleries and aisles, the more striking this impressive auditorium appears to our visitors.

The steps address, delivered by the President from Old North to a large crowd immediately after the formal ceremonies, was quite informal, a sort of heart-to-heart talk from one Princeton man to others. Here is part of it. The opening sentence, by the way, carries the peculiar atmosphere of much of his style; the flavor (or flavour) of an earlier century is in it. The last sentence shows the ideal of his attitude toward the rest of us Princeton men: "I have come from a place where I have been telling them what the ideals of Princeton are. The ideals of Princeton are contained in the men whom Princeton sends out, and I take it that the men who have been associated in the class comradeships in this place know the plan for this place. We are not afraid when we make plans, for we are making plans for men of affairs. And we know that the knowledge that goes into Princeton comradeships will be a knowledge that translates itself into power, because it is only by the conduct of men that learning propagates itself. It is only when men know how to be brothers to one another that comradeship gets its best expression. I believe the comradeship that shows itself in the field will show itself also in letters. I ask that you will look upon me not as a man to do something apart, but as a man who asks the privilege of leading you and being believed in by you while he tries to do the things in which he knows you believe."

The sod ceremony—to use a current colloquialism—then took place on the east lawn of Prospect, on the site selected for the new dormitory to be given by '79. Dr. A. W. Halsey, President of the class, made a speech on behalf of '79, and President Wilson made his third speech of that day,[3] speaking on behalf of the university. The spade with which he performed his first official act is an interesting implement. The haft of the handle is in the form of a recumbent tiger, containing exactly seventy-nine ounces of silver, the sides of the handle showing intertwined ivy leaves made also of silver. The silver is from the mines of a '79 man.[4] The blade is made out of copper from the mines of another '79 man.[5]

After this there were a number of luncheons; but as it was now two o'clock, and the Columbia game began at half-past, many of them were hurried unceremoniously. It may be of interest to know that the following men were invited to luncheon at Prospect: President Hadley of Yale, President Butler of Columbia, President Harper of the University of Chicago, President Harris of Amherst College, Dr. Patton, Governor Murphy, Mr. Cleveland, Mr. J. Pierpont Morgan, Mr. Samuel Clemens, Mr. Thomas B. Reed, Mr. H. C. Frick, Mr. Edmund Clarence Stedman, Colonel A. K. McClure, Mr. Robert T. Lincoln, and Mr. Wayne MacVeagh.

[3] No record of these remarks seems to have been made.
[4] Undoubtedly Daniel Moreau Barringer.
[5] Cleveland Hoadley Dodge.

President and Mrs. Wilson's reception after the football game, though very late, was crowded.

The '79 Dinner, in honour of their classmate, was held that evening at the Inn, and the President made his fourth and, '79 men maintain, his best speech of the day—though it was past midnight when he arose to respond to the various pleasant and enheartening things that they had spent the evening saying to him. Incidentally this speaks well for the endurance of our new executive head. There were about seventy men at the dinner out of seventy-eight—some claim seventy-nine—'79 men here during the day. The Rev. Dr. Halsey, the class president, acted as toastmaster. Cyrus McCormick responded to Princeton University; W. B. Lee to Wilson, the President; the Hon. Charles A. Talcott to the Class of Seventy-nine; Dr. Samuel Alexander to the College of New Jersey, and after the reading of letters and telegrams by William R. Wilder, the secretary, Robert Bridges spoke of Wilson, the Classmate.

They looked as though they were having a very good time, these '79 men. They had a gayly decorated headquarters, opposite the Inn, just as if it were a Commencement reunion. Friday afternoon they held a class golf tournament for cups presented by Adrian Riker '79 and P. A. V. Van Doren '79, which were won respectively by J. B. Waller '79 of Chicago, and John S. Baird '79 of New York. All of them marched impressively in the academic parade, as a division by themselves, taking precedence over all the other alumni. They filled the back row of the horseshoe in Alexander Hall, and they grinned all day long with pardonable complacence. . . .

Printed in the *Princeton Alumni Weekly*, iii (Nov. i, 1902), 83-86.

A News Item

[Nov. i, 1902]

President Wilson was a guest at a dinner in honor of the Crown Prince of Siam in New York the other night.[1] Being called on unexpectedly for a speech, he made a hit by quoting the following rhyme, which is by a well known and versatile member of the Princeton faculty[2] who is given to making verses at odd moments —when he isn't writing text books, planning new buildings, or developing new departments:

There was a young man of Siam,
Spent his time reading Omar Khayyam.
Said he, Old Omar,
You are my Homer;
Said Omar Khayyam I am.

Printed in the *Princeton Alumni Weekly*, III (Nov. 1, 1902), 87-88.
    1 Crown Prince Cha Fa Maha Vajiravudh, on a tour of the United States, was feted at the Metropolitan Club on October 27, 1902, by the Presbyterian Board of Foreign Missions in expression of its appreciation for the courteous reception given Presbyterian missionaries in Siam. The Crown Prince succeeded to the throne as Rama VI on the death of Chulalongkorn in 1910.
    2 That is, Wilson himself.

To Edith Gittings Reid

My dearest Friend,   Princeton, 2 Nov., 1902

    How can we get over the disappointment of your getting away on the twenty-fifth without our having so much as a single word with you! I looked at you again and again as we sat in the hall; but, though it was good to have sight of you, it was a cruel trial to miss speaking with you. It was delightful to see Mr. Reid and Miss Goodwillie at our reception, but it was a sore trial to have them bring the news they did of your indisposition. For hours afterwards we hoped and hoped that you would come here to "Prospect," as we begged, to be put to bed and taken care of. And how are you now? Please write and say that you are well again.

    We have run straight into troubled waters. Yesterday my Jessie and my sister Annie's little daughter[1] took to their beds with scarletina,—light cases, but the genuine thing. This house is so constructed that they can be perfectly isolated, with the nurse who is in charge; but for four weeks my friends will be suspicious of me; I cannot make calls, but must stick to mere business and fatigue, without so much as a weak thought of relaxation! The two patients are as light-hearted and content as may be, and the nurse we have seems both kind and competent,—so that we are hoping that all will go as well as possible;—but alack a-day, the dear ladies, the mothers, are at sore straits to keep heart!

    Ellen joins me in warmest love. When are you coming back to *see* us. After our quarantine is well past we shall compel you to come!

    As ever, with all affectionate messages to Mr. Reid,
                        Your devoted friend,   Woodrow Wilson

ALS (WC, NjP).
    1 Annie Howe, eleven years old.

From Daniel Coit Gilman

My dear Mr. President   Baltimore   Nov. 2 1902

The memory of my delightful visit to you, on that day of great significance, will be a lifelong possession to one of your oldest & most admiring friends. In common with the multitude, I enjoyed your speech, every sentence of it, & I enjoyed the tokens of respect & appreciation which were lavished upon you,—an earnest I am sure of the support you will receive from all Princeton in the arduous career upon which you are entering. In a different way, I had equal enjoyment in seeing Mrs Wilson and you at home, surrounded by those who are nearest to you. I was particularly glad to see your father, in his serene old age, casting the benediction of his presence upon the family circle, & your sister who came from such a distance to see the "coronation." To them all & to Mrs. White[1] I beg you to give my kindest remembrances. By a premature goodbye I was able to take the train leaving at 3'7 & so I reached Baltimore a few minutes after seven, while the other Baltimoreans missed a good connection of the trains & were not here until midnight. I look forward to the perusal of your speech in better type than that of the newspapers & then I shall see how carefully you hold the balance between conservatism & advancement. It is hard to say which is most important in the conduct of a university.

Once more, my dear friend, accept the heartiest congratulations of   Yours Sincerely   D. C. Gilman

ALS (WP, DLC).
[1] Probably a new nurse for Dr. Wilson.

To Daniel Coit Gilman

Princeton, New Jersey.
My dear Mr. Gilman: 3 November, 1902.

Your letter of yesterday has given me the deepest pleasure. I do not know of anything in my academic career upon which I look with more unalloyed satisfaction than my cordial relations with you, and your unbroken and affectionate friendship. It is a privilege to feel that I have entered into some part of the work which you have done so much to advance in this country, and I can only hope that in what I do, I shall prove myself a worthy Hopkins man, as well as a loyal son of Princeton.

Mrs. Wilson and I enjoyed most deeply your brief stay with us, and were delighted that you should be one of our first guests in

Prospect. The whole affair of the 25th was made so much the more enjoyable to us because we could have near friends at hand to give us their sympathy and generous support.

Pray give our very warmest regards to Mrs. Gilman, and tell her how sincerely we regretted her absence. Had she been here, our satisfaction would have been complete.

Most sincerely yours,   Woodrow Wilson

TLS (D. C. Gilman Papers, MdBJ).

To Clyde Weber Votaw[1]

My dear Sir: Princeton, New Jersey.   4 November, 1902.

In reply to your kind letter of the 1st, I would beg that you will excuse me from becoming an Associate Member of the Counsel of Seventy of the American Institute of Sacred Literature.[2] I do not feel that I am in a position as yet to give it the occasional counsel, which I feel my acceptance of such associate membership would entitle it to expect.   Very truly yours,   Woodrow Wilson

TLS (American Institute of Sacred Literature Papers, ICU).
   [1] Assistant Professor of New Testament Literature, University of Chicago.
   [2] The Council of Seventy was a group of prominent men selected to advise the American Institute of Sacred Literature. The Institute, founded by William Rainey Harper, President of the University of Chicago, was a correspondence school specializing in biblical studies. It was later merged into the University Extension Division of the University of Chicago.

From Robert Bridges

Dear Tommy: New York, Oct [Nov.] 5 1902

I have just been talking with C. C. [Cuyler] on the telephone, and am very sorry to hear that your children are both ill. I do hope that it is a light case. I can understand your anxiety.

I read the inaugural over carefully the other day and like it even more than I did when I heard it first. Everybody speaks of it with enthusiasm, and it is doing Princeton a lot of good. The English of it pleased me mightily. After all *that* is the real vitality of literature. It may be a lot of other things that we approve of—but if it has'n't a vital style it dies.

C. C. just told me of Cope's death.[1] It is very tragic—and I agree with you both that we should wait awhile.[2] I am in favor of very deliberate action anyhow. . . .

Pyne is on the Committee of grounds & Buildings and ought to be consulted.

However, your firm stand straightened it all out. I think that C. C.[,] you and I can do it *simply* without consultations outside.

Faithfully Yours   Robert Bridges

ALS (WP, DLC).
  1 Walter Cope, who had been designated as the architect for Seventy-Nine Hall, died on Nov. 1, 1902.
  2 That is, before choosing a new architect.

From the Minutes of the Princeton Academic Faculty

5 p.m. November 5, 1902

The Faculty met, the President presiding. . . .

Resolved, that all Committees of the Academic Faculty be hereby regarded as dissolved, with the understanding that the President is to take his time in the reconstitution of these Committees, and that in the meantime the old Committees continue to serve until the new Committees are appointed.

The Faculty then adjourned.

Attest   W. F. Magie
                                                     Clerk.

To Robert Bridges

My dear Bob: Princeton, New Jersey.   6 November, 1902.

Thank you very much indeed for your letter of yesterday. The children are doing finely. By the way, "the children" include but one of my own, and my sister's little girl who has just returned from Germany to meet with this inhospitable reception. The cases have been of the slightest possible, and nothing but the tedious convalescence and its dangers of cold catching seem now to be before us.

I cannot tell you how much I appreciate what you say about the inaugural address. It gives me the greatest possible comfort to know that you think its form as well as its substance will be effective in spreading good doctrine and in increasing the good name of the college. May our friends give us the means to live up to the doctrine!

Cope's death is indeed tragical. There is certainly no need for any extraordinary haste in choosing some one else to do the building for us. At the same time there seems to be a certain need for promptness, and the sooner we can hit upon a plan, the better. I hope that we can have a meeting as soon as possible after the 15th. For to break ground in March and to expect the building to be entirely completed by the following June is to allow very scant time for setbacks. The difficulty of obtaining material from the great combined industries of the country seems now the most serious, and may lead to indefinite delays, so that it seems to me the sooner we break ground, the better. No doubt we can manage to find a new architect, but I must admit that I do not now see who it can be.

     As ever,   Affectionately yours,   Woodrow Wilson

TLS (WC, NjP).

To Charles Bowdoin Fillebrown[1]

My dear Sir: Princeton, New Jersey.   6 November, 1902.

     Allow me to thank you for your letter of November 3.[2] I feel that I have long ago fallen out of the ranks of economists, and do not feel competent now to espress [express] myself with any sort of authority upon the interesting questions submitted by the league.[3] I hope that you will believe this to be not affected modesty, but the real truth of the matter, and that you will excuse me from an expression of opinion, such as you desire.

                 Very sincerely yours,   Woodrow Wilson

TLS (WP, DLC).
   [1] Boston merchant, manufacturer, and single tax devotee.
   [2] It is missing.
   [3] The Massachusetts Single Tax League, of which Fillebrown was a past president.

To Waterman Thomas Hewett[1]

                             Princeton, New Jersey.
My dear Professor Hewett: 6 November, 1902.

     Mr. Hendrix's[2] suggestion to me with regard to the possibility of your accepting a place here in German interested me very much, and I told him that I should certainly be disposed to give it my very cordial consideration.

     Professor Humphrey's death came so suddenly and so unexpectedly, and the effects of it are likely to lead to so radical a reorganization of the German department here, that as I told Mr. Hendrix, it is hardly possible for me as yet to say what the proper plan to pursue may be. We shall probably do nothing for the present year; but in the course of this academic year must plan very definitely what is to be done for the department; and it will give me very great pleasure while making those plans to remember that it is possible that if we can make the position attractive enough, we may have an opportunity of asking your consideration of it.[3]   Very sincerely yours,   Woodrow Wilson

TLS (WC, NjP).
  [1] Professor of the German Language and Literature at Cornell University.
  [2] Probably Joseph Clifford Hendrix, President of the National Bank of Commerce of New York and a trustee of Cornell.
  [3] Insofar as is known, Hewett did not receive the call from Princeton. See the Finance Committee's Report to the Board of Trustees, Oct. 14, 1902, n. 5.

A News Report of a Talk to the Philadelphian Society

[Nov. 7, 1902]

MURRAY HALL ADDRESS.
President Wilson Speaks on the Subject
"The True University Spirit."

The regular Thursday night meeting of the Philadelphian Society was addressed last evening in Murray Hall by President Wilson. Taking as a base for his address a part of the twenty-fourth chapter of Proverbs, President Wilson spoke on the true University spirit. In the course of his remarks he said that the book of Proverbs is an illustration of the true University spirit; the least spiritual book of the Bible, one which contains more worldly wisdom than any other, it shows us that wisdom cannot be divided, that what is wise is wise both spiritually and worldly. Thus the University is not merely a place where learning is to be secured for its own sake but represents the unity of spirit, whence a man cannot go out unaltered, but must have changed for either the better or the worse.

The true University is the spirit of enlightenment, of openness, of freedom. It is a place where men experience new feelings of life, where new things are unfolded to them. It is through the instrumentality of the University that men are stripped of wrong impulses, and are brought to see true conditions and true standards of life by means of research and investigation. There can be no end or limit to inquiry except in those phases and emotions of life, such as friendships, which do not allow of investigation. Thus a man who has sought out the mysteries of life, who sees the truth of things, who has heard many voices of counsel, will not be overcome by the voices of uproar in the day of adversity, but will be able to look beyond his immediate surroundings and see and know that an overruling Providence is above all things. Thus the power of the mind is transferred to the motives and emotions. The speaker likened knowledge to wine; when taken into the mind it invigorates the spirit and fills it with strength and power. The spirit of that man who wants learning and strives to obtain it, is equipped for the whole conduct of existence.

The keynote of the University spirit is, then, "What think ye of Christ?" Is He the centre and essential of the pattern of life? If he is not, if a life is entirely unrelated to Him, there are no means by which the character of life may be determined. Christianity is the only standard and category of the spirits and motives of mankind. Although a man may not have accepted Christ, he has been benefitted and helped through Christianity. He has thus borrowed and traded in that which is not his own, and to be a true man he must accept Christ personally.

If spiritual and worldly wisdom are inseparable, there is no place where the Light should shine so brightly as in the University in which all knowledge is centered.[1]

Printed in the *Daily Princetonian*, Nov. 7, 1902.
[1] There is a brief WWT outline of this speech in WP, DLC.

Notes for a Talk

Graduate Club   7 Novr., 1902
The Objects of Graduate Study

(1) *A limited object*: the attainment of an exact acquaintance with the materials and the results of scholarship.

This sufficient for the ordinary duties of the teacher, provided he keep abreast of the times and teach only tyros.

(2) *A larger object*: To become a master by being quit of masters: the attainment of independence

This the only object worthy of ambition.

Can be gained only by

(a) A knowledge of the subject studied in its large outline and its relation to an entire field.

(b) Imaginative exploration: the curiosity which runs beyond ascertained phenomena

(c) The *synthetic* habit and practice

The *apotheosis* of *Method*. The only supreme method, *Divination*[1]

WWhw MS. (WP, DLC).
[1] As is best revealed in Wilson's address, "The Variety and Unity of History," printed at Sept. 20, 1904, Vol. 15, he meant the use of imagination and intuitive perception in the reconstruction of the past.

Two News Items

[Nov. 8, 1902]

PRESIDENT WILSON ADDRESSES
THE GRADUATE CLUB.

The first regular meeting of the Graduate Club was held in Dodge Hall last evening. President Wilson addressed the meeting on "The Objects of Graduate Study." The speaker said that the chief object of graduate study is to secure an equipment for teaching. Although the field of research appears practically exhausted, there are some few men who arise in every age with new conceptions. The speaker dwelt upon the fact that the most satisfactory results are to be obtained when the student engages in some independent research and through the use of his scientific imagination is able to explore new fields.

Printed in the *Daily Princetonian,* Nov. 8, 1902.

◇

[Nov. 8, 1902]

President Wilson's first appearance, after the Inauguration, before his class in constitutional government, was made the occasion of a goodly demonstration by the 376 students in the course. The cheering lasted about four minutes, after which President Wilson remarked dryly, "Had I anticipated this I would have brought my inaugural address with me." But we trust they all have read it in The Weekly.

Printed in the *Princeton Alumni Weekly,* iii (Nov. 8, 1902), 116.

To Richard Heath Dabney

My dear Heath: Princeton, New Jersey. 10 November, 1902.

I am very glad to answer your letter of the 7th[1] most explicitly. Things certainly run riot in this topsy turvy world. It is true that the Presidency of the University of Virginia was offered to me, and in effect offered to me three times, as I would long ago have told you, if I had supposed that you did not know it, and strangely enough this very Mr. Miles about whom you speak was the active agent of the Board of Visitors in repeatedly urging the acceptance of the place upon me.[2] Nobody could have done more than he did in the matter. And inasmuch as my impression of the man was gained entirely in that way, I naturally have very pleasant impressions of him, and had supposed him a man unselfishly attached to the service of the University.

But it is absolutely untrue that I ever gave anyone to understand either orally or in writing that I would accept the position. It is necessarily false, therefore, that I withdrew my acceptance upon hearing that there was opposition on the part of the Faculty. I knew that there was no such opposition; I knew it both from you, and from what several other members of the Faculty had said to me. I understood the situation perfectly, namely, that while they were unwilling to have any President, if a President was to be given them, I would be more acceptable to them than any other person that could be chosen. It was my knowledge of that attitude on their part more than anything else that inclined me to take the matter seriously under consideration; and the reason why it did not go farther was simply that the men here were so overwhelmingly opposed, and so unmeasuredly generous to me, that I felt it would be mere ingratitude to leave them. That is absolutely the whole case, and you are at perfect liberty to say to anyone whom you please to say it to, that I did not learn or believe that there was any opposition to me in the University Faculty, and that I did not in any form or at any time, express a willingness to accept the position. The Princeton men made that impossible.

Now as to what you ask about my knowledge of Mr. Venable.[3] I am sorry to say I have none whatever,—only the very pleasant impression he has made upon me as a man during one or two very brief interviews. That impression has been better than the impression made on me by any of the other men whom you mention. There is in Venable a directness and simplicity and geniality, which I think strike even the most casual acquaintance at once as being the qualities of a straightforward and genuine man. I should not be surprised if he would do you real service in the office.[4] I feel like kicking myself that I cannot think of anybody whom I would be willing to recommend out of abundant knowledge of him. But the fact is so, and I must not try to make any suggestions outside of the ranks of those whom I know well.

With warmest regard, and with great regret that you should have been so distressed by a cock and bull story,

Cordially and Faithfully yours,   Woodrow Wilson

TLS (Wilson-Dabney Corr., ViU).

  [1] It is missing.

  [2] Wilson was not describing the offers quite accurately. In all three instances, he was offered the Chairmanship of the Faculty, together with a professorship in the Law Department of the University of Virginia. For the full story of the first

offer, the only one in which serious negotiations took place, see G. W. Miles to WW, March 21, 1898, and the ensuing documents relating to the subject through C. C. Cuyler to WW, May 16, 1898, printed *passim* in Vol. 10. For the second and third "offers," see G. W. Miles to WW, March 4, 1899, and G. W. Miles to WW, May 7, 1900, both in Vol. 11.

3 Francis Preston Venable, President of the University of North Carolina.

4 As this letter intimates, the University of Virginia was at this moment the scene of a power struggle between the Board of Visitors, who wanted to elect a strong executive head of the institution to be called the "President," and the faculty, who were reluctant to accept a president in place of the traditional Chairman of the Faculty and wished to restrict the powers of the new office. The conflict at this time centered around George Washington Miles, Headmaster of St. Albans School in Radford, Va., and a former member of the Board of Visitors, who avowed his candidacy for the presidency in the autumn of 1902. Most of the members of the Board supported Miles, while a majority of the faculty opposed him. The struggle was soon carried into the newspapers of Virginia, and various alumni groups took sides in the dispute. In the spring of 1903, the Virginia legislature adopted an enabling act to permit the creation of the presidency, but the Board of Visitors had by then concluded that Miles's candidacy was too controversial and postponed the election. In the following year, several prominent names were suggested, including that of President Venable, who was formally proposed by a majority of the faculty. However, on June 14, 1904, the Board of Visitors unanimously elected Edwin Anderson Alderman, then President of Tulane University. Alderman accepted and assumed his new duties in September 1904. See Philip Alexander Bruce, *History of the University of Virginia, 1819-1919* (5 vols., New York, 1920-22), v, 28-38.

From the Minutes of the Princeton University Faculty

4 p.m. November 12, 1902.

Special Meeting. The Faculty met, the President presiding. . . .

Resolved that the Standing Committees of the University Faculty be discharged, their discharge to take effect on the announcement by the President of the appointment of new committees. . . .

"Minutes of the University Faculty of Princeton University Beginning September, 1902 [and] Ending June, 1914," bound minute book (UA, NjP).

To John Grier Hibben

My dear Jack,   Princeton, 12 November, 1902

My heart rejoices over the vindication of your judgment by the Faculty's action this afternoon. You can no longer have the slightest vestige left of the feeling that your heart has discredited your head among your colleagues.[1]

As ever,   Affectionately Yours,   Woodrow Wilson

ALS (photostat in WC, NjP).

1 The cryptic minutes of this meeting do not explain this reference.

To Allan Marquand

Princeton, New Jersey.

My dear Prof. Marquand: 14 November, 1902.

Is there any money left to expend this year for Trask Lecturers?[1] If there is, I am very anxious to arrange for a lecture some time in the latter part of January by Mr. William Garrott Brown, a man who has won very great distinction in recent years as a writer upon American History, and who has also won his spurs as a successful lecturer. I would be glad to hear what you think about this at as early a date as possible.[2]

I note what you say about the dates for the meeting of the Archaeological Society, and Mrs. Wilson and I will be glad to give a reception to the members of the Society on the evening of the second day of the meeting, namely the 1st of January. We have fixed upon that day, rather than the first day of the meeting, under the impression that it would probably be more conveninet [convenient] for the Society, and there would by that time be a full attendance.[3]

Very sincerely yours,   Woodrow Wilson

TLS (A. Marquand Papers, NjP) with Marquand's hw notation on letter: "Nov. 1, 1902 $760.16."

[1] About this series, see the Princeton University Faculty Minutes printed at Dec. 2, 1896, n. 1, Vol. 10.

[2] Marquand must have thought well of the suggestion, for Brown delivered a Trask lecture on "Jackson and the New Democracy" on Jan. 15, 1903.

[3] A news report about this meeting and Wilson's address of welcome is printed at March 1, 1903.

From Edward Wright Sheldon

My dear Wilson: New York, November 19, 1902.

I have your letter of yesterday and take pleasure in handing you the enclosed check for $320.00 to the order of young Semple.[1] If you should think it wiser to give him the amount in instalments, or otherwise disburse it, for his benefit, I will make the check payable to your order. I could not think of taking your indorsement of his note for the amount. Indeed I hope you will never permit your generosity to carry you so far. Trusting that the career of the young man may justify your kindly interest in him, believe me, with warmest regards,

Yours as ever,   Edward W. Sheldon

TLS (WP, DLC).

[1] James Lithgow Semple, a sophomore of the Class of 1905. Sheldon's check was a loan to enable Semple to continue his education at Princeton. See James L. Semple to WW, April 21, 1904, ALS (WP, DLC).

From the Minutes of the Princeton Academic Faculty

5 p.m. November 19, 1902

The Faculty met, the President presiding. The minutes of the meetings of November 5 and November 12 were read and approved.

The President presented a plan for a new arrangement of Faculty meetings: It was

Resolved, that the University Faculty shall meet on the first Wednesday of the University year immediately after the opening exercises, and on the first Wednesday of each month of the University terms thereafter: that the Academic and Scientific Faculties meet on alternate Wednesdays throughout the University year, the first Wednesday of the year and the first Wednesday of each month excepted; it being understood that this action applies only to the meetings of the Academic Faculty. . . .

A Memorandum[1]

20 Nov., '02

Notes　　　*Revision of Academic Course of Study.*

Freshman Year—2 or 3 hours for general, descriptive *Physics.*

Groups:　I. Philosophy
　　　　　II. Classics
　　　　　III. Mathematics
　　　　　IV. English
　　　　　V. Modern Languages
　　　　　VI. Politics—History (a) (b)
　　　　　VII. Art—Archaeology
　　　　　VIII. Biology—Paleontology
　　　　　IX. Physics—Chemistry
　　　　　X. Geology

I.

Group I. *Philosophy.*

Sophomore:　Greek (2)　　Both terms
　　　　　　　Latin (2)　　　"　　　"
　　　　　　　German (3)　"　　　"
　　　　　　　History (2)　　"　　　"
　　　　　　　Logic (3)—Psychology (3)
　　　　　　　Biology (3) Both terms.

Junior: History of Philosophy, Both terms
Theory of Logic,—Symb. Logic & Theory of Prob.
Plato (2)—Aristotle (2)
Lucretius (2)—Cicero (2)
Politics (2)—Economics (3)
German (2)—German (2)
—Ethics (2)
Biology (3)

Senior: History of Philosophy, Both terms.
Physiological Psychology—Psychology of Logic
Epistemology,—Metaphysics
Experimental Psychology,—Experimental Psychology.
Adv. Gen. Psychology,—Adv. Gen. Psychology
Hist. Eng. Ethics,—Heredity and Descent
German,—German.

II.

Group II., *Classics.*

Sophomore: Greek (4)   Both terms
Latin (4)   "   "
German (2)   "   "
Chemistry (2)—Biology (2)
Logic (3)—Psychology (3)

Junior: Greek (4)   Both terms
Latin (4)   "   "
Eng. Lit (3)   "   "
History of Philosophy (2)   "   "
German (2)   "   "

Senior: Greek (4) (Sanscrit) Both terms
Latin (4)   "   "
Archaeology & Art (2)   "   "
English Lit. (2)   "   "
Politics (2)   "   "

VI.

Group VI. *Politics.*—History.

Sophomore:
Latin (4)   Both terms
Greek (2)   "   "

German (4)	" "
	Logic (2)
History (2)	
English (2)	Both terms

Junior:

History of Philosophy (2)	Ethics (2)
History (4)	Political Economy (3)
Politics (4)	History of Philosophy (2)
English (4)	History (4)
Juvenal	Politics (4)

Senior:

History of Philosophy (2)	Both terms
History (6)	Cicero (2)
Politics (6)	History (4)
	Politics (6)

WWhw MS. (WP, DLC).

¹ This memorandum seems to have represented Wilson's first attempt to put together his thoughts concerning revision of the undergraduate course of study. It is interesting that he was apparently thinking at this time in terms of a fully prescribed course program for concentrators in various fields, with no provision for electives.

Notes for an Address to the New York Society of Mayflower Descendants

21 Nov., '02

Mayflower Descendants

Now performing the judicial (?) functions to which we have been assigned by our responsible position as "Posterity."

Can we judge? Painfully aware of changed and changing conditions,—a new age unlike theirs. Have we forgotten that our ancestors also came into a New World, and *subdued it to old principles*?

The Scots-Irish more elasticity and gayety,—and I a recent importation. I've had no assistance in 'getting up' my patriotism,—as the Pilgrims had none. But the place and the task still generate it.

We are under obligations to let neither the faith nor the achievement flag

What we need is, not ideas, but *power*

1. The power of *steadfast conviction*
2.   "   "   "   unselfishness, so that the first question will not be *Will it pay?* but *What is best?*

3. The *spirit of reformers* without the professional temper of reformers.

Old woman who saw a man read thr. a 2-inch board.[1]
Two frogs in watered milk.
"The plaid o' thae lying McFechlans."
The robustious Tennessean Methodist.

WWhw MS. (WP, DLC).
[1] This and the following were cues for anecdotes.

A News Report of an Address to the New York Society of Mayflower Descendants

[Nov. 22, 1902]

Four hundred members and guests of the New York Society of Mayflower Descendants, enjoyed the eighth annual dinner of the organization last night at Delmonico's. The dining room and tables were elegantly decorated. Dr. Woodrow Wilson, president of Princeton University; District Attorney Jerome, the Rev. Ernest M. Stires, Assistant District Attorney Littleton, of Kings, and William W. Goodrich were the principal speakers.[1]

Dr. Wilson was the first speaker. He said he was not a descendant of the Mayflower, and that the only thing Puritanical about him was his face. The Pilgrim Fathers, he declared, applied old principles to new conditions.

"The question of the present day to solve," he went on, "is not what new principles discover, but what old ones apply. Every conviction that has been an achievement has been unselfish. It is not my business to teach men how to succeed in money making, but to put them out with inspiration and character to make their fortunes. We believe we have come into a new age and we must apply ourselves to newer principles. We are apt to be confused at this time at the principles of this age."

Printed in the *New York Daily Tribune*, Nov. 22, 1902; editorial headings omitted.
[1] William Travers Jerome, District Attorney of New York County; Rev. Dr. Ernest Milmore Stires, Rector of St. Thomas' Episcopal Church, New York; Martin Wiley Littleton, Assistant District Attorney of Kings County, New York; and William Winton Goodrich, Presiding Justice of the Appellate Division, Supreme Court of New York.

From Cyrus Hall McCormick

My dear Woodrow: Chicago   November 24th, 1902.

Our plans are being consummated for your visit to Chicago,[1] which we are looking forward to with deep interest.

I understand from David Jones that you are to arrive by the Pennsylvania "Special" at 8:55 A.M. Friday [November 28]. We are to have the pleasure of having you with us at our house, 321 Huron Street. On your arrival at the station be on the lookout for my brougham. The footman has maroon livery and will be waiting for you at the train, or at the gate—if they will not let him pass through before the passengers descend from the train. My carriage will bring you to our house. Give the checks that you may have to the footman.

As we are spending Thanksgiving at Lake Forest I will come in on the morning train which reaches the city just at nine, and I will either be at my house by the time you arrive or reach there a few minutes after. We will then plan for the rest of the day. David Jones wishes you to lunch with him Friday at the University Club, to meet some of the college men, and Friday evening we have the Princeton Dinner. If you will telegraph me as to any special plans you have in mind for Friday morning or Friday afternoon I will arrange them.

On Saturday David Jones and I are inviting some business men to meet you at the Chicago Club at luncheon; on Saturday evening occurs the Commercial Club dinner. Please wire me, if convenient, the train on Sunday by which you must depart so that I may have your accommodations reserved[.] I think I understood from David Jones that you had to leave on the Pennsylvania Special at 12 o'clock so as to be in Princeton Monday morning.

I am,   Very sincerely yours,   Cyrus H. McCormick.

TCL (C. H. McCormick Papers, WHi).

¹ Where he was to speak to the Princeton alumni of Chicago and the Commercial Club. See the news reports printed at Nov. 28, 29, and 30, 1902, and the text of his address to the Commercial Club, printed at Nov. 29, 1902.

From Fred Neher

My dear Dr. Wilson: Princeton University. 24 Nov., 1902.

In obedience to your request I have the honor to submit the following suggestions for the consolidation and co-ordination of the courses in Chemistry offered in Princeton University.

At present, as you are aware, the work in Chemistry is carried on by three distinct and practically independent "Departments" bearing the somewhat misleading titles of General Chemistry, Applied Chemistry and Organic Chemistry. These departments have separate quarters in the Chemical Building, separate stocks, separate storerooms, separate appropriations and separate staffs of instructors. None of the eight instructors renders assistance in any course lying outside the accidental boundaries of his particular department. This condition of affairs might be justified in a measure were the courses offered by the several departments at once distinct in character and co-ordinate in arrangement. As a matter of fact, under the present arrangement there is not only an unnecessary annual expenditure for equipment and a waste of increasingly valuable laboratory room, but a duplication and even triplication of certain courses and parts of courses with the consequent employment of a teaching force out of proportion to the aggregate results accomplished.

It should be clearly understood that the organization, equipment and manning of the courses in Chemistry suggested below are by no means ideal either in kind or degree. They are not worthy of Princeton University even in its present state of development. They represent merely one man's opinion as to how the existing plant, equipment and teaching force could be most effectively and economically used. The problem was treated as one of re-arrangement rather than one of extension and development. Yet it will be seen that the consolidation of existing courses would seem to make possible the practical recognition of the recent immensely important development of Physical Chemistry. Perhaps the most that may be said for the proposed plan is this,—that while it greatly reduces the number of existing courses, it provides more courses and more extended courses, yet at the same time more and better instruction for more men, both Academic and Scientific, than has ever been possible heretofore.

It will be remarked that no provision is made for the continued separate existence of the so called "Chemical Course"[1] though nearly all of the courses which it now includes reappear with some modifications in the proposed arrangement. The courses in Assaying and in Special Metallurgical Analysis are omitted from the plan as being too technical for recognition in a general Bachelor of Science course. At the same time, following present custom, very much less emphasis is laid upon work in Determinative Mineralogy (Blowpipe Analysis), which at present in the B.S. department is made a prerequisite for laboratory courses in Chemistry and is required of all students in the C.E. department.[2] For the latter, in the opinion of the writer, general Qualitative Analysis would be much more to the purpose. The introduction of such a course for C.E. students is not suggested in the proposed

[1] That is, a chemistry major in the School of Science.
[2] The Department of Civil Engineering.

arrangement, however, owing to lack of laboratory accommodations and instructors.

Nor does this plan make any provision for graduate courses as yet. Graduate students we have had who for the most part have simply taken work they might have taken equally well as undergraduates, but graduate courses in the strict sense have never been offered by any of us. We may hope for these higher things, it seems to me, only after we have set our house thoroughly in order for our undergraduates.

Naturally, in suggesting assignments of work under the proposed rearrangement of courses, I have at every step taken account of the personnel of our available teaching force. From 1888 as a student and since 1891 as an instructor I have had abundant opportunity to study the temperaments, tastes and equipments of the individual instructors, as well as the aims we profess, the ideals we hold and the methods we try to apply. So far as possible I have tried to distribute the proposed work in such a way as to make the most profitable use of our special aptitudes and attainments. To almost the same extent I hope the assignments would fall in with our individual inclinations. In this latter matter, however, I foresee a few serious difficulties due to a radical departure from our present method of dividing the work of administering the courses. I have long been convinced that in a well organized chemical department *all* of the acting instructors should devote a certain portion of their time to the instruction of students in the laboratory. Only thus can science teaching be made thoroughly effective. Needless to say, it is the wellnigh universal custom, whether the institution be large or small, for the older as well as the younger men in the chemical departments to appear at least daily in the students' laboratories. No divorce between classroom and laboratory instruction is tolerated. With us, however, but four of the eight instructors do laboratory teaching. Not a student has had laboratory instruction from either Professor Cornwall or Professor McCay[3] for more than ten years past. Professor Cornwall withdrew from all laboratory instruction or even inspection in 1891 when we moved into our present building. Since 1892 Professor McCay has had no laboratory in which to give instruction had he so desired. And yet both these professors are pre-eminently laboratory chemists and their presence in the laboratories in the old days was always an inspiration to the students. Putting the best interests of the students above all other considerations, I have therefore suggested such an as[s]ign-

[3] Professors Henry Bedinger Cornwall and LeRoy Wiley McCay.

ment of laboratory instruction both to Professor Cornwall and to Professor McCay as will best place their ripe experience in laboratory practice at the service of the students.

Further, I have in most cases assigned several instructors to the laboratory work in connection with each of the various courses, while making some one instructor responsible for the class work and general oversight of the course. In some cases I have even gone so far as to indicate that a junior instructor might claim the services of his senior in the laboratory, as in Quantitative Analysis (5) and Determinative Mineralogy (10) below. Perhaps this feature is not practicable before the millennium.

Finally, I realize that the successful carrying out of this plan, or indeed of any plan looking toward consolidation and co-ordination, would require the patient and wise supervision of a strong executive head with broad chemical sympathies and training. Lacking this, I fear the scheme is Utopian.

I would make the following specific suggestions:

A. STOCK AND EQUIPMENT. I am confident that several hundred dollars, as well as much space and time, could be saved yearly by placing the purchasing of apparatus and chemicals, the care of the stock, the equipment of the lecture rooms and laboratories, both professors' and students', the keeping of the students' accounts etc. entirely in the hands of a single officer.

Beside the stores for General Chemistry, which for the most part would best be kept near the main lecture room as at present, we have now four large storerooms in the basement and two storerooms on the third or laboratory floor. Certainly two, possibly three of these six rooms could be utilized for other purposes, should the separate stocks be combined.

We have now, scattered through our private laboratories, a large amount of expensive special apparatus[,] much of it in duplicate, of which no record is kept. Pieces become broken, mislaid or lost and no one is held responsible. We exchange or add to our equipment special pieces of apparatus without consultation with each other. There can be no question that the University should have some record of the many hundreds of dollars worht [worth] of apparatus now stored in our several private laboratories and in some ways regarded as our private property. Much of this special apparatus we use so infrequently that it would work little hardship to us if we had to apply for it at a central store as occasion for its use might arise. I should recommend therefore that the officer in charge of equipment be required to keep a record of all the stock in the professors', as well as the students' laboratories and that professors, like students, be required to sign applications for all general or special apparatus they may need for their private use. This would be in no way a more unreasonable demand upon us than is now very rpoperly [properly] made by the custodians of the University's books at the Library.

For these responsible duties I should recommend Mr. [John Stout] Van Nest, now Assistant in Chemistry and Mineralogy, who, being naturally methodical and businesslike, would undoubtedly find the position congenial. At the same time he is the one a portion of whose time could best be spared from teaching. With the help of the storekeeper at present allowed my department and of the janitor, Mr. Van Nest could, I think, take charge of all matters pertaining to equipment and stock and still be able to give six to eight hours a week assistance in the laboratory.

N.B. Our present combined outlay for equipment, not including gas and water, is something over $3,000 yearly.

B. *COURSES OF INSTRUCTION.*

1. *General Chemistry.* At present two courses, each consisting of similar experimental lectures, are given. The one course of three hours per week (previous to this year two hours per week) extending through both terms is required of all B.S. and C.E. students in their first year. After this year an equivalent may be offered for this course on entrance. The class is taken in two divisions, lectures being given by Professor McCay (4 hrs per week), recitations conducted by Dr. Foster[4] (2 hrs per week), Mr. Woodward[5] preparing the lecture experiments. The other course runs three hours per week through the second term and is given to two divisions as above. It is required of all Academic Sophomores. In both courses last year there were about 375 students.

This means that practically the same lectures are given four times each year, a state of things unparalleled in any other university so far as I know.

In place of these two courses I should suggest a single course of three hours per week extending throughout the year, required of all B.S. and C.E. men who have not offered Chemistry on entrance, but elective for Academic men in their Sophomore year.*

---

* I have consistently urged elective Chemistry for the Academic men for several years. Last year I got so far as inducing the now defunct Committee on Scholarship to incorporate a recommendation to this effect in their report. [Neher's note]

4 William Foster, Jr., Instructor in General Chemistry.

5 Truman Stephen Woodward, Assistant in General Chemistry.

With the number of men required to take Chemistry reduced on both sides, i.e., through entrance options and placing the subject on the elective list for Academic men, for some time to come from two hundred and fifty to three hundred would probably be in attendance on the course yearly. This number could be handled in two divisions in the present lecture room which seats about one hundred and sixty. This would mean for Professor McCay four lectures a week throughout the year as against four in the first term and eight in the second term under the present arrangement. A class of this size should be broken up into at least four to six divisions for weekly recitations (Foster).

It is now admitted on all hands that such a course should be *accompanied* by laboratory work on the part of the students and in fact there is scarcely a college or university of standing in the country where laboratory work is not given in connection with lectures and recitations on General Chemistry. For us unfortunately, with our present equipment and staff, provision for laboratory work for any such number of students as the above is obviously out of the question.

The work demanded in connection with this course would thus be

	1st Term	2nd Term
McCay	4 hrs	4 hrs
Foster	6 "	6 "
Woodward	Preparation of experiments etc. throughout course.	

2. *Laboratory Chemistry*, illustrating and reviewing General Chemistry and introductory to Qualitative Analysis. At present this course is represented only by my limited first term Academic (Junior) elective. Its object would be twofold; first to make good so far as is at present possible the lack of laboratory work in connection with our General Chemistry; second, to review General Chemistry and prepare the way for rapid and intelligent progress in Qualitative Analysis.

It should be allowed 4 hrs, or rather exercises, per week throughout the first term and be open as an elective to all men, B.S. and Academic, who have completed the course in General Chemistry satisfactorily. The number of applicants as matters now stand would probably be about one hundred (100) all told. My present course is limited to twenty men since I have but twenty desks in my laboratory, but during the first term there are at present and have been for years about fifty desks lying idle in the laboratory of the Department of Applied Chemistry. By utilizing this space and taking the class in two divisions for laboratory work, one hundred men could easily be accommodated.

I regard the present analogue of this course as by far the most important of the courses organized under my department and I have experimented with it for four years until I think I begin to know its limitations. For the present at least I should be glad to undertake the supervision of the extended course, but should require assistance, especially in connection with the laboratory work, from three or four other members of the teaching force, say from Mr. Sill[6] and Mr. Van Nest and from Dr. Foster and Mr. Woodward as well, for the latter at present give no laboratory instruction. Since this is a laboratory course for beginners it is necessary to give the students taking it a great deal of individual coaching, especially during the first half of the term. With two divisions the total laboratory hours would be twelve. There should always be at least three instructors present in the laboratory with each division. The examination of notebooks would require from ten to twelve hours each week, for I find I spend from two and one half to three hours each week in this manner with my present class of twenty.

The assignment of hours in connection with this course would therefore be

	First Term only	
	Class Room	Laboratory
Neher	1 or 2 (Lect.)	4
Sill	2 (Recitations)	12
Foster	____	8
Woodward	____	8
Van Nest	____	8
		—
		40

There would thus be three men present in the laboratory with each division at each exercise, while I should be present for one laboratory exercise each week with each division. I should put Mr. Sill practically in charge of the recitations and of the laboratory under my supervision.

3. *Qualitative Analysis*. At present two distinct courses are given, each four exercises a week throughout the second term. In the B.S. course Professor Cornwall gives the lectures and holds the recitations and examinations, while Mr. Sill with Professor

[6] Herbert Fowler Sill, Instructor in Analytical Chemistry.

Phillips[7] and Mr. Van Nest has charge of the laboratory work. About forty to forty-five men, Sophomores, take the course. In my department about twenty Academic Juniors each year, though the number of applications reaches nearly fifty. I have no assistance in carrying the course.

In the consolidated course of four exercises a week, second term, one hundred men could be accommodated in two divisions in the present B.S. laboratory, i.e., at the very desks used in the first term for Course 2 above.

I should distribute the work as follows:

| | Second Term only | |
	Class Room	Laboratory
Phillips, in charge,	3 (Lect. & Rec.)	8
Sill	——	8
Foster	——	8
Woodward	——	6
Van Nest	——	6
		——
		36

4. *Quantitative Analysis*, introductory course, four exercises per week in the first term. At present three such introductory courses are offered, two in Professor Cornwall's department and one in my department. The consolidated course should be open to all men who have completed courses 1, 2 and 3. I should hope to see it in charge of Professor McCay, as all the students, after a year spent in the laboratory since leaving the lecture room for General Chemistry, would hail with delight another opportunity of working under his inspiring guidance.

From twenty-five to thirty students could be accommodated in the large (B.S.) laboratory in addition to those taking Course 2 above. At present about twenty men all told are applying for the work each year.

The arrangement of hours would be

| | First Term only | |
	Class Room	Laboratory
McCay in charge,	1	about 5 all told
Phillips, assisting,	——	6

5. Quantitative Analysis, continued, four exercises per week during the second term. Direct continuation of above, intended

[7] Alexander Hamilton Phillips, Assistant Professor of Mineralogy.

for men wishing to specialize in either the theoretical or practical side of Chemistry. Here I would have Professor Phillips take charge, Professor McCay assisting. Fifteen to twenty men could be admitted.

Two such courses are at present offered.

The hours would be

	Second Term only	
	Class Room	Laboratory
Phillips	I	4
McCay	——	4

6. *Quantitative Analysis*, special and advanced course, four exercises a week during the second term, open to B.S. Seniors who have taken Courses 1, 2, 3, 4 & 5. This course would best be given by Professor Cornwall. The men might be given the option of spending the second half of the term on Organic Analysis under my direction. The hours would be [blank] Six to ten men could be cared for.

	Second Term only	
	Class Room	Laboratory
Cornwall	I	4 to 6
Neher	I	4 to 6 *for half term only*

7. *Theoretical Chemistry.* Second term, two hours (lectures) a week as at present. Open to any man who has taken Course 1 (and Course 2?). The course at present embraces about a dozen lectures on the outlines of Organic Chemistry which should be omitted since they parallel a portion of my introductory course on Organic Chemistry. Thirty to forty men in all.

	Second Term only
McCay	2 lectures

8. *Organic Chemistry*, as at present, two lectures a week throughout the year. Fifteen to twenty-five men in all.

	First Term	Second Term
Neher	2 lectures	2 lectures

9. *Organic Chemistry*, laboratory work, one or two terms, four exercises per week, open to all men who have taken Courses 1, 2, 3 and 4 and are taking Course 8. B.S. students could thus begin laboratory work in Organic Chemistry either in second term, Junior year, or in first term, Senior year, whereas the present ar-

rangement of the B.S. chemical courses debars them from work in the Organic Laboratory. Academic men, as at present, could take the work only in second term Senior year. About twelve men could be accommodated in my present laboratory after the Academic Juniors had been transferred to the main laboratory as proposed under 2 and 3 above.

	First Term	Second Term
Neher	Class Room 2	Class Room 2
	Laboratory 6	Laboratory 6

Unfortunately there is no one at present with us who could assist me in the supervision of this laboratory work. Should the demand for the work show any increase, I should need not only more laboratory room, which could easily be arranged, but an assistant as well.

10. *Determinative Mineralogy.* Elective, three (or four) exercises per week during the first term. At present given in the second term also for the C.E. students. Now conducted by Professor Phillips and Mr. Van Nest, formerly by Professor Cornwall and Professor Phillips. About forty men could be cared for in present laboratory.

I should make the following assignment of hours:

	First Term only	
	Class Room	Laboratory
Phillips	I	6
Cornwall	⸺	6

11. *Advanced Mineralogy.* First term, two hours a week in class room (now one hour a week each term). At present a small course including men taking the "Chemical Course."

	First Term only
Cornwall	Class Room 2

12. *Applied Chemistry* (as named at present), i.e., examination of water, foods, poisons etc. At present also includes elements of Organic Chemistry which could be discontinued, making the first term of my Organic Chemistry a prerequisite for this work. Two lectures a week during the second term. Now in first term.

	Second Term only
Cornwall	2 lectures

13. *Technical Chemistry.* Two lectures a week during the first term. Now *one* hour a week during the second term.

First Term only

Cornwall   2 lectures

14. *Physical Chemistry.* Two lectures a week during the sec- New course
ond term to supplement the course now given by Professor
Loomis[8] under the title of Chemical Physics.

Sill   2 lectures during the Second Term only.

15. *Physical Chemistry*, laboratory work, to accompany Course New course
15[14]. Two exercises a week during the second term. Possibly
there would be at first six to ten applicants for the work. Accommodations for this number at least could be provided in one of the
basement rooms.

Second Term only

Sill   4 hours in the laboratory.

SUMMARY OF THE ASSIGNMENTS (In hours per week)

	First Term		Second Term	
	Class Room	Laboratory	Class Room	Laboratory
Cornwall	4 (now 4)	6 (now none)	3 (now 3 or 4)	6 (now none)
McCay	5 (now 6)	5 " "	6 (now 8)	4 " "
Neher	5 (this year 4)	10 (recently 18)	4½ (formerly 5)	9 (recently 12)
Phillips	1 (now 3)	12	4	12
Sill	2	12	2	12
Foster	6 (now 2)	8 (now none)	6	8 (now none)
Van Nest, Equipment	8	——	6	
Woodward, Experiments		8 (now none)	——	6 (now none)

This plan, as is evident, involves a marked increase in the total number of hours service required of Professors Cornwall and McCay, Dr. Foster and Mr. Woodward, none of whom gives any laboratory instruction at present. At the same time it somewhat relieves Professor Phillips, Mr. Sill, Mr. Van Nest and myself, who now carry the entire burden of the laboratory instruction. The time saved in the cases of Professor Phillips and Mr. Sill is transferred to the class room, while the lightening of Mr. Van Nest's hours will make it possible for him to take entire charge of stock and equipment.

The following table of comparisons will show thw [the] rela- tive efficiency of the present and the proposed arrangements. In

[8] Elmer Howard Loomis, Professor of Physics.

calculating the efficiency of the present arrangement I have assumed the laboratory of my department to be operated to its fullest capacity with the aid of an additional instructor, i.e., that all the courses announced in the Catalogue at present and actually given by me single-handed in 1899-1902 again become operative each year. Laboratory courses only are co[n]sidered. All "Chemical Course" courses except Assaying *are included*.

		Number of Courses	Number of Instructors**	Number of Students	Average Hrs per week	Ratio of Students to Instructors
1st	Present Plan	6	10	102	3.72	10.2
Term	Proposed "	4	11	177	3.77	16.1
2nd	Present Plan	7	14	104	4.27	7.4
Term	Proposed "	5	11	157	3.87	14.3

So much for the possible efficiency of the proposed plan. Its economy is seen on considering that it dispenses with the services of an instructor otherwise absolutely necessary in my department and makes possible a saving of at least $500 yearly in expenditure for equipment.

Trusting that you will not hesitate to call upon me for such further statements or explanations as you may desire, I am

Yours very respectfully,   Fred Neher.

** By number of instructors is meant the sum of the number of instructors available for laboratory instruction in each of the courses. [Neher's note]

TLS (WWP, UA, NjP).

To Henry Cooper Pitney, Jr.

Princeton, New Jersey.

My dear Mr. Pitney: 26 November, 1902.

I note in going over my list of engagements that the 22nd of February next comes on a Sunday. I do not recollect whether in speaking of my promise to go to Morristown for the celebration of that day anything was said about shifting the celebration to Saturday or Monday. Will you not be kind enough to let me know what arrangement has been made in the matter? I am asking the question because of my desire to accept another invitation for Saturday evening, the 21st, if that does not conflict with your plans in Morristown.

With much regard,

Very sincerely yours,   Woodrow Wilson

TLS (Washington Association of N. J., Morristown, N. J.).

Notes for an Address[1]

26 Nov., 1902[2]
Chicago Alumni, 28 Nov., '02
The Future of the University.

No one can look upon such a company and not feel the abounding *life* of Princeton. There may be many things to do for the University, but there is at least no lack of vitality.

What has bred this Spirit?

The life of a *Place*. A university does not consist of buildings, but it does in large part consist of environment,—of the influence of sight and surroundings and comradeships and associations,—and these we shall enhance

Our dream of what is to be:

The scheme (ground plan) of material development.

Dormitories: the central college community.

Graduate School: a swarming community of men devoted to learning placed at the very heart of the comradeships of the friendly little town of reading men.

School of Jurisprudence:

Electrical School

Museum of Natural History: a home for such things as the unique Patigonian collection made by Mr. Hatcher.[3]

And all this that the spirit of the place may be transfused with the comradeships of letters[,] the home of reading men, inquiring men, conversing men, thinking men, in the place of thoughtless boys doing tasks.

The Tutors,—subjects, instead of stunts,—an introduction into the freedom of letters.

Therefore Equipment,—opportunities, companionships, tasks wh. will attract the most brilliant and ambitious men of all the teaching fraternity.

It is time we gave Princeton the position to which her traditions and her splendid spirit entitle her.

Her reputation must always be a by-product of the careers of her teachers and her sons.

The Cost, $12,500,000,—a sum so small that no other place could transform it into so much life and power,—a sum which must and will be got.

WWhw MS. (WP, DLC).

[1] A news report of this address is printed at Nov. 29, 1902.

[2] Wilson's composition date.

[3] John Bell Hatcher, Curator of Vertebrate Palaeontology at Princeton from 1893 to 1900, who led three expeditions to Patagonia between 1896 and 1899.

They secured a vast collection of palaeontological and ornithological specimens for Princeton University.

To Jenny Davidson Hibben and John Grier Hibben

My dearest Friends,   [Princeton, N. J., Nov. 27, 1902]

I hope you will not smile at the expense of your sentimental friend when you receive this letter. I find myself under the strongest impulse to write it, and know of no reason why I should resist it.

The burden of my thought this Thankgiving is of you. I have many things to be thankful for, but the cause of thankfulness which I find uppermost in my thought is that I have been given such friends as you have been to me,—so perceiving, so thoughtful, so sympathetic, in every time of need so tender and loving,— and always so unfailingly delightful, made to (Wordsworth).[1] How I can have attracted such affection I will not stop just now to think: it seems to relieve my heart in its present condition to tell you, though you must already know it, how profoundly grateful I am and thankful to God for your sweet and satisfying friendship. Even if you should find me out and cease to love me, I at least have the precious possession of the years that have bound us together.   Your devoted friend,   Woodrow Wilson

I did not get the chance at Mrs. Cleveland's last night until after dinner, but then I literally sat at her feet,—where every man of sense and taste must feel that he belongs. She is so fine, unusual, beautiful and delightful.

Transcript of WWshLS (WP, DLC).
[1] "(Wordsworth)" in WWhw. Wilson obviously intended to insert a quotation from the poet at this point when he transcribed his letter.

To David Laurance Chambers[1]

[My dear Sir,]   [Princeton, N. J., c. Nov. 27, 1902]

The gentlemen of the English department have just apprised me of the arrangements they advise for next year.

Mr. [Hardin] Craig, as you doubtless know, is to return. He is willing to take up again the work he did before leaving and the department is anxious to have him do so. They had hoped, as I had, that it might be possible to enlarge the force of instructors to three, but unhappily, as I explained to you the other day, the funds of the University do not yet permit the addition.

In determining what appointments to recommend, the department has chosen Mr. Craig and Mr. Long.[2] The choice between Mr. Long and yourself they made, I know, with the greatest reluctance, and with deep and genuine regret that they could not retain you. They have spoken to me in the highest terms of your work as well as of your character. They feel that in losing you they are losing a valuable man and colleague who had won their admiration and affection.

I am asked to say this to you with the greatest cordiality, and I do so with the greater willingness and pleasure because of my own great esteem for you and appreciation of your work. Please call upon me or upon any of us to assist you to get a place worthy of your powers and of your ambitions.

[Very truly Yours, Woodrow Wilson]

Transcript of WWshL (WP, DLC).
[1] Princeton 1900; Assistant in English at Princeton, 1901-1903.
[2] Augustus White Long, Instructor in English.

A News Item

[Nov. 28, 1902]

PRINCETON'S PRESIDENT HERE.
Woodrow Wilson Seeks Aid for University—
Banquets in Honor.

President Woodrow Wilson of Princeton university arrived in Chicago to-day on a mission, it is understood, of securing as much of the $12,000,000 desired for the needs of the university as he can encourage Chicago capitalists to contribute. Immediately on his arrival President Wilson went to the home of Cyrus H. McCormick, 321 Huron street, where several hours were devoted to discussing the needs of Princeton and the best methods of satisfying them.

President Wilson's time will be fully occupied during his stay in Chicago, which will probably extend over Sunday. The Princeton club, composed of alumni of the university, will claim the educator's attention first and will tender him a banquet this evening.

To-morrow morning President Wilson will be met by members of the Phi Kappa Psi fraternity of the University of Chicago and escorted to the university, where a reception followed by luncheon will be held in his honor. President Harper will then receive the easterner informally, after which he will become the guest of the Commercial club. A banquet given by this organization will follow in the evening.

Printed in the *Chicago Daily News*, Nov. 28, 1902.

A News Report of an Address to the Chicago Alumni

[Nov. 29, 1902]

OBJECTS TO BOOK WORMS.
President Wilson of Princeton
Addresses Graduates.

"I don't believe the natural, carnal man was ever meant to sit down and read a book."

In this manner President Woodrow Wilson of Princeton university startled 100 alumni of old Nassau into a consideration of his theory that American colleges should follow more closely the English system of education by tutors and make the university examination more of a judgment day for the students. He detailed his plan for devoting a part of the $12,500,000 that he wants for Princeton to the institution of the kind of tutoring in vogue at Oxford and Cambridge, but improved to correspond with American ideals.

President Wilson's address was delivered at a dinner given for him by the Princeton Alumni association of Chicago at the University club. A joyous evening of songs and cheers for alma mater led up to the speeches, which, for an audience of men who "felt like boys again," as Toastmaster J. C. Mathis put it, were fittingly dressed out in the negligee idiom of the campus.

It was upon the famous Princeton spirit and how little it owes to the mere matter contained in books and drawn out through examinations that Dr. Wilson dwelt in his opening remarks.

"Yes, I feel just that way about the reading of books after all my experience," continued the president. "I would rather walk out and talk to some man—see life through the eyes and feel it. The only reason we read books is that they can give us more experience than we would be able to get in any other way. We want to know what past generations have thought and done; we want to know what men are thinking whose environment is one that we shall never have the opportunity to feel in our own persons. But we want useful men, not men who have learning for learning's sake, and who think they are better than others because they have something in their heads which is useless."

Rapidly the speaker sketched the spirit of comradeship and

useful manhood that is derived from the wholesome college surroundings, from contact between man and man.

"Everyone gets by heredity," he went on, "the suggestion that comes from the Gothic style of architecture. I know that from the Tudor style of building one gets the spirit of the tradition of the old English learning. Now the old English tradition is not the tradition of the lecture room where students sit under the eye of the master. It is the tradition of the reading man, the man who gets the subject up for himself and in the end is put through his paces by the board of examiners. I believe that the student should read in his own way, consulting with responsible men as to the works best fitted for his purpose, and be given to understand that he is on his own responsibility, and will later be expected to know what he has been studying.

"Let these students at examination time come to a day of judgment and know that in the meantime they are not to loaf any more than every American citizen is entitled to under the constitution. I believe they should loaf a certain time each day, but how much I decline to say.

"Now, my hobby is this: when our friends get ready to give us that $12,500,000 I want $2,225,000 devoted to the maintenance of a body of tutors like the English tutors, but without their drawbacks. English tutors are appointed for life and go to seed. They make out their note books and consider that nothing more is to be discovered bearing on the subject in hand.

"I believe five years is long enough service for that kind of a man, and one year if he is not so good. By this system of tutoring I believe that students can be coaxed into becoming reading men. There is not a dry subject in the world—it is the fellow who is dry.

"Under the present routine of [a] college student an undergraduate forgets what he has learned as soon as the task is done. As a rule all he requires is two days to get ready for any examination and make it necessary for the instructor to pass him, but he forgets it all afterwards. We must make the students 'hump' to help themselves."

Dr. Wilson said that $12,500,000 was the minimum sum that Princeton needs for its contemplated scientific school, including an electrical school, a museum, and biological laboratories. He denied after the dinner that he had come to Chicago for the special purpose of raising this money. He came principally to make an address tonight at the dinner of the Commercial club. He is the guest of Cyrus H. McCormick. . . .

Printed in the *Chicago Daily Tribune*, Nov. 29, 1902; some editorial headings omitted.

An Address to the Commercial Club of Chicago[1]

[[Nov. 29, 1902]]

THE RELATION OF UNIVERSITY EDUCATION TO COMMERCE

Mr. President, and Gentlemen of the Commercial Club: I feel the honor, as I feel the embarrassment, of standing in this place, because I know how many really distinguished men have been your guests, and I know how far I am from having proved my right to stand in this place. But I take it that one of the encouraging signs of our age is that men have that catholic desire to interchange ideas which makes it a welcome thing to them to hear any man who speaks at any rate from conviction and out of a thoughtful mind. And so it is not a presumption on the part of a man placed in the position in which I have recently been placed, to ask leave of you to speak aloud some of the thoughts which have been passing through his own mind in respect of the relation and the responsibility of the university in regard to commerce.

I cannot pose as an authority on commerce. There are gentlemen in this room who know me, and in whose presence it would be embarrassing to pose as an authority on commerce. I should feel in the position of that unsophisticated woman, who, in a side show attached to a circus, saw, or supposed that she saw, a man read a newspaper through a two-inch board. She got up in great excitement, and said, "Let me out of this place. This is no place for me to be with these thin things on." (Laughter.) I should feel very much in her position if I should attempt to pose before you as an authority on commerce. But whether I am an authority on the relation of the university to commerce or not, I hope soon to qualify myself as an authority and I am trying myself off on you. This is my maiden trip in this capacity, and I want to read in your faces, if I may, whether I am right or wrong in the position which has seemed to my thought a valid position.

In the first place, it does not seem to me that a university is a place to give a man a business education. A druggist in a very small way at Princeton—all merchandise is in a small way in that small place—took me aside the other day, and told me now was

[1] A news report of this affair is printed at Nov. 30, 1902.

the opportunity to establish at Princeton a business education. And when I questioned him as to what he meant by a business education, I understood him to mean the keeping of accounts and the handling of commercial paper, and the technical duties of commercial transactions. I told him that it did not seem to me that we were quite ready yet to transform Princeton into a business college; and I believe that you will all agree with me that the real point of commerce is not the method of commerce, but the catholicity of its outlook. Commerce is great or small according to its horizon, not according to its detailed method. No man ever made a fortune out of method. No man ever extended commerce by method. He extends commerce, I take it, by vision; by an imaginative conception of places and of conditions which he never saw; by having what I may describe as a traveled mind, which has gone up and down the world and ascertained the conditions of men; and there never was a time, assuredly, when it was more necessary for the commercial mind to be a traveled mind than at the present day, when commerce is almost of necessity international in its scope; where no neighborhood marks its boundaries; where the men who are engaged in commerce can hardly set limits to at any rate the imaginative conception of what commerce will one day become. And when we address ourselves to questions like the Chinese question, we are really asking ourselves what is the means of entrance of western ideas into eastern countries. We know instinctively that the western ideas go in with the western goods, but that first of all the western goods must fit the eastern ideas; that you are not going to get your entrance into eastern markets by forcing at the outset western tastes upon the eastern buyers; but that you will get your eastern markets by understanding eastern tastes, so that your business as traders with the east is to understand not your own minds so much as the eastern mind, as the eastern taste, as the very religion of the east, so that you may know those prejudices which are hardened against change, those tastes which can be invaded only by a sort of sacrilege; those things which your thoughts must know and must match if you would achieve ascendancy in the markets of the east. And so it seems to me that it is true that it is the traveled mind that knows the markets.

One of the most characteristic things of modern trade, I suppose, is the commercial traveler. I don't know of any more impossible person than some commercial travelers that I have met. Because some commercial travelers—men without elasticity of mind who believe that they can through their single, individual

eye, read all the world as they travel—are more safely insured
against the introduction of knowledge than any class of men I
know of. (Laughter). A Yale professor of my acquaintance said
that the result of his twenty years' experience in teaching was
that the human mind has infinite resources for resisting the
introduction of knowledge (laughter), and I believe that those
resources are increased by knocking about the world with a dull
mind. The mind gets case-hardened. It gets smoothed over on the
surface. It gets all the ordinary touches of life exhausted upon
it, and a man thinks that his mind is complete because its surface
is fair, although its interior is empty, and he takes the hollow
sounds that come from it as being the real music of intelligence.

There are some commercial travelers of that sort. But there
are commercial travelers of another sort, who see through things,
as well as see the surface of things, and this casting up and down
the world, this familiarity with steamers that seek the other side
of the globe, this life upon the fleeting tides of what men are doing, is the characteristic feature of modern commercial undertaking. Everybody knows, of course, that modern industrial undertaking strains at the leash all the time to get into channels of
commerce, that commerce is the outlet of industrial undertakings
and that industrial undertakings are without significance unless
they have the outlets of commerce; that the commercial man, the
trader, is the middle man between the product and its freedom to
command the markets of the world, and that without the intelligence of the merchant the intelligence of the manufacturer goes
for nothing. So that these are the channels, it is trite to say, of
achievement. But look what that means. It seems to me that the
most statesmanlike occupation is commerce. It seems to me—to
put it otherwise—that the commercial man, the trader, must know
as much as the statesman of international conditions; and he
must know the international conditions more beneath the surface than the statesman knows them; and that is the reason
for the circumstance which Mr. Jones[2] has alluded to, that commerce has commanded policy, international policy. Tradesmen
have been inside the life of nations the outside of whose policy
statesmen have observed, and traders have been able to tell
statesmen the things which are necessary to control a policy,
and to dictate it, and to make it intelligent. It is a trader's business, in short, to know the world. Instinctively, therefore, men
who are engaged in commerce feel the pulse of affairs. They

---

[2] David Benton Jones, who introduced Wilson.

are singularly, as it were instinctively, sensible of approaching changes of weather. They will be able to tell you sometimes that a change is coming without being able to explain to you any of the indications of change. There is some subtle influence that comes to them, they know not whence, which apprises them of a change in the cast of the heavens, and one of the feelings that the merchant has, I take it, more distinctly than any other citizen, except the man who is at the right hand of the merchant, viz., the banker, is the necessity for a universal, sympathetic association so that there will be no miscarriage when it comes to the strain, in the shape of a misunderstanding between one class and another. I suppose that the merchant is more intimately interested, for example, in the questions of the relation between labor and capital than most other men, because the moment there is a derangement there, the whole machinery of exchange feels the influence of it, and the machinery of exchange is so sensitive that, when one part feels the influence, that influence is propagated and spread to the other parts, so that there must be a universal cordiality and intimacy of mutual understanding in order that the way of trade may be free and unobstructed.

One of the most interesting circumstances in our national history, gentlemen, is the circumstance that it was the commercial classes of this country more than any others who were dominantly influential in the adoption of the Constitution of the United States. A very minute and painstaking student of the conditions of that period, a neighbor of yours at the University of Wisconsin, has been at the pains to draw and color a map of the vote with respect to the adoption of the Constitution of the United States.[3] He has been at the pains, by examining every available record, to determine in which districts men were elected who were supposed to be favorable to the adoption of the Constitution, in which districts there were mixed delegations elected, some in favor and some against, in which districts those were elected who were opposed to the Constitution. The districts which were in favor of the Constitution he has colored red; those which were opposed to the Constitution he has colored—I suppose with a little malicious touch—green; those which were doubtful and distributed their vote between the two sides, he has given the intermediate color, yellow; and the interesting part in looking at that map is, that you instantly see that the red lines, the red

[3] The "student" was Orin Grant Libby. Wilson included a revised version of Libby's map, divided into two sections, in his *A History of the American People*, III, facing pp. 78 and 80.

surfaces, run down the coast; that the color thickens at the ports of entry; that it turns and ascends the valleys where the rivers run; that it is governed in almost every instance by the life of the community in respect to its communications with the outside world; in other words, that the roots of power for the constitutional party are the roots of trade. You have only to look at the map to see the demonstration of that statement. And that means this, that the commercial interests, then as now, felt the imperative necessity of political union. They knew that without political union there would be those interruptions of trade which were already manifesting themselves in so disturbing a manner, and which had brought about the agitation of the adoption of the Constitution,—when the State of Connecticut had a tariff against the State of New York, and the State of New York against firewood and the chicken's eggs out of Connecticut; when New Jersey—that interesting and most maligned portion of the country in which I live, which has been described as the intermediate state (laughter)—was experiencing the inconvenience of its position in having its port of entry on one side controlled by one state, and on the other by another, so that it was between the devil and the deep sea. You will notice that the delegation from New Jersey were the men who insisted upon giving the work of the convention of 1787 the widest possible scope and having not a mere patching of the Articles of Constitution [Confederation], but a new and substantial Constitution. They wanted to get out of a hole, and every community that felt restricted in trade, felt the absolute necessity of direct communication with the rest of the world, insisted upon having a common Constitution. Then you know what the subsequent constitutional history of the country was: how the independent race of men that went up and down the Mississippi said that if the people across the Alleghanies would not treat them squarely, they would have relations with somebody, even with England if it came to the pinch, and if not with England, why then with Spain; they would have some world connections which would release the great wealth and the great power of that valley. It was the voice of commerce, insisting that it was kin to the world, and that it was not to be shut up in little political pockets and kept away from the free outlet and inlet of energy.

You know, also, how large a part the commercial interests have played in questions like the tariff. The tariff is essentially a commercial question. It is a question on one side of how you are thinking to increase the internal wealth and energy of the country by fostering its resources, and on the other side of which you are thinking what you are going to do after you have done enough fostering and are in danger of tying up the resources which you have magnified. That, I take it, is the position we have arrived at at the present moment. That is what is causing some gentlemen of very well established party connections to examine their consciences. They are saying, "If you don't let something out the system will break, and it is time to consider whether we will not adjust our ideas between the internal fostering and the external outlet, because we are beginning to say after all, while we have all these years been bent on making the United States yield everything it contains under the best conditions, we have been forgetting that a time was coming, and we now know that it is coming, when what we want to do is to make all the world buy what we have got." The internal trade of this country, magnificent as it is in proportion, is not all that we want and is not sufficient to take the surplus product of this incalculably rich country, and we now want to know the reason why we cannot let our products go where they will and command the markets of the world upon their own merits—and we cannot command the markets of the world upon the merits of our products unless we can get something in exchange for them, for as Mr. Hughitt[4] and I were just now agreeing, commerce comes down, in the last analysis, to barter; you cannot do it on paper, you have got to do it with goods. And if you sell goods, you have got to buy goods from somewhere, and your external commerce is going to consist in bringing in balances of goods as well as sending out cargoes of goods. That is the hard matter of fact in the heart of the business that is now impressing us and which is making the commercial man the man of real international feeling in this country. You know that when some years ago Mr. Cleveland nearly gave us nervous prostration by the Venezuelan message, it was the commercial men who got on their hind legs, because they said, "If this match drops in powder, where are we going to be?" and for two or three days they didn't know whether it was going to drop into powder or into some very harmless place at Hatfield House, where Lord Salisbury was thinking the matter over. Lord Salisbury happened at that time to be thinking of enough things at a time to see the inconvenience of going to war with the United States. They say that the trouble with Lord Salisbury is that he does not ordinarily think of enough things at a time; he thinks of one thing at a time, and nothing is more fatal in this complex world than to think

[4] Marvin Hughitt, President of the Chicago and North Western Railroad.

of but one thing at a time. You have got to think of—by a minimum computation—at least a dozen at once, and Lord Salisbury
had his variety cap on that morning, and did not think that a
war with the United States was worth while, and so the commercial men of the United States were saved their nervous prostration. But you will observe it is a matter of nerves, and when you
say it is a matter of nerves you mean that it is a matter of sympathy, and a matter of sympathy is a matter of imaginative conception. I haven't any sympathy for a man if I cannot form some
imaginative conception of the contents of his head. If I don't
know what he is thinking about, I don't know what to think about
myself in addressing him. One of the most inconvenient things
that can happen to a man in my business—that is, of addressing
college classes—is to have a dignified and inscrutable stranger
enter the class room and sit down (laughter); then you begin to
say in your heart, "Who in thunder is that?" (Laughter.) "Is he
a merchant?" You can generally tell if he is one of the cloth. But
what is he, and what part of this lecture is going to interest him?
Because we have a more or less histrionic instinct and we all wish
more or less to appeal to the audience which we are addressing,
and we instinctively know that that man knows more than any
of these boys that are sitting here, and that if we are not particularly in good form that morning we had better brace ourselves up
to his standard and not count on the average ignorance of our
audience (laughter). And so it becomes a matter—a very acute
matter—of nerves in those circumstances. It is in every case a
question of imaginative perception as to how the other man feels
when it comes to a question of influence.

Now with all this elaborate setting out of the stage, I introduce the university to play her part. What part is the university to
play in preparing men—I won't say in preparing men, but in serving the community in respect of commerce? I have already said
that it does not seem to me any part of a university function to
give men a business education, to teach them, that is to say, the
methods of the business office. There is no touch of the university in that. It always must do something very different from that.
I have no doubt that technical schools of various sorts are extremely serviceable, but technical schools of the narrow sort do
not seem to me appropriate parts of a university. We are apt to
forget, gentlemen, that the university is not intended for everybody. The principle of power is a principle of differentiation. We
are in danger just now of supposing that a university must include every kind of education, and we are apt to lose distinctions

of thought and efficiency of result by confusing one sort of education with another. There must be various sorts of education, and
when I say that the field of the university is set apart, and peculiar, I am not meaning to imply that it is better, that it is more
noble, that it is more dignified than other fields of education. I
believe—as every man born on this soil, I take it, must believe—
that the dignity of toil with the hands, provided the heart goes into the work, provided the conscience gets translated into the product, is enough to dignify any man and give him a touch of nobility. There is no comparison in point of nobility, there ought to
be no attempt to compare, in point of nobility of work, the work
of the head and the work of the hands. It is not a question of
nobility, it is a question of division of labor, of the separation of
functions. It is a question of that differentiation upon which the
efficiency of the modern world depends. And upon that basis, not
upon the basis of comparison, I say that the business of the university is with the head and not with the hands; that the business of the university is something different from the business
of technical education, and if men are so impatient that their
sons should get to the immediate tasks by which they make
their living that they cannot allow them to spend the four
years necessary for a university education, the thing to do is not
to send them where they will be pretending that they are in
college, but to put them at the desk, and let them learn the
business like men. Don't put them in a technical school which
is called a university and then say that they are getting a university education. Not because they won't be getting something
valuable there, I repeat, but because you must not confuse ideas.
And the idea of a university education is different from the
idea of a technical education. It seems to me that the thing
that the university must do is to make men acquainted with
the world intellectually, imaginatively.

The business of the university is to cultivate intellectual
imagination. We do not enough emphasize that in our idea
of university work. We suppose that a university is a place
where the contents of certain books are extracted and inserted
into the minds of certain young men, and that the whole process
is a process of taking from one vessel and pouring into another;
that it is a process of filling, a process of cramming; that it is
a process of informing, informing by authority, of telling a
young man that a certain thing is so because it is said to be
so by an authoritative text book. That is a very mechanical
and a very mistaken idea of a university. Mind you, I don't say

that many universities don't do that. I am not saying that most universities don't do a great deal of it. Most of us do a vast deal of it, and it is a mistake to fill a young man's head with statements given him not upon proof but upon authority, for the thing in which you should pride yourself in the teaching function, it seems to me, is the liberation of the human mind from authority; the cultivation—to repeat the phrase I have already used—of intellectual, independent observation. For your purpose is to give these young fellows the freedom of the world of thought and the world of affairs. You will say there is no way of getting at the freedom of affairs except by mixing in affairs. How many men ever mix in many affairs? The most experienced man of affairs takes the knowledge of nine-tenths of the affairs that he knows anything about from the mouths of other men and from the books and official reports that he reads. I remember being very much impressed with that fact not long ago when Mr. Cleveland was writing a couple of papers on the quarrel which many of you will remember that he had with the United States Senate about dismissals from office and appointments to office in the early part of his first term as President.[5] In writing those papers he took occasion to read the congressional debates which occurred in connection with the quarrel, and as I had the privilege of being with him during a part of the time in which he was preparing these papers, he told me that he was beginning to find out a great many things with regard to the circumstances at that time and of those transactions which he had never known before, "because," he said, "in the daily pressure of executive business, men would come in and tell him that this, that or the other thing had been said in the Senate or in the House; that this, that or the other thing was being rumored on the street; that this, that or the other thing was being done, the shifting of this group and that group of men, and that he did not have time to read anything about it and so had only uncertain information which was brought him by word of mouth." Nobody stood more at the center of that particular transaction than Mr. Cleveland, and yet he knows nine-tenths of what he knows about it from the report of other men, and from the printed records of the debates of Congress. Ask yourselves, sitting in your office, how much you know of what is actually going on in your busi-

[5] Grover Cleveland's first two lectures at Princeton on the Henry Stafford Little Foundation, delivered on April 9 and 10, 1900. They were published under their original title, *The Independence of the Executive* (Boston and New York, 1900).

ness. You know it by the reports of the men under you. You know it by knowing that on previous days certain things were done, and the number of things that come under your direct observation as you sit in your office are absolutely insignificant as compared with the number of things which imaginatively come under your observation and are present in your thought as you see, as it were, the map of the business before you. And so it is that it is not idle to claim that the university can spread some portion of the map of life before men, and out of the credible evidence of men who have taken part in affairs, cultivate among men an intellectual and independent observation of the life of mankind. I am now, of course, talking about undergraduates. I am not talking about advanced students, who set themselves to master a specific task of scholarship. That is another story. That is a matter of the investigation of abstract truth. And I suppose that every intelligent man knows the service that that does. This wonderful instrumentality which is just now in its infancy and will presently run through every process of the globe —I mean electricity—would not have the practical uses that it has now if men had not in secluded places of investigation sought the laws of electrical force without so much as thinking for a moment of the significance of that force from a material and commercial point of view. Commerce has got the by-products of their mind as that mind has moved forward in its eager, unremitted pursuit of abstract truth, essaying to know the laws of nature and the laws of God. Commerce, I say, has stood on one side and picked up the droppings from the tables of these men, and has put it to use in the enrichment of a world—in the material enrichment of a world. That is the service that abstract scholarship does to the material undertakings of men. If men were not bent upon the essential things, the practical thing would not come into revelation at all. But I am not now speaking of that. That is another matter. That is a matter of the general progress of the world. I am now speaking of the administration of the world, and the administration of the world comes by letting men out upon the field of life imaginatively. There are only two ways in which to do that. There are some men who get out upon that field by their own genius, by their own acute power of observation, by the intensity with which they live. You can count those men on the fingers of two hands in any community. Even self-educated men—the men who have not stood in need of the university—would have been set forward faster, I take it, if their imaginings had been assisted by the right forces of university training. But they have had such intrinsic genius for observation that the university has not been indispensable to them. For the average man the university is indispensable. Not, it may be, to enable him to know these things before he dies, but to enable him to know these things at the outset. The university is, if I may express it in the language of the racetrack, the pacemaker for the mind. It shows the mind the pace that it must strike at the outset if it would keep a winning gait throughout all processes of endeavor. It is a process of informing men of the facts of life. And what we are most apt to forget is that one of the principal facts of life is thought, is the thinking process, is what men have conceived their lives to be,—the purpose that men have conceived to be contained in their lives. For when you think of it, gentlemen, the only imperishable thing that any one of you is creating is the conception of his business. The particular things which you manufacture or deal with are going to pass away from the sight of man; the things which you are creating are invisible. They are conceptions of business. You know that the great business mind is the mind which, when you lay before it certain elements, combines those elements in a situation and sees where to put the money and when to put the money. That is a purely abstract conception.

Nobody ever saw, for example, a government. I mean, with the physical eye. Well, I don't know that that is literally true, either. At one time when Richmond was evacuated, some gentlemen did see the Confederate government, I believe, on its way beyond the lines. But leaving that singular and exceptional instance out of view, I take it that nobody on any other occasion ever saw a government.

One of the most impressive things that was ever said, though when repeated in cold blood it sounds rhetorical, was what Mr. Garfield said when Mr. Lincoln was assassinated. I am told that at that time Mr. Garfield was at the Fifth Avenue Hotel in New York, and that when the news reached New York an excited crowd gathered in the square in front of the hotel ready for almost any outburst of frenzied excitement; that Mr. Garfield was asked to step up to the portico of the hotel and say something to quiet the crowd, and that this is what he said: "My friends, the President is dead; but the government lives and God omnipotent reigneth." And, as you may readily believe, the crowd was quieted. They knew, whether they analyzed it or not, that that abstract conception about which our loyalty gathers, the facts of law and of government, stood just as firm as if that man still lived; that though that rare spirit, which better than any other spirit then living could handle that government, was gone from among us, the government remained. And it steadied them with an abstraction.

Every man who fights under the flag of the United States fights under an abstraction. He fights for a thing he never saw and never can see. He fights for a poetic idea, and when we speak of the nation, we speak as men who are ignorant, unless we have some imaginative and sympathetic conception of the parts of the country in which we do not live.

You know, gentlemen, as well as I do, that the great incubus upon this country is its provincialism. I mean that this country is still not homogeneous in the makeup of its life, and consequently the makeup of its habits and conceptions, and that one part of the country is apt to look askance at another part; that when there thrills through the air such a question as, "What is the matter with Kansas?"[6] for example, something is wrong; that one part of the country should have to ask what is the matter with another part of the country and not know that it is just as reasonable for Kansas to ask what is the matter with the rest of the country. It is provincial. It is downright provincial not to have an imaginative conception of what the rest of the country is like, and that is the imaginative conception which the university is meant to give to men, not only in regard to the country in which they live, but in regard to the world in which they live. Because a cultivated man is, as I understand it, a man who knows what the work of the world is, and who consequently understands what the relation of his work is to the rest of the work of the world; who finds his zest not so much in the narrow road of daily routine in his office as in his knowledge of the relation which all of that bears to the whole burden of work which the world is carrying.

One of the most encouraging features of our day is that men like to get together and remind each other of the horizons that surround them; that men find business intolerable unless they can meet upon occasions like this and talk to each other of the general conceptions which run all through the lives which they are living. There is no other reason for the existence of an association like this than that. And the essential idea of an association like this is the university idea, that men get together to compare diverse opinions, to learn of diverse conditions, to give

6 From William Allen White's famous editorial in the *Emporia*, Kan., *Gazette*, Aug. 15, 1896.

each other the traveled mind. That is the business of the university.

Now there are certain specific things which the university can undertake by way of instruction, by way of definite information. For example, it can undertake the study of political and social conditions. And, as I was trying to expound at the outset of my remarks, political and social conditions are the gist of business; because, unless you understand the political situation, and more particularly the social situation, you cannot understand national taste and the processes of exchange, and you cannot be a successful merchant. You cannot know what kind of goods to send to what places unless you know a great deal about social conditions, and social conditions are often dominated by political conditions.

Now, mark you, I don't mean sociological conditions, because I don't know what sociology is (laughter); moreover I am convinced that there isn't a man living who does (laughter and applause); whenever a man is studying anything queer he calls it sociology (laughter). I guess that what is normal is good enough for me (laughter), and the best society not too good (laughter). But, for example, these people who call themselves alienists are at one of the centers of sociological inquiry (laughter). And the fellows who call themselves—I have forgotten what they call themselves,—the men who go around and live in penitentiaries and try to get the point of view of the convict, and get it so perfectly that they can never get it out of their heads afterwards. I had one of these gentlemen—one of the most expert and curiously learned of them—spend a whole evening with me in my study, and when the evening was over I was hypnotized; I felt exactly as though it would be congenial to me to go out and commit a crime (laughter); I felt a certain hunger for irregularity, and I examined my state of mind with the curiosity of a surgeon using the scalpel. Now these fellows are sociologists, and I am afraid of them (laughter); they get me in an abnormal condition; and sociology, as I understand it, is everything left over after the political economist and the student of politics are through (laughter and applause). The political economist is talking about something definite and something in particular; the student of politics is talking about something definite and something in particular; but the sociologist is talking about anything he darn pleases. He doesn't define or limit his scope in the least, and he takes all the irregular things as his special, pet product. Now I don't believe that we have anything to do with that in a commercial community. We are after the regular thing. We have a zest for the regular thing, because a large market depends on the regular thing and not on the irregular thing. We are not selling to the abnormal person, we are selling to the normal person; and so I am not speaking of the study of sociology, but the study of society and the study of social conditions. By that I mean what men wear, what they eat, what their tastes are, what kind of patterns they prefer in their coats, what kind of goods they prefer next to their skins, the kind of fashions that they have, the kind of prejudices that they have, the kind of old, wornout prepossessions that they have; all of that is pertinent to our imaginative conception of what the world is, and that is a subject matter of definite study, because men with their eyes wide open, men with the power of description and the power of explanation have gone up and down the world and found these things out for us. There is hardly a corner of the world into which at least a bicyclist won't go. There is hardly a part of the world into which some man won't go now out of sheer curiosity. He does not require any other or higher motive. He wants to go somewhere else, where nobody else has been, and the consequence is we are finding out a good deal about the dark corners of the globe. The light of information has gone into them, and there follows always the light of commerce. The moment the information comes, the commercial man is on tiptoe to know what he can sell to those people, and the moment that inquiry comes he is after his Consul and his Government to see to it that those doors that have been shut shall be open, and that commerce shall be allowed to get in there. He knows because he has read, and these fellows say, he has got something which these strange people want to buy. That is social study, and is susceptible of definite university treatment.

Then there is the study of political economy. I know that the study of political economy is not in as high repute as it once was, and that is the fault of the political economists, as Professor Laughlin[7] will admit. The political economists allowed themselves a self-indulgence. The most self-indulgent thing you can do when you get hold of a complicated study is to simplify it and say to yourself, "Now we are dealing with men in their economic relation, but it is too troublesome to bring in all the things they are likely to think about, and all the motives which

[7] James Laurence Laughlin, Professor of Political Economy at the University of Chicago.

are likely to move them: the taste of their wives; the preference they have for living in a particular region of the country; the predilection which they have for the trade of their fathers; all the sentimental things which come in; we cannot keep our books if we try to consider all those things; so we will simplify them and say that they will always follow the line of least resistance under the force of self-interest." That was the self-indulgence which the political economists allowed themselves. They said, we will reduce all this to a proposition of self-interest; all sorts of incalculable forces come into play which are not to be brought under the category of self-interest, and so political economy became an abstract science. So that one of its principal writers, John Stuart Mill, warned everybody that they were not for one moment to suppose that all of this was true in fact; that it was true in theory, but that it was not true in fact, and they were not to make the mistake of going out and passing acts of legislature according to the principles he put into his books. Men got into trouble by putting these abstract principles of political economy into statutes, because the limitation upon a statute is that it has to work; and if it is based upon too small a reckoning of human nature it is not going to work. We speak of ourselves as differing from the lower animals by reason of being rational creatures. But the rational process is the least thing about us. That is not, perhaps, a pleasant thing to think, but it is a fact. I take it that when we say that mind is king; we regard mind as one of the modern constitutional monarchs who reigns but does not govern. There is a great tumultuous House of Commons made up of the passions which really runs the government, and the Prime Minister is the principal passion of the moment. It may be the money-getting passion; it may be the humanitarian passion; but it is a passion, and it is not rationalistic. It is not based upon the processes of logic, and government in all its institutions is intended for human nature, of which, as Burke profanely said, "The reason is the least part." And so we must understand human life in its complexity by social study along with the economical study, the two pieced together, in order to make a complete man for our consideration.

There is another thing that we can study. We can study that very interesting thing which is of comparatively recent creation. I mean economic geography,—the geography which divides the world up according to its products, according to what its soils produce, according to the place where its minerals are deposited, according to the various uses which it makes of its woods, and of all the things which are native and natural to it. Economic geography is, as it were, the map of the world for the student of commerce. It is also the map of the world for the student of human life in general, because, although I believe and profoundly believe in the regnancy of the human spirit, nevertheless everybody must admit that the economic rootages are among the most vital rootages of human life, and that according to a man's environments so is his life; that his economic condition governs his thought in nine cases out of ten. I had a long conversation the other day with a gentleman who was one of the most interesting interviewers that I ever had visit me. He came to interview me, but I found that he liked to talk, and I interviewed him, and I think he went away with the impression that he had got my ideas, when he had only exploited his own. One of his ideas was this, that you can judge the reliability of a man by the latitude in which you find him. He maintained that lying was inevitable south of the 23rd parallel, and not knowing that I was from south of Mason and Dixon's line, he began to offer me his theory about the habits of mind of our southern people. He said, "Now you take a Southerner"—which interested me very much—"a Southerner has a self-indulgent habit of mind, which leads to his rhetorical use of language, because it is a great deal easier to state a thing vaguely and grandiloquently and with all the handsome flowers of speech than to state it precisely and come down to business. It costs a decided effort to make the mind a tool of precision, and your Southerner won't brace himself up to that effort, and so he fires at the mark, but he hits all around it as well as the mark itself. He fires with bird shot instead of with a rifle, and he brings down the game, but then he peppers the whole countryside in the process (laughter). That is a pure indication of indolence, and all you have to do is to increase that indolence a little bit, and you come to the belt of liars." (Laughter.) "For example, a Filipino cannot tell the truth, and it is for this reason. You ask him tonight, 'Will you do a certain job for me in the morning?' and, the line of least resistance is for him to say yes, because it saves him trouble. When the morning comes the easiest thing to do is not to do it, just to stay where he is. He is not deliberately lying; it is the condition of the climate. (Laughter.) The climate has taken out of him the snap that there is in the truth." A very interesting theory of the morals of our fellow men which goes Buckle just one better. Buckle thought that men were made by the mountains that were around them and the plains that spread about them, and the heat and the cold of the climate in which they lived, and he thought that the Italian was no less moral than the Norwegian, though he had different habits in respect to various matters; that it was altogether a question of the influence of climate. Well, now, it is not merely a question of the climate, but the climate has a tremendous lot to do with it; and all the economic conditions which the climate and the products of the soil produce have a great deal to do with it; and all of these things are susceptible of definite study.

But it seems to me, gentlemen, that there is one thing with which the university can govern all of these things. After all, I suppose that in our sober, reflective moments we know that the object of life is not merely to set forward any particular piece of business, but that all pieces of business dovetail and fit and consort together, and that the real task that every man has set for himself is to give himself integrity of spirit and of purpose. The most pleasing thing to me about university life is that men are licked into something like the same shape in respect of the principles with which they go out into the world; the ideals of conduct, the ideals of truthful comradeship, the ideals of loyalty, the ideals of co-operation, the sense of *esprit de corps*, the feeling that they are men of a common country and put into it for a common service. After all, when you have got that into a man you have got the root of the matter into him; you have got that one idealizing element which it is very difficult for the mere knockabout, hard experience of the world to give a man. If you put a man out into the world without first steadying him after that fashion, he is apt to think, is he not, that the hand of all the world is against him, and that the thing for him to do is to take every advantage against the world as the world seems to take every advantage against him? If he has never climbed some height of observation on which he can see the whole map of life, he is apt to stumble along its paths like a man without a direction and not to know what the end of his journey is. I believe that you will find that every great man of business has got somewhere, whether at the university or by his own birthright, a touch of the idealist in him, and that it is this touch of the idealist that makes the man, this conception of conduct as a whole, this love of integrity for its own sake, this idea of what he owes to the man in the other business, and to his rival or comrade in the same business, this feeling of the subtle linking of all men together, and behind it all the country itself, the country's welfare, the progress of America, and all the dear ideals which we are ready to leave our business for and give our lives to vindicate.[8]

Commercial Club of Chicago, *"The Relation of University Education to Commerce," Address by Woodrow Wilson, LL.D., President of Princeton University, November the Twenty-Ninth MCMII* (Chicago, 1902).
[8] There are two WWhw outlines of this address, both dated Nov. 29, 1902, in WP, DLC.

From Andrew Fleming West

Dear Wilson,   Rome Nov. 29 1902

Your very welcome letter, "machine-made" but autographic all the same, greeted me on arriving at the Eternal City.[1] Of course I realized the overwhelming mass of work that has fallen on you at the very start and hardly see where you found time to write at all outside the circle of your necessary engagements. So your good long letter was doubly appreciated. By the way don't mind this pen I am using. It is one of those soft-nibbed wobbling-pointed pseudo-gold pens, made of some base mixture of yellowish metals. By pushing down hard I can double it up any time.

But this is indeed a digression. I had a remarkable time in Berlin, of which I will tell you all when I get back. Only a few days, but so full of the richest experience. David Magie and George Howe came up from Halle and we had a capital time together for two days. Then I went to Leipzig and saw Professor Brugmann.[2] Then to Halle, where I stayed in the same house with our two gallant Princetonians—moreover, a house rendered forever sacred as the actual abode of Jesse Carter and [William Kelly] Prentice when they were in Halle. Professor Wissowa[3] is very genial, friendly and inspiring, and is full of goodwill and encouragement for our two classical representatives now there. Then I went to Nuremberg. How it riveted and rooted me fast! There is some spell over the place—the distilled essence of medieval romance, the Master Singers, Albert Durer, the Reformation, —all etherealized, impalpable,—but ever present. You turn a corner—and lo! a great round tower and the quaint old city walls—gray, with red tiled tops. Again you go in the busy market place—and there are the old booths with the picturesque peasant women selling their wares. Across the way is a richly decorated bronze fountain and back of all the twin-spired cathedral. Crooked streets, high peaked houses, substantial burghers. It is like a scene from the *Meistersinger*.

Then to Munich, then to Verona, the Lago di Garda, Bologna with its ancient University, Ravenna in desolate splendor, Rimini,—and now Rome. I am stunned by Rome. All else fades as the vision of the central city of history slowly re-forms as you gaze on the ruins. The long procession of events and influences that defiles into Rome from the older past,—converging, blending, re-arranging in new orders,—and then defiles out of Rome, diverging every whither into the medieval and modern world!

Who is sufficient for these things! Everywhere as you look at the place, the older city—the base and support of all the later periods—seems trying to push itself up to the light of modern day in a thousand places,—here fully emerging, there barely suggesting its presence by some inscription or fragment, and in many places still concealed. The old city is the material counterpart to all else—the stage and scenery, with the old actors gone,— or hovering around as memories, like the portraits of famous players that decorate the halls or *foyer* of some famous theatre. Now this is all trite, commonplace, flat and obvious,—but eternally true.

I have seen some very interesting men here—among them Father [Franz] Ehrle, the Prefect of the Vatican Library, Monsignor [Denis Joseph] O'Connell, formerly Head of the American Catholic College, Lanciani the archaeologist,[4] Rushforth, Director of the British School,[5] Huelsen of the German Institute,[6] and so on.

Tonight I start for Paris—stopping there a week. Then to London, where I sail December 11th on the *Minneapolis*, arriving in New York December 20th to 22nd.

I am glad to hear the Faculty Committees are to be reorganized. It is hopeless to do much till this step is taken. As for the Committee on the Graduate School I shall of course be glad to have you change that, if you think best. It is very good as it is, though perhaps it may be advisable to add one or two. I tremble as I think of the housecleaning that has been left for you to do. But in whatever way I can be of help, call on me for anything you want me to do, and you will find me ready.

I have kept notes during the journey, most of all on the Graduate College, and the tutorial question. But I have tried to keep an eye open for anything of use to Princeton from vines, trees, and flowers, to methods of teaching—and the secrets of professorial greatness.

Never have I seen so much in a short time—and never have I

had so good a chance to learn. I am glad you want twelve and a half millions. To want great things is the first step toward getting them. Let me help whenever I can. Remember me to Mrs. Wilson.

Ever yours   Andrew F. West

ALS (WP, DLC).
    1 It is missing.
    2 Karl Brugmann (1849-1919), Professor of Indo-Germanic Philology at the University of Leipzig.
    3 Georg Wissowa (1859-1931), Professor in the Philosophical Faculty at Halle.
    4 Rodolfo Amadeo Lanciani (1847-1929), Italian archaeologist and authority on ancient Rome.
    5 Gordon McNeil Rushforth (1862-1938), Director of the British School at Rome, a center for the study of classical history, art, and archaeology.
    6 Christian Carl Friedrich Huelsen (1858-1935), Secretary of the German Archaeological Institute at Rome.

From Henry Cooper Pitney, Jr.

Dear Mr. President: [Morristown, N. J.] Nov. 29, 1902.

I have duly received your kind letter of November 26th asking on what date our celebration will fall.

Our celebration will be held on Monday February 23d, which under the statute will be the legal holiday. So we shall expect you on Monday and not on Saturday.

It is our custom to report stenographically and print the address of this occasion for circulation among our members. I presume you will not object to our following this custom.

Anticipating the pleasure of your presence here,

I am,   Very truly yours,   [Henry C. Pitney, Jr.]

CCL (Washington Association of N. J., Morristown, N. J.).

A News Report of an Address to the Chicago Commercial Club

[Nov. 30, 1902]

WILSON WOULD BAR TECHNICAL COURSES
Says They Should Not Be Given Place
in Universities.

President Woodrow Wilson of Princeton university declared last evening in an address before the Commercial club, in the banquet hall of the Auditorium hotel, that in his opinion technical schools had no place in universities.

Coming from the head of one of the most important institutions of higher education in the country, this attack on the present tendency to bring almost every kind of school under university government startled the gathering of representative Chicagoans. In view of repeated attempts by President [William R.] Harper to bring about the affiliation of the Armour Institute of Technology with the University of Chicago, and of the plans of Northwestern university for the establishment in the near future of a school of technology and other departments of the kind, the statements of President Wilson had special significance to his auditors.

President [Edmund J.] James of Northwestern university and several trustees of that institution; J. Ogden Armour, the special patron of Armour institute, and Dean Harry Pratt Judson and other representatives of the University of Chicago, were among those who listened to the limitations laid down by President Wilson. It was apparent that they did not agree entirely with all the ideas expressed by the speaker. . . .

President Wilson was the speaker of the evening at the monthly dinner of the Commercial club. He sat at the right of President David B. Jones of the club, at the speakers' table. At the left of President Jones was the Rev. Dr. W. R. Notman, pastor of the Fourth Presbyterian church. President James of Northwestern university, President [Edward D.] Eaton of Beloit college, President [Richard D.] Harlan of Lake Forest university, and Professor [J. Laurence] Laughlin of the University of Chicago were also at the speakers' table. President Jones made a brief address in introducing President Wilson, and the Rev. Dr. Notman was called upon after the address of Dr. Wilson. . . .

President Wilson was entertained at a luncheon given at the Chicago club by C. H. McCormick and David B. Jones at 1 o'clock Saturday afternoon. Twenty guests were present.

Printed in the Chicago *Inter Ocean*, Nov. 30, 1902; some editorial headings omitted.

Francis Wayland Shepardson's[1] Review of
A History of the American People

[Dec. 1, 1902]

A NEW HISTORY OF THE AMERICAN PEOPLE*

President Woodrow Wilson's "History of the American People" is in many ways like an expanded and illustrated five-volume

* A HISTORY OF THE AMERICAN PEOPLE. By Woodrow Wilson. In five volumes, illustrated, New York: Harper & Brothers.

[1] Historian and Secretary to the President of the University of Chicago.

edition of Professor Goldwin Smith's "The United States." Such a statement refers, of course, in no particular to subject matter, but rather to method of treatment; the author's plan, apparently, having been not to enter into details regarding the occurrences in the western world between 1492 and 1900, discussing each one in chronological sequence, but rather to attempt to give a correct interpretation of important events, to give a judicial estimate of the relative value of particular topics, to declare the real influence of leaders of life, considering the four centuries as a part of the world's history.

If such a purpose on the part of the author be fairly assumed —there is no preface indicating any plan and the volumes must speak for themselves—then it is safe to say that this History will be much better appreciated by those who have read widely about American men and measures, who are more or less familiar with details, and therefore are better equipped to enjoy a philosophical analysis and review, than by those who will turn to it for first information about America. In other words one can not help feeling that the reader who is unacquainted with the details of wars and presidential administrations, party problems and personal prejudices, will find the History a disappointment, after the pleasure of examining the pictures is past.

By the former class, on the other hand, the five volumes will be studied with much satisfaction, giving as they do approved modern judgment of the great questions and great men of American origin, the scholarly character of the author lending weight to his carefully-worded sentences. The last portion, covering the years from 1865 to 1900, will not be accepted by every reader with the same grace accorded the earlier narration; but even sharp differences of opinion regarding estimates of measures and men of our own time, will not prevent general recognition of the success of the author's attempt to review the work of the four centuries in judicial language and lofty tone.

The most striking first impression from an examination of the work is that the illustrations are remarkable, both for variety and unvarying excellence. They embrace representative selections from almost every possible source. There are pictures of persons, contemporary prints, idealized scenes. There are facsimiles of documents and signatures, reproductions of the title-pages of famous books and pamphlets, or of rare campaign posters and tickets. There are views of the homes of many leaders, and pictures showing the progress of invention. There are excellent maps and interesting plans, all these making a great collection of nearly eight hundred illustrations, scattered unevenly throughout the volumes and combining to give powerful aid to the narration. Some of the pictures are far out of relationship to the immediate text, and two of them might well have been omitted, since the American people do not care to perpetuate the memory of features or names of those who assassinate presidents. It is unfortunate that the title "Cumberland Gap near Wheeling Virginia" should be used in one case (III, 241), an error closely associated with a statement (III, 245) that the national road was built through the Cumberland Gap to the Ohio, when long usage has attached that geographical designation to an opening in the mountains a good ways south of Wheeling and the course of the Cumberland road.

A second impression, and a strong one too, is that there is a lack of proportion in the History. There are five volumes, averaging three hundred and fifty pages, with 1689, 1781, 1829, 1865, and 1900 as terminal points. Of the eighteen hundred and forty-eight pages eight hundred and nineteen are taken up with the story of colonial times. One hundred and six pages (fifty-six of text and fifty of pictures) are used to describe the Revolutionary War: while the Civil War is passed in fifty-four pages, sixteen of these being given to illustrations. The Mexican War is finished in three pages. In the vista of years the operations of the Ku Klux Klan in Reconstruction times surely will not seem of commanding importance, and yet they are accorded three and a half pages,—the amount of text space taken to discuss the Jay Treaty of 1794, Burr's Conspiracy, Decatur's achievements in the Mediterranean, and the Missouri Compromise, all together. The Louisiana Purchase is described in fewer words than is Bryan's free silver campaign. The Trent affair, and the military movement culminating at Gettysburg in what has been called one of the world's decisive battles, are each given half a page, while the disturbance created by Sitting Bull commands as much space as these two together. And yet it must be said, that while the average reader will notice the scant treatment accorded certain events in their chronological sequence, the one who forgets details and seeks the philosophical analysis of history, the logical relationship of cause and effect, will find elsewhere in some chapter of summary review the points omitted in their natural order.

The earlier part of the narration seems most matured. There is a charm of style which is irresistible, the illustrations are very helpful, and it is doubtful whether there exists another so interesting account of the "swarming of the English" and the gradual approach of these English to the Revolution of 1776. The later part discusses topics of our own times upon which the minds of men are yet divided. The four million eight hundred thousand voters who favored Mr. Blaine in 1884 will hardly be satisfied with the treatment accorded him as compared with that of the one who, although elected, was credited with but sixty-two thousand more of the popular vote. The almost constant condemnation of the Republican party of a whole generation, and the evident leaning toward the Democratic policies and leaders, notably Mr. Cleveland, will not be relished by others, even by those who will accept as probably correct the judgments on Reconstruction measures of the Republican radicals. It is extremely difficult to be absolutely unbiased upon those themes associated with the actions and motives of men now living; and yet whatever the reader's personal view may be, the pages devoted to later American history will be found extremely interesting and suggestive.

In all likelihood the chapters which deal with the Jacksonian period will be considered the best of all. The dominating presence of masterful men is felt, and one catches the spirit of the times from the flowing sentences whose graceful words paint speaking portraits. Something of the charm of the style is shown in this characterization of Daniel Webster:

"Mr. Hayne's sentences rode high, upon rhetoric that sought often an adventurous flight; Mr. Webster used words as if he meant only to clarify and strengthen the thoughts he touched and cared nothing for cadence or ornament. And yet he spread them in ranks so fair that they caught and held the eye like a pageant. Beauty came upon them as they moved as if out of the mere passion of the thought rather than by the design of the orator. And he himself gave to the eye, as he stood, in his own person the same image of clean-cut strength, beautiful only by reason of its perfect action, so square was he, massive, and indomitable, and with a head and face whose mass, whose calm breadth above the deep-set slumbrous eyes, seemed the fittest possible throne for the powers he displayed."

But the beauty of the imagery does not give strength to the account of the Jacksonian era; it is rather the apparent justness of the judgments. Taking a dozen topics of the middle period and examining the treatment of each, the reader feels that the decision of history in the light of modern criticism is here rightly recorded. The story of the reign of King Andrew is splendidly told; the difference between the democracy of Jefferson and that of Jackson is clearly set forth; the certain catastrophe is strikingly described; and the survivals of the wreck are plainly marked for permanent mementos of a personal regime. If only Jackson had been scored unmercifully for the results of his career, the account would be perfect, but even now one seems to hesitate to blame him for actions which in any other man would lead to severest criticism.

Many other portions of the History might be mentioned in particular,—Jackson's view of the court, his view of the constitution, the explanation of his attitude toward South Carolina, the discussion of the effect of slavery upon the South, the splendid chapter reviewing the Southern Confederacy,—but enough has been said. Here are five volumes by a clear-headed student of American affairs which are suggestive and interesting, filled with striking sentences, and convincing in their thoughtful declarations. They make a notable addition to that variety of the literature of American history already rich in the contributions of writers like McMaster and Fiske and Rhodes.

FRANCIS WAYLAND SHEPARDSON.

Printed in the Chicago *Dial*, XXXIII (Dec. 1, 1902), 393-95.

Notes for an Address to the Presbyterian Union of New York[1]

Presbyterian Union   1 Dec., 1902

The Future of Princeton?
> You will not wish me to speak of her *material* future. I am to report on that next week to my constituents.[2]
> Its spiritual future?
>> Its *intellectual and spiritual* future
>> The age of battle is past, the age of peace and accommodation has come. Doubt is no longer militant,—neither is dogmatic belief.
>> Not because materialism has triumphed,—the swing of the pendulum is the other way, rather.
>>> Signs of the times.
Function of the University, mediation (other notes)
> A definite belief.
Natural Presbyterian alliance

WWhw MS. (WP, DLC).
[1] About this organization, see WW to N. C. Rogers, Nov. 24, 1901, n. 1, Vol. 12.
[2] When he was to speak to the New York alumni on December 9, 1902. The text of his address is printed at that date.

A News Report of a Dinner in New York

[Dec. 2, 1902]

PRESBYTERIAN UNION DINNER.

Nearly five hundred members of the Presbyterian Union sat down to the annual dinner of the organization in the Hotel Savoy last evening. It was "Princeton Night," and the exercises were arranged with a view to honoring Princeton University. That was because the Rev. Dr. Henry van Dyke, Moderator of the General Assembly,[1] is a Princeton man.

Dr. Van Dyke was absent, however, on account of the illness of his wife. Robert C. Ogden presided, and the speakers were President Woodrow Wilson of the university, President Francis L. Patton of Princeton Theological Seminary, and Dr. St. Clair McKelway of Brooklyn. Among those seated at the guest table were John Wanameker [Wanamaker], the Rev. Dr. W. H. Roberts,[2] the Rev. Dr. William K. Hall,[3] the Rev. Daniel Russell, Jr., Moderator of the New York Presbytery;[4] the Rev. Dr. S. Alexander,[5] Alexander P. Ketchum,[6] Warner Van Norden,[7] J. J. McCook, William N. Crane,[8] and James Yereance.[9]

President Wilson said that he did not know that a union of churches could be expected in the immediate future, but that a spirit of live and let live was coming, and that he saw the prospect of admitting, to the heathen at least, that we all worshipped the same God; that we were really all Christians, and not angry at one another; but that it was a spiritual amusement for us to split hairs. He said he thought that the university should give a free rein to inquiry in a reverent spirit.

Dr. Patton said that evangelical Christianity was the issue of the day; that the pendulum had swung far toward the metaphysical side, and that it would return toward the human or natural side of the various questions of theology.

Printed in the *New York Times*, Dec. 2, 1902; one editorial heading omitted.

[1] Of the Presbyterian Church in the U.S.A.
[2] Stated Clerk of the General Assembly of the Presbyterian Church in the U.S.A.
[3] Pastor of the First Presbyterian Church of Newburgh, N. Y.
[4] And pastor of the Harlem Presbyterian Church in New York.
[5] Actually, the Rev. Dr. George Alexander, pastor of the University Place Presbyterian Church in New York.
[6] Alexander Phoenix Ketchum, lawyer of New York.
[7] New York banker.
[8] Flour merchant of New York.
[9] Manager of the Equitable Life Assurance Society.

To Bliss Perry

My dear Perry: Princeton, New Jersey. 3 December, 1902.

It is very kind of you to wish to show me so interesting an attention while I am in Boston to speak to the Twentieth Century Club,[1] and, of course, I cannot resist such an invitation. The only thing that makes me hesitate is that I must be back as far as New York on my way home that evening. You will know the train times, as I do not. I believe there is a well known five o'clock train, is there not, which puts a man into New York in comfortable time for bed. If so, I will have to take that train. But that will leave plenty of time for a not too hurried luncheon, and I am sure that I shall enjoy it very much indeed. I have been so rushed of late that I have not had any conversation with Mr. Tedcastle about what he wants me to do when I am in Boston, but Mrs. Tedcastle's health is very delicate indeed, and I feel very sure that such an appointment as you suggest would not interfere with his plans.

I am pretty tired from the long jaunt that I have just made for the purpose of making two or three speeches; but I shall hope by the time January comes around to be fit again.

With warmest regard from us both to you all,

Faithfully yours,   Woodrow Wilson

TLS (B. Perry Papers, MH).
    [1] Notes for this address are printed at Dec. 29, 1902, a news report of it at Jan. 3, 1903.

To Elijah Richardson Craven

Princeton, New Jersey.
My dear Dr. Craven: 3 December, 1902.

So far as my own convenience is concerned, it would be perfectly agreeable to have the meeting of the Committee on the Curriculum, of which you speak, on the afternoon of Wednesday, the 10th, the day preceding the meeting of the Board.

A complete reorganization of the Committees of the Faculty is in progress, and while this does not, of course, include the special Committee which was appointed last year to confer with the Special Committee on the Curriculum,[1] it does involve what directly concerns the business of that Committee, namely, a reconsideration of the whole matter of the courses of study. You will remember that the Committee of the Faculty reached a definite set of conclusions with regard to the recommendations made last year br [by] Dr. Patton. These conclusions were presented at the last meeting of the Special Committee on the Curriculum. There has been no further discussion of the matter either in the Faculty or in its Committee, and I know that there is a very general desire on the part of the Faculty that these particular recommendations should be laid aside until the Faculty shall have had time for mature deliberation to present for the consideration of the Board a new scheme of studies. I should hope, therefore, that it would be possible, without disobedience to the instructions of the Board, to postpone the business of the Special Committee on the Curriculum indefinitely, or else to ask the Board for its discharge, in view of the radical change of the circumstances of the case.[2]

It seems to me very important that Committee meetings should not be held on the morning of the meeting of the Board, unless it is certain that no matter of importance is to come up for consideration. I know of no matter of importance awaiting the consideration of the regular standing Committee on the Curriculum, and, therefore, shall not urge that this time the meeting take place on Wednesday. I think it proper to add that I have just received a notice from Mr. S. Bayard Dod that there will be a meeting of the Committee on Morals and Discipline on the morning of the 11th, at ten-thirty.

With much regard,

Very sincerely yours, Woodrow Wilson

TLS (Trustees' Papers, UA, NjP).

[1] About the appointment and work of this Special Committee on the Curriculum of the Board of Trustees, see n. 2 to the Princeton University Faculty Minutes printed at Jan. 29, 1902, Vol. 12.

[2] As the note just mentioned points out, the Board of Trustees, at their meeting on December 11, 1902, approved the request of the Special Committee on the Curriculum that it be discharged.

A Tribute and an Address

[c. Dec. 3, 1902]

The Faculty of Princeton University.
In Reference to the Resignation of Dr. Patton
and the election of President Wilson.

Although the resignation of the Rev. Dr. Francis Landey Patton as President of the University and the election of Dr. Woodrow Wilson as his successor in office are events which have taken place in a region beyond the province of this Faculty; yet no portion of the academic body is more directly affected by them, and they call for an expression of sentiment on our part more intimate and more appreciative than any of the other tributes which they are evoking from the Alumni and from the general public.

The retirement of Dr. Patton in the midst of his labors and honors came simply as a surprise, not explained by anything in the cordial relations existing between himself and his colleagues and only relieved by his assurance, that he wished to be freed from administrative cares and enabled to devote himself to the more congenial work of a teacher and author in his chosen department of study. While we acquiesce in this view, as we must, we are made sensible of a loss, which cannot be easily estimated.

As President of the University during the past fourteen years, Dr. Patton has conducted an administration which has been both brilliant and successful. It has marked the epoch, when the college, after long periods of healthy growth, attained mature age at the sesquicentennial celebration in 1896, and with stately ceremony took its place among the Universities of Christendom. It has adorned the campus with such buildings as the new Library Hall, the new Literary Halls, Alexander Hall, The Dodd and The Brown Dormitories, Blair Hall, the two Stafford Little Dormitories, the Dodge Annex to Murray Hall, the Brokaw Memorial and Alumni Gymnasium. It has doubled the enrollment of students and more than doubled the number of Professors, including among them graduates distinguished as authors, thinkers and investigators. It has knit together the Alumni as one loyal body in a true republic of learning by making them sharers in the government as well as in the privileges of the University.[1] It has enriched the curriculum with a variety of new studies, equipped the Library with endowed Seminaries for special reading and completed the undergraduates Schools of Letters, of Science, and of Art, with a new Graduate School for the promotion of expert scholarship and original research. And it has kept aloft our traditional standard of sound learning[,] pure science and true philosophy above the empirical methods which are menacing the higher education of our day. Of all this large and rich development of academic life Dr. Patton has been the fortunate leader and exponent, and with his name it will ever justly be associated.

As President of the Faculty Dr. Patton has been distinguished by his unfailing courtesy to his colleagues, by his scrupulous fairness in conducting discussion and debate, by his skill and acuteness in sifting the complex educational problems which have come before us, by his liberal aims in combining the Literary with the Scientific courses and in expanding the elective studies, by his readiness to accept advice and cooperation within his own official sphere, and by his intelligent effort to keep the views of the Faculty in accord with those natural to his more public position and wider field of observation. He has favored a policy at once academic and practical, and without depreciating scholarship, has also valued the generous culture incident to University life.

As the Professor of Ethics and the Philosophy of of [*sic*] Religion he has shown rare logical skill, acumen, and familiarity with living issue; and has also begun to make valuable contributions, to this department which it is too soon to estimate. We congratulate ourselves that, in this important professorship, he is to continue among us as a colleague; and we also congratulate Dr. Patton as now the honored head of a neighboring institution, in which he may illustrate the orthodoxy of Princeton Seminary in harmony with the liberality of Princeton University.[2]

This record of his services should not be closed without acknowledging the notable manner in which Dr. Patton has represented us before the public especially by his eloquent sermons in the Chapel, by his stirring appeals at the Alumni meetings, and by the scholarly grace and charm of his addresses at academical functions. Nor should we fail to do honor to the moral self-conquest which has enabled him when he deemed the time for his retirement had come to place what he considered the good of the University above every other consideration.

The immediate accession of President Wilson, without a trace of friction in the process, has already been hailed with general approval in which the Faculty have special reason to join. We are welcoming to the Presidency, not merely a graduate with an enthusiastic following of the Alumni, not merely a scholar imbued with the Princeton spirit, but also a colleague who for ten years has shared our counsels and has been trained as one of ourselves in the service of his Alma Mater. And all the elements of the new leadership are in the line of our best traditions. A layman whose Christian faith can have no polemic mission, he simply expresses that catholicity which was potential in our very charter and was fitted to save us from any form of clericalism inconsistent with the University spirit. Of Southern birth and Northern training, with an academic experience gained in the Universities of Virginia, Connecticut, Maryland, Pennsylvania and New Jersey, he only joins a succession of Presidents who have represented the national indistinction from the provincial type of American learning. No mere recluse student, but already a distinguished author whose historical and political writings are known throughout the country, he illustrates afresh that public spirit which impelled the patriot Witherspoon to make Nassau Hall a school of statesman [statesmen] as well as a nursery of divines. With such precedents we may join him in the pledge, that "the men who spring from our loins shall trace their lineage to the founders of the republic."

The Faculty have pleasure in assuring President Wilson of their cordial support and co-operation and look forward confidently to a new era of prosperity under his administration.

Committee.
{
Charles W. Shields.
Henry B. Cornwall.
S. R. Winans.
Alexander T. Ormond.
Andrew F. West.[3]
}

HwS MS. (WP, DLC).

[1] A reference to the institution of alumni representation on the Board of Trustees. About this matter, see n. 1 to the notes for a talk printed at Nov. 21, 1901, Vol. 12.

[2] Patton had been elected first President of Princeton Theological Seminary on October 14, 1902.

[3] This tribute and address was spread on the Princeton University Faculty Minutes for Dec. 3, 1902, and was printed in the *Princeton University Bulletin*, XIV (Dec. 1902), 34-36. West's name was later stricken from the list of signers, presumably at his request, because he was out of the country at the time the document was written and had not seen or signed it before its adoption.

From the Minutes of the Princeton Academic Faculty

4 p.m. December 3, 1902

The Faculty met, the President presiding. . . .

The Committee to propose Rules of Order presented the following report, the recommendations of which were adopted:

"Your Committee appointed to propose Rules of Order for the Academic Faculty respectfully recommend that the Faculty adopt Reed's Rules of Order, with the following modifications:

§§ 205, 207. A motion to reconsider may be made at the meeting in which the original vote was taken, or at the next meeting by anyone present when the vote was taken who did not vote in the minority.

§ 40. The presiding officer shall have the same right of debate as other members, and need not yield the chair while speaking.

§ 215. The maker of a motion shall be permitted to close the debate on that motion even after the previous question has been voted.

§ 215. A member may speak a second time on a motion in order to clear a matter of fact or to explain himself in some material part of his first speech.

§ 87. When the Faculty goes into Committee of the Whole the officers of the Committee shall be those of the Faculty. The motion to go into Committee of the Whole is not debatable.

§ 46. Reports of Committees containing matters which should be of record shall be in writing. Unless otherwise ordered these reports shall be placed on file and only the recommendations in them which are adopted shall be recorded in the minutes."[1]

The Faculty then adjourned.

Attest.   W. F. Magie   Clerk

[1] The same action was taken later this same day by the University Faculty.

A News Item

[Dec. 3, 1902]

SHAKESPEAREAN READING

Dr. Horace Howard Furness, of Wallingford, Pa., will give a reading of Shakespeare's "Twelfth Night" in Alexander Hall this evening at 8 o'clock. Dr. Furness graduated from Harvard in the class of 1854, and has received the degrees of Doctor of Philosophy from the University of Halle, Doctor of Literature from Columbia, and Doctor of Laws from Harvard. Besides being an authority on legal subjects, Dr. Furness is considered the greatest Shakespearean scholar in the world, and is the editor of the "New Variorum" edition of Shakespeare of which eleven volumes have already been published. Each volume contains copious notes, together with a condensation of the best criticisms made by Shakespearean scholars, and the series is the most authoritative work of its kind. With his keen sense of humor, Dr. Furness will surely bring out effectively all the grotesque and humorous passages of the comedy which he has selected for his reading to-night.

Dr. Furness was especially asked to lecture before the University, by President Wilson, and will probably read the entire book of "Twelfth Night." . . .

Printed in the *Daily Princetonian*, Dec. 3, 1902; one editorial heading omitted.

A News Report of an Address to the Baltimore Presbyterian Union

[Dec. 5, 1902]

PRESBYTERIANS BANQUET
President Wilson, Of Princeton,
The Guest Of Honor.

The dinner given last night in the banquet room of Music Hall by the Presbyterian Union was voted an unqualified success in every particular by the participants. The union is composed of laymen among the Presbyterians of the city and is designed to promote sociability and fellowship among the members of the different churches. The union holds four meetings annually, two of which are dinners and one a supper. The fourth is the regular business meeting. The affair last night was the first dinner of the present year. . . .

In introducing the guest of honor President Woodrow Wilson, of Princeton University, President [Edward Herrick] Griffin[1] said that when the question of selecting a speaker for the occasion arose there was but one opinion among the members as to the most desirable person to obtain, and the general expression was: "If we can only get that man." President Griffin said: "We have got that man, and now I have the pleasure of introducing him to you."

As President Wilson arose the applause was spontaneous and loud and every member and guest arose to his feet and continued cheering for several minutes. When quiet was partially restored the speaker began. He received the most flattering attention during the whole of his address.

He spoke in part as follows:

"I am not yet familiar with the plans of Princeton University. No man can foretell its future. The immensity of that future and the tremendous capacity for action and momentum contained in the body of its alumni is something beyond the comprehension of the ordinary mind. There is no mistaking the plans and hopes of Princeton University. Under its charter there's no possibility of any intimate and organic union with the church. That instrument declares in its first clause that there shall be no denominational distinctions. It is a matter of duty not to recognize one creed above another. But it happened that the men who founded the university were for the most part of the creed of the Scotch and Scotch-Irish Church, and the institution was started with a definite purpose, and there is no danger that we will depart from that purpose. The day of the battle of creeds is past. Many say it is because the creeds of today are not of the militant quality. I do not so read the signs of the times. I do not think there is any subsidence of spiritual power, but there is a great metamorphosis. Men are known today and pointed out, not for the money they have made or success in business, but for what they have done for the cause of education and what they have given of their wealth for the uplifting of the human race.

"Some men are making a great effort to shorten the term in the colleges.[2] They say, and perhaps with truth, that the sophomore of the present has advanced as far in his studies as his grandfather had when he graduated, but the greatest part of what a man learns at college is not in the classroom. I sometimes think it is the least part that he learns there. A man cannot get the saturation of the atmosphere of the place that is the real education. The university is a place for free thought, not in the usual sense which I think should be called loose thought. A man to be completely educated should be put through a rounded representation of the pieces of knowledge. An exclusively classical education dwarfs a man, but so does an exclusively scientific one. Man is ruled by a tumultuous congress of his passions, and his master passion is the presi[d]ent of the congress."

Printed in the Baltimore *Sun*, Dec. 5, 1902; some editorial headings omitted.

[1] Wilson's old friend, Dean of the College Faculty of The Johns Hopkins University.

[2] Among them being Nicholas Murray Butler, new President of Columbia University. See n. 2 to the news report printed at Dec. 13, 1902.

A News Report of an Address in Newark

[Dec. 6, 1902]

WOODROW WILSON PRINCIPAL SPEAKER
AT HIGH SCHOOL TEACHERS' BANQUET
Education at a University

President Woodrow Wilson, of Princeton University, delivered an address on "The Meaning of a University Education" before the New Jersey High School Teachers' Association at the four-teenth semi-annual banquet of the society in the Continental Hotel last night. The attendance was large, and Dr. Wilson was received with enthusiasm. A reception in the hotel parlors pre-ceded the dinner. I. W. Travell, president of the association, in introducing Dr. Wilson, congratulated his hearers on the fact that they had an opportunity to listen to such an eminent edu-cator as the head of Princeton.

Dr. Wilson said that it was one of the privileges of his new office that he could make new friendships. He hoped, he said, that the friendships he would make among the members of the association to whom he was speaking would be lasting, as there was no difference in the professions to which they belonged in the educational world.

"I have delivered five addresses this week," said Dr. Wilson, "and so I ask your indulgence if I am not very forceful. I am reminded of Rufus Choate, who was asked, after some strenuous labors, whether he thought his constitution would stand it. 'Oh, bless you,' he said, 'I've exhausted my constitution long ago, and I'm now living on my bylaws.' So that is the way I feel; I am working on my bylaws to-night.

"There was an old minister down in Tennessee, a very power-ful, robust man, with a heavy voice. In church, one Sunday, he spent a quarter of an hour praying for power. After the service one of the deacons took the dominie aside and said to him: 'Look here, parson, you don't want to pray for power, you want to pray for idees.' And so to-night," went on Dr. Wilson, "I feel that I must pray for ideas."

"It is an age in which we must live by ideas as well as by ideals. I do not wonder, sometimes, that men think a college education a poor thing. They are men who have made great things of their lives without that college education, and they cannot see the need of it. It is easy to abuse things of which we know nothing. As long as men will do this, so long will there be the difference of opinion regarding the value of university training.

"The men who say that a college education is of no value are men who have never had a college education. How are they qualified to testify about it. They would not be admitted as wit-nesses in a court of justice to tell of something of which they knew nothing.

"I have every sympathy with a man who is hesitating about sending his boy to college. It is a serious matter to take four years out of a young man's life, between the ages of eighteen and twenty-two, if they are not to become years of preparation, years to be of service in the future.

"Some young men go to college for fun, and they have a great deal of it there. Others go because of social conventions. Their father went, their grandfather went and their great-grandfather went, and so they must go that the traditions of the family may be preserved. These are the men we have trouble in getting through.

"Many go to college for an education, and if they do not get it the effort is not worth the four years of time. We must show four years of a consistent and integral part of life to make the college education worth while. We must justify the existence of the university by showing it to be a part of the world.

"The universities used to be cloisters, places where men shut themselves away from the world that they might pore over books. But why should a man do this. I am more and more convinced that carnal man has [was] never intended to sit down and read books. I protest against the number of books I am compelled to read. I begin the perusal of a book unwillingly, but I read on until I am beguiled by some subtle power of the author, to proceed, by some spell which he has cast over the pages. I read to find the zest and pleasure that others found in the book.

"I positively resent some books that are thrust upon me; books that are mere tools, tools not written by real men, but that have the appearance of having been made by a dictionary, if a dictionary had the power of expressing thoughts. These are books with no men back of them. They have no pulses, no red blood. But we must read books to get something we cannot get in any other way. We cannot live in the past, and only by books can we learn what generations past did and thought and said, what lives, what pleasures, what experiences they had.

"Every man worth his salt must feel his own life a trifle too narrow for him. He must feel that he has some margin of power to expand into some wider field. He must look over the whole map of life. He must see the main roads of travel, as well as the bypaths. He must see how other men travel, see their joys, sorrows and tragedies. We want to know the real face of life, and that is why we go to college and send our sons there, for nowhere else can all this be obtained.

"We hear arguments now in favor of a shorter college term. It is said that the lessons of the first two years of college are learned in the high school now. Two years is enough for a college course, these persons say, so graduate the men when they have finished their sophomore year and give them their degree. Well, no man who ever knew a sophomore can use that argument. The sap is rising in the sophomore, but it has not got to his head yet. No one can handle a body of sophomores and say they are finished college men. Yet a few years ago our colleges graduated men with no more book learning than the present sophomore has, but, then, the graduates were men, and there is a difference between men and sophomores.

"Now, I am not saying a word against the sophomore. He is a very lovable chap, and I like him, but I do not dote on him as a trained and finished product of the university."

Mr. Wilson went on to say that an exclusive home life bred provincialism, but that at college a man came in contact with men of all countries and kinds, and felt something of the life that circulated in the world. The danger in the United States to-day, he said, was the danger of provincialism, the danger that one section of the country would not understand another section. The danger of provincialism or sectionalism, he said, was that there was a chance of creating a division of [the] country, a fundamental division, that of misunderstanding. Men of one section of the country would not understand the men of another section; they would have no sympathies in common. The associations of college life tended to break down these barriers, the speaker stated, and for that reason he wished that every Southern youth could attend a Northern college, and every Northern boy go to a Southern university.

Mr. Wilson advocated the throwing of the college man on his own resources, instead of letting him depend too much on the classroom and the instructor. The college man must find the fun there was in thinking his own thoughts.

"The way to learn is not to sit under a tutor all day, but to hump yourself and learn," said Mr. Wilson. "The use of a college professor is to show the students where to find things to learn. The highest compliment a college professor can have after he has delivered a lecture is to have a few men remain behind and tell him they don't believe a word he has said. That shows they thought for themselves."

Intellectual comradeship was the gist of the whole matter of the college education, Mr. Wilson said. A man must feel the intellectual sympathy and suggestion of those about him. He will know the power that is in him by feeling the power in others. This comradeship was not obtainable in a short time, the speaker said, and he stated that he did not see how it could be gotten in less than four college years.

At the conclusion of the remarks Mr. Wilson was given a rising vote of thanks.

Printed in the *Newark Evening News*, Dec. 6, 1902; some editorial headings omitted.

From Theodore Roosevelt

My dear President Wilson: Washington. December 6, 1902.

I have just finished your really notable address which I read for the first time in the Atlantic Monthly.[1] As a decent American I want to thank you for it.

Is there any chance of your getting down to Washington to spend a night with me at the White House this winter? There are many things I would like to talk over with you.

Faithfully yours,   Theodore Roosevelt

TLS (WP, DLC).
[1] "The Ideals of America," printed at Dec. 26, 1901, Vol. 12, which had just appeared in the *Atlantic Monthly*, xc (Dec. 1902), 721-34.

A News Report

[Dec. 8, 1902]

IMPRESSIVE EXERCISES
Commemorating the 25th Anniversary of Formation
of Student Y.M.C.A. Movement.

The commemorative exercises of the Philadelphian Society, to celebrate the twenty-fifth anniversary of the formation of the American and Canadian Student Young Men's Christian Association Movement, were held in Marquand Chapel on Saturday morning at 11 o'clock. Mr. Cleveland H. Dodge '79, chairman of the sub-committee on Student Work of the International Committee of the Young Men's Christian Association, and chairman of the Graduate Advisory Committee of the Philadelphian Society, presided, and opened the exercises with a few words, explaining the purpose for which the celebration was held.

Professor Henry van Dyke delivered the invocation, and J. E. Steen 1903, president of the Philadelphian Society, welcomed the delegates and invited guests on behalf of the society.

Mr. Luther D. Wishard '77, the first travelling secretary of the movement, delivered the first address of the morning upon the subject, "The Beginning of the Student Movement." He began by referring to Mr. William E. Dodge, in whose brain the Student Movement had its origin. While visiting his two sons, then undergraduates at Princeton, Mr. Dodge, in speaking of religious work, referred to immense good that might be accomplished by Christian men in college working together like the members of a football team. At the same time, Mr. Wishard said, no distinct organization was discussed, but the idea gained ground and a convention was held at Louisville, Kentucky, during December 1877, when the present movement was organized. At this convention there were present twenty-one delegates, representing twenty-five colleges in eleven different states. After speaking briefly of his experience as the first travelling secretary of the new movement, Mr. Wishard closed by narrating the history of the organization of the various departments of the student work: the Bible Study department, organized in 1885; the College Summer Conference, which began in 1886; the College Association Buildings, the first of which, Murray Hall, was erected in 1879; the General Secretaryship, which originated at Yale; the Student Volunteer Movement; and the Foreign Department.

Mr. John R. Mott, the second speaker, had as his subject "The Achievements of the Student Movement." He spoke of the important part which the universities and colleges play in moulding the sentiment of the world, and of the important position of the Young Men's Christian Association in the universities and colleges. Continuing, he showed the great improvement in the Young Men's Christian Association of to-day over the religious organization of twenty-five years ago, and illustrated his statements by statistics of the extent of the growth in the various departments of the Student Movement.

President Patton delivered the third address upon "The Significance of the Student Movement to the Church." He called attention to the fact that the Young Men's Christian Association is a refuge to the young man coming to college from a Christian home, and then showed how the religious work here in college prepares a man for its continuance in his later life. In conclusion he warned his hearers against ever letting the Student Movement drift into an institution teaching merely philanthropy, humanity, and morality, and urged the necessity of keeping up the religious zeal which inspired the founders of the movement.

President Wilson delivered the last address of the morning upon "The Significance of the Student Movement to the Nation." "The things," he said, "that bind the mind are spiritual, not intellectual, and men are governed by their passions." From this he urged that all should endeavor to make their purest passion the ruling one. He showed how this would tend to bring about a reign of purity and justice in our government. In conclusion, he expressed his absolute sympathy and confidence in the Student Movement.

Dr. Henry van Dyke pronounced the Benediction.

Printed in the *Daily Princetonian*, Dec. 8, 1902.

To Robert Bridges

My dear Bob: Princeton, New Jersey. 8 December, 1902.

I am sorry to find in looking over my calendar that it is really impossible, without the greatest imprudence, to find any date that would suit Mr. Smith for the Men's Association of the Brick Church.[1] It is a matter of real regret and disappointment with me, but I simply must draw the line this side of over-exertion.

Howard Butler, whom we are learning to think very highly of as an authority in such matters, has expressed to me the highest opinion of Morris,[2] as an architect and as a man of artistic taste and training. He has promised to tell me all he knows about him, and before we meet again, I think I shall be able to contribute something definite to the discussion of our choice.

In haste,   Affectionately yours,   Woodrow Wilson

TLS (WC, NjP).
[1] That is, the Brick Presbyterian Church of New York.
[2] Benjamin Wistar Morris III, architect of New York, who was in fact engaged to draw the plans for Seventy-Nine Hall.

To Julius Sachs[1]

My dear Sir: Princeton, New Jersey. 9 December, 1902.

Your kind letter of December 2nd[2] came while I was away from home, and I beg that you will pardon my delay in replying.

It would, I am sure, be very stimulating and delightful to be able to attend the next meeting of the History Association of the Middle States, and address it, as you suggest, but I am sorry to say that it is not possible for me to do so this season. Indeed, my executive duties have so absorbed me that I am not sure that I have anything to say to a History Association: I have ceased to be an historian, and have become a man of business. And my business is of so absorbing a character that, for the present at any rate, I must devote myself wholly to the learning of it.

With much regard and appreciation,

Very sincerely yours,   Woodrow Wilson

TLS (WP, DLC).
1 Professor of Secondary Education, Teachers College, Columbia University.
2 It is missing.

An Address to the Princeton Alumni of New York[1]

[[Dec. 9, 1902]]

Mr. Alexander[2] and fellow alumni: I am not vain enough to take this demonstration as an evidence of your admiration of me. I know what you have come here for. You have come here to express your gratification that a Princeton alumnus whom you know and have consorted with is now in command of the ship which we all man (applause). I know that the meaning of this company is that there is a life in the body of men who have gone out from Princeton that cannot be quenched, and which cannot be resisted. There are many things which Princeton needs, but she does not need life and vigor, she does not need the blood and the spirit of men to carry her standards and her cause forward.

You will readily believe me when I say that I have been deeply moved by the scene which I look upon to-night. I am ordinarily, gentlemen, a very witty man, but all wit has been subdued in me by the spirit almost of solemnity which this scene brings upon me. I do not doubt that we have entered upon a new era, not because of anything that is in me, but because of the spirit that is in you. If you feel any tithe of that combined power which you show in demonstrations like this to-night, we are sure of the future of Princeton University. I believe that the gentlemen who are with us from other institutions must have felt the pulse that is beating in this body to-night. No man can mistake it; no man can sit here and not feel it; and I suppose that those who do not know us have wondered what bred this spirit amongst us. How did it happen that men so diverse in age and occupation and condition, so different in the circumstances of their lives and the antecedents of their fortunes, are bound together by this common tie, like boys, and yet like men, with the feeling of boys and with the purpose of men? How did that happen? (applause). It

1 A news report of this affair is printed at Dec. 13, 1902.
2 James Waddel Alexander, the toastmaster, who introduced Wilson and the other speakers.

is a thing bred by the spirit of a place, a place which the memory of every man here keeps as a sort of a shrine to which all his happiest thoughts return; a place in which his comradeships, the dearest comradeships of his life, have begun; a place in which he remembers some of the best impulses of his life to have begun; a place where when we walk we feel that we have renewed a spirit of allegiance to the truth, to learning, to manhood, to that fair spirit of dealing man with man which makes the best part of the feeling of the American people.

All of this has been bred by life in a place the charm of which even strangers feel. I have marked how men who never saw that place before feel the spirit of it when they walk those streets and across that campus; how they say, "There is something in this place which we never felt anywhere else, some atmosphere which takes the imagination, which kindles enthusiasm, so that one can hardly leave here without feeling that he has been adopted in the Princeton family, and has partaken of the Princeton allegiance." No one fails to feel it. The Freshman feels it in the midst of his miseries; the Sophomore feels it in the midst of his pride; the Junior and the Senior in the midst of their leisure have time to feel it (applause). And by a simple device we have enhanced the spirit of the place. By the very simple device of constructing our new buildings in the Tudor Gothic style we seem to have added to Princeton the age of Oxford and of Cambridge; we have added a thousand years to the history of Princeton by merely putting those lines in our architecture which point every man's imagination to the historic traditions of learning in the English-speaking race. We have declared and acknowledged our derivation and lineage. We have said: "This is the spirit in which we have been bred"; and as the imagination, as the recollection of classes yet to be graduated from Princeton are affected by the suggestions of that architecture, we shall find the past of this country married with the past of the world and shall know with what destiny we have come into the forefront of the nations,—with the destiny of men who have gathered the best thinking of the world, and wish to add to the politics of the world not heat, but light—the light that illuminates the path of nations and makes them know the errors as well as the wisdom of the past.

Gentlemen, we have dreamed a dream in Princeton of how the charm of that place shall be still further enhanced. I need not tell you of the familiar map of that beautiful place. You know how naturally in the old historic campus there is slowly being formed into a sort of circle, a quadrangle, a great quadrangle, a little town. That little town will presently close its lines from the Brokaw Building back of Prospect to where the Infirmary now stands, and up Washington Road, and within that little town, girt about with buildings in the style that is historic, there will live the College of Liberal Arts, there will dwell all the high-spirited youngsters who represent us in the ball field, who represent us in the writing of the college periodicals, who carry the spirit and the go of the place in their veins. And then there will come in the midst of that friendly town another quadrangle, a smaller quadrangle, more beautiful than any that has yet been built, and in that quadrangle there will live a little community, a community of graduate students, touched by the life in the midst of which they live, sympathetic with it, dominated by it, and yet going in and out like men bent upon the errands of the mind, loving sport, but not following sport; sympathizers with the undergraduate life, but not taking part in the undergraduate life, rather seeming to remind men as they go to and fro that there are invisible things which men seek with the mind's eye, that there is a life which no man has touched, which no man has seen, that there is something that makes free—the very truth itself; and these men shall touch the spirit of the undergraduates, the youngsters shall wonder if there are not visions which are worth seeing, if there are not tasks in those closeted places that are worth doing, if there is not something immortal bred in the occupations of those men (applause).

Back of this little town, full of the visions of scholarship and of the diversions of sober, eager, ingenuous young men, there will stretch a fair garden open to the eye, where men shall see all the pleasant outlooks that that place commands; there shall be a girth of buildings down the avenue which leads to the woods below, and there shall run by those buildings a path which leads to the open quadrangles of the professional schools, upon which we shall look out from above, through the broad garden, as men look forward—look forward to their professional careers, look forward to the things in which they shall specifically serve the world; a quadrangle which shall house the men who are the students of jurisprudence, the students of law in all its scholarly outlooks, the men whose ambition it is not merely to seek their bread and butter by the practice of the law before the courts, but also to supply the courts with the principles by which they shall develop the law of the country; men who shall know the old and abundant rootages of the great system of jurisprudence under which they live, and who will be capable in moments critical and perplexing to give guidance to the development of the jurisprudence of this country; and beyond that a quadrangle for the men who handle that force which runs the modern world of industry, a School of Electrical Engineering.

The electrical engineer stands at the strategic center of the future industry of this country, and we cannot afford that the industry of this country should go without the touch of the Princeton spirit (applause). The Princeton spirit, I think I do not deceive myself in believing, is a spirit which is touched with the ideals of service, which is touched with those ideals which elevate professions from the lower grades to the grades in which they are conspicuous, the grades from which men reach achievement. There is a difference, gentlemen, between success and achievement. Achievement comes to the man who has forgotten himself and married himself and his mind to the task to which he has set himself; success may come to the merely diligent man.

And then where the woods close about, and all the fine outlooks are checked by the falling country, as it sinks away to the lower lands below, where the soil is fertile, where it invites to cultivation, there will stand the great Museum of Natural History, a museum which Princeton imperatively needs at once, to relieve the groaning receptacles of Old North, which hold priceless collections which no man can even examine because they cannot be handled, because they cannot even be classified, because they cannot be laid before the student—those evidences of the life of the globe which it is indispensable that man should explore if he would understand the life of nature or the progress of medical science.

These are the things which we dreamed of in our vision; and do we think of these things simply to enhance the charm of the place, simply to give ourselves new quadrangles and better and ampler architecture, simply to make some man's artistic fortune by saying, "Here is a place in which you can conceive the most complete and systematic body of academic buildings that can be erected anywhere in the United States"? Is this merely to please ourselves by adorning the place which we leave? No! I take this dream to have this at its center: That we want to transform thoughtless boys performing tasks into thinking men, fit for the work of the world. The trouble, gentlemen, with the modern undergraduate is that, though a lovable boy, he is a thoughtless boy. He is a boy who does his tasks sometimes merely because it is honorable for him to do them; generally because it is compulsory; because he wants something which when he does his tasks in that spirit really counts for nothing essential at all; he wants a paltry piece of parchment; he wants to escape the disgrace of saying that he did not graduate; but he is graduated when the end comes upon no scale of endeavor, he is graduated upon no scale of achievement, he is graduated upon hardly more than a scale of residence.

We have heard a great deal about shortening the college course, and a great many persons have talked as if all that you had to judge of when you try to answer the question, "When should a man graduate?" was how many times he had attended class. I have heard a great many discussions of this course which puzzled my non-mathematical head, because they said that in order that a man should graduate it was necessary only that he should have to his credit in the aggregate, sixty class exercises per week. It makes you dizzy to think about it. It is not required that he should attend all sixty in one week; he can spread these, if he have breath enough for the pace, over three years; if he has not breath enough for that he can spread them over four, if he chooses to be a gentleman of leisure he can spread them over five. But when he has sixty hours a week to his credit, why then he can graduate. What the hours thus spent count for is apparently for these gentlemen a matter of indifference; they simply want to reckon up so many pharisaical performances of a certain definite requirement and then put the self-righteous pupil to his graduation. It makes a great deal of difference, gentlemen, to a university whether it turns out thinking men or not. It does not make very much difference whether it turns out men who have attended lectures or not (applause). It would be a very nice test of university lecturers if the attendance were made optional. If a man had something to say the men would go, and if he didn't have anything to say the men would not go. I believe in my heart that any man who has something to say can get an audience; it may not be the same audience every day, but if he has something to put into the thought and the talk of the campus, somebody will be there to hear him lecture; and if he has not something to contribute to the talk and the thought of the campus, ought anybody to be there to hear him lecture? That is a nice question which I should not like to press too far.

Now, gentlemen, I do not believe that a man ought to work all time.

Several voices: Right! Good!

PRESIDENT WILSON: I know [knew] that would be a popular sentiment. I believe that the Constitution of the United States guarantees to a man a certain amount of loafing; otherwise we should come under the prohibition of cruel and unusual punishments. I am not going to propose that we compel the undergraduates to work all the time; but I am going to propose that we make the undergraduates want to work all the time (applause). And there is a way to do that. There is a way which I believe an infallible way. Mind you, there is no study in the curriculum of a university which is not of itself intrinsically interesting. There are no minds in a university to which some subjects in that university may not be made to seem interesting, and the only way I know of to make a man see that a subject is interesting is to get him on the inside of it. The only way to get him on the inside of it is to throw him on his own resources in becoming acquainted with it. I believe that there must come in this country a radical change in our conception of an education, and I believe that it must come in this way: That we shall give up the schoolboy idea that men are to be examined upon lectures and upon text books, and come to the grown-up idea that men are to be examined upon subjects. Let me take a concrete example, because I want to get into the substance of this thing. I want to be able to say, for example, to the undergraduates who choose that line of study, "You will at a certain date, which may turn out for you to be a fateful date, be examined on the subject of the constitutional history of the United States. Now, you can get up that subject in ways which we will point out to you, or you can get it up in ways which you discover for yourself, but if you don't get up that subject, we shall have the pain of parting company with you. We are not going to examine you upon what the lecturer in American Constitutional History said; we are not going to examine you in the particular text books which he put in the catalogue as associated with his lectures; you can get up your history of America in that way or in some other way, but get up the history of America you must." That makes a man of him, and it makes a man of him for this reason: that no man is a man who receives his knowledge wholly by instruction from somebody else; that man is a man who obtains his knowledge by his own efforts and inquiries.

Now, there is a way to do that, gentlemen. There are different sorts of subjects in a curriculum, let me remind you. There are drill subjects, which, no doubt, are mild forms of torture, but which every man must submit to. So far as my own experience is concerned, the natural carnal man never desires to learn mathematics. We know from a knowledge of the history of the race that it is necessary by painful processes of drill to insert mathematics into a man's constitution; he cannot be left to get up mathematics for himself, because he cannot do it. There are some drill subjects which are just as necessary as the measles in order to make a man a grown-up person; he must have gone through those things in order to qualify himself for the experiences of life; he must have crucified his will and get [got] up things which he did not intend to get up, and reluctantly was compelled to get up. That, I believe, is necessary for the salvation of his soul. But there are other subjects—subjects which are out of the field of the ordinary school curriculum, and which, I may perhaps be permitted to say, are more characteristic in their kind of university study. They are what I may call the reading subjects, like philosophy, like literature, like law, like history. In those subjects it is futile to try to instruct men by mere class-room methods. The only way to instruct them is to provide a certain number of men sufficiently qualified as scholars, who will be the companions and coaches and guides of the men's reading, just as if we supplied the university with a score or more, with fifty or more, reference librarians, whose business it would be to say to students, "If you want to get up such and such a subject, here is the central and most authoritative literature on that subject, these are the books to read; if there are hard places in them we will explain them; if you lose your compass in the journey we will find your whereabouts again; you may report to us from time to time, you may consort with us every evening; we are your companions and coaches in the business; we are at your service." Just so soon as you do that you invite men inside the subject that they are seeking to get up, and until you do that you cannot get them inside.

That, you will say, is the English tutorial system. Yes; but the English make an old-fashioned mistake about it; they appoint their tutors for life, and their tutors go to seed. No man can do that sort of thing for youngsters without getting tired of it. It makes it necessary that he should always be understanding the difficulties of beginners, and after a while, ceasing to be a beginner himself, the thing becomes intolerable to him. He wants to go on about independent research for which his beginnings have made him fit, and, therefore, I do not believe you can afford to keep an ordinary tutor for more than five years at that particular job. I said this same thing in Chicago the other night, and a newspaper reported that I had said that no man ought to be a professor for more than five years.[3] I did not say any such revolutionary

---

[3] The Chicago *Inter Ocean*. The headlines of its report of Wilson's speech to the Chicago alumni in its issue of Nov. 29, 1902, read "TEACHERS USELESS AFTER

thing as that. I said that no man ought to have this sort of a job
for more than five years at a time.

Gentlemen, if we could get a body of such tutors at Princeton
we could transform the place from a place where there are youngsters doing tasks to a place where there are men doing thinking;
men who are conversing about the things of thought, men who
are eager and interested in the things of thought. We know that,
because we have done it on a small scale. Wherever you have a
small class, and they can be intimately associated with their
chief in the study of an interesting subject, they catch the infection of the subject; but where they are in big classes, and simply
hear a man lecture two or three times a week, they cannot catch
the infection of anything, except, it may be, the voice and enthusiasm of the lecturer himself. This is the way in which to transform the place.

All of that, gentlemen, costs money. Now, I am coming to business. To start that particular thing fairly and properly would need
two millions and a quarter (whistles from audience). I hope you
will get your whistling over, because you will have to get used
to this, and you may thank your stars I did not say four millions
and a quarter, because we are going to get it (applause). I suspect that there are gentlemen in this room who are going to give
me two millions and a quarter to get rid of me. They will be able
to get rid of me in no other way that I know of. And then, gentlemen, in order to do these other things which I have dreamed of,
we shall need a great deal more than two millions and a quarter.
I have not guessed at any figure that I have uttered. I have calculated upon a basis that I think in business would be recognized
as a sound basis every cent that I have estimated that Princeton
will need, and the total is twelve millions and a half (applause).
What I want to say first of all about that sum of money is this,
that there is no other university in the world that could make so
small a sum go so far. There is not another university in the
world that could transmute twelve millions and a half into so
much red blood.

Now, why do all of this? Why not be satisfied with the happy
life at Princeton? Why not congratulate ourselves upon the comradeship of a scene like this, and say "This is enough; what could
the heart of man desire more?" Because, gentlemen, what this

FIVE YEARS   Princeton President Says They Soon Become Incompetent." And it
quoted Wilson as saying: "No teacher is qualified to instruct classes for over
five years. No matter what the subject may be, the teacher is incompetent after
those five years have rolled around."

country needs is not more good fellowship, what this country needs now more than it ever did before, what it shall need in the years following, is knowledge and enlightenment. Civilization grows infinitely complex about us; the tasks of this country are no longer simple; and men are not doing their duty who have a chance to know and do not equip themselves with knowledge in the midst of the tasks which surround us. Princeton has ever since her birthday stood for the service of the Nation.

I have heard, and my heart has echoed all the fine cheers of loyalty that have gone up for Princeton in this place, and in other places, and no man who hears those cheers can doubt the genuineness of the impulse that is behind them. But, gentlemen, cheers and good wishes will not make the fortunes of Princeton; these things will not give Princeton reputation. Nothing will give Princeton reputation except the achievements of the men whom she creates. The reputation of a university is not a matter of report. It is a matter of fact. You know that we hear a great deal of sentimental cant nowadays about cultivating our characters. God forbid that any man should spend his days thinking about his own character. What he wants to do is to get out and accomplish something, achieve something that is honorable, something that leaves the world a little nearer to the ideals that men have at their hearts, and his character will take care of itself. Your characters, gentlemen, are by-products, and the minute you set yourselves to produce them you make prigs of yourselves and render yourselves useless. I should despair of producing a character for Princeton by praising her. We are here to praise Princeton by serving our day and generation, by having some vision of the mind which we got in the comradeships of that place; and then these comradeships will mean for this country something that will assure her a noble future. A body of men like this can in a day of crisis save the country they live in if they have purged their hearts and rectified their ways of thinking.

This is the vision which we all have; and when we have completed the task that is before us, as we shall complete it, so far as any one generation can complete what must go on forever—then every man who has scholarship and public service at heart will feel that he must go first or last to worship at the same shrine with us (applause).

Printed in *Speech of President Woodrow Wilson of Princeton University at the Princeton Dinner Given at the Waldorf-Astoria December 9, 1902* (New York, n.d.).

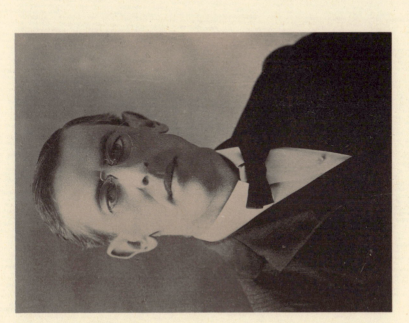

The two Purdy photographs of Wilson, taken in August 1902

The Wilson's house on Library Place, "For Rent"

Prospect, the residence of the President of Princeton

The entrance to Prospect

The academic procession entering Alexander Hall for the
inauguration of Wilson as President of Princeton

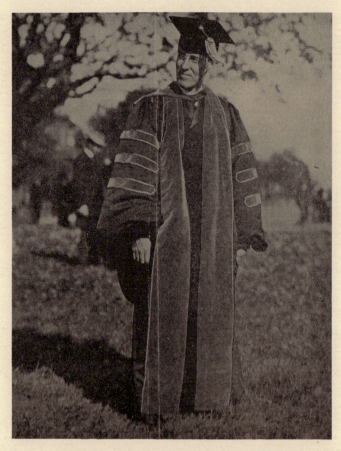

Wilson on the day of his inauguration

Mr. J. P. Morgan with the ladies of his party
attending Wilson's inauguration

Wilson speaking from the steps of Nassau Hall
after the inaugural ceremony

Breaking ground for Seventy-Nine Hall

From the Minutes of the Princeton Science Faculty

Wednesday December 10. 1902

The School of Science Faculty met at 5 pm in the Faculty Room, with President Wilson in the chair. . . .

The President announced the following Standing Committees of the Faculty:

Committee on Examinations and Standing:

    Professor C. G. Rockwood Jr.

    Professor A. H. Phillips

    Professor E. O. Lovett.

    Professor E. H. Loomis

    Professor F. Neher.

Committee on Special Students

    Professor W. M. Rankin

    Professor H. S. S. Smith

    Professor E. H. Loomis

    Mr. G. M. Priest. . .

"Minutes of the School of Science Faculty, 1898-1904, Princeton University," bound minute book (UA, NjP).

To Edith Gittings Reid

My dearest Friend,   Princeton, New Jersey, 11 December, 1902

You must have wondered what had become of the academic gentleman whom you so generously entertained a week ago.[1] The fact is, that he has been allowed, since you saw him, to remain at home only a few hours at a time,—only long enough to dispatch the absolutely necessary business of his responsible office.

This time the hours of his stay prove to be some thirty minutes longer than usual, and he can tell you that he reached home well and not exhausted on Saturday last,—to find all going well at home, and that he is never more content away from home than when staying with his dear friends at 608 Cathedral St. Mrs. Wilson joins me in all affectionate messages, and I am, as always

        Your affectionate friend,   Woodrow Wilson

ALS (WC, NjP).

[1] When he spoke to the Presbyterian Union of Baltimore on Dec. 4, 1902.

From Lawrence Cameron Hull[1]

Dear Dr. Wilson: Indianapolis, December 11, 1902.

Since I have come to Indianapolis I have heard on two or three occasions quite serious criticisms of the method of conducting the examinations here in Indianapolis for admission to Princeton. I know that you will be anxious if any possible scandal results like that of the Phillips-Andover examinations last year. I do not know how just the criticisms that I have heard expressed are; but it seems wise that I should report to you the fact in order that you may be able to take what action seems to you to be wise in order to avoid any further criticism. The charges made are that the supervisors have been extremely careless and that their criminal neglect of the candidates has made it possible for entirely unworthy students to pass the examinations. I have made no investigation of the case because it is, of course, clear that it is not my business; but I feel perfectly sure that you will consider this letter I am sending you as a wholly confidential matter.

Yours most sincerely,   Lawrence Cameron Hull

TLS (WP, DLC).
[1] Principal of the Shortridge High School in Indianapolis.

Samuel Ross Winans to the Board of Trustees' Committee on Morals and Discipline

GENTLEMEN: Princeton, N. J., 11th, 1902.

The period since my last report has been notably free from serious disorder. As far as my own observation goes, or reports have reached me, fairly normal conditions have prevailed in student life. For a similar period I have seldom known greater quiet and decorum on street and campus. There have been very few cases of formal discipline. And my report may be correspondingly brief.

Three men (two Juniors and one Sophomore) have come under discipline for drinking. There had been a considerable number of cases in the month previous. I have endeavored to let it be felt that no case of intoxication which is observed and reported can escape discipline, while the penalty should be proportionate to its gravity as a first or a repeated offence.

One student (a Junior Scientific) was found guilty of stealing plotting instruments from his fellow students. His father was allowed to remove him without formal expulsion. This has been the custom in these pitiful cases.

The four Sophomores reported last time as suspended for hazing were on recommendation of the Student Hazing Committee allowed to return November 14th, after four weeks suspension. While this penalty may appear too slight for the offence, it seemed to the Faculty wise in this instance to adopt the student recommendation, inasmuch as the penalty being thus imposed by the students themselves was taken the more seriously and might prove efficacious; in short, it was deemed best to try still further the plan of student control, as giving hopes of the best results, if the student interest can be quickened and sustained.

The annual Cane Spree wrestling, which last year came under some criticism for its methods, passed off this time without accident, under proper supervision.

As to *Attendance*. The attendance on Chapel, within the limits of the rules, has been better than in any period I have known,— especially in the lower classes. Not many pensums[1] for excess —and no suspensions—have been found necessary thus far.

Class Attendance has been generally good, although the classes thin out before holidays. Many of the best students save up their allowed absences for use at such times; others present excuses more or less sound, and many incur pensums.

Scholarship. The Freshmen, both Academic and Scientific, have been carefully looked after as to their work through the Division officers and the Class Committees. In all cases where there seemed danger of general failure at the term examinations, notice has been sent to the parent. A number of students have been put on special probation.

Four Freshmen have been dropped already,—*two* Academic and *two* Scientific. Three of the four were repeating the year, having been dropped last year from '05. I believe that Statistics would show that not more than one in three of men once dropped go on successfully in a lower class and graduate.

Respectfully submitted.   S. R. Winans   Dean

TLS (Trustees' Papers, UA, NjP).
1 A penalty, usually in the form of additional work.

Charles McLean Andrews'[1] Review of
A History of the American People

[Dec. 11, 1902]

Coincident with the inauguration of Dr. Woodrow Wilson as president of Princeton University appears a history of the American people from the pen of the professor thus signally honored.* Its appearance is timely from the publishers' point of view, for public interest has been aroused by the inaugural exercises at Princeton, just as it had been aroused before by the unusual circumstances attending Dr. Wilson's selection for the high office to which he has been called. Its appearance is timely from the reader's point of view, for there is great need of a compact and impartial history of the United States, written by a scholar, with an adequate sense of historical proportion and with a true appreciation of what history is and how it should be written.

His history of the American people is a sketch—brilliant and profound, but none the less a sketch—of the settlement, growth and expansion of the United States. It is not a study of the people in the sense made familiar by Professor McMaster. It does not portray their daily life, their habits and customs, their mental attitudes and traditions, in detail. Its underlying purpose seems to be to show the connection between the conditions of popular life and the forms and changes of governments; to elaborate Sir Henry Maine's axiom that social necessities and social needs are always more or less in advance of law conventions. Consequently the author's point of view is always that of the central government, whether in the colonies or the nation. He illustrates with a firm hand and an illuminating touch the habits and temperaments of the New Englander and the Virginian, of the Easterner and the Middle Westerner, of the Northerner and the Southerner, of the cultivated inhabitant of the more highly developed East and the farmer of the frontier plains, and he brings out with admirable clearness the influence of these men of many nationalities and varying grades of social and intellectual advancement in the upbuilding of the country. All these aspects he illustrates with broad sweeps of the brush; but he does so, not in order to portray

---

* A HISTORY OF THE AMERICAN PEOPLE. *By Woodrow Wilson, President of Princeton University.* Illustrated with portraits, maps, plans, facsimiles, rare prints, contemporary views, etc. In five volumes. New York: Harper & Brothers. $17.50 net.

[1] That Andrews, at this time Professor of History at Bryn Mawr College, was the author of this unsigned review is evidenced by the fact that he kept a copy of it in his personal papers—in the file of reviews that he had written—now in the Yale University Library.

the people as such, but rather to elucidate changes in governmental theory and practice and to explain the conditions attending the great crises of colonial and national history. Thus the story is, after all, the familiar one, narrated with all the genius of a clear thinker, a sound historical student and a stylist of unusual powers. We may not have here the life of the people properly so called, but we have an exposition of American history that has not hitherto been equaled in insight and attractiveness.

Dr. Wilson is at his best in the last two volumes, and the portions of those volumes which cover the period from 1828 to 1889. The matter before the first date does not possess the grasp and insight exhibited in the later period, while that which follows the second election of Harrison [Cleveland] seems lacking in unity and coherence. But in the middle period the writer is thoroughly at home. Here he has an opportunity to study men and parties, to balance the issues of Presidential campaigns, to discuss motives and to weigh the influence of public opinion. It is in this field that he had done his best work before, in the little volume of the Epoch series, entitled "Division and Reunion," and it is here that his knowledge is most complete and his temper of thought most in harmony with his subject. Public life is his theme, specific men, not abstract tendencies, his chief interest, and he dissects and criticises, probes and demonstrates with all the skill of a man of affairs, without any of the weaknesses or prejudices usually accompanying the comments of an actual participant in the events of the day. Perhaps at times he exaggerates the personal and takes too little account of deep and far-lying influences, the remoter causes that are not tangible and so frequently elude the historian. At times he certainly does fail to consider aspects of the case that others deem essential to a right understanding of the story. He has passed over entirely the growth of the democratic spirit in the proprietary and royal colonies and the ultimate victory of the legislative over the executive branch of the colonial governments. He makes no attempt to explain why Burgoyne lost the battle of Saratoga, the turning point of the war, because of the negligence of the Home Government. He fails to notice that public opinion had been a political influence in England twenty years before it began to work on the matter of the American Revolution, and he consequently misses an important point in the rise of the elder Pitt to power. He omits Paine's "Common Sense" from the place of its logical influence among the causes of the Declaration of Independence. He does not bring out clearly enough the changing relations in the legislative, executive and judicial departments of government during the years since 1790, tho at times he hints at the gradual shifting of their power. We think, too, that there are many fair-minded students of recent events who will not be satisfied with his account of America's share in the Venezuelan controversy and will not be ready to accept his unqualified admiration, we almost wrote glorification, of ex-President Cleveland. However, these are minor matters and hardly weigh in the balance as against the substantial merits of the work. For the chapter on the Confederate States all readers may be grateful, for there exists no such analysis of government and life south of Mason and Dixon's line as that which Dr. Wilson has here given us. Of exceptional usefulness, too, is the appendix to volume IV, containing in parallel columns the constitutions of the United States and of the Confederate States.

Another feature of this work strikes us as most admirable. This is the spirit in which it is conceived and written, the spirit of one strong in his love for his country and hopeful of its future. This work is full of optimism, life and courage, like the people of whom it treats, patient to bear, eager to persevere. The view is always forward, on to better things, guided by the experiences of those things that have been. The tone is instinct with enthusiasm, confidence and expectation. The history is, therefore, wholesome, the sort of work that will make a man sleep better, as did the Massachusetts men after Webster's reply to Hayne. There is nothing pessimistic or chicken-hearted here, and if there be "anti-imperialists" still abroad they will find nothing in this history to support their warnings of evil to come. Dr. Wilson anticipates evils, difficulties, crises, but he teaches us that as they have been met in the past so they will be met in the future. Such works as Rhodes's "History of the United States" and Wilson's *History of the American People* cannot fail to elevate the tone of the community and breed stronger and better citizens. We should like every young man to read all that is contained in these volumes, and wish that after the publishers have reaped their due reward they may find it possible to issue a single volume without the paraphernalia of pictures, at a relatively cheap rate. This could readily be done, as the entire work contains only about three hundred thousand words, less than many a single volume frequently issued. We believe in the cultivation of patriotism through the medium of such books as these. There is not a false or exaggerated note in all that Dr. Wilson has written.

We can add but a word regarding the illustrations, which form so large a part of the volumes before us. They are many of them of great value as throwing new and suggestive light upon the detail of the text. Some of them are, however, works of the imagination, and while doubtless historically accurate, are nevertheless open to the criticism of the careful student who prefers a contemporary print. Many of the illustrations have nothing to do with the text and some are inserted without regard to their proper place as adjoining the matter they illustrate. But one may easily be hypercritical in regard to these details of arrangement, and we do not believe that there is an illustration here, among the thousand or more that these five volumes contain, that will not prove of profit or pleasure to every reader. It is high praise when we say that they serve to enhance the value of a work that is destined to become, in its way, a classic among books on American history.

Printed in *The Independent*, LIV (Dec. 11, 1902), 2957-59.

A News Report of an Address at the Brooklyn Institute

[Dec. 12, 1902]

WOODROW WILSON ON A UNIVERSITY'S USE

President Woodrow Wilson of Princeton University, in the course of a lecture last night before the Brooklyn Institute of Arts and Sciences on "The Function of the University in the United States," rather startled the alumni of Columbia and various other universities located in cities by the positive statement that the university which was robbed by its urban location of the community atmosphere was a failure in the highest and best definition of the American university.

"The gist of the university," said Dr. Wilson, "is that it should be a community with all the wonderful advantages that that word conveys. I don't believe that, unless the students of the university are kept together, they can get the atmospheric advantage of the community.

"If the students, after they leave the lecture and class rooms of the university, can at once dive out into the street of a great city and become drifting and separate integral parts of urban life, they are not getting the benefit of a university. They are simply going to a day school. It is my firm conviction that the real effects of a university are wrought between the hours of

6 P.M. and 9 A.M. It is during those hours the all-powerful influence of association between mind and mind is exerted. Therefore, it is absolutely necessary that the American university should be a compact and homogeneous community. The individualistic spirit is not American."

President Wilson began his lecture with the statement that, being one of the very newest of college Presidents, he was probably better able to theorize regarding the functions of a university than an older President, who was handicapped by fact and experience. Entering upon his subject, he said that all citizens of this Republic were put under a certain compulsion of duty. "All the work of the country must be done by the ordinary citizen, and so we should make of the ordinary citizen a varied and as various a body as possible." This he said was the guiding thought in considering the function of the university.

The speaker said, however, that not all men should be trained alike and not all men were benefited by or should be given a university education. Neither should the university teach everything.

"There has been a tendency in recent years," said the speaker, "to the belief that the university should cover the whole field of learning, from handicrafts to abstract schools of philosophy. To do that it would be necessary to resort to the principle of average, and this is not for the really great university. For the university is, as much as anything else, lifting the spirits of men. It is in giving a man the capacity to look above the smoke and dust of his particular occupation in life and get a broad view of the world. And as I said, the university is not for every man. For one thing, it is not every man who could or would care to wait until his twenty-fourth year to go into business. The world must be served in various ways, and the university man alone is not able to serve in all.

"And furthermore, the universities turn out a good many failures, but men go to the universities from various motives. Some are turned out still in the raw state after four years' attendance, some are turned out who are acquainted with learning, but whose stock of it will not stand the wind and weather of life. And yet every man must get some little benefit from his university training. The human mind has an infinite capacity for resisting knowledge, but we have a system of dragooning students, and they are benefited somehow and in some ways in spite of all.

"The only way to kindle fire is with fire, and once it is kindled you may safely leave it to burn. It is the teacher's duty to lay before the pupil the compass and chart and show him where men have explored and where the dark continents of thought lay. The teacher is also to breed the temper of judgment, sanity, and tolerance. In an intellectual sphere there is poise and ease, and that is where the university differs from the common school. The boy learns to use his mind like a tool of precision. The great thing about our universities is their democracy. The only difference in them is in achievement. It may be intellectual, athletic, or social, but these are the only lines of demarcation among the students.

"And so the function of the university of the United States is the service of the Nation, the preparation of specialized minds, not in the sense of being narrowed, but in the sense of being tempered for hard and delicate use."[1]

Printed in the *New York Times*, Dec. 12, 1902; some editorial headings omitted.
[1] There is a brief WWhw outline of this address dated Dec. 11, 1902, in WP, DLC.

To Isaac Minis Hays

Princeton, New Jersey.

My dear Mr. Hays: 13 December, 1902.

I am in receipt of your notice that I have been chosen a member of the Committee on the General Meeting of the American Philosophical Society for April 1903. I am so engrossed just now in learning the duties of my new office as Preisdent [President] of Princeton that I clearly foresee that it will be impossible for me to take any active part in the work of such a Committee. If I can be of service here in Princeton by correspondence, I shall be happy to render such assistance as I can; but I am afraid that I ought really to be excused because of the practical certainty that I cannot attend Committee meetings. I very much appreciate the appointment as a real honor, but I do not think that I ought to accept merely nominal duties.

Very sincerely yours,   Woodrow Wilson

TLS (Archives, PPAmP).

From Augustus C. Buell's[1] Review of
A History of the American People

[Dec. 13, 1902]

SOME COMMENTS ON
PRESIDENT WOODROW WILSON'S NEW WORK.*

Several histories of the United States or of the American people have been written, varying in style, tone, plan, and aspiration, from the volumetric grandeur of Bancroft to the conscientious plodding of McMaster. In the main these histories have been more or less polemic, and in their pages constantly crop out with more or less vehemence the zeal and passions of political contests or of personal feuds long past and gone. For example, Mr. Bancroft seldom records an event, great or small, without arguing the case all over again ex parte, and deeply impressing the reader with his own views as to its causes and consequences; and in most cases he leaves his reader with the inference that Mr. Bancroft considered his own views and opinions more important than the event itself.

In like manner, though necessarily in lesser degree, other American historians have wrought, with result that the average reader of them is likely to emerge from their perusal with a pretty clear idea of what one on [or] the other side held and struggled for in this, that, or the other great political controversy; with an impression that those on one side were demigods and those on the other side demons; and in the end he will find himself wondering how the country has developed so well.

At last, however, we have a "History of the American People" which is something more than a belated campaign document. Its author is Prof. Woodrow Wilson, President of Princeton University, and it is published in five superb royal octavo volumes profusely and judiciously illustrated.

Prof. Wilson's plan is unique, from the conventional American point of view. It contemplates a straightforward narrative, without discussion or discursion, of the rise and expansion of the American people from the first permanent settlement to the end of the nineteenth century. The reader will instantly observe the almost total absence of footnotes, the whole volume of the work being in main text. This fact indicates two things, first, that Prof. Wilson felt sure of his ground all the way, and, secondly,

* A HISTORY OF THE AMERICAN PEOPLE. By Woodrow Wilson, President of Princeton University. In 5 vols. Illustrated. Library binding, gilt tops. New York: Harper & Brothers. $17.50 net per set.

[1] Civil engineer, journalist, and biographer.

that he aimed to hold the reader to the thread of his narrative, and to avoid distracting or diverting his attention by introducing correlative or even contributing matter.

The professor avoids also another common fault of both American and English historians. He does not forereach. That is to say, he manages to carry his narrative along in close array like a phalanx of events instead of running out a single line far in advance and then saying: "We will now return to so-and-so."

To do this in writing a history of complex events covering a long period and involving many shifts of scene is, as every book writer knows, the most difficult of all literary tasks, and it is the one which authors most often abandon in despair. But Prof. Wilson has accomplished it to a degree that we have seldom seen equaled. And not only that, but, while carrying all along together, he has kept the relation of each event to every other perfectly clear, and when he has done with a situation, no matter how important its bearing or how complex its details, his explication needs no analysis. The reader sees clearly why and how it happened, together with its consequence in the sum total.

We shall not tire the reader with comparisons. Suffice to say that Prof. Wilson has written of the American people on a plan and in a mode very like those on and in which Thucydides wrote of the Greeks and Livy of the Romans. . . .

On the whole, Prof. Wilson's "History of the American People" is the most important work that has fallen from the press in a long time. It may be read with equal pleasure and profit by scholar, statesman, man of affairs, and intellectually well-grown undergraduate alike.

Its plan is comprehensive, its arrangement convenient, its tone moderate and judicial, its literary style plain, fluent, and easy. It is quite likely to become a textbook on American history.

AUGUSTUS C. BUELL.

Printed in the *New York Times Saturday Review of Books and Art*, Dec. 13, 1902; several editorial headings omitted.

A News Report of a Meeting of the Princeton Alumni in New York

[Dec. 13, 1902]

If the number at the dinner and the enthusiasm of the diners may be taken as an indication of the attitude of the New York alumni toward our new President, we should think that when he arose to speak at their dinner to him on the ninth, he must have felt that the New York alumni were stanch backers, loyal comrades, warm friends. They are. Nearly six hundred of them were there, the greatest crowd ever gathered at a Princeton alumni dinner in New York, or any other city, and their enthusiasm was, we believe, greater than at any previous banquet of Princeton or any other alumni in the whole country. Even the Waldorf waiters were impressed by it. More could not be said. The spirit of the banquet hall (the large ballroom where the charity ball is held) swept out past the Astor galleries, echoed down the stairs, along the corridors, and penetrated the innermost recesses of the Waldorf, where typical looking Astorians were having a typical Waldorf-Astoria time, enjoying such very different things in such a very different manner.

Perhaps the most striking thing of all about this dinner was that every one seemed to have such a good time—even those who had to speak. Generally a great dinner is a great bore. Men go from a sense of duty and then look as though they had done so, all through a long and rather dreary evening. But besides the self-satisfying feeling that it was their pleasant duty to launch their new leader, our alumnus President, this dinner was made a grand foregathering of the classes. Instead of long L-shaped tables, small tables were scattered all over the room and each class with men enough had a table to itself, and a remarkable number had men enough. The tables were assigned according to academic seniority, so that besides having much of the charm of individual class reunions, there was the additional interest of seeing and visiting at the nearby tables the old freinds [friends] of neighboring classes.

The classes, old and young, lost no time in making themselves heard, class cheers and class songs echoed through the hall before the diners got through the fish, and by the time the dinner was finished they were all in good shape to sing the following to the tune of Mr. Dooley.[1] The author of the words modestly left his name out of the small song book which the eminently efficient committee furnished for the occasion:

> Her educated graduates
> Are Princeton's special pride.
>   To turn out just good business men
> Nassau has never tried.

[1] A popular song of 1902, inspired by the famous fictional character created by Finley Peter Dunne. The song came from a musical comedy, *The Chinese Honeymoon*, with book and lyrics by George Dance and music by Howard Talbot.

But tho' we all wear glasses,
And look sadly underfed,
We think in choosing Wilson
That we showed our business head.

Chorus

For Woodrow Wilson, Woodrow Wilson,
  He's one of us, a son of Nassau Hall,
It's Woodrow Wilson, Woodrow Wilson,
  It's Wilson, Wilson, Wilson—that is all.

We're fond of Dr. Patton,
And we're fond of Nassau Hall,
  Perhaps we like the faculty—
They're not half bad at all;
  And so we'll cheer for Princeton
With a tiger, siss, boom, ah!
  For the President of Princeton,
And the Ruler of Nassau!

Now Butler at Columbia
Has cut the course in two;[2]
  He must have quite forgotten
Both the football team and crew;
  But Wilson down at Princeton
Didn't stand for it a bit;
  It struck him right away that it
Would graduate De Witt.[3]

Tracy Harris '86, the President of the Princeton Club of New York, presided, and James W. Alexander '60 acted as toastmaster, introducing with the grace for which he is so famous, the following speakers in the following order: President Wilson [']79, ex-President Patton, Mr. Austen G. Fox, the representative for Harvard; Judge Henry E. Howland for Yale; the Hon. George

[2] In his first annual report as President of Columbia University, presented to the Board of Trustees in October 1902, Nicholas Murray Butler proposed that a shortened course program of two years be added to the existing four-year program of Columbia in order, for one reason, to permit those undergraduates who wished to do so to enter Columbia's professional schools two years earlier than before. His proposal was at this time under intense discussion both at Columbia and elsewhere. The final decision of the Columbia faculty, adopted in 1905, was to permit students to enter Columbia's professional schools after two (or, in the case of the Law School, three) years of undergraduate study. They would receive the A.B. degree after a total of four years of undergraduate and professional work.

[3] John Riegel De Witt '04, a football hero at Princeton.

L. Rives, corporation counsel of New York, for Columbia, and the Hon. Job E. Hedges '84 as the representative of the Princeton alumni. The other places at the guests' table were occupied by Gen. Adna Chaffee, looking quite as grim as in his pictures but more agreeable; Col. Albert L. Mills, Superintendent of West Point; Col. Richard W. Thompson, representing Annapolis; Alexander C. Humphreys, President of Stevens Institute; Prof. W. M. Sloane, of Columbia University; Morris K. Jesup, George Harvey, editor of Harper's Weekly; Col. John J. McCook, Prof. John H. Finley, Chancellor Magie '52, Hon. W. M. Johnson '67, Adrian H. Joline '70, John D. Davis '72, of St. Louis; Hon. Mahlon Pitney '79.

A clapper stolen from Old North—by the present freshman class, it was said—was used by the toast-master as a gavel. There is something quaintly humorous in turning over to the trustees a piece of property filched from a campus building. In the course of Mr. Alexander's brief speech he said:

"I was going to say to-night that the King is dead, long live the King, but I cannot, for here on the other side of me sits the ex-King, alive and not kicking. [Cheers for Dr. Patton.] Of our new President I want to say that he has spirit, brains, education and the support and respect of the alumni, to help him carry on his work. There is only one thing that he lacks and that is cash. Like all of us, he has heard of the man with the hoe, but what he wants to hear about is the man with the dough. Now the minute Dr. Patton went to the Theological Seminary an old lady died[4] and left the seminary $2,000,000, which it didn't need any more than a dog needs two tails. It is astonishing—the small mortality among those with bequests for the college. But we announce to-night that we don't insist on people dying before they can give us any money. We are willing to take the devise and postpone the demise."

Many were not surprised to hear President Wilson say that $12,500,000 was the sum he had decided to ask for, because he had already made this announcement at Chicago. But those who may have thought it merely a vague longing—with the five hundred thousand stuck on for artistic purposes—were convinced that he meant business. He has figured up the whole job, and that is the amount his carefully detailed budget calls for. He not only knows how much he needs, but exactly why. Moreover,

[4] Mary Gelston (Mrs. Henry R.) Winthrop of New York, who had died, presumably during the spring or summer of 1902, and had left her entire estate to Princeton Theological Seminary. The Seminary received $1,750,000 from this bequest in 1905.

he said "We are going to get this money," and he said this as if he meant it, too. And that is the best thing about it.

Job E. Hedges's ('84) hit, in responding for the alumni, was the more notable in that he was the last man to be called on, the hour was past being late, had begun to be early, and many were satiated with food, drink and oratory, while others were anxious to go over to the Princeton Club to enjoy more of each after a more informal fashion. But Mr. Hedges aroused interest and provoked merriment in both classes of his hearers and made a fine ending to a successful dinner.

Then the crowd, or much of it, went over to the Princeton Club. President Wilson was called upon for another and different sort of speech, and showed that he knew how to do it. Then President Humphreys responded for Stevens Institute, and Col. Richard W. Thompson, President of the Annapolis Military Academy Alumni, for Annapolis. After a few songs and other diversions, Dr. Samuel Alexander '79 was called for and gave a long speech after the manner of a certain reverend gentleman.[5] It was so cleverly done that it convulsed his audience. Only one thing could have made it more of a hit, and that would have been the presence of the reverend gentleman himself. For the latter would have appreciated it and enjoyed it as much as any of them.

Printed in the *Princeton Alumni Weekly*, III (Dec. 13, 1902), 195-97.
  [5] Undoubtedly a reference to Dr. Patton.

To Cyrus Hall McCormick

My dear Cyrus,   Princeton, New Jersey   14 December, 1902.

I have thought very often of the conversation we had just before I left Chicago a couple of weeks ago, and as often as I have thought of it I have admired the generosity which led you to promise, at a time when you are clearly less free than at any previous time to act in such a matter, to consider, with your brothers and your mother, the question (very pressing for the University) what you can do for Princeton. I have also thought again and again what I could do to render the thing easier for you and relieve you of the necessity of immediate action. It is about that that I write. This letter is not dictated; I am using the machine myself.

The necessity that the University should obtain very large sums of money becomes more and more painfully evident to me as I look into one matter after another. The business has been allowed to run down very seriously, and we must face the facts. It has occurred to me that, if I get large sums, as I confidently expect I shall, it will take us quite two years, at the least, to put up the buildings, select the men, get the apparatus, mature the plans which such gifts will make possible. In most instances the first thing to do will be to erect a building or buildings before men or apparatus can be used or plans put into execution; and if we can see the money by (say) 1905 which is to be spent in salaries for the new men and in the actual administration of the new work we can go forward with the rest as if we had it already in hand.

What I have to suggest, therefore, is this: that, since you feel that it would seriously embarrass you to give away any considerable sum during the next two years, during which everything is involved in the reorganization of your business on the new basis,[1] you take the matter of a gift to Princeton under consideration in this shape: What can we authorize the University to look to us for in (say) 1905? I beg you to consider it in that light, in order both that your own embarrassment may be relieved and your power to be generous may be increased.

You know me, my dear Cyrus, well enough to know that I would not take the liberty of offering this suggestion if I were not sure of my ground with you. I feel obliged to be frank in these matters, and to throw myself on the indulgence of my best friends because I know the desperate needs of Princeton and feel all too profoundly my responsibility for relieving them.

My warmest regards to Mrs. McCormick.

As ever,

Faithfully and cordially Yours,   Woodrow Wilson

WWTLS (C. H. McCormick Papers, WHi).
[1] That is, the reorganization of the family firm of the McCormick Harvesting Machine Co. into the larger International Harvester Co. through the incorporation of other farm machinery companies.

To Cleveland Hoadley Dodge

My dear Cleve.,   Princeton, 14 Dec., 1902

I am to be in New York on Thursday evening, the 18th, to attend the Bankers' dinner.[1] Will you be at leisure some time the next day (the 19th) to see me for a talk about the University? Appoint any hour that will suit your convenience best.

Thank you for Miller's letter.[2] I shall have something to say about it when I see you. A talk is better than a letter.

As ever,

With warmest regards

Faithfully Yours,   Woodrow Wilson

ALS (WC, NjP).
    1 See the news report printed at Dec. 19, 1902.
    2 This letter from Lucius Hopkins Miller '97, at this time a student at Union Theological Seminary, is missing. As later correspondence reveals, it concerned the matter of continuing courses in biblical literature at Princeton. See WW to L. H. Miller, March 18, 1903.

To Robert Bridges

My dear Bobbie: Princeton, New Jersey.   15 December, 1902.

Thank you for your letter about Mr. Morris. C. C. [Cuyler] had told me that he (Morris) would come up on Wednesday. I had hoped that you would arrange to come with him, so that we could go over the ground together, with a full knowledge of your previous conversations with him. Could you not still manage to do so? It would be a great pleasure to see you.

As ever,   Affectionately yours,   Woodrow Wilson

TLS (WC, NjP).

Ellen Axson Wilson to Mary Eloise Hoyt

My dearest Mary,   Princeton, Dec. 15, 1902

I have been meaning for weeks and weeks to write and *beg* you again for the children's bill of expenses! Of course you know you never sent it. What I sent amounts to just $5.00 a week for them while with you; the trips to Phila. and all other incidentals are still unpaid because you *won't* send the bill! Arn't you ashamed to be so unbusinesslike!

We have had a hard time since you were here with your girls. With Jessie I am thankful to say all has gone well, though she is still in quarantine because the peeling is so slow; it looks as if the feet would scarcely be peeled before Xmas. We are still shut off from them both, but I have seen her through the door and she scarcely looks pulled down at all. Little Annie did just as well as regards the fever but in the third week she developed some of those terrible "sequela" and was very ill for two weeks. It was a heart trouble—inflamation of the pericardium;— and also a *very* painful swelling in the veins of the legs. Sister Annie was *perfectly* frantic! The child is quite relieved now, but will be an invalid all the rest of the winter. She is a nervous wreck,—had nervous prostration last winter in Germany.

Poor father has failed frightfully since we moved. He can't stand up alone now or even feed himself; he has to be attended exactly like a baby, and has one of those terrible attacks about every fourth day. He seems to suffer constantly and when coming out from his stupors moans and cries—even screams,—for hours, exactly, the nurse says, like a person who has been under the influence of ether. It is simply harrowing. I wish the children had not to see and hear so much of it; it is bad for their nerves. We have an attendant for him now who takes beautiful care of him. Not a "trained nurse" but a very kind & experienced middle-aged woman.

I am *very* glad that Woodrow is out of the house and out of the town so much about his business that he sees very little of it and can't even *think* of it very much. He *made* me go last week to the great Alumni dinner in New York and it is wonderful how much it helps to have ones thoughts forced into other channels for a few hours. I thought I had nerves that could be depended on, but I regret to say I have developed a habit of lying in bed awake half the night and holding myself!

But the dinner was *magnificent*—615 alumni gathered from all the country to do Woodrow honour; and the enthusiasm over him and his speech was enough to turn anybody else's head. The similar dinner to Hadley[1] was only 350 though they have so many more graduates. It was the largest alumni dinner ever held in America. The women of course only went to hear the speeches, sitting up in the boxes. I had a sort of "state box" assigned and was treated something like a queen, all the men crowding up to be presented, &c, &c. We stayed at the Cuylers, she giving me a woman's dinner beforehand.

Be sure to send that bill *at once*, also all the news about dear Florence and the rest of you. With devoted love from all to all.

Ever fondly yours   Ellen

It seems as if we will have no Xmas this year,—it seems impossible to get off for shopping! And by the way Margaret says you would have liked the little girl[2] to come up for Xmas, but of course you would not want her here as things are. All normal life is rather out of the question for us. Do excuse this scrawl!

ALS (in possession of William D. Hoyt, Jr.).
1 Arthur Twining Hadley, President of Yale University.
2 She is unknown to the Editors.

From Edward Dowden

My dear President Wilson,   [Dublin] Dec 16, 1902.

I heard with deep satisfaction that you were chosen—& in a way which showed so clear a conviction as to what was right—to preside over the life & work of Princeton University. My happiness in this appointment was really more for the sake of the University than for your own sake; but I felt too how a great task & a great responsibility would bring you the best summons & challenge, & that you would make a worthy response to such a challenge. And I felt also that Mrs. Wilson would rejoice in seeing you placed where your powers would have full play, & I could not help thinking how well she would fill her part, & help you in your task. We have to thank her for various papers about which I suppose my wife will write. We both read your Address with a hearty assent, & knew that it came out of your whole self.

I must congratulate you on the American History which I shall see that our National Library gets. We in Trinity Coll. Dublin lose Professor Bury,[1] who—you have seen—succeeds Lord Acton at Cambridge—a serious loss to us. We had great pleasure lately in reviving Princeton recollections when Professor West paid us a visit. And from him we learnt much that interested us as to educational ideals & also the visible & material growth of Princeton since the [Sesquicentennial] Celebration.

Today I have another link with Princeton—for the book I have had for hours in my hand—Professor James's Gifford Lectures[2] reminds me of the conferring of Degrees at the Celebration.[3] A most interesting book it is.

Give our kindest regards & congratulations to Mrs. Wilson.
                    Ra, Ra, Ra, Siss, Boom, Ra
                    Wilson, Wilson, Wilson, Tiger Tiger, Ra!
—which may not be quite correct, but relieves my feelings.
                    Ever sincerely yours   E. Dowden

ALS (WP, DLC).
1 John Bagnell Bury, who was leaving the position of Regius Professor of Greek at Trinity College, Dublin, to become Regius Professor of Modern History at Cambridge University.
2 William James, *The Varieties of Religious Experience: A Study in Human Nature, Being the Gifford Lectures on Natural Religion Delivered at Edinburgh in 1901-1902* (New York and London, 1902).
3 William James had received an honorary degree from Princeton along with Dowden and others at the Sesquicentennial Celebration in 1896.

Charles William Leverett Johnson[1] to
Susannah Batcheller Johnson

Dear Mama,   Princeton, Wednesday 17 Dec. 1902

Today I marched myself off to "Prospect" at 3 o'clock and had my interview with the President. It was hard for me to come to the point of going, but I am glad it is over and satisfactorily done. I began by telling him my feeling of uncertainty and what I hoped to make of myself and detailed the circumstances of my coming.

I think I did as well as I could—not at great length but I don't think I omitted any important point. He listened very attentively and explained how things stood. It came to about this: That the university was living up to its income, he had found on taking office, and was prevented from making many changes that were demanded. He spoke as if he really expected soon to get a larger revenue. But meanwhile he had come to the conclusion that it was due to the younger men here to state to them what was the expectation they might have of advancement. He wanted to be able to say to men that promotion would come to them in course of time, the time being dependent upon the success of the efforts made for an enlarged endowment. Accordingly he is going to gather all the information he can in regard to men's work from the professors in the departments. He was very tactful in his way of putting things—quite assuming the attitude that I was one who deserved promotion, without committing himself. As to Greek, his policy will be to get someone of note from the outside. That disposed of the possibility of a place in that department. I am sure it was wise to see him, as the consideration of my claims must be the more thorough by reason of it. . . .

Your loving son,   C.

ALS (C. W. L. Johnson Coll., NjP); P.S. omitted.

1 Instructor in Latin at Princeton.

From the Minutes of the Princeton Academic Faculty

5 p.m. December 17, 1902

The Faculty met, the President presiding. The minutes of the meeting of December 3 were read and approved.

The President announced the membership of the following Committees:

Committee on Examinations and Standing: Professors Fine, Thompson, Westcott, Prentice, Finley, Vreeland.

Committee on Special Students: Professors Westcott, Daniels, Harper, Prentice.

Professor Robbins was appointed to act as Chairman of the Committee of Instructors of the Freshman Class.

A News Item

[*Dec. 18, 1902*]

FOOTBALL BANQUET AT PRINCETON.

PRINCETON, N. J., Dec. 18.—Tiger Inn, one of the large upperclass social clubs of the university, last evening tendered a banquet to ex-Capt. Ralph Davis and Captain-elect John R. De Witt of the football team. The dinner was held at their clubhouse, on Prospect Street. In all forty men sat down at the tables, among whom were, besides the two guests of honor, President Woodrow Wilson, Prof. J. B. Fine of the Advisory Committee,[1] Prof. Henry B. Fine of the Faculty Committee, H. G. Duffield of the Graduate Committee, Jesse Lynch Williams, W. J. George of Lawrenceville, Prof. J. Grier Hibben, and G. R. Murray, the athletic Treasurer. The others were the members of the club and the managers and Captains of the various athletic associations. F. C. Fairbanks, 1903, of Indianapolis, Ind., son of Senator Fairbanks, acted as toastmaster.

President Wilson made the principal address of the evening. He expressed admiration for the conduct of Capt. Davis on the field, and his attitude both toward the team and the Faculty. He commended the election of De Witt, asserting that the new Captain would ably fill the place of Davis. Other addresses were made by Profs. J. B. and H. B. Fine and the two Captains.

Printed in the *New York Times*, Dec. 19, 1902; one editorial heading omitted.
[1] About this group, the Graduate Advisory Committee of the University Athletic Association, see Jesse Lynch Williams to WW, Sept. 25, 1891, n. 2, Vol. 7.

From Cyrus Hall McCormick

My dear Woodrow: [Chicago] December 18th, 1902.

I thank you for your kind letter of the 14th, and whenever I am able to make progress in the important matter which you have suggested I will advise you. For the next two or three weeks I shall be too much occupied with some special matters I have in hand to take the question up, but will put it on our docket as soon as I can.

I am,　Very sincerely yours,　Cyrus H. McCormick.

CCL (C. H. McCormick Papers, WHi).

A News Report of Remarks to the New York State Bankers' Association

[Dec. 19, 1902]

CURRENCY TALK AT DINNER.

To insure elasticity in the currency, the national banks should issue notes for more than the par value of the bonds deposited by them, according to the address delivered last evening to the bankers of New-York by William B. Ridgely, Controller of the Currency, at the annual dinner of Group VIII of the New-York State Bankers Association at the Waldorf-Astoria.

Dr. Woodrow Wilson, president of Princeton University, spoke on "The Relation of the University to Business"; the Rev. Dr. Robert S. MacArthur discussed "Bankers—the Promoters and Conservators of Civilization"; Major General Adna R. Chaffee, U.S.A., told of his experience with banks and bankers, and John S. Wise gave his views on "Some Things Which Bankers Don't Know." Dr. Adolf Lorenz, who came late, was also called upon for a few words.

The other guests were Dr. E. R. L. Gould, City Chamberlain; James Stillman, president of the New-York Clearing House Association; Archbishop [John Murphy] Farley, Frederick D. Kilburn, Superintendent of the Banking Department, New-York; Jacob H. Schiff, J. Sloat Fassett, Morris K. Jesup, William Sherer and Stephen M. Griswold, president of the New-York State Bankers' Association. . . .[1]

The next speaker, President Wilson of Princeton, began by saying that a college man was well able to discuss the currency, because he never saw it. He continued:

But the college man is needed in such affairs, for he should bring to them clear, sound, true thinking and because he is able to view them in their entirety, to decide upon them with a better idea of their proportions, without too much personal bias. The college man brings light, not heat. It is, therefore, desirable that a man like the college professor, who is not concerned with the active endeavor of getting money, should give his views upon financial subjects.

The danger of this country is provincialism. The trouble is that the small country banker doesn't know what Wall Street wants—he doesn't see the great forces that control the movements of currency. Our business in the college is to show the community of interest that exists throughout the nation. To do this national thing the university should draw its students from all over the nation. The more regions of the country you have represented, the safer an instrument for the service of the country is the university.

There is provincialism of the mind in respect to the subject. The difficulty is that laws are made by people who have not visited that region of thought. The mission of the university is to make its students citizens of the world of thoughtful men.

Printed in the *New York Daily Tribune*, Dec. 19, 1902; one editorial heading omitted.

¹ The individuals not identified in this report or in this and earlier volumes were the Rev. Dr. Robert Stuart MacArthur, author, editor, and pastor of Calvary Baptist Church in New York; Major General Adna Romanza Chaffee, commander of the Department of the East, U. S. Army, and formerly military commander of the Philippines; John Sergeant Wise, lawyer of New York and former congressman from Virginia; Adolf Lorenz, M.D., Austrian orthopedic surgeon, at this time visiting the United States; Jacob Henry Schiff, banker and head of the firm of Kuhn, Loeb & Co.; Jacob Sloat Fassett, lawyer, financier, and politician, at this time a banker in Elmira, N. Y.; and William Sherer, Manager of the New York Clearing House Association.

Notes for an Address

Brooklyn   Lafayette Ave. Church (Dr. David Gregg)¹
Sunday evening, Dec. 21, '02

The University and the Country

Our pride in the past of our race and country, not so much because of individual achievement as of the *motive* of individual achievement,—*idealistic common effort*, unselfish and for the whole

"*Public spirit*" our word.

Voluntary combination for a common object our method.—Every man put upon his honour and challenged to service.

Efficient combination our boast.

The University has served these ideals and methods

By being a *communitas* of ideals. Not learning so much as the *Spirit of learning* has made our universities seed ground. They stand beside the Church as *vehicles of spirit*

It propagates—

(1) The influence of individual idealists.

(2) National rather than provincial sympathies.
(3) The Spirit of affairs.
(4) The central religious idea of *service*

WWhw MS. (WP, DLC).
[1] Pastor of the Lafayette Avenue Presbyterian Church of Brooklyn.

A News Report of a Talk at the Lafayette Avenue Presbyterian Church, Brooklyn

[Dec. 22, 1902]

AMERICANS BORN LAWYERS.
No People So Able to Form Combinations,
Says Woodrow Wilson.

Forefathers' Day was observed last night at the Lafayette Avenue Presbyterian Church, Brooklyn, when President Woodrow Wilson of Princeton University spoke on "The University and Our Country." The speaker was introduced by the venerable Dr. Theodore L. Cuyler,[1] formerly pastor of the church, as "the first president of Princeton born on American soil."[2] President Wilson said in part:

The motive of the forefathers of our nation was that of religious faith and independence. This motive has become national. I do not say there is no other motive, but this dominates and permeates the nation. Because [The cause] of the motive is the achievement of the American vision of the idealistic for public service.

I believe in the utmost freedom of combination in a free country. There is no people so able to form combinations as the American people. We are born lawyers. There is no race that produces a people so capable of self-government, because there is an inborn sense of the power of combination—always under parliamentary rules.

I have heard denunciations and the expression of fear at the concentration of interests. The doubts extend to a plan for a concentration of government with a one man head. I should pity the man who undertook such a government. The inborn parliamentarian and the independence of thought of the race would make his lot a hard one. He would need to place a policeman at the elbow of every man, and then he wouldn't be sure of the policeman.

The American has no patience with inefficiency. We haven't time to put up with it. I know a great many uncomfortable things are said about our city governments. It is even customary for us when asked about them to say that we haven't time to discuss them; but we ought to discuss them. But we ought also to know what the trouble is, and the time will come when we shall know.

President Wilson then went on to say that the broadening education given by the universities would go a long way to help solve the problem.

Printed in the *New York Daily Tribune*, Dec. 22, 1902.

¹ The Rev. Dr. Theodore Ledyard Cuyler, Princeton 1841; pastor of the Lafayette Avenue Presbyterian Church, 1860-90; pastor emeritus, 1890-1909.

² Dr. Cuyler was in error, even if he meant that the American colonies were British, not "American soil," before 1776. John Maclean, Jr., tenth President of the College of New Jersey, was born in Princeton in 1800.

A News Report of an After-Dinner Talk at East Orange, New Jersey

[Dec. 23, 1902]

WILSON TALKS ON EDUCATION
Head of Princeton University Is Given
an Enthusiastic Reception at Dinner.

For the thirty-third time the New England Society of Orange last night commemorated and fostered the virtues of the fathers of New England and cultivated social relations among its own members in a Forefathers' Day dinner. For this 282d anniversary of the landing at Plymouth Rock the Orange descendants of the Pilgrims hied themselves to Commonwealth Hall, East Orange. . . .

Led by Franklin W. Fort, a number of Princeton men sang "In Praise of Old Nassau" as President Wilson rose to speak. The new head of the university was given an enthusiastic reception, for which he expressed his appreciation. His toast was "Forefathers' day," but he permitted himself the latitude allowed after-dinner speakers and discussed mainly educational thoughts. President Wilson said that as a Scotch-Irishman, born in Virginia, he never felt entirely at home in a function of the sort being observed. He gave a humorous account of the ability and shrewdness of the New Englander to "get ahead of the game," as he called it. He reminded his hearers that Virginia was settled thirteen years before the Pilgrims landed at Plymouth, and he insisted that the Pilgrims did not intend landing in Massachusetts, but proposed going to Virginia. Continuing, he said:

"In the hurry of our lives we are apt to forget the principles in the life of the nation, if we do not stop deliberately to recall them. A nation must recollect its years of experience, must consider what it has gone through with, its vicissitudes, its friends, its enemies, its errors. The function of a university is to preserve its memorials, to keep in the recollection of the youth the principles, the traditions, the impulses of race, to act as a sort of clearing-house where the indebtedness is cancelled, where the fine balances of thought must be thought out. When men quarrel with the university for reviving ancient learning, I reply that if we do not know the old thoughts how are we to distinguish the new ones? The old thoughts are indispensable parts of the record of human experience. I have come to believe that the real effects of university life are not wrought out in the classroom, but I would fain believe that they are wrought in the hours between 6 P.M. and 9 A.M., during the hours of comradeship.

"I have been to college, and I know that in these hours the students do not discuss deep matters, but a boy can't stay in college four years and resist the infection of fine thought. He resists it as much as he can. But a lad can't stay in college and not have something important creep into his thoughts. That is the whole gist of the matter when it is suggested to shorten the college course. We are told that when our boys become sophomores they have learned as much as our grandfathers had when they were graduated. But when our grandfathers were graduated they were seniors, and when our youngsters get as far as our grandfathers were they are sophomores, and any one who proposes that a sophomore shall be graduated doesn't know a sophomore. The sap of manhood is rising in a sophomore, but it hasn't got to his head. The atmospheric pressure, the subtle influence of comradeship, is a great deal, but the best thing that is happening is that some sort of comradeship is arising between the faculty and the students. What is greatest about the university is not the learning it imparts, but the spirit of openness of mind, of fairness, of openness to new impressions, the distrust of prejudice, the desire to canvass the field and to know the elements of judging before passing judgment, and that is the spirit which most young fellows get unless their case be hopeless.

"There is a double function for the university. It has to remind men that all titles to dignity are stored in the records of the race, and also that the records are not closed, and that this generation and the next generation must go on writing records which will show no decline. Every man must do his own thinking, and the one who doesn't will fall out of the race. The man who isn't bred to the temper of affairs, the processes by which men have controlled by their actions, has no place in a nation like this. This nation is a nation of captains, and the most difficult task is to fit men to be captains. Any man can follow in the ranks, but in this age he who can read the key to the battle and give battle and say which way the fight wins and which way the force shall be applied, is what is needed."

Printed in the *Newark Evening News*, Dec. 23, 1902; some editorial headings omitted.

From Theodore Roosevelt

My dear President Wilson: [Washington] December 23, 1902.

If you are to come on the 5th of February,[1] can you not arrange to leave on the afternoon of the 4th, take dinner and spend the night with me? If this is impossible, can you not come down the morning of the 5th and take lunch with me? In either case you see you would have your own dinner and night free at the time of the Alumni dinner.

Faithfully yours,   Theodore Roosevelt

TLS (Letterpress Books, T. Roosevelt Papers, DLC).
  [1] President Roosevelt had obviously read about Wilson's engagement to speak to the Princeton alumni in Washington on February 5, 1903. This speech was canceled on account of the death of Joseph Ruggles Wilson on January 21, 1903.

From Charles Scribner

My dear President Wilson: [New York] Dec. 23, 1902.

It is evident that you are overwhelmed with engagements at present and I do not wish to add to their number and I know that what you have most at heart is the success of your work in strengthening the University. But as I have read your addresses in various parts of the country and see the great interest in what you have to say about university education in connection with the state and business, the question of the length of the university course and its relation to professional schools, et-cetera, it has seemed to me that it would be a good thing to gather into one volume such articles and addresses as seem to you of the most importance. In this way you could place clearly before everyone what you most wish to say and I do not think it is possible in any other way to secure the thoughtful attention of those whose opinion you would most care for. There is a certain definiteness and responsibility attached to a book which is almost always wanting in an occasional address. If this suggestion interests you and you have no other engagements in the matter, we should be delighted to publish the book for you and should regard its publication not so much a business question as an opportunity to be of some service to Princeton.

Yours sincerely　　Charles Scribner

TLS (Letterpress Books, Charles Scribner's Sons Archives, NjP).

To Charles Scribner

Princeton, New Jersey,

My dear Mr. Scribner:　　　　　　　　24 December, 1902.

Your suggestion that I should collect in a volume the addresses I have been making this winter is a most interesting and acceptable one and I sincerely wish that I could follow it, but the truth is that only two of those addresses have been reported with any degree of fullness or in a form which I could work up into permanent shape. My speaking engagements are so many that it has proved out of the question for me to make more than a skeleton of the briefest sort of each address and I have found by experience that it is not possible for me after an address has been delivered to reproduce anything approaching a likeness of it.

I am afraid that the preparation of a book would mean nothing less than a preparation of a number of essays on the subjects which I have been discussing and that amidst my present rush of duties is out of the question.

I need not tell you how much I appreciate your thought and wish in this matter or how much I regret that it is not feasible for me to do the interesting thing you suggest.

With warm regard,

Very sincerely yours,　　Woodrow Wilson

TLS (Charles Scribner's Sons Archives, NjP).

To James Waddel Alexander

Princeton, New Jersey,

My dear Mr. Alexander:　　　　　　　24 December, 1902.

I cannot tell you how much gratified I have been by reading your letter of December 19th,[1] which came while I was away from home. It is delightful to know that you think my speech before the Bankers a decided success. I certainly feel that I made on that evening a great many interesting friends.

As for reproducing the address I very much fear that that is impossible. I had the barest skeleton outline and since that evening I have spoken on somewhat the same line on two other occasions. I feel quite sure that I could not disentangle that particular speech from the others; moreover I have reproduced a speech before and have found that what I dictated had only the merest ghostly resemblance to the subject. The singular mistakes of the press with regard to what a man actually says on such an occasion are provoking enough, but with my method of preparation and of speaking I really feel that I am helpless in the matter. Some of these days I may learn how to prepare a brief beforehand which will guard against such things, but with the present rush of engagements even that seems clearly impossible.

With warm regard and appreciation,
    Very sincerely yours,   Woodrow Wilson

TLS (WC, NjP).
[1] It is missing.

From Thomas Roseberry Good[1]

Dear Dr. Wilson   [Princeton, N. J.] Dec 24. 02

The past term's work has been so full of helpful influences to me, and your personal character and example have been so full of inspiration, I trust I may without offence, at this happy Christmas time, send you a word of grateful appreciation.

The tiger-lilies on this little card grew wild in the foot-hills of the Rocky Mountains, and bring you the greetings of one of your Western students.

May your Christmastide be blessed with health and peaceful joy, and the New Year bring you ever deepening satisfaction in your work and opportunity.

Believe me,   Respectfully & gratefully   T. R. Good

ALS (WP, DLC).
[1] Of Denver, at this time an academic special student at Princeton. He received the A.B. with the Class of 1904.

To Charles Henry Marshall[1]

My dear Sir: Princeton, New Jersey, 26 December, 1902.

A somewhat extended absence from home has prevented my acknowledging sooner your kind letter of the 22nd,[2] notifying me of my unanimous election as a member of the ROUND TABLE CLUB.[3]

I am deeply gratified by the election and accept it with a great deal of pleasure. I shall hope to be present at as many meetings of the Club as my engagements will allow and shall look forward to them with real zest.

With much regard,

Sincerely yours,   Woodrow Wilson

TLS (Papers of the Round Table Dining Club, NHi).
  [1] Chairman of the New York Board of the Liverpool & London & Globe Insurance Co., Ltd.
  [2] It is missing.
  [3] A private dining club, organized in 1867-68, which met monthly in the rooms of the Knickerbocker Club of New York. Among the members at the time of Wilson's election were Charles Francis Adams, John Lambert Cadwalader, Joseph Hodges Choate, Grover Cleveland, Edwin Lawrence Godkin, William Dean Howells, John La Farge, Alfred Thayer Mahan, Silas Weir Mitchell, Frederic Law Olmsted, and William Graham Sumner. Also elected in 1902 were Joseph Bucklin Bishop, Nicholas Murray Butler, Thomas Jefferson Coolidge, Arthur Twining Hadley, and Augustus Saint-Gaudens. *The Roster of the Round Table Dining Club, New York* (New York, 1926).

To Grace Parish Dodge[1]

My dear Mrs. Dodge,   Princeton, 26 Dec., 1902

I did not reach home till Tuesday,—very much tired out with my round of speech-making. Since my return I have been a little under the weather, out of sheer reaction; but I am now all right again, and able to appreciate to the full how delightful were the intervals *between* speeches, when I was with you and Cleve. and when I was with the Cuylers. It was truly delightful to catch a glimpse of your most attractive home, to see the children,[2] to meet Mr. and Mrs. Dodge[3] in so informal a way, and to feel the warm comradeship of real friends. I shall not soon lose the relish of it. My warmest regards to you all.

Sincerely Yours,   Woodrow Wilson

ALS (WC, NjP).
  [1] Wife of Cleveland Hoadley Dodge.
  [2] Elizabeth Wainwright Dodge, born Aug. 10, 1884; Julia Parish Dodge, born Jan. 5, 1886; and Cleveland Earl Dodge and Bayard Dodge, born Feb. 5, 1888.
  [3] Cleveland Hoadley Dodge's mother and father, William Earl Dodge and Sarah Hoadley Dodge.

To Andrew Carnegie

                                        Princeton, New Jersey,
My dear Mr. Carnegie,   27 December, 1902

I am sincerely obliged to you for your thoughtful kindness in sending me a copy of your Rectorial Address at St. Andrews.[1] It came while I was away from home, and I found it lying on my desk upon my return.

I have read it with the greatest interest. It has cleared my thought upon many things. I wish we might have such addresses at Princeton. My ambition is to make our men reading and thinking men and to keep their thoughts upon real things, so that the University may be directly serviceable to the nation. The Scots blood that is in me makes me wish to renew the traditions of John Witherspoon's day in the old place.

I was particularly struck by the concluding passage of your address. The men who command the thought and the emotions of the world are, after all, its masters,—and that is what every man who has the guidance and training of young men should keep constantly in mind.

I hope that you are fully restored to health and that we can at some not too distant day induce you to pay Princeton another visit. It would give me real delight to have you as my guest here at "Prospect."

With warm regard,

Sincerely Yours,   Woodrow Wilson

ALS (A. Carnegie Papers, DLC).
  1 *A Rectorial Address Delivered to the Students in the University of St. Andrews, 22nd October, 1902* (Edinburgh, 1902).

Notes for an Address to the Twentieth Century Club of Boston[1]

29 Dec., 1902

State Education: Its Relation to Political Life and Development.

Has not stopped short, amongst us, with *popular* education (i.e. the rudiments) but has gone on to the handicrafts and the University.

Popular education ⎱
Manual training ⎰   To familiarize the mind with the tools of thought,—language, mathematics; and with its environment,—history, geography, the elements of the physical universe

To familiarize the hand with its tools of precision.

We have expected too much of this first process
    Order, diligence, obedience, perception the only *moral* effects reasonably to be expected

Only the wide surveys and high topics of university discussion
bring the *spirit* into training,—and even they serve political
life and development only if they be made the instruments of
something more than information and training,—of enlightenment.

Seats of *learning*?

  Seats of the *catholicity* of learning, of the *spirit* of learning,
    from which may be had the wide and general view which
    will prepare men for the general life of society.

  Society is not saved by efficiency, but by judgment, sanity, de-
    votion, and the *statesmanship of the mind.*

  A body of specialists not the best jury.

Political life, a universal adjustment of *relationships*

Political development a progressive betterment of the adjustment;
  and the adjustment as much a matter of mutual understanding as of individual intelligence

Plain,.·., how education may serve political life and development
  1) By producing reading and thinking (observant) men
  2) By adding to these the social consciousness and conscience,
     which can be done only by a common life and the spirit of
     a place
  3) By keeping learning free from pedantry and making it
     seem an instrument of life

This can be done better by a private than by a State institution—
  an institution where particular ideals breed from generation to
  generation after their own kind,—and where the object is not
  the utilitarian object loved of the tax-payer, but the ideal object
  loved of men of vision

WWhw MS. (WP, DLC).
  [1] A news report of this address is printed at Jan. 3, 1903.

A Calendar

[Jan. 1-Dec. 31, 1903]

Printed calendar entitled *Year Book   Your Memory in Cloth Covers
1903*, with WWhw entries about lecture, professional, and personal
engagements.

Printed calendar (Wilson Library, DLC).

A Pocket Notebook

[c. Jan. 1, 1903-c. Dec. 31, 1904]

Inscribed "Woodrow Wilson 1903," with WWhw lists of potential
donors, notes, reminders, etc., relating mainly to the affairs of Prince-

ton University; also names and addresses, personal reminders, brief memoranda, etc.

Pocket notebook (WP, DLC).

To James Phinney Munroe[1]

My dear Sir,   Princeton, New Jersey, 1 January, 1903.

Your kind letter of yesterday has just been handed to me, and I am sincerely obliged for all its kind suggestions. But I must beg that you will give yourself no concern about me while I am in Boston. I am a good deal of a Bohemian in my going about on errands of this kind. You may count on my turning up at the Colonial Theatre at the right hour, enough beforehand to relieve you of anxiety; and I am promised for lunch afterwards to Mr. Bliss Perry, who is to have a few friends meet me at the University Club.

With much regard and appreciation,
                    Sincerely Yours,   Woodrow Wilson

WWTLS (WC, NjP).
    [1] Treasurer of the Munroe Felt & Paper Co. of Boston; author and lecturer on education and history; and chairman of the Education Committee of the Twentieth Century Club of Boston.

George McLean Harper's Review of
A History of the American People

[Jan. 1903]

Before reading a large historical work it is important to know what the scope and purpose of it are—what limitations the author has deliberately fixed for his endeavor. Is a given book mainly intended to bring to light new material? Then it may serve as a source, but only by rare chance will it be of direct use to the general reader. And again, some histories are valuable chiefly as books of reference; the facts, even minute particulars, are to be found in them, but no one cares to read them from beginning to end. They lack cohesion or informing unity. Books of these two classes need possess no marked literary excellence; there is not necessarily behind them a strong personality, determining by its pitch and compass the direction and validity of their effect. A third class comprises histories which are really essays on a large

A HISTORY OF THE AMERICAN PEOPLE. By Woodrow Wilson, Ph.D., Litt.D., LL.D., President of Princeton University. In five volumes. Illustrated. New York. Harper & Brothers. 1902.

scale. In them the character, temper, and antecedents of the author are everything. A dominant note sounds in them throughout. They may, without the slightest impairment of accuracy or judicial integrity, be warm with artistic ardor, not to say personal feeling. One rises from reading them with a clear sense of having observed a drama unroll, of having heard a high argument pleaded. These are not books merely to put on the shelf for reference, but they are books to read, if it may be, in a day or a week of complete absorption. In such a book no episode can be as thrilling as the whole; the parts are subordinated, and a general spirit pervades the particulars.

President Wilson's "History of the American People" is obviously of this character. Whatever excellence it possesses as a scientific work is incidental and tributary to its main interest, which is literary. Its purpose—what the author attempts and what he does not attempt—lies patent on every page. It is a history of the American people, the people of the United States and their ancestors on this continent, in what pertains to the national life. Except in discussing the periods of early exploration and settlement, where the details of social life possess fundamental importance, the national idea is not only foremost, but exclusive. Not that it is conceived in a doctrinaire spirit or with a display of prophetic fervor, as if the creation, development, and maintenance of the Union were a matter of destiny now at length made manifest. Nor is the book a mere study of constitutional law. Dr. Wilson secures unity of effect by assembling his material around the one idea that certainly is central and organic in the life of the nation. His book is therefore more of a political history than are Professor McMaster's "History of the People of the United States" and J. R. Green's "Short History of the English People." If, for example, inventions are referred to, it is chiefly for the purpose of showing how the cotton gin increased the hold of slavery or how the expansion of the West accompanied the building of railroads; and the rise of the modern kind of newspaper is mentioned chiefly in connection with party politics. Rigid discrimination has evidently been necessary in marshalling the vast mass of facts. Many important but not central fields of interest have been left outside the sphere of the work. Among these are State politics and State constitutions, municipal politics, and the growth of cities. Some attention, though not much, has been paid to the development of present political methods, the boss, the caucus, the primary, the convention. The interesting issues connected with the distribution of population in the last sixty or seventy years are only mentioned. The growth of our public school system, the transformation of higher education, the evolution of public and private charities, the present status and proportions of religious bodies—all these are scarcely so much as touched upon. No doubt such subordination of detail was a necessary part of the author's plan. Matters of this kind, previous to the Revolution, call for full notice because of their position in a formative period, but as the interests of the country grow more complex, a less ample treatment becomes imperative. As events crowd thick upon the calendar, events of wide diversity and showing no signs of convergence, it is no doubt wise to direct the reader's gaze only to what bears immediately upon the collective life of the nation.

In one important respect, however, Dr. Wilson has permitted himself greater freedom, and the reader may rejoice: the work abounds, even to its close, in descriptions of notable men, drawn to a generous scale and warmly colored. Among the most striking of these are the figures of William Penn, James Blair, Washington, Jackson, Lincoln, Grant, Lee, and Cleveland. They, and many others, particularly from early Virginia days, are depicted with rare skill. In no other detail of the work is so much excellent literary finish manifested, and surely the reconstruction of personality is an essential in historical writing of this kind.

To accomplish the task thus broadly sketched, the work, which contains in all about 1,700 pages, is arranged as follows: Volume I. narrates the exploration of our coasts and the arrival and establishment of English settlers down to the end of the seventeenth century; Volume II., the drawing together of the English colonies in common activity against the French and the Indians and for other purposes, with the approach of the Revolution and its consummation; Volume III., the establishment of a national government and its working, down to the election of Jackson, in 1829; Volume IV., the Democratic revolution, with the accompanying financial and social changes, also the extension of slavery and other causes of the civil war, with its course and termination, including a novel and extremely interesting account of the Southern Confederacy; Volume V., reconstruction chiefly, with a rapid survey of subsequent events, especially in national politics. Thus the record runs from 1492, or more particularly 1607, to the beginning of the twentieth century. Every chapter ends with a bibliography of resources and authorities for the period with which it has dealt, a significant distinction being thus made between crude material and historical literature more or less finished and fitted for general use. The illustrations, including maps, plans, and reproductions of old documents and prints, and especially portraits of distinguished men, are of great interest. Some of the imaginative drawings are less apposite, and the vignettes of modern celebrities, made from photographs, are less attractive, though possibly more truthful, than the portraits of older worthies, drawn from oil paintings and engravings.

The scope of the work and its main outlines being thus defined, it remains to observe, first of all, its structural qualities. And here, it may be, is its most solid claim to eminence, namely, its admirable proportions, its nice adjustment of emphasis, its breadth, fairness, and catholicity. It is a notable history of the United States written by a Southerner born, and yet no history of the United States breathes a finer spirit of appreciation for all the elements that have contributed to build the nation, to hold it together, and to make it great.

So thorough, indeed, is the blending of sympathies, so harmonious is the union of deep-rooted local pride with strong national sentiment, that the book may fairly be termed unique in the centrality of its point of view. A singular exception to its high merit in this respect is the fine-spun argument in palliation of the Ku-Klux movement. Otherwise the reconstruction period is treated in a temper and with a fulness which make the chapter devoted to it more valuable perhaps than any other in the book.

A novel fairness and an unusual breadth of conception mark the account of Andrew Jackson and his two administrations. As to the pre-revolutionary times, they are described with uncommon picturesqueness of phrase and extreme carefulness of manner. Here the effort to produce an artistic effect is more evident than in the later volumes. The resulting difference of style is very marked. The plainer and swifter narrative style in which the life of the Republic is told is more normal and on the whole more lastingly attractive. Yet when the highly wrought phrases come less frequently they are very effective, and we linger with delight over the consummate portraits which, even in the fifth volume, retain something of the leisurely elaboration of the first two.

As a test of the judicial temper that pervades the work, we have only to turn to the discussion of Tory sentiment and conduct. Here for once adequate consideration is bestowed upon the loyalists of the Revolution. The facts about them are for once frankly set forth. But, in this case, detachment may at this late day be reasonably expected of every historian. And one of the pleasantest elements of Dr. Wilson's history is his profound spirit of race. Most Americans of the better sort were glad to call themselves English until separation from the mother country became inevitable; and the qualities of blood that brought on the struggle were the strong English traits to which we owe much of what is best in our national life still. Dr. Wilson makes willing acknowledgment of all this. He also gives due prominence to the fact that it was only by a turn of the dice that our opponent in the War of 1812 was not France, rather than England. Few of our older historians possessed the detachment or were sufficiently removed in time from those early years to give either a true report of these facts or enough weight to them when once ascertained.

With respect to the questions of slavery and its consequences, President Wilson gives proof of a higher quality even than passive receptivity of truth; he shows a conscious, active determination to seek the truth and behold it steadily. A strong desire to be fair is a great element of charm in a man. It will serve, if need be, as a substitute for many showier virtues. It is also a source of charm in any book where its reassuring presence is felt.

Finally, a reader who has submitted himself to the power of President Wilson's history rises conscious of a few large and perhaps fresh thoughts astir within him. He cannot help being sensible, perhaps for the first time, of the really considerable antiquity and venerableness of our country and its institutions. We are much older as a people than the nation which we have created in the third era of our life on this continent. Again, he will be profoundly impressed with the consistency of our general character from almost the beginning down to the very present. There is encouragement in this thought. Considerations only second to these are the esssential and still vital relation of parentage between Great Britain and the nation to which she gave birth, and the happy isolation of our national life in other directions—our good fortune in avoiding hitherto almost all foreign entanglements.

Printed in the New York *Book Buyer*, xxv (Jan. 1903), 589-92.

A Newspaper Report of an Address
at Lowell, Massachusetts

[Jan. 3, 1903]

WOODROW WILSON
Talks on What it Means
to be an American

President Woodrow Wilson of Princeton university lectured on "What it Means to be an American," before the Middlesex Women's club yesterday afternoon. He spoke for more than an hour and the lecture was characteristic of the man, scholarly and impressive.

He said in part:

"There is no nation now talked about with so singular a mixture of fear and admiration as the United States. There is hardly a conference of ministers or an international convention, in which the chief topic discussed, in private if not in public, is not the effort made against Europe, in the growing supremacy of the United States. We ourselves are pleased with the supremacy. A party of lawyers was once discussing who was the leading lawyer. 'I am,' said one. 'How do you prove it?' asked another. 'I don't have to prove it,' he replied. 'I admit it.['] So with ourselves. We feel that we are no longer called upon to prove our supremacy. We admit it. With that admission has come an added touch of self-consciousness. We have always been a self-conscious people, but until now it has been the self-consciousness of the young fellow who believes that he will some day make conquest of the world. Our question, to all newcomers to our shores, has been, 'What do you think of America?' and we have shown almost absurd sensitiveness as to the answer. We have now the self-consciousness of assured power. The question now comes, what are we going to do with the powers which we have acquired.

["]The typical American does not now live on the Atlantic seaboard. He has gone west. The men in Boston and New York have sat at the receipt of customs and taken toll from typical Americans who were moving on.

"After the revolution we spent another century making a nation. The nation did not feel the full national consciousness until the Spanish war.

"We do not talk constitutional questions any more. We are grown. The question now is, what shall we do with our strength. That is what has happened since 1898. It means that another century at least, lies before us with a great question mark. We have to face this century with the qualities and powers which we got from the last century.

"You know, we have built a constitution which has proved admirably elastic. It was feared that a written constitution was too rigid; but we are good lawyers, and a lawyer can always read any possible meaning into a document.

"I am not quarrelling with this. I was bred a lawyer myself. I believe it is necessary that a constitution should be adjusted to suit conditions. I do not believe that anyone can say that the principles of the constitution have been ignored. But we have learned to be builders, have learned to give elasticity and adaptability to the things that we are to use.

"Again: We have learned to be frontiersmen. I do not know whether you understand what that means. Benjamin Franklin would have been an admirable frontiersman, because what he did not find, that he needed, he would have invented. I have my doubts whether John Adams would have stood the test. He was a man made for regions where politics live. I mean by politics, the art of combining and managing your fellowmen. There are not any politics on the frontier; there is nothing but work.

"The political committee meeting condition of affairs is the condition in which most of our American statesmen have belonged. That is not the frontier.

"We used to think that there was a peculiar brand of human nature, known as the American. We now know that American human nature is exactly like any other human nature. We have had a special American past, but what that past has taught us, is that we are of the same blood as the rest of mankind.

"You know, we pride ourselves on the character of our government; but we do not go into details. We do not mention our city government. We speak of the principles, and we teach the children in the schools to perform genuflexions to the national flag. That is all very graceful, and serviceable; but in the meantime, how about the government of the cities? How does it happen that there are model city governments in European monarchies and very few model city governments in free America? That is something for our private digestion, something which we do not talk about outside of the family. Bpt [But] it is a matter for reflection and we must remind ourselves that the job is not finished.

"For my part, I believe that a good deal can be done by education. I have not the Utopian hopes about education that some people have, because I have taken part in education. I believe, with a Yale friend of mine, that the human mind has infinite capacity for resisting the introduction of knowledge, and that therefore a man need not flatter himself that all he has got to do, to get the truth accepted[,] is to state the truth. I have always believed that the best work of a college was done between the hours of 6 in the evening and 9 in the morning, when the men worked their effects upon each other. I have noticed that even the dull fellows cannot get away from the place without catching something. One of the valuable services which college life performs is to keep men from the follies which result from segregation.

"It is not necessary for a man to be cultured, in order to be educated. A man is educated, who can, without a supreme effort, interest himself in things which he does not touch and handle every day. Americans are more amenable to interest in general topics than men living elsewhere, because, under their institutions and organizations, they are mixed with the affairs which are not their own; and the constant interchange gives them malleable[,] serviceable, adjustable minds.

"Such, therefore, are the men who must face the 20th century. Being an American myself, I cannot help hoping that we will do something very good with it. I have never been able, even through the processes of indigestion, to make myself a pessimist. I have never lost my faith in the essential soundness and wholesomeness of this nation."

Printed in the *Lowell* (Mass.) *Sun*, Jan. 3, 1903.

A News Report of an Address in Boston on State Education

[Jan. 3, 1903]

FUNCTION OF UNIVERSITIES

However little the auditors of Dr. Woodrow Wilson, president of Princeton University, who lectured in the Twentieth Century Club course in the Colonial Theatre, this morning, may have learned about the first part of his subject, "State Education," they certainly did learn something about the second part, "the relation of education to political life and development." Moreover, they learned some of the doctor's opinions on the greatly-debated topic of the day—shortening the college course to less than four years, and received a new idea on the raison d'etre of the university. Arguing that the province of the university is to develop the spirit of learning, and holding that this is a process rather than a method, the speaker made the following statement, which sets forth clearly his opinion on the college course: "I can't for the life of me see how a man can expect to graduate a sophomore, who ever saw a sophomore. They are lovable fellows: the sap of manhood is rising in them but it hasn't reached their heads."

Dr. Wilson faced a good-sized house when he was presented by James P. Monroe of the education committee of the Twentieth Century Club. He began his discourse by outlining the province of the public school. The public school, he said, is designed to supply the child with the tools of thought and the environment of thought. It is the field of information, but is not the field of inspiration. In the old time country school the two were combined, the pupil received inspiration as well as information; but in these latter days, when the children are gathered together in great masses, under a military drill and discipline, the spirit of education cannot be infused into them. Order, diligence, obedience and perception are all that are to be expected from the public school. A training in citizenship such as was to be had in the old country school is not to be had in the great schools of the present. Manual training has been added, but that only does in the practical sphere what the grammar school does in the intellectual sphere. The public school cannot determine what use the pupil will make of his mind when he leaves the school.

What we really want to get at is not the child's mind, but his soul, and the real route to that is through the things that are beautiful. Mathematics is a necessary experience, like the measles, for it keeps us from association with others of our kind. History, on the other hand, releases us into the broad field of companionship.

It is to get at the spirits of men that the university is created; to my mind it is not to make scholars. No undergraduate can be made a scholar in four years, and it is of them that I am speaking. In the graduate school we have to make scholars. The average undergraduate doesn't get learning, perhaps, but he does get the spirit of learning—that open mind hospitable to learning, that catholicity of spirit that is not prejudiced, that is amenable to argument, and that knows the broad horizon of the world of thought. Much of the spirit of learning is to be got in the classroom from the instructor, by the straight influence and sympathy of minds, but the very best effects of university life are wrought between six and nine o'clock in the evenings, when the professor has gone home, and minds meet minds, and a generating process takes place. In the classroom the man is on his guard against allowing anything to enter his mind, and it takes almost a surgical operation to get anything into some men. But with his fellows the man is off his guard and he allows things to creep into his mind unawares. This is not a method but a process, and requires time. For one, I am against shortening the process by reducing the number of years of a college course.

The community life in a university, too, has a great influence upon the men. It eradicates the provincial manner of thought and the provincial mind, which is one of the greatest dangers of education. The State Legislature and Congress act the same way. Many a man has gone to Washington with the thought of a county and returned with the thought of a country. What the country needs is not so much efficiency—no nation was ever saved by efficiency—but sanity, devotion, statesmanship of the mind. For only so long as there are judicial minds at the head of the nation will it be safe.

Political life consists of the adjustment of the various elements in society, and political development comes with the betterment of this adjustment. What most reformers do not know is their place in this adjustment. They isolate themselves in their minds, and announce that they will overthrow existing conditions by the sole power of truth. Their audacity is to be admired, but the whole body politic cannot be changed in a generation. The instrument of the reformer is wrong. What he wants is not compulsion, but persuasion, demonstration of his ideas and not law. Until the reformer has made the major part of the community see the need of his proposal there is no use in getting a law. As Henry Ward Beecher said: "A prohibitory law works everywhere but where it is most needed." A law is no use unless it is enforced, and an enforceable law must be backed by the majority.

Americans have known how to find their place in the adjustment of society better than others. They make things elastic. Take the constitution, for example. Its wording is just the same as when it was written, and it is the same, with the addition of some amendments, as the original document, but how changed is it in the reports of the Supreme Court. In fact, it isn't the law that governs, but what we read into the law. I don't believe that wisdom lies between the covers of a book (no man who has written a book can), but books are our only way of keeping our reckoning. By means of them we know which way we are going, and one of the greatest uses of education is to make the mind travel up and down the routes of the past as revealed in books.

To secure this desirable community of spirit in a university, I think that a location in a country place, where it is the whole

thing, is better than a location in a city where the students have
to travel back and forth on the cars. In the country college the
men are there all the time and the influence of the community is
soaking into them steadily. The university can make learning
seem not a pedantic thing, but a vehicle of life. Much is said
about the cultivation of character. Do not cultivate character;
cultivate virtue and highmindedness, and character will take
care of itself. The man who goes about making his own character
makes a prig of himself. I believe that the curse of the age is the
man who spends so much time thinking of himself. The enlightenment of study must take this out of a man. How can he conceive himself to be the centre of the universe or even a considerable personage in it, when he is in the presence of the
accomplishments of the ages?

Perhaps you do not see what all this has to do with State education. But I am speaking of the best education and that ought to
be good enough for the State to pay for, since only the best education subserves the State. The taxpayer is of necessity a utilitarian.
He cannot see the use of teaching his son anything that he cannot see the use of. Therefore, he isn't willing to pay for "seeing
visions," the only thing that really emancipates the human mind.
Education is meant to be a motive and not a cramming power.
It is not designed to fill the vessel but to give it power.

I have seen public school pupils make genuflections to the
United States flag, and repeat passages, the meaning of which
they did not know. They were led to believe that the flag stands
for acquiescence in the Government. On the other hand, it does
not stand for acquiescence, but for the biggest "kick" on record,
for the right to think for ourselves. If we can get Legislatures to
pay for giving men the right to think for themselves, we have
justified "State Education," for I do not know of any better way
of making a good citizen than by making a good man.

Printed in the *Boston Evening Transcript*, Jan. 3, 1903; some editorial headings
omitted.

To Martha Carey Thomas

Princeton, New Jersey,

My dear President Thomas,   5 January, 1903.

I take real pleasure in introducing to you my friend Miss Mary
Anderson of Red Springs Seminary; North Carolina. Miss Anderson is a most cultivated and charming woman whom I am glad

to make known to you as my friend. She is interested in all really interesting things, and is desirous of seeing Bryn Mawr on the inside.   Sincerely Yours,   Woodrow Wilson

ALS (President's Files, PBm).

Edward Graham Elliott's Memorandum of a Conversation with Wilson

[Princeton, N. J.]   Jan. 5th 1903.

I went to Prospect about 8.30 p.m. to consult W. about my course for the second term.[1] I had made out a partial list of subjects to be treated, such for example as the canal questions, Suez and Panama, China in 1900, the Monroe Doctrine &c. He expressed his approval of my choice and said he would leave the further determination of topics to my discretion. In reply to my suggestion that I had thought he might consider these topics as encroaching on the field of Politics, he gave me a very clean boundary line as a limit to my discussion of that phase of the questions: which was the following—some knowledge of world politics was necessary to a grasp of the subject, and so much & no more ought I to give,—in other words enough politics to elucidate the law in the case, but always maintaining the legal standpoint in the supremacy.

The question of conflict with other courses, particularly Finley's,[2] came up and while he said that in principle he was not opposed to parallel or competing courses being offered, yet he thought it inadvisable with so limited a corp of instructors—competition as the life of trade, he thought applicable to lecturers as well as business. In this connection he proceeded to give me in some detail his ideas regarding lecture courses: he considered that there were but two kinds of lectures: the one general, outlining disquisition upon a subject the object of which was to stimulate interest or excite curiosity so that the students would be impelled to further investigation. Under no circumstances was the imparting of knowledge to be considered an object of a lecture course. The second kind was of the nature of a minute and careful presentation of some very limited portion of a subject, which

---

[1] A second-term senior elective, "Some Unsettled and Current Problems of International Law."

[2] A second-term senior elective, "The Expansion of Europe," the description of which reads as follows: "Following the overflow of European peoples into other continents, considering the problems incident to this expansion and examining the methods of colonial administration."

was to serve as a model to the students of how scholarly investigation should be carried on. Upon neither of these should the student be examined, but upon the *subject*—and he should be given to understand that it wasn't possible to master the subject by reading any *one* book or syllabus of a book or lecture. His strictures on the use of syllabuses were most severe—he condemned them in unmeasured terms. Speaking further on the subject of lectures, he said perhaps I was not aware that he would be in favor of having those lectures of the first kind held in Alexander Hall and have the attendance optional—in that case the lecturer would have no one to blame but himself, if [he] had no audience; his opinion was that it would work wonders in the character of lectures delivered. It would put the bug on the lecturers, he said and laughed in that engaging way of his at the humorous thought of the plight in which it would put some of my colleagues.

In the course of the conversation regarding my second term elective it was agreed to restrict it to those men who have elected this term's work in International Law. I told him I would like to work with about ten or a dozen men, and he said that is what we would all like to do, but we mustn't be selfish, and spoke at some length of the desirability of work of that character, not neglecting to mention his tutorial system as recently outlined in his Chicago and New York speeches.

Due to my suggestion that I hoped he would call on me to help him in his work consequent on the examinations, a discussion arose upon the new courses he has developed since my undergraduate days, viz. the Elements of Politics & Constitutional govt. He gave me his definition of constitutional govt. in some such words as these—"a reasonably definite arrangement between governor and governed"—and then went into a short analysis of the course, how it was attempted to show what were the incidentals and what the essentials of constitutional govt.—e.g. the question of representation. In short it had as background the constitutional history of England, the home of constitutionalism, but did not neglect the variants as seen upon the continent. The discussion of his idea of liberty was most interesting to me, presenting the question in a somewhat new light. I had remarked that Jellinek had at one time given a most delightful excursus on that subject in his seminar and I should be very glad to hear his lectures on that topic. With that he proceeded to expound to me at some length his views on the subject. Liberty in its last analysis is to him a frame of mind; it is that comfortable adjustment of the relations between governed and governor, which leaves the former contented; it is a state in which he is not galled by the restrictions of government. He illustrated his view by a bird that is caged—so long as the bird does not come to a realization of its imprisonment, so long as the bars are not sensible barriers against which it beats in its desire for larger action, just so long is that bird free. He stated it in about these words—"As long as he does not feel himself unfree, I can not think of him as not enjoying liberty." He quoted Burke to the effect that those are free who think they are. I questioned him regarding the Russian peasants who, while being ground down by the strong arm of oppression are yet intensely loyal to the Czar. He replied that so long as this peasant was not conscious of the restrictions imposed upon him,—by that I mean, knew nothing else and had no ideals of anything better, and hence was satisfied with his condition, so long was he free. *Liberty* therefore was something relative, dependent upon the mental attitude of the individual. *Constitutional liberty* however was different. Here it is that our idea of the participation of the individual in the acts of government finds its proper place. This might be called institutional liberty and it was his object to separate the two concepts of liberty and institutional or constitutional liberty.

He told me, much to my surprise, that his mind was not philosophical—that as soon as he felt that, in pursuing a thought[,] his mind was leaving the solid basis of fact, he at once "shied off," as he expressed it. I had always thought him very philosophical and told him so, but he protested no & went to some pains to prove to me that I was mistaken. He said he could not follow men into their philosophical discussions, as e.g. the subject of law, and for this reason Burke was the only writer he read with complete satisfaction, remarking that Burke had never been philosophical except in his [blank] and he didn't care for that. (Laughing)

For this reason, he said, he never cared for the German writers on Jurisprudence. Jellinek, Gesetz & Verordnung, he said was an exception—he had not read Das Recht des Modernen Staates & so did not know whether he could follow Jellinek's discussion of law therein contained or not. I had remarked that Jellinek was philosophical in his turn of mind & writings, having first been a student of philosophy and later turning to law. We had a discussion as to the meaning of the word philosophical, as he thought perhaps I was using it inexactly,—he had previously used *sanction* as applied to law in a loose sense & I had been bold enough to bring it to his notice—indirectly of course. He rejected as philosophizing the gathering together of a body of facts and erecting out of them a theory—that was mere generalization, not philosophy. To him philosophizing seem[s] to be typified in the procedure of the higher mathematician and the physicist, who postulate an unreality, as e.g. that a straight line is the shortest distance between two points or that a body, elevated above the earth, if allowed to fall, will do so at a constantly increasing rate of speed, while all the time they say there is no such thing as a straight line and that it is only in a vacuum that the law of falling bodies holds true. But given these, and similar postulates, then, say they, we can construct for you the sciences of mathematics and physics.

For the same reason he said that purely theoretical political economy did not appeal to him. When Mill, for instance, takes his man in a vacuum so to speak, and disregarding the influence of family and locality, which to give but the single instance impedes the free distribution of labor, and tho' expressly saying that his vacuum-man does not and can not exist, still constructs from him, a system of political economy, then, said W., I lose interest.

The above discussion arose from his having said that his mind was too strongly legal in its constitution, to allow him to accept of International Law as law in the sense used in the courts. I took the position that it was law as much as any other body of rules so-called, that, if you will, it was an undeveloped or rather a not fully developed system, but nevertheless law. "Oh," said he, "that is my stumbling block—it is undeveloped and I feel the need of some other word to express what is meant by Int. Law." He finally agreed that it was a question of definition in the end. Definition was of use only to those who did not need it—who had thought the thing out for themselves, at the end properly, as text in the beginning. He defined law as that body of rules "which somehow gets itself enforced," having previously used the word sanction in the limited sense of punishment, whereas I defined law as those rules of human action whose enforcement was guaranteed, maintaining that sanction or penalty was only one of the guarantees, to which he acquiesced. Upon my questioning if he didn't believe that the social forces were strongest guarantees he said yes, undoubtedly, but still he was not disposed to accept International Law as law in the ordinary sense—he was more inclined to compare it to social laws which a man dare not break for fear of ruining his career. He admitted that the whole tendency of modern thought was toward the adoption of the view that International Law was law of the truest sort.

In the discussion of philosophy, he remarked that the philosopher was inclined to rationalize—to take his premise and then build up his theory, rather than to take his facts and make a generalisation—and in this connection he drew an illustration from Jellinek, Gesetz und Verordnung, to the discomfiture of my statement that Jellinek was a philosopher. He said that in reading that book he came to a statement which made him know Jellinek knew whereof he spoke: it seems that Jellinek was discussing the adoption of English constitutional forms in Germany—after a long exposition of how almost by chance and accident and without premeditation, the introduction of all money bills had been firmly established as within the province of the House of Commons, he remarks that this feature has been adopted in almost every lower house in Germany. The Germans, he said, had attempted to rationalize and *therefore* this meaningless adaptation. Others, W. said, might have admitted the attempted rationalization *and* that the adaptation was meaningless, but that J. was the only one who would use the *therefore*. W. quoted again from Burke to the effect that "Politics (in its broadest sense) is the development of institutions in which reason plays but a small part."

This I admitted was all very true and was exactly the position Jellinek assumed—thereby removing him from the field of philosophers according to W.'s definition—and furthermore that I could never run mad after a theory and follow it into inconsistencies or disregard of facts, whereat he remarked "Now, you are speaking like a member of your race." He had earlier remarked that the Anglo-Saxon mind was legal in its character. He agreed with Sir Henry Maine in believing that the reason why the Americans had been so successful in setting up their govt and developing their institutions was because they had been so long subject to a king. He then touched upon the ideas as set forth in the Atlantic for Dec. 02, in the article, American Ideals. I said that I had read the article with much pleasure, as I had long wished to know his views regarding the Philippines. He asked if I did not think his solution of the question more reasonable than that of the anti-Imperialists. I told him most decidedly,—that I didn't see how students of constitutionalism or institutional history could adopt the anti-imperialistic views which would confer upon the Philippines a constitutional government. He said that he would like to believe they couldn't, but it was like personal vanity, which he characterizes as the most contemptible of all characteristics—he would like to believe it couldn't exist in a great man, but we had too many examples where it had.

I told him I had been much interested in Jellinek's view that imperialism must lead to a strengthening of the central govt. and a loss of individual liberty as it has hitherto existed in America. W. asked why so? and cited England as a case in evidence of imperialism, strong central govt. and a wide measure of individual liberty. He spoke of the inherent Rights of Man and he indicated his disbelief in such rights when written in capitals. He told me of a very interesting discussion on the subject with [William M.] Sloane, who, having heard that W. had told his class there were no rights of property except as developed by the law, brought him to task, but without changing his views. W. said he might admit that a man had the right to as much of this world's goods as might be necessary for subsistence and as might be acquired without damage to the same right of his fellow man, but that man had the natural right of storing up these acquired goods, he could not accept. Sloane he said, was incapable of discussing the question calmly.

He recounted to me his experience with Henry van Dyke at a dinner given at the Ivy Club by [Walter A.] Wyc[k]off in honor of White,[3] a pro-Boer. Wycoff it seems gets all such in tow. Wilson was about the only pro-English one of the party and their sentimental twaddle made him boiling mad. The discussion naturally drifted to the discussion of our own colonial possessions; Vandyke spoke up in his "expansive" way, saying he *knew* that democracy could not exist with over-sea possessions. Wilson turned on him at once,—"Henry, how do you *know* it can not? Can you give me an instance in history where a democracy like ours has had colonies?" He was compelled to admit that he could not, and W. continued,—"I am perfectly willing to discuss the likelyhoods in the case, as to what will or will not be the effects, but *you* don't *know* and *I* don't *know* what the result will be." I asked him what happened to that despicable quality, personal vanity, and he laughed heartily, adding that it may have been a bit brutal to treat V. so, but sought to palliate the severity of his conduct by alleging his extreme disgust at having been drawn into something, with which he was entirely out of sympathy.

W. said there was about as much reason in what they said, as there was in[4]

Hw memorandum (H. M. Robinson Papers, CSmH).
  [3] The Editors have been unable to identify him.
  [4] Elliott stopped in mid-page and for some reason never completed this memorandum.

From the Minutes of the Princeton University Faculty

5 p.m. January 7, 1903.

The Faculty met, the President presiding. The minutes of the meeting of December 3, 1902 were read and approved. . . .

The President reported the appointment of the following Committees:

On Entrance: H.D. Thompson, Chairman, S.R. Winans, J.B. Carter; J.P. Hoskins, T.M. Parrot, J.H. Coney, E.H. Loomis.

On Course of Study: The President, Chairman, C.F. Brackett, C.A. Young, A.F. West, A.T. Ormond, W.B. Scott, S.R. Winans, H.B. Fine, G.M. Harper, W.M. Daniels, F. Neher.

On Library: C.A. Young, Chairman, C.F. Brackett, S.R. Winans, W.B. Scott, H.B. Fine, L.W. McCay, E.C. Richardson, G.M. Harper, W.M. Daniels, J.G. Hibben, P. van Dyke, J.B. Carter, T.M. Parrot, J.S. Morgan.

On Graduate School: A.F. West, Chairman, C.F. Brackett, W.B. Scott, H.B. Fine, W.F. Magie, G.M. Harper, H.D. Thompson, J.G. Hibben.

On Discipline: The Dean, Chairman, H.B. Fine, A.T. Ormond, J.G. Hibben, S. Axson, E.O. Lovett, H. McClenahan.

On Attendance: E.Y. Robbins, Chairman, the Dean, the Registrar,[1] H. McClenahan, J.H. Coney, A.H. Wilson,[2] G.M. Priest.

On Schedules: H.D. Thompson, Chairman, H.S.S. Smith.

On Catalogue: W.F. Magie, Chairman, H.D. Thompson, H.S.S. Smith.

On Teachers and Schools: H.D. Thompson, Chairman, J.H. Westcott, W. Libbey, F. Neher, S.R. Winans.

On Sanitation: C.F. Brackett, Chairman, W.F. Magie, W. Libbey, The Curator.[3]

On Out Door Sports: W.B. Scott, Chairman, H.B. Fine, C.F.W. McClure.

On Non Athletic Organizations: W.F. Magie, Chairman, J.G. Hibben, W.M. Rankin, S. Axson.

On Music: A. Marquand, Chairman, L.W. McCay, W. Gillespie.[4]

On Trask Lectures: The President, Chairman, A. Marquand, H. van Dyke, J.H. Finley.

On Examinations and Standing.

　Academic: H.B. Fine, Chairman, H.D. Thompson, J.H. Westcott, W.K. Prentice, J.H. Finley, W.U. Vreeland.

　Scientific: C.G. Rockwood, Jr., Chairman, A.H. Phillips, E.O. Lovett, E.H. Loomis, F. Neher.

On Special Students:

    Academic: J.H. Westcott, Chairman, W.M. Daniels, G.M. Harper, W.K. Prentice.

    Scientific: W.M. Rankin, Chairman, H.S.S. Smith, E.H. Loomis, G.M. Priest.

Instructors of Freshman Class.

    Academic: E.Y. Robbins, Chairman.

    Scientific: C.G. Rockwood, Jr. Chairman. . . .

[1] Henry Nevius Van Dyke.
[2] Albert Harris Wilson, Instructor in Mathematics.
[3] That is, James MacNaughton Thompson.
[4] William Gillespie, Instructor in Mathematics.

From W. M. Jackson[1]

My dear Sir,   Campbellsville, Ky., Jan. 10, 1903

A few weeks ago I bought your History of the American People and I want to thank you for the pleasure and satisfaction I have had in reading it. We at last have an impartial narrative of our country's history, just to all sections, and I feel that the South especially owes to you a deep debt of gratitude in that you have portrayed her in a just light and yet have not detracted from any other section.

With highest esteem, I am

           Very truly,   W. M. Jackson

ALS (WP, DLC).
[1] Principal of the Campbellsville, Ky., High School.

To W. M. Jackson

My dear Sir: Princeton, New Jersey. 13 January, 1903.

Allow me to thank you very warmly indeed for your letter of January 10th. I do not know any praise of my History that I would rather hear than that which you bestow, that it is at once frank and just, and certainly there is no region from which I would rather have that praise than from the South. One of my chief objects in writing the History was to do justice to the region in which I was bred and which I love, the region which, I think, also I understand and can without presumption speak for. I am indebted to you for a warm act of kindness.

          Very cordially yours,   Woodrow Wilson

TLS (Wilson Letters, Vi).

From Azel Washburn Hazen

My dear Dr. Wilson   Middletown, Conn. 16 January [1903].

I must tell you in what a delightful way I became the happy possessor of your History of the American People. Ever since your charming courtesy to *us three* in Princeton,[1] Maynard[2] has shared his parents' fondness for you. Hence it was entirely his own idea, while during the Holidays he was earning a little money in his uncle's store, to purchase these noble books as a Christmas gift to his father. Thus I am reading them with a tenfold happiness.

What a beautiful and royal Inauguration you had. Let me thank you once more for the pleasure you gave me in allowing me to witness it. Yet to me the choicest moments of the day were the few spent in your home. Your warm greetings, and those of Mrs. Wilson will never be forgotten.

Now when you come to Middletown in June[3] will you not *both* be our guests while here? If affection for you constitutes a claim, there is none stronger than ours.

Mrs. Hazen unites with me in genuine love for you all.

Believe me always

Most Sincerely Yours   A. W. Hazen

ALS (WP, DLC).
[1] See A. W. Hazen to WW, April 15, 1901, Vol. 12.
[2] His son.
[3] When Wilson was to give a bicentennial address on John Wesley. The text of this address is printed at June 30, 1903; a news report of it at July 1, 1903.

To Emma C. Spenser[1]

                                    Princeton, New Jersey,
My dear Miss Spenser,   19 January, 1903

I have been away from home and am able only just now to reply to your kind note of the sixteenth.[2] It is a most acceptable thought to a man of letters that intelligent people care to talk of his life and writings; but I do not know what to say to the Kenilworth Club of Passaic except that I thank them most sincerely for stopping to think of me. You ask about my name. I was christened Thomas Woodrow Wilson; but my mother wished me to use the two family names and I did not like the form T. Woodrow Wilson. I therefore incontinently dropped the Thomas altogether—and have almost forgotten it.

With much appreciation,

Sincerely Yours,   Woodrow Wilson

ALS (PP).
¹ Kindergarten teacher in the Passaic public school system.
² It is missing.

To Augustus Thomas

Princeton, New Jersey.

My dear Mr. Thomas: 19 January, 1903.

I am sincerely sorry to say that I am to be so tied up on the 21st, that it will not be possible for me to be present at the dinner and annual meeting of the National Institute of Arts and Letters. I should particularly like to hear Professor Loundsbury,¹ but it turns out to be impossible for me to come.

Very sincerely yours, Woodrow Wilson

TLS (WC, NjP).
¹ Thomas Raynesford Lounsbury, Professor of English at and Librarian of the Sheffield Scientific School of Yale University.

A Memorandum by Henry van Dyke

Princeton University January 22nd, 1903.

Memorandum for President Wilson in regard to the views of the English Department on Sophomore English.

(1) It is the unanimous and clear judgment of the department that, if possible, arrangements should be made for two hours required English throughout Sophomore year. It is suggested that the class should be divided into two parts, as nearly as possible equal in size, but the division to be made, if possible, according to the preference of the members of the class. In the first term, part one should take the General Survey of English Literature under Professor Axson; part two, a course in Argumentative Composition under Professor Covington. In the second term, the parts should be reversed, and the course in Argumentative Composition should be somewhat modified, and called Advanced Composition, under the instruction of Professors Covington and Harper.

(2) In case an arrangement should be made for two hours of sophomore English required in the first term, and elective in the second term, the arranged should be the same as above, except that in the second term the choice between the General Survey and Advanced Composition should be altogether elective.

Respectfully submitted on behalf of the Department,

Henry van Dyke

HwS memorandum (WP, DLC).

From Edith Gittings Reid

My dear Mr. Wilson   [Baltimore, c. Jan. 22, 1903]

I am so, so sorry for you in your sorrow.[1]

I know you are dear to many—thank God—and many are dear to you. But you will miss your father so, and with our nearest we are hardly ever ready to say "it is best" or that the time has come.

My love to Mrs. Wilson. I wish you could bring her down here to me for a few days rest. Can't you?—or *won't* you? It will always be a regret to me not to have known your father.

Your very faithful friend   Edith Gittings Reid

ALS (WP, DLC).
[1] Dr. Wilson died in Prospect on Jan. 21, 1903.

A News Item

[Jan. 24, 1903]

The Secretary of '79 writes to tell us in confidence "the Real and Genuine Coronation of President Wilson, in comparison with which the celebration of October 25 appeared tawdry," took place on Friday, January 16, at the semi-annual '79 dinner at William B. Isham's house in New York.[1]

Printed in the *Princeton Alumni Weekly*, III (Jan. 24, 1903), 262.
[1] Another of the famous Isham dinners, about which see WW to EAW, May 6, 1886, n. 1, Vol. 5.

A News Item

[Jan. 24, 1903]

REV. JOSEPH R. WILSON, D.D.

The venerable Rev. Dr. Joseph Ruggles Wilson, father of President Woodrow Wilson and one of the most distinguished ministers of the Southern Presbyterian Church, died at Prospect on Wednesday of this week, in the 80th year of his age. Dr. Wilson has been in feeble health for two or three years and has lately made his home in Princeton with his son. . . .

A brief service was held at Prospect, Thursday noon, conducted by the Rev. J. Hendrik de Vries, D.D., and Prof. Dr. John Grier Hibben, after which the remains were taken to Columbia, S. C., where the interment was made.

Printed in the *Princeton Press*, Jan. 24, 1903.

A News Report

[Jan. 24, 1903]

FUNERAL SERVICES OF THE LATE
DR. JOS. R. WILSON.
They Were Held at the First Presbyterian Church
Yesterday Afternoon—Burial in Churchyard.

The funeral services of the late Dr. Joseph R. Wilson were held in the First Presbyterian church yesterday afternoon at 2 o'clock, the body having arrived here in the morning. The service was conducted by the Rev. Dr. [Samuel Macon] Smith assisted by the Rev. Dr. [William Thomas] Hall, who is at present moderator of the southern Presbyterian general assembly and Dr. J. Wm. Flinn, chaplain of the South Carolina college and a special friend of the family.

Dr. Smith read the psalm and announced the hymns. Dr. Flinn read the lesson from 1 Cor. XV, and Dr. Hall offered the prayer.

The hymns used were "Lead Kindly Light" and "How blest the righteous when he dies." The choir rendered two beautiful pieces also. The pall-bearers were as follows:

Honorary—Rev. W. M. McPheeters, Rev. R. C. Reed, Rev. W. T. Hall, Rev. H. A. White, Rev. J. Wm. Flinn, Mr. W. A. Clark, Mr. Douglas McKay, Mr. W. R. Muller.

Active—Messrs. T. S. Bryan, D. R. Flenniken, J. S. Muller, D. L. Bryan, C. H. Baldwin, Jr., A. C. Squier, S. B. McMaster, Thornwell Muller.

Printed in the Columbia, S. C., *State*, Jan. 24, 1903.

A Tribute to Joseph Ruggles Wilson

[Jan. 24, 1903]

JOSEPH RUGGLES WILSON.

Rev. Joseph R. Wilson, D.D., LL.D., who died in Princeton, N. J., and whose funeral was conducted from the First Presbyterian Church yesterday, was a man whose "passing" deserves more than casual mention.

He belonged to a somewhat large class of men who were born and reared in the north but who came south in early manhood and became thoroughly identified with the section of their adoption. Dr. Wilson made Virginia his home just ten years before the great civil strife was joined. At the actual outbreak of the war he was a resident of Augusta, Ga., and pastor of the First

Presbyterian church of that city, one of the leading churches of the south. It was in this church, in that memorable year 1861, that the Southern Presbyterian church was organized by the presbyteries lying within the territory of what was then the Confederate States of America, and which has ever since preserved its separate existence in spite of all the many and manifold inducements offered to it to unite again with the Presbyterian Church in the United States of America, popularly known as the Northern Presbyterian church. The leading spirit in that organizing movement was the brilliant South Carolina genius, teacher and orator, James Henley Thornwell; the moderator of the assembly was Benjamin M. Palmer and the clerk of the body was Joseph R. Wilson, pastor of the church in which the meeting was held.

It was inevitable, therefore, that Dr. Wilson should have a prominent part in moulding the character and shaping the course of the organization just starting on its career in such critical troublous times. It was a juncture that called for the guidance of ecclesiastical statesmen, men acute, able and discreet; men wise to discern the times; men who were master builders. The men needed were not wanting and the papers then adopted amid all the travail of those times, in the storm and stress of passion unparalleled, remain models of moderation to this day, monuments whose inheritors feel no call to modify or amend, and to which after forty odd years they still point with pardonable pride.

The position Dr. Wilson took in that initial assembly he held with growing influence till increasing infirmity led to his retirement a few years ago. From 1861 to 1898 he was the clerk of the General Assembly, present annually at every meeting. This fact gave acquaintance with the church in all its sections, and a familiarity with its history, and an understanding of its precedents not shared by any one else and made him easily one of the most influential men in the whole denomination.

He was a man rarely qualified to maintain such a position: highly gifted by nature, he was one dowered with scholarly instincts, developed and enriched by ample culture, crowned with the wisdom that comes from ripe experience as a man of affairs, and with all his rich resources ready for instant use in facile, fluent speech, he would have been a leader in any body to which he belonged, a leader by the divine right of royalty.

As a writer he had few equals and possibly no superior in ecclesiastical circles. There was nothing flamboyant in his rhetoric, his taste was far too fastidious for the bizarre to any degree or in any direction; but for a style clear, perspicuous, chaste, individual without eccentricity and beautiful without weakness he was remarkable. He prepared his discourses with great care and was listened to with great delight by large audiences of the most cultured people; his sermons would bear printing simply as specimens of pure, lofty literature.

He was an ornament to any circle, courtly and courteous, genial and affable, sparkling in epigram, overflowing with exuberant bonhommie, he was a companion to beguile the longest, weariest hours and give life to their most leaden feet. His personal presence was eminently fit for the man: in his prime he was as handsome a specimen of magnificent manhood as one would find in a day's journey, one among a thousand.

In all the positions and relations of life he was highly favored; few of his fellows have had the rich wine of existence in fuller measure than he, and now that he is gone it is pleasant to think that the gloaming gathered about him in such an ideal situation—that his last hours should be spent in the thoroughly congenial home of the distinguished son in whom his love and his pride found such open and just joy, ministered to by his tenderly loved and loving daughter and surrounded with every influence that could mitigate the approach of that inevitable hour that was to round out 80 years of fruitful life.

One by one the great men who have made our history in church and State are leaving us, and it is most fitting that in such cases the youth of our southland should be asked to pause and consider the men the mantle of whose mission is falling on their shoulders and recognize and appreciate the character which alone can prove worthy to wear such mantles.

Printed in the Columbia, S. C., *State*, Jan. 24, 1903.

To Betty Brese Blodget

My dear Miss Blodget,   Princeton, 26 Jan'y, 1903

I cheerfully comply with your request for my autograph. It is a small return for your kindness in desiring it.

Sincerely Yours,   Woodrow Wilson

ALS (in possession of the University Cottage Club, Princeton, N. J.).

To Edwin Anderson Alderman

Princeton, New Jersey.

My dear Dr. Alderman: 29 January, 1903.

I have been very much interested in your letter of January 23rd,[1] but I must admit that the task it sets me quite daunts me.

I have again and again tried in my own thought to answer the question about what specific influences and traits of character the South has contributed to the general variety of the nation; but I have never been able to formulate a satisfactory answer, and I have come to the conclusion that my mind was not fit for that sort of analysis. I have no doubt that it would be possible, in a series of say a dozen biographies, to give the best types of southern life in the old regime, and I sincerely hope that you will do it. But it seems to me that the only way in which the distinct contribution of the South can be brought out in biography would be by making the picture of each man an intimate view of personal and social relations which would reveal the society in which he lived, which would show him both as a partaker in that society and as an originative force in the determination of its character. Literary skill and minute portrayal, it seems to me, would do more in such a case than philosophical analysis.

With apologies for my incapacity in such matters,

Very sincerely yours,   Woodrow Wilson

TCL (RSB Coll., DLC).

[1] Neither the original nor a copy of Alderman's letter is in the Wilson Papers or the Alderman Papers. However, Alderman had sent identical letters to a number of writers and scholars in both the North and the South, saying that he was about to undertake a biographical study of southern contributions to the American character and requesting his correspondents to tell him what they thought these contributions were and to suggest the names of the half dozen historical figures who best symbolized them. Dumas Malone, *Edwin A. Alderman: A Biography* (New York, 1940), pp. 155-56.

To Cleveland Hoadley Dodge

My dear Cleve: Princeton, New Jersey.   29 January, 1903.

I shall be very glad to take up the matter about which Lucius Miller has been writing you just as soon as I get around to it. I will then ask him to come to see me. His ideas do not fit mine by a good deal, but his suggestions have enough elements in common with my plans to make me feel confident that we can hit upon something that will be agreeable to both of us.

Always cordially yours,   Woodrow Wilson

TLS (WC, NjP).

To Cyrus Hall McCormick

My dear Cyrus: Princeton, New Jersey. 30 January, 1903.

Bridges, Pyne, Cuyler and I have all seen the plans and sketches made by Benjamin Wistar Morris for the '79 dormitory, and we are all equally pleased. We left Mr. Morris with the understanding that he was to forward the plans and sketches to you, and I hope you will like them as much as we did. We have had several consultations with Mr. Morris, and the plans have been several times modified in accordance with our suggestions. In each of the interviews we have found Morris of the right stuff, not only artistic and quick to appreciate what was needed, but also very sane and reasonable in following instructions. It seems to me we have found the right man.

I hope that you are all well, and that you will give my warmest regards to your mother, Mrs. McCormick, and your brothers.

Faithfully yours,   Woodrow Wilson

TLS (WP, DLC).

To Nicholas Murray Butler

Princeton, New Jersey.

My dear President Butler: 30 January, 1903.

I have been peculiarly touched by your kindness in expressing your sympathy for me in the loss of my father.[1] The more so because, though I several times drew paper to me to do it, I could never suit myself with any expression of sympathy for you in your still more intimate and overwhelming loss.[2] I want you to know, though I cannot express it, my warm sympathy for you, and my deep appreciation of your thought for me.

Most sincerely yours,   Woodrow Wilson

TLS (N. M. Butler Papers, NNC).
[1] Butler's letter is missing.
[2] His wife, Susanna Edwards Schuyler Butler, had died on Jan. 10, 1903.

To James Woodrow

Princeton, New Jersey,

My dear Uncle James,   30 January, 1903.

Thank you very warmly indeed for your letter, accompanying the undertakers' receipted bill. I did not quite understand from the wording of your letter whether you had yourself paid the bill or had simply asked them to receipt it for my convenience.

I enclose a cheque which, unless you paid the bill yourself, I will ask you to endorse over to them.

I have felt the reaction of our long period of anxiety and its distressing end very strongly since I got back. I was of course plunged at once into the arrears of work which had accumulated on my desk. I have only just now worked my way out to a breathing space. And the work itself was very wholesome for me. But it has brought unusual fatigue.

I am glad to say that I keep well, hovever [however], and that we are all well. It has been a great pleasure to tell the dear ones here of my visit to you. That at least was all pleasure, despite the sad errand. I shall not forget how sweet you all were to me. Your affection was a real restorative, and I am deeply grateful.

All join me in loving messages.

Affectionately Yours,   Woodrow Wilson

This is not dictated. I use the machine myself.

WWTLS (in possession of James Woodrow).

To Peyton Harrison Hoge[1]

My dear Dr. Hoge: Princeton, New Jersey.   31 January, 1903.

Allow me to thank you most warmly for your kind letter of sympathy which reached me this morning.[2] The blow of my father's death has been very hard to me, and my spirits come back with difficulty; but I try to remember that it is far better for him, and that even though he is gone in person, I still have all that is best of my long association with him to live upon as spiritual capital.

With much regard,

Very sincerely yours,   Woodrow Wilson

TLS (photostat in RSB Coll., DLC).
   [1] Pastor of the Warren Memorial Presbyterian Church of Louisville, Ky., and Dr. Wilson's successor as pastor of the First Presbyterian Church of Wilmington, N. C.
   [2] It is missing.

A News Report about the American Rhodes Scholarships

[Jan. 31, 1903]

The President and Dean West '74 represented Princeton at a conference in Philadelphia this week, with Dr. Parkin,[1] the agent of the Rhodes trustees, who is consulting with American educational leaders, before preparing his recommendations on the best method of assigning the Oxford scholarships for the United States, bequeathed by the late Cecil Rhodes. President Remsen of Johns Hopkins University and Provost Harrison and two deans of the University of Pennsylvania[2] were the other members of the conference, which represented New Jersey, Pennsylvania, and Maryland. Three points were agreed upon by way of advice to Dr. Parkin, namely, that candidates for the Rhodes scholarships from these three states must have had at least two years in an American colleges [college], that they must be between nineteen and twenty-three years of age, and that they must represent the state of their legal residence—not their college residence. It was also agreed to advise that there be an appointing committee in each of these states, the President of Johns Hopkins to be the chairman of the Maryland committee, the Provost of the University of Pennsylvania to be chairman of the Pennsylvania committee, and the President of Princeton to be chairman of the New Jersey committee. In this the conferrees simply followed the example of the Massachusetts, Rhode Island and Connecticut conferences.

Printed in the *Princeton Alumni Weekly*, III (Jan. 31, 1903), 275-76.
[1] George Robert Parkin (1846-1922), Canadian-born educator, advocate of British imperial federation, and first Secretary of the Rhodes Scholarship Trust.
[2] Charles Custis Harrison, Provost of the University of Pennsylvania. The two deans were probably Josiah Harmar Penniman, Dean of the College Faculty, and William Romaine Newbold, Dean of the Faculty of Philosophy.

To Theodore Roosevelt

Princeton, New Jersey

My dear Mr. President,   1 February, 1903

I have just learned that, out of thoughtful consideration for me, in view of the death of my dear father only ten days ago, the Princeton men in Washington have postponed for a few weeks the dinner they were to have given on Thursday evening next.[1] I had meant to attend the dinner, of course, as an official duty, not a private pleasure, and I had also looked forward with the greatest gratification to spending the previous night, the night of the fourth, with you. But I must confess that, though I would not have asked for the postponement of the dinner, it jumps with my feelings. I am for the time being in no spirits for pleasure. I feel, therefore, that I am relieving you of a sad guest in asking you not to expect me on Wednesday, and in begging that you will pardon my seeming lack of appreciation in doing so.

Of course you were making no special arrangements for my entertainment. I hope, therefore, that I am causing you no inconvenience. It goes hard to deny myself the pleasure of seeing you and of speaking with you about things which I am sure hold the thoughts of both of us; but I know that you will understand and approve.

With warmest regard and appreciation,

Faithfully Yours,   Woodrow Wilson

ALS (T. Roosevelt Papers, DLC).
  1 The meeting was held on March 27, 1903. See the news report of it printed at March 28, 1903.

George Louis Beer's[1] Review of
A History of the American People

[Feb. 1903]

The introduction of the critical spirit in historical research was a prominent phase of the development of thought in the nineteenth century. It was part of the general movement of intellectual scepticism, which would not accept of the truth of any statement without first carefully testing its accuracy. In historical work this spirit demanded that all the sources of knowledge be examined. *Ne quid veri non audeat historia* came to be the cardinal principle on which every scholarly historian worked. So rigidly was this principle insisted upon that only recently a French historian, Seignobos, asserted that it was impossible to write a scientific history of the nineteenth century, because no individual, during the normal span of life, could personally examine the enormous mass of available material.[2] This prevailing view led inevitably to great specialization in historical research; investigation was confined to necessarily narrow limits. It brought about also, in some instances, a false perspective, one in which the method came to appear as an end, not simply as a means. A great mass of purely antiquarian matter was produced; few had the courage to oppose the current of scientific thought and to produce large synthetic works, resting on the labors of specialists. The horizon was narrowed, broad views were lost

"A History of the American People." By Woodrow Wilson. Harper, 5 vols. $17.50.

  1 Businessman and historian. At this time, he was on the verge of retiring from the business of importing tobacco to devote himself to the historical studies of the British colonial system that made his reputation.
  2 Charles Seignobos, *A Political History of Europe Since 1814*, trans. Silas M. Macvane (New York, 1899), p. v.

sight of. Though the unity of history was insisted upon, there were few books the reading of which made this fundamental truth self-evident. We had accumulated, as Lamprecht said, *"Eine tote Masse in sich wohlzubereiteten Stoffes."*

In recent years there set in against this attitude a marked reaction, one sign of which were those co-operative histories in which specialists joined forces to produce works of broader scope. Such are Traill's "Social England," Lavisse's "France," Helmolt's "Weltgeschichte."[3] Another form of compromise to meet the well-recognized evil were the various historical series published. President Wilson's book is a product of this reaction, unique in the respect that it is the first attempt, in recent years, of an American scholar to cover in a formal manner the entire field of American history. It is characteristic of him to make the attempt, for already a number of years ago, in his charming essay on Adam Smith, he deplored the narrow specialization of the day, claiming that "our thinking needs . . . men to fuse its parts, correlate its forces, and centre its results." "Without them and their bold synthetic methods," he said, "all knowledge and all thought would fall apart into a weak analysis."[4] The utility, even the necessity of such broad works is undeniable. They unquestionably demand a higher order of ability than that manifested by the specialist. To write a satisfactory work of broad scope requires pre-eminent attainments,—a comprehensive and firm grasp of facts and a large mental outlook. It involves also an immense amount of labor, for the secondary material, on which it must to a large extent be based, has accumulated rapidly; and finally, it requires a complete mastery of method, as this secondary material has to be tested in the same rigid way as was the original material on which it rested. When success is so difficult, it is no wonder that failures are so frequent.

It was sound advice that a brilliant English critic gave, when he told us to estimate a book for what it is, and not to find fault with it because it is not something else. Obviously, it is impossible to adopt the same standpoint in evaluating a text-book, a self-confessed compilation, a scientific monograph, and a formal general history. Usually, the preface gives us some clue to the author's intentions. Here, however, unfortunately the preface is wanting. So, perforce, we have to rely on the publisher's circular

---

[3] Henry Duff Traill (ed.), *Social England: A Record of the Progress of the People* . . . (6 vols., London, 1893-97); Ernest Lavisse (ed.), *Histoire de France depuis les origines jusqu'à la Révolution* (9 vols., Paris, 1900-11); Hans Ferdinand Helmolt (ed.), *Weltgeschichte* (9 vols., Leipzig and Vienna, 1899-1907).

[4] See Wilson's essay, "An Old Master," printed at Feb. 1, 1887, Vol. 5.

and on the clue furnished by the title. From these it is legitimate to infer that Wilson has sought to do for American history what Green did for English history. Bagehot served as model in Wilson's work on Congressional Government; Green performs the same function now. While in his former work Wilson followed very closely Bagehot's spirit and method, his "History of the American People" differs radically in execution from Green's "English People." Green maintained that "political history, to be intelligible and just, must be based on social history in its largest sense," and this view he carried into practice. Priest, reformer, scholar, poet, and scientist figured in his pages side by side with warrior, statesman, and king, each in his way as an exponent of great forces in the nation's life. Not so with Wilson; his is a political history in which England and the colonial governments, and later Washington, always occupy the centre of the stage. Green gave us a history of civilization; Wilson has given us merely a history of political life, which is merely one phase of a people's activity. Beyond an occasional enumeration of names, no space is devoted to literature, art, science, religion, or scholarship. The book has unquestionably been misnamed; it is not a history of the American people.

There are in general two ways in which the political life of a people can be treated by the historian. He can, by an analysis of social forces and institutions, show how the past gave birth to the present. The interest in this method is centred on the state, on the people organized into a racial, religious, and economic entity. This is the scientific or philosophical method, and appeals primarily to the understanding. On the other hand, in some writers whose scientific impulse is less strong than is their artistic sentiment, we find a desire to visualize the past, to reconstruct it, and, by putting themselves in the place of the protagonists in the story, to get at the innermost workings of their minds. To such men history is primarily literature, closely akin to the epic, drama, and romance. The past appeals to them, not so much because it explains the present, but on account of the great men which it contained. Such historians were Carlyle and Froude, and such, on a more modest scale, is Wilson. He is pre-eminently an artist, not a scientist. He has reconstructed past politics as they appeared to people of the day, and his pages in consequence glow with life. He appeals through the emotions, and thus only mediately, to the intellect.

The question arises, whether or no such a narrative, life-like and vivid though it be, leads to an understanding of the past.

In a certain sense it does, for it arouses our imagination and sympathy, and we are better able to understand the immediate reasons for certain measures and acts. But in a higher sense it explains nothing. The immediate and self-confessed motive for an act is rarely the underlying one. We may realize why men acted in a certain manner, but what were the great social and natural forces which conditioned their every action, of this it tells us nothing. It emphasizes the ephemeral and accidental, and ignores the permanent and normal features. Wilson is a political historian, and such historians, as Morley said, always seek "the superficial and immediate causes of great trans-actions."

In his effort to get at the standpoint of the time, he inevitably judges events with the eyes of the well-informed statesman of that day. He voluntarily abandons the vantage ground which the lapse of time affords him. One result of this attitude is his general tone of placid impartiality. In the great conflicts of the world there is but little to choose between the individual morality of either victor or loser. When we study the men and not the movements, we naturally find little to blame. Wilson is neither a chauvinist nor a partisan. Nay, so far is he carried by his sym-pathy with the motives influencing men that in one instance, at least, he condones an attitude which seems clearly immoral. The treaty which recognized the independence of the United States contained certain clauses intended to secure the payment of debts due to English merchants and also to secure the restora-tion to the Loyalists of their confiscated property. After men-tioning in detail the amount of the debt incurred by the Colonists in supporting their long war for independence, he says:

> No wonder the men in responsible charge of public affairs in America rejected with a touch of bitter passion the demand of the treaty of peace, that they should in addition to all this, re-store to the loyalists the property they had lost, *and pay to British merchants debts which antedated the war.*

As already stated, a mastery of method is not essential to the specialist alone, but also to the general historian. We do not ex-pect such a writer to have an intimate acquaintance with all the sources, but we do demand of him a complete grasp of the sec-ondary material. He must have digested and assimilated the mass of well-prepared material that is on hand. There's no excuse for misstatements based on a misunderstanding of a broad series of facts, and there is no excuse for purely mechani-cal reliance on other people's work. Let us cite an instance illustrating what we have in mind. Speaking of the early history of North Carolina, Wilson says (vol. i., pp. 252, 253):

> Worst of all, the governor whom the proprietors had sent them sided with the King's officers in enforcing the Navigation Acts, whose enforcement would spoil their trade. They sold their timber and their cattle very freely to shrewd skippers out of New England, who brought them what they needed from the ports of the Puritan colonies, got their timber and cattle, disposed of them in the West Indies, and came back again thence with good cargoes of sugar, rum, and molasses, for which they took tobacco, to be sold at home for export into England,— all without license from the crown and in plain defiance of the Acts.

This statement is remarkable, not only because all the transactions mentioned were in no way in contravention of the Navigation Acts, but also because a few pages farther on Wilson gives a fairly accurate outline of the commercial legislation that bound together the Colonies and the mother country. He either wrote this passage without thinking,—unfortunately, the writing of history requires thought,—or he does not understand the economic relations that existed between England and her American plantations. Though Wilson has no footnotes and furnishes us with no guidance, it will be interesting to go farther, in order to see the origin of this passage. In Prof. William J. Rivers's account of the Carolinas, published in Justin Winsor's "Narrative and Critical History"[5] (vol. v., part. i., p. 295) we read:

> The New Englanders, with their characteristic enterprise, had long been sailing through the shallow waters of the Sound in coasting vessels, adapted to such navigation, and had largely monopolized the trade of North Carolina; buying or trafficking for lumber and cattle, which they sold in the West Indies, and bringing back rum, molasses, salt, and sugar, they exchanged these for tobacco, which they carried to Massachusetts and shipped thence to Europe without much regard to the navigation laws.

This selection (itself taken almost literally and without acknowledgment from Hawks's "North Carolina,"[6] vol. ii., p. 470; *cf.* also *ibid.*, p. 264) bears close resemblance to the excerpt from Wilson. The difference, however, between the two should be noted. Rivers, or rather Hawks, is accurate. The clause "without much regard to the navigation laws" refers only to the tobacco being

[5] William J. Rivers, "The Carolinas," in Justin Winsor (ed.), *Narrative and Critical History of America* (8 vols., Boston and New York, 1884-89), v, 284-335.
[6] Francis Lister Hawks, *History of North Carolina* (2 vols., Fayetteville, N. C., 1857-58).

shipped to Europe, which is here used as opposed to England. It was legal to ship tobacco to England, in fact it had to be shipped there; it was illegal to ship it to the Continent. Wilson, by substituting England for Europe and by making the illegality refer to all the transactions, distorts the whole meaning. At first glance it would appear that the connection between the two is a close and immediate one; we have reason, however, to believe that it is only indirect and mediate. In John Fiske's "Old Virginia and Her Neighbors"[7] (vol. ii., p. 281) we read:

> Ships from Boston and Salem brought down to Albermarle Sound all manner of articles needed by the planters, and took their pay in cattle and lumber, which they carried to the West Indies and exchanged for sugar, molasses, and rum. Often with this cargo they returned to Albermarle and exchanged it for tobacco, which they carried home and sent off to Europe at a good round profit, in supreme defiance of the statutes.

John Fiske was likewise a scholar whose capacity for assimilation was greater than was his power of production; he also, at times, relied mechanically on the results of his predecessors. Though he does not cite Rivers or Hawks as an authority, the connection between the two passages is patent. This has, however, no bearing on the question at issue now. It appears from a close examination of the three excerpts that Wilson's statement was derived from Hawks or Rivers through Fiske. This is apparent from the general context and from the fact that the construction of Wilson's and Fiske's statements is similar. In addition, both omit the commodity "salt," which appears in Hawks's and Rivers's statements. There is, besides, other evidence for taking this view. In the reign of Charles II, a statute was passed in virtue of which certain colonial products could be exported only to England and her colonies. These were the so-called "enumerated" commodities, and among them was "cotton-wool," the ordinary term of the day for raw cotton. By omitting the hyphen and putting in its place a comma, Fiske (op. cit., vol. ii., p. 46) adds another commodity to the list. Instead of "cotton-wool," we have cotton and wool. Wilson (vol. ii., p. 16), evidently relying on Fiske, goes one step farther, omitting cotton and mentioning only wool. He is a great admirer of Adam Smith, and could have avoided this error by a closer study of those pages wherein the great economist explained the principle underlying the policy of enumeration.

It is not necessary to comment on this method of writing

[7] John Fiske, *Old Virginia and Her Neighbours* (2 vols., Boston and New York, 1897).

history. It reminds us forcibly of the *bon mot* made at the expense of a well-known French historian, that he wrote with his pen in one hand and Sismondi's work in the other. It is such slipshod mechanical, uncritical work that subjects American scholarship to the unfortunately all too just strictures of a Münsterberg.

Having now seen in general the nature of Wilson's work, let us turn to his handling of the different periods. As a whole the treatment of the colonial period is the weakest. Here we find the loosest control of facts, not alone from the standpoint of accuracy, but also from that of literary form. The narrative is at times involved and confused, and many of the sentences are poorly constructed. The period from the recognition of independence to the election of Jackson is, on the other hand, by far the most satisfactory. In this section we have some brilliant character drawing. Jefferson's nature has never been so tersely summed up as it is in the following words: "He deliberately practised the arts of the politician and exhibited oftentimes the sort of insincerity which subtle natures yield to without loss of essential integrity." Equally commendable is Wilson's account of the War of 1812. This episode is treated in proper perspective to the larger contest, the great duel between England and France, on which the fate of civilization seemed to hang. Barring verbal changes, the fourth volume, covering the years 1829 to 1865, is nearly identical with the text-book entitled "Division and Reunion" that Wilson published a decade ago. There is, however, one important addition to it, the chapter on the Confederate States, which is the only social history which the work contains. This chapter seems to be based primarily on Professor Schwab's scholarly monograph.[8] It was well worth while to instil a breath of life into that heap of material, thus rendering Professor Schwab's labor of years accessible to the general reading public. The last volume takes us from the Civil War through the Reconstruction era down to the second election of McKinley. These years, however, hardly lend themselves to historical treatment. We are beginning to get ready to look upon Reconstruction impartially; we have hardly approached that attitude when we arrive at events so recent as is the Spanish War.

We have still left for discussion the question whether or no Wilson contributes anything to the already existing knowledge of the subject which he treats. This is, after all, the final test of a

---

[8] John Christopher Schwab, *The Confederate States of America, 1861-1865: A Financial and Industrial History of the South during the Civil War* (New York, 1901).

book. While, from an abstract standpoint, the whole course of historical development does exist absolutely outside of our perception of it, still all our knowledge of this development is subjective, and, as each historian has his individual characteristics, it follows that each history must inevitably bear the imprint of the author's mind. As has been crudely, but forcibly, said, history must have at least one "twist." Minds with any elements of originality and force must necessarily view the same facts in a slightly different light, and we must expect from such men, reviewing the whole course of our national development, some new ideas, some new grouping of facts, an accentuation of some line of development peculiar to each one. It would be difficult to point out anything new in view-point or in ideas for which we are indebted to Wilson. Beyond a slight shading here and there, the prevailing views reappear unaltered in their fundamentals and in their details.

We have stated above that Wilson is primarily an artist. He is already known for his remarkably attractive style. To him a book, above all else, must be readable. He strongly believes in the "literary method," as he calls it, not alone in scientific works, but also in the lecture-room. The aphorism of a French critic, *"le style, c'est l'homme,"* has a sound substratum of truth, for a man's style, if it really be a style, must inevitably correspond with the character of his intellect. Wilson's style is that of the man of letters, of the artist, not that of the scientist. It closely resembles the French classical manner of writing, what Taine calls *"le style oratoire, régulier, correct, tout composé d'expressions générales."* Wilson is by birth a Southerner, and his style appears to be typically Southern, with its characteristics reinforced by many years of lecturing. Like the French classical, the Southern style is a result of pre-existing social conditions. In the South before the war oratory was practically the sole medium of intellectual expression. The essence of successful oratory lies in appealing to the emotions, to sentiment, rather than to cold reason. This is the fundamental characteristic of Wilson's writings. It corresponds closely to his intellectual nature, and is admirably adapted for the description of the human element that is in past politics, and this is the subject which seemingly interests him most. He suggests, rather than defines; we gather impressions, not clear-cut conceptions. He gives us the atmosphere rather than the sharply drawn general lines. What his style lacks is precision; he seems unable to formulate a conception concisely. It is a style ill-adapted for the treatment of legal, institutional or economic questions, but these questions Wilson does not discuss in his book. It will be apparent that such a style has a distinct charm. Its very vagueness, its tendency toward general rather than specific statements, and the consequent absence of detail make Wilson's work preeminently comprehensible and readable.

Printed in the New York *Critic*, XLII (Feb. 1903), 172-76.

From Helen Woodrow Bones

My dear Cousin Woodrow—   Chicago, February 2 [1903].

My not having written you before this certainly does not mean that you have been out of my thoughts for very long at a time, since Margaret's letter came telling us of your trouble. I know I do not have to assure you of my most loving sympathy.

This has been a sad winter for you all, and especially hard for you. It must be such a comfort to be able to feel you did so much to make your father proud and happy. I know there never was a better, more loving son than you have been, and surely never was a father prouder of his son than Uncle Joseph was of you. I shall never forget his delight the day we heard you were to be President —it was the best thing to remember of a very happy day.

I wonder if you are going to be able to rest at all, now. It does seem as though a man couldn't stand the strains you have been under ever since your election. I wish the College could do something of itself—you seem to have the whole thing to do!

We were so glad to hear from Margaret that the little girls are well again. She said nothing about herself, but I do hope her throat has quite got over the effects of this vile Chicago climate. It was mighty nice to have her here, and I am counting on getting her back in the spring.

Please give Cousin Ellen and Cousin Annie—indeed, each member of the family—my love. With a great deal for yourself
                    Yours most affectionately   Helen

ALS (WP, DLC).

From Theodore Ledyard Cuyler

My dear Mr. President   Brooklyn   Feby 2nd   1903

Allow me to add my grain of sand to the *mountain* of honest commendation that is greeting your superb "History of the American People."

To me as to many others the *4th volume* is of the most absorbing interest as coming from a native Virginian—& the pathetic chapter on the "Confederate States" will touch thousands of hearts most deeply.

It required some *courage* to write the 112th page of the Vth volume; but yours will be the verdict of posterity on Gen. Grant as a *President*. I *thank* you for your every word on heroic Grover Cleveland.

If you should find a spare hour for my recently published "Autobiography,"[1] you will see in the 1st chapter my intense loyalty to dear old *Princeton*—& in the 11th chapter a few items in regard to "Lincoln & the Civil War" that may not have been familiar to you. To what I say of Dr. *McCosh* on the 237-239th pages, you will doubtless say *"Amen."*

While congratulating you on your splendid History—let me sympathize with you in the departure of your noble and venerated *Father*. I see now what hands have *moulded* the man who is to *mould* young men in our great training-school of Princeton.

May God's guiding hand never be lifted from you!

Lovingly Yours   Theodore L. Cuyler

P.S. Your good *wife* must have given you an extra kiss for that charming *"Dedication"* of the "History."[2]

ALS (WP, DLC).
   [1] *Recollections of a Long Life: An Autobiography* (New York, 1902).
   [2] "To E. A. W. in loving acknowledgment of gentle benefits which can neither be measured nor repaid."

To Edith Gittings Reid

My dearest Friend,   Princeton, New Jersey, 3 February, 1903

You must not be angry with me,—you must sympathize with me,—when I tell you that I must spend Friday night, when the Princeton men dine,[1] with Mrs. Bird.[2] It is to keep an old lady who loves me very much from being hurt to the quick,—hurt beyond cure. I would give my [right arm?] to stay with you and Mr. Reid instead, but this is a case of a sort I do not know how to manage. I mean to see you by hook or by crook, though my stay must be brief, as, alas! always.

It was very sweet of you to write as you did of my dear father's death. It comforted me not a little to have your sympathy,—so direct and genuine. But it has quite taken the heart out of me to lose my life-long friend and companion. I have told you what he was to me. And now he is gone and a great loneliness is in my heart. No generation ahead of me now! I am in the firing line. The more reason to be steady and attend to the fighting without repining.

Mrs. Wilson joins me in all affectionate messages to you both. It cheers me to think that I am to see you so soon.

As always   Faithfully Yours   Woodrow Wilson

ALS (WC, NjP).
¹ A news report of the dinner of the Princeton Alumni Association of Maryland, held in Baltimore on Feb. 6, 1903, is printed at Feb. 14, 1903.
² Sarah Baxter (Mrs. William Edgeworth) Bird, Wilson's old friend in Baltimore.

From Henry Cooper Pitney, Jr.

Dear Mr. President: Morristown, N. J.   Feb. 3, 1903.

I beg to offer assurance of my sincere sympathy in the loss of your venerable father.

We are confidently expecting your presence here on Monday the twenty-third of February instant. Please come by the train leaving New York at 11.10 A. M. and Newark at 11.35 A. M., arriving at Morristown at 12.55 P. M. Attached to this train will be three parlor cars for the comfort of our members and guests. The same cars will leave Morristown going east at 4.23 P. M. Kindly let me know that you will come by this train.

I would like very much to have you spend Monday night here. Can you arrange to do so?

I am,   Yours very truly,   [Henry C. Pitney, Jr.]

CCL (Washington Association of N. J., Morristown, N. J.).

From Theodore Roosevelt

My dear Mr. Wilson: [Washington] February 4, 1903.

I am greatly grieved to learn of the death of your father. Pray accept my profound sympathy.

Perhaps a little later in the year you can come on and give us the pleasure of having you as our guest at the White House.

Faithfully yours,   Theodore Roosevelt

TLS (Letterpress Books, T. Roosevelt Papers, DLC).

From the Minutes of the Princeton University Faculty

5 p.m. February 4, 1903.

The Faculty met, the President presiding. The minutes of the meeting of January 7 were read and approved. . . .

The Committee on the Course of Study was requested to take into consideration the average standing required of candidates for Fellowships.

The Committee on the Course of Study made a report, containing the following recommendations, which were adopted:

To authorize a course in Municipal Government, Senior Elective, first term, offered by Professor Finley.

To authorize a course on Some Current and Disputed Questions in International Law, Senior elective, second term, open only to those Seniors who have taken the first term course in International Law, offered by Dr. Elliott.

To authorize an extension for ten lectures of the course on Personal Hygiene for the Academic Freshmen, offered by Colonel Woodhull, on condition that satisfactory schedule arrangements can be made.

To authorize an optional course of ten lectures to Academic Seniors, offered by Colonel Woodhull; and to authorize such a course as a Senior elective, if the full number of hours are given.

The schedule hours of Politics 8 were changed to 4 p.m. Thursday and Friday. . . .

To Henry Cooper Pitney, Jr.

Princeton, New Jersey.

My dear Mr. Pitney: 5 February, 1903.

I am very much obliged to you for your letter of February 3rd, and shall take pleasure in adopting your suggestion about the train which I am to take on the 23rd inst. I shall look forward to the occasion with a great deal of pleasure.

Allow me to express also my warm appreciation of your kind words about the death of my father.

I am sorry to say that I cannot spend Monday night away from home because of duties here early Tuesday morning.

Very sincerely yours,   Woodrow Wilson

TLS (Washington Association of N. J., Morristown, N. J.).

William MacDonald's[1] Review of
A History of the American People

[Feb. 5, 1903]

It is, perhaps, not wholly unnatural that an elaborately illustrated historical work, written in the first instance for a popular magazine, should be viewed by many with some suspicion. It is so easy, by means of heavy paper, large type, wide margins, numerous pictures, and fine binding, to give an air of importance to what is, after all, of but minor value that the critic, particularly if his taste be that of the scholar rather than the general reader, is prone to look upon all such undertakings as presumptively wanting in merit. Here, for example, is a work in five large volumes, handsomely printed and bound, profusely illustrated, and making, in general, an appearance of which any booklover might be proud. It professes to be a history of the American people from the discovery of the continent to the very present. Yet it contains only about two-thirds as many words as Green's 'Short History.' Unquestionably, the predisposition of the critic is not likely to be favorable.

Nevertheless, subject to some rather important qualifications, the general verdict on President Wilson's book must, we think, be commendatory. The author has not thus far been especially prominent as an historian, but has won repute rather as a keen observer of political and governmental conditions, a successful popularizer of scholarly knowledge, and an essayist with a peculiarly vivid and picturesque style; and it is in these same capacities that he appears in this his latest book. The student who is searching for a concise and comprehensive narrative of historical events, a careful marshalling of facts and weighing of evidence, or a bringing together of tested and assured information from monographs and documents, will not find any of these things here. No existing history of high quality will be superseded by President Wilson's work, nor need any would-be writer of American history on a large scale be deterred from prosecuting his undertaking to its completion. What the author has given us is, rather, a brilliantly written essay summarizing the general course of events, with only so much of selected incident as is needed to

A History of the American People. By Woodrow Wilson. In five volumes. Harper & Brothers. 1902.

[1] Professor of American History at Brown University and a frequent contributor to the New York *Nation.*

hold the narrative together and make the reader feel that he knows what the author is talking about.

The defects are, naturally, those of the qualities. It is inevitable that, in writing of this character, comment and opinion should preponderate over fact, and that, so far as the average reader is concerned, much should throughout be taken for granted. The inquirer who should turn to President Wilson's pages for what the author himself might call "mere information," would hardly succeed in finding a great deal of it; but if he have his information well in hand in advance, he will find much to admire and not a little worth thinking about in the broad outlines, the sweeping generalizations, the keen judgments, and the illuminating comments with which the pages abound. Further, with a writer as interesting as President Wilson, there is at times the feeling that something has been sacrificed to form and grouping, that events were not always quite as clear as they are made to seem, and that the emphasis is often as much personal as historical. One must not be disturbed, for example, at finding the witchcraft delusion disposed of in half a page of text, or at seeing Garrison shot suddenly into the field, and for the first time, in 1845. In other words, President Wilson's work is to be commended as a useful stimulant for those who already know a good deal about American history, but hardly as a safe "short cut" for those who begrudge the acquisition of knowledge in the old-fashioned way. To say that the generalizations and summaries are, as a rule, both safe and informing and that the apportionment of space does not, in the main, greatly distort the relations of things, is only to say again that the achievement is praiseworthy.

A well-known writer and teacher declared, a few years ago, that no one might now expect to live long enough to write, on a large and comprehensive scale, a history of the American people. President Wilson has not, as we have said, attempted this alleged impossible task in the way which the speaker had in mind. There is nothing in either the matter or the manner of his book to indicate any extensive first-hand acquaintance with the subject; but the important secondary literature seems to have been industriously used, while numerous references or statements show that the monographic work of specialists has not been neglected. Occasionally there is a slip, as where the old charge that Braddock "walked into an ambush" is given another lease of life; but such errors, so far as we have noted, are rare. In one respect especially the treatment is notable. Throughout the whole of the colonial period President Wilson is constantly calling attention to the course of events in Europe, and to the inseparable connection between European history and American history. The history of the Navigation Acts, in particular, is followed with unusual closeness, and again and again recurred to, with the conclusion that their influence on American trade was not disastrous, and that England was obviously as much interested in developing the colonial trade as in taxing it. This point of view, not as yet very generally taken, helps to clarify very much this part of the subject. Similarly, the handling of the causes of the Revolution is broad and firm, without going to either of the extremes which such writers as Mr. Lodge and Mr. Trevelyan may be taken as representing. Readers of the author's 'Division and Reunion' will recognize the same general attitude in the account of the earlier Constitutional period here. Coming down to recent events, the brief account of the war with Spain foreshadows the more critical temper which will not honor as heroes all who participated in that struggle, while the characterization of President McKinley may well give somewhat of a chill to the admirers of that subservient leader. It was difficult for a president of Princeton to write at once truly and discreetly of President Cleveland, but President Wilson has acquitted himself with rare tact and reserve.

In the selection of the hundreds of illustrations, President Wilson acknowledges his indebtedness to Mr. Victor H. Paltsits of the New York Public Library. For the selection and mechanical reproduction of the pictures there can be, in general, nothing but praise. It is a pity, however, that fancy pictures, save, perhaps, the few that are in themselves notable works of art, could not have been excluded, and that a fuller indication of origin could not have been given than is afforded by the oft-recurring ascription, "from an old print." It was a happy thought to present, as the frontispiece of the first volume, the fine photogravure of Sir Edwin Sandys, than whom no man better deserves recognition as the friend and aider of American colonization. Occasionally an illustration is out of place—thus, in volume ii., the picture of the Plains of Abraham, on page 86, is inserted in the account of Braddock's campaign; and the picture of Washington and Rochambeau at Yorktown, on page 306, precedes by twenty pages the account of the operations depicted. A picture of Carpenter's Hall, Philadelphia, is set into page 11 of volume iv., although the text relates to the beginning of Jackson's administration. The picture (vol. iv., p. 184) of the Dunker Church "where John

Brown preached the night of the raid," is a curious lapsus, since the incident referred to did not occur.

Appended to the several divisions of the narrative are select bibliographies giving the titles of both primary and secondary works. We cannot imagine that any considerable number of those who will read President Wilson's volumes will have use for the bibliographies, but it is the fashion to have them even in popular works, and they at least suggest the possibility of further study. The lists are laudably free from worthless books, and the range is fairly comprehensive. There are unexpected omissions, of course. The bibliography of Carolina, for example, makes no mention of Mr. McCrady's history,[2] nor does that of Virginia include Bruce's 'Economic History' or Brown's 'First Republic in America.'[3] The most extraordinary omission is that of Parkman, who is not mentioned in the list of authorities (vol. ii., p. 96) on the French and Indian wars. With the numerous references to sources in the bibliographies, further, one does not expect to find the texts of a few appended documents reprinted from Preston's collection[4] instead of from some authoritative source.

Printed in the New York *Nation*, LXXVI (Feb. 5, 1903), 117-18.

[2] Edward McCrady, *The History of South Carolina under the Proprietary Government, 1670-1719* (New York and London, 1897); *The History of South Carolina under the Royal Government, 1719-1776* (New York and London, 1899); *The History of South Carolina in the Revolution, 1775-1780* (New York and London, 1901); and *The History of South Carolina in the Revolution, 1780-1783* (New York and London, 1902).

[3] Philip Alexander Bruce, *Economic History of Virginia in the Seventeenth Century* (2 vols., New York and London, 1895), and Alexander Brown, *The First Republic in America: An Account of the Origin of this Nation . . .* (Boston and New York, 1898).

[4] Howard Willis Preston (ed.), *Documents Illustrative of American History, 1606-1863* (New York and London, 1886).

From Henry Cooper Pitney, Jr.

Dear Mr. President: Morristown, N. J.   Feb. 6, 1903.

I have your kind letter of Feb'y 5th and am glad to know that you will be here on the 23rd.

We hope you can visit here and see our town and country at your leisure on some future day.

We shall desire to print your address in a form approved by you. Will you be able to give me the text of it in writing. It will be published in a pamphlet for our members. Before publishing I will submit the printer's proofs to you.

The Masters of the Morristown School desire, as perhaps they have written you, to have you visit and see their school on the 23rd. The school is a little more than a mile east of our building on the same road. If you have time to spare after our meeting, the Masters propose to take you to see the school, which will interest you.   Very truly yours,   [Henry C. Pitney, Jr.]

CCL (Washington Association of N. J., Morristown, N. J.).

A News Report of an Address to the Trenton Y.M.C.A.

[Feb. 9, 1903]

President Woodrow Wilson, LL.D., of Princeton university, was the speaker at the men's meeting in Association hall yesterday afternoon under the auspices of the Y.M.C.A.

It was the most notable service of the season. General Secretary Fry[1] presided and the hall was crowded. The association symphony orchestra played three selections and led the singing. The appearance of President Wilson on the platform was the signal for a vigorous outburst of applause. Seated with him on the platform were Dr. James M. Green,[2] president of the State schools, and President John A. Campbell and several directors of the association. Dr. Green offered prayer. Mr. Campbell, an alumnus of Princeton, class of '77, presented Dr. Wilson to the audience as an "eminent author, historian and educator, who was distinguished as a typical American." President Wilson's theme was "God is Love."

His first words were as striking as was the address throughout. He said in part:

"Why should man do right? We know the right is not palatable. Our nature does not correspond with what society demands of us, so why not follow nature? That is how the question appeals to us. But ask the question concerning some other fellow and then we see it differently.

"We never bestow the title 'noble fellow' upon a man we know is doing wrong.

"A man may be strong, famous, powerful or rich, but if he is not doing right he is not noble. The man entitled to be called noble is he who forgets himself and serves others. Every man realizes there is more in him than he ever uses. We cannot satisfy our nature without multiplying it. There is an instinct in every one to reach out after better things. A man's ability to do things constitutes his capital in life. In proportion as he uses his capital for others is he a noble man.

"The world always has honored self-sacrifice—sacrifice for home, neighbor or country, the spirit in a man that causes him to forget the life in him for the life in them.

"No man can laud the honor of the United States and be dishonorable.

"Sentiment runs the world, not intellect. A man goes to college to learn how to get his sentiment into the right channels. Love is the real driving power of every man. There are only two motives to strenuous lives. The first is self-aggrandizement. This is the selfish spirit that wants money to get power. In the afternoon of life what good is power?

"The other motive is service. Service either for a person or a cause. The one motive for service is love. If you would know the true spirit of love, love something greater than yourself and catch its glory.

"No man knows what he is born for until he 'comes to himself' as did the prodigal son. When a man really finds himself he discovers his relation to the rest of the world.

"To help men to find themselves you must lay yourself alongside them. Then get the spirit that loves to overcome. Do things for the sake of the perfection of the task. The culmination of the whole matter is to love somebody higher and nobler than yourself. A man ought not to love the Lord Jesus just to be saved. That is selfish. It should be not love for salvation's sake, but service for love's sake. Jesus Christ presents the only perfect example of service for love's sake. Love Jesus Christ and learn from Him the love that could never push a brother man to the wall, but rather, if need be, would get in the gutter to let another man pass."

Printed in the Trenton *Daily True American*, Feb. 9, 1903; editorial headings omitted.
   1 Wilfred W. Fry, General Secretary of the Trenton Y.M.C.A.
   2 James Monroe Green, Principal of the New Jersey State Normal and Model Schools.

To Henry Cooper Pitney, Jr.

Princeton, New Jersey.

My dear Mr. Pitney: 10 February, 1903.

In reply to your kind letter of February 6th, I would say that my address is not written, and I shall have to depend on you to procure an expert stenographer, if it is your wish to publish what I say.

I shall hope to be able to meet the wishes of the masters of the Morristown School; but I dare say it will depend on circumstances how much time I will have for a visit to the school.

With much regard,

Very sincerely yours, Woodrow Wilson

TLS (Washington Association of N. J., Morristown, N. J.).

From Adolfo González Posada[1]

Monsieur,   Oviedo, Espagne, Fev. 10/1903

J'ai reçu votre lettre du 13 Janvier. Je vous remerci beaucoup votre autorisation pour traduire votre livre *The State*.[2] J'ai reçu aussi une lettre de M. l'Editeur D. C. Heath et Comp. Il est d'accord avec votre autorisation.

Je suis déjà au travail de traduction. J'ai l'intention d'écrire un étude préliminaire pour l'édition espagnole de votre ouvrage.[3]

Agréer Monsieur l'expression de mes sentiments très élevés.

Adolfo Posada

ALS (WP, DLC).

[1] Professor of Law at the University of Oviedo, prolific writer in the fields of public law, Spanish constitutional law, international law, municipal government, comparative government, administration, and other branches of political science.

[2] His translation, Woodrow Wilson, *El estado; elementos de política histórica y práctica . . . con una introducción de Oscar Brownin* [Browning], trans. Adolfo Posada (2 vols., Madrid, 1904), appeared as a volume in the series entitled *Biblioteca de derecho y de ciencias sociales*.

[3] Posada's introduction, "Estudio Preliminar," pp. xxxix-lxxxiii, was a long review essay on modern literature in political science relating to the state. At the beginning and the end, it was highly complimentary to Wilson's own work, but it made no effort to relate *The State* to other writers or schools of political science. Hence it will not be printed in this series.

A News Report of an Address at the Peddie Institute

[Feb. 13, 1903]

PRESIDENT WILSON EXPLAINS COLLEGE TR[A]INING'S WORTH

Hightstown, Feb. 13.—President Woodrow Wilson delivered an address on "The Meaning of a College Course" last evening at Peddie Institute on the occasion of the celebration of Founder's Day, the birthday of the late Hon. Thomas B. Peddie of Newark, for whom the school is named.

Beginning with an answer to the customary criticisms of college training by "self-made" men who claim to be eminently practical, President Wilson said in part:

"Few men would object to the muscular training afforded by the gymnasium and yet the dumb bells and parallel bars play no part in the counting room or the office. Everybody knows that the gymnasium makes good red blood and fits a man to fight the physical battles of life. It is equally true that the other branches of training in college life fit a man to fight the battles and meet the problems that require more than physical fitness.

"Some people would like to cut Latin out of the college course, and others would discriminate against something else, but all the studies have their place in the development of a man's faculties whether he ever uses them in his business or not.

"The college is a little world in a truer sense than any neighborhood can be and it gives a man a more practical introduction to the great world than he can gain otherwise.

"If the eastern young man has regarded the prairies as a benighted part of the world and referred to them with scorn, it will do him good to go to college and meet a man from Kansas and very likely the man from Kansas will make a formidable impression on him that he will not soon forget. The college shows a man that there are people from all parts of the country who are his equals or superiors in body or in mind.

"College life shows a man that there is no patent rule or pet philosophy by which he can solve all the problems of life. It rids him of his prejudices and prompts him to earnestly seek the broadest culture.

"In some indefinable manner it is easy to distinguish a freshman from a sophomore, a sophomore from a junior and a junior from a senior. College brings about a transformation by degrees and makes the student a free man.

"Hazing is considered a terrible thing by many people. I disapprove of many of the methods of hazing, and yet it is a good thing for a man to be brought to realize how little he amounts to as he emerges from his narrow surroundings and goes into a progressive community of students with ignorance of the amenities to which he must learn to pay heed. It helps a man to find his bearings among his fellows.

"There is a kind of hazing that a man is likely to undergo if he does not go to college, and it is worse than mere physical torture. It is the bitter experience that causes the mind to suffer, and this experience visits in greater or lesser degree all who go unprepared and unfitted into the affairs of the world. It is for the purpose of avoiding this pain and helping a man to find himself in the surest and best way that the college exists."[1]

Printed in the *Trenton Times*, Feb. 13, 1903; some editorial headings omitted.
¹ There is a WWhw outline of this talk, dated Feb. 12, 1903, in WP, DLC. It discloses that Wilson also gave this talk at the Bordentown, N. J., Academy on March 14, 1903. No newspaper report of the Bordentown affair can be found.

A News Report

[Feb. 14, 1903]

THE BALTIMORE REUNION

Baltimore alumni report that the eighteenth annual reunion and dinner of the Princeton Association of Maryland, held in that city on February 6th, was the best they have had. Over a hundred alumni and guests were present, and they sang the old and new songs, including the one ending "Wilson, Wilson, that is all," as sung with great success at the New York dinner, and another to the tune of Pretty Molly Shannon, with this chorus:

> How would you like to be me
> And have a job as fat as he?
> I can tell you, boys,
> There's none compares with him,
> He is the only one in his class,
> There's no president he can't surpass
> Woodrow, Woodrow Wilson—
> He is the real, real thing.

The Hon. Stevenson A. Williams '70 was toastmaster and President Wilson '79 responded for Princeton University.

The President started a hurrah by asking the company if they had heard why the ground hog went back into his hole this year. The answer was, he said, because the ground hog was afraid the President of the United States would put a "coon" in.¹

President Wilson deprecated the endeavor of some reformers to shorten the college course. He expressed the belief that to shorten it would be sure to result in leaving out something of real value. He believed, he said, that each of the four years gave its distinctive touch, and that no one of the years could be dispensed with without distinct loss; that the typical college graduate was a man who had the complete impress of college life upon him.

The President said that there was at Princeton a programme of progress rather than of reform. He would not call it reform, he said, because he believed the place essentially sound and its methods essentially good, but progress, he thought, was needed in every department, and the progress should take the direction of extending and broadening the field of scholarship in its processes. He hoped, he said, that the time would never come at Princeton when the intellectual life of the place was held between the covers of books; that study should itself be a means of companionship and regarded as part of the general training of the world—part of the process of becoming efficient. He did not expect, of course, to make undergraduates learned men, but he did expect to impart to them a spirit of scholarship, a spirit, that is, of candid inquiry, of right judgment, and of catholic sympathy. He did not think, as some seem to think, that the four years of college life are the best of a man's life. The best years, he said, are not those of preparation, but those of achievement, and the preparation should have achievement in view. Such preparation would not only enhance the Princeton spirit, but immortalize it. He spoke with confidence of raising the twelve and a half millions needed for Princeton within a reasonable length of time, and said that he felt sure that every Princeton man might feel confident of her future.

Printed in the *Princeton Alumni Weekly*, III (Feb. 14, 1903), 311-12.
[1] A reference to President Roosevelt's appointment of Negroes to political offices in the South, particularly of Dr. William D. Crum as Collector of the Port of Charleston, S. C., and of Mrs. Minnie M. Cox as postmistress of Indianola, Miss. Mrs. Cox had just resigned under local white pressure and threats, and Roosevelt had closed the Indianola post office.

From Abbott Lawrence Lowell

Dear Mr. Wilson   Boston   Feb. 15, 1903

I want to tell you how much Mrs. Lowell and I sympathise with you in the loss of your father. At the time of your inauguration, he looked frail, and I suppose his death was not altogether unexpected; but it must have come as a shock to you, and as a wrenching of memories of the past. It must have been a gratification to him to have lived to see his son at the head of a great university.

We are both sorry to miss the pleasure of having Mrs. Wilson here as we had hoped.[1] I should like to have a few gentlemen connected with our educational institutions meet you quietly at dinner if that would be agreeable to you, and for that reason I want to ask how long you can be with us. You have engagements already I believe for the evenings of the fourth and fifth of March.[2]

With kindest remembrances to Mrs. Wilson, I am,
                    Yours sincerely,   A. Lawrence Lowell

ALS (WP, DLC).
  [1] Wilson was scheduled to speak at the annual dinner of the Princeton Alumni Association of New England in Boston on March 5, 1903. His earlier correspondence with Lowell about his Boston trip is missing.
  [2] Wilson's Boston engagements were canceled on account of the death of his father.

To Cyrus Hall McCormick

My dear Cyrus: Princeton, New Jersey 16 February, 1903.

  I am very much obliged to you for the copies of your suggestions to Cuyler and Bridges about the dormitory. I have read them with a great deal of care, and quite agree with several of them. I do not think that I do agree with those which concern the outside architectural features; but I think that they too ought to be given the most careful consideration, and I have no doubt that the [we] can arrange to have the matter carefully canvassed. We have certainly to thank you for a most thorough and business-like examination of the whole thing. I will take it up with Cuyler at the earliest possible moment.

                    Very sincerely yours,   Woodrow Wilson

TLS (WP, DLC).

A News Item

                                                    [Feb. 16, 1903]

PRESIDENT WILSON'S APPOINTMENT.

  President Woodrow Wilson has been elected vice president from New Jersey of the Thomas Jefferson Memorial Association. The object of the association is to erect at Washington a memorial to Thomas Jefferson. Admiral Dewey is chairman of the organization.[1]

Printed in the *Daily Princetonian*, Feb. 16, 1903.
  [1] Very little is known about the activities of the Thomas Jefferson Memorial Association of the United States. Admiral George Dewey, on February 1, 1903, issued an appeal to the American people for funds for an appropriate memorial to Jefferson. *New York Times*, Feb. 2, 1903. Moreover, there was a Jefferson birthday dinner in Washington on April 14, 1903, at which William J. Bryan and George F. Hoar spoke. The appeal for funds was not productive, and the plan for a memorial was abandoned. Merrill D. Peterson, *The Jeffersonian Image in the American Mind* (New York, 1960), pp. 292-93. The Association does not seem to have held any meetings after the spring of 1903, and it issued no reports whatsoever. However, it did sponsor Andrew A. Lipscomb and Albert Ellery Bergh (eds.), *The Writings of Thomas Jefferson* (20 vols., Washington, 1903), which Professor Julian P. Boyd, Editor of *The Papers of Thomas Jefferson*, has characterized as "the worst edition of Jefferson's papers ever produced."

A Preface to Dean West's *The Proposed Graduate College of Princeton University*

Princeton, New Jersey, 17 February, 1903.

On the side of University growth, a Graduate College is undoubtedly our first and most obvious need, and the plans for such a college which Professor West has conceived seem to me in every way admirable. To carry them out would unquestionably give us a place of unique distinction among American Universities. He has conceived the idea of a Graduate School of residence, a great quadrangle in which our graduate students will be housed like a household, with their own commons and with their own rooms of conference, under a master, whose residence should stand at a corner of the quadrangle in the midst of them. This is not merely a pleasing fancy of an English college placed in the midst of our campus; but in conceiving this little community of scholars set at the heart of Princeton, Professor West has got at the gist of the matter, the real means by which a group of graduate students are most apt to stimulate and set the pace for the whole University.[1] I hope that the privilege of building and developing such an institution may be accorded us in the near future, in order that in carrying out our plans the scope and efficiency of the University may be assured from the very outset.

WOODROW WILSON,
President of Princeton University.

Printed in [Andrew F. West] *The Proposed Graduate College of Princeton University* (Princeton, N. J., 1903), p. 3.

[1] In view of the later bitter controversy between Wilson and West over the location of the Graduate College (Wilson wanted it situated in the heart of the campus; West, on a site considerably removed), it might be pointed out that in this sentence Wilson was only warmly endorsing West's own plans and purposes as he had expressed them in *The Proposed Graduate College of Princeton University*. The Dean made much of the point that one of the chief benefits of a strong graduate college would be its stimulating, invigorating, and elevating effects on the undergraduates (p. 11). "To every graduate who lives within its quadrangle," he also said (p. 14), "and to every undergraduate who passes it in his daily walks, the College should, in its very beauty and in the completeness of its appointments, be a visible symbol of the nobility of the truth and knowledge that are fit to dwell there, and the very fact that there is within the college world such a body of men devoted to high and serious work should quicken all good purposes."

A News Report of an Address in Harrisburg, Pennsylvania

[Feb. 20, 1903]

WOODROW WILSON TALKS TO ALUMNI

Last night was Princeton night at the Harrisburg Club and the cheers and songs of the sons of old Nassau and those who had gathered to do honor to them and their distinguished president resounded through the banquet hall. . . . That remarkable Princeton spirit was manifested by the diners and college songs were sung with vigor and old time feeling. . . .

President Charles H. Bergner, of the Association, in beginning the speechmaking, referred to the growth of the University from a college where every man knew each other by his first name to a great university working for the good of the world. Speaking of the joy of reunions he said that the gatherings were happy events, eagerly looked forward to by many alumni scattered throughout the whole world. The toast was "Princeton University, Great in the Past, Greater in the Future."

President Wilson, in responding, spoke of the great happiness he felt in his reception and paid high tribute to the University spirit, the Princeton sentiment. Appreciating the gravity of his position he declared the sense of cooperation made him strong in his work. He said he did not believe that the four years of college were the most enjoyable of life, but the happiest years were those in which a man achieved something. "College life must fit a man for achievement or it is nothing. Heaven lies about us in infancy, in old age we lie about ourselves."

The President said we have reached the end of the era of experimentation and there has been for twenty-five years a riot of doing as you please in college courses. The elective system was the invention of a lazy man, for it certainly helps the lazy man and as it is a hard job to combine studies they let it be, go as you please. Certainly ingenuity and originality of choice are afforded and the college student being a son of Adam takes the line of least resistance. It is time to turn about and organize studies for a purpose.

Among other things Dr. Wilson said: Uniformity in universities is not desirable. Privately endowed institutions should preserve individuality, as a nation takes power from variety, not from following a single pattern. We should have rivalry, not many standards. In Princeton we have the highest development of residential college work and comradeship in studies.

Touching upon the questions of the day, Dr. Wilson said this is not a country of classes, not even the cultivated class rule it. The business of the world is devolving more and more on college bred men. We are deceived sometimes in contemplating the great captains of industry, but what would the great combinations amount to if they did not have men of science to carry forward the processes, thereby creating places of investment for capital. The great enterprises which are controlled in Wall street could not be carried on except through the agency of trained intelligences.

There are always places for thoughtful men, but no man ought to put all of his thought into his task; he should use some for the benefit of his fellow men. A man should be a citizen as well as a workman, but should not be a visionary reformer ahead of possibilities. There is a special responsibility upon college men, trained men, for as no man can be absolute in this country, the man who would be at head must be a leader, who would be tolerant, who would walk ahead and beckon on. Dr. Wilson declared with emphasis that we have been Germanizing too much in this country's institutions of learning. We have been specializing to too great an extent, which is not wise in a democratic country.

In this country we are confronted with serious problems, said Dr. Wilson. One of these is whether we will consent to the establishment of a system which will scale all labor to the capacity of the least skillful. Are we willing to rate the capacity of our men by the man below the average or the man above the average? We have won the leadership of the world by encouraging extraordinary men and shall we lose it by holding to the level of the ordinary man. The speaker frankly confessed that he knew of no remedy for conditions and said that as labor had as much right as capital to combine, he saw no more danger in one than in the other. He suggested that both sides should be taught by one man in colleges.

Teaching, declared Dr. Wilson, should have reality. There is too much lecturing and class room work, he said in advocating the idea of making men read for themselves. He urged that students should be left to their own resources and not be spoon-fed by text books and syllabi, for when men used their own minds they grew to know how good it felt. Let teaching have reality, not cobwebs: divest it of technicalities and teach sense. The Doctor said that every man wakes up and to find oneself on his own resources will bring about the awakening.

Men, said he, just before closing, are kept children by being set tasks. Let them have intellectual liberation and assistance in their search for themselves. In his peroration Dr. Wilson paid a high tribute to the spirit of American patriotism as exemplified by the college men of to-day.

Printed in the Harrisburg, Pa., *Patriot*, Feb. 20, 1903; some editorial headings omitted.

To William Brewster Lee[1]

My dear Chang: Princeton, New Jersey.   23 February, 1903.

You know how hard it is to say no to anything that you ask, but really the work of the year has been so overwhelming, and my calendar of engagements is so chock full, that I really have not the vigor to add another, feeling very sure besides that it would be a great imprudence to do so. I have spoken to one or two Presbyterian Unions, and the task is peculiarly difficult. No doubt another winter I shall have more leisure, and therefore more energy in such matters, but this winter I am sure that I have gone to the limit.

I know that you will be generous enough to explain this to the gentlemen interested, and that they will in the circumstances be willing to excuse me.

It would be the greatest possible pleasure if I could come and be with Mrs. Lee and you; but I am doing, not what I want to do this winter, but what I must, and pleasures unhappily must wait.

Mrs. Wilson joins me in warm regard, and in the hope that you are all as well as possible.

Always faithfully yours,   Woodrow Wilson

TCL (RSB Coll., DLC).
[1] Wilson's classmate, a lawyer in Rochester, N. Y.

To Varnum Lansing Collins

Princeton, New Jersey.

My dear Mr. Collins: 23 February, 1903.

I don't think that I can do what you ask about my History, though I am sincerely obliged to you for asking it. I feel that it would be impossible for me to dictate such a description of the objects and scope of my History as would be suitable for your use. I would inevitably drift into a sort of essay in exposition of what I deem to be the proper method of writing history.

It will be no loss to the Bulletin[1] to go without a notice of the work. Indeed it would be my preference that it should omit it. An analysis of so long a work is impossible, and anything else would look like a sort of advertisement.[2]

Hoping that you will agree with this view of the matter,

Very cordially yours,   Woodrow Wilson

TLS (WC, NjP).
  [1] That is, the *Princeton University Bulletin*, an official publication.
  [2] The notice was never printed in the *Bulletin*.

An Address on Patriotism to the Washington Association of New Jersey

[Feb. 23, 1903]

Mr. Chairman and Gentlemen:

I am not going to commit myself to you by delivering a discourse on Washington. I believe everything that is to be said about Washington, and which can be proved, has been said and proved, and I am not a candidate to say that which is not proved. Moreover, I do not know any task so difficult as the task of analyzing the character of that incomparable man. There is a symmetry about that character that seems to defy the hand of analysis, so that we are tempted to say there is a separate quality of greatness consisting of a certain poise and proportion of moral and intellectual quality which cannot be described, except by example. We recognize the greatness of such a man, but we cannot set it apart in its elements, and therefore it seems to me, rather than undertake a task well nigh impossible, it were better on an occasion like this to select the field which his name suggests above every other name of a man in this country. I am going to ask your leave to stop for a little while to-day to speak on the subject of *Patriotism*.

I am very well aware, as I remember the word, that there are some words in our language which seem to have the quality of living things, which seem to speak as if they had inherent qualities of their own. The word *liberty* is such a word, one which I suppose constitutes a greater part in the imaginations of men than any other word that comes from our lips; a word which sends a thrill along the blood; a word which has been stained by some of the most cruel expressions that men have ever uttered, and which has been illustrated by some of the finest stories of self sacrifice and self devotion that history affords; in fine, one of those words which one cannot look upon with coolness, remembering the hopes of men, the daring of the race, the deeds of reform and liberation that have gone into its history.

Patriotism is another word of that sort, a word which lives with the quality which has been in men, with the quality which has been in the history of great races. I believe that we make a mistake in thinking of patriotism as a sentiment. It breeds a sentiment no doubt, but I do not myself think of it as a sentiment. It is rather a principle in life, a principle of action. It is a certain energy of character acting outside the narrow circle of self interest.

It is a very interesting circumstance that we reserve the word *noble* for the description of men who do not center their powers upon themselves. We describe many a man who has centered his power upon himself, upon the advancement of his own material interests and upon the acquisition of power and fortune, as *great* but we do not describe him as noble. We therefore reserve the fine adjective *noble* for the man who has loved his fellow men, who has exercised a quality of character outside of his own personal fortunes and who has had a splendid free capital of character to introduce into the general enterprises of the world. This is the sort of men we describe as noble and it is of this quality that patriotism is made. A man is *not* patriotic because he serves the country, provided he serves it for his own aggrandizement. He *is* patriotic if he serves the country because he *loves* the country and is ready, if the time comes, to sacrifice himself for the advancement of the race and the advancement of that particular organization of the race into which he has been born and in whose advancement he believes.

I conceive patriotism to be of the quality of *friendship* upon a higher scale. No man is a true friend who will not sacrifice something for the friend whom he loves; no man is a true friend who will not sacrifice something for a friend at the risk of personal blame in order to serve him. I am not a true friend if I do not study my firend's [friend's] qualities and try to serve him according to his manhood. I am not his friend if I put myself always to the task of pleasing him, provided I can serve him better by displeasing him for the time being. I would count myself a cowardly friend if I did not risk my friend's good will to apprise him of a fault. And so I believe we are sometimes on the wrong cry when we say that because a man preaches to his country its faults he is therefore unpatriotic. I have found myself in a similar condition recently. I am of the class of men who are described as *imperialists*, and yet I have had such an intense sympathy with the men on the other side who are getting sat upon that I could almost have wished that my opinions were different that I might join their ranks. They have just as much right to say what they think as I have to say what I think; and if they are in the minority because of greater courage, you may depend upon it they are not serving themselves by saying what they think; and that is considered the test of true devotion. Patriotism is a principle, not of taste—not because we like this country more—,but it is a principle of *devotion*. It is a principle of *consecration*; and if you think the country is wrong you are not patriotic, you are no patriot, if you dont stand up and say so. And so it seems to me we do not give these gentlemen the full courtesy of the arena. We are not at liberty to cry they are wrong because they differ with us in opinion.

I know there has been some mistaken comparison of the flag of the United States in recent years with the national emblem of the German Empire, as a result of which some fun has been made of the German flag. This is not right. The emblem of the German Empire stands for the *power* that is concentrated in the German Government; but the flag of the United States stands for the biggest *kick* on record. It stands for deliberate nonconformity; it stands for the thing which men who are resisting authority stand for. When I look at that flag, I sometimes think that its stripes are alternating stains of blood on old parchment. On the old parchment in white stripes are written the immemorial principles of individual liberty, and the red stripes are streaks of blood which have sealed those principles. And you have just as much right to be devoted to the white stripes as the red; just as much right to be devoted to the old principles of liberty as the new; for you understand they are devoted to the memory of the men who fought for those principles. I honor both things alike. I should certainly not consider a man patriotic who did not stand up for the white stripes as well as for the red, for they are both there and they are both parts of the integral conception of the national emblem.

And so it seems to me that we are in this case in this country; we live in a country where it is a man's obligation to think political thoughts out for himself, because that is the example of the history of this country, and then we are under the obligation to stand up for and speak the conclusions we have arrived at. I, myself, would not give a pepper-corn for the principles that were not worth fighting for and that could not stand fighting for. I believe with Dr. [Charles] Hodge that "truth is no invalid." . . .[1]

Because this fight is to the finish—not with the fist, not with the sword, but with the head,—and the fight that is to the finish with the heart and head is the fight that is going to bring the truth triumphantly to the end. That is the principle not of depression, but of peace and progress, that men shall not be afraid to examine into the justness of the position which they hold and that they shall not be afraid to have the other side heard. These are the principles of peace and progress. And if I mistake not, that is what this country stands for.

And so it seems to me, we ought to realize that we should love the country for the sake of its character, for the sake of the things which we expect to accomplish and by means of the things which must be used for that accomplishment. I do not believe that character is the object of the individual. I think that a man is a prig who is always thinking about his character. If he will do honest work and achieve great advancement, his character will take care of itself. Character is a bye-product. It is the result of the life that men live; and the object of that life is not to create character but to accomplish great things and let character be created incidentally. I ask you if a man who is always thinking about himself is an agreeable companion. The man whose thought is upon himself ought really to be read out of co-operative society, because so certain as he centers his thoughts upon himself the less he thinks of the relation of common interests. If I am in a desert, my difficulty is not to place myself. I am there, yet I am lost and I haven't found myself until I have found the other things around me. I haven't found myself until I have discovered my relations with the geography thereabouts. And in life a man has not found himself until he has found his relation with other people and with the world. His relation to the world at large is a relation of this sort. He is contributing to the kind of thinking and the kind of achievement that will make the reputation of a nation. So it is in some degree proved that the object of national life is character. And so, it seems to me, a man ought to purify his thinking according to this principle, that he wishes to contribute to the pure repute of the nation to which he belongs, and that therefore he cannot afford to contribute *ignoble* things to a total which he wishes to be *noble*. He must therefore realize that the only immortality of a nation must be on this side of the grave, and for the nation as such there is no future world. It is

[1] This ellipsis and following ones by the stenographer, Joseph P. Lukeman, to indicate that he had missed portions of the address.

regenerated or damned on this side of the grave; and its damnation is that it walks straight to a grave which is the condemnation of history. The degeneration of peoples is the degeneration of the individual aggregate of character. And therefore the man who presumably contributes to the total is an essential part of the grand result. And therefore patriotism puts him under compulsion to be a *pure* man. We are as it were upon our honor. Our liberty to act and to achieve is conditioned upon our acquiescence in the general standards of high morality; so every man is put upon his honor to be a man and to contribute to the manhood of the race.

I long ago found that some of the best political principles are to be found not in the systems of writers on political science but in the poets who are supposed not to know anything about political science. If you would get at the spirit of people you must take in that spirit through those sympathetical powers which the man with poetic gifts has and which the man without poetic gifts lacks. Every man who would understand a race of people must have something in him in order that there may be transmuted something of the spirit of the race for which he speaks. And it seems to me that I have found in certain lines of Tennyson so many texts for the consideration of such a subject as this:

"A nation yet, the rulers and the ruled;
　　Some sense of duty, something of a faith;
Some reverence for the laws ourselves have made;
　　Some potent force to change them when we will;
Some civic manhood firm against the crowd."[2]

I do not know where you will find so much material to think about in the field of politics as in those few lines. A nation bound together by common ties and common duties; under the obligation to understand each other, and under the obligation to co-operate with each other. When you see the sectional misunderstandings that sometimes mar the progress of affairs in this country, it is well to repeat that line of the poet's—"A nation yet, the rulers and the ruled,"—notwithstanding the differences of opinion, notwithstanding the differences in the stages of economical development.

One of the most important questions in this country was the famous question—What is the matter with Kansas? No man

2 From "The Princess: Conclusion."

should be permitted to answer until he knows and if he doesn't know he ought to go and see. And if he thinks that because he cannot understand Kansas that therefore he is superior to the men of Kansas, he will find himself a fool when he meets the men of Kansas. Let him go and lay his mind fairly up alongside a Kansan mind. He will find that one stage of economical development is different from the other and that there are men in this country thinking at exactly the same point at which his father thought or his grandfather thought. And I think, therefore, you might make an intellectual history of this country by keeping in line with all the different stages of economical and intellectual development. You cannot afford to despise those men unless you despise your grandfather or your father. They have established a cult now for respecting our fathers and grandfathers. If that cult is to be maintained, we must also reverence and respect these contemporary ancestors of ours, these men who are just at the stage that the conditions of their life are what the conditions of our ancestors' lives were. Moreover, this country is not run for us in this particular period; and if we cannot compound these differences we have not entitled ourselves to the name of citizens; we have not entitled ourselves to the name of patriots; because until this love of country is based upon a common understanding and a common sympathy and until these sectional differences are obliterated, in our imaginations and in our affections at any rate if not in fact, we have not realized the first line of my text, "A nation yet," nor the other part, "the rulers and the ruled."

There is a notion abroad in this country that the people are the rulers in this country. I may not have read history deeply enough, but I know of no instance in which the people were the governors of any country. If they are governors, they are like the God Baal. They must be asleep and it may be necessary to call louder and wake them. We have made ourselves laws to awake them at stated intervals. These are the election laws, which are the peremptory laws of the nation. We are permitted to sleep in between elections, but on that day we must exercise the privilege of peremptory, ultimate popular sovereignty.

Two sets of candidates are proposed. One man says, "I hadn't anything to do with the choosing of these two sets." "Of course not, that was done while you were asleep." Then he adds, "you are simply to take A or B; one is a Republican and the other a Democrat." ["]Well, what do these men propose?" "Why, it is presumed they propose what their conventions have proposed, and their conventions met while you were asleep. We will have to ask you to just assume that these are the candidates, and then take your choice between them."

There is nothing that gives a man more profound belief in Providence than the history of this country. It is undoubtedly a providential system, and there is no doubt about it, that we have governors in this country, and ourselves are governed just as liberally; just as constantly and consistently, as the people of any other country in the world. But we dont always act that way. We call the President of the United Dates [States] by his nick-name. We go into the White House and say we own the premises. There is no secret about it, but in our reflective moments we speak of the President as a magistrate embodying the laws of the nation. We haven't very much reverence or respect for our rulers until we get into trouble, and then if circumstances are favorable we dont always get into trouble. Notwithstanding, the whole stamina of the nation, whether we speak of it lightly or solemnly, is in the laws and in the men who by process of change are put in the place of governors where the laws are made and administered. We ought to have more of the temperament of people that are governors. If we once realized that we are not the rulers, but simply chose the masters, I think we would be more careful in the choice. We realize that we have put governors over ourselves and we have no voice in respect of the exercise of their powers. We had better learn the lesson soon than late that there is no prerogative so important to us as the chance to study the ordinary lessons of history and of political science.

The processes of a government as constituted are not necessarily processes which render it a government after it is constituted; and because it is a government we ought to look upon it as something which we have put over ourselves and to which we have rendered ourselves obedient. So that the whole of this nation—"the rulers and the ruled"—ought to sink into our consciences, if we would have the true conception of our national life. "Some sense of duty" should sustain us; "some reverence for the laws ourselves have made"; so that we shall not regard a statute as something exterior to ourselves but as something strongly part of the national life; and yet we need some strength of will, some character, "some potent force to change" these laws when we will. It is all right to observe the matter of constantly keeping in mind a sense of nationality; always keeping immersed in the conditions which apprise us that the nation is all one; that it is a body politic; that it is an organic thing; that it cannot be several things, but one; that it cannot have several senses of duty, but one; that it must look upon its laws critically, not as things to be played with; but when these laws show themselves to be wrong they must be changed and the processes of change must not be created from the temper of change. No nation is safe, which has the temper of change; which believes that governments are provisional without intended permanency,—with whom everything is voluntary, everything common, no people secure[,] everything susceptible of momentary transition. No nation is fit to be free unless it has some unchanging underlying principle. There ought to be a sense of permanency. It is often said that the majority of people are too volatile and therefore incapable of self government because they think of something new to do every morning.

An Englishman once answered an argument by saying "I have never heard of such a thing in my life." (And the fact that you dont smile makes me think that you never did either.) (Young men should not be trusted. They have too many new ideas and ought to be suppressed, for they are too smart.) We really have our reliability because of that temperament. We have the idea that anything out of one's line is ridiculous—like the Englishman who thought it was absurd for a Frenchman to call "bread" "pan" [*pain*]. We have the idea that things are what we call them, and it is an absolute thing.

Tom Sawyer said [blank]

And yet there is in this race a sort of glacier movement which makes the mass move slowly; and it has established the principle that the man who stands in the way is sure to get crushed. So that it is necessarily a trait among ourselves, something that has not always been too common—I mean that "civic manhood firm against the crowd," so that a mwn [man] will not be afraid to stand up by himself in a company of men and defend his principles, in favor and out of favor, until men, out of sheer respect for his moral weight, have stopped to hear him. When Mr. Beecher waited for an hour to say something in a famous meeting in Liverpool;—I was then a young Southerner, but, no matter where I was born or bred, I stand to admire the splendid triumph of that man on that day, when, against the howling opposition of a great body of ill-mannered Englishmen in that great hall, he waited calmly, waited serenely, until they shouted their dull throats hoarse, and then went in [on] to win their cheers before he was through.

As I said at the outset of my address it doesn't make any differ-

omit3

omit
omit

omit

---

3 This "omit" and following ones by Wilson.

ence[,] he "is a man for a' that." And so that "civic manhood firm against the crowd" must be cultivated among us.

There is a love of popularity in this country which sometimes undermines character. A man wants to be with the procession. And there isn't any other country in the world in which individual opinion asserts itself less. This is not an original statement, but I believe it to be true. I believe that in a crowd of five Englishmen, or five Frenchmen, or five Germans, you will be more apt to find five different opinions upon general questions of public discussion than you are to find two opinions in a crowd of five Americans. They are affected by the newspapers they have read. They are told that things are going this way; and the weather signs are out, and they are trying to get under cover.

There is a temper of acquiescence which is bred by the democratic air of the country, and therefore you can find the big man by this "civic manhood." Individuality in this country is all the bigger, when you get it, because it takes such a big individuality to assert itself, and therefore we have bred a few giants in every generation; men who dont stop to calculate the effect of their principles, or to employ them in order to suit the general taste. We are dependent upon a few great men with training to train the minds of men for political conditions. They speak because God gave them energy to do so. For, when you think of it our polity is an intellectual polity. One of the most interesting things that can be remarked about our institutions is, that they require more knowledge, more nice discrimination, more good temper on the part of the people than any other institutions in the world. There are some nice, intricate, delicate points to be understood in this polity, and yet we count upon the people at large to understand them. And therefore we are dependent, as we ourselves realize, in this world upon the public school,–. . . some system which gives us a chance to use the mind with discrimination in order that men may be able to sustain the tests of the practical life which we live; the test of judgment; the tests of understanding and of discrimination. It is an intellectual polity and you must have a high grade of intellectual power.

This is exemplified by Chief Justice Marshall in his judicial work. When the court would meet for consultation, the Judge would suggest a line of reasoning to sustain a particular decision, and then ask what the other Judges thought. They usually acquiesced. Then he would turn and say: "Story, I wish you would see if there are any authorities for that?" If you will examine Marshall's opinions, you will find he doesn't cite many authorities. He takes the essential principles of our systems and reasons them out. It is purely an intellectual process: a historical process among English speaking people; the drawing out and building up from a particular document of the whole organization of our institutions.

And John Marshall's opinions are more typical of the American polity than anything else in writing in this country. That is the substance of the reasoning out of which the institutions of this country have been built up. And because it is an intellectual polity, it is the business of every one to study the national life. I dont believe that any man can conscientiously use his powers against the general formation of the national life which is bred in our practice, in our books, in conversation and in our conception of this country.

omit

Moreover, I believe that every man ought to study the science of practical politics in this country. Politics have fallen into unmerited disrepute in America. We have an idea that no man is a politician unless he goes in for office. This is a familiar mistake we make. We ought to pray that every thoughtful man might be a politician, and if the men who dont go into office would be thoughtful, the men who did would be thoughtful also. They would have to be thoughtful, because a man cannot afford to be thought about unless he does some hard thinking. You know one of the reasons Mr. Roosevelt is now President of the United States. He was a man of independent means and he went into politics in earnest and the politicians found this out. At the convention which named him for Vice President it was known among all the politicians that he could not be cast aside and buried politically, for he had enough energy to run three nations, and would be at every party convention, in every party caucus, and heard upon every party matter. This is the reason he became a giant in their sight. There was no known method of getting rid of him. The consequence was that that happened which happens in every case. The politicians said to themselves, the only way we can quiet this man is by putting him in one of the highest offices and seeing what he can do. You see it was inevitable; you cant afford to have a man like that running loose.

I believe we all, in proportion to our abilities, ought to make some impression upon the politicians. We are going to be at the meetings and we are going to speak our minds. We are going to let the country at large know that the right sort of man can be a power in this world. And it wouldn't take many men of this kind to reform the politics of this country. If more men would act along this line the country would be safer. If more men would study practical politics there would be fewer reformers who could not reform anything. A reformer of the type I am speaking of is a man who sets himself out for an object, whether it is practical or not, and puts his head down and runs after it. A man who can[not] compromise, who can[not] accommodate and [can]not accomplish, is not a real friend of society. (I am not speaking of moral questions) Therefore, as a man of the world, I suppose Savonarola would be the most conspicuous example, who preached in a time when men did not believe what some day men would come to believe about the principles of justice; about the principles of character; about those things that lie at the very center of character, whether that be individual or national character. But that is not what I am talking about. I am not talking about the practical reforms which must be transacted in the great cities. And those things can in no case advance to their consummation except through the agency of those who are studying the conditions of practical politics.

What are the conditions of practical politics? The politician has got to compound differences with the other members of the board and the committee. Whatever time he may have to devote to it, he will wait and try to get it,—by the next meeting, or whether he waits twenty years or not. Pushing in this direction and setting out for a goal until it is achieved is the art of leadership; and nothing but leadership accomplishes anything. The man who can adjust the opinions of others to his own opinions by slow persuasion and who can carry the mass along with him is a leader. For unless you do carry the mass you don't gain your object.

Take every novel idea that has been worked over so thoroughly with old ideas and in old phrases that it wont look new. Then it will look as if it had been handled; and it will be put in old words which they have heard time out of mind, and they will get the impression that there is nothing new about them at all. The art of persuasion is to mingle the old with the new, and thus do away with the prejudice against new things. A man may study the conditions of practical politics and be a partizan of that which is right. It is not well to be lukewarm about anything, except the style of one's clothes; and if you are lukewarm, get into you the energy of partizanship, for it isn't a bad thing to be a partizan of that which is right. Make profession of principle; it wont do you any harm. . . .

On the contrary, go into it on the principle that Solon tried to omit

put in his laws when he said it would be against the law of Athens not to take sides in politics. He wanted to make it a positive law of the land that a man [blank]

And if you could enforce such a law it would not be a bad law. The men of whom I am afraid are not the men who vote, but the men who dont vote. If you could pass a law making men take part in every campaign it would be a good thing, for non-voting men are a danger to the community. I nearly lost a friend recently in New York. He was condemning Tammany, and I said to him —"Did you vote in the municipal election before the last?" "No," says he, "what was the use?" "Oh, well," I said, "I dont care to discuss the matter with you any longer until you get to voting." He didn't vote and yet was astonished that Tammany got in. That is the kind of astonishment that means imbecility. And there is another principle which often dwells in my thoughts. I believe we ought to be fearless in criticism and yet fearful of change.

omit

We ought to use what [blank] described as a [blank] Go into a thing heart and soul, but be sure where you strike. And, while fearless in criticism, we ought to be fearful of bringing too much change in the course of our criticism. We ought to be nice in our discrimination of what is the most central place to strike, in order to accomplish our object, and it seems to me that it can be accomplished in this way. . . .

I most seriously believe what I am about to expound. You know a book is a very symmetrical thing. When a man writes a book he cannot picture it as conforming with life itself, unless it is complete in every part. And therefore (says he) I will gloss over the different parts, so that the surfaces will look alike. Then I will make the other parts look just the same. And I shall hope no one will step on the weak part. And to make it complete, some parts must be supplied from imagination. The book ia [is] not an image of life, because I cannot command in my thought the whole image of life.

You nust [must] remember that a man doesn't get the whole thing in books. You must correct the doctrines of books with the experiences of life. The same kind of men whom you meet every day write these books. The same kind of men lived under the old doctrines that live under the new generation. You may test the old doctrine just as well as you may test the new by knowing it, and therefore you must correct the ideas that you get from books with the ideas that you get from experience. Men most often object to a college education in that we do not at one and the same time give the youngsters a knowledge of books and of life. I do not know anything but life itself that can give a knowledge of life. Sensible fellows will find the things that cannot be gotten in books by experience in the world, and that is the practice of every man who lives in this world. I am beginning to fear I shall not live long enough not to be imposed upon by the parents of students who are in trouble. The genuineness of their feeling misleads me into accepting the genuineness of their reasoning. They are not absolutely in error and I am expected to deal with erratic people. But if these people would only feel out their position. . . . And therefore I must learn the art of allowing his head to be turned and his hand left untouched. . . .

omit

And that is part of the experience of life you come in contact with in dealing with the passions of men. We speak of this as a world in which mind is supreme. Mind is one of those things that run, but this governs. The real government of this world is in the House of Commons composed of the passions; and the strongest passion is prime minister; and that House governs life. And the one way in which you can purify life is by having the purest passion of your life at the helm of state. You must therefore remember that during nine tenths of your time you are not thoughtful beings. You have strong hopes, fears and conceptions of what will serve the people best; of what will help them to make a place of safety and happiness for themselves, and you are feeling out their position. If you are not to be duped by men, you must meet their passions with reason and abide by the consequences. Aim to have your purest passions at the helm of state and then you will be good citizens.

The best citizens are not necessarily the most brilliant men but the men who stand the test of life and keep themselves sweet and unstained and who are nevertheless guided by but one wish and that is to follow the goal towards which they set themselves in their youth when they stood by their mother's knee and saw the path of life before them like a simple journey. These men who have the courage of their convictions are not to be put down or thrown aside. They may lose themselves for a while, but they will find themselves again. And the reason that a democratic nation is safe is, that it is a good judge of character, though it is not always a good judge of policy; and you can depend upon it to pick out the men upon whom it can rely, because, whether they make mistakes or not, their purpose is straight and clean. Some of the most illiterate men in this country have been the most intelligent men in this country. Men forget what is said and done and there emerges above all the confusion simply that quiet figure of a man who sought to keep himself right and did not yield to temptation.

We do not think ourselves governed by sentiment, but we ought to be governed by sentiment. The only art of loving in a man is in his affections. If we do not love that which is good we cannot achieve that which is great.[4]

T MS. (Washington Association of N. J., Morristown, N. J.).
    [4] As future documents will reveal, there was considerable controversy over the authenticity of this text, and Wilson eventually repudiated it. Lukeman obviously missed some sentences and garbled others; however, there can be little doubt that he rendered substantial portions of the text as Wilson delivered them.

From Charles William Dabney[1]

Temporarily in New York,
My dear President Wilson,   26 Feb. 1903.

It was my great privilege as a boy to see your father upon his frequent visits to Hampden Sidney and to hear him talk and preach. My father[2] and mother admired and honoured him greatly and he was usually a guest in our home, so that I had a rare opportunity to see and hear him. Most of the good and great men of the South came there in those days, and the best part of a lazy boy's education was obtained in this intercourse with them.

Is it not the best kind of education that any kind of a boy can have? All the great preachers and elders of the Southern Presbyterian Church came together there from time to time. The princes among them were Dr. Hoge[3] and Dr. Wilson—Hoge the superb orator and Wilson, the clear-cut scholar. As a mere lad I sat silently at the feet of these men and drank in, in deepest reverence the wisdom and devotion which they gave forth.

Indeed it was a privilege. I regret that I did not improve it better!

Your father impressed me as the clearest thinker and strongest scholar of them all. His scholarship was like a granite building, strong and massive, but clean-cut and beautiful. His discourses were at once overpowering and delightful, so tremendous was their logical power and so beautiful their form. He was a master of strong, pure, splendid English.

But you know all this. I only felt moved to make a little acknowledgment of my debt to your great father.

I need not remind you of his services to the Southern church, or tell you how my father honoured and loved him.

Your father and Dr. Hoge and my father—all gone from us! How we shall miss them! What an honour to be their heirs according to the flesh, at least, and what a responsibility to be their heirs according to the Spirit!

Very cordially yours   Chas W Dabney.

ALS (WP, DLC).
[1] President of the University of Tennessee.
[2] His father, the Rev. Dr. Robert Lewis Dabney, was Professor of Church History at the Union Theological Seminary of Virginia, then located at Hampden-Sydney, Va., from 1853 to 1883. Dr. Dabney also taught occasional courses at Hampden-Sydney College and was co-pastor of the college church from 1858 to 1874. Charles William Dabney was born on June 19, 1855.
[3] The Rev. Dr. Moses Drury Hoge, pastor of the Second Presbyterian Church of Richmond, 1845-99.

To the Editor of the *Daily Princetonian*

[Dear Sir:]   [Princeton, N. J., c. Feb. 27, 1903]

In the recent action of the Faculty in regard to dropping men conditioned in a half or more of their work,[1] two or three cases were excepted upon a legal ground, which seemed with the Faculty imperative. After full deliberation, the Faculty decided that they were not at liberty, in applying the accumulative rule with regard to back conditions, to go back of the date at which the present rules were promulgated, since to apply the rule to conditions incurred before that date would be to attach a penalty to them which was not attached at the time they were acquired.

WOODROW WILSON.

Printed in the *Daily Princetonian*, Feb. 28, 1903.
[1] See the news item printed at March 7, 1903.

From William Edmond Pulsifer[1]

Dear Dr. Wilson: New York   Feb. 27, 1903.

I have just finished the fourth volume of your excellent series of the History of the American People. I feel under such great obligation to you for preparing this history and have received so much pleasure from the critical reading that I have given it, that I feel like expressing my thanks to you for this valuable contribution to historical literature.

I regard this history as the best in the English language. It is, for the ordinary reader, better than Bancroft, for it is written in such an attractive style as to hold the attention like a romance from beginning to end.

I have been particularly interested in your treatment of the State Rights question, the Slavery question and the skillful and eminently fair and just way you have treated them. I shall take the greatest pleasure in recommending these books to my friends, feeling sure that I am conferring a favor upon them by so doing. If you never do anything else in a literary way during your life you have, it appears to me, erected a monument by the creation of this series to your literary talent, and I may say genius, which will be enduring so long as letters exist.

Most cordially and respectfully yours,   W. E. Pulsifer

TLS (WP, DLC).
1 Treasurer and later president of D. C. Heath and Co.

From Charles Williston McAlpin

My dear Dr. Wilson: [Princeton, N.J.] February 27, 1903.

. . . Mr. Robert R. Henderson of your class writes me that a friend who has been reading a novel, Hope Loring, tells him that a statement is made therein that under the Charter of Princeton University no negro can graduate at the University.[1] I am advising Mr. Henderson that the Charter contains no reference to negroes.

I remain,

Very sincerely yours,   [C.W. McAlpin] Secretary.

CCL (McAlpin File, UA, NjP).
1 Lilian Lida Bell, *Hope Loring* (Boston, 1903), p. 3: "He [John Loring, father of Hope] was a graduate of Princeton, as were his father and grandfather before him, it having been an ancestor of his who was responsible for that clause in Princeton's charter which, unless altered, would for ever prevent negroes from graduating from that famous university, and which has made it such a favourite for Southern gentlemen."

From Isaac Minis Hays

My dear Sir: [Philadelphia] February 27th [190]3.

The Committee charged with the arrangements for the General Meeting of this Society in April next has requested me to ask you if you will not respond to the toast of "Our Universities" at the Dinner to be given on the evening of Friday, April 3rd, at the Hotel Bellevue.

I trust that this may be agreeable and convenient to you, and remain

Very faithfully Yours   I. Minis Hays, Secretary

ALS (Secretary's Letterpress Books, PPAmP).

A News Report about the Conferral of an Honorary Degree

[Feb. 28, 1903]

This was Dr. Horace Howard Furness' presentation of President Wilson for the degree of Doctor of Laws from the University of Pennsylvania, at their notable Washington's Birthday celebration in Philadelphia last Saturday. Dr. Furness, it will be recalled, was the recipient of one of Princeton's honorary degrees at the Sesquicentennial celebration:

> We have invited to be present here to-day Woodrow Wilson, because from his youth upwards, he has chosen to "scorn delights and live laborious days" in devotion to a self culture, whereof the fruits are destined to elevate and refine all who come under their influence. An early legal training imparted to his mind a bent which, in maturer years, led him, and we hope will still lead him, to send forth to his fellow citizens, from time to time, treatises of deep import, and "rich with the spoils of time," on politics, government and literature. In these later days the past lives anew, with its warning or its cheer, in the vivid and thoughtful pages of his Histories and Biographies. He has been recently appointed to the most august position in the gift of a farfamed university, our sister and nearest neighbor; and has already, in his new sphere, given promise of every quality which the needs of the highest standard of education demands, or sympathy with ardent youth can exact, or the most devoted son of Princeton can desire. Well may his fair mother exult in such a son! This high office crowns his career with the assurance of that enduring fame, which is,
> > "—no plant that grows on mortal soil
> > But lives and spreads aloft by those pure eyes,
> > And perfect witness of all-judging Jove."[1]
> Therefore do we, the Trustees, present him to the Provost that he may receive the honorary degree of Doctor of Laws.

Four other honorary degrees were conferred, D.Sc. upon President [Alexander Crombie] Humphreys of Stevens Institute, and LL.D. upon Principal [William] Peterson of McGill University; John S. Sargent, the portrait painter, and General Leonard Wood.

Printed in the *Princeton Alumni Weekly*, III (Feb. 28, 1903), 341.
[1] From Milton's "Lycidas," lines 78, 81, and 82.

To Isaac Minis Hays

My dear Mr. Hays: Princeton, New Jersey. 28 February, 1903.

I seem to be fated never to be allowed to accept an invitation to speak before the American Philosophical Society. The evening of April 3rd is already spoken for on my calendar[1]—indeed it would be hard to find an evening that was not, so many have I had to promise away this university year.

Please express to the Committee my sincere appreciation and genuine regret.

Very sincerely yours,   Woodrow Wilson

TLS (Archives, PPAmP).
[1] He was scheduled to attend the Round Table Club in New York on this date.

A News Report

[March 1903]

GENERAL MEETING OF THE ARCHAEOLOGISTS
IN PRINCETON

One of the features of the winter season in Princeton was the meeting of the Archaeological Institute of America, which convened here on December 31st and remained in session until noon of January 2nd. . . .

The first session was opened on Wednesday at 2:30—Professor John Williams White, of Harvard, President of the Institute, presiding—by the address of welcome which was delivered by President Woodrow Wilson of the University. In welcoming the members of the Institute to Princeton, President Wilson assured them that they had made no mistake in choosing this stronghold of classical studies for their place of meeting, and his remarks upon Princeton's position in these matters were heartily applauded by his audience.

Printed in *Princeton University Bulletin*, XIV (March 1903), 37-38.

From Moses Taylor Pyne

My dear Woodrow   Princeton, N. J.   Mch 5/03

I want to thank you very much for your kind letters.

The sympathy and affection of our old friends & companions mean much to us at this time.[1]

I hope that as you feel stronger you will not jeopardize your health by attempting too much. You are too valuable to Princeton and to us to risk the work of the next twenty years for a single speech or journey.

Mrs. Pyne joins me in thanking you

Sincerely yours   M Taylor Pyne

ALS (WP, DLC).
[1] Pyne's son, Robert Stockton Pyne, died on Feb. 25, 1903, at the age of nineteen.

A News Item

[March 7, 1903]

Forty-six Princeton students were dropped from their classes at the recent mid-year examinations,—twenty-four from the Academic Department and twenty-two from the School of Science. To the undergraduates these figures look very large, especially as some good athletes were swept out at this semi-annual faculty house-cleaning. The campus view of it seems to be that with the new administration a Draconian policy has come in. The Tiger[1] is coming out with a cartoon of the President, representing him sitting alone on the steps of Old North in the year 1910, with the inscription "Wilson, That's All"[2] below.

Printed in the *Princeton Alumni Weekly*, III (March 7, 1903), 355.
  [1] An undergraduate magazine of humor. The cartoon appeared in the March 1903 issue on pp. 158-59. It is reproduced on the following page.
  [2] The slogan of a whiskey popular at the time.

A News Report of an Address to the Alumni of Western Pennsylvania

[March 8, 1903]

SONS OF OLD NASSAU HELD A BRILLIANT BANQUET LAST NIGHT

The twenty-ninth annual banquet of the Princeton Club of Western Pennsylvania, held last night at the Union club, in the Frick Building, far surpassed any previous event of a similar nature held by the association. Over 180 sons of "Old Nassau," representing classes of over half a century, gathered around the festive board, and during the course of partaking of a sumptuous repast, engaged in singing their old and time-honored college songs and made the banquet hall resound with Princeton yells, recalling their own student days and reminiscences of the time they spent at their alma mater.

The occasion was a particularly notable one, since the gathering was honored by the president of Princeton University, Dr. Woodrow Wilson, as well as many other guests of national reputation. This is President Wilson's first visit to Pittsburg since he was placed at the head of the university. Many of the alumni of the institution present at the banquet had left the institution years before Dr. Wilson was made president, and they were enthusiastic in meeting the newly-inaugurated head of their alma mater. . . .

1910
That's All!

President Wilson was then presented, and after an appropriate anecdote at the outset of his address, said:

"If we can go on perpetuating the spirit of Princeton University we can afford to be one of the lesser universities in number if we are one of the foremost in power and quality. With good quality we can be perfectly indifferent in reference to quantity. I believe we can also ignore what is called the practical test of education. Latin and Greek are said to be not practical, while mathematics are, but much of our mathematics are entirely theoretical, in the air, as it were. Is the practice in the gymnasium practical? No, this exercise is simply to make the body a suitable habitant for a strong mind. Therefore I shall not discuss the practicability of an education such as afforded at Princeton University.

"It seems to me the object of a college education is to give a man a little world in which to live. It should give a man a world in little, which should be a copy of the world in large. He should be able to wend his pathway along the lines mapped out by previous leaders of thought, profiting by their experience.

"I find the greatest lessons in the lines of the poet, and not the extremely practical man. Were it not for the ideals upheld by these men, the history of our country should never have been written. So do not despise the dreamer. He occupies an invaluable position in the economy of life."

He then showed how the ideal and theoretic aspect of man's development applies in the sphere of business. He said that the successful business man must be able to think in terms of alien races. He must know of the climatic conditions of other countries and the customs and manners of their people. He must be a universal man.

"But," he continued, "we must do more for the undergraduate of the university. He must be made observant; then he must be made reasonable. There are few unreasonable [reasonable] men in the world. Few look at a proposition in an impersonal sense, and many think a proposition is reductio ad absurdium if he says that he has never heard of the thing before. Then a man must be discriminating. I sometimes wish that a universal system of ethics could be established in our colleges. Sometimes the student will put his brain in action when in the laboratory but adjourn his mind as soon as he leaves the laboratory and are [is] ready to take any rumor as a positive truth.

"Then, again the college man must have a Catholic mind—not necessarily a Roman Catholic mind. I mean by this a man who is not afraid to take up new ideals and put them to use.["]

The speaker then turned to a discourse of what Princeton is doing for training young men and the hopeful outlook of the university in the future. "Our ideal," he said, "is not to excel, nor to see how much better we may be than others, but to give young men high ideals. I believe the things we have to do at Princeton are indispensable to the country. It is to be a place of outlook upon the world at large, to give a sweep around the horizon. May it not lose this high ideal."[1]

Printed in the *Pittsburg Press*, March 8, 1903; some editorial headings omitted.
[1] There is a WWhw outline of this address, dated March 7, 1903, in WP, DLC.

From John Glover Wilson[1]

Dear President Wilson: Cumberland, Md., March 9, 1903.

My visits to Pittsburg seem to be prolific of inspiration from you. Last spring a year ago, after the base-ball game with Yale, I went over there and heard the fellows talking of your "When a man comes to himself."[2] This year I heard your speech of Saturday night, and I cannot resist the impulse to write and thank you for it. I rejoice that we Princeton men have a leader who stands for such high ideals—which at the same time are concrete and practical enough to be of help in daily life and work.

I am sure you would have been pleased if you had heard the expressions of unqualified approval of your speech afterwards from that usually irreverent crowd with which I was seated.

With kindest personal regards and renewed good wishes for the continued success of your administration, believe me,
          Very Faithfully and Loyally,   John G. Wilson

ALS (WP, DLC).
[1] A friend and former student, Princeton 1892, who was at this time state's attorney for Allegheny County, Md.
[2] Printed at Nov. 1, 1899, Vol. 11.

From John Grier Hibben

My dear Woodrow   Princeton   March 10/03

I find that there are still depths in your generous friendship which I had not fathomed. Your letter, its contents and enclosure,[1] and above all the thought which prompted you to surprise me so delightfully, I appreciate with all my heart. If you do not have the Board of Trustees "on your hands" this afternoon, we shall hope to see you at five oclock.

Ever affectionately yours,   John Grier Hibben

ALS (WP, DLC).
1 They are missing.

From Goldwin Smith[1]

Dear Sir,   Toronto   March 10th 1903

I have just finished my perusal of your most valuable and I think monumental History of the American People. I am particularly impressed with what you say towards the close about Mr. Cleveland. Some years ago I was among the representatives of sister Universities who attended your University celebration.[2] After the academical exercises, Mr. Cleveland, then President, delivered an address to a large and mixed audience. I was greatly struck by the manner in which he was received and the impression which his address made; the more so as the address was not rhetorical either in composition or delivery, so that the impression was evidently personal. To me as an onlooker Mr. Cleveland seems to be the one man, with the possible exception of President Roosevelt, who has a real hold on your people. Why, then, is he shelved, and at a time of manifest danger, political and industrial, when personal leadership is most needed? If this is necessary, does it not point to a practical defect in your institutions?

Yours very truly,   Goldwin Smith

TLS (WP, DLC).
1 Author and journalist of Toronto, Canada.
2 That is, Princeton's Sesquicentennial Celebration in 1896. Smith represented Oxford University.

A News Report

[March 11, 1903]

FIFTH ANNUAL BANQUET
Of the Daily Princetonian Given at the
Inn Last Evening.

The fifth annual banquet of THE DAILY PRINCETONIAN Board was held last evening at the Princeton Inn. The dinner began about half past eight and closed with the toast by President Wilson. At intervals during the banquet selections were rendered by a quartet from the Glee Club consisting of O. A. Hack 1903, J. R.

Miller 1903, J. R. Truesdale 1904, A. Jagger 1904, and a quartet from the Banjo Club, consisting of C. W. Hall 1903, J. Cecil 1904, R. S. Crocker 1904, and J. L. Grimes 1905.

The list of toasts was as follows:

"The Retiring Board," John G. Armstrong 1903.

"The Incoming Board," Francis W. Dinsmore 1904.

"*The Yale News*," E. W. Clucas.

"*The Harvard Crimson*," J. A. Field.

"The Faculty," Professor J. B. Carter, '93.

"Eastern and Western College Journalism," Professor J. H. Finley.

"The College Man in Journalism," Mr. Talcott Williams.

"Princeton University," President Woodrow Wilson. . . .

The last toast, "Princeton University," was responded to by President Wilson. He spoke of the common feeling that there are great differences between members of the faculty and students, and expressed a desire that this feeling might be abolished. In speaking of college papers he said that there was something in college journalism which is higher than that expressed in daily papers, for the latter are bound by party ties, whereas college papers endeavor to express non-partisan sentiments. "There should be a real comradeship between faculty and undergraduates. It is your duty from now on to be picked, representative men of Princeton. In order to show that universities are necessary to the life of a nation you must show that you as university men are better than other men in carrying on its life and in lifting its ideals high above sordid suspicion."

Printed in the *Daily Princetonian*, March 11, 1903.

To the Board of Trustees of Princeton University

[Princeton, N. J., c. March 11, 1903]

The Committee on Honorary Degrees recommends that at the Annual Commencement in June the Honorary Degree of LL.D. be conferred on

The Rt. Hon. Sir Michael Henry Herbert, British Ambassador at Washington; William Earl Dodge, of New York; William Milligan Sloane, Seth Low Professor of History in Columbia University.

The committee also recommends that the Honorary Degree of Litt.D. be conferred at the same time on

Hiram Corson, Professor of English Literature in Cornell University; Thomas Frederick Crane, '64, Dean of the Faculty of Arts and Sciences and Professor of the Romance Languages and Literature in Cornell University.

The committee further recommends that the Honorary Degree of A.M. be conferred at the same time on Mr. James Hazen Hyde[1] of New York.

Respectfully submitted,   Woodrow Wilson
Chairman.

TRS (Trustees' Papers, UA, NjP).

[1] Harvard 1898; Vice President of the Equitable Life Assurance Society of the United States and officer or director of many other large business concerns.

Samuel Ross Winans to the Board of Trustees' Committee on Morals and Discipline

GENTLEMEN: [Princeton, N. J.] 12th March, 1903.

The period covered by this report, December to March, generally furnishes more disorder than the other seasons of the Academic year, as it includes the breaking up and reassembling before and after the holidays, the term examinations with the subsequent relaxation, and the festivities of Washington's Birthday. The record this year, I am happy to state, shows a comparatively small number of discipline cases. And apart from this freedom from petty disorder, we may congratulate ourselves on the more significant advances made in student tone and sentiment in that certain grave evils of long standing have been quietly abolished. The Sophomore-Freshman feud in its various manifestations at this season has disappeared:—the snow-balling, the reading of translations at examination times, the revival of "horsing" at Washington's Birthday. And on the other side the Freshmen have refrained altogether from painting, and we may hope that this senseless vandalism will never be revived. These customs, some of them have existed a score of years, and silly and outrageous as they seem to older persons, they have made part of the cherished body of student customs. The impulse in this movement has distinctly been a loyal desire on the part of the student body to promote the best interests of the University and to do their part at this time in advancing its reputation and prosperity. This was the most quiet and orderly Washington's Birthday known in many years. I am sorry to note that a group of recent graduates more or less intoxicated furnished the only disorder.

The outlook in general for a real cessation of Sophomore-Freshman annoyances is, I think, more hopeful than ever before. The students propose to limit the "guying" of Freshmen strictly to a few days at the beginning of the term.

There have been since my last report twenty-two (22) cases of discipline, against thirty (30) in the same period last year, and forty-seven (47) in the year before. Last year, however, thirteen (13) were Freshmen implicated in painting; and the year before a number were suspended for excess of chapel absences,—a policy since changed. By classes, there were seven (7) Seniors, six (6) Juniors, six (6) Sophomores, three (3) Freshmen; of this twenty-two (22), fifteen (15) were in the School of Science. As the ratio of numbers in the two departments is not quite five to seven (5 to 7) the disproportion of discipline cases is marked, and this disproportion manifests itself constantly in these statistics. The drinking cases were fourteen (14),—the same number as last year; they were twenty-two (22) the year before. Eight (8) of the fourteen (14) again were Scientific Students. Ten (10) were suspended,—for repeated or aggravated offense.

One Junior implicated in an affair with women was sent away for one year, but on account of his previous good conduct will be allowed ultimately to return.

One Freshman guilty of several forgeries and other dishonesty was dismissed.

Two Freshmen found guilty by the Student Investigating Committee of dishonesty in an examination were promptly and finally dismissed. The immediate sense of ostracism which these men experienced and the general tone of the student discussion of the matter has made plain that the Honor System is a living and operative system which the students are proud of and thoroughly determined to maintain. This is the first case of observed dishonesty in several years.

The students dropped for deficient scholarship after the examinations (including several withdrawn for this cause earlier in the term) number fifty six (56),—twenty eight (28) in each department. The number is somewhat larger than hitherto, especially in the School of Science. There was some increase in the number of conditions given, particularly in the Sophomore and Junior years. It is to be noted that twelve (12) of the fifty six (56) had already been dropped back a class; while a dozen more had been heavily conditioned and then allowed further trial for special reasons. In six (6) cases only—(five Sophomores and one Junior)—was the dropping due to the Faculty rule, adopted two years ago, by which neglected arrearages of work are added to the total of deficiency. The scholarship rules have been applied with firmness and consistency, and the effect must be salutary.

I append tabular statements[1] of the discipline cases and of the men dropped, adding the figures for two years preceding.

Respectfully submitted,   S. R. Winans
Dean of the Faculty.

TLS (Trustees' Papers, UA, NjP).
 [1] They are not printed.

To Goldwin Smith

My dear Sir: Princeton, New Jersey. 13 March, 1903.

Allow me to thank you for your letter of March 10, with its very kind reference to my History of the American People.

The point you touch upon in respect of Mr. Cleveland is certainly a most interesting and important one. It has always seemed to me a serious practical defect in our political arrangements that a man of personal force, once lifted to the top of our Government, cannot be kept there, but must be thrust aside for other men after a definite term of service. Mr. Cleveland undoubtedly has a great hold upon the American people, and only a preverse [perverse] tradition keeps him from resuming the leadership which I believe he himself does not desire, but which thoughtful men throughout the United States would cordially desire to see him have.

With much appreciation and regard,

Very sincerely yours,   Woodrow Wilson

TLS (G. Smith Papers, University Archives, NIC).

From Charles Williston McAlpin

My dear Dr. Wilson: [Princeton, N. J.] March 13, 1903.

Mr. W[alter]. K[napp]. Tompkins of the Senior Class has just been here to see about some additional assistance; he rooms in North College [Nassau Hall] and has a part managership in a Club paying what remains of his board bill direct and not through the Office. His total bill at the Office at present amounts to $79.08 which includes $30.08 due from last term.

I know nothing about him except that he is a second group man and seems to be very pleasant. I am writing to you to see if there is any money in the Loan Fund at the College Offices with which to help him. If there is not or you think it inadvisable to assist him from that source I have a sufficient balance in the funds that I administer here to advance enough to clear him at the Offices. I have asked him to call again on Monday and if you can let me know your decision in the matter by that time I shall be very glad to give him a definite answer.

I remain,

Sincerely yours,   [C. W. McAlpin] Secretary.

CCL (McAlpin File, UA, NjP).

To Charles Williston McAlpin

My dear Mr. McAlpin: Princeton, New Jersey. 14 March, 1903.

I know nothing of Mr. W. K. Thompkins but what is favorable to him. He has been one of the steady men of the class, and I should think that you would be perfectly justified in advancing to him the money which he needs to make him square at the University Offices. I am sorry to say that the small loan fund at the College Offices is already long since exhausted.

Very sincerely yours,   Woodrow Wilson

TLS (McAlpin File, UA, NjP).

From William Earl Dodge

My dear Prest. Wilson   New York.   March 14 1903

Secretary McAlpin of the University has informed me of the great honor suggested by the Trustees in proposing my name for an honorary degree at the next Commencement

I very deeply appreciate their kindness but am in doubt as to my duty in accepting it because as a layman without any literary pretension or position I fear it might be misunderstood.

I have already declined this honor from another College where I had no association, but it would be a great pleasure to have a direct connection with Princeton for which I have a warm regard and where my sons graduated.

May I ask you confidentially, if you think such an appointment would be well received by those who feel degrees should only go with scholarship to which I have no pretension[.] I am

With sincere regards   Yours cordially   W. E. Dodge

ALS (WP, DLC).

To William Earl Dodge

My dear Mr. Dodge,   Princeton, 15 Mar., '03

Your letter of yesterday does you great honour as an additional proof of your genuine modesty,—and I thank you most sincerely for the compliment you pay me in asking my advice in a matter in which I may be regarded as a party in interest. I will try to prove myself worthy of your confidence by an equal frankness in reply.

I never knew an honour of this kind conferred with greater heartiness and unanimity and it received my warmest support. You probably do not realize how universally you are regarded as the representative, as well as the patron, of all that college men like to be thought to stand for. There is a learning and experience got outside universities for which the degree of Doctor of Laws is as appropriately given as for the more formal acquirements of scholarship,—and that eminence, which is of public service and of wide acquaintance with men and books you represent in a most unusual manner. Last year we had the pleasure of conferring the degree on Mr. Morris K. Jesup; we should be deeply disappointed could we not add your name to our highest roll. I speak simple truth when I assure you that alike in judgment and in feeling I deeply approve the choice.

Since beginning this letter I have received the sad news of the death of Mrs. Wm. E. Dodge, Senior.[1] Will you not permit me to express my heartfelt sympathy, and my deep appreciation of the beauty of the life that is just ended?

With warmest regard
Cordially and Faithfully Yours,   Woodrow Wilson

ALS (WC, NjP).
[1] Melissa Phelps Dodge died on March 15, 1903. She was the wife of William Earl Dodge (1805-83) and the mother of the addressee of this letter.

To James Hazen Hyde

My dear Mr. Hyde: Princeton, New Jersey.   16 March, 1903.

I have read your letter of March 13th with the most genuine pleasure. It is very gratifying indeed to learn that the action of our Board, taken I can assure you with great cordiality, is acceptable to you. I am sorry that we shall not have the pleasure of seeing you here in June, but glad to learn that it is only a pleasure deferred, and that you will be able to come to receive the degree in October.

With much regard,

                    Very sincerely yours,   Woodrow Wilson

TLS (NHi).

From Henry Cooper Pitney, Jr.

Dear Mr. President: Morristown, N. J.   Mar. 16, 1903.

Your recent favor about revision of notes was duly received.

In another parcel I send by mail to you today the stenographer's transcript of his notes. In this some omissions occur for which gaps are left. The star marks indicate an omission of matter which should be supplied in order to introduce what next follows. One or two latin phrases were likewise lost.

Will you kindly revise the notes as well as your time will permit and fill the omissions as far as you can.

Mr. Lukeman will be very glad to call to see you, and take your dictation of any corrections and amendments in case you would like to have him do so.

On return of the notes revised by you I will commit them to the printer and later send you the printer's proofs.

Hoping you will be able to revise the notes soon, I am with good wishes,   Yours very truly,   [Henry C. Pitney, Jr.]

CCL (Washington Association of N. J., Morristown, N. J.).

To Hugo Münsterberg

                              Princeton, New Jersey.

My dear Professor Munsterberg: 18 March, 1903.

I take pleasure in giving you the following list of men in the Princeton Faculty, who might very properly be called upon for papers at the International Congress or [of] Arts and Sciences to be held in St. Louis next year.[1]

In the mathematical field—Prof. H. B. Fine, H. D. Thompson, E. O. Lovett.

In the classical languages and philology—Professors A. F. West, S. R. Winans, J. H. Westcott, E. Y. Robbins, J. B. Carter.

In the political sciences Professors W. M. Daniels and W. A. Wyckoff.

In art–Professors Allan Marquand and A. L. Frothingham.

In astronomy, Professor C. A. Young; in physics, Professors C. F. Brackett and W. F. Magie; in geology and paleontology Professor W. B. Scott; in chemistry Professor S[L]. W. McCay and Professor F. Neher; and in biology, Professor C. F. W. McClure.

In the mental sciences, Professor A. T. Ormond, J. G. Hibben, J. M. Baldwin.

In English literature, Professors G. McL. Harper and S. Axson.

In history, Professor J. H. Coney, and in the practical, Professor J. H. Finley.

Very sincerely yours,   Woodrow Wilson

TLS (H. Münsterberg Papers, MB).

¹ The International Congress of Arts and Science was to be held in St. Louis from September 19 to September 25, 1904, in conjunction with the Universal (or Louisiana Purchase) Exposition. Planning for the Congress had begun in September 1902. Münsterberg had at that time suggested that the Congress should be organized around a central theme and had outlined a scheme of organization which was subsequently adopted. The distinguished astronomer, Simon Newcomb, was appointed president of the Congress; Münsterberg and Albion W. Small of the University of Chicago, vice-presidents. These three men did most of the actual work of organizing the Congress and of securing participants, both in the United States and abroad.

The unifying theme was to be "The Progress of Man since the Louisiana Purchase." The organizational scheme provided for the arrangement of all learned studies in seven "Divisions": Normative Science, Historical Science, Physical Science, Mental Science, Utilitarian Science, Social Regulation, and Social Culture. These divisions in turn were divided into "Departments"; Historical Science, for example, was divided into Departments of Political and Economic History, History of Law, History of Language, History of Literature, History of Art, and History of Religion. The departments were subdivided into "Sections"; for example, the Department of Political and Economic History included sections in the History of Greece, Rome, and Asia, Mediaeval History, Modern History of Europe, History of America, and History of Economic Institutions.

After the opening ceremonies on the first day of the Congress, the morning of the second day was to be devoted to meetings of the seven divisions, with one major address at each meeting; the departments were to meet the afternoon of the second day, with two speakers at each meeting. Up to this point, all the speakers were to be Americans, to emphasize the contributions of the United States to the learned disciplines. The remaining five days of the Congress were to be devoted to meetings of the sections, with two major speakers at each. In these meetings, both American and foreign scholars were to participate.

As it turned out, Wilson himself gave the address to the meeting of the Division of Historical Science on September 20, 1904. It is printed at that date in Vol. 15 of this series. Of the Princeton faculty members mentioned in the above letter, only four actually took part in the Congress. James Mark Baldwin (who had by then left Princeton to go to The Johns Hopkins University) addressed the Department of Psychology. Alexander T. Ormond spoke before the Section on Metaphysics of the Department of Philosophy. Andrew F. West was chairman of the Section on Classical Literature of the Department of the History of Literature. And William Berryman Scott was chairman of the Section on Paleontology of the Department of the Sciences of the Earth.

For further details relating to the Congress, see Margaret Münsterberg, *Hugo Münsterberg: His Life and Work* (New York and London, 1922), pp. 95-117, and Howard J. Rogers (ed.), *Congress of Arts and Science, Universal Exposition, St. Louis, 1904* (8 vols., Boston and New York, 1905-1907), especially Volume I, which includes a history and plan of the Congress.

To Lucius Hopkins Miller

My dear Mr. Miller: Princeton, New Jersey.   18 March, 1903.

I wrote to Colonel McCook and have his answer.[1] I am sorry to say that he thinks it unsafe to count upon any funds from Mrs. Brown's estate[2] for the next academic year. We are, therefore, apparently shut in to postponing the arrangement about Bible study until 1904-05.[3]

I may say, by the way, that in the argument we had the other day about putting Bible in our curriculum, you went a good way toward converting me to your view.

I need not tell you how much I regret the postpon[e]ment of our plans.   Always cordially yours,   Woodrow Wilson

TLS (Selected Corr. of L. H. Miller, NjP).
  [1] His letter is missing.
  [2] McCook was the executor of the estate of Susan Dod Brown, who had left the bulk of her estate, worth about $223,000, to Princeton University. Under the terms of her will, ex-President Patton was to decide how her bequest should be used. He stipulated that $35,000 should be added to the endowment of the chair in moral philosophy held by his son, George Stevenson Patton, and that the balance should be used to provide income for faculty salaries.
  [3] President Patton, George Stevenson Patton, and other members of the faculty had given courses in biblical literature for many years through the academic year 1901-1902. These courses were dropped in 1902 and were not given again until 1905, when Lucius Hopkins Miller was appointed Assistant Professor of Biblical Instruction.

To Landonia Randolph Dashiell

My dear Madam: Princeton, New Jersey.   19 March. 1903.

I am deeply gratified that the Virginia Society of Colonial Dames should desire me to make an address on their Field Day at Yorktown in May, and I can assure you that it would give me the greatest pleasure to do so if it were at all possible; but my engagements for the rest of the academic year are positively prohibitive of new promises of this kind. I am caught fast for every remaining week until our Commencement in June.

Pray express to the Committee of the Society my very warm appreciation of the honor they have done me, and my very sincere regret.   Very truly yours,   Woodrow Wilson

TLS (Berg Coll., NN).

To Robert Bridges

My dear Bobby: Princeton, New Jersey. 21 March, 1903.

I am distressed to find that April 3rd is preengaged. I shall be in New York on that evening, but unhappily at another dinner, the dinner of the Round Table Club. Evidently I am so entangled with engagements that it would be out of the question for you to have both me and Halsey, as Halsey is equally embarrassed, and it is much more necessary to have him than to have me. Wont you please go ahead without me? It would be delightful to be there; but after all it is not necessary, and the rounding up of the dormitory should not be delayed. I need not tell you how disappointed I am, but really you ought not to wait for me.

Yes, the lions are temporarily out of business.[1] They were made of plates joined together with a metal cement, which had in the course of years disintegrated; and what happened the other night was not a piece of vandalism at all, but an accident. One of the men tried to pull himself up onto the pedestal of one of the lions by pulling on the lion's head, and the whole fore part of the animal gave way. Nothing was done which had not been done a hundred times before; and the newspaper reports were an instance of what we suffer from reporters who do not investigate.

Always affectionately yours, Woodrow Wilson

TLS (WC, NjP).
[1] The lions which flanked the steps at the main entrance to Nassau Hall had been given by the Class of 1879 as its decennial gift to the college. The lion was a symbol of the House of Orange-Nassau, for which the building was named. The lions were replaced in 1911 by the bronze tigers (also a gift of the Class of 1879) which still adorn the entrance to Nassau Hall.

To James Bryce

My dear Mr. Bryce, Princeton, New Jersey, 23 March, 1903

I am taking the liberty of sending you, under another cover, a copy of the address which I delivered at my inauguration as President of Princeton.

I am expecting to sail for England, with Mrs. Wilson, on the first of July, and am looking forward with pleasure to the possibility of seeing you when in London.[1]

With much regard,

Sincerely Yours, Woodrow Wilson

TLS (Bryce Papers, Bodleian Library).
[1] The first indication in the documents that the Wilsons were planning to go

abroad during the summer of 1903. As will become evident in future documents, they made an extended trip through Great Britain and the Continent. Jenny D. Hibben to WW, Aug. 16, 1903, discloses that Wilson did see Bryce in London.

To Charles Williston McAlpin

Princeton, New Jersey.

My dear Mr. McAlpin: 24 March, 1903.

. . . I have just received a letter from Mr. William E. Dodge,[1] in which with some modest hesitation, he accepts our invitation to receive a degree at Commencement.

Sincerely yours,   Woodrow Wilson

TLS (McAlpin File, UA, NjP).
   [1] This reply to Wilson's letter to Dodge of March 15, 1903, is missing.

From George Robert Parkin

Dear President Wilson: Washington, D. C., March 24, 1903.

I have now nearly got through my long tour of the United States and I have only a conference at New York on Thursday next at Columbia University to complete my work on this Continent. It has occurred to me that it would be very interesting to my trustees if in my report to them I should be able to mention the names of the Committees of Selection recommended in each State in the Union with their official position. I suppose it will be as easy for you to name this Committee[1] now as at a later time and if you have no special objection to doing so I would be very glad if you would think the matter over and send me a list of the names in accordance with the decision which we reached at our conference.[2] A letter will reach me on Thursday at Columbia University and till Friday night at the Parker House, Boston. I am sailing on the following day by the Commonwealth for Genoa as I am trying to avoid the bad weather in crossing by taking this route. I have had a profoundly interesting tour and I have every reason to feel that in carrying out our scheme we shall have the sympathy of almost every leading educational man in America. With kind regards, believe me,

Yours sincerely,   George R. Parkin

TLS (WP, DLC).
   [1] That is, the committee for New Jersey.
   [2] Wilson's reply is missing, but the New Jersey Rhodes Scholarship Committee consisted of Wilson, chairman, President Austin Scott of Rutgers College, and Henry Burchard Fine of Princeton.

To Lucius Hopkins Miller

My dear Mr. Miller: Princeton, New Jersey.   26 March, 1903.

I have read the letters which I return with this with genuine interest, and am very much obliged to you for letting me see them. I am afraid we are shut in to making no plans at all for next year, but I have a feeling that your experience at the Hill School will be of service both to you and to us.

It was not at all necessary for you to pay for the telegrams I have been sending, and I shall take pleasure in handing the money which you enclose to the Treasurer of the Philadelphian Society.

With warm regard,

Sincerely yours,   Woodrow Wilson

TLS (Selected Corr. of L. H. Miller, NjP).

A News Item

[March 27, 1903]

PRESIDENT WILSON'S ADDRESS.

President Wilson addressed the regular weekly meeting of the Philadelphian Society in Murray Hall last evening. He took his text from the nineteenth Psalm, his principal theme being the "Laws of the Lord."

As President Wilson said, the text contains the elements of strength, wisdom, and happiness, the three things for which every man longs. Men prefer, first, however, to try the ways of the world and only afterwards learn to turn towards God. There is a great reaction taking place in the way the world regards religion. In its literary aspects it is striving after spiritual realities such as are seen in the text, which shows that the simple can be made wise only by means or [of] the truths of God. The chief attraction of the Bible is its simple, wonderful appeal to the instinct.

President Wilson showed that a man rejoices in his heart not because of worldly triumphs, but because of a true adjustment of his relations to God. Only the law of the Lord can bring peace.

In conclusion, President Wilson spoke of the power of sympathy in a man's life by which he may attract friends to himself.

The Reverend D. S. Morris '93, a missionary in China, will deliver an address on next Thursday evening, which will be illustrated by stereopticon views.

Printed in the *Daily Princetonian*, March 27, 1903.

A News Item

[March 28, 1903]

Fifty alumni foregathered at Albany, N. Y., on March 19th, at the annual dinner of the Princeton Club of Albany. Dean Andrew F. West '74 represented the University. President Wilson '79 had been expected, but a sore throat kept him in Princeton. He sent a letter and telegram of regret, which were read at the dinner. A correspondent writes that "Professor West most graciously consented to act as substitute, at the eleventh hour, and delivered an address that will be long remembered 'in these parts.' "

Printed in the *Princeton Alumni Weekly*, III (March 28, 1903), 409.

A News Report of an Address to Princeton Alumni in Washington

[March 28, 1903]

Washington Alumni Receive a Message from Alma Mater.
PRESIDENT WILSON'S ADDRESS

More than three-score sons of Nassau, members of the Princeton Alumni of the District of Columbia, gathered round the banquet board at the New Willard last evening in observance of their annual reunion and dinner, and, as is customary in the reunions of the alumni of that honored university, there numbered among the members and invited guests many whose names have become familiar in both national and international affairs. Seated at the right of the presiding officer of the evening, Gen. James M. Johnston,[1] was the guest of honor, Dr. Woodrow Wilson, president of Princeton University, who came to Washington to meet those who have turned their backs upon the class-rooms of Nassau, and to tell them of the progress of their alma mater. . . .

As President Wilson arose, it was the signal for the entire alumni, who gave three standing cheers, and closed with the "Sis! Boom! Ah!" "Tiger!" which has heralded so many victories and soothed the sting of so many defeats. President Wilson said, in part:

"It is a great pleasure for me to be with you on this occasion, for the reason that, in contrast to former visits, I will now be held responsible for what I may say, and there is a wholesome satisfaction that is attendant upon responsibility. But I always find it extremely difficult for me to address men who know me. I know that it is useless for me to attempt to appear anything other than what I am, and consequently I will not put on any airs, but will try to be, as some of you used to know me, a plain professor, talking to his class.

"I have been asked to give a full account of the university as it is, but I am not equal to the task. It is only within the past year or so that I have begun to find out what the university really does possess. In course of time I hope to be able to tell you the full result of my study, but not now. Suffice it to say that we are going to do greater things in the future. It is, however, one of the worst things a man can do to say what he is going to do, and therefore I will confine myself to generalities.

"Generalities are good things to stick to, particularly in matters of education. And that leads me to the inquiry, 'What does education amount to?' or, even further than that, 'Why do university men become apologetic when discussing the educational methods in vogue in their own particular alma mater?' It is regrettable that in our country to-day we have so many who are decrying the methods of this institution or that institution, and who declare that this system should be modernized, or that system eliminated altogether. My answer to such people is, 'Keep your sons away from those institutions, if you don't like them, and stop trying to graft your own ideas upon the powers that rule any other institutions.' A man came to me recently complaining that Princeton was behind in certain lines of education, and cited a rival institution of learning, where things were up to date, according to his idea. He said to me: 'Why don't you do as that university does?' My Scotch-Irish temper got the better of me, and I told him that Princeton did not follow in the footsteps of any university, but beat her own trail as she saw fit, and that if he didn't like the way we did things he could withdraw his son, and send him to the rival school. That is the way I feel about it, and that is the policy of Princeton.

"There is a little college down in Kentucky which in sixty years has graduated more men who have acquired prominence and fame than has Princeton in her 150 years.[2] But we must not allow ourselves to be fooled by this practical test. The best college is the one where the faculties are generalized. The man who aspires to a restricted technical task, is not the man for a university. In formulating your policy for life you should find out what you want, form your ideal, and then stick to it. Characters should not be changed, as a general rule, but appreciated. Find out what you have, and cultivate along the best lines conducive to its greatest success. There is to-day a false sort of rivalry among the universities—the rivalry of imitation. There is a tendency to keep within the beaten path. But Princeton is noticeable because of her individuality, because she stands for something different, and when you reflect that she has 150 years behind her you may rely that her course is a safe and solid one.

"One of the greatest evils we have to deal with in this democratic country is similarity. We are under the oppression of opinion, and he is a leader of men who can display the courage of his convictions. There is too much 'do as the other fellow does,' and we must inaugurate a fight against this tendency to level men's views. That is why I say that the university is not for everybody, but for the few who are seeking to cultivate their minds through that particular channel.

"What is the principal object of a liberal education? It is to liberate men from the dull round of one idea, to broaden their minds and their ability to conceive. The university is a little world of thought and action where we fit men for the larger world. People sometimes say that when a man goes through college he is ready to tackle the world. That is wrong. He has already tackled the world, on a small scale, when he has completed his course at college. The university is a world in miniature, and the larger the university the easier may this idea be realized.

"Again, I believe that the residential college, the college where the students rub shoulder to shoulder, both in school time and play time, is the only proper institution. You cannot go to college on a street car, and know what college means. When the students are residents, it is possible for the professor not only to lecture to them, but to give them something to talk about between times. Education, after all, is chiefly the interchange of ideas, and the best way to cultivate the mind is by subsequent discussion. This is almost impossible when the university course is secondary to some major occupation. The student and professor must be comrades. That is our plan at Princeton to-day, and we are not going to stop until we have worked it out.

"As to the length of the course, four years is far too short to make a scholar, and even forty years may be spent in learning new things every day. The best a university can do at all events is to instill the proper spirit in its graduates that it may develop in later life. We want men to-day who can read, who know how to read, and who, through reading, possess a traveled mind. No one who has not gone to that grand tour of the world, either actually or through the pages of good books, can conceive the possibilities of business. We need the men also who not only perceive what they see, but the significance of what they see; who have an observant eye, the eye to really see what you observe. Those are the successful men.

"Then there is the discriminating mind, which sees the bearing of things and how one proposition stands as compared to another, whether it be physical, social, or mental phenomena. The university teacher has discovered the kind of reading that will produce such minds as these, and that will produce in the mind of the graduate that valued faculty of reasonableness. The man is bound to be a successful man who knows he doesn't know everything; who is hospitable to suggestions, and who is ready to change his mind when shown to be wrong. This age is practical. It is the concert of power that carries the world forward. We must know each other and form ourselves into armies of peace, armies of thought, armies of ideals, that are ready to shed their life's blood toward its realization."

Printed in the *Washington Post*, March 28, 1903; some editorial headings omitted.

¹ James Marion Johnston '70, Vice President of the Riggs National Bank of Washington and President of the Princeton Alumni Association of the District of Columbia and Southern States.

² In this somewhat curious statement, Wilson was presumably referring to Centre College of Kentucky.

To Robert Bridges

My dear Bobby: Princeton, New Jersey. 30 March, 1903.

Unhappily I do not know any man to suggest to the Amherst people for their chair of English Literature, and my adviser in such matters, Axson, is away ill. I have handed your letter on to Harper, however, in the hope that he will be able to make some suggestion.   Always cordially yours,   Woodrow Wilson

TLS (WC, NjP).

To the Schoolchildren of the Eighth Grade, Indianapolis Public Schools

Princeton, New Jersey

My dear young friends: March 31, 1903

It seems perhaps a novel thing to write a letter on the subject of "Patriotism." A great many fine words are spoken about patriotism; but, after all, when one comes down to sober thinking about it, it is not a thing which needs big words to describe it; one should love his country as he should love his friend. You love your friend not for your own sake, but for your friend's sake; and you do not love him well unless your desire is to be helpful to him, and to serve him in a way in which he needs to be served. Something besides affection is necessary in our friendships; we must be willing to make sacrifices for our friends, and to tell them their faults, and to make every effort to set them in the right way of being happy, and that may involve much that is difficult and disagreeable to us.

Our love for our country ought to be a larger sort of friendship —loyal affection for all who are our fellow citizens, and for the governments which are set over us, and willingness for self-sacrifice in the service of the country, and a steady courage to tell it when we think it wrong, as well as to applaud it when we think it right.

Do you not think that this is, after all, the pleasantest idea of patriotism? Does it not give us something definite to think about, and does it not please us with the knowledge that there is something for every one of us to do in keeping the country the pure and admirable place we all wish it to be?

Your sincere friend,   Woodrow Wilson

TCL (RSB Coll., DLC).

To Charles William Leverett Johnson

My dear Dr. Johnson,   Princeton, 7 April, 1903

I promised you some time ago to tell you very frankly what your prospects here were likely to be, and I have delayed all too long about doing so. I have waited for the mature and united advice of the Latin department. That I now have, in unanimous form.

The men of the department all speak in the most cordial terms of your scholarship and all unite in the admiration which I am sure every one who knows you must feel for your personal qualities; but we have very restive, skittish colts in our Freshman and Sophomore classes and the Latin men feel that your hold on these youngsters has grown weaker rather than stronger. They do not feel, therefore, that they can renominate you for next year.

I feel that I must accept their judgment in such a matter; and yet I feel the very deep regret which I know they also feel in coming to this decision. We all feel that this argues nothing as to your success or failure elsewhere, and I am sure that you may count upon our most cordial assistance in backing you for an appointment elsewhere. I wish the conditions here were less peculiar and less exacting,—both for your sake and for ours.

Believe me

Most Sincerely and Cordially Yrs.,   Woodrow Wilson

ALS (WC, NjP).

To Isaac Minis Hays

My dear Mr. Hays: Princeton, New Jersey. 8 April, 1903.

Allow me to acknowledge with sincere appreciation your notification of my appointment to serve as a member of the Committee of the American Philosophical Society to make arrangements for a[n] appropriate celebration of the Two Hundredth Anniversary of the Birth of Benjamin Franklin. It will give me pleasure to serve on the Committee, and to take such part in its action as may be possible in the midst of my other engagements.[1]

Very sincerely yours,   Woodrow Wilson

TLS (Archives, PPAmP).
[1] For further correspondence concerning this matter, see WW to G. F. Edmunds, June 2, 1903; and WW to E. F. Smith, Nov. 25, 1904, Vol. 15.

From the Minutes of the Princeton Academic Faculty

5 p.m. April 8, 1903.

The Faculty met, the President presiding. The minutes of the meeting of March 18 were read and approved.

The President presented the case of Herbert Webb Hopkins, '03, a student of very high standing, who has been ill since the end of the first term of the Senior Year. It was *Resolved* that Mr. Hopkins be recommended for the degree of Bachelor of Arts at Commencement. . . .

From John W. Cornell[1]

My Dear Sir: Trenton, N. J. April 11, 1903.

Your favor of the 7th. instant, with Inventory, received during my absence from town. I do not consider it will be necessary for you to exhibit your receipts and render an accounting as is usually legally required of executors,[2] provided of course your sister and brother who are equal residuary legatees with you are entirely satisfied. I would *suggest* however, for your own protection, (and of your family, in case of your death), that release or releases should be executed and recorded here from all who receive a beneficiary interest under the will, showing thereby the settlement of the estate, the law requiring a settlement by executors. The proper legal requirement of a release to be recorded is that it should be executed as a deed before any one authorized to take acknowledgments of deeds. The release or releases from the legatees of $250. each[3] should merely acknowledge the receipts of the legacies. The one to be signed by your sister and brother should set forth briefly the terms of the will as to the residue of the estate, your appointment, amount of estate, amount paid out for debts and expenses, balance for distribution, and receipt of one-third from each, saying they have examined your accounts and are satisfied therewith. Now of course this will entail some little expense (only a few dollars however, say $2.25 to $2.50 for drawing, acknowledging and recording each release), and if you prefer not to do it, we will not require it; it is only as I said before, to show by the records that you have made a settlement in accordance with the statute.

Enclosed please find bill for recording Inventory &c.

Very truly yours,   J. W. Cornell

Enc. please find bill for proving recording filing Inventory Reg fees

TLS (WP, DLC). Enc. missing.
    [1] Surrogate of Mercer County.
    [2] Wilson was the executor of his father's estate. Dr. Wilson's will, a WWT MS. dated Sept. 11, 1902, is in WP, DLC, along with a printed inventory form with WWhw entries showing a valuation of the estate of $19,412.50.
    [3] Belle R. Robinson of Wilmington, N. C., and Hattie Taylor Tennent of Spartanburg, S. C.

From Louis Dyer[1]

My dear President,   Oxford   Saturday, April 11th 1903.

Your letter of March 23rd greatly pleased me as did the beautiful publication which soon followed it. I have had much pleasure in rereading your inspiring address and in renewing my agreement with it.

It was doubly pleasant to hear from you because your letter came but shortly before the arrival of our common friends Professor and Mrs. Toy,[2] who have been intimates of mine ever since he settled at Harvard & made me acquainted with Mrs. and Miss Sanders.[3] They are spending a few weeks here, and I do not despair of finding them still in Oxford when I return from Scotland whither I go to join Mrs. Dyer three weeks hence.

You hold out a pleasant prospect in announcing your intended visit in July with Mrs. Wilson to the hour [honor] of whose acquaintance we shall all aspire. Our term will end about June 25th & so by starting on July 4th, you will arrive after term has been closed three weeks. For a week or ten days after that time (the end of term) the majority of the University magnates linger on but will for the most part I fear be scattered, though not far, by the date of your landing. Still the men who are vigorously in harness, the younger fellows & tutors stay on for the most part through July and you would see them. Our especially valued friend Professor [Albert Venn] Dicey will, I hope, be in Oxford through July. Mrs. Dicey's health has of late exiled her and him, except for his necessary lectures; but there is hopeful talk of Mrs. Dicey being well enough to come home in June. I fancy, if once back, she & he may be slow to move. A. L. Smith[4] the history teacher at Balliol,—a man of great power who was Jowett's[5] right hand for many years,—will be here, and I fancy you will like to talk collegiate organization over with him. I know no one more powerful, hopeful, & progressive upon that topic.

Thanking you for your kind gift and most delightful letter, I remain   Yours very sincerely   Louis Dyer.

ALS (WP, DLC).
    [1] A gentleman scholar, resident in Oxford, whom Wilson had met there on August 5, 1899. See WW to EAW, Aug. 6, 1899, n. 1, Vol. 11.
    [2] Crawford Howell Toy and Nancy Saunders Toy. Toy was Hancock Professor of Hebrew and Other Oriental Languages at Harvard.
    [3] That is, Nancy Saunders and her mother. Toy came to Harvard in 1880 but did not marry Miss Saunders until 1888. Dyer was Assistant Professor of Greek and Latin at Harvard from 1881 to 1887.
    [4] Arthur Lionel Smith, Tutor in Modern History at Balliol College.
    [5] Benjamin Jowett (1817-93), Master of Balliol and Regius Professor of Greek.

From Edmund Clarence Stedman

My dear President Wilson: Bronxville, N. Y.   April 12th. 1903

My thanks to you and the Secretary of the University for this copy of the private reprint of your noble Inaugural Address. As I listened to it, last October, I was elevated by its wholesome doctrine, and gained refreshment and content—as always in the case of any address or writing composed by you—from its force and vigorous English style.

                Sincerely yours,   Edmund C. Stedman

ALS (WP, DLC).

A News Report of an Alumni Dinner in Philadelphia

[April 15, 1903]

OLD NASSAU'S SONS GATHER

The Tiger of Old Nassau came out of his lair among the elms of Princeton last night and counted the children of his rearing who make their home in the good city of Philadelphia and its vicinity.

He counted them in the foyer of Horticultural Hall, from the gray old graduate of '61 to the beardless youth who became a baccalaureus artium in 1902, as they stood around the banquet board and sang, with eyes that saw all young again, the same old anthem that for years puts strength in the hearts of the sons of the Orange and the Black as it rings from stand and bleacher.

He counted them afterward in the great auditorium beyond, as they flocked up the stairs with matron, maid and many a distinguished guest to meet in a vast gathering of a thousand and more in the reception which followed the dinner.

And when the review was over, the last carriage gone and good-night said the Tiger growled a pleased "well done" to the committee and members of the Princeton Club of Philadelphia, whose first "annual dinner and reception to President Woodrow Wilson and the Board of Trustees of Princeton University" was the occasion of his visit.

And well he might be pleased for the sons of the venerable college of New Jersey proved a brilliant and impressive gathering as they sat grouped around the distinguished scholar who leads the fortunes of their alma mater, or as they wandered through the hosts of guests on the floor of the reception room.

But at table or in hall there was one man on whom all eyes were centered, whose single personality dominated the entire assemblage.

That man was Woodrow Wilson, thirteenth president of Princeton University, who, while yet a young man, has gained fame by his warm and sympathetic government of the college over which he presides and has won a place in the hearts of its sons which bids fair to be cherished as is that of the revered McCosh.

The dinner guests assembled shortly after 7 o'clock and soon were seated at the tables in the foyer beneath a huge tiger of Royal Bengal breed, which, with gleaming teeth and tawny fur, overlooked the banquet from a raised platform.

In the absence of Judge [John Craig] Biddle, '41, who was detained till the time of the reception, Alexander Van Rensselaer acted as toastmaster. To his right sat President Wilson and Rev. Dr. Charles Wood, while on his left was Judge [John Lambert] Cadwalader, of New York, and John Cadwalader [Richard McCall Cadwalader], of this city.

Many songs enlivened the discussion of a short but admirably-selected menu, the most striking being to the tune of "Mr. Dooley," which ran as follows:

There is a man in Princeton Town and he is wondrous cute,
He's known to every Princeton man, from Lawrenceville to Butte:
He knows so very many things that we know naught about,
But each alumnus knows enough to join in hearty shout.

CHORUS.

'Tis Woodrow Wilson, Woodrow Wilson,
He's one of us, a son of Nassau Hall;
'Tis Woodrow Wilson, Woodrow Wilson,
'Tis Wilson—Wilson—Wilson—that is all.

You cannot find his equal as a teacher of the law.
In all his batch of writings you can never find a flaw:
Queer things have lately happened at Old Princeton, so it's said,
And the latest news that reached us is "the lion's lost his head."
O'er Woodrow Wilson—

He's not as fat as Grover and he's not as thin as Pat:
And sure his head is not too large to fit the average hat.
For all the grads of Harvard and the wearers of the Blue
Admit that in the colleges there are but very few
Like Woodrow Wilson—

He's chasing round the country now to hunt a little dough,
For he found the Princeton treasure increasing mighty slow:
So he thought he'd strike the capital and tackle Uncle Sam
"If you'd like an introduction," quoth the Raven, "ask the man."
'Tis Woodrow Wilson—

We recently have learned that forty-six men have been dropped,
To keep the college running, 'xaminations must be stopped.
If at the college services the roll they go to call,
The only one who answers will be Wilson, that is all.
'Tis Woodrow Wilson—

As the coffee came on Mr. Van Rennselaer rose and in a few words expressing the loyalty of the alumni to the university and its president, introduced Dr. Wilson.

With a ringing tripple cheer and a shout of "Hats off!" in memory of college days, the banqueters greeted the speaker. He said in part:

"I feel some hesitation in speaking to so many of the older men who have known me for the last twelve years and more, not as president but as I am. I feel like the old woman who went to the circus and saw, or imagined she saw, a man read a newspaper through a two-inch board. 'This is no place for me,' she cried, 'with all these thin things on,' and that is how I feel.

"But, since being president I have contracted some habits that go with the office. There are times when I feel extremely dignified. I have also contracted the habit of speaking from a text and I will talk from one to-night. It is this—

"It is conceivable that an institution with millions of money and numberless students will not do as much for science and learning in ten years as Johns Hopkins does in two months or as much for citizenship and manliness as Princeton does in a week.[1]

"There is a little of the academic attitude about Princeton. It is not a place apart, but is a part of the world: one of the sweetest and pleasantest parts of the world, but still a part of it.

"When I see a man who says he is learning for learning's sake I write him down an unserviceable man. There is no learning that I have seen that is worth learning for its own sake. It is that we shall know so as to grope no more in the darkness mystified by superstition.

"The danger to Princeton is the danger of a big, numerically big, university. The greatest good in education is close and personal contact. The portraits of seven Princeton graduates hang in Independence Hall. They all graduated under John Witherspoon, a little group of men gathered around a great personality.

"By standing close to their college they gained what they gained, and so today Princeton men must stand by the old mother who breeds men and statesmen."[2]

Printed in the *Philadelphia Press*, April 15, 1903; some editorial headings omitted.
[1] Wilson was apparently quoting from his own text.
[2] There is a WWhw outline of this address, dated April 14, 1903, in WP, DLC.

From Isaac Wayne MacVeagh

Dear Mr. President: Washington, D. C. Apl. 16, 1903.

I beg to thank you for a copy of your inaugural address last fall which I had the great pleasure of hearing in person, and also to thank you very warmly for the admirable warning you have just given at Philadelphia. I have been anxiously waiting for the head of some great university to say just what you so well said.   Sincerely yours,   Wayne MacVeagh.

TLS (WP, DLC).

Charles William Leverett Johnson to
Susannah Batcheller Johnson

Dear Mama,   Princeton   Thursday, 16 Apr. 1903

I have had my talk with the President. We nerve ourselves, don't we? I had of course made up my sentences in thinking it over and formulating my line of procedure, but Mr. Wilson, began by going over the matter which was in his letter[1] and so the conversation took somewhat different course from what I had expected. He was very skilful in putting the conversation on a pleasant basis. But I said all I wanted to say, and nothing omitted. It would appear that he does not intend his phrase to be thought to mean *discipline* but mastery or control over the minds of the of the [sic] men, so as to *make* them work. Well, I can understand how it would take a very strong will to do that and I don't feel that there is after all quite so serious a criticism. But all the same the reason seems to me quite as inadequate. The president explained how he was guided entirely by the Latin faculty. Prof. Westcott left memoranda and it seems that the president called on Carter and West for comments and they agreed to Westcott's views. I clearly indicated how it was easy to agree to a third man's opinion. The opinion is about as I've given it above.

I really think I will arrive Friday night 9.45 I think and then can talk about it all.   Your loving   C.

ALS (C. W. L. Johnson Coll., NjP).
   [1] WW to C. W. L. Johnson, April 7, 1903.

To Andrew Carnegie

                                        Princeton, New Jersey.
My dear Mr. Carnegie: 17 April, 1903.

We are forming plans for a new Princeton in which, I venture to believe, you will be interested,—if only because we mean to make the new Princeton like the old Princeton of John Witherspoon's day and yet of the modern age, with its new interests, studies, methods, and undertakings. Witherspoon made Princeton an instrument of patriotic public service; we mean, if we can, to make her the same again.

You have been kind enough to express your interest in Princeton as, what I believe she really is, the most American of our colleges, the college most saturated with the traditions and political beliefs which have made America great and democracy triumphant. She has been largely made by Scotsmen,—being myself of pure Scots blood, it heartens me to emphasize the fact,—and she is thoroughly Scottish in all her history and traditions in matters educational. One can feel it in the air of the place. It is because I know how you value these things that I venture to lay what follows before you. I do so in the confidence that a really great Scotsman who knows what Princeton has been will wish to know what we mean to make her in the future.

I have set forth the most immediate needs of the University in the report to the Board of Trustees which I take the liberty of sending you with this letter.[1] That report shows that, if we would make Princeton again the dominant power and influence she once was, we must attempt nothing less than her re-endowment; but it is a document written for those already acquainted with the institution on the inside. It strips facts to the bone and presents a mere skeleton of bare necessaries. There are some parts of the plan which it gives in broad outline which I would like, if you will permit me, to explain a little more fully.

If the paragraph about a Graduate College of residence interests you, as at least a hint of the place where men might be made fit, as we have not now the means to make them, for the tasks of the Carnegie Institution,[2] I have in print a full explanation of the plan which I would be glad to send you.[3] But there are other parts of our scheme of development which I think I can elaborate here without being prolix.

The plan which lies at the centre of my most interesting hopes for Princeton is that for a School of Jurisprudence and Government, such a school as the revolutionary traditions of the place would make most characteristic of it. We can imagine Witherspoon himself realized again in the spirit of such a school better and more completely, perhaps, than in anything else that could be added to the University. My idea would be to make it a school of law, but not in any narrow or technical sense: a school, rather, in which law and institutions would be interpreted as instruments of peace, of freedom, and of the advancement of civilization: international law as the means and guarantee of cordial understandings between the nations of the world, private law as the accommodation of otherwise hostile interests, government as the means of progress. No doubt it would be wise, too, as immediately collateral matter, to expound the part which commerce and industry have played, and must increasingly play, in making for international as well as national peace and for the promotion of all the common interests of mankind.

Of almost equal consequence seems to me the proper manning and equipment of our School of Science, which at present languishes under a grossly inadequate endowment. There should unquestionably be added to it at once, besides an adequate general endowment, a Museum of Natural History worthy of our collections and of the possibilities of biological and geological study here in view of those collections. We have superb collections, in many features quite unique, which can now not even be seen for lack of space and of proper places in which to classify and exhibit them.

The old-fashioned academic studies have heretofore very greatly preponderated in our course, and must continue to do so until we have a much larger endowment for the scientific branches. And yet we have done a great deal with nothing to do it on. Under the direction of Professor Brackett, a man better qualified, I venture to believe, than any other man in the country to plan and successfully administer a great school of electricity, we have, on no endowment at all, already won an enviable reputation for the exceptional quality of the electrical engineers we have sent out. It is part of my ambition to add to our general School of Science a fully equipped School of Electricity.

Over and above all these things and in aid of the influence and efficiency of the entire University radical changes in our methods of instruction are imperatively necessary. I believe that the only vital method of teaching is that which brings teacher and pupil into immediate contact and constant intercourse with one another; and, if this be true, it is essential that the whole machinery of recitations and lectures should be modified so as to make the University a place where undergraduates and graduates alike would be made reading men rather than mere pupils under masters, taking instruction on authority. Imagine a great body of reference librarians turned into a body of teachers acting in concert with one another for the purpose of guiding the reading of the men under them in the most intelligent manner possible, systematizing it, and making it a means of development which should give them minds and purposes of their own and you have in the rough my conception of the tutorial system mentioned in my report. Sensible, unpedantic men with whom I have taken counsel think nothing better worth trying than that, if we would change college students from boys into men with the true impulse and spirit of investigation, the true power to put themselves and keep themselves into communication with their age. With fifty such reading guides, who should also be the constant advisers and companions of the men in their use of the libraries, we could institute the most interesting, far-reaching, hopeful reform of the age in education; with one hundred, we could, I veritably believe, work a profound revolution.

In my report to the Board of Trustees I have estimated the cost of these things at a minimum in order to make my figures modest, my total as little startling, as possible; and I was well aware, of course, in doing so, that I was embodying in my recommendations much less than was to be desired. In the case of the Museum of Natural History, for example, I have set down nothing more than the cost of the building ($500,000), without equipment or endowment; and the $212,000 which I have added for additional instruction in biology would give us men only, not materials. I very keenly realize that, without an endowment for its support and development, the Museum might very well prove a burden to us. But I need not explain that to you. Your own experience in such matters puts you in a position to judge of that even better than I can.

In the case of the School of Law and Government, the estimate in my report provides for no building except such as would suffice at the outset to contain the library and lecture halls of the school. In order to make it the unique institution it should be it ought to have its own quadrangle of dormitories and conference rooms and its own distinctive life as a separate college of residence, with its own name and character. Only in that way can the close contacts of intercourse and study between students and teachers be brought about which produce the most vital results,—those invaluable results of direct personal influence which show so plainly and so significantly in James Madison's utterances concerning his training under Dr. Witherspoon. Such a quadrangle of residence would add $600,000 to the cost of carrying out the plan.

I have written a long letter; but not longer, I am sure, than your interest in such matters warrants. I have taken counsel far and wide upon these matters, and I can say with the utmost confidence and candor,—a candor which, I am sure, you will pardon in such a cause,—that nothing seems to me worthier of the great reputation for intelligent and useful giving which you have made and are destined to make than any or all of these things built upon the patriotic foundations already laid here at Princeton. And the establishment of your name here would seem only like one more, in this case a crowning and incomparable, service by a great Scotsman rendered to the cause of education at a place filled with the best spirit of citizenship from both sides of the water. Witherspoon and McCosh received their fame from what they did at and for Princeton; in this case there would be a difference,—her latest and greatest Scottish benefactor would give to her his name and fame as well as memorable and inestimable service.

I have spoken plainly,—pardon me, if I have spoken too plainly. I felt confident that you would wish me to speak so. I should be delighted to have an opportunity to explain any part of the matter of this letter to you in person, should you at any time desire it. It would make Mrs. Wilson and me very happy if you would be our guest here, to see Princeton from the inside. It would be a great personal pleasure as well as a great honor to Princeton. If you could make it convenient to come to us while the Spring lasts we would have the added pleasure of showing you the place in its full beauty.

Most sincerely yours, Woodrow Wilson[4]

TLS (A. Carnegie Papers, DLC).

[1] That is, a copy of his report to the Board of Trustees printed at Oct. 21, 1902.

[2] The Carnegie Institution of Washington, established in 1902 by Carnegie's gift of $10,000,000 for the purpose of encouraging "investigation, research and discovery" in "the broadest and most liberal manner."

[3] West's *The Proposed Graduate College of Princeton University.*

[4] A WWsh draft of this letter, dated April 8, 1903, and a WWT undated draft, with extensive WWhw emendations, are in WP, DLC.

A News Report of an Address in Philadelphia on National and University Life

[April 18, 1903]

"The National and University Life" was the subject of a lecture delivered last night by Professor Woodrow Wilson, president of Princeton University, at Association Hall, under the auspices of the Princeton Club. The earnest and impressive manner of the lecturer and the depth of thought shown by him held the close attention of the audience.

Professor Wilson began his address by referring to the greatness of national life in this country, and how its character can be set forward in many ways by the universities. He spoke of the motive of advancement that characterizes the English peoples, and said: "The heart of this race has expanded as the hearts of others have not. And then we are also proud of the method of achievement. It has been voluntary achievement."

He spoke of the faculty the boys of America possess in conducting a meeting. They all seemed to have the right idea as [to] how it should be done, and he added that French and German boys do not possess this faculty.

"There is an instinct of co-operation and voluntary combination in our people that can be found nowhere else," Dr. Wilson continued. "When gold was discovered in California the Spaniard sought to hold to himself. With the American he immediately looked about for four or five partners.

"We pride ourselves not only on our public spirit and voluntary combination, but also upon our efficient combination. We have men who command the policy of the world, because they command the trade of the world. Some of these men seem to be born with an instinct. They cannot tell how they do it.

"In the midst of this life the university stands and asks what it can do. In no other country is the university called upon to do this. The business of the English university up to the present time has been to train the privileged classes. One thing that has made Oxford uneasy about the Rhodes scholarship has been those ninety Americans. 'How will they conform their manner? Will they throw a lasso and ride a broncho?' There will undoubtedly be a breaking up of the old order."

Dr. Wilson spoke of the university in this country preparing generalized men who will be fitted for anything the country may need them for.

"I love to think of a university in this country as a community of ideals. The same ambitions, the same attitudes towards the national life. You cannot do this without a community life."

He referred to the men in a university as coming from all parts of the country and said what is wanted is to create in a university a national type of men.

He spoke of John Witherspoon, the founder of Princeton, as a man who made statesmen in spite of themselves. "Such spirits as these propagate like spirits."

In public affairs he said the university man has learned discretion.

"And," he added, "discretion is the better part of valor in public affairs. Learning can be made the instrument of manly force. It can get the same spirit in the man of affairs, and can elevate the man who has not drunk at those refreshing fountains."

Printed in the Philadelphia *North American*, April 18, 1903; editorial headings omitted.

To Robert Bridges

My dear Bobby: Princeton, New Jersey.   20 April, 1903.

Of course I am greatly disappointed that the dormitory cannot be made suitable to the original plans because of the difficulties of the grade; but if the plan as Morris now outlines it is indeed necessary, I of course yield, and beg that you and Cuyler will go forward with the matter as rapidly as necessary. Will you not be kind enough to thank Morris for his letter,[1] for me, and tell him that I of course acquiesce. I have not time to write as many letters as I should like before leaving for the West.

          Always affectionately yours,   Woodrow Wilson

TLS (WC, NjP).
    [1] Morris's letter is missing.

To Mrs. Christian S. Baker[1]

My dear Mrs. Baker: Princeton, New Jersey.   20 April, 1903.

Mr. [Jesse Lynch] Williams brought me your letter of April 11th,[2] and I have read it with the greatest interest and appreciation. What you recall of the early days of my father's residence is Staunton is very vivid, and makes for me very delightful reading.

My father's last years were somewhat painful because there came with old age a thickening of the arteries, which resulted in a slow clogging of the action of the organs, and resulted finally in blood poisoning; but he kept to the last his fine spirits, and his mind was at no time in the least clouded.

My dear mother died in 1887 [1888], and during the latter part of his life my father had moved rather restlessly from place to place because his children were all married, and his home broken up.

I wish very much that he had been able to see these lines of yours before he went; it would have cheered him very much to know how he was remembered, and to have the old days recalled.

          Very cordially yours,   Woodrow Wilson

TLS (Wilson Letters, Vi).
    [1] There are no Staunton city directories extant for this period, hence it is impossible to identify Mrs. Baker.
    [2] It is missing.

To Ellen Axson Wilson

My own darling,   Ann Arbor, Mich., 21 April, 1903

I arrived safe and well, and on schedule time, to-day, at 12.30, after a not too fatiguing journey, to find President Angell[1] waiting for me at the station. We came right up to his (very delightful) house, had lunch at one with Mrs. Angell; and at two he went off to a lecture (*he*, at any rate, keeps up his class-room work,—two hours a week,—saying that he *must* have *some* fun, do *some*thing he loves to do, amidst all the weary round of dull administrative labour!), and I, after half an hour's talk with Mrs. A., came up to my room, where I have been ever since, sleeping, thinking of my address, dressing, and, now, writing. I shall not go down, unless called, until six, when dinner will be ready. Is not that exemplary? Could you wish me to take better care of myself?

How keenly I feel this separation, my darling; how entirely, now that I sit down to this letter, do I feel like your lover,—your *exiled* lover, his heart suspended till he can see you again! My body is here, but my whole life is with you, my whole heart engrossed by your anxieties, my whole thought absorbed into your life. It is a pity that a college president with his constant duties abroad should be so deep, so preoccupied a lover. No doubt Stock is better, healed by your dear love (ah, what a lovely sister you are, my Eileen!) and will presently be off to Virginia ready to enjoy its quiet southern air and sights and associations like a sweet renewal of his boyhood, but how do I *know* that he is? There's the rub! And what am *I* doing to sustain my loved one's spirits? Well, I am at least loving her with all my heart. She must know how inexpressibly dear she is to me, that she is my life and hope, my all in all. May God bless and keep her always!

My love to Stock, to the dear chickens, and to the Hibbens. Always and altogether   Your own   Woodrow.

I am perfectly well.

ALS (WC, NjP).
    [1] James Burrill Angell, President of the University of Michigan.

A News Report of an Address at the University of Michigan

[April 22, 1903]

THE PRINCETON PRESIDENT
Delivers an Inspiring Address
on Patriotism.

Woodrow Wilson, the president of Princeton University, one of the leading historians of this country, delivered his most forceful and inspiring lecture on "Patriotism" last night in University Hall. President Wilson voiced the beliefs of the new element in civic development exemplified by President Roosevelt. His lecture was delivered in perfect form—diction and delivery were delightful, and his audience gave him the closest attention throughout. His exposition of patriotism was especially valuable to a student audience, made up as it is largely of young men soon to assume the burdens of citizenship.

President Wilson, after being introduced by Dr. Angell, said that in speaking of "Patriotism" he felt somewhat presumptious, as though he were posing as one qualified to teach his fellow citizens the essence and qualities of Patriotism: that to attempt to do so to Americans especially was perhaps out of place, but his conception of patriotism was different from the popular idea of the meaning of the term.

"Patriotism" brings up visions of so many things a man loves and believes that one should be careful in dealing with the subject not to allow sentiment to overcome reason. It is hard to hold one's country off at arms' length and analyse it; hard to suppress sentiment and exercise reason only. Patriotism is not a sentiment; it breathes sentiment, and may affect our sensibilities as only an emotion can, but it is founded on calm, deliberate thought. Patriotism is a principle of action which expresses itself in a display of energy outside of selfish interest. A noble man is not he who forgets, but he who remembers his neighbors—one ready to loan his power to others. It is friendship large as the country itself, embodying not only one's neighbors, but his fellow citizens. As one serves his friends, so should he serve his countrymen. Sometimes one's service to his friend is one of pain to both; faults must be corrected, and it is hard to both make and hear criticisms. When you love your friend, you must at times hurt him, and thus must we serve our country. The destiny of a nation is in this world, not the next. Here shall our nation rise or fall, grow or decline. Each generation affects this destiny, and is a factor in the game of national existence. Therefore we must not trust some vague prosperity to bring our nation safely through, but we are responsible individually and as a people. Our children in the schools should honor and worship the flag for what it stands for. It stands for the biggest kick on record—the American revolution. Then the minority thought, then acted, and forced the majority to both respect its opinions and accede to its demands. The flag's white stripes represent lines of parchment declaring constitutional liberty, her red bars the blood which flowed in that declaration's victory. The child must realize that every man must judge for himself, not accept the opinions of others without question. The flag stands for independent opinion, not weak conformity. Here every man is potentially both president and laborer. He may be called to any office, for any duty. Therefore ours is an intellectual polity, and men must think. You must go not to books, but where the pulses of the nation beat, and there study our institutions and national character. We are a nation, yet have we the full national feeling? Are there no sectional differences, no tolerances? During the war a flame of feeling rushed through the country, but after the war did we not hear "What is the matter with Kansas?" It is not a nation where one part asks whether another section has gone mad. Not Kansas, but the interrogator was mad. The different sections vary in development and he is the true patriot who makes allowances for this in thought and spirit. We should not speak of our executive as "Teddy." It is the old spirit of Andrew Jackson's time over again, the feeling of disrespect and desire to make everything common property. What regains the stability of our polity is the determination and persistency of the minority who insist on being heard. The chief duty of a patriotic man is to study his nation and its temper, and above all, see both sides. Our state legislatures are in a degree bad because we take it for granted they are. I do not say they are made up of wise men entirely, but the majority are men who wish to do well for their country. Men do not at once rise to an idea in or out of a legislature.

It is the stolidity of the masses that steadies our polity. An English speaking race expects to go on forever doing what it now does. We believe only one thing at a time, and we learn slowly. We must teach our legislatures if they wish to learn. There is a great deal of Phariseeism in our intellectual classes. They think their wares are too good for those who wish to buy.

The law of political life is the law of compromise—you must

see things as others see them. Every man should go into politics, not to run for office, but to watch those who do. When a critic, not a contestant, your hands are clean and your judgment free. Go in, but leave the offices alone. Break up the machine, and if forced into office you are free to accept with a clean conscience. Do your own thinking, and tie to and die for good men. Be a partisan, one without a side is a nonentity. Use your mind. Think hard, good compulsive, impulsive thinking. So I come back to my definition of patriotism, and urge you to devote your energy to your civic duties, not for self, but your fellow countrymen, and you will in the highest sense be patriotic.

Printed in the *Ann Arbor Daily Argus*, April 22, 1903; one editorial heading omitted.

To Ellen Axson Wilson

The Congress Hotel

My own darling,   Chicago   22 Apr. 1903

The lecture went off very well indeed last night, to an audience of, I should say, nine hundred or so; I spent this morning seeing the little there is to see of the University of Michigan; left Ann Arbor at half-past one, and reached this hurly-burly half an hour ago,—at nine. I shall probably get upbraided to-morrow by both McCormick and Jones[1] for coming to a hotel, but it is the most convenient thing to do at this time of night.

I shall go first thing in the morning to McCormick's office,—chiefly to see if there is any mail from home,—then take a look in on Jones, and then go out to Edgewater,[2] where I shall invite myself to lunch. In the evening I must start for St. Paul. It is an all-night journey, and more, I believe.

I had considerable "freedom" in speaking last night (I am reading Wesley's Journal as I go,[3] and may be permitted to speak as a Methodist!), partly, no doubt, because I was far away from home and could use illustrative and other material (I spoke on *Patriotism*) long ago familiar in the latitude of Princeton and had to "make up" very little; and I must say that the audience seemed fooled to the top of my wish. Their stillness and attention at points were really delightful.

The Angell's were most kind to me, and I have come away liking and admiring him as I did not before. It is worth while to see a man in his own home. I dare say I myself appear to greater advantage at home than elsewhere!

Alas, how long a time it seems since my darling was in my

arms,—and how intolerably long till she shall be there again!
I do not see that I get in the least used to this business. Never
mind—wait until we go off *together*, on a second honey moon,
this summer! That will make up for many, many things! How
delightful it is to dream of it!

Good night, my sweet one. May God keep and bless you. Unbounded love to all. I am perfectly well—and fresh.

Your own   Woodrow

ALS (WC, NjP).
  [1] David Benton Jones.
  [2] To visit his cousin, Jessie Bones Brower, and her husband, Abraham Thew H.
Brower.
  [3] In preparation for his address on John Wesley, printed at June 30, 1903.

From Ellen Axson Wilson

My own darling,   Princeton   April 22 [1903]

I am afraid I can't get off much of a letter today for Stockton
is having a bad day again and I *must* be with him practically all
the time. He tried walking out early which enabled Mr. Whight-
man[1] & I to get through with the correspondence comfortably.
Yesterday he was so very bright that I began to hope the battle
was won but he went to New York and found that something
was wrong with his kidneys, and that upset him again completely. He does'nt know at all how serious it is; the doctor told
him it was "nothing to fret about" but at the same time looked,—
he said, very grave. I wrote to him myself last night demanding
to know what it is, for I *must* keep steady myself and uncer-
tainties are always—to me—more hard to bear than anything
else. Stockton is making a splendid fight for self-control and so
far he has not lost it today—that is since he got up.

We are all well and there is no news. I went into Phila. yesterday & finished my shopping,—got a beautiful hat! The weather
continues wonderful. I am so thankful for that. With inexpressible love,   Your devoted little wife,   Eileen.

ALS (WC, NjP).
  [1] Wilson's part-time student secretary, McQueen Salley Wightman.

To Ellen Axson Wilson

My own darling,   Chicago, 23 April, 1903

I hoped to find a letter from you at Cyrus's office this morning,
telling how you have fared, but there was none, and I am trying
to think that no news is good news.

I have had hard luck again about finding Jessie. She was off playing golf, as usual; there was not even a servant at the house because this is *the* maid's "day off"; and Helen [Bones] is off on a visit to the Pacific coast,—returns to-morrow morning! These things I found out from Cousin Abe at his office here in town. Jessie, it seems, has now taken to amusing herself by *teaching* all the young women of her acquaintance how to play!

And so I have had nothing to do half the day but wander idly about the noisy, uninteresting town. I could not venture even to go to a "continuous performance" to wile the time away. I looked in on Cyrus and the Joneses.[1] I am to dine with the latter to-night, and then, at ten o'clock take a train for St. Paul, where I shall be, if my train is on time, to-morrow morning at half-past nine. I have declined rides and lunches at St. Paul and mean to take the day as quietly as may be, so as to be fresh for the evening.

I am *very* well and have not so far felt any unusual fatigue at all. Isn't that a fine record? It makes me so happy to tell you just because I know how it will please you. The most delightful, the most wholly joyful and profitable thing in my life, is that you are *glad* when all goes well with me,—that it makes a *difference* to you,—that you *love* me. And, ah, my sweetheart, how I love you in return,—with what a rush of joy I think of you! It is my life to be your lover and your husband!

Love to the chicks and to Stock. and the whole heart of

Your own   Woodrow

ALS (WC, NjP).
[1] David Benton Jones and his brother, Thomas Davies Jones.

From Ellen Axson Wilson

My own darling,   Princeton, April 23 [1903].

I postponed writing until late today so that I could write something definite as to our plans. It was almost decided last night that Stockton would go to Va. tomorrow and I would go with him to stay until Monday, getting Miss Finley[1] to sleep here. But it couldn't be settled until Stockton went in to see his doctors again. He went on the special and got back at three, I being very busy in the meantime with preparations for the journey. But when he reached Dr. Hayes[2] he was (fortunately perhaps) at his very worst. It was borne in upon them how serious his condition is and it ended with their insisting on his coming to N. Y.

and staying in their house for a week at least—in Dr. Van Valzeh's[3] room. The doctor himself will be there in two weeks probably, so this plan will enable Stockton to see him. Of course I am deeply thankful that affairs have taken this turn, for it becomes daily more evident that he is in no condition to go alone among strangers. He will hardly go to Va. at all now but join the Tedcastles on their fishing trip if he is well enough by the 10th of May. Dr. Hayes says the kidney trouble is really not serious,— ought to pass off of itself as his general condition improves. This is no letter of course, darling, but I [am] too desperately tired to . write more tonight. Tomorrow it will be different. Mr. Hibben has been perfectly lovely to us!

I hope for a letter from my darling tomorrow. With love beyond words.   Your own   Eileen.

ALS (WC, NjP).
   [1] Anna J. Finley, who lived with Prof. and Mrs. John H. Finley at 90 Bayard Lane.
   [2] William Van Valzah Hayes, M.D.
   [3] Dr. William Ward Van Valzah, Princeton 1873. Hayes and Van Valzah both specialized in diseases of the digestive system and had their offices at 10 E. 43rd St. in New York.

To Ellen Axson Wilson

My own darling,   Minnesota Club, St. Paul.   24 April, 1903

After dinner with the Joneses last evening, I took the ten o'clock train and, after a very comfortable night's journey, which my steady sleeping made seem very short, I reached St. Paul this morning at half-past nine. To my great satisfaction I found it raining. There is no excuse for forcing me out "to see our city," and I am left here alone, to write and rest and follow my own devices. At half after one (it is now eleven) some Princeton men are coming in to lunch with me.

McCormick came in to dinner at the Joneses last night. Mrs. McCormick and the children are down in New Mexico. How are rich people's children ever educated? Can we wonder that they find the steady, unbroken, long continued routine of college irksome and next to impossible? Mr. and Mrs. Bancroft[1] were also there, suddenly summoned to meet me. Bancroft is the young Chicago lawyer who, Finley thinks, would be the ideal man for the chair he is vacating,[2]—and certainly he is most interesting and attractive. Probably he would not leave a rising career at the bar for the economies of a professorship.

I did not tell you of the cousin I found at Ann Arbor, uncle Thomas Woodrow's youngest son, Herbert. I did not realize that he was old enough to be in college, but he is a Junior. Tom, his next older brother, also graduated at Ann Arbor. Aunt Helen moved there then to be with him, and kept house; and Herbert tells me he has been there ever since,—first in school and then in college, though Aunt Helen has gone back to Chillicothe. I liked the boy very much. In appearance he is a singular and most interesting mixture of Aunt Helen and Uncle Thomas.

I am perfectly well. The constant movement has not proved a strain on me yet. Our love for each other acts like a constant tonic on my thoughts and spirits. I am what I am because I am

Your own   Woodrow

ALS (WC, NjP).
1 Probably Edgar Addison Bancroft and Margaret Healy Bancroft. He was at this time Vice President and General Solicitor of the Chicago & Western Indiana Railroad and the Belt Railway of Chicago. Born and reared in Galesburg, Ill., Bancroft was graduated from Knox College in 1878 and had practiced law in his home town from 1884 to 1892. Finley presumably had known him when he, Finley, was President of Knox College in Galesburg.
2 Finley had recently been elected President of the College of the City of New York.

From Ellen Axson Wilson

My own Darling,   Princeton, April 24 [1903]

Your two dear letters came this morning and I cannot tell you how good it was to get them. No doubt they arrived in due time yet somehow it seems to me *weeks* since you left! They were such satisfactory letters too! It is delightful to know that you enjoyed the Ann Arbour visit so much, and that the lecture went off so well. In short the letters have been a real tonic to me, *dear love*!

All is going well here; Stockton got off this morning in rather good shape, declaring positively that he meant to be quite rid of his trouble in another week. He is certainly making a splendid fight,—poor, dear fellow.

It has been a glorious day and that has helped me not a little to be cheerful and hopeful. I have been extremely busy too picking up loose ends as regards the spring sewing,—for of course I have had to let May go on as best she could for the past week. So you see everything is very peaceful and normal again and you have nothing to worry about as regards me, dear heart. Mr. and Mrs. Hibben have both been in to see me today and Miss [Henrietta] Ricketts made a long visit,—almost spent the morning,—and I have been out myself too. So you see I have not been *too* busy after all! But the result of these various diversions was that I have had to spend the evening writing business letters and have so much less time for my dear.

By-the-way, did you pay Mr. Phillips[1] for the deer's head? She[2] was calling yesterday and told me that it was done, so I should not like to delay much longer paying for the "skin."

I love you sweetheart—ah *how I* love you! You *are* doing *everything* for me, dear; absence makes, I cannot of course say *no* difference, for there is magic in the warm touch,—but no essential difference in that.

Yours in every heart beat,   Eileen.

ALS (WC, NjP).

[1] Alexander Hamilton Phillips was an amateur taxidermist as well as Assistant Professor of Mineralogy.

[2] That is, Mrs. Phillips.

To Ellen Axson Wilson

My own darling,   Minnesota Club, St. Paul.   25 April, 1903

It racks my heart to be away off here while my sweet one spends her days under a cruel strain of anxiety. I feel like a man unfaithful to the strongest principal in him,—his love for those who constitute his life. I have just read the dear anxious letter in which you tell of Stock's visit to the doctor and of the disturbing symptoms pointing to trouble with the kidneys. You were right, of course, to ask the doctor for a statement of the plain truth. I hope with all my heart that he has answered promptly and that you will presently be relieved of the suspense. That— alone almost—is intolerable. Ah, my love, my love, what would I not give to take you in my arms and hold you close till you could look in my eyes and smile,—the happy smile you can *always* give me, no matter what betides, whenever I can make you *realize* my love for you! It passes all expression, sweetheart, my Eileen. It fairly possesses me whenever anything touches your happiness. I feel then more than at any other time that my very life is wrapt up in you.

I am perfectly well, and going through with my engagements with wonderful ease and absence of fatigue. The dinner[1] went off last evening here in the pleasantest, most informal manner,— some forty at the board, more by fifteen than they had ever assembled before. One or two came on from North Dakota to be present! They gave me the most cordial reception, and my speech, while it seemed to me rather below the average, seemed to give them a great deal of satisfaction. This afternoon I go over to Minneapolis.

God bless and keep you, my Eileen, and give you strength and comfort in the same abundant proportion that you have the tender, passionate love of   Your own   Woodrow

ALS (WC, NjP).
[1] A news report of this meeting of the Princeton Alumni Association of the New Northwest is printed at May 2, 1903.

A News Report of an Address in Minneapolis

[April 26, 1903]

The Lecture Platform

Woodrow Wilson, president of Princeton university, who lectured in Plymouth church last evening in the New Century course on "What it Means to be an American," was gracefully and graciously introduced by President Northrop,[1] who said that Princeton had conferred an honor upon Prof. Wilson by making him president, and that Prof. Wilson had also conferred an honor upon the position, because of his scholarly attainments and deep culture.

Woodrow Wilson is, in many ways, the typical American of whom he had so much to say in his lecture. He is tall and lank, like Abraham Lincoln and Uncle Sam, with a touch of the awkwardness that one associates with the sons of New England. But he has the compensating qualities, equally typical and obvious, of determination, thoroughness, self-reliance, and intelligence.

His lecture was delightfully informal and his choice of words such that a child might understand him. But as a skillful, cultured architect constructs from ordinary materials a building of symmetry and beauty, so does Prof. Wilson wield his strong, pure, meaty English into sentences and paragraphs of vivid strength and thoughtful significance.

His enunciation and pronunciation are correspondingly perfect and unaffected and the result is delightful and convincing in the extreme.

The lecture was a masterly and thoughtful analysis of the causes and methods of the marvellous growth of this country which included, of necessity, an analysis of the complicated American character, or rather, various types of character.

None but a thoughtful, fair-minded American could have written such a masterpiece of analysis and deduction, and no report of the lecture, short of a complete reproduction, can transmit its force and interest to those not fortunate enough to hear it.

CARYL B. STORRS.

Printed in the Minneapolis *Sunday Tribune*, April 26, 1903.
[1] Cyrus Northrop, President of the University of Minnesota.

From Ellen Axson Wilson

My own darling,   Princeton, April 26 1903

I was distressed to know from your letter yesterday that you did not find a letter from me in Chicago, but I still hope it reached you before you left that night. It ought to do so for I wrote the day after you left,—Tuesday night,—could not write earlier in the day, you know, because I was in Phila. However the poor little note brought you small comfort when it *did* reach you, so it is all one! Things were not going well then. The only trouble now is that I don't know *how* they are going, but my incorrigible optimism is doing me good service and I feel very hopeful. I was disappointed of course at not hearing from Stockton last night, but still it was natural he should not write the very day he left. I am rested and "perfectly all right" again myself,—have had quite a pleasant day. Mrs. Hibben came to see me after church, (Mr. Hibben is away, you know) then in the afternoon I went to see her and we went together to see the Ricketts, where we made a long and *very* pleasant visit.

It certainly was too bad that you missed Jessie again; you will have to write or telephone hereafter. I am more happy than I can say to hear that you are feeling so well and fresh, *dear* one! Indeed I *am* glad when all goes well with you; nothing in the world can make me *so* glad as that! You are the very life of me. Everyone I meet tells me they think you are looking *so* well again now,—so much better and less tired than you did a few weeks ago and their remarks are cheering me up inexpressibly; and now I am beginning to hope that this trip may on the whole be more pleasant than fatiguing.

Dr. Stephenson[1] gave us on the whole a very good sermon to-day,—one part of it we did not like much. He is not remarkable at all,—very far from being such a preacher as Dr. Purves. Oh, I forgot to mention that I sent him to the Inn after all because, you know, I expected to be in Va. over Sunday. Mrs. Purves invited him to her house but he preferred the Inn.

I told Miss Ricketts in confidence yesterday, about the classical department having wanted George [Howe] so long and of our various phases of feeling in the matter. Of course I did not speak of the matter in detail,—of the possible vacancy this year, &c. She was much excited about it and I must say I was greatly impressed by what she said, and feel as if I did not want you to let George come after all. She said she could not *bear* for people to have any such opportunity to question your motives however unjustly. She said she knew better than we could how people feel about you now,—their enthusiasm, their reverence for your "almost romantic disinterestness",—even people that were of quite an opposite character themselves. Of course a reputation like that is a great power for good and should not be risked except at a very obvious call of duty; it is very different from mere popularity. Can't something more be done to find that boy a place elsewhere? Do let us *try* Fiske,[2] or whichever is the best agency. It would certainly do no harm. Perhaps if you *saw* Harper or Shorey[3] you could get him a little berth, just to begin with, at Chicago.

You see I do not need to confess, dear, that my mind has changed completely on this matter. I even feel thankful for having told Miss Ricketts about it,—as if it might be the means of escaping a pit-fall. Of course I *knew* all this before but I seem to have got a different perspective,—to feel that you were to have been in a sense sacrificed to George.

A letter from Sister A. says her Fla. friend was to be in Charleston to talk over with her the Fla. land deal. They were both well. No other news. We are all quite well and all love you. As for your little wife she loves you, dearest, simply to distraction.

Your own   Eileen.

ALS (WC, NjP).

[1] The Rev. Dr. Joseph Ross Stevenson, pastor of the Fifth Avenue Presbyterian Church of New York, and later President of Princeton Theological Seminary, preached in Marquand Chapel at the morning service on April 26.

[2] The Fisk Teachers' Agencies, established in 1884, with offices in several cities, including New York.

[3] William Rainey Harper, President of the University of Chicago, and Paul Shorey, Professor of Greek at the same institution. The latter was an old friend of the Wilsons from Bryn Mawr days.

To Ellen Axson Wilson

My own darling,   Chicago.   27 April, 1903

Here I am in McCormick's office, passing through Chicago for the second time. I find your second letter here. It reads as if there were one between it and the first which had not reached me, but I trust not. They are very careful here.

Ah, my pet, my sweet, poor pet! How my heart aches as I read, between the lines, of the time of dreadful anxiety you have been passing through! How hard it is to go doggedly on my way and not turn homeward at once to you! I shall not soon forget this trip nor easily leave you again. I shall fairly *cling* to you when once I get you in my arms again. My precious one, my incomparable, indispensable darling! How could any one fail to love you, and how could any one who has once loved you do without you? You are more to me than words or deeds can ever express.

I spent yesterday in Madison, most of the time with [Frederick Jackson] Turner. It was a truly delightful lull in the *business* of the trip and refreshed me not a little,—though my heart wondered all day long what letter was waiting for me here from my love. I was simply taken possession of for the whole day and had not ten minutes to myself, so that when I got to bed about midnight I was thoroughly tired out. But I was not too tired and it was a wholesome fatigue. I arrived in Madison at about half-past eight in the morning (having left Minneapolis the night before at 10:20); went to the hotel (for I had not told anyone I was coming), shaved, had breakfast, and went to church. At church the minister recognized me, and one of the chief citizens of the town, whom I had known before, got hold upon me and carried me off to dinner. After dinner Turner came in, summoned by telephone, with the president-elect of the University, Dr. [Charles Richard] Van Hise, and I presently went off with them—called on [Richard Theodore] Ely and [Reuben Gold] Thwaites,—took tea with the Turners,—and altogether put in a full day enjoying my friends.

I *talk* of these things, my pet; but my heart is not in them! It is with you,—its love and yearning inexpressible, almost unendurable.

Always, with all the love my nature can ever give
Your own   Woodrow

ALS (WC, NjP).

From Ellen Axson Wilson

My own darling,   Princeton   April 27, 1903

I am so happy over this good letter from Stockton that I must hurry it on to you,[1] for I know it will relieve your mind too. It is certainly a white letter day that has brought me two such letters as this and the one from you this morning. I could almost hug the postman. That was truly a wonderful letter of yours, sweetheart. Ah, *how* I love you,—for it and for everything! I am sure it *would* make me happy to think of your love in any extremity of trouble.

I am also very happy at the repeated good reports from you;—it is delightful to feel that you are really enjoying it, and that it is all so successful.

But I must not write long today (I sent a *document* last night!) for I have been very busy with the mails and the sewing, and now I am anxious to get away (was interrupted here by a visitor (!)) before people begin to call, and enjoy this wonderful day. It is now or never for that walk! With love and haste.

Your own   Eileen.

Keep Stockton's letter for me.

Got caught after all—have had four visitors since signing this!

ALS (WC, NjP).
[1] This enclosure is missing.

To Ellen Axson Wilson

My precious darling,   St. Louis, 28 Apr. '03

The letter I find waiting for me here has brought me peace of mind again! Ah, *what* a relief to have this breath of quieted thought and normal conditions come back breathe through your sweet letter! God bless you with every blessing, my sweet one. Your love, your strength, your divination of what is right and full of comfort for those who love and trust you fill me with unutterable happiness and thankfulness. You bring a blessing upon me every day of your life, as you bring a blessing also upon dear Stock. and upon all whom your heart includes!

I arrived here this morning at a few minutes after eight. Lionberger Davis[1] was at the station to meet me, and I was in time to join the family at breakfast. I am now (11 o'cl.) supposed to be composing my address to the University Club this evening on "The Expansion and Character of the United States"![2] Immediately after writing you yesterday I went out to Edgewater. Helen was at the house, just back from a visit to Colorado. Jessie came in, from the dentist's, at about five o'clock, and we had a delightful evening together. Marion and her husband[3] were telephoned to and came hurtling out in their automobile to dinner. At ten o'cl. they took me into town at what *they* thought a slow pace, which fell just short of scaring me to death. At 11:40 (when I was already asleep in my berth) my train pulled out for St. Louis.

It was a delightful *family interval* in my travels and, if I could have had quieter thoughts of you, would have been altogether healing and delightful. I shall see them again when I go to Chicago on the 4th. I am perfectly well, not too tired (indeed scarcely tired at all), and, after reading your letter, very happy! With unspeakable love,   Your own   Woodrow

ALS (WC, NjP).
    [1] John Lionberger Davis, Princeton 1900, the son of the trustee, John David Davis, at whose home Wilson was staying.
    [2] A news report of this address is printed at April 29, 1903.
    [3] Marion McGraw Bones and her husband, whose name is unknown to the Editors.

From Ellen Axson Wilson

My own darling,   Princeton, April 28 1903

I myself answered the enclosed letter[1] yesterday telling him that you had nothing suitable which was not already in print and could not *possibly* prepare anything in time. But I get a letter[2] from him today (written of course before receiving mine) begging me to forward his to you,—so I do it to satisfy him! He *knows* how busy you are and I feel indignant with him for teasing you with such requests.

By the way did you get your salary checks, and did you sign and return them to the bank? I note that your account when you left was $305.00. I have had to pay $200.00 in physical culture bills, $32.00 to Prof. Phillips,[3] besides a number of smaller bills; so unless that money has been deposited I have overdrawn the account. But I have about $30.00 in cash. There are only two signed checks left so I will send a few for signature in case of need. One item was an advance to Maggie [Foley] of half wages because they are building a house on Bank St. which is to be rented to a *professor*! Does'nt it seem funny? Have just had a note from Miss Hopkins[4] in answer to mine asking what I owed her for my private lessons; she says she did not give me lessons but only *advice* & "advice has cost nothing since the world began,"—rather neat, eh?

There is no further news from Stockton indeed no news of any sort. The wonderful weather still lasts and I *will* get out today and enjoy it. Yesterday afternoon was really farcical—six visitors while I was trying to scribble that little note to you. I finally escaped at six o'clock! What a comfort it will be to have a "day" next winter! It must give one a delicious sense of security when one is at work.

No letter from my darling this morning but I can hardly expect regularity under the circumstances.*

All well and *very* cheerful, and I love you, love you with all my soul.   Your little wife   Eileen.

*Did not notice this until me letter was begun[5]

ALS (WC, NjP).
   [1] This enclosure is missing.
   [2] The forwarded letter is also missing.
   [3] That is, for the deer's head.
   [4] The Editors have been unable to identify her.
   [5] A word at the bottom of the page, which she had written earlier and crossed out.

A News Report of an Address to the University Club of St. Louis

[April 29, 1903]

DR. WOODROW WILSON GUEST OF CLUB MEN
Talked Last Night on "The Expansion and
Character of the United States."

Dr. Woodrow Wilson of Princeton college entertained last night at the University club one of the most representative audiences ever gathered in the club. He gave a talk on "The Expansion and Character of the United States," and in developing the subject he pointed out that the recent expansion in the Philippines and Porto Rico was really due to the same adventurous impulse which created English America in the first place.

It illustrated the same impulse of extension as the purchase of Louisiana. That purchase expressed the impatient force of the settlers of the country east of the Mississippi and the impossibility of confining them within the bounds of the original territory of the United States.

He said that a century seemed to be the dramatic unit in the history of the country. There had first been a century of colonization, then a century of war to be rid of the French and gain independence from England, then a century of nation making, and that we had now finally, come to the century in which what we had done was to be tested and made good.

The new expansion, although, as natural, as inevitable, as characteristic as the old, showed a radical difference in character and seemed likely to test everything that had gone before: our political character, our political capacity, our political principles, even our political organizations.

The new field of action showed two things which distinguished it from the old. There was in our new possessions a great native population to be handled such as our old possessions had not at first contained. Our new possessions also brought us into international relationships which had to be defined and which would call for the best statesmanship. It seemed likely that in these new fields the old character of our constitution would be tested, not only in its operation, but in its very principles.[1]

Prof. Wilson arrived yesterday morning from Chicago and during his stay in the city will be the guest of John D. Davis. He will be entertained with a dinner by the Princeton club at the University club to-night and after participating in part of the dedicatory ceremonies[2] will leave Friday evening.

Printed in the *St. Louis Globe-Democrat*, April 29, 1903.
  [1] A WWhw outline of this address, dated April 28, 1903, is in WP, DLC.
  [2] See n. 1 to the following letter.

To Ellen Axson Wilson

My own darling,   St. Louis, 29 April, '03

I find myself a good deal upset by your complete change of mind about George's appointment. I had allowed the Latin men to make their arrangements on the assumption that they were to have him. Perhaps you had better send for Jessie [Jesse] Carter and advise him to be looking for another man in view of a probable change of plans. No doubt you are right; but we must not be too selfishly careful of my reputation. There is deep selfishness in that as well as in the other.

By all means pay Mr. Phillips, my pet, what we owe him; and at once, because they are to be off presently for Europe.

Will you not have the enclosed cheques deposited, making out the deposit slip and having the proper entry made in my bank book?

The affair at the University Club last night went off very easily and successfully. I spoke on "The Expansion and Character of the United States" and found that I had sufficient momentum and self-confidence to do it in reasonably good form. I spoke only half an hour and stopped before my welcome had grown cool.

I fear I shall have no time to write to-morrow. The day is to be filled from morning to midnight with "functions" connected with the dedication of the Fair in which, as "an official guest," I shall be expected to take part; and I cannot courteously break away.[1] How *much* I should prefer to sit quietly here and write to my darling, who seems more indispensable to me with every hour that passes! "Where'er I roam, whatever realms to see, My heart, untravell'd, fondly turns to thee"[2] my incomparable darling!

I am well and am standing the pace in fine shape. If only I could have sight of you, and touch of your sweet lips I could be happy! Everybody is as kind and generous to me as possible. With love that overflows my heart,

Your own   Woodrow

ALS (WC, NjP).

[1] Although the Exposition in St. Louis was not to open until April 30, 1904, dedicatory exercises were held a year earlier to commemorate the centennial of the Louisiana Purchase.

[2] From "The Traveller," by Oliver Goldsmith.

From Ellen Axson Wilson

My own darling,   Princeton April 29 1903

Your dear letter written in Mr. McCormick's office came today; ah, how I wish that you could have got my later letters at the same time so that your anxiety might be promptly relieved! It *hurts* me so to think of you anxious and distressed on my account, especially since at the very time you were reading it things were already going *much* better with us. I cannot understand why the letters are so slow in reaching you. I sent *four* letters to Chicago, and three to St. Louis.

I have had another very cheerful letter from Stockton today; he said he was just ending the best 24 hours he had had since this thing began. I am really *happy* about him today.

Madge[1] sails for New York today and will reach here Friday or Saturday. Had a letter from Sister Annie today too. She says the Fla. man who was telegraphing about her land was sent to the insane asylum the other day! Strange! is'nt it? Perhaps it is a case like Uncle Wills.[2] She has also discovered that she has only *one* thousand acres.

Dr. Jones[3] could not preach on May 17, neither could Dr. Upham;[4] it is his commencement Sunday. So I went this afternoon to consult with Mr. Hibben, and he recommended Dr. Stevenson of Schenectady;[5]—knows him to be a good preacher. I have therefore just written inviting him in your name! Odd how often I have to settle this pulpit question; I shall be escorting them to the pulpit next! We are all perfectly well & happy. I was charmed with your account of the pleasant day at Madison. With love unspeakable.   Your own   Eileen.

ALS (WC, NjP).
    [1] Her sister, who was probably returning from a visit with Axson relatives in Savannah.
    [2] William Dearing Hoyt, M.D.
    [3] The Rev. Dr. John Sparhawk Jones, pastor of Calvary Presbyterian Church in Philadelphia.
    [4] The Rev. Dr. Samuel Foster Upham, Professor of Practical Theology at Drew Theological Seminary.
    [5] The Rev. Dr. Alexander Russell Stevenson, pastor of the First Presbyterian Church of Schenectady, N. Y.

A Pocket Notebook

[c. April 30-c. June 30, 1903]

Inscribed "Woodrow Wilson Europe, 1903," with WWhw addresses of hotels, pensions, and things to see, addresses of friends, possible itineraries, and brief financial records relating to the settlement of the Estate of Joseph Ruggles Wilson.

Pocket notebook (WP, DLC).

A News Item

[April 30, 1903]

PRINCETON DINNER AT UNIVERSITY CLUB
Ex-President Cleveland a Guest of
Honor—Prof. Wilson's Address.

The Princeton club of St. Louis gave its twenty-sixth annual dinner last night at the University club.

Prof. Woodrow Wilson, president of the college, was the chief speaker, and honored guests were ex-President Grover Cleveland, now a member of the board of curators of Princeton college, and Prof. Andrew F. West, the dean.

Prof. Wilson explained, as one of the reasons that he had asked for $12,500,000 by which to promote the growth of the institution, that a privately endowed institution could maintain its own individuality.

Ex-President Cleveland made a short talk, in which he said that one reason why he became connected with the college after retiring from the presidency was the favorable impression made upon him by the Princeton people while attending the sesquicentennial anniversary celebration of the college.

Printed in the *St. Louis Globe-Democrat*, April 30, 1903.

To Ellen Axson Wilson

My own darling,   St. Louis, Mo., 30 April, 1903

Here I am, after all, a prudent boy, sitting quietly in the house instead of spending the day, as I was expected to do, at the Fair Grounds. It has blown off piercingly chill, and, after trying the reviewing stand (without a seat) for about a hour, I took flight. The program would have been tremendous and alarming enough in any weather. We (the official guests) were expected to ride out to the grounds in carriages; sit behind the President for an hour and a half to see a review of troops (some 12,000) go by; take a cold, standing lunch in a windy tent; hear some two hours' speaking and "dedicating" in the Liberal Arts building; and sit out a long formal dinner! I was glad of an excuse (namely, anxious thought for my health) to run from April-turned-November and celebration-run-mad, and come back to the empty town and deserted house. I was not made for "functions," but for equable work that tells and long, refreshing chats with those whom I love. How I hate show and the crush of spectacles! How I love the quiet enjoyments that strike deep and set the heart at ease! What a chap to be put to playing public character! I get solid comfort, at any rate, out of this escape and indulgence. What a luxury it is to love *you*, my Eileen. I can love you so entirely without reserve and can so satisfy every taste that is in me by the sweet indulgence. What powers and what capacities of enjoyment have you not released in me! I never feel so fully that I am expressing myself as when I give full leave to my love for you. Never for a moment lose hold of me, my precious love,— never for a moment lose consciousness of *possessing* me, of being the *medium* of my life by the genius and power of love. In proportion as you realize all of this will you intensify our sense of union and my joy in living,—and your own, too, will you not? Is it not a chief part of your life that I am

Your own   Woodrow?

Two of the cheques you sent were the *signed* ones! What a sweet letter from Stock, and how you deserve it!

ALS (WC, NjP).

From Ellen Axson Wilson

My own darling,   Princeton April 30 [1903]

Your letter describing your visit to Jessie came this afternoon and was delightful. It was a relief to *my* mind to know that *yours* had been relieved by the receipt of my later letters. I had another letter from Stockton today,—it is still cheerful and confident though he confesses that he still has bad times; that it is "a simple case of nervous prostration" and the doctors say will "take time." To my great disappointment the Maine fishing trip has fallen through. He wrote to Mr. Tedcastle telling him about his depression, and that he was doubtful about imposing himself on them in such case. Mr. T. answered that Dr. Wood thought the Maine lakes too exciting for nervous patients on account of the altitude so he "would not press him to go," and invited him to visit them at Clifton later. It is too bad because in Maine there would have been something interesting to *do*;—and there isn't in Va.,—that is the weak point in the latter plan. He thinks he will try it however next week,—since the doctor says he must not go to the backwoods alone,—and he wants to know if I can go with him for a few days. I suppose I *must*,—so don't be surprised or alarmed if you hear that I have run off! I should like to send Madge with him for *she* could stay,—and perhaps I will send her. Only, unfortunately, Stockton confessed to me in Phila. that he was'nt very well acquainted with Madge, thought her rather cold-hearted, and in short didn't love her as much as he did me and you and Ed! But "she's all right" at bottom and an experience like this would probably make a woman of her. At any rate she will be here to stay with the children. We are all quite well and in *excellent* spirits.

I must tell you something amusing—in a way. Jessie came in to dinner very red and embarrassed because she had been putting some wreaths of flowers on the grave of "Catherine Bullock"[1]—one or two other girls standing by—when a party of students passed and laughed at them very heartily. It was rather pretty in them to think of such a thing—wasnt it?

No news except that Dr. Patton's son Frank married today[2] and I actually remembered to send cards! Oh! and your check for over $7,000 from Harpers came tonight.[3] I will keep it until you return.

I love you, dear, tenderly, passionately unutterably.

                                        Your little wife,   Eileen.

ALS (WC, NjP).

1 She was the niece of Col. George Morgan, eighteenth-century gentleman farmer whose home was located on the site of the present Prospect. Her grave stone was the last one still visible in the old Prospect burial ground, now covered by the southern end of Seventy-Nine Hall. "Around it had grown a cruel and utterly false legend connecting her name and Colonel [Aaron] Burr's." The grave was moved to the Princeton Cemetery when Seventy-Nine Hall was constructed. Varnum Lansing Collins, *Princeton: Past and Present* (Princeton, N. J., 1931), p. 68.

2 Francis Landey Patton, Jr., married Jessie Campbell McIntyre in New York on April 30, 1903.

3 In WP, DLC, there are royalty statements from Harper and Bros. dated Dec. 31, 1902, showing $7,039.75 due on May 1, 1903, from sales of *A History of the American People* and $94.28 due May 1, 1903, from sales of *George Washington*.

To Ellen Axson Wilson

My own darling,   St. Louis, Mo.   1 May, 1903

I am here a day longer than I expected and so shall be obliged to go without a letter to-day. It is "Diplomatic Day" in the three day series of dedicatory exercises in connexion with the World's Fair, and Mr. Davis, as one of the distracted managers, is off to look after his part of the undertaking. I have begged off, as I did yesterday,—not because I am not up up [*sic*] to it, but because I hate it all and eagerly welcome an opportunity to rest. I am becoming a wise bird in my old age!

We start (the St. Louis delegation[1] and I) for Cincinnati to-night at about nine o'clock. We reach there in the morning about seven, and such a full programme has been arranged for the day that you need not be surprised if forty-eight hours go by before this letter is followed by its successor. I shall *try* to write, of course, but I may not be my own master.

As I sat here alone last night waiting for dinner to be far enough away from bed-time, I read, in *Littell*, my sweet one, of a delightful woman, the mother of Anatole de France, who had "the heavenly patience and joyful simplicity which belong to those who have no business in the world but love,"[2]—and it set me musing upon the wonderful little lady who has given her life to me. Stock. would think of the same person, with glad tears in his eyes, should the words come his way; but he does not know the wonder and beauty of it as I do! Some of the sweetest and most attractive women in the world have *only* the power of love and it is no marvel that they make it their business; but *you* have *every* power and *yet* make love your business! And so love is enhanced, adorned, made transcendant by the service of a mind and nature with wealth and resources for any enterprise. There is profound gratitude as well as lasting delight, therefore, in the devoted love of   Your own   Woodrow

ALS (WC, NjP).
¹ That is, the delegation from the Princeton Club of St. Louis to the meeting of the Western Association of Princeton Clubs in Cincinnati on May 2, 1903.
² Paul Mantoux, "Anatole France on Childhood," *The Living Age* [formerly *Littell's Living Age*], ccxxxvi (March 28, 1903), 820-22.

To Cyrus Hall McCormick

My dear Cyrus,   St. Louis, Mo., 1 May, 1903

Will you not be kind enough to have Mr. Stewart¹ send such mail matter as may come for me, or such as may have come, to Mr. Jones's, #141 Astor St., to await me there?

Are you going to be able to get off and attend the convention of Clubs in Cincinnati to-morrow? I sincerely hope so. At any rate, I shall see you on Monday.

Always   Faithfully Yours,   Woodrow Wilson

ALS (WP, DLC).
¹ Frederick A. Steuert, McCormick's confidential secretary.

From Ellen Axson Wilson

My own darling,   Princeton, May 1, 1903

It pleases me to write "May," at the head of this letter for it seems to bring the time of your home-coming nearer. I hope you have kept well during the last two days in St. Louis in spite of the fatigues of the occasion, and the extreme changes of temperature. We are having the same here, a little later,—intense heat yesterday, and a high cold wind today.

The "corner Wilsons"¹ had a may-pole &c. as usual, and all the children had to dance around it in their heavy winter cloaks. I went down partly to see it, chiefly to ask Mrs. Paxton and Mrs. Magie² for money for the Infirmary. It was horrible! I don't think I was cut out for that business. Yet they were both kind and Mrs. Paxton really cordial.

By the way, there was an operation for appendicitis at the Infirmary last night,—a junior,—Harold Smith from Chicago. It was a complicated case but he is doing very well. He is a friend of the Pynes and they were there until after midnight—also dear, good Mr. Hibben who simply saw the bright light in the operating-room, and went over to see what was wrong and if he could help. I saw the mother today.

I wrote to Bishop Talbot[3] days ago but have had no answer,—
suppose he was not at home. But I assume he will stay here; I
tried to get the Hibbens to help me entertain him Saturday night,
but this is the week when "the brother-in-law,[4] comes" so at their
suggestion I have asked Dr. Shields, who has accepted.

No news!—except that the new verses to the Faculty song are
all horrid except yours.[5] This class must be peculiarly spiteful.
The one on Frothingham *is* funny though. He has evidently taken
a very *noticeable* brace. I think I can repeat them.

> Heres to Frothy our latest find,
> He's gentle and easy to drive and kind
> He had to make his courses hard
> Or he couldn't play in Woodrow's yard.

My hand shakes so that I can hardly write just from walking
all over town holding up my heavy dress, I think. So I will stop
scrawling. I am *so* happy over the continued good news from my
darling. In every heart-beat—   Your own   Eileen.

ALS (WC, NjP).
    1 She was referring to the Frederick Newton Willsons, who lived at the corner
of the Lawrenceville Road and Stony Brook.
    2 Caroline Sophia Denny (Mrs. William Miller) Paxton of 20 Library Place
and Mary Blanchard Hodge (Mrs. William Francis) Magie of 78 Library Place.
    3 Ethelbert Talbot, Protestant Episcopal Bishop of Central Pennsylvania, who
was to preach in the Chapel on May 3, 1903.
    4 William Newcomb Davidson, of Elizabeth, N. J., Mrs. Hibben's brother.
    5 "Here's to Wilson our President,
    "On raising millions he's quite intent,
    "Square and loyal, firm and true,
    "A man we honor thro' and thro'." *1903 Campus Songs* (n.p., n.d.)

Claude Halstead Van Tyne's[1] Review of
A History of the American People

[May 1903]

President Wilson has chosen a title for his work very similar to
that of Professor McMaster's "History of the People of the United
States." In these two works we have represented the two schools
of historic writers. Their methods of treating their subject stand
at the remotest corners of the field of history. Taking the two
works as typical of the two schools, the first striking difference is
in the scope of the two undertakings, one covering the four hun-

A History of the American People. By WOODROW WILSON, Ph.D., Litt.D., LL.D.
    In five volumes. Price $17.50. New York and London: Harper & Brothers, 1902.

────────

    1 At this time, Instructor in History at the University of Pennsylvania.

dred years from Columbus to the late war with Spain, the other dealing, as far as completed, with the forty years from the adoption of the Constitution to the Jacksonian era. The difference in spirit and method is even greater than the difference in scope. Mr. Wilson deals with abstractions and broad generalizations which seek to give us the whole essence of an historical period without our going to the wearisome trouble of viewing the facts from which these abstractions are presumably made. Mr. Mc-Master gives us those details, and so arranges and groups them, that the reading compels the mind to accept the opinion that the author holds but does not express. What we carry away from Mr. Wilson's book is the pleasing phrase in which he has given us his judgment. Mr. McMaster allows the reader to see the facts and arrive at an opinion by the logical process of deduction.

The comparison of the schools as represented in these two authors might be carried on indefinitely, for never were two authors more antithetical in the execution, as well as in the whole conception, of their work; but perhaps it will be more profitable to compare Mr. Wilson's work with its title. It promises a history of the people, and yet it is but a history of the politics of the people. We look in vain for anything but names on the subjects of religion, art, literature and science. Legal, economic and institutional questions of the greatest interest are ignored or slighted. Social forces that are of the greatest moment in the history of a people are not noted. The author's interests are with men and their political activities, and in the portrayal of these he proves himself an artist.

In the summary treatment of the several historical periods, the specialist recognizes that the facts often lie behind opinions and comments, but the untrained reader is not permitted to see them. This method of writing is Mr. Wilson's ideal of historical production. The reader has only to accept the results, while the historian does the work, which is satisfactory enough if one is simply interested in conclusions and generalizations and could be sure that the data of the field had been well considered. The very size of the undertaking, however, assures us, in this case, that the data have not been well considered. The original matter that must have been consulted in order to warrant such generalizations is too vast.

Still, there was another method of work which was left open to the author, if he wished to be the great synthetic and philosophical historian of the American people. He might have availed himself of the numerous monographs written by men who have gone to the original sources, but although we have evidence in some cases of familiarity with the more prominent workers in special fields, we do not feel that Mr. Wilson has given us more than a small measure of the results of analytical scholarship in American history. Too often the first-hand information has filtered through several secondary histories before it reaches Mr. Wilson's work, and has had its meaning reversed in the process of filtration.

The work is an able summary of American political history. As evidence that Mr. Wilson is abreast of the historical scholarship of the day bearing on political aspects, it is to be noted that he has embraced the lately advanced opinion of Professor Osgood, of Columbia, that the colonial history must be studied from the European side, and that the colonies were only a phase of the European history of the age.[2] Especially in the treatment of the navigation acts has he seized upon the recent theories of Professor Osgood, and shown the harmlessness of the restrictions in actual practice. He accepts the conclusions of Egerton and Mellen Chamberlain[3] that there was no intentional tyranny on the part of the British ministry, but only an insistence upon constitutional and legal forms rather than a statesmanlike acceptance of existing facts. "They did not know whereof Mr. Burke spoke when he told them that the colonial assemblies had been suffered to grow into a virtual independence of Parliament, and had become in fact, whatever lawyers might say, co-ordinated with it in every matter which concerned the internal administration of the colonies; and that now it was too late to ask or expect the colonists to accept any other view of the law than that which accorded with long established fact." Of King George, Wilson says, "The nature of the man was not sinister. Neither he nor his ministers had any purpose of making 'slaves' of the colonists. Their measures for the regulation of the colonial trade were incontestably conceived upon a model long ago made familiar in practice, and followed precedents long ago accepted in the colonies. Their financial measures were moderate and sensible enough in themselves, and were conceived in the ordinary temper of law-making. What they

[2] Van Tyne probably was referring to Herbert Levi Osgood's paper, "The Study of American Colonial History," *Annual Report of the American Historical Association for the Year 1898* (Washington, 1899), pp. 63-73. The first of Osgood's monumental volumes on the American colonies in the seventeenth and eighteenth centuries did not appear until 1904.

[3] Hugh Edward Egerton, *A Short History of British Colonial Policy* (London, 1897), and Mellen Chamberlain, "The Revolution Impending," in Justin Winsor (ed.), *Narrative and Critical History of America* (8 vols., Boston and New York, 1884-89), VI, 1-112.

did not understand or allow for was American opinion. What the Americans, on their part, did not understand or allow for was the spirit in which Parliament had in fact acted. They did not dream with how little comment or reckoning upon consequences, or how absolutely without any conscious theory as to power or authority, such statutes as those which had angered them had been passed; how members of the Commons stared at Mr. Burke's passionate protests and high-pitched arguments of constitutional privilege; how unaffectedly astonished they were at the rebellious outbreak which followed in the colonies." Thus the author has softened somewhat the harsher judgments of the more scientific, though less artistic and sympathetic, special students who have, of late, tended to swing too far in the opposite direction from the old, excessively patriotic writers like Bancroft.

The bearing of Mr. Wilson as an historian is admirable. He is suave and not easily drawn into passionate denunciation or invective, and yet he does not lack in boldness of judgment. In the treatment of the history after the adoption of the Constitution there is an admirable balance between extreme Northern and Southern views, a position such as few men beside Wilson could have taken. There is a democratic bias, if any, but imperturbable fairness in spite of natural sympathies.

Mr. Wilson has declared, as his theory of writing history, that the historian must select from among the mass of events that which is characteristic, and then he must throw all the light upon that event that his sources will permit.[4] Such a canon of selection is of value only to the artist, and the thing selected will be determined by the tastes of the historian rather than by his reason. In the history before us the events that are emphasized are often only the personal interests of Mr. Wilson, and not the historically most important or characteristic matters. He often subordinates because the general reader will not be attracted by the theme, and expands because there is limited human interest, though perhaps great economic and institutional importance. Mr. Wilson's method of study gives an uneven effect. His intention is to study closely what he decides is important, but, in this way, he often fails to realize what is important.

Occasionally there is such a treatment of a period as suggests incomplete mastery of the subject. There is no adequate approach to the War of 1812, and when the reader is plunged into that war he feels aggrieved that the transition had not been plainly enough

[4] In "The Truth of the Matter" or "On the Writing of History," printed in this series at June 17, 1895, Vol. 9.

indicated to have avoided the shock. The author seems to have greater interest in immediate than in ultimate causes. But even this hypothesis will not explain some of the faults of proportion. Why should the Mexican War and the Ku-Klux Klan each be allotted three pages? Does the Revolution get twice as much space as the Civil War because Mr. Wilson knows more about the former? Why is the Missouri Compromise notably slighted, while Bryan's free silver campaign is spun out to an inordinate length? The Trent affair and the Gettysburg campaign both dwindle as compared with Sitting Bull.

The literary execution of the work is of a high character, but hardly equal to that of the masterpiece of biography, Mr. Wilson's "Life of George Washington." It is, however, bold, dignified and archaic, never losing its historical tone in unhistorical passion. The use of archaic words and phrases is especially effective in lending a fitting atmosphere to the treatment of colonial matters. None but a true man of letters could have given the work its fine literary flavor and form.

The make-up of the book renders it far more imposing than it really is. It may be stated, the five volumes could easily be reduced to two, but the heavy paper, the deep margins, a wilderness of injudiciously chosen pictures, for which Mr. Wilson is not responsible, and a sumptuous binding, produce a volume so ponderous as to be unwieldy. There is an unfortunate predominance of fancy pictures rather than representations of real historical objects.   C. H. VAN TYNE.
Washington, D. C.

Printed in the *Annals of the American Academy of Political and Social Science,* XXI (May 1903), 473-76.

A News Report

[May 2, 1903]
President Wilson in the Northwest

This Saturday is the date scheduled for the third annual convention of the Western Association of Princeton Clubs. So far in his Western trip President Wilson has attended alumni reunions in St. Paul and St. Louis. For the following account of his reception in the Northwest we are indebted to James D. Denegre '89:

"President Woodrow Wilson was the guest of the Princeton Alumni Association of the Northwest at their annual dinner at the Minnesota Club in St. Paul, on the evening of April 24th. Over ninety per cent. of the alumni of Minnesota and North and South Dakota were present to greet him. This is especially significant of President Wilson's popularity in the Northwest; several alumni journeyed three or four hundred miles, all the way from the Dakota frontiers, to attend this meeting. Every Princeton alumnus in St. Paul was present, and Minneapolis sent over all of her Princeton men, except two or three who were out of the city or kept away by illness, and Duluth, Winona and the other larger Minnesota towns were also represented. It was the largest gathering of Princeton men the Twin City association has ever been able to muster together.

"President Wilson was warmly greeted and his address on the Princeton system was received with enthusiasm. In the course of his remarks he said: 'A university which one goes to in a street car cannot, it seems to me, fulfil the true ideal of what a university should be. The true university should stand for something of its own, should be something different from other universities and colleges, and in order to develop this institutional spirit a community of interest and life is necessary. The educator has no business to be trying new things. It is his business to gather the best of the past and present it in forms which have the sanction of time instead of running after new fads and theories. The purpose of culture, which is the end of the university course, is the opening of the student's mind to what is best in the great minds of the past. While curious speculation may be valuable as mental gymnastics, it has no part in the method of the educator. The private institution has the advantage of the state institution in that it is able to preserve its characteristics and is not obliged to seek the changing favor of politicians and of the uninformed who have a say in the running of the latter institutions."[1]

Printed in the *Princeton Alumni Weekly*, III (May 2, 1903), 492-93.
[1] There is a brief WWhw outline of this address, dated April 24, 1903, in WP, DLC.

A News Report about Wilson in Cincinnati

[May 2, 1903]
President Wilson Is Queen City's Guest.

The fourth annual meeting of the Western Association of Princeton clubs was held at the Grand hotel Saturday [May 2], the attendance numbering about fifty delegates. The clubs represented were the Princeton club of Western Pennsylvania, Princeton club of Chicago, Princeton club of St. Louis, Princeton Alumni association of Northern Ohio, Princeton club of Louisville, Rocky Mountain club of Princeton university, Princeton Alumni association of Omaha, Princeton Alumni association of New Northwest, Princeton Alumni association of Indiana, and the Princeton association of the District of Columbia and the Southern States. Dr. Woodrow Wilson, president of the Princeton university, arrived with the St. Louis delegation at 9 o'clock Saturday morning. He was taken to the Queen City club, where he will be the guest of the association. The banquet will be given at the Queen City club and promises to be a brilliant event.[1]

Ex-President Grover Cleveland, who was expected, informed President Wilson that he could not attend. Mr. Cleveland will pass through Cincinnati Saturday evening, on his way East. Dr. Wilson predicts a great future for Princeton university. He said the attendance was increasing each year, and numbered fourteen hundred the present season. He believes that a law school will be added to the university in the near future. Dr. Wilson is a thorough college man, believes in a moderate amount of athletics as the best stimulant for healthy mental exercise. He will remain in the city until Sunday evening, speaking at the Y.M.C.A. Sunday afternoon.[2] During Saturday afternoon he and the visitors are to be shown the Zoo gardens and other points of interest about the city.

Printed in the *Cincinnati Times-Star*, May 2, 1903; one editorial heading omitted.
1 See the second news report printed at May 3, 1903.
2 A news report of this talk is printed at May 4, 1903.

To Ellen Axson Wilson

My own darling,   Cincinnati, Ohio, 2 May, 1903

What do you think of the company your husband keeps,—in print,—and on the first page of an afternoon paper?[1]

I have been rushed about from place to place, as I expected, and am writing now with the dinner company waiting down stairs, to break off at any moment and finish to-morrow.

May 3 They gave us a day of it: in the morning, a business meeting of the Association—at which a speech, of course; after that a ride out to a truly beautiful park where we had lunch,—the whole crowd of delegates (about 50); then back to town, to make ready for dinner. I met a reporter by appointment at the Queen City Club, where I am staying, and where the dinner was given, and dictated to him the substance both of the speech I had made in the forenoon and of the speech I was to make in the evening.[2] Then I went up stairs, took an hour's snooze, dressed, began this letter, was called down to dinner, spent a really delightful evening with a most diverting company, made a decent speech, very high pitched and solemn, and was in bed by one o'clock. I feel rested and fresh this morning; shall go to church presently, then dine with a new friend,[3] then speak at the Y.M.C.A. at three o'clock, go out for tea to a suburb,[4] and thence take a train, at about 8, for Chicago. Do not be alarmed. It is not at all a killing pace. I am fresh and well and having as good a time as any poor devil of a college president can expect to have. It is not ideal, but it is quite supportable. At Chicago I stay with the Joneses, and there is no speech till Tuesday night,—the last of the series, heaven be praised![5]

I shall hear from you again at Chicago and be happy. Nothing keeps me really *happy* and light-hearted but thoughts of you, my Eileen. They are the breath of life to me. I saw West at St. Louis and he delighted me by reporting how well you seemed, the colour back in your cheeks. Ah, that was tonic to me. My little wife, my little wife, you are all the world to me, and I am in all things and altogether   Your own   Woodrow

ALS (WC, NjP).
    [1] This enclosure is missing, but it was a clipping of the front-page news report in the *Cincinnati Times-Star*, May 2, 1903, printed as the preceding document. "The company your husband keeps" referred to sensational headlines reading: "SHOOTING CAUSED PANIC IN CHURCH," "PRIEST ARRESTED ON CHARGE OF HAVING MURDERED WOMAN," and "DOZEN PEOPLE KILLED IN EXPLOSION IN FACTORY."
    [2] Wilson was undoubtedly referring to a reporter from the *Cincinnati Times-Star* and to his story referred to in n. 1.
    [3] The Rev. Paul Clement Matthews, Princeton 1887, at this time rector of St. Luke's Episcopal Church in Cincinnati.
    [4] At the home of James Harlan Cleveland '85, Professor of Law at the University of Cincinnati.
    [5] A news report of this affair is printed at May 6, 1903.

A News Report of a Meeting of the Western Association of Princeton Clubs

[May 3, 1903]

Western Association of Clubs
Entertained by Alumni.

The Princeton Alumni Association of Cincinnati and vicinity entertained as their guests yesterday the members of the Western Association of Princeton Clubs, which held their fourth annual meeting in this city. There were about 100 members of the association, and they were entertained in a most hospitable manner. The day's festivities began with a business meeting at the Grand Hotel, in which President Woodrow Wilson, of Princeton University, was a guest of honor.

The object of this meeting was pleasure and the advancement of the interests of the Princeton University in the educating of young manhood.

After the meeting was called to order President Wilson spoke upon the object of the meeting, his subject being, "What Can Be Done By the Western Association of Princeton Clubs For the Furtherance of the Interests of the University?"

Other business of the association followed Mr. Wilson's talk, after which an election of officers was held. . . .

The meeting then temporarily adjourned, and the visitors were invited by members of the local association to join them in a trolley ride. The handsome special cars of the Cincinnati Traction Company, Atlantic, Baltic, and Honolulu, arrived in front of the hotel, and the party were shown the many interesting sights and scenes of Cincinnati as seen from the street railways for about an hour, when the Zoo was reached. Here luncheon was served in the promenade of the pavilion, and several hours were spent in short talks by members of the association and in music. . . .

About 4 o'clock the party returned to the special cars and were shown the residential parts of the city via Walnut Hills, where they enjoyed the beautiful scenery of Cincinnati. After concluding the ride they adjourned in a body to the Grand Central Depot to greet Grover Cleveland, ex-President of the United States and his party, who were expected to be special guests of the meeting, but had to decline on account of important business matters needing Mr. Cleveland's attention. They met this distinguished gentleman, who is a Trustee of Princeton University, and gave him and his party a royal welcome with the Princeton yells.

Printed in the *Cincinnati Enquirer*, May 3, 1903; some editorial headings omitted.

A News Report of an Address in Cincinnati

[May 3, 1903]

PRINCETON MEN ENJOY DINNER

The sons of Old Nassau shouted themselves hoarse last night in greetings to President Woodrow Wilson, of Princeton, their University, at the annual dinner, which was given at the Queen City Club. This dinner is a National affair tendered by the

Alumni Association of this city to the Western Association of Princeton Clubs, and the gathering last night was composed of representatives from the East, the West, the North and the South, and from all classes from '41 to '91.

Judge O. B. Brown, of Dayton, O.,[1] acted as toastmaster and introduced President Wilson, who spoke on "The College, and Its Value to Society." President Wilson is a magnificent speaker, and he treated his subject with a clearness and logic that time and time again filled the banquet hall with the reverberating echoes of applause. He spoke of the differences between the university and the technical school and the needs and demands of the world of today. In referring to the fact that the heads of great institutions are in few instances thorough college-bred men, he said that you can make a man like Charles M. Schwab President of the United States Steel Corporation, but he leads only the result of work of college-bred men, who toiled and studied with their knowledge to make his position possible.

He referred to the education as it is received by some today, and said, as an instance, he would not give diplomas to many of the graduates of our law schools who get them upon their ability to memorize old cases and not to think for themselves and their equipment to meet new conditions. Such he characterized as "rope" ["rote"] lawyers, and he said that if he gave such a lawyer a diploma he would feel guilty of giving an award to a quack.[2]

Printed in the Cincinnati *Commercial Tribune*, May 3, 1903; one editorial heading omitted.

[1] Oren Britt Brown, Princeton 1876, Judge of the Court of Common Pleas, Second District of the State of Ohio.

[2] There is a brief WWhw outline of this address, dated May 2, 1903, in WP, DLC.

A News Report of a Talk to the Cincinnati Y.M.C.A.

[May 4, 1903]

Before an audience of several hundred men, young and old, President Woodrow Wilson, of the Princeton University, yesterday spoke at Sinton Hall, in the Y.M.C.A. Building. The address, as announced, was to young men, with no particular subject, but the twenty-minute talk that the distinguished educator gave was of a nature that could be only beneficial to all who heard him. Dr. Wilson was introduced by Judge Ferdinand Jelke, who announced him as one of the men whose business it is to create active, energetic and real young Christian Americans.

The reception accorded Dr. Wilson was evidence of the esteem felt for him in this city. His remarks, while general, were along the line that the mere material prosperity should not be the aim of the young man of today. He pointed out in eloquent manner the truth that the noblest attribute of man is self-sacrifice. The man who serves most and loves most the noble things of life, the speaker said, will bring out of himself most of what is noble and true. He urged self-sacrifice instead of material gain, pointing out that real contentment and happiness are not from outside circumstances, but from within. Selfishness was characterized as one of the greatest evils, and always unsatisfactory. The deepest and noblest self-indulgence, the speaker said, is always the highest self-sacrifice.

While the address was supposed to be for men only, so much interest was there in what President Wilson might have to say that a number of women also attended the meeting. Yesterday he was the guest of Harlan Cleveland, and this morning he starts for Chicago, where he is to deliver an address.

Printed in the Cincinnati *Commercial Tribune*, May 4, 1903; editorial headings omitted.

To Ellen Axson Wilson

My own darling,   Chicago, 4 May, 1903

I left Glendale, a suburb of Cincinnati, where I took tea with Mr. Harlan Cleveland and a classmate of his of '85, at half-past nine last night, and reached Chicago at 7.30 this morning. There is nothing on the programme to-day in the speaking kind. I take luncheon at the University Club with the Joneses[1] and a pleasant group of gentlemen whom I have met before, and there is to be a little dining here this evening at which, I am promised, I am to meet some interesting people whom I have not met before. The meeting of the Twentieth Century Club at which I am to speak is to take place to-morrow evening. I find that I need not stop in Pittsburgh on my way back. I shall leave here, therefore, on Wednesday at noon and be in Princeton the next afternoon I cannot say just when, I hope about half-past four—two days sooner than I expected. Isnt that delightful? To-morrow will be my last letter day—to-morrow's letter will be followed by my*self*! Ah, how happy I shall be! The mere sight of you, the mere touch of your lips will rest me and refresh me enough to blot out all the fatigues of the trip. Its *longings* I do not wish to have wholly blotted out. They reveal to me so much of myself and reveal to me so exactly the seats of my happiness! They all centre on you. They discover to me the essential secrets of my life, the grounds, the immutable grounds, of my love. I wish I had some language in which to interpret them to you!

My day went off as scheduled yesterday. I was recognized and palavered at church, lunched with an Episcopalian dominie of '87, spoke (at a greater cost of strength than any alumni or lecture function demands) at the Y.M.C.A., and then took an hour and a quarter ride on the trolley to Glendale.

To-day I am well and hearty, thank you. Your letter has made my heart sing, and I am in all things

Your own   Woodrow

ALS (WC, NjP).
¹ That is, David Benton Jones and Thomas Davies Jones.

From Ellen Axson Wilson

My own darling,   Princeton   May 4, 1903

I did not find any free time to write yesterday as I had hoped,—thought I would be able to do it in the evening, while the Bishop preached at Trinity,¹ but Mr. McEwan² did not go to church so I could not leave him. I am writing instead just after breakfast hoping to catch the usual train.

The Bishop turned out a splendid fellow,—a genuine *man*, th[r]ough and through, with no nonsense about him. His sermon was good and sensible, manly and straightforward, but neither intellectual nor moving. He preached entirely without notes. I rather think the boys liked it very much. He is a superb looking man, very large and deep-chested, with fine head and extraordinarily handsome face of the square Roman type, massive yet at the same time very finely chiselled. He was a missionary bishop in the Dakotas for some years; when he mentioned that I said, laughingly, "why, you might be the original of Owen Wister's 'Bishop,'³—you look the part!" and he confessed that he was! I was quite interested, and pleased at having made so good a guess. Wister's bishop is quite his best character—very strong and manly,—meeting the rough men on their own ground as it were, and winning their affection, yet deeply devout. I am sorry you missed him; he seems to have the most intense interest in *you*; you would be amused at the innumerable questions he asked about you. He was very easy to entertain because he is so simply and sincerely interested in everything and especially *everybody*. Dr. Shields and Dr. McEwan were at dinner Saturday night, and Paul Vandyke and Mr. Baker[4] came afterward. After church Mr. Vandyke walked with him about the campus &c. I had Mr. Fine to dinner and then he and the Bishop took a long walk and were immensely pleased with each other. Mr. Dullas[5] was at tea and Mr. West called after church, his train did not arrive in time for him to come to tea. Dr. McEwan is staying here too,—leaves after his trustee meeting today.

It was very good to get such direct news of you from Mr. West. He says you are looking *very* well and not at all tired. *How* good it is to have actually reached the last week of this long separation! I can't tell you, darling, how indescribably eager I am to see you. It seems a month. I love you, dear, beyond all words—I am altogether   Your own   Eileen.

I am *so* glad you did not sit out the parade! Madge comes today and possibly Stockton. Havn't heard from him again about the Va. plan.

ALS (WC, NjP).
    [1] Bishop Talbot preached at the evening service in Trinity Episcopal Church in Princeton after preaching in Marquand Chapel in the morning of May 3.
    [2] The Rev. Dr. William Leonard McEwan, pastor of the Third Presbyterian Church of Pittsburgh, who was in Princeton for the commencement meeting of the Board of Directors of Princeton Theological Seminary.
    [3] The "Bishop of Wyoming" appears in "How Lin McLean Went East," the first sketch in Owen Wister's *Lin McLean* (New York and London, 1898). Bishop Talbot, who had served as missionary bishop to Wyoming and Idaho (not the Dakotas) from 1887 to 1898, was indeed the model for Wister's bishop. See Talbot's autobiographical work, *My People of the Plains* (New York and London, 1906), p. 137.
    [4] The Rev. Dr. Alfred Brittin Baker, Princeton 1861, rector of Trinity Episcopal Church in Princeton from 1866 to 1914.
    [5] Joseph Heatly Dulles, Librarian of Princeton Theological Seminary.

To Ellen Axson Wilson

My own darling,   Chicago, 5 May, 1903
    So I am not to find you at home, after all, when I get back, but you are to be in Virginia with Stock! Ah well: all right. Of course you are doing perfectly right, and I should be a selfish churl should I complain. I will be unselfish and be glad that poor Stock. is so blessed. I hope it will not be wrong to envy him, though. *That* I *can*not help!
    Last night we had a most agreeable dinner. May I write here a list of the guests? Mr. and Mrs. Cyrus McCormick, Mr. and Mrs. Harold McCormick,[1] Mr. & Mrs. Waller ('79),[2] Mr. and

Mrs. Professor Hale (University of Chicago),[3] Mr. and Mrs. Martin,[4] Mr. and Mrs. Slosson Thompson,[5] Mr. Brownell, the critic,[6]—besides the Joneses.[7] A congenial and even jolly company, with lots of good talk.

This morning, immediately after breakfast, I went out to Edgewater, found Jessie and Helen, and spent nearly three hours with them, quietly and most delightfully. Then I came into town again and took lunch with a group of old acquaintances at the Chicago Club,—so that here I am (4 o'clock), writing my last letter till I reach home and find out what your Virginia address is. I dare say you are there, or on your way there, as I write. There is no further news. To-night the Twentieth Century Club, and then freedom to turn to the neglected work at home.

Jessie and Helen sent you messages big with love. *My* love for you may be the death of me yet.

Your own   Woodrow

ALS (WC, NjP).

[1] Harold Fowler McCormick, Princeton 1895, a younger brother of the second Cyrus H. McCormick. His wife was Edith Rockefeller McCormick, a daughter of John D. Rockefeller.

[2] James Breckinridge Waller and Elizabeth Wallace Waller. He was in the insurance and real estate business in Chicago.

[3] William Gardner Hale and Harriet Knowles Swinburne Hale. He was Professor and Head of the Department of Latin at the University of Chicago.

[4] The Editors have been unable to identify them.

[5] Slason Thompson and Julia Dickinson Watson Thompson. He was a journalist of Chicago.

[6] Probably William Crary Brownell, art and literary critic and editor and literary advisor for Charles Scribner's Sons of New York.

[7] He was referring only to the two Jones brothers. David B. Jones was a widower, and Thomas D. Jones never married.

A News Report of a Speech in Chicago

[May 6, 1903]

WHY OFFICE SEEKS ROOSEVELT.
Dr. Woodrow Wilson Tells Twentieth Century Club in Lecturing on Patriotism.

"President Roosevelt owes his high position to the fact that he was a politician who did not want to hold office," said Dr. Woodrow Wilson last evening in addressing the annual meeting of the Twentieth Century club in the Fine Arts building. The subject of the address was "Patriotism."

"Roosevelt was a thorn in the side of the politicians," continued the speaker. "He attended their meetings and became one of them, but if things did not suit him he said so. He was so sure he knew how it ought to be done and he was so much trouble to the politicians that they gave him a position to get rid of him.

"If you think you know so much about it go in and try it your-self," they said.

"If men would study politics, not striving for office, it would change the face of affairs all over the country. The danger of our age is not partisanship, but that our thoughtful men will belong to no party. Don't form yourself into a third party. Don't isolate yourself. Go into the arena and take your active part."

Printed in the *Chicago Daily Tribune*, May 6, 1903.

To the Secretaries of Various Classes of Princeton University

[Dear Sir:]   [Princeton, N. J., c. May 10, 1903]

I take the liberty, as president of the University, of writing to you about a matter which I am sure you will agree with me in regarding as of greatest importance to all of us. Your class, I am glad to hear, is to have a reunion at commencement. The only thing which gives any of us serious concern in connection with class reunions is the use of beer and liquors at class headquarters. It makes the headquarters the center of a sort of excitement, carried far into the night[,] which creates in the minds of the hundreds of visitors who flock to Princeton at commencement time a very false impression of the meaning and significance of the whole season, a false impression concerning the alumni themselves. It creates, too, as those of us know who live here the year round, a false and unpleasant impression in the minds of the undergraduates also and breeds a serious demoralization among the more reckless and susceptible of them.

It is distressing to say anything to mar the success and fine loyalty of class reunions. They are to every alumnus one of the most delightful and characteristic features of our present day commencements, and we are all alike interested in putting them beyond criticism in order that they may be a permanent element among the enjoyments of the commencement season. I am sure that no one with right feelings would wish to put any unreason-able or puritanical restraints upon them or take away from them any feature of the real, even thoughtless, enjoyment; but the way in which liquors are used obviously involves the good name both of the University and of the several classes.

Several ways of controlling the matter have been suggested. The most effectual is the entire exclusion of drinking from the class headquarters, so that members of the class may make it a place of gathering but not a drinking place. Several classes have tried this with perfect success. It involves little inconvenience to men who want to drink, because they can easily be supplied elsewhere, and it avoids the serious abuses of "free beer." Another is to surround the use of liquor at the class headquarters with careful restrictions. No undergraduate ought ever to be invited or permitted to drink there; that is the minimum restraint required by prudence and consideration for the morals of the young men. General invitations to come to headquarters for drinks can be avoided and only individuals here and there invited, the use of the place for that purpose being confined for the most part to members of the class. Various ways of minimizing the dangers of the practice occur to every man who has ever had any experience in such matters.

It is not my purpose to suggest specific measures of reform or restriction but I have the matter very much at heart, and I wish very earnestly to call your attention to it, in the hope that, in conferences with the executive committee of your class you may be able to do something effectual to safeguard the reputation of the great institution to which we have all pledged our deepest affection and loyalty. I know that I need not urge you to give it your most careful consideration.

Respectfully and cordially Yours,   Woodrow Wilson

73, 78, 83, 88, 93, 94, 96, 98, 00, 02.[1]

Transcript of WWshLS (WP, DLC).
[1] The classes holding reunions in 1903.

To Walter Augustus Wyckoff

Princeton, New Jersey.
My dear Professor Wyckoff: 12 May, 1903.

Perhaps you have already heard from Daniels the result of my consideration of your request for an extended leave of absence.[1]

I am sincerely sorry that you are disappointed in the matter of Mr. Katzenbach,[2] and was a little surprised also until I read your letter[3] and was clear in the recollection that in the conversation we had before you sailed we had found ourselves entirely of one mind in the matter of his retention, agreeing that though a man of ability, he had not the refinement and the qualities as a man, which made it desirable that we should offer him a permanent place on the University staff, and I thought it only fair to come to a clear understanding with him in that matter. I am sorry that he is not willing to remain another year, but I think he is taking the best course for himself.

Unfortunately no other man is in sight who is capable of doing the work. Daniels and I will certainly do all we can to find a suitable man; and if adequate provision can be made for giving courses in some degree equivalent to those which you would give if you were here, I shall be very glad indeed to ask the Trustees to extend your leave of absence. If it should prove impossible to do so, I hardly see how I could consistently with my duty to the University advise you to remain longer than the opening of the next college year.

I know how serious a matter this is for you, and I need not tell you that only with the greatest reluctance and under the pressure of real necessity shall I come to this conclusion; but I dare not leave the department at 6's and 7's as it would be left, should we be unable to find a substitute. Either Daniels or I will keep you informed as to the progress of our search, and I shall certainly hope to have good news for you before the college year is over.[4]

What you tell me of your work interests me very much indeed, and I shall hope that in any event what you have planned will not be seriously or permanently interferred with.

With warm regard,

Very sincerely yours,   Woodrow Wilson

TLS (WC, NjP).

[1] Wyckoff, who taught the sociology courses in the Department of Political Economy and Sociology, was abroad at this time, studying conditions of the working classes in Great Britain and on the Continent.

[2] Edward Lawrence Katzenbach, Princeton 1900, Instructor in Political Economy, 1902-1903.

[3] Wyckoff's letter is missing.

[4] Wyckoff did get his second year of leave. Arthur Cleveland Hall, a recent Ph.D. graduate from Columbia, was brought in to serve as Instructor in Economics and Sociology for the year 1903-1904.

A News Report

[May 15, 1903]

LAST MEETING OF PHILADELPHIAN SOCIETY
ADDRESSED BY PRESIDENT WILSON.

The last weekly meeting of the Philadelphian Society, held last night in Murray Hall, was addressed by President Woodrow Wilson. The subject of the talk taken from the eighth chapter of Romans, was contained in the text "To be carnally minded is death; to be spiritually minded is life and peace." Taking the word "spiritual," President Wilson showed first in what way this state of mind caused life in contrast with death. He showed that life itself is not of the body but a result of a condition of the mind. Taking nature as an example, he explained that it is not the outward appearance of the beauties around us that bring us pleasure, but the ideas and feelings they produce, the spirit present in them.

In referring to peace as a result of spiritual-mindedness, President Wilson said it is only the right adjustment and perception of the spiritual faculties that can bring peace. Men who reject Christ find no zest or satisfaction in doing their work, since they have no positive conception of their hopes and destinies. Such ideas blind a man's soul for all time and prevent his breathing the air of reality and diminish his realization of peace.

President Wilson, in his closing remarks, spoke of the peace resulting from a reading of the Scriptures.

Printed in the *Daily Princetonian*, May 15, 1903.

To Henry Hopkins Kelsey[1]

My dear Mr. Kelsey: Princeton, New Jersey. 15 May, 1903.

I have received and read with the greatest gratification the kind letter signed by yourself, Dr. [Melancthon W.] Jacobus, and Mr. Coffin,[2] inviting me to accept an election as a member of the corporation of "The Hartford School of Religious Pedagogy."[3] You have certainly bestowed upon me an honor which I very greatly appreciate, and I wish most unaffectedly that it were possible for me to accept it.

But I have so clear a conviction of what a man ought to do who accepts such a position, that it does not seem to me that I ought, for the present at least while the duties of my office remain so multitudinous and so engrossing, to undertake the responsibility of labors elsewhere. My absorption in my tasks here is so great, and must for a long time remain so great, that I am certain not to have the time to perform the duties you ask of me with conscientious thoroughness, and I must beg in the cirsumstances [circumstances] that you will excuse me. I could not get my own consent to be merely a nominal member of a body which will have such important work to do.

Very sincerely yours,   Woodrow Wilson

TLS (CtHC).

[1] Pastor of the Fourth Congregational Church of Hartford, Conn.

[2] Fulton Johnson Coffin, Professor of Old Testament at the Hartford School of Religious Pedagogy, soon to become Principal of the Presbyterian Theological College in San Fernando, Trinidad.

[3] This letter is missing. The Hartford School of Religious Pedagogy was an outgrowth of the Bible Normal College of Springfield, Mass., founded in 1885 to train Sunday School workers and pastors' assistants. It was moved to Hartford in 1903 where it was located near, and closely associated with, the Hartford Theological Seminary. The Bible Normal College was incorporated under its new name at the session of the Connecticut legislature in January 1903. It was this incorporation which required the election of new members of the corporation. Curtis Manning Geer, *The Hartford Theological Seminary, 1834-1934* (Hartford, Conn., 1934), pp. 190-201.

An Interview

[May 16, 1903]

Dr. Wilson has given the following interview to The Weekly, in response to a request for the most vivid impressions of his Western trip: "Two impressions remain with me which seem to take precedence of all the rest. In the first place, I found the greatest enthusiasm everywhere, and it seemed to be an enthusiasm the sources of which were very deep. The men evidently came together from a real, spontaneous love for Princeton, and while they were together seemed like a genuine band of brothers, so that my trip was like moving from one family group to another. In the second place, what most impressed and delighted me was to find that what the men who came together at the various gatherings desired was not light, playful after-dinner speaking, but a serious discussion of Princeton's plans and ideals. They wanted to hear about the matters of serious moment to the University; what she needed, what she meant to do, and how she meant to do it. They responded to nothing so quickly as to what touched upon the deeper meaning of Princeton's life and the methods by which she was to serve the country as a center of intellectual enlightenment and sound principles of conduct."

Printed in the *Princeton Alumni Weekly*, III (May 16, 1903), 529-30.

A News Report of an Address to the Newark Alumni

[May 16, 1903]

PRINCETON MEN HONOR WILSON.

Something of the very spirit which its particular guest of honor dwelt so proudly upon pervaded the annual dinner of the Princeton Club in the New Auditorium last night. That guest was President Woodrow Wilson, of the university, and the function was the first real chance the local alumni had had to entertain him since his ascension to Dr. Patton's position. The spirit showed itself at every one of the twenty round tables that covered the floor, and left comfortable room for good service. In proportionate measure it disported at the crescent-shaped board, under the shadow of the proscenium arch, where sat the speakers and the invited guests. . . .

When Dr. Wilson got up he had first to listen to a specially dedicated chorus which had during the dinner been going the rounds of the tables. This time every table and the guests in the gallery took it up. It followed the air of "Mr. Dooley." There were four verses, and the particularly significant last ran in this fashion:

> "Her educated graduates
>   Are Princeton's special pride;
> To turn out just good business men
> Nassau has [n]ever tried.
> But tho' we all wear glasses,
>   And look sadly underfed,
> We think in choosing Wilson
> That we showed our business head."

Chorus—
> "For Woodrow Wilson, Woodrow Wilson,
>   He's one of us, a son of Nassau Hall.
> It's Woodrow Wilson, Woodrow Wilson,
> It's Wilson, Wilson, Wilson, that is all!"

Various other forms of greeting delayed considerably the inception of the speech, but when he could begin Dr. Wilson said:

"I don't know many of your faces, but your manners are certainly familiar. I don't know that I can countenance great levity now that I have been lifted to the august position I occupy, though I saw much of it and managed to live through it for many years. I suppose that now I should look upon it with a certain amount of condescension, but somehow I can't exactly feel that way. It is a very difficult matter to educate everybody. Just how difficult I can hardly say. There is a growing disinclination to be educated and there have got to be seasons of the day when I really don't care if anybody is educated. If they don't want to be it is their funeral, but after all there isn't going to be any funeral at Princeton.

"I find that there is a very consistent difference between what men demand and what men need. I find that where a good many men demand good booze, that what they really want is good advice. The great trouble in this matter of educating people, I find, is that there is a tendency to reduce education to a commercial basis. Only recently I heard a distinguished educator refer to education as a commodity. Now I dissent from that proposition, at any rate, so far as to take the position that it is not the business of education to study the opinions of people who don't know anything about education, who never had an education and would not know one if they saw it. They are not the kind of people we should go to for advice. But I would not be misunderstood. There are, of course, a great many kinds of educations besides university educations, that are valuable and indispensable, but our business as graduates of a university is to determine just what is a university education.

"On my recent Western trip I visited two or three of the most distinguished State universities in the land,[1] and I found there a distinct growth of commercialism. And as a result of continued observation I say that technical education is swamping us, this being forbidden to take things that are characteristic of a university. Why, the heads of two or three of these State universities I have referred to tell me that they envy the man who is at the head of an institution where he can follow the endowed inclinations and purposes of the real university life and curriculum. I believe in technical and in industrial education to its proper extent and in its place, but I do say that technical skill is the business of the employe and not of the employer. It is not given to many men to lead, but it must, however, be given to many men to understand, else we would come upon catastrophe.

"We must be guided and controlled by men with minds that understand the whole world as a single community, and at the same time are filled with the idea that the world is bigger than a single understanding. Why, some of the least intelligent men I've met have been men whose minds are confined to a single thought. They are the men I'm afraid of in almost any capacity, commercial or governmental. Recently I met such a one and he asked me why we at Princeton did not get an endowment to erect on the campus—the most beautiful campus in the world—a great flagstaff to be endowed sufficiently to fly silk flags of the nation through good weather and bad. His idea was that, there being so much labor troubles, with the disposition to riot growing out of them, his ever-flying flag scheme would serve as a symbol to disaffected ones, of the majesty of the law.

"I told him that we constantly flew a national emblem from the top of one of our most honored buildings, and I asked him if he didn't think it better that our university, or any other, should be endowed for the study of the social situation and the understanding of the spirit of law and order: to have a university a place of power rather than a place where the flag of the United States flew as a symbol of law and order but was not understood."

Continuing, Dr. Wilson spoke of a general tendency among universities, nowadays, to imitate, to run after each other like sheep, as he similized. It was time, he thought, that each institution determined for itself what it stood for. The time had come, in his opinion, when a university should apply its money and brains to something in particular rather than everything in general. He asked his hearers to look at the catalogue curriculum of almost any university and see if it didn't answer to the description of a miscellany rather than of a system.

"When I was in Cincinnati recently an alumnus asked me what the West could best do for Princeton. I told him that the best service any part of the country could render would be to stop its miscellaneous endeavors to turn every boy's steps toward Princeton, to pause and consider first what the pace was and then to send only the choice spirit, the most useful all-around Christian gentleman, who has the stuff to make the place. I don't want any better description of the sort to send to Princeton than Cecil Rhodes gives in his provisions for Oxford scholarships. He said that in the first place competitors must be scholarly boys, but boys with red blood in their veins; competent boys who expect leadership and achievements; boys capable of characters larger than are needful to expend on their particular breadwinning cots [lots]. Boys that have that spirit will perpetuate the spirit of Princeton."

As the speaker resumed his seat there were loud demands for "Old Nassau," and, in keeping with the oldest traditions, every one, upstairs and down, as they had sung "My Country, 'Tis of Thee" half an hour before, stood and for about the ninth time went through the favorite Princeton anthem. There were several triple cheers, ending in a repetition of the "Old Nassau" refrain.

Printed in the *Newark Evening News*, May 16, 1903; some editorial headings omitted.

[1] The Universities of Michigan, Wisconsin, and Minnesota.

To Cyrus Hall McCormick

My dear Cyrus: Princeton, New Jersey. 18 May, 1903.

Mr. Bayard Henry has just sent me the $100 which you were generous enough to contribute to the payment of Chapel preachers. I am sincerely obliged to you, and am sorry that it should have been necessary to call upon you in this matter, all the more because you are so ready to be generous.

Very cordially yours,   Woodrow Wilson

TLS (C. H. McCormick Papers, WHi).

To Robert Randolph Henderson

My dear Bob: Princeton, New Jersey. 25 May, 1903.

I have just heard with the greatest distress of your mother's[1] death, and write to assure you of my heartfelt sympathy.

I know that the last months of her life were months of suffering, and it may be that her death was a release for her, but I know that that can hardly lessen the burden of your grief. My own recent loss enables me to realize very keenly what this separation must mean to you, and I can assure you, my dear fellow, that you have my sympathy in a sort which is very deep and genuine. May God bless you and comfort you.

Affectionately yours,   Woodrow Wilson

TLS (WC, NjP).
[1] Rebecca Magruder (Mrs. George) Henderson.

A News Item

[May 26, 1903]

MONDAY NIGHT CLUB MEETING.

President Wilson addressed the final meeting of the year of the Monday Night Club[1] last evening at 9 Lower Pyne. He took as his subject "Sir Henry Maine, a Lawyer with a Style," and first dwelt at some length upon the various events that took place in the life of Sir Henry Maine, tracing their influence upon his works. President Wilson then spoke with some detail about the works of Sir Henry Maine and their importance in the field of contemporary literature.[2]

Printed in the *Daily Princetonian*, May 26, 1903.
[1] About this organization, see n. 1 to the news report printed at Oct. 9, 1894, Vol. 9.

² He apparently read them the lecture on Sir Henry Maine printed at Feb. 25, 1898, Vol. 10, and published in the *Atlantic Monthly*, LXXXII (Sept. 1898), 363-74.

To Charles Williston McAlpin

My dear Mr. McAlpin: Princeton, New Jersey. 27 May, 1903.

. . . I hand you also the enclosed letter from the United States Philippine Commission. I see no possible objection to the admission of such Filipinos as may be sent us, and of course we should be willing to make the same concessions in the matter of tuition to them as to others in need of assistance. Will you not be kind enough to reply to the letter?

Very truly yours,   Woodrow Wilson

TLS (McAlpin File, UA, NjP).

To Elijah Richardson Craven

My dear Dr. Craven: Princeton, New Jersey. 27 May, 1903.

I find that next week is much complicated for me by an engagement to be present at an important celebration at the Mercersburg School.[1] This renders it necessary for me to exercise some ingenuity in finding times at which it will be possible for me to meet the several Committees of the Board.

I write therefore to ask if you will not be kind enough to call a meeting of the Curriculum Committee here in Princeton for Friday afternoon, June 5th, at 3.15? The only other time that seems available in view of imperative engagements is Saturday evening after dinner, but I fear that that would prove a very inconvenient time for you. It would be a real convenience to me if the meeting can be called at [t]he hour on Friday which I have suggested. I have a good deal of very important business to lay before the Committee, and am anxious to find a time when I shall be able to present it fully.[2]

With warm regards,

Sincerely yours,   Woodrow Wilson

TLS (WWP, UA, NjP).
¹ Wilson was to participate in the celebration on June 3, 1903, of the tenth anniversary of Mercersburg Academy (before 1893, it had been a college) and of the headmastership of William Mann Irvine, Princeton 1888. Wilson took part in the ground-breaking ceremony for a new dormitory during the day and spoke in the evening on "What It Means to Be an American." See the editorial printed at June 5, 1903, and H. M. J. Klein, *A Century of Education at Mercersburg, 1836-1936* (Lancaster, Pa., 1936), pp. 494, 500.
² The committee's report to the Board of Trustees is printed at June 5, 1903.

From Grover Cleveland

My dear President Wilson: Princeton   May 27, 1903

I am asking the members of the Committee to recommend Standing Committees of the Trustees of Princeton University, to meet next Tuesday June 2d at 11.30 A.M., in the University Library rooms.

Can you not meet with us?

                                        Grover Cleveland   Chairman

ALS (WP, DLC).

From Cornelius Cuyler Cuyler, with Enclosure

My dear Woodrow: New York. May 27/03

The enclosed letter was handed to me by John Kilpatrick who is one of our younger alumni and deeply interested in all that pertains to the University. Naturally I do not feel competent to pass on the matter but it seems to me that it is one which merits more than a passing notice.

We are preparing to close up the Dormitory matter on the basis of $105,000. after much negotiation and revising of bids. With extras the cost may run to $110,000. or even $115,000. It is going to be a great labor to get in this money and I have written Cyrus very fully my views stating that I must depend on the loyal support of all our men in this large undertaking. I refer now entirely to the direct negotiations with architect, contractors &c., the bulk of which must of necessity fall on me. Hoping to see you next week I am with kind regards

                                  Yours faithfully   C C Cuyler

ALS (WP, DLC).

ENCLOSURE

William Belden Reed, Jr., and John Douglas Kilpatrick to the Princeton Board of Trustees

Gentlemen: New York, May 15, 1903.

The under signed Graduates in Civil Engineering, at Princeton,[1] desire to call the attention of the Authorities to conditions at present prevailing in that Course, in the hope that something can be done to improve the same.

We desire to quote the following figures, taken from the Catalogue, which will show the increase in the numbers taking the C.E. Course, during the past two years.

1902—Seniors 12   Juniors 30   Soph. 40   Freshmen 76
1903—   "   27   "   32   "   39   "   68

We learn that for the use of this number of men, there are now, 8 Levels, 9 Transits, 7 Compasses, in good condition. In addition to the number of men above, there are now 46 B.S. Juniors, and 8 or 10 Academic Students, electing the Course in Geodesy. This number of instruments for use by so many men, makes it necessary, that such a number of men, be assigned to each instrument, that no man can receive the proper drill in the use of any instrument. We have therefore decided to request that the number of Transits be increased from 9 to 14, as soon as possible, and that two new additional Levels be bought to satisfy an immediate need. And that this number be increased from year to year, to replace those which are constantly giving out, and to provide for increased wants, so that within a year or two the Course shall be sufficiently equipped to allow each man to receive his proper instruction.

These instruments we estimate would cost about $1,000.00., and we trust that these suggestions may be given due consideration with the result that we desire.

In addition to this equipment in Geodesy, there are for the Course in Constructions and Strength of Material, only two testing machines, one for cement and one for testing small wire. The Course in Construction due to latter day practice in the use of concrete and steel is lamentably weak, as there is no opportunity for the Professor in charge to go into these most important features of Engineering practice, for lack of testing facilities.

There should be provided for this Course sufficient apparatus to give the Students the drill they need in making tests in various Construction materials.

We have also noticed that certain Professors in the Engineering Course have as high as 36 Exercises per week between Class Room and Field Work. It can be very readily seen, that this leaves very little time for out side work and investigation, which is absolutely necessary in these days, for a man to keep up with the times. We also find that certain Professors, in spite of this increased amount of work, receive the same salary as they did as instructors. It seems to us, that they should receive such an increase in salary, as to compensate them properly for their work.

The Civil Engineering Course at Princeton is doing good work for the University. About fifteen years ago this Course ranked twenty sixth in the estimation of the Pennsylvania Engineers. Today this same Company goes first to Princeton to fill any vacancies which it may have. This condition of affairs is due primarily to the fact that the Course in Geodesy is one of the best offered in any College in this Country, and in a vast majority of cases the Student upon graduation finds his first employment in the application of the principles taught in that Course. This Course is also made effective by the fact that the Professor in charge of it[2] allows himself to come more closely in contact with the individuals in his Classes. But this is only one feature of an Engineer's preparation. He should be carefully prepared in all the other branches including the fundimental practice in the operation of a steam engine.

We believe that we have stated sufficiently some of the matters which require immediate attention, so that this Course which is the only one in the University, that enables a man immediately upon graduation to earn living wages, should be given the proper amount of consideration.[3]

A list of some of the recent Graduates, with their respective positions might be compiled to show that many are advancing rapidly, and are in a fair way to establish records for themselves.

Respectfully yours,   William B. Reed Jr. '96.
John D. Kilpatrick '96

TLS (WP, DLC).
[1] Of the Class of 1896.
[2] Walter Butler Harris, Professor of Geodesy.
[3] There is no evidence in the documentary record that their recommendations were discussed or acted upon. Perhaps the needed equipment was given by a private benefactor.

From George Howe III

Dear Uncle Woodrow,   Oxford[1] 28 May 1903.

Just a note to thank you for letting me know so promptly of my good fortune in N. C., and more particularly for all you have done to secure it for me. Mother sent me Pres. Venable's letter, and, so far as I can judge, it seems almost a settled thing that I am to have the position. At least, I cannot help counting on it as a certainty. I hope I am not laying myself open to disappointment.[2]

I shall leave it to you to imagine with what joy I received the news, & how much it excited me. I am very eager to begin work and put myself to the test to see whether I am worthy of your backing and expectations. I am a little tired too of only preparing myself, instead of doing something more active, so to speak. At the same time I confess to a sort of dread of the beginning and fear of the responsibility of being answerable for all the Latin of the department. But of this & many other things, later, when I come home.

Did Mother write you about my suggestion to take the girls South with me?[3] I sail by the Barbarossa on June 14th & reach New York—if on time—June 24th. I shall stop in N. Y. a day and night to see Wilson[4] & then run over to Princeton, provided you will have a few minutes to spare in between times. I thought that, if you have not decided to send the girls South before my arrival, you might let them go with me. I could look after baggage, tickets, changes & perhaps make them more comfortable in other ways. I hope they will not have gone before I get there.

I have only two weeks more in Oxford, and each day I grow more impatient to be off. Sometimes it is all I can do to sit still at all. But it will be over at last & very soon I can thank you in person. My best love to all, yourself very much included from

Your affectionate nephew   George H.

If, for any reason, you wish to have a letter reach me before I leave New York, you can safely address it either c/o Wilson (746 St. Nicholas Ave.) or to the German Lloyd steamer Barbarossa.

ALS (WP, DLC).
  [1] Howe had been studying at Oxford for several months, after receiving the Ph.D. from the University of Halle.
  [2] He was not disappointed. He was soon appointed Professor of the Latin Language and Literature at the University of North Carolina.
  [3] That is, the Wilson girls. They were to stay with Annie Wilson Howe at Skyland, N. C., near Asheville, while the Wilsons were abroad during the summer.
  [4] His brother, James Wilson Howe, a clerk in Baker & Williams, bonded warehouses, New York.

To Melancthon Williams Jacobus

My dear Dr. Jacobus: Princeton, New Jersey.   1 June, 1903.

I am very glad to avail myself of the suggestion of your letter of May 25, and name a member of our Faculty for membership of the Corporation of the Hartford School of Religious Pedagogy. I think much the best man would be Professor John Grier Hibben. His influence and usefulness grow every year, and I do not think that the School could have a more useful adviser or a man better suited to turn students in its direction. It gives me the greatest pleasure to nominate such a man. I do so of course with his consent.

It interests me very much that we should have the opportunity to connect Princeton with the interesting pland [plans] you are making for the School.[1] I wish it the most substantial success, and shall hope myself indirectly to be of use to it.

Very cordially yours,   Woodrow Wilson

TLS (CtHC).
[1] See WW to H. H. Kelsey, May 15, 1903, n. 3.

To Alfred James Pollock McClure

My dear McClure: Princeton, New Jersey, 1 June, 1903.

I am sorry to have been so long in reporting on the matter of assistance to your sons.[1]

I have been disappointed in one or two of the men I applied to, but $125 has come in which I take pleasure in sending you. I send it in two separate cheques simply for convenience of account.

I confidently hope to be able to send you at least as much more in the autumn, and sincerely hope that this amount though small will be welcome relief to your strained finances. I trust that Mrs. McClure is better,[2] and that your domestic horizon is clearing up of difficulties. It gives me real pleasure to do this, I only wish I could conveniently do more.

With warm regard,

Always faithfully yours,   Woodrow Wilson

TCL (WP, DLC).
[1] About this matter, see A. J. P. McClure to WW, June 10, 1902, Vol. 12.
[2] Mrs. McClure had recently undergone a brain operation.

From Cyrus Fogg Brackett

Dear sir: Princeton, New Jersey, June 1 1903.

At the close of the present academic year I shall have completed thirty years of service in this institution. In a few days thereafter I shall have reached the age of seventy years. In consideration of this latter fact I feel constrained to place my resignation of the office of instruction which I have so long held in your hands asking that the Board of Trustees deal with it as seems best for the interests of the University.

This occasion appears to be a proper one on which to express my gratitude for the kindly consideration which I have always received at the hands of the Trustees and for the confidence which they have reposed im [in] me.

Very sincerely yours.   C. F. Brackett.

TLS (WP, DLC).

To George Franklin Edmunds

My dear Sir: Princeton, New Jersey. 2 June, 1903.

In reply to your letter of May 29th, informing me of what was done by a minority of the Committee of the American Philosophical Society charged with the duty of preparing a plan for celebrating the bi-centennial of the birth of Franklin,[1] I would say that I heartily approve of the nomination of a sub-committee made, and hope that it will go into effect.

I sincerely regret that official duties prevented my attending the meeting.   Very sincerely yours,   Woodrow Wilson

TLS (Archives, PPAmP).
[1] See WW to I. M. Hays, April 8, 1903.

From the Minutes of the Princeton University Faculty

5 p.m. June 3, 1903.

The Faculty met, the Dean presiding in the absence of the President. The minutes of the meetings of May 6 and May 28 were read and approved. . . .

A report was received from the Committee on the Course of Study, containing the following recommendations, which were adopted:

I. that Mr. L. Frederick Pease[1] be authorized to offer the following elective courses during the year 1903-1904:

    1. General History of Music: Junior Elective, two hours, Second Term.

    2. Harmony, Senior Elective, two hours, both Terms.

    3. Counterpoint, Senior Elective, two hours, Second Term.

Any modification of this arrangement to be left to the President.[2]

II. that Mr. Howard Crosby Butler be authorized to offer the following elective course:

    Architectural Drawing, Senior elective, two hours, both Terms, open only to Seniors electing Architecture 1, 2.

III. that Mr. Bayard Tuckerman[3] be authorized to offer the following elective course during the year 1903-1904:

Eighteenth Century Prose, restricted Senior Elective, two hours, Second Term.

IV. that Dr. E. G. Elliott be authorized to offer the following elective course:

History of Modern Political Theories, Senior elective, two hours, First Term.

V. that the restatement of Latin 5, 6, in the School of Science schedule, as proposed by Dr. C. A. Robinson,[4] be authorized.

VI. that Applied Chemistry 7 in the School of Science be open to Academic Seniors.

VII. that Mineralogy 17, 18 be opened in the First Term to such Academic Juniors as intend to elect Physical Geology in the Second Term.

VIII. that the University Faculty accedes to the suggestion conveyed in the letter of Professor Jacobus that Hartford Theological Seminary indicate to this University the particular courses in our Catalogue which will be of advantage to candidates for the ministry who are to pursue their theological studies in Hartford Theological Seminary. . . .

[1] Lewis Frederic Pease, Princeton 1895. After a period of ranching in the West, he studied music at Harvard, 1899-1900, and in Germany and France, 1900-1903. He was Lecturer on Music at Princeton during the academic year 1903-1904.

[2] Princeton had had several "Lecturers on Music" previously, most recently Ernest Trow Carter, Princeton 1888, who held that position and also served as organist and choirmaster from 1899 to 1901. In 1900-1901, Carter had given the first formal course in music ever offered at Princeton, a two-term junior and senior elective in harmony. However, with Carter's resignation in 1901 to become a free-lance musician in New York, music was dropped from the curriculum until Pease arrived in 1903. Apparently the experiment in offering something like a full program in music during 1903-1904 was not a success, most probably because very few students took the courses. Pease left Princeton at the end of his first year to become organist and choirmaster of the North Avenue Presbyterian Church in New Rochelle, N. Y., and no more courses in music were offered at Princeton during Wilson's presidency.

[3] Lecturer on English Literature.

[4] Charles Alexander Robinson, Instructor in Latin.

An Editorial about Wilson at the Mercersburg Academy[1]

[June 5, 1903]

WOODROW WILSON

All who were fortunate enough to be present at Keil hall at Mercersburg academy on Wednesday night [June 3] when Dr. Woodrow Wilson, president of Princeton University, delivered his address on the subject, "What it Means to Be An American," must have left with that feeling of ample satisfaction that follows a profitably spent hour. They had listened to an address that for scholarship, length, breadth, depth and originality has seldom been equaled in Franklin county.

In speaking of the "artistic temperament" Dr. Wilson said that it sounded like a useless article, and yet, he insisted, it is essential to the perfection of any work. A person with the artistic temperament is not satisfied until his work is perfectly finished and adorned. If Dr. Wilson's address on Wednesday night is a sample of his work he possesses the artistic temperament to a marked degree. It was a finished work, rounded out, complete, adorned; a perfect whole, to which, as it seemed to the careful listener, nothing remained to be added, from which nothing could be taken without marring its symmetry.

Dr. Wilson is too big a man to be measured at one sitting. Fortunately, however, what he is and what he has done are matters of such public knowledge that an estimate of him is possible. There are many men of great learning; many eminent scholars; many who can rattle off facts of history, science, religion, art; but the majority of them are utterly lacking in originality and a working knowledge of practical affairs. Was not a shining example of this large class adroitly pointed out by Dr. Wilson when he said that an exception to the good qualities of Pennsylvanians is the belief of many that the state government needs no improvement? Among the great scholars there is occasionally found one who is also an original thinker. Such a happy and useful combination is Dr. Woodrow Wilson. His scholarship is manifest in everything that he utters. His originality appears both in his thought and in his expression of it.

His idea that mankind is ruled by sentiment rather than by brain is born of deep study of humanity. As nearly as we can remember it this was one of his expressions in this connection. "It is a popular belief that the brain is monarch. It is a monarch like modern kings and queens who reign but do not govern." Here was independent originality of thought and of expression. And again, "every man is ruled by his strongest passion. Pray God that your strongest passion may be your purest."

Dr. Woodrow Wilson forces upon one the impression of that perfect balance which the vast majority of mankind lack.

Printed in the Chambersburg, Pa., *Public Opinion*, June 5, 1903.
  [1] This is the only notice extant of Wilson's address at the Mercersburg Academy on June 3, 1903.

The Curriculum Committee to the Board of Trustees of Princeton University

Princeton, New Jersey. 5 June, 1903.

Your Committee on the Curriculum would report that, at a meeting held in the University Library on Friday, the fifth of June, 1903, the following actions were taken, which are hereby recommended to the Board for its adoption:

That Dr. Max F. Blau, of Brooklyn, New York, be elected Assistant Professor of German, in the place of Professor Willard Humphreys, deceased.

That Mr. Fred Neher and Dr. Alexander Hamilton Phillips, now Assistant Professors, be advanced to the rank of Professors.

That the following new courses and modifications of existing courses, recommended by the University Faculty, be authorized:

I That Mr. L. Frederick Pease be authorized to offer the following elective courses during the year 1903-1904:

1. *General History of Music*
   Junior Elective, two hours, second term.
2. *Harmony*
   Senior Elective, two hours, both terms.
3. *Counterpoint*
   Senior Elective, two hours, second term.

Any modification of this arrangement to be left with the President.

II That Mr. Howard Crosby Butler be authorized to offer the following elective course:

Architectural Drawing
   Senior Elective, two hours, both terms.

Open only to seniors electing *Architectute [Architecture]* 1, 2.

III That Mr. Bayard Tuckerman be authorized to offer the following elective course during the year 1903-1904:

Eighteenth Century Prose
   Restricted Senior Elective, two hours, second term.

IV That Dr. E. G. Elliott be authorized to offer the following elective course:

History of Modern Political Theories
   Senior elective, two hours, first term.

V That *Applied Chemistry* 7 in the School of Science be opened to Academic Seniors.

VI That *Mineralogy* 17, 18 be opened in the first term to such Academic Juniors as intend to elect *Physical Geology* in second term.

That the President of the University be authorized to organize the work of the Faculty under Departments and departmental heads at his discretion, and that he be authorized to do this even when it may prove necessary to create departments which shall include instructors on both the Academic and Scientific sides of the University.[1]

Professor Cyrus F. Brackett, after thirty years of distinguished service in the University offers his resignation, in view of the fact that at the end of the present academic year he reaches his seventieth birthday. Your Committee recommend that this resignation be declined, that Professor Brackett be requested to retain his place on the teaching staff of the University, and that the President be authorized to express to Professor Brackett the Trustees' sense of his eminent services and of his great and continuing value to the University.

That the leave of absence granted to Professor Walter A. Wyckoff be extended one year in view of his ill health during the greater part of the year originally granted.

The President of the University reports the following appointments:

In the Department of Latin, Mr. Edwin Moore Rankin and Mr. Howell North White as Instructors and Mr. Robert Patton Anderson and Mr. Thad Weed Riker as special teaching Fellows.

In the Department of English, Mr. Hardin Craig and Mr. A.W. Long as Instructors.

In the Department of Chemistry, Mr. William Foster, Jr., as Instructor.

In the Department of Mineralogy, Mr. John Stout van Nest as Instructor.

In the Department of Mathematics, in the Academic Department, Mr. John G. Hun, and in the School of Science Mr. Carl Ebin Stromquist as Instructors.

In the Department of Geology, Mr. Gilbert van Ingen as Assistant in Geology and Curator of the Museum of Invertebrate paleontology.

In the Department of Economics, Dr. A. Cleveland Hall, as Instructor in Economics and Sociology, to supply the place of Professor Walter A. Wyckoff.

TR with WWhw emendations (Trustees' Papers, UA, NjP).

[1] At a meeting of the University Faculty on December 2, 1903, Wilson announced that he had reorganized the Princeton faculty into eleven departments, each with a chairman to be appointed annually. For details of the reorganization, see Wilson's memorandum printed at Nov. 30, 1903; the extract from the University Faculty Minutes printed at Dec. 2, 1903; and Wilson's report to the Board of Trustees printed at Dec. 10, 1903, all in Vol. 15.

A News Report of an Alumni Meeting at the Lawrenceville School

[June 6, 1903]

LAWRENCEVILLE HONORS
Reunion of Hamill Academy Students and Alumni Now United in One Organization.
BRIGHT EPOCH YESTERDAY

Yesterday was a bright spot in the history of Lawrenceville school when the alumni of the institution and the graduates of the old Hamill school[1] were united in one organization, both respecting the same alma mater, as the Hamill institution is generally looked upon as the beginning of the present Lawrenceville.

The exercises incident to the reunion were perhaps the most interesting of the commencement period, bringing together many prominent men, headed by President Woodrow Wilson, of Princeton university. Yesterday was given over to the alumni, and in response to the calls which had been sent out, many of the old graduates, who had not visited the school in years, returned, and the meeting took more the form of a general reunion.

The business meeting of the graduate bodies of the two institutions took place at 12:45 in the auditorium. . . . After the meeting the alumni were entertained at luncheon in the gymnasium, after which toasts were responded to by President Wilson, Henry W. Green, '87, president of the board of trustees, Dr. Simon McPherson, the head master of Lawrenceville schools; Dr. Joseph Duryee, '68; Roland S. Morris, '92, and Frederick W. Ritter, '03, president of the senior class. . . .

President Wilson's address was an appeal to the members of the graduating class to always hold dear the memories of their "prep" school days. The same training which had been imparted to them while preparing for college he wanted them to carry into the university. President Wilson said that the benefits to be derived from a thorough preparatory school education could not be estimated. He showed examples by comparing the results in college of young men with a broad preparatory school training and those whose education was limited to the narrow confines of a private school, or at the hands of a tutor.

Printed in the Trenton *Daily True American*, June 6, 1903.
[1] The Lawrenceville Classical and Commercial High School, the predecessor of the Lawrenceville School; Samuel McClintock Hamill and his brother, Hugh Hamill, were co-principals from 1837 to 1883.

To the Board of Trustees of Princeton University

Princeton, New Jersey. 8 June, 1903.

Your Committee appointed to consider the proposed gift of the Rev. George Wells Ely, of Columbia, Pennsylvania, of a scholarship in the University in memory of his step-father, Mahlon Long,[1] would report as follows:

Mr. Ely first proposed to convey to the University the title to five small houses in Minneapolis, Minnesota, at a valuation of $5000 and the title to a house in Jersey City, New Jersey, valued at $2000, and to add to these gifts the sum of $3000 in cash, in order to make a total sum of $10000, with the request that the University bind itself to pay the beneficiary of the scholarship thus founded the sum of $400 a year, the interest at 4% on the total amount of the gift.

Your Committee thought it unwise to make this guarantee of a definite income; and upon their representation to that effect, Mr. Ely has consented to the following modification of his gift, namely, the conveyance of the five houses in Minneapolis at a valuation of $6250 and of the house in Jersey City at a valuation of $2500, together with a gift of $1250 in cash, to make an estimated total of $10000, the actual net income from which the University shall agree to pay to the beneficiary of a scholarship to be known as the Mahlon Long scholarship.[2]

Your Committee recommends that the gift be accepted upon these terms, and that the thanks of the Board be conveyed to the Rev. George Wells Ely for his generosity in making this useful addition to the funds of the University.

Respectfully submitted,   Woodrow Wilson,
Chairman

TRS (Trustees' Papers, UA, NjP).
[1] Princeton 1839.
[2] The Mahlon Long Scholarship was first listed in the catalogue of 1903-1904 with an endowment of $10,000.

From John Huston Finley

Princeton, New Jersey
My dear President Wilson,   June 8, 1903

I have, with great regret, to ask you to present to the Board of Trustees my resignation of the Professorship of Politics to which I was three years ago elected. You have been acquainted with the circumstances which led to my acceptance of another position and I need not rehearse them here; but I beg you will assure the Board that it has been only under the compulsion of an opportunity which could not be put aside that I have taken the step which now obliges me to make this request for release.

My deep regret in quitting the happy relationships into which my connection with the University has brought me, is increased by the fact that I have made but a beginning in the work to which I was, through your confidence in me, appointed. I can only hope that this my service, the first in the Chair of Politics, brief as it has been, may give foundation for a better service by others—a service which shall exert a lasting and wholesome influence upon the life of the University and our nation.

Sincerely yours,   John H. Finley

ALS (Trustees' Papers, UA, NjP).

Samuel Ross Winans to the Board of Trustees' Committee on Morals and Discipline

GENTLEMEN: Princeton, N.J., June 8th, 1903.

The record of discipline for the closing quarter of the year shows few serious cases and a comparatively small total.

One man (a Freshman) was dismissed for stealing. He stole and sold clothing of his classmates. This is the second case of the kind this year, and at least one such thief is discovered every year in the body of our fourteen hundred students.

One Freshman, who had been dropped last year, was required to withdraw before the final examinations for persistent neglect of his work and duties.

Five students were suspended for a short period for failure to do promptly the penalty work, or pensums, imposed for excessive absences.

Twenty-one men have come under discipline for drinking: 3 Seniors, 3 Juniors, 9 Sophomores, 6 Freshmen. In few, if any, of these cases was there gross excess. Two small groups among them consisted of men found drinking beer in their rooms, and were noisy rather than intoxicated.

A summary of all the cases by classes shows—3 Seniors, 3 Juniors, 10 Sophomores, 12 Freshmen. In the total of 28, 21 were Scientific Students,—and of these 9 were in the C.E. department, which constitutes only a third of the Scientific side. A disproportion of this sort constantly appears in these statistics, although it is unusually great in this instance owing to the fact that in two affairs small groups of classmates were concerned.

While it is too early to speak of the order at this Commencement as a whole, so far, I am happy to say, there has been a marked improvement over recent years.

The annual parade by the nascent Sophomores passed off without disorder.

Since the class and club banquet festivals have become concentrated on Friday night, that night has been increasingly marked by intoxication and boisterousness at late hours,—and parties of graduates it is not easy to restrain or control. An earnest request from the President[1] to the Secretaries of classes holding reunions—that undergraduates be not admitted and given drink at the class headquarters is, I am told, being generally heeded. This custom had become a great evil.

The problem of drinking is the perennial one for Dean and Faculty. Faithful proctorial report of all excesses and the inevitable sequence of some penalty graded to the particular offence, not over severe but sure,—will keep the evil within bounds. The cure—or the hope of an improved condition, where a total eradication cannot be looked for—lies, I believe, not in stringent regulations which it is impracticable to enforce effectively, but in the development of a better, saner, manlier tone and sentiment in our undergraduate life. I hope to see the time when drinking shall be a less extensive custom, when fewer begin to drink at College, when students with social and class ambitions will not feel it essential to be convivial in order to be clubable, when more men who do not drink shall share the coveted fellowship of the various clubs, and when all excess either of degree or of habit shall be under the ban of student reprobation, and become unpopular as being ungentlemanly.

The Academic year now closing, as a whole, has been the most quiet and free from serious disorders that I have known during my Deanship. I may take myself credit for this only so far as the steady and persistent application of discipline in previous years may have contributed to the improvement. The gain is due in no small measure, I feel, to the temper of the student body itself and the quickened, expectant interest they are taking at this time in the expansion and prosperity of the University.

As to Sophomore-Freshman relations, the outlook is hopeful. Some teasing of Freshmen will doubtless always persist, but a decided improvement was made this year, and the student body now inclines to restrain still further Sophomore license. The painting nuisance, for one thing, vanished this year,—I trust for good.

The fact that practically all the Freshmen and not a few Sophomores do not find rooms in our dormitories, but are scattered in private houses throughout the town, may well cause serious concern from the side of discipline and good order. In some places they are practically under no oversight, and in others the landladies are lax and inefficient in the control of their roomers. Certain houses become conspicuous for the number of men unsatisfactory in their work and conduct. The matter calls for present attention, and perhaps some sharp restrictions will be found necessary. Dormitory life, while apparently giving greater liberty, would, nevertheless, under the oversight of our officers and the resident instructor, be more wholesome.

In concluding this report I would emphasize again my belief, based on my experience and close observation, that the most effective way—while the least conspicuous and causing least unpleasantness and friction—to purge the University of its undesirable element is the firm and steady enforcement of the scholarship rules. The delinquent list always contains a large percentage of those who have bad habits or who are notorious idlers.

In the larger matters of University order, without the petty machinery of a student court, we have in effect much of the spirit and reality of student self government. Not a few men of prominence in undergraduate life are found ready to give valuable help in guiding student opinion and action. And the student body as a whole, when rightly addressed, is quick to respond to appeals to loyalty and Academic patriotism.

Respectfully submitted,   S. R. Winans
Dean of the Faculty.

TLS (Trustees' Papers, UA, NjP).
1 WW to various class secretaries, May 10, 1903.

A Report to the Board of Trustees of Princeton University on the Club Situation

[Princeton, N. J., c. June 8, 1903]

The Committee appointed to confer with a representative of each of the existing Clubs upon the whole question of the relation of these Clubs[1] to the University and its life Respectfully Report:

After a full consideration and investigation your Committee[2] are of the opinion that the present club or society system in Princeton is a better one both to the Clubs and the University than the system in vogue in other Universities. With us the members are not chosen until after Easter Sunday in their Sophomore year. This enables each Club to select a harmonious section, as the new members are well and thoroughly known to those who elect them and to each other. In many other Colleges, such for example as Columbia, Pennsylvania and Cornell and in practically all the smaller colleges boys are pledged in advance before entering College and for the whole of their college life they are compelled to belong to a society which may be filled with uncongenial or distasteful members which being sharers in the secrets of the society they cannot exchange for another. This leads to the breaking up of a Class into small cliques and much of the value of the College life is lost.

In Yale and Harvard there is a gradual weeding out by the passing upwards from one society to another, so that in Senior year very few out of a Class succeed in making a society. This is a great abuse at Yale where three Senior Societies—the Scull & Bones and Scroll & Key and Wolf's Head select fifteen each out of a Class of several hundred men, and the influence of these societies is so potent that it touches all college interests, sometime, it is said, even affecting the choice of members of the Faculty.

At Princeton, however, not only is the period of selection deferred until the men are well known and friendships made, but should a member of one Club be elected to another there is nothing to prevent his changing. In fact, especially at the end of the Sophomore year, such a change is by no means unusual.

The Clubs are in no wise secret societies. The houses are open by invitation to every one, except to members of the two lower classes and guests are frequent at meal time. Each Club is required to have two members of the Faculty on its rolls. Luncheons, Dinners, Teas, etc., to ladies are of very frequent occurrence and as at any time ladies may be brought into the houses there is a tendency towards refinement of manners. Gambling

---

[1] Ivy (1879), University Cottage (1886), Tiger Inn (1890), Cap and Gown (1891), Colonial (1892), Cannon (1895), Elm (1895), Campus (1900), Charter (1901), Quadrangle (1901), and Tower (1902).

[2] For the appointment and membership of this committee, see C. W. McAlpin to WW, Oct. 24, 1902, and n. 1 to that letter.

and the use of spirits or wine or malt liquors in the Club houses are positively prohibited and this rule is strictly lived up to with the one exception that at Annual Dinners, as will be shown later, the service of wine has long been allowed.

No undergraduate is permitted to room in the Club houses. This ruling was made many years ago to prevent the breaking up of the Class and College into cliques and has proved a very effective preventative as the student body is practically only separated on Club lines at mealtime. And as these eleven clubs are all situated on adjoining lots on one street and the Club houses are open to visits from one to another the democratic spirit of the University continues to exist, so that except for the natural striving for members for a short time each year there is little class or college politics affected by the Clubs.

As the Clubs, unlike secret societies of other Colleges, have no ties with other Universities the whole interest of their members is concentrated in Princeton, the class spirit is unbroken and the Clubs are made subservient to the interest of the University.

There is a noticeable improvement in the tone of the students commencing with their Junior year. This is in great measure due to the influence of the Clubs. The change from the crudeness of the average sophomore boarding houses to the dignity and refinements of the upper class clubs exercise an elevating effect on the individual.

A censorship of morals and actions is held over the underclass man which in many cases produces a beneficial result. The best way to bring a freshman or sophomore to reason if he shows signs of dissipation is to tell him that his course will, if persisted in, (to use the common expression) "queer him with the Clubs." No form of legislation, however drastic, will produce so good a result.

The Clubs are managed with intelligence and a considerable amount of business ability. They are ordinarily each governed by a Board of governors composed of graduates while the interval matters are regulated by an undergraduate body who correspond to the House Committee of a Club. Each year more care seems to be shown in the selection of officers of the Clubs.

The honour of a Club is rated very high and severe discipline is sometimes meted out to offending members. Last year one Club expelled three members for dissipation.

While the Clubs are by no means perfect your Committee repeats that it believes our system to be the best one and that

Princeton is unusually fortunate in that the problem has worked out along the present lines and that this is due in great measure to the wise policy of President McCosh and his faculty which has been continued along the same lines by his successors in so guiding the students that the present system has developed.

Among the objections which could be raised is the fact that each year a number of men fail of election to a Club. This is the case in every College and is a serious question, for while the majority of these men either from lack of means or for other reasons do not desire or expect an election, yet the fact remains that every year a few men are left over who ought from every point of view to be elected. Generally these men are gentlemanly, studious, quiet, refined retiring fellows who sometimes for some petty reason but generally because they are not known to their own classmates, have been passed over. The best remedy for this, in our judgment, is the increase in the number of Clubs. There are eleven now in existence and we believe that one other Club could be with advantage organized this year. Some of the alumni have for this reason done their best to form new Clubs and with great success. This year a new Club "Tower" was organized which will undoubtedly be permanent, last year Charter and Quarrangle [Quadrangle] were started, the previous year Campus, two years earlier Cannon, two years previous to that Elm, two years earlier came Colonial and a year earlier than that Cap and Gown. Thus it will be seen that of late there has been a new Club formed every year or two, and as the University grows in number so will the Clubs increase. It must be remembered that the formation of each new Club gives thirty students each year the comfort of a pleasant club house with its good food, comfortable surroundings, library and fellowship and that the cost to the members is but little greater than the same men would have to pay at an ordinary boarding house without any of the Club accessories.

With the exception of one Club, the new one, each Club now owns its own house and ground. All these houses are beautifully situated on Prospect Street and each house contains a dining room, sitting rooms, billiard room, a library, a writing room, a private dining room, a ladies reception room and bed rooms for the graduates, the latter are yearly returning in greater numbers on account of the Clubs. Some of these houses are free of debt, but the greater number are mortgaged for more or less of the cost. The interest is always paid and the principal generally reduced a certain amount each year.

Another objection might be taken that the Freshmen and Sophomores have a hard and rugged life with poor food and surroundings, and that the Clubs should take men in at an earlier period of their course. This remedy your Committee do not recommend. They believe that the present dividing line is the best, but they do recommend that special attention be given by the Board to the amelioration of the condition of the underclassmen, which is a crying need of Princeton today. The food and surroundings of the average boarding house is undermining the constitution of many a boy and laying the seeds of future weakness if not disease. An attempt is being made to remedy this in part by the opening for the third time of University Hall as a Commons. This time it is done without cost or risk to the University as a private enterprise, but we reserve to ourselves the right of oversight of the food served. Should this prove a success a good start will have been made, but its evil will not be fully cured until the freshmen boarding houses are taken out of the hands of private keepers and the sophomores can have clubs of their own or so controlled that the quality of food can be regulated.

Another evil which promised some four or five years ago to upset the whole theory of the upper class clubs arose when some clubs, in their eagerness to obtain members, began to pledge sophomores and freshmen in advance. Had this custom crystallized a club election would have ceased to be an honour and the underclassmen would have soon had the privilege of choosing their own club out of the whole number. The control, therefore, which the upper classman, with his maturer judgment exercises over the younger men would have been lost in a chase for members. Fortunately this was prevented by a treaty entered into at first by the more prominent clubs and finally agreed to by all, by which the pledging of members is absolutely prohibited until a certain day in the second week after Easter, when all the elections go out together.

While the Clubs allow no gambling nor the use of any wines or spirits in their buildings an exception as [we] have said has been made in the case of the Annual Dinner on the Friday before Commencement. At this time it has been customary for most of the Clubs to serve wine at the dinner, it being the time when great numbers of the Alumni return to Princeton. This use of wine has been allowed without restraint for at least fifteen years and possibly a longer period. This being the case your Committee consider it inadvisable to endeavor to stop it absolutely, but it was distinctly and clearly put before the representatives of the Clubs and as clearly understood by them that no excesses whatever can be tolerated and that any excess would probably result in drastic legislation next year.

The Club officers at the meeting unanimously professed themselves thoroughly in harmony with the views of your Committee in this matter and each one promised to use the most careful supervision and restriction at their dinners this year.

Your Committee understand that the President has communicated with the Secretaries whose Classes are to hold reunions this year suggesting that the undergraduates are to be absolutely prevented from visiting the various headquarters. The President's suggestions were received with the hearty accord of these Secretaries and we believe that a very great improvement has already shown itself this year.

[Moses Taylor Pyne, Chairman]

TR (Trustees' Papers, UA, NjP).

Two News Reports

[June 10, 1903]

BACCALAUREATE SERVICE.
Extracts from Dr. van Dyke's Sermon and
President Wilson's Address.

Dr. Henry van Dyke chose as his theme for the Baccalaureate sermon "The Battle of Life." . . .

Immediately after the sermon President Wilson addressed the class saying:

"Whatever your course may be we sincerely pray you will not bring disgrace on this, your beloved university, but that all you do may redound to her glory. We know the capacity with which you are graduated and we are aware of the spirit that has been installed into each of you. You know as well as I do that there is no sound learning without true religion. As you enter life's hard paths do not seek after success, but strive for honor, remembering that honorable success is the only real success. Strive not to serve yourselves, but your generation. You may not have wealth or great influence, but you have got the knowledge of Christ's power and love, so there is no excuse for not seeing what is your duty and doing what is right."[1]

[1] There is a brief WWhw outline of these remarks, dated June 7, 1903, in WP, DLC.

ALUMNI DINNER
Held in the New Gymnasium Yesterday.
President Wilson and Others Speak.

The Annual Alumni Dinner was held yesterday afternoon at 1 o'clock in the new gymnasium.[1] The procession formed by classes shortly before 1 o'clock in front of Nassau Hall and marched to the gymnasium where preparations had been made for about six hundred guests. The speakers were seated at a table on a platform on the west side of the building from which radiated nine tables for the accommodation of the alumni. After the serving of the luncheon, Judge David T. Marvel '73, who acted as toastmaster, welcomed those present to the opening of the new gymnasium and followed his welcome with a few remarks on the growth and policy of the University. Mr. Marvel mentioned the rapid growth of Princeton and said that the improvements made during recent years were only a begin[n]ing of greater things. The substance of his short address centered about the important question of curriculum changes. Concerning this subject, Mr. Marvel said that the object of the University is to furnish opportunities for a broad and liberal education and that it was his desire that Princeton be slow to turn from that policy which furnishes a liberal education and turns out broad-minded men. "May Princeton not follow precedent because memorial, but may she follow that policy which has turned out broad and liberal minded men. Let Princeton not be afraid to stand, even if she has to stand alone."

Judge Marvel then introduced President Wilson as the next speaker.

President Wilson said in part that he thought he had the support of the graduates not because they particularly believed in him, but because they believed in the University and its ideals, and knew that he believed in it. In his travels of the past year among the alumni, he had found them a body of thoughtful men. Their dinners were not merely for enjoyment but also for the purpose of hearing a serious discussion of the business of the University and of what it is to be. He had found them intelligently interested in questions of the policy of the University; they had a distinct individuality in regard to their ideas as to what has been and what is to be done. Education in the University field is a branch of statesmanship. It is the business of Princeton to supply the citizenship of this country with thoughtful men who will stand behind the statesmanship. The policy [polity] of this country is not commercial, not political, but fundamentally intellectual. It is the part of the American people to have the power to sympathize with and understand all classes and divisions of society, and to do this they must have broad and intellectual minds. If therefore the University is to lose the distinction between itself and the technical school and is merely to produce skill, it will lose its intellectuality and its power to turn out men who are leaders. Not every man that goes out from Princeton is fit to be a leader but every man is fitted to understand and choose a leader. Princeton is a place not for the purpose of giving mere skill of hand but to impart an elevation and a higher outlook of learning. This does not mean the exclusion of any new thought but binding and unification of thought as a whole.

President Wilson then announced the election of Professor Henry B. Fine as Dean of the Faculty, to succeed Dr. Samuel R. Winans, who will devote all his attention in the future to teaching. In closing, President Wilson spoke of the gift of the gymnasium as a fitting expression of the love and enthusiasism [enthusiasm] of the graduate to-day, for Princeton.[2]

Printed in the *Daily Princetonian*, June 10, 1903.

[1] Made possible by the contributions of alumni, the new gymnasium was begun in February 1902 and used for the first time for the annual alumni luncheon on June 9, 1903. Its total cost was approximately $300,000. Designed by Walter Cope to harmonize with the Gothic style of Blair Arch, Blair Hall, and Stafford Little Hall, the gymnasium contained rooms for a variety of athletic activities, an elevated running track, locker accommodations for nearly 2,000 men, and, in its central portion, unobstructed floor space measuring 166 feet by 101 feet.

[2] There is a WWhw outline, dated June 9, 1903, of this address in WP, DLC. For a fuller report of Wilson's remarks about Winans and Fine, see the second news item printed at June 13, 1903.

To Harry Augustus Garfield[1]

My dear Mr. Garfield: Princeton, New Jersey. 11 June, 1903.

By the resignation of Professor Finley of our Faculty, who is just leaving us to assume the Presidency of the College of the City of New York, our chair of Politics has become vacant, and I am taking the liberty of writing to you to ask if you would be willing to consider a call to fill it?

It is, I believe, the only chair of Politics in the country. It was given that name rather than the chair of Political Science because of our desire to have instruction given which should differ in some essential points from that usually given in Political Science. Professor Finley was the first to fill the chair, and I selected

him for the position because he seemed to me to afford a delightful combination of man of the world and man of letters. I myself
am very much averse from symmetrical theories in matters of politics, and from all teachings derived exclusively from books. Politics, whether on its institutional or on its active side, seems to me
so essentially a matter of life and experience that I should hesitate
to entrust teaching in such fields to men wholly academic in their
training and point of view.

Professor Finley has offered such courses as Contemporary
Politics, a study of the present political institutions and of the
recent history of parties in Europe and the United States; Contemporary State Legislation, a study of the scope, nature and
trend of recent and current legislation in the commonwealths of
the United States; Municipal Government, a study of municipal
administration and its problems; and the Expansion of Europe,
that is a consideration of the overflow of the European people into
other continents and the study of the problems incident to this
expansion and the methods of colonial administration. This will
show you what so far the field of the chair has been. His successor would not be bound to this programme. My own idea is,
however, that these courses indicate clearly the character and
general field of instruction. I myself lecture on the theory of
politics, and yet I hope do not make the theory too theoretical.

I know that my question as to whether you would be willing
to consider a call to such a chair will come to you as an entire
surprise; but I hope that if you have the slightest inclination in
this direction, you will not put it aside without serious consideration. I my [may] say frankly that a man of your type is just the
sort we are looking for, and we should be seriously disappointed
if we had to confine ourselves in making the choice to the academic field.

The salary of the chair is $4000. This, as you know, is large
as college salaries go, but by every other standard small. The inducements for such work certainly do not lie in the direction of
money, but only in the opportunity for what is, I myself believe,
one of the most interesting forms of the intellectual life, and
yet in a case like this also a form of public life.

With much regard,
                    Very sincerely yours,   Woodrow Wilson

P.S. Perhaps I ought to add that the question of the time at
which the duties of the chair would be taken up might easily be
accommodated to your plans and convenience. It is not neces-

sary that the work should be entered upon at the beginning of the next college year.   W. W.

TLS (H. A. Garfield Papers, DLC).
    [1] Born Hiram, Ohio, Oct. 11, 1863, son of President James Abram Garfield. A.B., Williams College, 1885. Teacher of Latin and Roman History, St. Paul's School, Concord, N.H., 1885-86. Student at Columbia University Law School, 1886-87. Read law at All Souls College, Oxford, and at the Inns of Court, London, 1887-88. Practiced law as a member of the firm of Garfield, Garfield & Howe of Cleveland, 1888-1903. Professor of the Law of Contracts, Western Reserve University Law School, 1891-96. An organizer, 1896, and later president of the Municipal Association of Cleveland. Professor of Politics, Princeton University, 1903-1908. President of Williams College, 1908-34. U.S. Fuel Administrator, 1917-19. Died Dec. 12, 1942.

To Winthrop More Daniels

My dear Daniels: Princeton, New Jersey. 12 June, 1903.

I send you with this Dr. Hall's scheme of courses for next year.[1] He told me that it already had your approval, and it seems to me very excellent indeed. Will you not be kind enough to see that it is put in the proper form into the catalogue?

It was a great surprise to see Wyckoff in town, and to learn that he is immediately to be married.[2] It makes me the more glad that we were able to find him a substitute and thus set him free for what he had promised himself.

With much regard,

Cordially yours,   Woodrow Wilson

TLS (WWP, UA, NjP).
    [1] Hall assisted Daniels in Political Economy 2, the elements of economics, and gave courses in theories of social reconstruction and modern industrial organizations.
    [2] Wyckoff married Leah Lucile Ehrich in New York on June 25, 1903.

Two News Items

[June 13, 1903]

Things are at a pretty pass when the President of the University himself, from his seat in the grandstand, has to call upon a baseball official to suppress the objectionable blatancy of a young person who is permitted to stand out in full view of the Commencement throng and bawl through a megaphone at the old and young men and women in the grandstand, ordering them in a raucous, juvenile voice to "Talk up there! We got him up in the air last Saturday; we can do it again."[1] It is needless to add that such exhortations were unauthorized, but it is eloquent of the spirit which prompts much of the noise at many baseball games.

1 The occasion was the second game, played in Princeton on June 6, 1903, of the annual championship baseball series with Yale. Princeton won by a score of 10 to 6.

❖

The first official announcement of the resignation of Dean Winans '74 and the election of Dean Fine '80 was made by President Wilson '79 at the alumni luncheon on Tuesday afternoon. The President spoke of Professor Winans' extraordinary faithfulness and promptitude in the exercise of his functions during the four years he has served the University as Dean; he referred to the depletion of the Greek faculty by the withdrawal of the elder men of that department and said that ever since Professor Winans "came into our teaching body he has been one of the most successful teachers in this place"; and said that he had now consented to return to his teaching functions exclusively, where he is so much needed and appreciated.

In announcing Professor Fine's appointment, the President referred to a football dinner at Tiger Inn during the winter[1] at which an undergraduate manager had advised his successor to "tie to Harry Fine." This sentiment the President endorsed, adding: "He is, in the vernacular, white; he is stern sometimes; he speaks his mind with a refreshing frankness; but there is behind that frankness no touch of acid, no bitterness, no vindictiveness."

Printed in the *Princeton Alumni Weekly*, III (June 13, 1903), 612, 607-608.
1 A news report of this affair is printed at Dec. 18, 1902.

From Harry Augustus Garfield

My Dear Mr. Wilson: [Cleveland] June 13, 1903.

Your letter of the 11th inst., presents a question which I am unable to decide without most careful consideration. What you propose comes indeed as a surprise, and awakens desires which appeal to me most strongly. I would not have you assume that my answer probably will be in the affirmative, but if a little delay will not prove an embarrassment, I will give the subject my earnest and immediate attention.

A business engagement will take me to New York next week, and, if agreeable to you, I will come to Princeton to see you. I shall probably leave here Wednesday afternoon, and my address in New York will be University Club.

Whatever may be the outcome, please believe that I am most appreciative of the honor you propose.

Very sincerely yours,   H. A. Garfield.

TLS (Letterpress Books, H. A. Garfield Papers, DLC).

From Moses Taylor Pyne

My dear Woodrow   Princeton, June 13/03

I asked Mac Thompson what it would cost to move the 1st Church, provided the street were wide enough. He said that $15,000 would do it. Of course this is a mere guess yet it shows that we had better look pretty carefully into the matter as a new church would cost many times that sum.[1]

Another matter. During the past few years our "Literary Bureau" has been practically dormant, while other colleges—notably Columbia—have been very active. I know all about the latter's methods and work since it was copied from the "Bureau" which J. W. Alexander & I started in the early eighties, when we got a good share of notice in the papers. Of late years we have grown older & become too busy to follow these matters up and some one ought to be charged with the obtaining and dissemination of proper news for the papers. I had hoped 1st that Jesse Williams and then that Charlie McAlpin would take this up, but they seem unfitted for it. Do you think that Norris of the Alumni Weekly[2] could do it? It would be worth our while to pay him some small sum to get him to do it, if he seem to be the right man.[3]

We also need a handbook of Princeton—descriptive, historical and illustrated. The pictures should be good, so that those who have not seen Princeton should be impressed. Who can do this?[4]

When you are ready please let me know your London address. I shall be glad to see you if we are there about the same time.

Sincerely yours   M. Taylor Pyne

ALS (WP, DLC).

[1] The First Presbyterian Church, one of the masterpieces of the Princeton architect and builder, Charles Steadman, was neither moved nor destroyed, to the continuing benefit, it might be added, of the beauty of Princeton. Wilson and some of the trustees had been discussing the possibility of moving the church in order to open an approach from Nassau Street to Alexander Hall.

[2] Edwin Mark Norris '95, Associate Editor of the *Princeton Alumni Weekly*.

[3] A Princeton University Press Bureau was organized in the autumn of 1906 under the direction of Harold Griffith Murray and with the assistance of Maxwell Struthers Burt and Ivy Ledbetter Lee.

[4] *The Handbook of Princeton* (New York, 1905) was prepared by John Rogers Williams, part-time assistant in the Secretary's office and General Editor of the Princeton Historical Association. Wilson's introduction to the volume is printed at Aug. 1, 1904, Vol. 15.

To Harry Augustus Garfield

Princeton, New Jersey.

My dear Mr. Garfield: 15 June, 1903.

Allow me to thank you for your kind letter of June 13th, and to say that I expect to be in Princeton all the latter half of this week, and will be glad to see you at any time that may be convenient for you to come. If my plans should change, I will let you know by telegram to the University Club.

Very sincerely yours,   Woodrow Wilson

TLS (H. A. Garfield Papers, DLC).

A News Report of an Address at Brown University

[June 17, 1903]

CONTINUATION OF COMMENCEMENT AT BROWN.
An Address by President Wilson of Princeton.

. . . At 4 o'clock [on June 16] an audience of considerable size gathered in Sayles Hall to hear the address of President Woodrow Wilson of Princeton University before the Phi Beta Kappa. His subject was "Patriotism." President Kellen[1] presided, and the meeting was opened with prayer by President Faunce.[2]

President Wilson said in part: "I feel that you will expect of me first of all a justification for my theme. Have you been remiss in your duties to the nation that I should come to remind you of them? No. My object this afternoon is a very different one.

"We sometimes consider that patriotism is a sentiment, but it is not a mere sentiment; it is bred upon a principle. It seems to me to belittle patriotism to consider it a mere emotion. I have conceived of patriotism as a larger sort of friendship. It is friendship writ large, large as the life of the nation. I am not a true friend unless I take the pains to understand the character of my friend and to assist him according to his character. I am a true friend when I have learned to serve him according to his character.

"Patriotism is the service of a country according to the character of the country. Patriotism in a monarchy is different from patriotism in a republic. Being citizens of a republic, we are to serve the nation according to the character it has gained from the citizens that preceded us.

[1] William Vail Kellen, Boston lawyer and legal scholar, trustee of Brown University, and president of the university's chapter of Phi Beta Kappa.
[2] William Herbert Perry Faunce, President of Brown University.

"It used to be a very simple matter to be patriotic in the United States. It was a simple nation then. All the rough task of clearing this country from ocean to ocean was a patriotic duty. But with the passing of the frontier patriotism takes a new form.

"When we look at some of our city governments we begin to ask ourselves if there isn't a practical side of government which even we haven't understood. Are we as sure as we used to be that we know the forms individual liberty should take in order that the country may be a free country?

"It is imperative in the present day that we should be thoughtful. The artist who puts the finishing touch on a piece of work must have a more skilful hand and a more skilful eye than he who has rough hewn the work. We have done the rough hewing and have a new task before us. We are come into a new sphere. The whole world is as conscious of our existence as we have always been.

"The first thing for America to do on facing the world is to get together. This country is still sectionalized. Consider that phrase 'What's the matter with Kansas?' When used in that tone in which it is sometimes uttered it means that we of the East think that Kansas is benighted. It means the East against the West. It's the fundamental misunderstanding which exists between the different parts of the nation.

"Again, the men whom we have put in places of authority are our rulers and deserve our respect. There is a tendency in this country which militates against that. A nation which calls its chief executive 'Teddy' is not in a way to take itself very seriously. While our executive is President of the United States it ought not to be possible to call him by a nickname.

"We must be obedient to our laws. There are as many jails in the United States as in monarchical countries and they are as commodiously occupied. Most of our laws are older than any living man and we're obedient to the past. We are subjects though we sometimes call ourselves rulers. It is because the laws are the embodiment of what we conceive to be right that we are subject to them.

"The only reason we fear the Socialist or the Anarchist is because he would throw a bomb at our feet to overcome our opposition. We are afraid of these men because they will not see the right. It is not because we do not wish to change the laws in a proper way. Public opinion must consistently sit as a great board of conciliation.

"Even if you assumed that you had a multitude of knaves to govern, I can conceive how you can have good laws if you have enough men. If you get men enough you can keep some cool while others are hot. You can't get great nations to burn all at one time. So some men keep cool to judge others. We can, therefore, insist on the temperate way of changing laws if we be big enough as a nation and patient enough.

"Men in America are less inclined to resist a crowd than they are elsewhere. We have been indoctrinated with the idea that the crowd represents sovereignty. There are some men who are willing to stand out against the crowd, but they are as a rule so effervescent that we can't take them seriously. We look on them with a touch of intolerance. We say: 'Why have this horrid row? Why not take it coolly? Why not hire a hall?' It is a characteristic of America that after the voting is done and the votes are counted the fight's over. You've all got to make up your minds that the truth's no invalid, and that you needn't be afraid of handling her roughly.

"In conclusion, let me say that we ought first, every one of us, to acquaint ourselves with our country as a whole. Every man who has crossed the continent slowly enough knows that there are men of the same kind from ocean to ocean. There isn't any part of this country in which it isn't worth while keeping awake.

"Secondly, it is our duty to study the conditions of success in practical politics. The difficulty with politics in this country is that so many have despised politics and left it to men of limited capabilities. It's one thing to stand outside and say what ought to be done and another thing to stand inside and prove that what you think is the best thing to do, is the best thing to do. The man who doesn't give himself an insight into practical politics is like a man with an excellent principle who doesn't put himself into a position to put it into practice.

"Why do we smile at the word reformer? It is because a reformer is a very engaging man who doesn't know what he is about. They are intolerant of the very men among whom they would work.

"In this world we are between two things. It's necessary to read books, but it is dangerous to read books only. It is necessary to know men, but dangerous to know only the men with whom we are acquainted.

"No book is wholly systematic, because no man knows enough to make it so. Life itself is not systematic. It is full of fruitless experiments, full of things that didn't turn out as they were expected to. The book that makes a system of life presents a false image of life.

"The men you like best are those with the most engaging manner, but don't let them dupe you. Learn to love and follow good men. Learn to follow men whose moral and intellectual stuff can stand the weather. Then follow them with partisanship and ardor. You can't run about by yourself and conquer the world. You must tie to leaders, and if you don't tie to worthy men, who are tested and sincere, to whom can you tie?

"The world is governed by a tumultuous 'House of Commons,' made up of the passions, and the strongest passion is the Prime Minister. Our desire is that the best shall be strongest and that which shall be right for the country that we love."

Printed in the Providence *Evening Bulletin*, June 17, 1903; some editorial headings omitted.

A News Report of the Conferral of an Honorary Degree by Brown University

[June 17, 1903]

SUN SMILED ON BROWN COMMENCEMENT DAY.

The weather this morning on Commencement Day was an improvement on the days that had preceded, yet the week as a whole has been one of the stormiest Commencement weeks in the history of Brown University. As President Faunce remarked in his Class Day address, 1903 entered college during a torrent of rain and has finished its course at the university in the midst of a series of showers approaching a deluge.

To-day in the crowded auditorium of the First Baptist Church the time-honored custom of delivering the orations of the graduating class was carried out with the conferring of degrees, the announcement of prizes and the gathering of alumni. . . .

President Faunce, in conferring the honorary degrees, spoke a few words in praise of each of the persons so honored. His words were, in order, as follows. . . .

"Woodrow Wilson, Southern gentleman and Northern scholar, student of history and government, lucid writer, inspiring teacher, leader of old Princeton into the new day. . . ."

President Wilson of Princeton, when the hood was placed on his shoulders, received an ovation from the audience that crowded the church. He turned about and spoke briefly after bowing his acknowledgment. He said in part:

"As an imperative engagement prevents my attending your banquet today it would seem niggardly on my part did I not say a word at departing. I wish to convey a greeting from Princeton to Brown. Brown is in a sense a child of Princeton. A Princeton man[1] had the honor of taking part in the founding of Brown University. This historic connection between the two universities gives me a feeling of kinship to your college. I feel as I come into this gathering of college graduates that I am in a typical American gathering.

"As education is a characteristic of America, educated men are characteristic Americans. To an educator in America is presented the task not only of scholarship, but of statesmanship, for with the leadership of educated men the country is ruled. I, therefore, seem to myself to be standing among a company of men, not only sons of a college, but typical sons of a great country."

Printed in the Providence *Evening Bulletin*, June 17, 1903; some editorial headings omitted.
    [1] The Rev. Dr. James Manning, College of New Jersey 1762, first President of the College of Rhode Island, later Brown University.

To Henry Cooper Pitney, Jr.

My dear Mr. Pitney: Princeton, New Jersey, 20 June, 1903.

I am sorry to say that the thing is impossible.[1] I have tried my best to make something out of the address as you sent it to me, but really it cannot be successfully done without changing the whole character of the address. I must ask you to indulge me by not printing it.

I am very much distressed that I should have to make this request but under the circumstances I think it is only fair to myself to do so. I would rather have the men who heard the address to retain a pleasant recollection of it than read a poor report of it.

    With much regard,
                    Very sincerely yours,   Woodrow Wilson

TLS (Washington Association of N. J., Morristown, N. J.).
    [1] That is, that he could not reconstruct his address to the Washington Association of New Jersey on February 23, 1903, from the stenographer's transcript.

Two Letters from Henry Cooper Pitney, Jr.

Dear Doctor Wilson,   Morristown, N. J. June 22, 1903.

Your letter of June 20' is duly received.

I am sorry that you have so much difficulty in revising our report of your address of February 23.

The notes were taken, under some difficulties, and were transcribed by the stenographer with great pains under my supervision and as quickly as he could under my urgent pressing and before March 16.

It is necessary for us to print something to represent the address.

On February 23 I was instructed to print the address, according to our unvaried custom; and I have already received many inquiries for it. It is quite certain that the members will not be content with the pleasant recollection of those who heard it.

It may be fair to say that addresses, delivered in like circumstances, are never exactly reproduced. This is confirmed by my observations of parallel reports, in separate journals, of single addresses. I think it applies to other addresses made by you last winter, which I have heard and afterwards read in the "Alumni Weekly" and other journals.

I expected that the present report, with a few omissions supplied, would pass as a fair reproduction in the circumstances. Is it not practicable for you to connect the threads and discard what you do not recognize and so leave the report to be printed?

I am willing to subjoin an editorial note saying that the address is not rendered *verbatim*.

Very truly yours,   [Henry C. Pitney, Jr.]

CCL (Washington Association of N. J., Morristown, N. J.).

My dear Sir,   Morristown, N. J. June 24, 1903.

Let me add to my note of June 22,—that the publication need not be restricted to the matter which was actually delivered. In parliamentary phrase, there is "free leave to print."

You may strike out whatever paragraphs you please and may insert whatever matter you choose. This has been all the while intended; and we shall print with pleasure whatever you supply.

I trust you will have not too much trouble in eliminating the defective parts and introducing matters which you approve.

Very truly yours,   H. C. Pitney, Jr.

Mr. Lukeman, the stenographer, will gladly go to you at Princeton and take whatever notes you will give.

H. C. Pitney, Jr.

TCL (Washington Association of N. J., Morristown, N. J.).

To Henry Cooper Pitney, Jr.

My dear Mr. Pitney: Princeton, New Jersey, 27 June, 1903.

Once more I have tried to make something out of the report of my address at Morristown and once more it has proved impossible. I am sorry to have to withdraw my consent to the publication of the address, but it is necessary that I should do so and I hope that you will lay the matter before the proper officers of the association so that you may be released from your obligation to print.

I could not consent that this should go forth as my address and I cannot undertake to write something by way of substitution for it. I am leaving the country on the 1st of July.

I am much obliged to you for the note about a classical master for the Morristown School.[1] I am afraid that it is too late in the year to obtain the proper sort of man, but I realize the importance of the matter and have put it in the hands of the chairman of a committee which will certainly do something with it if possible.

Very sincerely yours,   Woodrow Wilson

TLS (Washington Association of N. J., Morristown, N. J.).
[1] It is missing.

To Charles Williston McAlpin

My dear Mr. McAlpin,   Princeton, New Jersey, 28 June, 1903.

For fear I should not have a chance to see you again before I sail, I must send you a few lines about University business.

I am going to instruct Mr. [Henry Nevius] Van Dyke, the Registrar, to refer to you and to Professor Fine, as Dean, respectively, all questions regarding schola[r]ship or administration that may arise during my absence; and I have authorized Fine, as I now authorize you, to decide them in my stead. You need not hesitate to forward to me any matter which you think of too great moment to be decided without consultation, but there is little reason to expect such questions to come up during the summer, and I shall have perfect confidence in your judgment. The past year has given me good reason to have.

My address will be *Care British Linen Co. Bank, 42 Lombard Street, London.*

I have taken the liberty of instructing the Post Office to deliver all letters destined for Prospect at your office. I hope that you will not think it an imposition. Will you not be kind enough to give instructions that all letters addressed to Margaret, Jessie, or Nellie Wilson, to Dr. George Howe, or to Mrs. Annie W. Howe, be forwarded to *Mineral Springs Hotel, Skyland, North Carolina;* that all addressed to Mrs. Wilson be sent to our foreign address; and that all addressed to me be laid on your desk for your inspection?

I would be deeply obliged to you if you would open all addressed to me? Perhaps it would be simplest to reply to all which can wait for my return with a printed slip saying that I am out of the country and will reply on my return. Many of them,—I dare say most of them,—can be disposed of in your own office: you may take any in hand that you choose. Those that are purely personal must, I suppose be sent after me to the other side, and you may use your discretion as to others.

Please ask Miss Thompson[1] to put five cent stamps on those forwarded, and keep a memorandum for me.

I hope with all my heart that this will not prove burdensome. I do not see any other proper way of disposing of the President's mail; and I am very anxious that no matter of business should suffer from my absence.

I trust that, in spite of the burdens of office, you may have a refreshing summer. How much lighter the task is by reason of our love for the place and the University.

Please give our warmest regards to Mrs. McAlpin. Mrs. Wilson joins me also in all cordial messages to yourself.

Cordially and Faithfully Yours,   Woodrow Wilson

WWTLS (McAlpin File, UA, NjP).
[1] Stenographer in McAlpin's office.

To Stockton Axson[1]

My dearest Stock.,   Princeton, 28 June, 1903

Here's good-bye, and may God bless you! Our address will be *Care British Linen Co.'s Bank, 41 Lombard St. London.*

The children got off on Thursday and reached Skyland (near Asheville), N. C., their destination, on Friday afternoon, joining sister, George, and Miss Flynn.[2]

We are quite well and comfortably near being ready to start. Ellen is about to drop you a line also.

I enclose Mrs. Hibben's memorandum of Jack's addresses during the summer.[3] Ellen said that you wanted them.

I put your Cent. of Ga. 2nd income bonds into the hands of Webb and Prall, #49 Wall St., N. Y. They said that they would hold them for a day or two, in hope of a little better price, and then remit to you direct, at Bryn Mawr.*

Be sure you keep your present pace and show us great progress in the Autumn. With heartfelt love

Affectionately   Woodrow Wilson

* I also sent the S. W.[4] script to Palmer Axson with a letter of explanation, as you desired.   W. W.

ALS (WC, NjP).

[1] Axson was in the Bryn Mawr Hospital in Bryn Mawr, Pa.

[2] Most probably Margaret Smyth Flinn, daughter of the Rev. Dr. John William Flinn, Professor of Philosophy and Chaplain at the University of South Carolina. George Howe married Miss Flinn on October 27, 1903.

[3] It is missing.

[4] The Southwestern Railroad Co. of Georgia.

From Charles Williston McAlpin

My dear Dr. Wilson: Princeton, New Jersey   June 29, 1903.

I was sorry to miss you today but I shall try to see you at the Steamer on Wednesday morning, if I do not let me take this opportunity of wishing you and Mrs. Wilson bon voyage and a very happy summer.

I accept gladly the responsibility that you place upon me in your kind letter of the 28th. I consider it a privilege to serve the University and I esteem it not only a privilege but a pleasure to serve you in any way that my abilities may enable me to do.

If you do not feel that I can perform my duties satisfactorily by coming to Princeton once a week please do not hesitate to say so and I shall regulate my plans according to your advice, but I feel that in my absence Mr. [John Rogers] Williams and Miss Thompson are well able to attend to all the routine matters that may come up and I shall always be where they can reach me should occasion arise.

I shall see that your mail is attended to as you request and forwarded to the right addresses.

Two or three matters have come up upon which I would like your advice before you leave.

When the Trustees adopted the suggestion of the Finance Committee that the sum of $2500 should be required with which to endow a scholarship Mr. Pyne told me to draw up the resolution and incorporate in the Report of the Finance Committee. I have done this and submit it for your approval on sheet "A."[2] You will notice in the first resolution I have stated that scholarships for students in *any* undergraduate department may be founded. Have I exceeded my authority in this matter?

I feel very strongly that a few scholarships in the School of Science would be a great help as there are some very worthy students in that department. If you approve of my suggestion is it necessary for me to submit it to Mr. [Henry W.] Green?

A C.E. man, Ford Smith, a member of next years Senior class, has been working his way through college and hopes to send his brother here after graduation. I have him in mind as the first incumbent of the PATTON SCHOLARSHIP[3] in case you approve and Mr. Patton has no objection.

I have sent a vote of thanks to Mr. Ely, but do not know what to do with the papers marked "B." Shall I keep them with the report of your committee or shall I refer them to the Treasurer?

Under the head of "C" I send you the first draft of the Minutes of the June meeting.[4] The second paragraphs marked "B" and "A" are for insertion in the Minutes where I have noted. If you see anything that needs correction will you be kind enough to note it?

I shall endeavor to keep just as much business as possible from you this summer in order that you may have nothing to do but enjoy yourself and forget that such a thing as an Alumni Dinner ever existed.

With kindest regards to Mrs. Wilson and yourself in which Mrs. McAlpin joins me, I remain,

Faithfully yours,   C. W. McAlpin   Secretary.

TLS (Trustees' Papers, UA, NjP).

[1] WWhw, as are all following marginal comments.

[2] This enclosure is missing.

[3] The John Linn Patton Scholarship, founded in 1903 by Mr. and Mrs. William D. Patton with an endowment of $2,500, in memory of their son, John Linn Patton '03, who died on Oct. 6, 1900.

[4] That is, of the Board of Trustees. This enclosure is missing.

From Henry Cooper Pitney, Jr.

Dear Doctor Wilson: Morristown, N. J.   June 29, 1903.

I am in receipt of your letter of June 27, saying that you cannot revise the address as reported, and that you cannot undertake to write something by way of substitution for it.

I am very sorry that you have this feeling about the address. Your request that we refrain from publication was laid before the Officers of the Association on June 24. They all agreed in the decision that they must publish something to represent the address, stating editorially if necessary that the matter published was not a full and verbatim report.

To prepare for such action, I have gone over my copy of the report again carefully with another of the Officers, and marked all those passages which are doubtful or unsatisfactory to us,— these passages to be entirely omitted and indicated by stars, with a note subjoined that they were not reported or the like.

I have hoped all the time since last March that you would be able to supply the matter for publication in a form entirely satisfactory to yourself. I have been willing to do everything in my province to facilitate such a result. But now, since it appears that you have not time to edit the report, I am decided in the opinion that it is our duty to make a publication in the manner above indicated.

Nothing less than a fair attempt to render the address from the material which we have will satisfy either our Officers or our members.

I thank you for your attention to the quest of a classical Master for the Morristown School.

Wishing you a pleasant vacation abroad, I am,

Yours very truly,   [Henry C. Pitney, Jr.]

CCL (Washington Association of N. J., Morristown, N. J.).

To Henry Cooper Pitney, Jr.

New York, Jun 30th [1903]

I earnestly protest against the injustice and discourtesy of publishing against my will what I did not say.[1]

Woodrow Wilson

T tel. (Washington Association of N. J., Morristown, N. J.).
[1] For the denouement, see H. C. Pitney, Jr., to WW, Nov. 4, 1903, and subsequent correspondence in Vol. 15.

An Historical Address[1]

[[June 30, 1903]]

JOHN WESLEY'S PLACE IN HISTORY

John Wesley lived and wrought while the Georges reigned. He was born but a year after Anne became queen, a year before the battle of Blenheim was fought; while England was still caught in the toils of the wars into which her great constitutional revolution had drawn her; when Marlborough was in the field and the armies afoot which were to make the ancient realm free to go her own way without dictation from any prince in Europe. But when he came to manhood, and to the days in which his work was to begin, all things had fallen quiet again. Wars were over and the pipes of peace breathed soothing strains. The day of change had passed and gone, and bluff Sir Robert Walpole ruled the land, holding it quiet, aloof from excitement, to the steady humdrum course of business, in which questions of the treasury and of the routine of administration were talked about, not questions of constitutional right or any matter of deep conviction. The first of the dull Georges had come suitably into the play at the centre of the slow plot, bringing with him the vulgar airs of the provincial court of obscure Hanover, and views that put statesmanship out of the question.

The real eighteenth century had set in, whose annals even its own historians have pronounced to be tedious, unheroic, without noble or moving plot, though they would fain make what they can of the story. They have found it dull because it lacked dramatic unity. Its wars were fought for mere political advantage,—because politicians had intrigued and thrones fallen vacant; for the adjustment of the balance of power or the aggrandizement of dynasties; and represented neither the growth of empires nor the progress of political ideals. All religion, they say, had cooled and philanthropy had not been born. The thinkers of the day had as little elevation of thought as the statesmen, the preachers as little ardor as the atheistical wits, whose unbelief they scarcely troubled themselves to challenge. The poor were unspeakably degraded and the rich had flung morals to the winds. There was no adventure of mind or conscience that seemed worth risking a fall for.

But the historians who paint this sombre picture look too little upon individuals, upon details, upon the life that plays outside the field of politics and of philosophical thinking. They are in

[1] A news report of this address is printed at July 1, 1903.

search of policies, movements, great and serious combinations of men, events that alter the course of history, or letters that cry a challenge to the spirits. Forget statecraft, forego seeking the materials for systematic narrative, and look upon the eighteenth century as you would look upon your own day, as a period of human life whose details are its real substance, and you will find enough and to spare of human interest. The literary annals of a time, when Swift and Addison and Berkeley and Butler and Pope and Gray and Defoe and Richardson and Fielding and Smollett and Sterne and Samuel Johnson and Goldsmith and Burke and Hume and Gibbon and Cowper and Burns wrote, and in which Wordsworth, Coleridge, Byron, Shelley, and Keats were born, cannot be called barren or without spiritual significance.

No doubt the wits of Queen Anne's time courted a muse too prim, too precise, too much without passion to seem to us worthy to stand with the great spirit of letters that speaks in the noble poetry with which the next century was ushered in; but there was here a very sweet relief from the ungoverned passions of the Restoration, the licentious force of men who knew the restraints neither of purity nor of taste; and he must need strong spices in his food who finds Swift insipid. No doubt Fielding is coarse, and Richardson prolix and sentimental, Sterne prurient and without true tonic for the mind, but the world which these men uncovered will always stand real and vivid before our eyes. It is a crowded and lively stage with living persons upon it; the eighteenth century can never seem a time vague and distant after we have read those pages of intimate revelation. No doubt Dr. Johnson failed to speak any vital philosophy of life and uttered only common sense, and the talk at the Turk's Head Tavern ran upon preserving the English Constitution rather than upon improving it; but it is noteworthy that Mr. Goldsmith, who was of that company, was born of the same century that produced Laurence Sterne, and that "She Stoops to Conquer" and the "Vicar of Wakefield," with their sweet savor of purity and modesty and grace, no less than "Tristram Shandy" and "Tom Jones," with their pungent odor, blossomed in the unweeded garden of that careless age. Burns sang with clear throat and an unschooled rapture at the North, and the bards were born who were to bring the next age in with strains that rule our spirits still.

A deep pulse beat in that uneventful century. All things were making ready for a great change. When the century began it was the morrow of a great struggle, from whose passionate endeavors men rested with a certain lassitude, with a great weariness and longing for peace. The travail of the civil wars had not ended with the mastery of Cromwell, the Restoration of Charles, and the ousting of James; it had ended only with the constitutional revolution which followed 1688, and with the triumphs of the Prince of Orange. It had been compounded of every element that can excite or subdue the spirits of men. Questions of politics had sprung out of questions of religion, and men had found their souls staked upon the issue. The wits of the Restoration tried to laugh the ardor off, but it burned persistent until its work was done and the liberties of England spread to every field of thought or action.

No wonder the days of Queen Anne seemed dull and thoughtless after such an age; and yet no wonder there was a sharp reaction. No wonder questions of religion were avoided, minor questions of reform postponed. No wonder Sir Robert sought to cool the body politic and calm men's minds for business. But other forces were gathering head as hot as those which had but just subsided. This long age of apparent reaction was in fact an age of preparation also; was not merely the morrow of one revolution, but was also the eve of another, more tremendous still, which was to shake the whole fabric of society. England had no direct part in bringing the French Revolution on, but she drank with the rest of the wine of the age which produced it, and before it came had had her own rude awakening in the revolt of her American colonies.

Great industrial changes were in progress, too. This century, so dull to the political historian, was the century in which the world of our own day was born, the century of that industrial revolution which made political ambition thenceforth an instrument of material achievement, of commerce and manufacture. These were the days in which canals began to be built in England, to open her inland markets to the world and shorten and multiply her routes of trade; when the spinning jenny was invented and the steam engine and the spinning machine and the weaver's mule; when cities which had slept since the middle ages waked of a sudden to new life and new cities sprang up where only hamlets had been. Peasants crowded into the towns for work; the countrysides saw their life upset, unsettled; idlers thronged the highways and the marts, their old life at the plow or in the village given up, no settled new life found; there were not police enough to check or hinder vagrancy, and sturdy beggars were all too ready to turn their hands to crime and riot. The old order was breaking up, and men did not readily find their places in the new.

The new age found its philosophy in Adam Smith's "Wealth of Nations," the philosophy of self-interest, and men thought too constantly upon these things to think deeply on any others. An industrial age, an age of industrial beginnings, offers new adventures to the mind, and men turn their energies into the channels of material power. It is no time for speculations concerning another world; the immediate task is to fill this world with wealth and fortune and all the enginery of material success. It is no time to regard men as living souls; they must be thought of rather as tools, as workmen, as producers of wealth, the builders of industry, and the captains of soldiers of fortune. Men must talk of fiscal problems, of the laws of commerce, of the raw materials and the processes of manufacture, of the facilitation of exchange. Politics centres in the budget, and the freedom men think of is rather the freedom of the market than the freedom of the hustings or the voting booth.

And yet there are here great energies let loose which have not wrought their full effect upon the minds of men in the mere doing of their daily tasks or the mere planning of their fortunes. Men must think and long as well as toil; the wider the world upon which they spend themselves the wider the sweep of their thoughts, the restless, unceasing excursions of their hope. The mind of England did not lie quiet through those unquiet days. All things were making and to be made, new thoughts of life as well as new ways of living. Masters and laborers alike were sharing in the new birth of society. And in the midst of these scenes, this shifting of the forces of the world, this passing of old things and birth of new, stood John Wesley, the child, the contemporary, the spiritual protagonist of the eighteenth century. Born before Blenheim had been fought, he lived until the fires of the French Revolution were ablaze. He was as much the child of his age as Bolingbroke was, or Robert Burns. We ought long ago to have perceived that no century yields a single type. There are countrysides the land over which know nothing of London town. The Vicar of Wakefield rules his parish as no rollicking, free-thinking fellow can who sups with Laurence Sterne. Sir Roger de Coverley is as truly a gentleman of his age as Squire Western. Quiet homes breed their own sons. The Scots country at the North has its own free race of poets and thinkers, men, some of them, as stern as puritans in the midst of the loose age. Many a quiet village church in England hears preaching which has no likeness at all to the cool rationalistic discourse of vicars and curates whom the spiritual blight of the age has touched, and witnesses in its vicarage a life as simple, as grave, as elevated above the vain pursuits of the world as any household of puritan days had seen. England was steadied in that day, as always, by her great pervasive middle class, whose affections did not veer amidst the heady gusts even of that time of change, when the world was in transformation; whose life held to the same standards, whose thoughts travelled old accustomed ways. The indifference of the church did not destroy their religion. They did not lose their prepossessions for the orderly manners and morals that kept life pure.

It was no anomaly, therefore, that the son of Samuel and Susanna Wesley should come from the Epworth rectory to preach forth righteousness and judgment to come to the men of the eighteenth century. Epworth, in quiet Lincolnshire, was typical English land and lay remote from the follies and fashions of the age. There was sober thinking and plain living,—there where low monotonous levels ran flat to the spreading Humber and the coasts of the sea. The children of that vicarage, swarming a little host about its hearth, were bred in love and fear, love of rectitude and fear of sin, their imagination filled with the ancient sanctions of the religion of the prophets and the martyrs, their lives drilled to right action and the studious service of God. Some things in the intercourse and discipline of that household strike us with a sort of awe, some with repulsion. Those children lived too much in the presence of things unseen; the inflexible consciences of the parents who ruled them brought them under a rigid discipline which disturbed their spirits as much as it enlightened them. But, though gaiety and lightness of heart were there shut out, love was not, nor sweetness. No one can read Susanna Wesley's rules for the instruction and development of her children without seeing the tender heart of the true woman, whose children were the light of her eyes. This mother was a true counsellor and her children resorted to her as to a sort of providence, feeling safe when she approved. For the stronger spirits among them the regime of that household was a keen and wholesome tonic.

And John Wesley was certainly one of the stronger spirits. He came out of the hands of his mother with the temper of a piece of fine steel. All that was executive and fit for mastery in the discipline of belief seemed to come to perfection in him. He dealt with the spirits of other men with the unerring capacity of a man of affairs,—a sort of spiritual statesman, a politician of

God, speaking the policy of a kingdom unseen, but real and destined to prevail over all kingdoms else.

He did not deem himself a reformer; he deemed himself merely a minister and servant of the church and the faith in which he had been bred, and meant that no man should avoid him upon his errand though it were necessary to search the by-ways and beat the hedges to find those whom he sought. He did not spring to his mission like a man who had seen a vision and conceived the plan of his life beforehand, whole, and with its goal marked upon it as upon a map. He learned what it was to be from day to day, as other men do. He did not halt or hesitate, not because his vision went forward to the end, but because his will was sound, unfailing, sure of its immediate purpose. His "Journal" is as notable a record of common sense and sound practical judgment as Benjamin Franklin's "Autobiography" or the letters of Washington. It is his clear knowledge of his duty and mission from day to day that is remarkable, and the efficiency with which he moved from purpose to purpose. It was a very simple thing that he did, taking it in its main outlines and conceptions. Conceiving religion vitally, as it had been conceived in his own home, he preached it with a vigor, an explicitness, a directness of phrase and particularity of application which shocked the sober decorum of his fellow ministers of the church so much that he was more and more shut out from their pulpits. He got no church of his own; probably no single parish would have satisfied his ardor had a living been found for him. He would not sit still. The conviction of the truth was upon him; he was a messenger of God, and if he could not preach in the churches, where it seemed to him the duty of every man who loved the order and dignity of divine service to stand if he would deliver the word of God, he must, as God's man of affairs, stand in the fields as Mr. Whitefield did and proclaim it to all who could come within the sound of his voice.

And so he made the whole kingdom his parish, took horse like a courier and carried his news along every highway. Slowly, with no premeditated plan, going now here, now there, as some call of counsel or opportunity directed him, he moved as if from stage to stage of a journey; and as he went did his errand as if instinctively. No stranger at an inn, no traveller met upon the road left him without hearing of his business. Those he could not come to a natural parley with he waylaid. The language of his "Journal" is sometimes almost that of the highwayman. "At

Gerard's Cross," he says, "I plainly declared to those whom God gave into my hands the faith as it is in Jesus: as I did the next day to a young man I overtook on the road." The sober passion of the task grew upon him as it unfolded itself under his hand from month to month, from year to year. He was more and more upon the highways; his journeys lengthened, carried him into regions where preachers had never gone before, to the collieries, to the tin mines, to the fishing villages of the coast, and made him familiar with every countryside of the kingdom, his slight and sturdy figure and shrewd, kind face known everywhere. It was not long before he was in the saddle from year's end to year's end, always going forward as if upon an enterprise, but never hurried, always ready to stop and talk upon the one thing that absorbed him, making conversation and discourse his business, seizing upon a handful of listeners no less eagerly than upon a multitude.

The news got carried abroad as he travelled that he was coming, and he was expected with a sort of excitement. Some feared him. His kind had never been known in England since the wandering friars of the middle ages fell quiet and were gone. And no friar had ever spoken as this man spoke. He was not like Mr. Whitefield; his errand seemed hardly the same. Mr. Whitefield swayed men with a power known time out of mind, the power of the consummate orator whose words possess the mind and rule the spirit while he speaks. There was no magic of oratory in Mr. Wesley's tone or presence. There was something more singular, more intimate, more searching. He commanded so quietly, wore so subtle an air of gentle majesty, attached men to himself so like a party leader, whose coming draws together a company of partisans, and whose going leaves an organized band of adherents, that cautious men were uneasy and suspicious concerning him. He seemed a sort of revolutionist, left no community as he found it, set men by the ears. It was hard to believe that he had no covert errand, that he meant nothing more than to preach the peaceable riches of Christ. "The spirit of the Lord is upon me, because he hath anointed me to preach the gospel to the poor; he hath sent me to heal the broken-hearted; to preach deliverance to the captives, and recovery of sight to the blind; to set at liberty them that are bruised, to proclaim the acceptable year of the Lord,"—this had been the text from which he preached his first sermon by the highway, standing upon a little eminence just outside the town of Bristol. It described his mission,—but not to his enemies. The

churches had been shut against him, not because he preached,
but because he preached with so disturbing a force and directness, as if he had come to take the peace of the church away and
stir men to a great spiritual revolution; and uneasy questionings
arose about him. Why was he so busy? Why did he confer so
often with an intimate group of friends, as if upon some deep
plan, appoint rendezvous with them, and seem to know always
which way he must turn next, and when? Why was he so restless, so indomitably eager to make the next move in his mysteri-
ous journey? Why did he push on through any weather and
look to his mount like a trooper on campaign? Did he mean
to upset the country? Men had seen the government of England
disturbed before that by fanatics who talked only of religion and
of judgment to come. The puritan and the roundhead had been
men of this kind, and the Scottish covenanters. Was it not possible that John Wesley was the emissary of a party or of some pre-
tender, or even of the sinister church of Rome?

He lived such calumnies down. No mobs dogged his steps
after men had once come to know him and perceived the real
quality he was of. Indeed, from the very first men had surren-
dered their suspicions upon sight of him. It was impossible, it
would seem, not to trust him when once you had looked into his
calm gray eyes. He was so friendly, so simple, so open, so ready
to meet your challenge with temperate and reasonable reply, that
it was impossible to deem him subtle, politic, covert, a man to
preach one thing and plan another. There was something, too, in
his speech and in the way he bore himself which discovered the
heart of every man he dealt with. Men would raise their hands
to strike him in the mob and, having caught the look in his still
eye, bring them down to stroke his hair. Something issued forth
from him which penetrated and subdued them,—some suggestion
of purity, some intimation of love, some sign of innocence and
nobility,—some power at once of rebuke and attraction which he
must have caught from his Master. And so there came a day
when prejudice stood abashed before him, and men everywhere
hailed his coming as the coming of a friend and pastor. He became not only the best known man in the kingdom,—that of
course, because he went everywhere,—but also the best loved and
the most welcome.

And yet the first judgment of him had not been wholly wrong.
A sort of revolution followed him, after all. It was not merely
that he came and went so constantly and moved every countryside with his preaching. Something remained after he was gone:

the touch of the statesman men had at first taken him to be. He was a minister of the Church of England. He loved her practices and had not willingly broken with them. It had been with the keenest reluctance that he consented to preach in the fields, outside the sacred precincts of a church, "having been all my life," as he said, "so tenacious of every point relating to decency and order that I should have thought the saving of souls almost a sin if it had not been done in a church." He never broke with the communion he loved. But his work in the wide parish of a whole kingdom could not be done alone, and not many men bred to the orders of the church could be found to assist him; he was forced by sheer drift of circumstances to establish a sort of lay society, a sort of salvation army, to till the fields he had plowed. He was a born leader of men. The conferences he held with the friends he loved and trusted were councils of campaign, and did hold long plans in view, as his enemies suspected. They have a high and honorable place in the history of the statesmanship of salvation. It was a chief part of Wesley's singular power that everything he touched took shape as if with a sort of institutional life. He was not so great a preacher as Whitefield or so moving a poet as his brother Charles; men counseled him who were more expert and profound theologians than he and more subtle reasoners upon the processes of salvation. But in him all things seemed combined; no one power seemed more excellent than another, and every power expressed itself in action under the certain operation of his planning will. He almost unwittingly left a church behind him.

It is this statesmanship in the man that gives him precedence in the annals of his day. Men's spirits were not dead; they are never dead; but they sometimes stand confused, daunted, or amazed as they did amidst the shifting scenes of the eighteenth century, and wait to be commanded. This man commanded them, and kept his command over them, not only by the way he held the eye of the whole nation in his incessant tireless journeys, his presence everywhere, his winning power of address, but also by setting up deputies, classes, societies, where he himself could not be, with their places of meeting, their organizations and efficient way of action. He was as practical and attentive to details as a master of industry, and as keen to keep hold of the business he had set afoot. It was a happy gibe that dubbed the men of his way *Methodists*. It was the method of his evangelization that gave it permanance and historical significance. He would in any case have been a notable figure, a moving force in the history of his age. His mere preaching, his striking personality, his mere presence everywhere in the story of the time, his mere vagrancy and indomitable charm, would have drawn every historian to speak of him and make much of his picturesque part in the motley drama of the century; but as it is they have been constrained to put him among statesmen as well as in their catalogues of saints and missionaries.

History is inexorable with men who isolate themselves. They are suffered oftentimes to find a place in literature, but never in the story of events or in any serious reckoning of cause and effect. They may be interesting, but they are not important. The mere revolutionist looks small enough when his day is passed; the mere agitator struts but a little while and without applause amidst the scenes and events which men remember. It is the men who make as well as destroy who really serve their race, and it is noteworthy how action predominated in Wesley from the first. The little coterie at Oxford, to which we look back as to the first associates in the movement, which John Wesley dominated, were as fervent in their prayers, in their musings upon the Scripture, in their visits to the poor and outcast, before John Wesley joined them as afterward. Their zeal had its roots in the divine pity which must lie at the heart of every evangelistic movement,—pity for those to whom the gospel is not preached, whom no light of Christian guidance had reached, the men in the jails and in the purlieus of the towns whom the church does not seek or touch; but he gave them leadership and the spirit of achievement. His genius for action touched everything he was associated with; every enterprise took from him an impulse of efficiency.

Unquestionably this man altered and in his day governed the spiritual history of England and the English-speaking race on both sides of the sea; and we ask what was ready at his hand, what did he bring into being of the things he seemed to create? The originative power of the individual in affairs must always remain a mystery, a theme more full of questions than of answers. What would the eighteenth century in England have produced of spiritual betterment without John Wesley? What did he give it which it could not have got without him? These are questions which no man can answer. But one thing is plain: Wesley did not create life, he only summoned it to consciousness. The eighteenth century was not dead; it was not even asleep; it was only confused, unorganized, without authoritative leadership in matters of faith and doctrine, uncertain of its direction.

Wesley's own Journal affords us an authentic picture of the time, mixed, as always, of good and bad. He fared well or ill upon his journeys as England was itself made up. The self-government of England in that day was a thing uncentred and unsystematic in a degree it is nowadays difficult for us to imagine. The country gentlemen, who were magistrates, ruled as they pleased in the countrysides, whether in matters of justice or administration, without dictation or suggestion from London; and yet ruled rather as representatives than as masters. They were neighbors the year around to the people they ruled; their interests were not divorced from the interests of the rest. Local pride and a public spirit traditional amongst them held them generally to a just and upright course. But the process of justice with them was a process of opinion as much as of law. It was an inquest of the neighborhood, and each neighborhood dealt with visitors and vagrants as it would. There was everywhere the free touch of individuality. The roads were not policed; the towns were not patrolled,—good men and bad had almost equal leave to live as they pleased. If things went wrong the nearest magistrate must be looked up at his home or stopped in his carriage as he passed along the highway and asked to pass judgment as chief neighbor and arbiter of the place. And so Mr. Wesley dealt with individuals,—it was the English way. His safety lay in the love and admiration he won or in the sense of fair play to which his frank and open methods appealed; his peril, in the passions of the crowds or of the individuals who pressed about him full of hatred and evil thoughts.

The noteworthy thing was how many good men he found along these highways where Tom Jones had travelled, how many were glad to listen to him and rejoiced at the message he brought, how many were just and thoughtful and compassionate, and waited for the gospel with an open heart. This man, as I have said, was no engaging orator, whom it would have been a pleasure to hear upon any theme. He spoke very searching words, sharper than any two-edged sword, cutting the conscience to the quick. It was no pastime to hear him. It was the more singular, therefore, the more significant, the more pitiful, how eagerly he was sought out, as if by men who knew their sore need and would fain hear some word of help, though it were a word also of stern rebuke and of fearful portent to those who went astray. The spiritual hunger of men was manifest, their need of the church, their instinct to be saved. The time was ready and cried out for a spiritual revival.

The church was dead and Wesley awakened it; the poor were neglected and Wesley sought them out; the gospel was shrunken into formulas and Wesley flung it fresh upon the air once more in the speech of common men; the air was stagnant and fetid; he cleared and purified it by speaking always and everywhere the word of God; and men's spirits responded, leaped at the message, and were made wholesome as they comprehended it. It was a voice for which they had waited, though they knew it not. It would not have been heard had it come untimely. It was the voice of the century's longing heard in the mouth of this one man more perfectly, more potently, than in the mouth of any other,—and this man a master of other men, a leader who left his hearers wiser than he found them in the practical means of salvation.

And so everything that made for the regeneration of the times seemed to link itself with Methodism. The great impulse of humane feeling which marked the closing years of the century seemed in no small measure to spring from it: the reform of prisons, the agitation for the abolition of slavery, the establishment of missionary societies and Bible societies, the introduction into life, and even into law, of pity for the poor, compassion for those who must suffer. The noble philanthropies and reforms which brighten the annals of the nineteenth century had their spiritual birth in the eighteenth. Wesley had carried Christianity to the masses of the people, had renewed the mission of Christ himself, and all things began to take color from what he had done. Men to whom Methodism meant nothing yet, in fact, followed this man to whom Methodism owed its establishment.

No doubt he played no small part in saving England from the madness which fell upon France ere the century ended. The English poor bore no such intolerable burdens as the poor of France had to endure. There was no such insensate preservation of old abuses in England as maddened the unhappy country across the Channel. But society was in sharp transition in England; one industrial age was giving place to another, and the poor particularly were sadly at a loss to find their places in the new. Work was hard to get, and the new work of pent-up towns was harder to understand and to do than the old familiar work in the field or in the village shops. There were sharper contrasts now than before between rich and poor, and the rich were no longer always settled neighbors in some countryside, but often upstart merchants in the towns, innovating manufacturers who seemed bent upon making society over to suit their own interests.

It might have gone hard with order and government in a nation so upset, transformed, distracted, had not the hopeful lessons of religion been taught broadcast and the people made to feel that once more pity and salvation had sought them out.

There is a deep fascination in this mystery of what one man may do to change the face of his age. John Wesley, we have had reason to say, planned no reform, premeditated no revivification of society; his was simply the work of an efficient conviction. How far he was himself a product of the century which he revived it were a futile piece of metaphysic to inquire. That even his convictions were born of his age may go without saying: they are born in us also by a study of his age, and no century listens to a voice out of another,—least of all out of a century yet to come. What is important for us is the method and cause of John Wesley's success. His method was as simple as the object he had in view. He wanted to get at men, and he went directly to them, not so much like a priest as like a fellow man standing in a like need with themselves. And the cause of his success? Genius, no doubt, and the gifts of a leader of men, but also something less singular, though perhaps not less individual,—a clear conviction of revealed truth and of its power to save. Neither men nor society can be saved by opinions; nothing has power to prevail but the conviction which commands, not the mind merely, but the will and the whole spirit as well. It is this and this only that makes one spirit the master of others, and no man need fear to use his conviction in any age. It will not fail of its power. Its magic has no sorcery of words, no trick of personal magnetism. It concentrates personality as if into a single element of sheer force, and transforms conduct into a life.

John Wesley's place in history is the place of the evangelist who is also a master of affairs. The evangelization of the world will always be the road to fame and power, but only to those who take it seeking, not these things, but the kingdom of God; and if the evangelist be what John Wesley was, a man poised in spirit, deeply conversant with the natures of his fellow-men, studious of the truth, sober to think, prompt and yet not rash to act, apt to speak without excitement and yet with a keen power of conviction, he can do for another age what John Wesley did for the eighteenth century. His age was singular in its need, as he was singular in his gifts and power. The eighteenth century cried out for deliverance and light, and God had prepared this man to show again the might and the blessing of his salvation.[2]

Printed in 1703-1903, *Wesley Bicentennial, Wesleyan University* (Middletown, Conn., 1904), pp. 157-70.
    [2] There is a WWsh draft of this address, dated June 30 [1903], in WP, DLC, along with two typed copies, both with WWhw emendations.

A News Report of a Wesley Bicentennial Celebration in Middletown, Connecticut

[July 1, 1903]

WESLEY IN HISTORY.
Address by Woodrow Wilson
of Princeton.
LARGE AUDIENCE HEAR HIM.

President Woodrow Wilson of Princeton university was greeted by a very large audience at the North church,[1] Tuesday night, when he delivered an address on "John Wesley's Place in History" in connection with the Wesley bi-centennial celebration. Every seat in the church was taken and many were obliged to stand.

There was a distinguished company on the platform and when it entered the auditorium there was prolonged handclapping. The members of it were Secretary of the Treasury Leslie M. Shaw, Governor [John Lewis] Bates of Massachusetts, Governor [Abiram] Chamberlain of Connecticut, ex-Governor [Owen Vincent] Coffin, President [Charles William] Eliot of Harvard, President Wilson of Princeton, President [Ira] Remsen of Johns Hopkins, President [Bradford Paul] Raymond of Wesleyan, and Bishop Hendrix.[2]

Governor Chamberlain presided with dignity and before introducing the speaker presented Governor Bates to the audience. President Wilson was greeted with hearty applause. He spoke in part as follows.[3] . . .

Printed in the *Middletown*, Conn., *Tribune*, July 1, 1903; one editorial heading omitted.
    [1] The First Congregational Church of which Wilson's old friend, the Rev. Dr. Azel Washburn Hazen, was pastor.
    [2] The Rev. Dr. Eugene Russell Hendrix, Bishop of the Methodist Episcopal Church, South, and a graduate of Wesleyan University in the Class of 1867.
    [3] Here follows a long summary of Wilson's address.

Frederick Jackson Turner's Review of
A History of the American People

[July 1903]

In his *History of the American People* President Woodrow Wilson of Princeton University has given us a survey of our entire history in the brief compass of about 300,000 words, apparently desiring to do for this country what Green in his single volume did for England; but the latter took something like 100,000 more words for his task. It is easy to see that while Green was more deeply affected by interest in the economic and social life of the people, Wilson's keenest interest is that of a critic of politics, more at home in characterizing political leaders and the trend of events than in dealing with the deeper undercurrents of economic and social change. The work is often brilliant in style; the author has read widely and has aimed rather to fuse the facts of American history into artistic literary form than to make investigative contributions to the facts of our development. His work is that of interpretation.

The first impression which the student will receive is, perhaps, that the narrative, with all its finish, lacks saturation with facts and fails somewhat to produce the effect of reality—or, in the phrase of the art critics, it lacks in "tactile values." This first impression is not altogether well-founded. In so compressed a treatment much has to be sacrificed to conciseness, and the author's literary fusion of his material presents the essence of many facts in sentences that run so gracefully and buoyantly that the reader easily overlooks the burden which they bear. The difficulty of this achievement is apparent to the student who knows the facts, but the general reader suffers a loss by the very success with which the author has substituted the well-phrased formulae that express many facts for the more concrete and less artistic materials themselves. This impression of something like tenuosity is exaggerated by the ornate and bulky form in which the publishers have presented the work. Green used to call his own history "Little Book." In this case "Little Book" is stretched by large type, heavy paper, and a profusion of illustrations into five volumes of nearly 350 pages each. The effect is that the stream of narrative too frequently runs like a rivulet between the illustrations. The excellence of most of these pictures must

A History of the American People. By Woodrow Wilson, Ph.D., Litt.D., LL.D. In five volumes. (New York and London: Harper and Brothers. 1902. Pp. xxvi, 350; xix, 369; xvi, 348; xv, 343; xii, 338.)

be recognized, although the process of artistically redrawing old prints and portraits is objectionable to the critic who is sensitive in the matter of the inviolability of sources; but even when the pictures are above reproach in this respect, and when they are appropriately placed, they continually distract attention from the narrative. The frequent irrelevancy of the illustrations is also to be regretted. Why Alexander Stephens should look out from the narrative of Jackson's war on the bank; why Cyrus McCormick should intrude in a discussion of the independent treasury; while Whittier's gentle smile plays above the story of McCormick's invention of the reaper; and why many similar incongruities exist could doubtless be answered by the expert in the composing-room. But these are difficulties that future editions can modify, and it is to be hoped that a single-volume edition will sometime allow the readers to see the work in its most effective form.

In the matter of general perspective and proportion President Wilson has shown good judgment. He has skilfully and pleasingly woven together the difficult and isolated pieces of seventeenth century colonial history in a single volume. To the eighteenth century and the Revolution another volume is given. Here one finds a lack of attention to the important facts of economic and political significance that were so powerful in shaping the sections during that period, in preparing the way for American political parties and institutions, in shaping the conditions that affected the Revolution, and in creating the forces that expressed themselves in American expansion. But this is the period that has suffered at the hands of all our historians. The French and Indian wars and the Revolution itself are so picturesque that they obscure the other facts of this important era of Americanization. A third volume carries the narrative from the treaty of peace to the election of Jackson,—by grace of over-heroic compression. In the fourth, President Wilson reaches the period with which he had before skilfully dealt in his little text-book, *Division and Reunion*, and carries the history on to the close of the Civil War. The fifth volume spans the years between Reconstruction and the close of the Spanish War. Whatever criticisms may be offered, it is impossible to find in similar compass or by another single author so sustained and vital a view of the whole first cycle of American history that rounded itself out with the nation's completion of the conquest of the west, and its step overseas into colonial empire.

Aside from matters of judgment the author has not fallen into more errors of fact than are common to first editions. The statements (III. 242) that the minimum provision of the tariff of 1816 applied to woolens as well as to cottons; that Jackson's declaration of opposition to the bank was made in his inaugural address (IV. 19, 43); that George Rogers Clark consulted Madison (Mason), and that he marched across the frozen *forests* from Kaskaskia (II. 293, 296) are typical of some actual errors. It is certainly a mistake to say that there is no doubt that Texas was a part of the Louisiana purchase, as recent students of Spanish claims to the region have shown. Willing's force did no such execution as the author credits it with on the lower Mississippi in the Revolution (II. 297). One doubts the accuracy of attributing pioneer settlement to Kentucky as early as 1730 (II, 61), and that Englishmen were building huts beyond the Alleghanies "as men who mean to stay," before the close of the seventeenth century (II. 9). The references to Cumberland Gap in connection with the national road, and the photograph of Cumberland Gap near Wheeling (III. 202, 241) will certainly confuse the reader in locating the celebrated gateway of the pioneers to Kentucky. Not all the members of Monroe's cabinet were shocked at Jackson's exploits in Florida (III, 258). Monroe's attitude toward internal improvements at national expense is inaccurately stated (III. 260). The select bibliographies that follow the various chapters are generally well chosen, but some striking omissions occur, such as the failure to cite McCrady's *South Carolina*, and the omission of Parkman's works in the references on the French wars. The student will be puzzled to know why the appendix containing the treaty of 1783, the Ordinance of 1787, the Constitution, and the Virginia and Kentucky Resolutions is taken *by permission* from Preston's *Documents*!

Perhaps the most significant thesis of President Wilson (himself of Southern antecedents), is that in insisting on the doctrine of state sovereignty the South, "unaltered from of old," adhered to the Union as it was in "that first generation whose life and thought she kept." "There had been," he says, "no amendment of the fundamental law. Could the law change because men's thoughts had changed and their interests?" Mr. Wilson admits that in her reaction the South "stiffened the old doctrines and exaggerated them," but this is a very important admission, which goes far toward vitiating the underlying idea of his theory. In fact the South had changed profoundly. Cotton had revived the decaying institution of slavery, carried it over the old farming area of the Piedmont, and lodged it among the new commonwealths of the Gulf, where it finally bred a more drastic and aggressive spirit of sectionalism. The idea of divided sovereignty and the idea of the beneficence of revolution prevalent in the period of the Revolutionary War help explain the conditions at the origin of the Constitution, but the presidencies of Virginians like Jefferson, Madison, and Monroe, and the decisions of the Virginian Chief Justice Marshall had erected strong barriers against disintegrating tendencies. Nor had the South as a section adhered to the Virginia and Kentucky doctrines (confessedly less rigorous than Calhoun's later exposition of them) in the day of their promulgation. Moreover Madison and Jefferson had given interpretations of these doctrines quite at variance with the theory of Calhoun, and Calhoun himself at the close of the War of 1812 was a nationalist. It would be more correct to say that the generation of 1787 framed a Constitution sufficiently elastic to adjust itself to growth, and sufficiently indefinite as to sovereignty to permit dispute, and that the South, after its economic and social transformations, followed Calhoun in an interpretation of the Union that was at least as novel as the doctrines defended by Webster and assented to not only by the North, but even, in the days of South Carolina's nullification, by the new southern states on the Gulf.

President Wilson is by no means a partizan, however, and he has the advantage that he is the first Southern scholar of adequate training and power who has dealt with American history as a whole in a continental spirit. Northern writers have hardly hitherto given a thoroughly appreciative, not to say sympathetic, presentation of the slaveholding region in our history. President Wilson, born and reared in the south, educated at Princeton, the University of Virginia, and Johns Hopkins, and disciplined by professorships in Pennsylvania and Connecticut, as well as at Princeton, has acquired a catholicity of view that is certainly worthy of mention. Although one gathers the author's friendliness for Mr. Cleveland's type of Democracy in his last volume, even here he is moderate and careful in his judgments.

Frederick J. Turner

Printed in the *American Historical Review*, VIII (July 1903), 762-65.

Notes for a Speech on Shipboard

R.M.S. "Oceanic." "Remarks" 4 July, 1903

Wound up? No place to get religion.

Interesting and gratifying to celebrate the day under the British
flag.

This ship typifies the intercourse wh. has made this possible

Indicates no relaxation of principle but a better and truer understanding

The present attitude of English historians.

Recent events, and our new self-consciousness as Americans.
We seek a new sort of distinction based upon national achievement.

Legend

Patriotism.

WWhw MS. (WP, DLC).

From Jenny Davidson Hibben

The Red Bridge Farm,
Seybertsville, Luzerne Co.,

My dear Mr. Wilson,   Pennsylvania.   July 5 [1903].

Your good-bye note written on the Oceanic was indeed welcome. Jack wrote to you sending his letter to the steamer, but
I am afraid it was too late.

We have followed you both over the sea daily—& doubt not
that yesterday the "favorite orator" delivered a patriotic address
in mid-ocean. *I* had a private celebration of my own. In the morning my host who is a physician took me into the living room, &
after looking through the book shelves, & rejecting "China Collecting in America,"[1] & "A Woman's Hardy Garden,"[2] & all frivo-
lous novels, selected as most appropriate "The Highway of
Fate"[3]—took my wrist—gave it a resounding whack—& the horrid
lump disappeared!

We have had a happy visit in this lovely valley with our dear
old friends, & I am so glad now that we made the effort, although
at one time it seemed a hugh [huge] one, to come here. Already
Princeton seems miles & miles away, & one week ago, *months.*
Jack preaches in a tiny village church this afternoon, & tomorrow
we go to Redfield.

When this reaches you, you may be in Edinburgh. The very
name brings to my mind such happy days there—its an *enchant-
ing* city to me.

It will be lovely for us when we begin to have your letters telling of yourselves & your travels. We miss you very much, & send our warmest love to you & Mrs. Wilson, our dear travellers.

Ever yours,   Jenny Davidson Hibben.

ALS (WP, DLC).
[1] Alice Morse Earle, *China Collecting in America* (New York, 1892).
[2] Helena Rutherfurd Ely, *A Woman's Hardy Garden* (New York and London, 1903).
[3] Rosa Nouchette Carey, *The Highway of Fate* (Philadelphia, 1902).

A Record of a European Trip

[July 10-Sept. 22, 1903]

European a/c—Woodrow Wilson

Liverpool—Chester to Furness Abbey	[$]24.00
Furness Abbey to Ambleside	11.71
July 11th	
Photos	3.25
Dove Cottage	.36
Rydal Mount	.56
Laundry bag	.48
July 12th	
Church collection	.60
July 13th	
Kirkstone Pass (refreshments)	.66
Ullswater, lunch	1.14
Ullswater, gondola	1.14
" Driver	24

Brt. forward	$44.14
July 14th	
"Our Country's Flowers"[1]	1.14
Arnold's Wordsworth[2]	.60
Map, Lake Dist.	.48
Photo	.18
15 July	
Stamps & post cards	1.11
Telegram	.16

[1] William John Gordon, *Our Country's Flowers and How to Know Them* (London, 1891). A copy of this book is in the Wilson Library, DLC.
[2] Probably a reprint of Matthew Arnold (ed.), *The Poems of Wordsworth* (London, 1879).

1903

European a/c — Woodrow Wilson

Liverpool — Chester	
to Furness Abbey	24.00
Furness Abbey to	
Ambleside	11.71
July 11th	
Photos.	3.25
Dove Cottage	.36
Rydal Mount	.56
Laundry bag	.48
July 12th	
Church Collection	.60
July 13th	
Kirkstone Pass (refreshments)	.66
Ullswater, lunch	1.14
Ullswater, gondola	1.14
" Driver	.24

Brt. forward	$44.74
July 14th	
"Our Country's Flowers"	1.14
Arnold's Wordsworth	.60
Map, Lake Dist.	.48
Photo	.18
15 July	
Stamps & post cards	1.11
Telegram	.16
16 July (leaving Grasmere)	
Waitress	.48
	.48
Maid	.60
Hd. Boots	.48
Boots	.60
Wythburn Church	.12
	50.57

The opening pages of Wilson's record of expenses
of the European trip in 1903

16 July (leaving Grasmere)

Waitress	.48
"	.48
Maid	.60
Hd. Boots	.48
Boots	.60
Wythburn Church	.12
	———
	50.57

Brt forward,	50.57
Skinpan boys	.07
Driver to Keswick	.48

Bill (Rothay [Hotel], Grasmere) including Ullswater trip, 15 s., special conveyance to Keswick, 15s., and laundry, 9/6	45.82
Crosthwaite church	.24
Hack driver	.10
Newspaper	.02
17 July	
Buttermere Hotel lunch (on drive)	1.52
Crummock water boat	.60
Buttermere driver	.12
	99.54

Brt. forward	99.54
18 July	
Maid, Keswick	.24
Waiter "	.24
Hd. waiter "	.24
Boots (2)	.48
Bill[3] (including cab to Crosthwaite ch., 3/6, and trip to Buttermere, 12/)	16.74
Fare Keswick–Edinburgh,	11.30
Cab, Edinburgh	.48
Porter	.12
19 July (Sunday)	
Free St. George's coll.	60
Trams,	16
	130.14

Brt. forward	130.14
20 July	
Thr. the Trossachs	12.56
Lunch,	1.02
4 o'clock tea	.72
Telegram	.24
Porter	.12
Shawl strap,	.36

[3] For £3-9-9 from the Keswick Hotel. Receipted bill dated July 18, 1903 (WP, DLC).

21 July
    To Melrose & return   4.08
    Carriage   1.92
    Lunch   1.38
    Abbotsford   .48
    Photos   .60
    Dryburgh   .24
    Melrose   .48
    Chocolate   .24

                                      $153.48

Brt. forward   153.48
22 July
    Carriage 3 1/2 hours,   2.64
    Castle guide   .24
    St. Giles,   .12
    Grayfriars sexton,   .06
    Jno. Knox's house,   .24
    Waterproof coat,   23.52
         "   " , Ellen,   9.60
    Davidson bag,   1.32
    Necklace,   6.24
    Tax on draft,   .25
23 July
    Edinburgh to London,   27.60
    Handkerchief,   .47
    Jewelry,   20.94
    Exhibition,   .36

                                      $247.08

Brt. forward   247.08
    Maid   .60
    Hd. porter   .60
    Boots,   .60
    porter   .24
    Hd. waiter   .24
    Boy,   .12
    Left luggage   .08
    Boy, (Including laundry)   .06
    Bill (Cockburn Hotel)   22.20

24 July (Durham & York)

Cathedral	.24
Chocolate,	.24
Bill (Royal County Hotel)[4]	5.64
Waiter,	.12
Box biscuit,	.48
Boots	.12
	$278.66

Brt. forward	$278.66
Porter (Durham)	.12
Porter (York)	.12
Cab (York)	.48

25 July (York)

Minster	.48
Drive	1.44
Merchant Adventurers' Hall &c.,	.36
Toll bridge	.02
St. Denis church	.05
Photos	.78
Chocolate	.24

26 July (Sunday)

Minster collection,	.72
Surgeon, Ellen's leg,	5.04
Stamps,	24
	$288.74

Brt. forward,	288.74

27 July (York, Lincoln)

Maids	.48
Boots,	.36
Hd. waiter	.48
Bill, (Harker's Hotel)	18.46
Porter,	.12
Cab, York,	.48
Cab, Lincoln,	.48
Porter,	.12

[4] In Durham.

Left luggage (Lincoln)	.08
Cathedral	.24
"Laird's Luck" by Q.[5]	1.08
Rubber bands	.06
Borax,	.02
28 July,	
Photos.,	.72
	—————
	$311.22

—————

Brt. forward	$311.22
Etching	.72
Castle (Lincoln)	.10
Cab,	.48
Bill (White Hart [Hotel])	6.72
Waitress,	.24
Maid,	.12
Boots,	.12
Porter (Lincoln)	.12
" (Ely)	.12
29 July.	
Telegram	.13
Bill, Lamb Hotel (Ely)	4.86
Waiter,	.12
Boots,	.12
Porter (Ely)	.11
Cathedral	.36
	—————
	$325.68

—————

Brt. forward	325.68
Porter (London)	.24
Maid (Ely)	.12
Cab (London)	.84
Cable (to H. A. Garfield)[6]	3.60
Burner and stand,	.32
Inkstand (travelling)	.72

[5] Arthur Thomas Quiller-Couch, *The Laird's Luck and Other Fireside Tales* (London, 1901).
[6] It is printed at July 29, 1903.

30 July (London)

Cab,	.48
"	.48
Bus,	.08
Nat. Portrait Gallery (E.)	.24
Top hat	5.04
Cab,	.36
Royal Acad. Ex[hibit] (included catalogue)	.72
Cab,	.36
	$339.28

Brt. forward	$339.28
Theatre, W.W. (Beaucaire)[7]	2.76

31 July (London)

Cab,	.36
Nat. Gallery (E.) admission and catalogue	.24
Cab,	.36
Cab,	.36
Cab,	.36
Witch Hazel (qt.)	1.32
Bus	.02

1 August (London)

Cab	.36
Cab	.36
Royal Academy	.48
Cab,	.36
Bus rides	.24
	$346.96

Brt. forward	346.96

2 August (Sunday)

Cab (to Temple church)	.48
Cab	.48
Bus	.04
Stamps	.60

[7] *Monsieur Beaucaire* was a dramatization by Booth Tarkington and Evelyn Greenleaf Sutherland of Tarkington's novelette, "Monsieur Beaucaire," which first appeared in *McClure's Magazine*, XIV (Dec. 1899 and Jan. 1900), 158-71, 247-54. The play opened in Philadelphia on October 7, 1901, with Richard Mansfield in the role of Beaucaire. Wilson saw it in London at the Comedy Theatre, with Lewis Waller in the lead.

3 August (London)

Cab	.48
Cab	.48
Cab	.48
Chocolate	.24
Cab	.60
Cab	.36
Theatre (Adm. Crichton)[8]	5.28
Cab	36
Cab	36

$353.20

Brt. forward, $353.20

4 August (London)

Cab,	.36
Wallace Collection,[9]	.30
Bus rides	.10
Travelling box,	14.76
Linen Co. Bank (exchange)	.38
Cab,	.36
Haircut	.12
Silk scarfs,	12.52
Cab	.36
Cab	.36
Bus	.14

5 August (London)

Cab	.36
Cab	.36
Bus	.08

$383.76

[8] *The Admirable Crichton* by James M. Barrie, playing at the Duke of York's Theatre with Henry Brodribb Irving in the lead.

[9] The Wallace Collection was accumulated by several generations of the Seymour-Conway family, particularly by Richard Seymour-Conway, the fourth Marquis of Hertford and his heir, Sir Richard Wallace. Housed at Hertford, the family home on Manchester Square, the collection was given to the government in 1897 and was opened as a national museum on June 20, 1900. It contains a magnificent group, many of them by the great masters, of nearly eight hundred paintings, drawings, and pieces of sculpture; an outstanding collection of Sèvres porcelain, French decorative furniture, and eighteenth-century snuff boxes; a unique collection of European arms and armor; and many other objets d'art.

Brt. forward	$383.76
Cab	.36
Cab	.36
Bus	.02
Theatre (Bishop's Move)[10]	5.28
2 Overcoats	60.48
Hotel Bill to 4th[11]	57.74
Pair braces	.84
Cab	.36
Cab	.36
6 August (London)	
Cab	.36
Cab	.36
Baedeker's *Paris* and *Switzerland*	3.06
Bus,	.04
Hotel bill to date	14.40
	$527.78

Brt. forward,	527.78
Burning spirits	.08
Empty 6 oz. phial,	.06
Hd. waiter	.60
Waiter	.60
Maid	.72
Hd. boots	.60
Boots	.72
Elevator boys	.48
Door boy	.24
Cab to Liverpool St. [Station]	.72
Porter " "	.24
Tickets to Cambridge	4.20
"Sir Richard Calmady"[12]	.60
Left luggage, Cambridge	.08
Porter, "	.12
Bull Hotel bus	.24
	$538.08

[10] A comedy by John Oliver Hobbes [Pearl Mary Teresa Craigie] and Murray Carson, playing at the Garrick Theatre with Arthur Bourchier and Violet Vanbrugh in the leads.

[11] From the Buckingham Palace Hotel. Wilson did not save his receipted bill for this stay; however, he did save the next one from this hotel, for £3-1-6 for August 5 and 6, 1903 (WP, DLC).

[12] Lucas Malet [Mary St. Leger Kingsley Harrison], *The History of Sir Richard Calmady* (2 vols., London, 1901).

Brt. forward,	538.08
Bull Hotel porter	.04
7 August (Cambridge)	
Mending shoes	.04
Cab to Jesus College	.36
Fee, Jesus chapel	.12
Boat	.36
8 August (Cambridge)	
Fees: St. Johns	.24
Girton	.12
Cab (Girton-Newnham)	1.08
Catalogue, Fitzwilliam [Museum],	.12
Hat brushes,	.48
Chocolate	.24
9 August (Sunday) no ex.	
10 August (Camb.-Warwick)	
Photos. & post cards	1.44
	$542.32

Brt. forward,	$542.32
Bill (Bull Hotel)	27.84
Hd waiter	.24
Waiter	.24
Maid	.24
Boots	.24
Bus to Station	.36
Tickets to Warwick	7.08
Porter at Cambridge	.12
" " Bletchley,	.12
" " Rugby	.06
Cab, Warwick	.72
11 August (Warwick)	
Castle fees	.48
Boy, Guy's Cliffs,	.02
Views " "	.36
Kenilworth Castle	.30
	$580.74

Brt. forward,	580.74
Driver to Kenilworth	.12
Leicester Hospital,	.32
Glass of milk	.04
12 Aug. (Stratford)	
Shakespeare's House	.48
Anne Hathaway's house	.24
Church	.24
Guildhall	.24
Pictures	1.56
Lunch,	1.92
Driver	24
Bill (including drives to Kenilworth, $2.28, and Stratford, $5.04)	15.60
Waitress	.24
Maid	.24
	$602.02

Brt. forward,	$602.02
Hd. boots	.60
Boy	.24
Porter at Warwick	.12
Tickets to Oxford	3.48
Porter at "	.12
Bus to Mitre [Hotel]	.36
Porter at "	.12
13 Aug. (Oxford)	
Clothes bag	.47
Fees,	.28
Bus, (tram)	.08
Map of Oxford	.24
14 August (Oxford)	
Stamps	1.00
Jug cream,	.12
Shelley Mem. (Univ. College)	.12
	$608.97

Brt. forward,	608.97
Sheldonian Theatre	.12
Strolling band	.12
Telegram	.12
15 August, (Oxford)	
Jug cream	.12
Students handbook	.60
Mem. book	.02
Cabs,	.76
Bodleian [Library]	.12
Divinity School,	.16
Pictures	.72
Cab	.48
2 Jugs cream	.24
Band	.12
Telegram	.12
	$612.79

Brt. forward	612.79
16 Aug. (Sunday, Oxon)	
Newspaper	.02
Collection, St. Mary's	.12
Ellen, church collection	.24
17 August (Oxford)	
Jug cream	.12
Charge on money drawn	.24
Ironing hat,	.36
Etchings	1.08
Photos.	6.00
Cab,	.48
Exeter porter	.24
Flaxseed	.06
Telegram	.12
18 August (to Wells)	
Bill, Mitre Hotel	48.02
	$669.89

Brt. forward	$669.89
Hd. waiter	.48
Waiter	.24

Maid	.48
Boots	.60
Novels	.24
Cab	.60
Porter (Oxford)	.12
" (Didcot)	.12
" (Swindon)	.04
Tickets (2nd., to Wells)	4.56
Guard, Chippenham,	.08
Cathedral	.12
Bishop's palace garden	.12
4 pair half hose	.96
	$678.65

Brt. forward	$678.65
19 August (Wells)	
Glastonbury Abbey	.24
Boy	.02
Glastonbury views	.24
Driver to Glastonbury	.24
Wells pictures,	1.16
To cathedral tower	.12
20 Aug. (Wells)	
Ink	.02
Postcards	.08
Telegram to London	.14
Cathedral	.24
Chocolate	.24
21 Aug. (to Salisbury)	
Bill, Swan Hotel, Wells,	23.04
	$704.43

Brt. forward,	$704.43
Waitress	.24
Maid	.36
Boots	36
Ticket to Salisbury,	3.92
Porter, Wells	.12
" Glastonbury	08

" Templecombe	.12
" Salisbury	.12
" "	.12
Cab,	.48
Cathedral	.24
" guidebook	.24
Cab,	.60
Lunch, Salisbury,	1.68
Tickets to London,	4.20
	$717.31

Brt. forward,	717.31
Left luggage, Salisb.,	.24
Cab, London,	.48
Porter, "	.12
22 Aug. (London)	
Bus,	.10
Cab,	.48
"	.48
Brit. Linen Co. Bank	.32
Cook's circular ticket[13]	91.52
English-French dict.	.48
Cook's for draft	.12
Bus,	.10
Photos	.96
Soap	.60
Cab,	.24
"	.36
	$813.91

Brt. forward	$813.91
Catalogues, Nat. Gal	.36
23 Aug. (London, Sunday)	
Cab	.36
Bus	.12
Telegram	.32
Bus	.02

[13] For part of the Wilsons' continental journey.

24 Aug. (Amiens, Paris)

Bill, Brown's Hotel,	24.78
Hd. waiter	.24
Waiter	.48
Maid	.36
Boots	.24
Boy	.12
Cab	.72
Porter	.24
Weigher	.12
	$842.39

Brt. forward	842.39
Overweight on luggage	2.32
"Spectator,"	.12
Dover porter	.24
Calais porter	.40
" officer	.24
" lunch	1.10
" Lavatory	.10
" Waiter	.10
Amiens porter	.10
" Consigne	.08
" cathedral	.20
" porter	.10
" supper	1.16
Paris porter	.20
" "	.20
" customs porter	.04
	$849.09

Brt. forward	849.09
Cab,	.90
25 August (Paris)	
Cab, general ride	1.50
Bus	.06
"	.12

26 Aug. (Paris)

Cab,	.60
Notre Dame	.10
Picture cards, Sainte Chapelle,	.16
Cab,	.36
Bus	.12
Catalogue, Louvre,	.24
" "	.25
Cab,	.36
Bus	.03
"	.12
	———
	$854.01

——————

Brt. forward,	$854.01
Cab,	.50
"	.50

27 Aug. (Paris)

Bus	.12
"	.03
Gloves	.95
Cab,	.36
Stamps	.30
Telegram	.48
Bus,	.12
Cab,	.40
Catalogue, Luxembourg,	.15
Cab,	.55

28 August (Versailles)

Cab (Gare des Invalides)	.40
Tickets to Versailles	.54
	———
	$859.41

——————

Brt. Forward	$859.41
Herald	.03
Fee, Grand Trianon	.03
Cab	1.10
Lunch, Versailles	1.10
Gratuities	.04
Fees, Palais, Versailles	.50

Tram	.08
Tickets to Paris	.54
Incidental	.04
Cab,	.36
"	.50
Bus,	.06
29 Aug. (Paris)	
Laundry	2.51
Cab,	.40
Pantheon	.40
	$865.10

Brt. forward	865.10
Eglise St. Etienne	.02
Cab,	.40
Bus,	.12
"	.06
Cab,	.40
Victory (bronze)	14.00
Bus,	.03
Dog (bronze)	4.00
Bus	.12
Cab,	.45
30 Aug. (Paris, Sunday)	
Cab	.35
Collection, American church	1.00
Tram,	12
31 Aug. (Chartres)	
Tram	.12
	$886.14

Brt. forward	$886.14
Ret. ticket to Chartres	5.96
Picture cards, "	.26
Cab	.35
Bus	.06
Postage	.06
Liberty scarfs,	3.80
Gloves	1.80

Ruch[e][14]	1.55
Photo	1.25
Cab,	.40
Cab,	.36
1 Sept. (Paris–Basle)	
Painting (Roses)	2.00
Cab,	.40
Sleeping berths	7.66
	$912.45

Brt. forward,	912.45
Stamp	.03
Cab,	.35
Telegram	.63
Flaxseed (farine de lin)	.10
Bill, Mrs. Van Pelt's[15]	43.20
Maid " " "	1.00
Guillaume	.20
Jean Marie	.60
Cab	.60
Porter, Gare de l'Est	.20
2 Sept. (Basel, Luzern, Pilatus–Kulm)	
Porter, Basel,	.20
Breakfast, en route,	.80
Porter, Luzern,	.20
Cab, "	.40
	$960.96

Brt. forward,	$960.96
Trams,	.15
Tickets (Pilatus–Kulm)	10.84
Railway Time Table (Cook)	.30
Porter, Pilatus–Kulm,	.10
3 Sept. (Pilatus–Luzern)	
Maid, Pilatus–Kulm,	.10
Pilatus–Kulm, extras	.50
Porter, Pilatus–Kulm	.10

[14] Lace frill for a dress.
[15] For 216 francs from Mrs. E. L. Van Pelt's Pension, 4, Square de Latour-Maubourg, Paris. Receipted bill dated Sept. 1, 1903 (WP, DLC).

Pears, Alpnach,	.16
Porter, Alpnach,	.10
Cab, Luzern,	.35
Tram,	.06
Telegram, Bellagio	.36
4 Sept. (Luzern)	
Trams	.18
Cyclorama	.40
	$974.66

Brt. forward,	$974.66
Necklaces,	4.80
Pin	1.60
Diorama,	.40
Tram	.06
Tickets to Fluellen	2.12
Lunch on boat,	.58
Tram	.06
5 Sept. (Luzern–Como)	
Maid, Luzern,	.20
Bill (3 days)[16]	18.34
Concierge	20
Boy	10
Hotel Porter	.09
Station "	.20
Paris *Herald*	.04
Tickets to Como,	12.02
	$1015.47

Brt. forward,	$1015.47
Lunch, en route,	1.80
Bus to boat, Como,	.28
Flowers,	.04
Tickets to Bellagio,	2.04
Refreshments	.40
Porter, Como,	.20
" Bellagio	.08

[16] For 91.60 francs from the Tivoli Hotel and Pension. Receipted bill dated Sept. 5, 1903 (WP, DLC).

6 Sept. (Bellagio–Sunday)

Refreshments, Villa Serbelloni,	.60
Waiter, Hotel	.40

7 Sept. (Bellagio–Luzern)

Bill, Grand Hotel, Bellagio,	17.60
Waiter,	.20
"	.20
Maid,	.20
	——
	$1039.51

Brt. forward,	1039.51
Concierge	.40
Post cards	.28
Porter, Bellagio	.20
" Como	.20
Lunch "	1.80
Porter "	.20
" "	.20
Cab,	.40
Herald,	.08
Ticket, Como–Luzern	12.04
Station porter, Como,	.20
" " Luzern	.20
Cab, Luzern	.40

8 Sept. (Luzern–Geneva)

Bill, Tivoli,	6.38
Trams	.45
	——
	$1062.94

Brt. forward,	$1062.94
Telegram to Geneva,	.13
Hair-cut	.30
Cailler's Chocolat-au-lait,	.30
Pillow (F.G.C.)[17]	5.12
Pins,	.80
Cloth	.42
Concierge, Tivoli	.20
Porter, "	.20
" "	.20

[17] Identified in Jenny D. Hibben to WW, Aug. 9, 1903, n. 3.

Station porter, Luzern,	.20
Herald	.05
"	.05
Porter, Geneva,	.20
9 Sept. (Geneva)	
Tram	.30
Tickets, boat, Nyon & ret.	1.20
	$1072.61

Brt. forward,	$1072.61
Herald	.05
10 Sept. (Geneva-Paris)	
Tram	.12
Cab	.40
Sleeping car reservation	19.60
Concierge,	.40
Laundry,	.60
Rent, field glasses,	.20
Maid	.32
Photos & cards,	.46
Walking staff,	3.00
Bill [Grand Hotel], Beau Rivage,	17.15
Hd. waiter	.40
Waiter	.20
Elevator boy	.20
Hotel porter	.20
	$1115.91

Brt. forward,	1115.91
Hotel porter with 'bus,	.40
Station porter	.20
11 Sept. (Paris)	
Porter, Gare de Lyon	.20
Cab	.60
Bus	.24
Loss on bad coin,	.60
Gloves,	.75
Bus,	.06
Incidental (E.)	.02

Cab,	.60
Bus,	.15
Photos.,	3.00
12 Sept. (Paris)	
Bus	.21
Laundry	2.12

$1125.06

————————

Brt. forward,	$1125.06
Bus	.12
Collars (E)	.50
13 Sept. (Paris—Cherbourg)	
Bill, Mrs. Van Pelt's	11.80
Guillaume	.10
Jean Marie	.20
Porter, Mrs. Van Pelt's	.10
St. Lazarre	.40
Baggage man	.10
" overweight	1.50
Cab,	1.10
Porter, Cherbourg,[18]	.20
" "	.30
Evian water	.25

$1141.73

————————

Brt. forward	$1141.73
16 Sept. (At sea)	
Shave	.25
19 Sept. (At sea)	
2 steamer chairs,	2.20
Charges on trunk sent to Cherbourg	4.65
Music,	1.25
21 Sept. (At sea)	
Table waters	.85

[18] The Wilsons sailed as first class passengers aboard the Norddeutscher Lloyd liner *Bremen* on September 13, 1903. Printed passenger list dated Sept. 12, 1903 (WP, DLC).

22 Sept. (New York)

Table steward	5.00
Boot "	1.25
Room "	3.00
Deck "	1.90
Room stewardess	2.50
Porters	.80
	$1164.88

Brt. forward	$1164.88
Import duty	23.75
Dock to R.R. station,	5.25
Station porter	.25
Ticket to Princeton (E.)	1.50
Lunch	1.25
	1196.88
Fees (outward bound)	20.00
	1216.88
Steamship tickets	250.00
	200
	1666.88

Pocket notebook (WP, DLC).

From Charles Williston McAlpin

My dear Dr. Wilson: [Princeton, N. J.]   July 13, 1903.

I enclose some papers of a personal nature and wish to ask your advice about one department of your correspondence. Several requests for lectures and addresses next winter have been received and I have answered them to the effect that you were abroad and would attend to them upon your return. Some of the gentlemen wish to know your foreign address in order to write to you this summer, but I have refrained from giving it stating that you directed me not to do so. If you wish me to discriminate I shall be very glad to do so, but I imagine you will be glad to escape all these appeals for a season.

I have written to Mr. Hughes, whose letter I enclose,[1] that you would not return until the fall, but his request seems so personal that I enclose it for your consideration.

An invitation to the President, Fellows and Trustees to attend the Installation of Professor Finley as President of the C.C.N.Y. has been received. I thought I could transfer the responsibility of answering it to the Dean, but he said the faculty had nothing to do with it and suggested that I accept stating that you would represent the University and asking for a ticket for Mrs. Wilson. As the installation is to take place on Tuesday, September 29th, I do not know whether you will have returned and if you do not expect to be here may I ask you to appoint a delegate?[2]

Mr. Carnegie has sent you a copy of his Presidential Address[3] which I have acknowledged with fair words. In your absence I have had the pleasure of thanking Mr. Frick for his contribution of $20,000 to the Gymnasium[4] and have also acknowledged the gift of $5,000 from Tom McCarter,[5] which is to be used subject to your direction.

We are having typical summer weather here which means a combination of all sorts.

I forgot to mention that I have received a cheque for $250, a gift from the Estate of George W. Brown, Jr., '77.

Trusting that you are having a pleasant time, believe me,

Very sincerely yours,   [C. W. McAlpin]

CCL (McAlpin File, UA, NjP).

[1] It is missing.

[2] Wilson returned in time to attend Finley's inauguration. For his comment on the affair, see WW to EAW, Sept. 30, 1903, Vol. 15.

[3] This copy is missing, but it was a reprint of Carnegie's presidential address to the British Iron and Steel Institute in London on May 7, 1903. It is printed in the London *Journal of the Iron and Steel Institute*, LXIII (1903), 32-48.

[4] Henry Clay Frick, father of Childs Frick '05. This was the first of many substantial donations to the university by the steel manufacturer.

[5] Thomas Nesbitt McCarter '88.

From Harry Augustus Garfield

Newstate P.O., Berkshire Co., Mass.

My dear Dr. Wilson: July 14, 1903

I have held your letter of June eleventh longer than I intended without answer, but a brief rest seemed necessary to a right conclusion.

I have decided to accept your call to the chair of Politics, & expect to be ready to take up the work at Princeton in February.

If convenient to you, I prefer that at least until my return home, about August first, no public mention of my acceptance be made.

With kindest regards, I remain,

Sincerely Yours,   H. A. Garfield

ALS (WP, DLC).

From Charles Williston McAlpin

My dear Dr. Wilson: [Princeton, N. J.]   July 17, 1903.

I enclose copy of a letter received from Mr. Garfield the receipt of which I have acknowledged. I shall not mention the subject to anyone until I receive word from you to do so. I also enclose a voluminous letter received this morning[1] the contents of which will interest you.

What do you wish me to do about bills that come to you, shall I forward them to you or simply send a postal similar to the enclosed?

We are having delightful weather this week, very similar to the weather that prevailed last summer, but the heat last week was intense.

Good progress is being made on the '79 dormitory and University matters, so far as I am cognizant, are quiet and in good shape.

I remain,   Very sincerely yours,   [C. W. McAlpin]

CCL (McAlpin File, UA, NjP).
1 This letter is missing.

Two Letters from Jenny Davidson Hibben

"The Braes" Redfield, N. Y.

My dear Mr. Wilson,   July 17, 1903.

Your letter written from the steamer was more than welcome last night. How lovely a thing a voyage must be without seasickness. I am delighted that you & Mrs. Wilson escaped it. If I may find fault, *why* didn't you tell me *where* you were going first. I do love to know of plans of travel in advance—so that *I* may travel too, but now I have no idea as to whether you went first to the lovely English lakes, & so to Scotland, or to London. I beg of you let me know something occasionally of your plans in advance.

My dear brother[1] sails to-morrow on the Etruria. He has a charming plan if he carries it out. After a few days in Ireland, (where I coaxed him to go, against his will) he goes to Skye, Lewis & the Orkney Islands—then down to Edinburgh & London where he has friends—Devonshire to see a cousin of ours & so home by the latter part of Sept.

I enclose a clipping from the Sun about Mr. West's Boston address[2] which to quote Mrs. Cleveland "judging from the reverberations must have been a great success." When does the Dean take that "quiet hour by the quiet lamp" *himself*, Jack & I ask—certainly not in the evening!

We have had a lovely visit here with my father.[3] Jack has had superb trout fishing & Beth & I have spent hours in the beautiful forest seeing many birds & hearing[—]most lovely sound of all[—] the Hermit Thrushes sing! We almost wish, all three of us, that we were going to Gorham again, as the time draws near, for us to go to Vermont.

I have had wonderfully flattering pictures taken, serious, & gay—the latter too much so. When you see them you & Mrs. Wilson must choose which you like best.

We leave on Monday, going to Vermont by way of Boston. Warmest love for you & Mrs. Wilson from Jack & myself

Ever yours,   Jenny Davidson Hibben

Pardon envelope.

[1] William Newcomb Davidson.

[2] This clipping from the New York *Sun* is missing. However, it was a report of an address by Dean West to the National Educational Association in Boston on July 6, 1903, on "The Present Peril to Liberal Education." West also spoke, along with President Eliot of Harvard, President Harper of Chicago, and President Butler of Columbia, on the following day on "The Length of the College Course." West's addresses are printed in *Present College Questions: Six Papers Read before the National Educational Association, at the Sessions Held in Boston, July 6 and 7, 1903* (New York, 1903), pp. 29-44, 63-75.

[3] John Davidson, of Elizabeth, N. J.

My dear Mr. Wilson,   Greensboro, Vermont   July 26, 1903.

Your letters make me feel really, as if I were taking a trip abroad myself. The one from Grasmere reached me Friday, & with it the photograph of that lovely little church. The Sunday we spent there is one of the happiest in my life. I know that Mrs. Wilson's enjoyment of the English Lakes must have been beyond all words. I am almost sorry that it did not come the last of your stay in England, rather than first.

We have just come back from church—a little *orthodox* church, with a shrill choir, & a plain, sincere, clergyman, old fashioned hymns, *dear* old hymns, & a clock ticking loudly all the time. After listening for a time I gave my mind up to wanderings, & I thought of my dear boy in Ireland going to some lovely cathedral service (Jack says "not at all—he was probably in a jaunting car going to the Lakes of Killarney"!) & you & Mrs. Wilson in St. Giles Cathedral with those splendid bare legged Highlanders about you, & probably you were in Durham or York, & I was all wrong!

I am reading *you* and Fiske. I have stopped you for a time until Fiske's charming old Virginia[1] shall catch up with you. You are both delightful & I am grateful for my books that "my author friend" as Jack calls you, gave me for this summer. Jack's work is going on well—a *proper* & appreciative criticism in "The Dial" of his book[2] has soothed me in regard to that Post article.[3] The weather is most unsettled but we tramp in spite of that, through rain or shine. Mrs. Perry is more lovely than I thought her. I feel as if I had not fully appreciated her before. Mr. Perry comes up to-morrow.

We wonder sometimes if we *ever* lived in Princeton, & fussed over gardens & went to games, & delivered lectures & went to faculty meetings & chapels & charming little dinners! & had our dear friends & neighbors! Be perfectly sure that we miss you both. You must have been away *months* already. Warmest love from us for you.

Ever yours,   Jenny Davidson Hibben.

ALS (WP, DLC).

[1] John Fiske, *Old Virginia and Her Neighbours* (2 vols., Boston and New York, 1897).

[2] Arthur Kenyon Rogers, Professor of Philosophy and Education at Butler College, Indianapolis, commented favorably on Hibben's *Hegel's Logic: An Essay in Interpretation* (New York, 1902) in "Aspects of Philosophic Thought," a review of three books on philosophy in the Chicago *Dial*, xxxv (July 1, 1903), 11-13.

[3] She referred to a sharply critical review, "Hegel's Logic Interpreted," by Charles Sanders Peirce of Harvard in the New York *Evening Post*, May 30, 1903.

To Harry Augustus Garfield

London [July 29, 1903]

Letter just received sincerely delighted.

Woodrow Wilson

Hw tel. (H. A. Garfield Papers, DLC).

To Harry Augustus Garfield

London. Buckingham Palace Hotel.

My dear Mr. Garfield,   29 July, 1903

Mrs. Wilson and I, after a week's wandering at too rapid a pace to ask our letters to keep pace with us, from cathedral town to cathedral town, have reached London (a few hours ago) to find a pile of mail awaiting us, but nothing so welcome or delightful as your letter announcing your willingness to accept the call to Princeton. I have just cabled my first expression of gratification, and send this to say more explicitly how deeply pleased I am. I am sure all connected with the University will be; and, as for myself, I shall look forward to many years of most enjoyable friendship and close association in work. I am sure that you will enjoy the life at Princeton. It is natural, simple, cordial, and there are many good fellows to supply flavour to the intercourse.

We are expecting to be back by September 21st. If you wish my advice in any matter, or if you or Mrs. Garfield should wish information upon any matter either from me or from Mrs. Wilson, we hope that you will not think it an intrusion upon our vacation to write to us before our return. Until about the 22nd of August our address will be c/o British Linen Co. Bank, London; after that, until Sept 12th, c/o Credit Lyonnais, Paris.

With cordial regard and pleasure,

Sincerely Yours,   Woodrow Wilson

ALS (H. A. Garfield Papers, DLC).

To Charles Williston McAlpin

London. Buckingham Palace Hotel.

My dear Mr. McAlpin,   31 July, 1903

We have reached London, after a sojourn in Scotland, and find your letters of the 13th and 17th here.

It is delightful to know that things are being so thoughtfully looked after, and I thank you most sincerely.

You are handling lecture invitations, as other matters, in exactly the right way. It would cause trouble to make exceptions.

Please send the postal in response to bills, as you suggest.

I am glad you did as you did with regard to Finley's inauguration.

I am delighted with the news about Mr. Garfield. He is an ideal fellow, and will, I am confident, prove quite a card. I think no news of the matter should come from us until the Trustees act in October.

I enclose a letter[1] which I commend to your favourable consideration.

We are very well indeed, and are being much refreshed by our outing

Mrs. Wilson joins me in warmest regards to Mrs. McAlpin and yourself, and I am, as always,

Cordially & faithfully Yours,   Woodrow Wilson

Letters which are to reach this side after the 20th should be addressed *Crédit Lyonnais, Paris.*

ALS (McAlpin File, UA, NjP).
  [1] It is missing.

From Charles Williston McAlpin

My dear Dr. Wilson: [Princeton, N. J.] August 3, 1903.

About ten days ago an invitation from the Trustees of the Carnegie Institute of Pittsburg to you to deliver the principal address at the Eighth Anniversary of Founders Day, November 5th, 1903, was received at my office. The invitation contained expressions of the esteem in which you are held in Pittsburg, allowed you the liberty to choose anything for a subject and invited you to bring Mrs. Wilson to Pittsburg. A postal was sent in answer to this stating that you were abroad. A telegram received from Mr. Church,[1] Secretary of the Institute, a few days later is as follows:

"Will you kindly return to me today my letter to President Wilson? In view of his prolonged absence we must make other arrangements. Please answer."

The letter of invitation was returned and with it a note expressing our willingness to forward any communication from the Institute. On Saturday, August 1st, the following letter from Mr. Church was received:

"Secretary Princeton University

My dear Sir: New York, July 31, 1903.

I desire to see Dr. Woodrow Wilson in Europe and will be greatly obliged if you will write me where I can probably meet him, or at least address him, from August 10th to say the

25th. Will he be in London in that period? Kindly address reply to me at Hotel Portland, Oxford Street, near Marble Arch, London, England.

Sincerely yours,   S. H. Church.

I sail tomorrow."

Feeling that this is too serious a problem for me to solve I have taken the liberty of sending the address of your London bankers to Mr. Church at his London address.[2]

If you are still enjoying yourselves as much as you did in the Lake District (I refer to Mrs. Wilson's letter to Mrs. McAlpin) you must be having a magnificent summer. We have been very comfortable on this side of the water thus far having had no very hot weather.

Mrs. McAlpin and I expect to start for the Yellowstone and Pacific coast on the 11th. It is our plan to make a hurried trip of three or four weeks returning by way of the Canadian Pacific railway.

I am making fair progress in the arrangements for supplying the Chapel pulpit. Dr. Henry van Dyke pad [had] promised to preach in New York September 27th but is endeavoring to change the date in order to occupy the College pulpit the first Sunday of the term. I have asked Dr. Patton to preach October 4th and January 31st, but have not heard from him. If Dr. van Dyke cannot give us September 27th I shall try to secure Dr. Patton for that date.

Drs. Upham, Charles Cuthbert Hall and Richards and Butler and Father Huntington and Mr. Janvier have all accepted.[3]

With kind regards to Mrs. Wilson in which Mrs. McAlpin joins, I remain,

Faithfully yours,   [C. W. McAlpin] Secre[t]ary.

CCL (McAlpin File, UA, NjP).

[1] Samuel Harden Church, railway official, prolific historian, and trustee and Secretary of the Carnegie Institute of Pittsburgh.

[2] Church probably saw Wilson in London, for Wilson gave the Founder's Day address at the Carnegie Institute on Nov. 5, 1903. Entitled "The Statesmanship of Letters," it is printed at Nov. 5, 1903, Vol. 15.

[3] The Rev. Dr. Charles Cuthbert Hall, President of Union Theological Seminary; the Rev. Dr. William Rogers Richards, pastor of the Brick Presbyterian Church in New York; the Rev. Willis Howard Butler, pastor of the First Congregational Church in Williamstown, Mass.; the Rev. James Otis Sargent Huntington, founder and Superior of the American Order of the Holy Cross, Westminster, Md.; and the Rev. Caesar Augustus Rodney Janvier, pastor of the Holland Memorial Presbyterian Church in Philadelphia.

Two Letters from Jenny Davidson Hibben

My dear Mr. Wilson,   Greensboro, Vermont.   August 9, 1903.

Your letter written from York was most welcome & *refreshing* —with your scorn of Englishmen & manners, only don't I beg, say *British*, for the Scotch are a "kindly people," as a Scotchwoman once said to me, & I think they are lovely to strangers. English people in their homes I think quite different from *travelling* English. Jack simply revelled in what you said. Perhaps you remember that he was so wrought up over them, that he answered a horrid contemptuous article in an Oxford paper about Americans.

Many thanks for the photograph of York Cathedral. It is perfectly beautiful, & I hope one day, that I may see it. Your summer is very different from ours. One lovely day here is exactly like another [—] the sweetest August days! The country is at the very height of beauty—the goldenrod & asters are in bloom—late haying is going on—& the mountains & woods are perfect—& the lake lovely in sunlight & moonlight. I am very peaceful & happy, & not rushing about as I often do, most foolishly. Jack, & Beth & I have found some one in whom, for different reasons, we are interested—a Mr. William Lord[1]—a clergyman & brother of my own dear Miss Lord.[2] He is an enthusiastic ornithologist & tells us much that we wish to know about birds—& he is more than that: a man of most lovely & unselfish life—a little man with no body—but much brain & heart & soul—& my other admirations are an old lady[,] Mrs. Perry's mother, who is a *dear*—& a pretty young married woman, the latter I like *because* she is pretty! Mrs. Perry is intense & sweet, Mr. Perry full of charm, & *sometimes* I seem to know him. Occasionally on a walk, he will let himself *go* & then I feel that we see him. Jack is well & splendidly brown, & Beth the picture of health & sweetness.

Your books will return to you much worn I am afraid for I carry them about, & they see different kinds of weather. I wonder how much you agree with Fiske & if you approve of what he says of the Scotch Irish, & I'm sure Mrs. Wilson & you would *not* agree with him about the settlement of North & South Carolina. I don't know enough about American history to question him, but Jack does. I'll have many questions to ask when you come home. I am deeply interested in your History & I think I am reading it in exactly the right way,—I mean for my own pleasure & benefit. Tell Mrs. Wilson I have cheerful letters from

Mrs. McCosh & happy ones from Mrs. Cleveland—about her "sweet baby," whose name may be Francis, she says.[3]

My dear brother had a horrid crossing & was desperately ill. He was on his way to the Lakes of Killarney & I hope his bad times are over.

Warmest love to you & Mrs. Wilson

Ever yours,   Jenny Davidson Hibben.

P.S. I have been rather troubled about an address, that I *think* I gave you, in Paris, the Hotel Chatham. My Father & I were there years ago & it was then a pleasant place, with a charming courtyard, good table & rooms. But it may have changed, so do not depend upon what I have said, but ask about other places. How I hope you enjoy the Continent too! Your letters are a very great pleasure—we are having two summers!   J.D.H.

[1] The Rev. William Rogers Lord, pastor of the Unitarian Society in Rockland, Mass. He was a lecturer on bird life and had published a handbook on the birds of Oregon and Washington compiled during an earlier pastorate in Portland.
[2] A daughter of Daniel Minor Lord; her first name is unknown to the Editors.
[3] Francis Grover Cleveland, born at Buzzards Bay, Mass., on July 18, 1903.

My dear Mr. Wilson,   Greensboro, Vermont.   August 16, 1903.

This is written at the end of a lovely Sunday. This morning we heard a *perfect* sermon from Dr. Duhurst of Chicago[1] & Jack hopes some time you will have him for one of the University preachers, & this afternoon we, with the Perrys rowed to the end of the lake, & then walked through a lovely wood road & pastures & climbed to the top of a hill & saw the sun set behind the mountains. The Perrys are delightful companions, & are so sweet and kind to us that we have grown very fond of them.

On Friday Jack & I started early, for an all day tramp up Blodgett Mountain, Mrs. Perry & Beth following with our lunch in a carriage. They were kind enough to bring our mail, & on the top of the mountain, while Mrs. Perry & Jack and Beth cooked our meal, I luxuriously rested & read my letters—one happy one from my dear Will from Oban, just as he was starting on his Highland trip, & the other from you, from London. You can not imagine how far away it seemed from that quiet mountain to the Royal Academy & Mr. Bryce & The Temple & Westminster Abbey. I can very well imagine Mrs. Wilson's delight in the beautiful pictures. I wonder if in the Tate Gallery she came across a picture I loved—"The Boyhood of Sir Walter Raleigh" by

Frank Dicksee, I believe. I only saw it once, & couldn't find a photograph of it.

We are glad that you are so happy over Mr. Garfield's acceptance. We have told no one, & Mr. Daniels is not here. He & Mrs. Daniels have been in Maine, all summer. We leave on the 28th for Bristol [R. I.]. I am very sorry, for I love this sweet, quiet place, & we shall probably be in Princeton by the 8th. Many thanks for all the dates of your changes. I thought of you both to-day in the Church of St. Mary the Virgin in Oxford, & when this reaches you, you will be on the Continent, perhaps in Holland! My reading continues to be a delightful occupation. Pardon this untidy letter, but my portfolio is on my lap. Beth's room is gay with postals from you & Will. You are so kind to send them to her. I hope Mrs. Wilson's ankle is quite well. Dear love for her and you.   Ever yours   Jenny Davidson Hibben

ALS (WP, DLC).
[1] The Rev. Frederic Eli Dewhurst, pastor of the University Congregational Church of Chicago.

From James Mark Baldwin

Dear Dr. Wilson,   New York   [c. Aug. 18, 1903]

I write to let you know that I have promised to take charge of a new department in the Johns Hopkins Univ[1] & have said I'd give one course at least this coming term (Oct.). I shall be able to do some Princeton work* tho' not all—if indeed such haste do not seem to you unseemly! If you do not find the suggestion irrelevant—I should be able to give my senior & graduate courses, if the Junior required[2] were taken off my hands. As Prof. Hibben has the scientific section of that class already, possibly he would assume it—or Prof. Warren.[3] If, however, for any reason you prefer to have me do so, I may present my resignations absolutely for the fall term.

In case I do some work (while you are getting matters adjusted) until 2nd term the question of salary may be arranged as seems proper when you return.

Kindly treat the matter as confidential until an announcement is made. Of course private communication to those interested must be made & I myself am informing the members of the Department at Princeton. I shall send to you for the trustees a personal note later on. I hope you are having a restful & healthful time.   Sincerely Yours   J. Mark Baldwin

* But only until Feb. (2nd. term) when my resignation is to be absolute.

ALS (WP, DLC).

1 Baldwin had accepted a professorship of philosophy and psychology at The Johns Hopkins University. It was hoped that he would revive the study of psychology at the Hopkins, which had languished since G. Stanley Hall departed in 1888 to become the first President of Clark University.

2 "Psychology. Elementary Course. Junior Required; first term."

3 Howard Crosby Warren, Professor of Experimental Psychology.

From Harry Augustus Garfield

My Dear Dr. Wilson: Cleveland, Ohio.   Aug. 19, 1903.

Your very cordial letter of July 29th reached me just after my return from the Berkshires. The breaking of ties here has its compensation in the friendship and association I shall have with you in your work.

Mrs. Garfield and I were in Princeton last week and had the pleasure of meeting Mr. Fine who impresses us both as most charming. You will perhaps be interested to know that I have arranged with him for the rental of his house,[1] and that we expect to come to Princeton as soon after November 1st as possible. I desire to be there long enough before beginning my work to familiarize myself with what you are doing, as well as to secure leisure for preparation which I find to be impossible here.

I avail myself of your permission to intrude upon your vacation to inquire whether what lies in my mind as the best work for me to undertake at the outset, meets with your approval and will properly supplement your work. I am impressed so strongly with the necessity of starting men on the right road in their civic life that, unless in other courses the field is sufficiently covered, it seems to me desirable to direct attention first of all to party government and activities. In my experience, men fresh from the universities too often regard themselves as apostles of an economic theory, and confuse means with ends. In the hurly-burly of municipal activities, one is easily forced into associations which, however congenial they may be, tend to alienate one from those politically inactive citizens who, if inspired to activity, carry enormous weight because of their association with the business enterprise of the city. A perspective created by a clear understanding of the course of party activities, here and in England especially, will, I think, enable one intelligently to analize existing situations and to exert an influence without loss of effectiveness or sacrifice of principle. For example, an understanding of the influence of the Tractarian movement, the young England party, the invectives of Carlyle and the Christian socialism of Kingsley and his friends upon the politics of the time is, I think you will agree with me, necessary to an appreciation of the Manchester movement, and the political activities from then to the present time. With the perspective well established, the burden of the work would consist of an analysis of the status and trend of political parties today, and so equip men as that the margin of activity over and above that required for establishing themselves in business or professions can be wisely and effectively devoted to public affairs.

It occurs to me that I have perhaps gone faster than I should. Possibly some further action is necessary before I am in a position to regard myself as formally engaged.

With very kindest regards, I remain

Sincerely yours,   H. A. Garfield.

TLS (WP, DLC).

[1] At 49 Library Place. The Fines were moving into the Dean's house on the campus.

Two Letters from Jenny Davidson Hibben

My dear Mr. Wilson,   Greensboro, Vermont.   August 21, 1903.

This will reach you in Paris, & I can not but wonder how you & Mrs. Wilson will like it. I have been there twice, but only for a week at a time, & I really know very little about it. I hope you surely go to Versailles, & there is a charming little palace in Paris, the Hotel Cluny that is very lovely, as I recall it twenty years ago!! I hope you have had my letter too, begging you not to take my recommendation of the Hotel Chatham for it too belongs to that same far distant time. A lovely letter from Mrs. Westcott told of their pleasant luncheon with you & the delightful afternoon at the Tate Gallery. I am glad that you see how truly charming she is. . . .

We are taking last favorite walks & rows. The leaves are turning very quickly now & the country is even more lovely than before. Jack is impatient to be in Princeton again, & we shall probably be there about the 8th & then we'll see your daughters & Beth & "the Wilson children" will have happy times to-gether, & we shall wait with impatience the return of the travellers

The reading of American history goes with a delightful rush

& I hope to keep it up through the winter. It has been a very real pleasure to me this summer.

Jack joins with me in warm love to you both.

Ever yours, Jenny Davidson Hibben

My dear Mr. Wilson,

Blithewold Bristol, Rhode Island
Aug. 30, 1903.

As you see by the heading of this letter, we are making our last visit of the summer & by Friday Sept. 5 we hope to be in Princeton. Just as we were leaving Greensboro, letters came from you from Oxford & from Will from the Orkney Islands. We really were very sorry to leave that lovely place. Jack found some men in whom he delighted & they were as sorry as he to part. They had camped & fished & golfed & studied to-gether & had delightful times. Now we are in a quite different place. The house is most lovely & with a green lawn that is perfectly beautiful going down to the bay, & our hostess is dear & sweet as ever & our host most kind. . . .

This will be my last letter before we see you. We shall follow you & Mrs. Wilson with our loving wishes as you cross the sea back to us again. With love & good bye,

Ever yours, Jenny Davidson Hibben

P.S. No, not good-bye quite yet, until I speak of Mr. Baldwin's resignation. Are you sorry or glad or a mixture of both![1] Now good-bye & a safe & happy voyage! J.D.H.

ALS (WP, DLC).

[1] J. G. Hibben to WW, Jan. 18, 1901, printed as an Enclosure with Jenny D. Hibben to WW, Jan. 18, 1901, Vol. 12, suggests that both Hibben and Wilson shared a low personal opinion of Baldwin.

To Harry Augustus Garfield

My dear Mr. Garfield,

Mrs. E. L. Van Pelt's Pension,
4, Square de Latour-Maubourg,
Paris 1 Sept. 1903

Your letter of August 19th reached me this morning, just on the eve of my leaving Paris for a few days in Switzerland. I hasten to answer it.

The course you suggest giving strikes me as excellent and an admirable supplement to what I am trying to do in the class room, viz., clear up the chief fundamental conceptions of law and government; I sincerely hope that you will undertake it. It will, I am sure, prove just the right introduction to what I most desire for the men: a course in *practical* politics, which is yet based on ideals,—and all the more practical because it takes hold on the spirit. The only ideal politics, to my mind, is that which is real,— which takes men as it finds them, and finds them spirit as well as matter, and so discovers the best men both to themselves and to the world. Follow out the lines you indicate, and I shall be delighted. We will talk it over more particularly when I have the pleasure of seeing you again.

I am very much pleased that you have secured so comfortable a house as Fine's—and that you like him so much. He is an old chum of mine and as fine a fellow as is made.

No, you are not going too fast at all. Of course the actual election of professors rests with the Board of Trustees, which will not act until its next meeting, Oct. 21st. But the selection of men rests with the President, and in this case the thing is as good as done. I shall, out of deference to the Board, say nothing to friends, of the matter; but a miscarriage is quite inconceivable.

Your decision has added greatly to the pleasure of my vacation, and I am sincerely glad that you can arrange to be in Princeton so soon. We shall have good times plotting the whole thing out.

Mrs. Wilson joins me in kindest regards to you both.

Cordially yours, Woodrow Wilson

TCL (H. A. Garfield Papers, DLC).

ADDENDA

To Charles Augustus Young

My dear Professor Young,   Princeton, 8 December, 1892

I am ashamed to have left your note of Nov. 26 so long un-answered. Both a continuous pressure of engagements, out of town and in town, and an inability to find an answer to your question have contributed to delay my reply most unreasonably.

I am sorry to report that our little collection of economic books does not afford any data on the point about which you ask. I am hardly surprised, for the collection is ridiculously inadequate, except in general treatises; but I am none the less disappointed that I cannot serve you. The only book that gave me any help was Rogers' "History of Prices";[1] but, since there was a great fluctuation in prices, because of the debasement of the coinage, at almost the very time which your question concerns, it would be next to impossible to determine by calculation the normal purchasing power of money then—and Rogers seems to contain nothing directly to the point.

I shall keep on the lookout for the point; but for the present I am foiled. None of the general histories yield me anything.

Sincerely Yours,   Woodrow Wilson

ALS (C. A. Young Papers, Archives, NhD).
    [1] James Edwin Thorold Rogers, *A History of Agriculture and Prices in England from the Years after the Oxford Parliament* . . . (7 vols., Oxford, 1866-1902).

Two Letters to Thomas Raynesford Lounsbury

Princeton, New Jersey,
My dear Professor Lounsbury,   30 October, 1896.

Pardon me for writing in this fashion; I have been threatened recently with writer's cramp, and have been bidden use the pen as little as possible.

I appreciate your kind letter[1] with all my heart. It was generous in you to write it, and it has heartened me mightily to read it. The great success of the oration surprised me more than I can say; but I am enjoying the surprise to the top of my bent. It is but another illustration of the fact that a man is always liked for saying what he really thinks, and always says it better than he could say anything else.

It was a great pleasure to have you in Princeton, and to make your acquaintance under the easy and genial conditions supplied by Professor Raymond's[2] table. I shall remember it all with keen relish; and shall hope that it will not be necessary to remember it very long before our intercourse is renewed.

With warm regards,

Most cordially Yours,   Woodrow Wilson

[1] T. R. Lounsbury to WW, Oct. 25, 1896, Vol. 10.
[2] George Lansing Raymond, Professor of Aesthetics at Princeton.

Princeton, New Jersey,

My dear Professor Lounsbury,   14 January, 1897.

Pray pardon this machine made letter: I have been threatened lately with writer's cramp and forbidden the use of the pen.

I am mightily attracted by your kind invitation,[1] and heartily wish I could accept it; but the truth is, that I shall be lecturing in Baltimore through all of February, completely tied by the leg; and that, after I get back and have met the engagements away from home already indiscreetly made, I shall have barely time enough to do a job of a book revision I am contracted for before the college year runs out.[2] In short I am already mortgaged over head and ears, and must not go further into debt.

And yet I am in debt to you for wanting me and saying so so kindly. I thank you most heartily, and am, with warm regard,

Faithfully Yours,   Woodrow Wilson

WWTLS (T. R. Lounsbury Papers, CtY).
[1] It is missing.
[2] The revision of *The State*, about which see D. C. Heath to WW, March 15, 1897, n. 2, Vol. 10.

To Franklin Henry Giddings

Princeton, New Jersey,

My dear Professor Giddings,   6 April, 1900.

You have certainly been very kind. The list you send is most interesting.[1] I had thought of all the men on it except Mr. Loos; I am therefore the more interested that you should have hit upon them also. If Ford had a little stronger physique and a little more emphatic personality (I have met him), he would be more to my mind than any of the rest.

It looks now as if we might be fortunate enough to get a scholarly man who has also had some experience in affairs; and that would be our decided preference, if we did not have to take a pronounced partisan.

Thank you most sincerely and heartily for the help, and the well considered help, you have given us.

With warm regard,

Most sincerely Yours,   Woodrow Wilson

WWTLS (in possession of Margaret Giddings).
[1] See F. H. Giddings to WW, April 4, 1900, Vol. 11.

From Arthur Twining Hadley

My dear Mr. Wilson: [New Haven, Conn.] June 10th, 1902.

I was greatly surprised, and yet more greatly pleased, to hear the news which last evening's wire has brought concerning your election to the presidency of Princeton. Changes have been wonderfully rapid in the last few years. With you and [Nicholas Murray] Butler and myself in our new positions, we certainly have old friends working all together.

I cannot begin to tell how great is the personal pleasure of having a man on whose clearness of vision I rely so much, and above all things, whom I think of as an old and trusted friend, in a position like the one which you are to occupy.

Faithfully yours,   [Arthur T. Hadley]

TCL (Hadley Letterbooks, Archives, CtY).

From Thomas Raynesford Lounsbury

Dear Mr. Wilson: London, June 24, 1902.

I have just chanced to see for the first time the notice of your election to the presidency of Princeton, & I feel that I must give vent to my own personal feelings, by expressing to you my intense gratification at the fact, though I doubt not that you have been already overwhelmed with congratulations. I was with some Princeton graduates when I heard the news, & it was a great pleasure to me to observe that, surprised as they were by Dr Patton's resignation, they were more than delighted by your election. I stop here because I do not wish to intrude upon your time, & I carefully refrain from giving my address, so as to save you the bother of even a perfunctory acknowledgment: now I don't believe that among the members of what may be called the outside public, any one is more gratified by your election than I.   Sincerely Yours,   T. R. Lounsbury

ALS (WP, DLC).

INDEX

NOTE ON THE INDEX

THE alphabetically arranged analytical table of contents at the front of the volume eliminates duplication, in both contents and index, of references to certain documents, such as letters. Letters are listed in the contents alphabetically by name, and chronologically within each name by page. The subject matter of all letters is, of course, indexed. The Editorial Notes and Wilson's writings are listed in the contents chronologically by page. In addition, the subject matter of both categories is indexed. The index covers all references to books and articles mentioned in text or notes. Footnotes are indexed. Page references to footnotes which place a comma between the page number and "n" cite both text and footnote, thus: "624,n3." On the other hand, absence of the comma indicates reference to the footnote only, thus: "55n2"—the page number denoting where the footnote appears. The letter "n" without a following digit signifies an unnumbered descriptive-location note.

An asterisk before an index reference designates identification or other particular information. Re-identification and repetitive annotation have been minimized to encourage use of these starred references. Where the identification appears in an earlier volume, it is indicated thus: "*1:212,n3." Therefore a page reference standing without a preceding volume number is invariably a reference to the present volume. The index supplies the fullest known forms of names, and, for the Wilson and Axson families, relationships as far down as cousins. Persons referred to in the text by nicknames or shortened forms of names can be identified by reference to entries for these forms of the names.

A sampling of the opinions and comments of Wilson and Ellen Axson Wilson covers their more personal views, while broad, general headings in the main body of the index cover impersonal subjects. Occasionally opinions expressed by a correspondent are indexed where these appear to supplement or to reflect views expressed by Wilson or by Ellen Axson Wilson in documents which are missing.

INDEX

Abbotsford, Roxburgh, Wilsons at, 524
Abner Daniel (Harben), 72
academic costume, 143, 191
Acton, John Emerich Edward Dalberg, 1st Baron, 295
Adams (mountain in Presidential Range), 111
Adams, Charles Francis (1835-1915), 306n3
Adams, John, 315
Adamson, Penrhyn Stanley (Penrhyn Stanlaws), 59-60,n1
Addison, Joseph, 503
Aiken, Charles Augustus, Mrs. (Sarah Elizabeth Noyes), 36-37,n3
Aimone's Manufacturing Co., New York City, 10,n1, 17
Albany: Princeton alumni dinner, 400
Albertson, Charles Carroll, 114
Alderman, Edwin Anderson, 205n4, 334
Alexander, Alexander John Aitcheson, 97n3
Alexander, Charles Beatty, 130,n1, 131; Mrs. (Harriet Crocker), 130
Alexander, Claude Aitcheson, 97,n3
Alexander, George, 253
Alexander, James Waddel, 144, 168n1, 268,n2, 289, 290, 304-5, 490
Alexander, Samuel, M.D., 187, 195, 291
Alpnach, Switzerland, Wilsons at, 539
Ambleside, Westmorland, Wilsons at, 521
American and Canadian Student Young Men's Christian Association Movement, 265-67
American Citizenship (Brewer), 136,n1
American Commonwealth (Bryce), 14
American Epoch Series, 281
American Historical Association, *Annual Report for 1898*, 443n2
American Historical Review, 519n
American Institute of Sacred Literature, 198,n2
American Philosophical Society, 285, 380, 381, 405, 470
American Revolution, 352, 445, 517
Americans (Münsterberg), 76,n1
Amerikaner (Münsterberg), 76,n1
Amherst College, 403
Amiens: Cathedral, 535; Wilsons in, 535
Anatole France on Childhood (Mantoux), 440n2
Anderson, Mary, 319-20
Anderson, Robert Patton, 474
Andrews, Charles McLean, 280-83,n1
Angell, James Burrill, 418,n1, 419, 421; Mrs. (Sarah Swope Caswell), 418, 421

Ann Arbor: WW at, 418, 425; WW lecture, 419-21
Ann Arbor Daily Argus, 421n
Annals of the American Academy of Political and Social Science, 445n
Anne, Queen, 502, 503, 504
Antique Furniture Exchange, New York City, 7,n7, 9
Apollo Belvidere (statue), 79, 85, 97
Archaeological Institute of America, 206, 382
Aristotle, 208
Armour, Jonathan Ogden, 248
Armour Institute of Technology, 248
Armstrong, John Gassaway, 388
Arnold, Matthew, 521,n2
Articles of Confederation, 232
Atlanta: Atlanta Lecture Association, 20n1
Atlantic Monthly, 33, 54, 265,n1, 324
Augusta, Ga.: First Presbyterian Church, 331-32
Axson, Benjamin Palmer, first cousin of EAW, *2:557n2; 499
Axson, Edward William, brother of EAW, *2:372,n2; 4,n2, 438; Mrs. (Florence Choate Leach), 4,n2
Axson, Margaret Randolph (Madge), sister of EAW, *2:417n1; *3:118n1; 4-5n1, 7, 9, 12, 15, 17, 22, 35, 39, 53, 65, 68, 72, 74, 90, 95, 97, 98, 99, 101, 103, 108, 111, 435,n1, 438
Axson, Stockton (*full name*: Isaac Stockton Keith Axson II), brother of EAW, *2:386n1; 25,n2, 44, 95, 138, 139, 187-88, 326, 329, 395, 403, 418, 422, 423-24, 425, 426, 428, 430, 431, 432, 435, 437, 438, 439, 453, 498,n1

Babcock, Oliver B., 129
Baedeker, Karl, 529
Bagehot, Walter, 13, 340
Baird, John Stuart, 195
Baker, Alfred Brittin, 453,n4
Baker, Christian S., Mrs., 417,n1
Baldwin, C. H., Jr., 331
Baldwin, James Mark, 126,n1, 127, 128, 395, 395n1, 553, 556,n1
Balfour, Arthur James, 1st Earl of Balfour, 27,n2
Baltimore: Music Hall, 260; Presbyterian Union, 260, 277n1; WW addresses, 260-61, 358-59
Baltimore *Sun*, 261n
Bancroft, Edgar Addison, 424,n1; Mrs. (Margaret Healy), 424,n1
Bancroft, George, 286, 379, 444
Bar Harbor, Maine, 92
Barbarossa, S.S., 468
Barrie, Sir James Matthew, 528n8

OPINIONS AND COMMENTS

I didn't know [Henry Cabot Lodge] was so rich; he seems to be, like Roosevelt, one of fortune's all round favorites, 8

READING

William Nathaniel Harben, *Abner Daniel*, 72
Algernon Charles Swinburne, 101
Edward Noyes Westcott, *David Harum*, 72
Owen Wister, *Lin McLean*, 453,n3

TRAVEL

Summer vacation at Clifton, Mass., July 1902, 4-5n1, 7-8, 11, 15-16, 18-19, 21, 25, 28, 31, 36, 41, 42-43
Vacation trip to Britain and the Continent with WW, July 10-Sept. 22, 1903, 521-43, 545, 546, 547, 548, 550, 551, 552, 553, 555, 556

WOODROW WILSON